POLITICS AND SOCIETY
IN
CONTEMPORARY AFRICA

POLITICS AND SOCIETY IN CONTEMPORARY AFRICA

Naomi Chazan
Robert Mortimer
John Ravenhill
Donald Rothchild

Lynne Rienner Publishers • Boulder, Colorado

Published in the United States of America in 1988 by
Lynne Rienner Publishers, Inc.
1800 30th Street, Boulder, Colorado 80301

Library of Congress Cataloging-in-Publication Data

Politics and society in contemporary Africa / Naomi Chazan . . . [et al.].

   Includes index.
   ISBN 0-931477-16-6 (lib. bdg.) ISBN 0-931477-17-4
(pbk.)
   1. Africa—Politics and government—1960-   2. Africa—Social
conditions—1960-   3. Africa—Economic conditions—1960-   4. Africa
–Foreign relations.   I. Chazan, Naomi, 1946-

JQ1872.P635 1988
320.96—dc19   87-34700
                                                           CIP

Printed and bound in the United States of America

5   4   3   2

■ Contents

■ Tables

■ Maps

■ Acknowledgments

This volume was conceived by Lynne Rienner several years ago in response to the need for a comprehensive and comparative overview of contemporary African politics and society. From the outset, it was designed as a joint venture, since it was generally agreed that no single individual could encompass, either geographically or thematically, all the main issues that such a book needed to address. The authors met initially to outline the book late in 1983, and have since communicated regularly despite the fact that they reside in three different continents. Thanks to the warm hospitality of Edith and Don Rothchild, the first draft was dissected at a week-long meeting in early 1987; since then several other meetings have taken place to go over various revisions. Subsequent drafts benefited substantially from the meticulous comments provided by Thomas M. Callaghy and Frank Holmquist. Throughout the writing and the revision of the manuscript this has been a most rewarding cooperative effort. We feel that the final product justifies the team approach; moreover we note that each of us has learned a great deal in the process.

Naomi Chazan owes particular thanks to Radcliffe College and its president, Matina S. Horner, for providing a most congenial atmosphere for writing. The Center for International Affairs at Harvard University, where she was a visiting scholar between 1985 and 1987, furnished additional facilities and stimulation. Nozipo Marraire and Katya Azoulay assisted in gathering some materials, and Allison Friedman processed multiple drafts. The Harry S. Truman Research Institute of the Hebrew University, Naomi Chazan's home base, continued its support for this project throughout. Robert Mortimer thanks Adeline Taraborelli, Sharon Nangle, and Marguerite Wagner for their expertise and unfailing good cheer in the task of preparing the manuscript. He is grateful to the Wayne Aspinall Foundation, which sponsored a stimulating term at Mesa College in Grand Junction, Colorado, in the spring of 1986, and to Haverford College for leave and travel support. John Ravenhill would like to thank Liz Kirby for research assistance, and the Department of Government at the University of Sydney for research and travel support. Donald Rothchild wishes to express his appreciation to the University of California, Davis, for financial support and to its Department of Political Science for secretarial assistance. In addition, Caroline Hartzell did exemplary work in editorial matters.

We would all like to thank Beverly Armstrong, who copyedited the manuscript, and Steve Barr, who has managed this complicated project. The authors are grateful to Liz Kirby for the superb job that she did in preparing the tables and index for the book. Above all, however, our deepest gratitude goes to Lynne Rienner, who has given us unstinting backing and support during the last few years.

■ Changes in Country Names

Present	Previous
Benin	Dahomey
Botswana	Bechuanaland
Burkina Faso	Upper Volta
Burundi[1]	Ruanda-Urundi
Cameroon	French Cameroons and British Southern Cameroons[2]
Cape Verde	Cape Verde Islands
Central African Republic	Oubangui Chari
Congo	French Congo; sometimes referred to as Congo-Brazzaville
Côte d'Ivoire	Ivory Coast
Djibouti	French Territory of the Afars and Issas
Equatorial Guinea	Spanish Guinea
Ghana	Gold Coast and British Togoland
Guinea-Bissau	Portuguese Guinea
Lesotho	Basutoland
Malagasy Republic (still often referred to as Madagascar)	Madagascar
Malawi	Nyasaland
Mali	French Soudan
Namibia	South West Africa
Rwanda[1]	Ruanda-Urundi
Saharan Arab Democratic Republic[3]	Spanish Sahara; sometimes referred to as Western Sahara
Somali Democratic Republic (Somalia)	British Somaliland and Italian Somaliland
Tanzania[4]	Tanganyika and Zanzibar
Togo	French Togoland
Zaire	Belgian Congo; subsequently Congo; sometimes referred to as Congo-Leopoldville or Congo-Kinshasa
Zambia	Northern Rhodesia
Zimbabwe	Southern Rhodesia; Rhodesia

1. Ruanda-Urundi was a Belgian-administered trust territory that became independent in 1960 as two separate states.
2. The Southern Cameroons, a British-administered UN trust territory, joined the Republic of Cameroon following a plebiscite in 1961; the people of the Northern Cameroons opted for integration with Nigeria.
3. Morocco has claimed this territory, a claim contested by the Polisario Front (the national liberation movement). Polisario refers to the territory as the Saharan Arab Democratic Republic (SADR).
4. The United Republic of Tanganyika and Zanzibar came into being on 26 April 1964, as a consequence of the union between Tanganyika and Zanzibar; the name "United Republic of Tanzania" was officially adopted a year later.

Source: Adapted from William Tordoff, *Government and Politics in Africa* (Indiana University Press 1984).

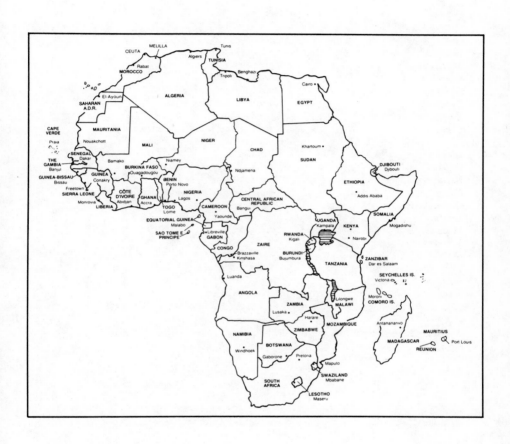

■ Introduction

The excitement of the struggle for independence still permeates the African continent. Nevertheless, current traumas regarding economic survival and effective political rule have taken a heavy toll; Africans, their governments, and the international community continue to grapple with economic adversity, political uncertainty, and social inequities. How have these constraints on growth and opportunity influenced the African political experience? What options exist in these circumstances? What political and economic choices have been made and what are their implications? The answers lie not in a single isolated variable but in the complex interconnections between politics and society, between domestic and external forces, and among historical legacies, available resources, and future prospects.

The purpose of this introduction to African politics and society is to depict in broad strokes the complexities and diversities of the African world since independence and to investigate new paths to understanding its intricate dynamics. Besides offering an initial acquaintance with contemporary Africa, we seek to provide a basic knowledge of political events and a closer comprehension of major problems, processes, and trends. By suggesting different ways of looking at issues, we raise a range of explanations for past occurrences and possible directions for theory. The book, therefore, constitutes a preliminary exploration into the multiple forces that make up present-day Africa.

In Chapter 1 we analyze different approaches to the study of African politics and present the main elements of a political choice method for the investigation of political structures, processes, and change. In Part 1 we focus on the building blocks of African politics. Chapter 2 is devoted to the study of government institutions. We examine the colonial legacy, the manner of transition to independence, and the structural foundations of the new states. We also trace

1

institutional changes since independence and pinpoint the differences that have emerged among African states since the 1960s. The third chapter is focused on the varying social groups that operate within the African setting. We look not only at cultural, kin, religious, racial, and geographic agglomerations but also at socioeconomic formations and their competing interests. Chapter 4 is concerned with the interaction of class, ethnicity, and the state in various African countries, highlighting differing patterns of cooperation, conflict, and exchange.

Part 2 centers on the study of the political process. In Chapter 5 we present a typology of regime forms and discuss their evolution. In Chapter 6 we examine how leaders have attempted to govern: We look at ideologies and at the linkages between rulers and ruled. Chapter 7 is devoted to political conflicts evident since independence. In Chapter 8 we analyze the mechanisms, the direction, and the nature of political change, summarizing common political themes, indicating diverging trends, and underlining the diverse dynamics of state-society relationships.

Part 3 concerns the political economy. In Chapter 9 we analyze the differing contexts of development and underdevelopment and examine several major policy issues. Building on this base, in Chapter 10 we study the relationship of Africa to the world economy, probing the ways in which global economic currents impinge on African choice and the differing strategies adopted by African governments and groups to enhance their capacity to manage and progress in such settings.

In Part 4 we delve into the international facets of the African experience since independence. In Chapter 11 we look at how external and domestic constraints have guided relations within Africa and in Chapter 12 we review Africa's ties with the outside world and its activities in the international arena. Diverging foreign policies are therefore conceived of as the outcome of the exercise of choice within the context of powerful common constraints.

In Chapter 13 we examine the special case of white minority rule and black opposition in South Africa. We look at the peculiar structures and processes of this dual society in order to understand the explosive situation in the southern part of the continent. In Chapter 14 we draw together the lessons gleaned from the study of the many dimensions of politics on the continent, reviewing major patterns, discussing ongoing trends, and advancing some tentative ideas as to the choices ahead for Africans as they continue to deal with the exigencies of scarcity, institutional fragility, dependency, and sociocultural diversity.

In each chapter we present the historical background, give an overview of developments since independence, and depict the differing manifestations of each topic and issue. Because it is impossible to go into detail for all fifty-one states in Africa, we conduct a comparative analysis of processes that exemplify emerging patterns on the continent. On this basis, special attention is devoted to Nigeria, Ghana, Guinea, Côte d'Ivoire, Cameroon, and Senegal in West Africa; Algeria and Morocco in North Africa; Chad and Mali in the Sahel; Ethiopia and the Sudan in the Horn of Africa; Zaire and Zambia in Central Africa; Kenya, Tanzania, and Uganda in East Africa; and Angola, Mozambique, and Botswana in southern Africa. We conclude each chapter by extracting the major patterns that emerge from the data; we discuss various explanations and raise further questions for thought and action.

In this textbook, unlike others on African politics, we concentrate on the period of independence in order to expose existing problems in greater detail and to explore the possibilities that emanate from the need to confront these difficult realities. The politics of contemporary Africa are as vibrant as they are diverse. Since independence, new dimensions of political life have unfolded that defy conventional wisdom and demand a reformulation of concepts and expectations. We offer this volume as an induction into this often confusing, constantly challenging, always fascinating, and ultimately questioning world.

The Diversity
of African Politics:
Trends and Approaches

The African continent encompasses a rich mosaic of peoples, cultures, ecological settings, and historical experiences. Africa's vast expanse of 11,677,240 square miles (30,244,050 square kilometers) stretches from the Mediterranean in the north to the meeting point of the Atlantic and Indian oceans in the south. The 450 million people of Africa (roughly 10 percent of the globe's population) are as diverse as the terrain they inhabit. The blacks and Arabs who live on the continent (together with small concentrations of Asians and whites) speak more than eight hundred languages, belong to hundreds of ethnic groups, and over the years have embraced many animist belief systems as well as all the great religions (most notably, Christianity and Islam). Although 70 percent of the continent's people live in the rural areas and make their living as farmers and pastoralists, rapidly growing ancient and new cities are also sprinkled over the map of Africa. Subsistence agriculture is sustained alongside hi-tech industries; the world's greatest mineral reserves are to be found in regions of the most abject poverty; universities thrive where illiteracy still prevails.

The political map of Africa captures the complexity that is the essence of the continent. Africa's fifty-one states are the product of conquest and separation, amalgamation and continuity. Ethiopia and Egypt are among the oldest political entities known to human history. But most of Africa consists of new states carved out by the imperial powers. Nigeria, with its population of 100 million, contrasts sharply with tiny Comoros or Gambia. Massive Zaire is bordered by the small republics of Rwanda and Burundi. Swaziland is a nation-state (that is, ethnically homogeneous). It is surrounded by some of the most heterogeneous, multiethnic countries in the world today. Africa sustains monarchies and dictatorships, military regimes and civilian governments, revolu-

4

tionary systems and democracies, populist administrations and authoritarian modes of rule.

African politics constitute a microcosm of political forms and contents, experiences and patterns, trends and prospects. To focus on the contemporary politics of this continent is therefore to contemplate some of the most basic issues of human survival, organization, change, and growth. This book provides an introduction to the central themes of political life in independent Africa.

■ INDEPENDENT AFRICA: TRENDS AND PATTERNS

The first wave of independence in Africa commenced in the 1950s with the emergence of North Africa and then Ghana from colonial rule. The year 1960, generally considered *the* year of African independence, witnessed the dismantling of the French colonial empire as well as the attainment of sovereignty by Nigeria—black Africa's foremost power. By the mid-1960s over thirty new states had undergone the process of decolonization.

The second, and generally more violent, wave of independence began in 1974, following the revolution in Portugal. The lusophone (Portuguese-speaking) states of Guinea-Bissau, Cape Verde, Mozambique, and Angola finally overcame 400 years of colonial domination. In 1975, Spain withdrew from the western Sahara, setting in motion a period of still unresolved strife over control of the territory. And in 1980 the struggle against white rule in Rhodesia was crowned with success: The independence of Zimbabwe brought the British colonial presence in Africa to an end. Namibia and South Africa are the last, and most recalcitrant, remnants of the colonial presence in contemporary Africa.

The heady expectations that accompanied the transfer of power have, in the first postcolonial generation, of necessity given way to a more sober view of domestic and international realities. The meaning of independence, nevertheless, has varied from place to place on the continent. Different states, individuals, and groups have undergone quite distinct experiences in a variety of spheres, rendering Africa far more heterogeneous in the late 1980s than it was on the eve of the transition from colonial rule.

In economic terms, the performance of many African countries has fallen far short of the vision of progress and well-being held forth by the leaders of anticolonial movements (see Table 1.1). In 1985, for example, twenty-two countries could not feed their growing population; agricultural production in the first part of the 1980s had actually declined. Economic growth rates per capita during the 1970s and the early 1980s, with a few exceptions, were stagnant if not negative. The foreign debt of most African states has increased precipitously since the late 1970s. Yet, some countries recorded substantial economic achievements (Botswana, Algeria, Gabon, and Côte d'Ivoire, for example) and others had taken significant steps to avert further economic deterioration (Ghana, Zimbabwe). Certain amenities, such as clean water, electricity, latrines, and feeder roads, are now generally more available than at the close of the colonial era. Some Africans have enriched themselves in the course of these years; for others the exigencies of absolute poverty have continued to shape their existence.[1] Although economic trends have highlighted a widespread malaise, the economic paths of African countries and specific groups have diverged markedly during this short time span.

Social gains in some areas have come together with social dislocation and glaring inequalities in others (see Table 1.2). Most African countries have made impressive advances in education and primary health care. Nevertheless, infant mortality rates are high (in some cases 50 percent of those born do not survive until the age of five), and life expectancy is still below fifty years. Access to much-needed services is uneven. The gap between the city and the countryside persists and has, in many places, been exacerbated. Elite-mass strains are pronounced. In Nigeria, for example, successful entrepreneurs and professionals fly around in private jets, while peasants line up for a portion of rice. Many rural areas have not been electrified; urban dwellers frequently have their own generators. In the countryside, wealthier landowners can control large tracts of land, while small farmers scratch out a living from depleted soil.

Social groups throughout the continent have become more aware, over the years, of their own particular circumstances. Ethnic groupings, incipient classes, and a variety of local communities, professional associations, trade unions, women's organizations, and religious movements have organized to forward their specific interests. In some instances, formal channels of participation have facilitated ongoing communication; in others, indirect avenues have been established to raise demands and to distribute benefits (patron-client relationships are a good example); and in other cases politicization has increased while access to the political center has been severely circumscribed. The opportunities for involvement in decision making have therefore varied.

Conflicts have been an integral part of the independence experience, as have the ongoing quests for national coherence. Political violence, unquestionably, has proliferated. Ethnic and nationality conflicts (in Ethiopia, Chad, Nigeria, Zaire, Sudan, and Angola) persist. Civil dissension has risen in Mozambique, Zimbabwe, and Uganda. Religious riots, virtually unheard of in the 1960s, are in evidence today. Interstate conflicts have also erupted: The Somali-Ethiopian conflict, the ongoing Chad-Libya dispute, the Zaire-Angola skirmishes, and the border wars between Burkina Faso and Mali are just some examples. From a most personal point of view, in some countries individual security has been threatened. Armed bandits roam through Uganda; in Nigeria, highway robbery is commonplace. But violent confrontations have been less widespread than could have been expected given the multiplicity of ethnic and linguistic groups and the growing socioeconomic discrepancies apparent throughout the continent. Indeed, with few exceptions, some form of national consciousness has evolved over the years. And in many countries norms of social interaction have been formulated and a modicum of civic order established.

Socioeconomic malaise is reflective of endemic political problems. In the early postcolonial years, most African leaders, in an effort to gain control, centralized power. Kwame Nkrumah of Ghana and Ahmed Sekou Touré of Guinea were among the first leaders to establish one-party states; they were followed by most of their peers. Centralization came with the personalization of power and with a heavy reliance on bureaucratic structures. The trend toward unitary government was almost uniform in the first two decades of independence. Yet, Nigeria developed a sophisticated federal system; Gambia, Botswana, and Mauritius have been able to sustain multiparty politics into the 1980s; and, most recently, Senegal returned to competitive elections. These countries constitute important examples of a possible shift away from the convention of centralized nonparticipatory politics.

African leaders have also experimented with many ideologies and political philosophies. African socialism, adopted in such countries as Tanzania, Ghana, Mali, Guinea, and Zambia, proliferated in the 1960s. In the mid-1970s Afro-Marxist regimes, more closely aligned with Marxist-Leninist principles, developed in Ethiopia, Mozambique, and Angola. In the early part of the 1980s, Jerry Rawlings in Ghana and Thomas Sankara in Burkina Faso introduced an African brand of radical populism. Throughout the past thirty years democratic ideas have proliferated alongside decidedly personalistic concepts of rule, and although ideological fads have come and gone, pragmatic values have prevailed in many countries.

Ideologies aside, authoritarian politics have dominated the domestic scene. Competition over access to and control of state resources has nurtured an instrumental view of politics in which the public domain is seen as a channel for individual or partisan enrichment. Zero-sum patterns of interaction (one side's gain is another side's loss) have led to the muzzling of loyal oppositions and to an intolerance of dissenting opinions.

Under these conditions, the military has become an important mechanism for bringing about political change. Virtually every African state has been subjected to an attempted coup. The armed forces rule in almost half the states of the continent. At least a third of the countries in the Sub-Sahara have had several military takeovers. The move from civilian to military rule and back again has become an essential part of the rhythm of politics in postcolonial Africa. In some countries, however—Cameroon, Zambia, Kenya, Côte d'Ivoire, Botswana, Senegal, Malawi—the army has not taken over, and some have witnessed orderly political succession. Patterns of political transition, therefore, have varied widely.

Governmental capacities have not improved markedly during these years. In many countries, top-heavy administrations run by civilian or military leaders wield very little authority, and the power of their governmental institutions has

TABLE 1.1
Basic Economic Characteristics of African States

	Area (thousands of square kilometers)	Population (millions) 1984	GDP (millions of dollars) 1983	GNP per Capita Dollars 1984	GNP per Capita Annual Growth Rate 1965–84 (percent)	Distribution of GDP 1983 (percent) Agriculture	Industry	Manufacturing[a]	Services	Debt (millions of dollars) 1984	Debt-Service Ratio as Percentage of Exports of Goods and Services, 1984
Algeria	2,382	21.9b	58,180b	2,550b	3.6b	8b	48b	11b	43b	13,664.0	33.3b
Angola	1,247	8.4	n.a.	n.a.	n.a.	n.a.	n.a.	n.a.	n.a.	860.0	n.a.
Benin	113	3.9	930	270	1.0	40	14	n.a.	47	581.5	9.3b
Botswana	600	1.0	890	910	8.5	10	43	n.a.	48	276.1	3.8
Burkina Faso	274	6.6	930b	160	1.4	41	19	n.a.	40	407.5	8.7b
Burundi	28	4.6	1,020	220	2.1	58	16	11	26	334.4	7.5b
Cameroon	475	9.9	7,220	810	2.7	24	32	n.a.	45	1,737.9	8.9
Cape Verde	4	0.3b	n.a.	430b	5.0b	n.a.	n.a.	n.a.	n.a.	n.a.	n.a.
Central African Republic	623	2.5	600	270	0.1	37	21	8	42	224.4	11.7b
Chad	1,284	4.9	320b	n.a.	-2.3b	n.a.	n.a.	n.a.	n.a.	109.0	1.7
Comoros	2	0.5b	n.a.	240b	-0.3b	n.a.	n.a.	n.a.	n.a.	n.a.	n.a.
Congo, People's Republic of the	342	1.8	2,110	1,120	3.5	7	55	6	38	1,395.6	20.5b
Côte d'Ivoire	322	9.9	7,090	610	1.0	27	24	13	50	4,834.6	21.3
Djibouti	22	0.4b	n.a.	n.a.	n.a.	n.a.	n.a.	n.a.	n.a.	n.a.	n.a.
Egypt	1,001	48.5b	30,550b	610b	3.1b	20b	31	n.a.	49b	18,501.0b	33.6b
Equatorial Guinea	28	0.4b	n.a.	n.a.	n.a.	n.a.	n.a.	n.a.	n.a.	n.a.	n.a.
Ethiopia	1,222	42.0	4,270	110	0.5	48	16	11	36	1,384.2	13.8
Gabon	268	0.8	3,120	3,480	3.2	7	63	5	30	724.5	11.4
Gambia	11	0.7	220	260	1.4	27	14	n.a.	59	160.9	7.7b
Ghana	239	13.4	3,720	350	-2.1	53	7	4	40	1,122.5	13.2
Guinea	246	5.9	1,910	300	1.1	38	23	2	39	1,168.2	n.a.
Guinea-Bissau	36	0.9	145	180	-1.5b	43	11	n.a.	46	149.4	11.8b
Kenya	583	19.7	4,940	300	2.3	33	20	12	46	2,633.4	22.9

Lesotho	30	1.5	300b	530	6.3	23	22	6	55	134.3	5.0
Liberia	111	2.1	980	470	0.8	36	26	7	38	756.7	8.6
Libya	1,760	3.8b	25,420b	7,170b	-1.3b	4b	57b	5b	39b	n.a.	n.a.
Madagascar	587	9.7	2,850b	270	-1.2	41	15	n.a.	44	1,636.4	24.3b
Malawi	118	6.8	1,330	210	2.2	n.a.	n.a.	n.a.	n.a.	730.6	20.3b
Mali	1,240	7.3	980	140	1.2	46	11	n.a.	43	960.0	8.0
Mauritania	1,031	1.7	700	450	0.3	34	21	n.a.	45	1,170.6	10.0b
Mauritius	2	1.0	910	1,100	2.8	14b	25	17b	61	354.2	14.8
Morocco	447	21.9b	11,850b	560b	2.2b	18b	32b	n.a.	50b	n.a.	n.a.
Mozambique	802	13.4	n.a.	160	n.a.	35	11b	n.a.	53b	1,042.0	n.a.
Niger	1,267	6.3	1,340	190	-1.2	33	31	n.a.	37	677.9	18.3b
Nigeria	924	96.8	64,570	770	3.2	26	34	5	40	11,815.4	25.5
Rwanda	26	5.9	1,560	270	2.3	n.a.	n.a.	n.a.	n.a.	243.9	3.3
Sao Tome and Principe	1	0.1b	n.a.	320b	0.8b	n.a.	n.a.	n.a.	n.a.	n.a.	n.a.
Senegal	196	6.4	2,570	380	-0.5	21	26	17	54	1,555.1	7.2
Seychelles	(-)	0.7b	n.a.	n.a.	n.a.	n.a.	n.a.	n.a.	n.a.	n.a.	n.a.
Sierra Leone	72	3.7	950	300	1.1	32	20	5	48	341.6	n.a.
Somalia	638	5.2	1,540	260	-0.8c	50	11	6	39	1,233.0	28.9
South Africa	1,221	32.4b	67,710b	2,010b	1.1b	5b	45b	23b	50b	n.a.	n.a.
Sudan	2,506	21.5	6,850	340	1.3	34	15	8	51	5,658.9	11.0
Swaziland	17	0.7	n.a.	800	2.6	n.a.	n.a.	n.a.	n.a.	178.0	5.4
Tanzania	945	21.5	4,550	210	0.9	52	15	9	33	2,593.6	14.1
Togo	57	2.9	720	250	1.1	22	28	6	50	659.2	26.3
Tunisia	164	7.1b	7,240b	1,190b	4.0b	17	34b	14b	49b	4,688.0b	n.a.
Uganda	236	14.3	3,360b	230	-4.4c	n.a.	n.a.	n.a.	n.a.	675.1	21.1b
Zaire	2,345	30.6	5,440b	140	-1.3	36	20	2	44	4,083.7	7.7b
Zambia	753	6.5	3,350	470	-1.3	14	38	19	48	2,778.7	11.3
Zimbabwe	391	8.2	4,730	740	1.5	11	32	21	57	1,445.7	20.0

Sources: World Bank, *Financing Adjustment with Growth in Sub-Saharan Africa 1986–1990* (Washington, D.C.: World Bank, 1986); World Bank, *World Development Report 1987* (N.Y.: Oxford University Press, 1987).

a Manufacturing is part of the industrial sector, but its share of GDP is shown separately because it typically is the most dynamic part of the industrial sector.
b Figures are for years other than those specified.
c Figures are for 1965–1983, not 1965–1984.

TABLE 1.2
Basic Social Characteristics of African States

	Life Expectancy at Birth 1983 (years)	Annual Growth of Population (percentage) 1973–83	Percentage of Married Women of Childbearing Age Using Contraception 1982	Urban Population as Percentage of Total Population 1983	Population per Physician 1980	Population per Nursing Person 1980	Daily Calorie Supply per Capita as Percentage of Requirement 1982	Percentage of Male Primary Age Group Enrolled in School 1982	Percentage of Female Primary Age Group Enrolled in School 1982	Percentage of Secondary Age Group Enrolled in School 1982	Percentage of 20–24-Year-Olds Enrolled in Higher Education 1982
Algeria	61[a]	3.3[b]	7[a]	43[a]	n.a.	n.a.	n.a.	106[a]	83[a]	47[a]	6[c]
Angola	43	2.6	1[a]	23	n.a.	n.a.	87	146[a]	121[a]	12[a]	2[c]
Benin	48	2.8	18	16	16,980	1,660	101	87	42	21	2[a]
Botswana	61	4.5	29[a]	11	n.a.	n.a.	94	94	110	23	n.a.
Burkina Faso	44	1.9	1	2	48,510	4,950	79	28	16	3	1[a]
Burundi	47	2.2	1	2	45,020	7,310	95	41[a]	25[a]	25[a]	1[a]
Cameroon	54	3.1	11	39	13,990	1,950	91	117[a]	97[a]	19[a]	2[a]
Cape Verde	63[a]	n.a.	n.a.	n.a.	n.a.	n.a.	n.a.	n.a.	n.a.	n.a.	n.a.
Central African Republic	48	2.3	n.a.	44	26,750	1,740	97	92[a]	50[a]	14[a]	1[a]
Chad	43	2.1	1	20	47,640	3,860	68	n.a.	n.a.	3	(·)[a]
Comoros	55[a]	n.a.	n.a.	n.a.	n.a.	n.a.	n.a.	n.a.	n.a.	n.a.	n.a.
Congo, People's Republic of	63	3.1	n.a.	55	5,510	790	113	n.a.	n.a.	69[a]	6[a]
Côte d'Ivoire	52	4.6	3	44	n.a.	n.a.	115	92[a]	60[a]	17[a]	3[a]
Djibouti	48[a]	n.a.	n.a.	n.a.	n.a.	n.a.	n.a.	n.a.	n.a.	n.a.	n.a.
Egypt	61[a]	2.8[b]	32[a]	46[a]	760[a]	790[a]	n.a.	94	72[a]	58[a]	21[c]
Equatorial Guinea	45[a]	n.a.	n.a.	n.a.	n.a.	n.a.	n.a.	n.a.	n.a.	n.a.	n.a.
Ethiopia	47	2.7	2	15	69,390	5,910	93	60[a]	33[a]	12[a]	1[a]
Gabon	50	1.4	n.a.	39	3,030	n.a.	88	n.a.	n.a.	n.a.	n.a.
Gambia	36	3.6	5	30	12,310	1,770	86	71	41	16	n.a.
Ghana	59	3.1	10	38	7,160	770	68	85	66	34	1[a]
Guinea	37	2.0	1	26	17,110	2,570	86	44[a]	22[a]	16	3[a]
Guinea-Bissau	38	4.3	n.a.	26	8,840	980	68	119	57	15	(·)

Kenya	57	4.0	8	17	7,890	550	88	114	94	20[a]	1[a]
Lesotho	53	2.5	5	13	18,640	n.a.	100	95	129	20	2[a]
Liberia	49	3.3	n.a.	38	8,550	2,940	98	82[a]	50[a]	20[a]	2[a]
Libya	60[a]	3.9[b]	n.a.	60[a]	620[a]	360[a]	n.a.	n.a.	n.a.	n.a.	11[c]
Madagascar	49	2.6	n.a.	20	10,220	3,670	114	n.a.	n.a.	14[a]	3
Malawi	44	3.0	1	11	41,460	3,830	97	73[a]	51[a]	4[a]	()[a]
Mali	45	2.5	1	19	22,130	2,380	74	35[a]	20[a]	9[a]	()[a]
Mauritania	46	2.2	1	25	14,500	2,100	97	43[a]	23[a]	10[a]	n.a.
Mauritius	67	1.4	51	55	2,010	610	128	107	105	51	n.a.
Morocco	59[a]	2.5[b]	27[a]	44[a]	18,600[a]	900[a]	n.a.	97[a]	62[a]	31[a]	8[c]
Mozambique	46	2.6	1	17	39,140	5,610	79	119	72	6	()
Niger	45	3.0	1	14	38,790	4,650	105	29[a]	17[a]	5	()[a]
Nigeria	49	2.7	6	22	12,550	3,010	104	n.a.	n.a.	16[a]	3[a]
Rwanda	47	3.4	1	5	31,340	9,790	95	72	67	2	()[a]
Sao Tomé and Principe	65	n.a.	n.a.	n.a.	n.a.	n.a.	n.a.	n.a.	n.a.	n.a.	n.a.
Senegal	46[a]	2.8	4	34	13,780	1,390	101	58[a]	38[a]	12[a]	3
Seychelles	69	n.a.	n.a.	n.a.	n.a.	n.a.	n.a.	n.a.	n.a.	n.a.	n.a.
Sierra Leone	38[a]	2.1	4	23	17,520	2,040	85	n.a.	n.a.	12[a]	1[a]
Somalia	45	2.8	1	33	15,630	2,550	91	38[a]	21[a]	11[a]	1[a]
South Africa	55[a]	2.5[b]	n.a.	56[a]	n.a.	n.a.	n.a.	n.a.	n.a.	n.a.	n.a.
Sudan	48	3.2	5	20	8,930	1,430	96	61[a]	43[a]	18[a]	2[a]
Swaziland	55	3.4	n.a.	18	7,900	1,040	96	111	111	42	n.a.
Tanzania	51	3.3	1	14	17,740	3,010	101	101	95	3	()[a]
Togo	49	2.6	n.a.	22	18,100	1,430	94	129	84	27	2[a]
Tunisia	63	2.3	42[a]	56[a]	3,900[a]	950[a]	n.a.	127[a]	105[a]	32[a]	6[c]
Uganda	49	2.8	1[a]	7[a]	26,810	4,180	78	69	51	8	1[a]
Zaire	51	2.5	3	38	13,940	1,810	98	104[a]	75[a]	23[a]	1[a]
Zambia	51	3.2	1	47	7,670	1,730	89	102[a]	90[a]	16[a]	2[a]
Zimbabwe	56	3.2	22	24	5,900	940	89	134[a]	125[a]	23	1[a]

Source: World Bank, *Financing Adjustment with Growth in Sub-Saharan Africa 1986–1990* (Washington, D.C.: World Bank, 1986).

[a]Figures are for years other than those specified.
[b]Figures are for years 1980–1985.
[c]Figures are for percentage enrolled in higher education; no age group given.

remained weak. Instability—a surface expression of a more profound inability to maintain political control—is indeed a common theme throughout the post-colonial period. It should not, however, obscure important instances of stable government nor minimize the prevalence of efforts to form meaningful frameworks for political interchange.

Perhaps the greatest achievement of African states since independence has been the fact that they have endured. Even in cases of apparent collapse, most notably Chad and Uganda at the beginning of the 1980s, governmental structures have persisted.[2] But survival has frequently not meant enhanced political efficacy. In the mid-1980s, the most pressing political challenge facing African governments and citizens was to forge a *modus vivendi* between the wielders of state power and their subjects, to align government institutions more closely to socioeconomic processes, to regularize state-society relations.

The corollary of domestic political uncertainty has been greater external dependence on foreign powers and international economic agencies. The International Monetary Fund (IMF) and the World Bank have been involved in extensive operations to bail African as well as other economies out of their economic morass. But the price for this support has been the forfeiture (with some partial exceptions) of control over certain facets of economic decision making.

Under these conditions, the role of continental institutions has vacillated. The Organization of African Unity (OAU), an important pivot of inter-African relations in the late 1960s and 1970s, almost collapsed at the beginning of the 1980s. It is slowly being reorganized in an attempt to deal more directly with the problems of economic rehabilitation. As gross inequalities between African states have come to the fore, many efforts at regional cooperation have stumbled. The Economic Community of West African States (ECOWAS) was in some distress ten years after its creation in 1975. Its experiences, and those of other groupings such as the Southern African Development Coordination Conference (SADCC), suggest that the road to fruitful regional collaboration, however enticing, is still a long one.

The African world on the eve of the 1990s is thus quite different than that at mid-century. The common trends of economic adversity, political unrest, and external dependency have evoked a variety of responses and generated a great deal of experimentation. African politics have become "dehomogenized" in the process.[3] The rules of the political game in Nigeria, Kenya, Cameroon, Côte d'Ivoire, or Zambia differ from each other and from those in Botswana, Ethiopia, or Zaire. Some African countries have exhibited a remarkable stability (Côte d'Ivoire and Botswana, to name but two); others have been shaken by constant political turmoil (Uganda and Ghana). As the independence generation is slowly withdrawing from the political scene, the surface similarities of yesteryear are giving way to more readily apparent differences. The specific social makeup of each African state is putting its stamp on the politics of that country. In this sense, at least, an Africanization and localization of politics has begun to take place.

Common problems and experiences, therefore, should not obscure the fact that there is not one but many Africas. The continuity of separate heritages, coupled with different experiences and patterns of change, have worked to differentiate African states from one another.[4] Behind the general processes, therefore, it is possible to discern intricate variations that have developed over the years. We shall examine not only the achievements and failures of African politics but also the diverse political mechanisms that have evolved over the years.

■ APPROACHES TO THE STUDY OF AFRICAN POLITICS

It is clear that there is no consensus among analysts on how to probe the complex interconnections between politics and society in Africa. Old certainties on the relevance of legal, formal-institutional (legislatures, executives, parties, judiciaries), psychocultural, and purely historical frameworks have largely disappeared, seemingly inadequate and incomplete in their insight into the new hegemonic (monolithic, state-dominant) orders that gained ascendancy in most of Africa. Thus, social scientists have had little alternative but to undertake a search for new conceptual frameworks that would afford a fuller insight into the dynamic processes unfolding on the continent.

In broad terms, this quest has revolved around several well-defined approaches. The first, centered on the concept of *modernization,* emerged in the early 1960s. Echoing the heady mood of the initial years of independence, modernization theories presented a hopeful general framework of progressive development toward "modern" statehood, conceived largely in a Western mold. By the close of the decade, however, it was apparent that these notions were at best only a partial guide to understanding the political and economic conditions prevailing on the continent. The second approach—*dependency*—came to the fore in the 1970s. Preoccupied with explicating the causes of Africa's underdevelopment, studies grounded in dependency analysis highlighted the external constraints imposed on African societies and focused attention on emergent class conflict. As the somewhat grim and deterministic implications of dependency ideas became more explicit, as their theoretical limitations were realized, and as conditions in Africa reached crisis proportions, a third approach—the *statist*—gained currency. To comprehend the extent of the African malaise in the early 1980s, it became necessary to reassess the role of the state and to pinpoint the effects of political frailty and mismanagement.

At the present time an integrative tendency is beginning to take shape that seeks to bring together what has been proven to be useful in the modernization, dependency, and statist conceptual frameworks. It stresses the choices that policymakers and societal groups have made and the complex dynamics of their interaction. This framework, which we term *political choice,* utilizes appropriate ideas from a variety of contemporary thinkers and theories to forge an eclectic method for understanding the relations between the historical, political, social, and economic dimensions of the contemporary African experience. Our textbook is cast in this mold. By expanding the field of political vision beyond the formal and the visible to the interactive and dynamic, it offers additional insights into the rhythm of politics on the continent.

☐ The Modernization School

Early studies of African nationalism and African politics were written mostly from a modernization, or political development, perspective. The basic premise behind this approach was that African societies are in the process of becoming modern rational entities in which efficiency and scientific logic replace traditional values and belief systems. In economic terms, modernization was seen as commensurate with mechanization, rapid industrialization, and growth; in social terms, its goals were defined as increasing individual mobility, controlling the political importance of communal identities, and establishing procedures for equitable resource allocations. In political terms, modernization implied institutional expansion, the rationalization of the government apparatus, power concentration, some measure of political participation, and an augmentation of capacities in order to meet growing demands.[5] Modernization was seen as providing a foundation for African countries to achieve, first, some measure of stability and autonomy and, ultimately, a pattern of convergence with the Western industrialized world.

Modernization theories emanated from the West and were closely related to developments in U.S. political science in the 1950s. Its analysts assumed that a focus on transformation from traditional to modern environments would lead to a generalizable theory of political development. The concerns of many of the first works on African politics, therefore, centered on one or several of the six challenges of political development that were identified as facing countries in their attempt to achieve modernization.[6] The first challenge was defined as one of identity: fostering a common sense of purpose among culturally diffuse groups.[7] The second challenge was viewed as one of legitimacy: arriving at a consensus on the valid exercise of authority (the most visible instrument for legitimation, the political party, became the object of intense research).[8] The third was that of participation, the need to guide public demands for inclusion in the decision-making process into constructive—and controllable—channels. The fourth was one of penetration: the quest to secure an effective government presence throughout a given territory. The fifth challenge was one of distribution: balancing the public's demand for goods and services with the government's obligations to provide such general welfare objectives as economic growth, resource mobilization, and national defense.[9] The final challenge addressed in this literature was that of integration: the creation of a coherent set of relationships among the many groups and interests competing for access and control within the new state framework.

In the modernization perspective, the task of politics was to create the conditions for equitable growth by ensuring social quiescence and stable government. If African countries faltered on this path, then surely these shortcomings could be attributed either to poor judgment, to mistaken ideologies, to the conflict between competing goals, or to an inability to overcome cultural impediments deeply rooted in African societies. When, by the mid-1960s, it was abundantly clear that many of the objectives of the modernization vision were not being fulfilled, its upholders turned their attention to isolating the sources of political inefficiency, explicating contradictions in development processes, and examining the role of the military in the political arena. They engaged, at this juncture, in documenting the manifestations of political decay.[10]

Early studies of African politics varied widely, both in terms of quality and in terms of explanatory theories. Nevertheless, they had in common a tendency to favor domestic rather than external explanations for political occurrences, and sociocultural rather than structural and economic factors in political analysis (for this reason, they are sometimes referred to as pluralist approaches). The utility of the modernization models was, however, increasingly questioned in an Africa frustrated by its incapacity to maintain previous gains, let alone progress toward the desired goals of societal betterment.

Critiques of the modernization school have clustered around several key themes. First, studies conducted within this framework could account for only a segment of the realities they sought to convey. Emphasis on industrialization, theoretically of some interest, seemed of peripheral relevance given the central role that agriculture plays in African economic life. Social change and education are undoubtedly important targets, but once again, the focus on these issues tended to overlook the ongoing roles of traditional institutions and norms. Although parties were a part of the transition to independence, more vital aspects of that political era, especially processes of bureaucratization, were frequently neglected. Social currents, inequalities, and conflicts were often glossed over. These theories of political development may, therefore, have fostered misplaced emphases and failed to reflect many crucial processes taking place on the ground.

A second set of criticisms, no less compelling, has related to the priorities built into these theories. The stress on economic growth, without a concomitant delineation of the beneficiaries of this economic activity, was subjected to severe scrutiny by the late 1960s. The bias toward equilibrium and harmony was similarly challenged. The tendency of some development theories to support elitist and status quo orientations was found to be particularly troubling.[11] And the supposition that the Western model of development was both feasible and desirable smacked of a type of arrogance not easily acceptable in countries that had only recently emerged from a period of colonial rule.

A third series of criticisms revolved around the tools of analysis generated by scholars of political development. Few instruments were designed to examine how transformations could take place or to evaluate the implications of ongoing processes. Thus, many analyses were extremely static. The external context of African politics was virtually overlooked. Issues critical to Africans, such as racial justice, pan-Africanism, negritude, and socialism, were not treated with the degree of seriousness that they deserve.[12]

In retrospect, however, modernization theories did provide a significant foundation for the analysis of postcolonial African politics. They helped to identify some of the principal problems faced by African political systems and nurtured a series of basic works on the dilemmas of independence.[13] But by the late 1960s, it became painfully apparent that these approaches, centered as they were on the achievement of ideal goals, could not keep up with the rapid and problematic pace of events in Africa. At the beginning of the second decade of independence, the search for alternative conceptual frameworks—overviews more likely to provide a challenge to an increasingly unacceptable status quo—became inevitable.

☐ The Dependency and Underdevelopment Schools

Theories of dependency and underdevelopment came into vogue as a reaction to the premises and the sources of political development theory and were based on the opposite assumption that African progress has been, and continues to be, impeded by forces (international and/or domestic) bent on the ongoing exploitation of the continent and its resources. These, primarily capitalist, interests could only be held at bay if the global system underwent a fundamental change that would alter the structural relations between the Third World and the industrialized world (underdevelopment) or between the masses and the dominant classes within Africa (dependency). Thus, in stark contrast to the modernization approach, these theorists have focused not on the process of development but on the roots of underdevelopment. They have shunned what they claimed to be empty objectivity in favor of an avowedly committed and activist approach and have rejected the seeming benevolence that underlay modernization analysis. They have asserted that if Africans have remained impoverished, then this condition is a result of circumstances that have enabled others to benefit at their expense.

Underdevelopment theory originated in Latin America and mirrored the Third World concerns of its designers. Dependency approaches, which contain an underdevelopment component, were rooted in neo-Marxist political theory. The tools employed by this school were quite different than those developed by the pluralists. In the first place, these studies adopted a purposefully historical perspective in an effort to trace unequal relations within Africa and between the continent and the rest of the world over time. Second, the units of analysis of the dependency and underdevelopment approaches were not the individual and the state but classes and/or the global system. Third, these studies were concerned primarily—but by no means exclusively—with the political economy. Economic structure and economic trends were highlighted, and the object of analysis moved more squarely to material matters such as trade relations, capital flows, and modes and relations of production. Finally, these analyses began with an assumption of inequality and disequilibrium. They sought to uncover the sources and illuminate the manifestations of Africa's scarcity in these terms.

In this view, the beginnings of Africa's systematic impoverishment were linked to imperialism, which, these analysts posit, not only brought Africa into the global economy but did so in a structurally unequal manner. Colonial economic policies perpetuated this institutionalized vulnerability to external economic trends and constrained the freedom of movement of Africa's new leaders on the eve of independence. [14]

Much attention has been given to the economic factors that continue to delimit Africa's options. In brief, the present pattern of global economic relations results in asymmetrical exchange: The benefits of these ties are shared unequally between core (the industrialized center of the world economy) and periphery (the less-industrialized countries of the Third World). Because of the superior information, technological know-how, wealth, and market advantages at its disposal, the core remains at a decided advantage in its exchange encounters with the African countries in the periphery.

The question of change is consequently central to dependency theory. For Immanuel Wallerstein, "it is not possible theoretically for all states to 'develop simultaneously.'"[15] In his opinion, because global relations are closed and rigorously structured, if one country or area advances, then the progress of others must, perforce, be impeded. Economic prospects in today's world may be less predetermined than such an approach would admit. Writers imbued in the more classical Marxist tradition, in which much of dependency theory is ensconced, have suggested that capitalism is still an important precondition for the emergence of socialism and that capitalist global and domestic relations are therefore a necessary, if painful, step in the process of transformation.

Whatever their approach to change, dependency and underdevelopment theorists have viewed politics as a reflection of global and economic relations. Explanations for political actions have been couched in historical and material terms. Political analyses shifted from the domestic to the international and from the idiosyncratic to the structural. In contrast to pluralist approaches, then, dependency and underdevelopment theories present politics in terms of resources and control rather than management.

Dependency theory has furnished potent insights into the nature of constraints on African development. Its vitality lies, first and foremost, in the importance it attributes to external factors in the explication of Africa's present predicament. By highlighting international structural variables, dependency analysts have placed specific policy actions in proper perspective. The second strength of this approach rests in its insistence on studying politics within a socioeconomic context. It has effectively outlined some historical, economic, and external limitations that operate in the African political environment. Third, dependency and underdevelopment theories have, relentlessly and accurately, illuminated the premise of inequality that underlies African political activity. Such theories have, therefore, added important dimensions to the analysis of African politics, even if they have not been accepted as a guiding theoretical framework, but have succumbed to severe criticisms from both Marxist and non-Marxist scholars.

The first weakness of underdevelopment theory (but not necessarily of its dependency counterpart) stems from the uniformity it imposed on the study of contemporary Africa. The distinction between exploiters and exploited, core and periphery, good and evil, did not always permit refined analyses of variations, degrees, and specific trends and patterns. Dependency scholars, in response to such criticism, spawned a growing literature on the meaning of various kinds of bourgeoisies. Studies of the peasantry came into vogue.[16] Arguments about precapitalist, capitalist, and mixed modes of production raged. But insufficient attention was devoted to the determined nationalism of many African leaders, to the ongoing significance of ethnicity, or to the intricacies of the political upheavals that engaged the continent during the course of the 1970s and 1980s. As a result, even the analysis of foreign relations frequently lacked finesse: There developed an inability to identify the changing patterns of links between African states and specific countries in the industrialized world. Thus, although it highlighted previously neglected factors in the study of African politics, dependency theory nevertheless remained aloof from many of the significant processes taking place on the continent. Its adherents' grasp of African realities was as skewed, albeit for very different reasons, as that of the modernization writers whom they treated with such contempt.

A second major difficulty with the dependency and underdevelopment schools relates directly to their assessments of African futures. While it successfully dispelled the false optimism of the modernization approach, dependency theory has been almost uniformly pessimistic in its evaluation of the prospects for the continent (an anomaly, given the reformist thrust of its practitioners). In this view, Africa is entrapped in a morass not of its own making, and from which it is virtually incapable of extricating itself.[17] Barring revolution or total global structural transformation, dependency theory provided precious few indications of possible guidelines for action in local arenas. By dichotomizing conflicts and envisaging outcomes in static terms this mode of thinking has had the effect of limiting choice, even at the margins.

A third criticism stems directly from the fact that underdevelopment notions are fundamentally atheoretical and also, quite surprisingly, apolitical. Dependency ideas possess greater explanatory power but have sacrificed a close study of ongoing events and processes in favor of debates over theory. African political processes are external in their derivation, execution, and implications. By removing autonomy from African actors, this approach inevitably stymies analytic growth and forecloses further inquiry. In this respect, the work of some dependency analysts, returning to more detailed research in the Marxist mold, has remained closer to the African experience.[18]

Hence, for quite different reasons and in very different ways, both the dependency and underdevelopment schools, although pointing to significant trends, have been unable either to advance significantly the understanding of the complexities of Africa's present predicament or to trace accurately the dynamics of the processes the continent is undergoing in the 1980s.

☐ The Statist School

Both the underdevelopment and the modernization schools have undergone considerable internal revision since the late 1970s. The pluralists have taken external and historical factors into consideration in their analyses, underdevelopment scholars have become more sensitized to the importance of internal sociocultural forces, and dependency theorists have moved from abstract debates to the application of models in the field.[19] By the late 1970s, therefore, both Marxist and liberal researchers, working from parallel, albeit inverted, paradigms, made an attempt to reorient their work so that it would focus more squarely on specific processes occurring within Africa. They were joined by a group of (mostly African) scholars who concentrated on studying African events from an African nationalist point of view.[20] These efforts began to yield a wealth of new material that, significantly, converged on one central point: the importance of the state and state actions in grasping the roots of the political and economic crises of the third decade of independence. What has emerged as a result is the beginnings of a third, coldly realistic and Africa-centric, school of analysis.

In the statist approach to the study of African politics, the state is viewed as a primary motor force behind social and economic occurrences on the continent, and state leaders are held responsible for the political and economic deterioration of the early 1980s. Unlike its predecessors, the modernization and dependency schools, and in contrast to ongoing materialist studies, this school has broken out of existing molds and placed political factors at the center of investigation and analysis. For scholars working within this framework, state structures are the key to coming to grips with contemporary African processes.

Those writing in this mode have concentrated on studying the state apparatus, its expansion, its uses (and abuses) of power, and its relations with domestic groups and the international economy.[21] They have presumed that the state is more than a descriptive entity; that it is an actor with interests, capacities, achievements and, of course, frailties. These analysts do see the postcolonial state as autonomous, at least to some extent, and hence as an entity in its own right.

Political scientists working within this framework have sought to uncover the characteristics of African states in the independence period. They have studied patterns of institutionalization, examined leadership styles, and devoted a great deal of attention to isolating the mechanisms of patron-client relations and identifying patterns of personal rule. The trends highlighted by writers in this school are of no mean consequence: The gradual enfeeblement of the state apparatus in many parts of Africa has been noted, as have the repressive predilections that have accompanied the reduction of systemic power.

The concept of politics that emerges from these studies is extremely instrumental. Power holders, it is claimed, have created structures of domination that have enabled them to misuse their offices to reap personal gains at the expense of the pressing needs of the bulk of the population. If Africa is undergoing a process of impoverishment, then the leaders of the new states bear much of the blame for this state of affairs. The food crisis of the early 1980s, the debt crisis of the middle of the decade, and the ensuant crisis of governability are the outcome of an extractive view of politics that has guided African ruling classes for over a generation.[22] The neopatrimonial statists have thus combined the domestic emphasis of modernization theory and elements of the structural and external analysis of dependency theory to depict a view of Africa that is simultaneously well documented and brutal.

The main contribution of the statist approach has been its stress on the inner workings of power politics within Africa. Nevertheless, the structural statist framework has not been able to come to terms with some issues that are central to its overall thrust. The definition and conceptualization of the state has proven to be elusive, and the distinction between it and specific governments frequently confused. State-society relations have not been studied with the precision they warrant. The relationship between state and class, especially when the state is in disrepair, is still obscure. What is more problematic is that the emphasis on personal rule and systems of domination has hampered a close analysis of the role of the state in the actual (and not just the formal) political economy. The limits of state power have yet to be defined and its relative significance adequately assessed.

The statist approach has, therefore, somewhat ironically, highlighted the external supports and the personal character of the postcolonial African state at the expense of a closer analysis of state organization and interactions. Although patrimonial relations and authority structures have been scrutinized at some length, the connection between public institutions and specific social groups has yet to be fully explored. Indeed, statist analysts have generated innovative and significant questions; their somewhat deterministic outlooks do not shed much light on African trends in the years to come.

The focus on the state in patrimonial terms just when the state in Africa may be undergoing significant changes highlights a problem common to all schools of political analysis in Africa: the propensity of political scientists to employ a top-down approach to the study of politics on the continent. Political processes and political conflicts have been interpreted as revolving exclusively around the formal state structures, either separately or in their international context. Politics in Africa, however, cannot be reduced so easily to the activities of actors on the national scene. State institutions intersect with nonformal structures; social organizations relate, or do not interact, with governments depending on changing conditions; and power constellations are not entirely state-centric. A new synthesis, which builds upon the strengths of previous approaches and, at the same time, goes beyond the weaknesses they have exhibited, has slowly begun to take shape.

■ THE POLITICAL CHOICE FRAMEWORK

This synthesis, which casts the political net widely to capture the choices that people actually do face, goes beyond the limitations of existing schools of thought, each of which contains important insights developed at various points in Africa's recent history, and attempts to concentrate more directly on the complex processes and factors at work on the continent.[23] We call this analytic framework, which is by no means a separate school, a political choice perspective.

This framework presumes that the state-society relationship is central to understanding the political dynamic of Africa today. Individuals and governments are constrained by a variety of demographic, technological, ideological, global, historical, and social factors. Changing conditions define available options at any given historical moment.[24] It is within this range that decisions are made, not only by political leaders and state officials, but also by external actors and domestic social organizations. By looking at the interaction of social forces, economic activities, formal institutions, and prevalent values, we may better grasp the meaning and direction of the diverse patterns that have evolved in Africa since independence.

The political choice approach, therefore, focuses on identifying the multiple factors at work on the African political scene and tracing their diverse dynamics over time. Those adopting this perspective commence their inquiry with an examination of the key components of African politics, assuming that its sphere is far broader than the formal state domain and the international state system. Official institutions, as in the statist approach, are, indeed, significant actors, but so, too, are individuals, social groups, traditional authority structures, trading networks, and multinational corporations. The study of the interests, organization, and capacities of these entities affords a better view of the processes by which they interrelate. Political competition encompasses struggles over material and normative resources, over identity and interests, over institutions and symbols. Power—the capacity to control these valued goods—and authority—the right to do so—may legitimately be vested in a variety of structures. Power vectors and the search for empowerment take on different meanings in this context. Structure and process are a precondition for understanding outcomes: economic policies and circumstances, social dynamics, and foreign relations. By studying the many dimensions of political interaction and modes of interchange, it may be possible to trace more accurately shifting political patterns in Africa and their ramifications for social and economic processes and political options in the years to come.

In the political choice framework, political factors account for many social and economic realities but are themselves informed by historical, demographic, cultural, ecological, ideological, and international factors. Politics are, therefore, perceived as interactive, the manifestation of the exercise of choice by multiple actors within existing parameters. This perspective, unlike the managerial view of the modernization school, the exploitative emphasis of dependency approaches, and the instrumental notions of statist writers, highlights the fluidity of politics and attempts to trace the vacillating political course. Thus, although this research strategy may help to account, together with existing theories, for the changing fortunes of many countries on the continent through its focus on the diversity of civil society, it is less concerned with assessing the reasons for past errors than with uncovering the components of ongoing processes and elucidating future opportunities and constraints.

☐ The Constraints upon Choice

The world of African politics and political choice is delimited by constraints imposed by the environment and history. Some of the most fundamental limitations to which African countries are subject arise from their geographical location in the tropics. Tropical climates affect all parts of Africa except the Republic of South Africa and the Mediterranean countries north of the Sahara. As Andrew Kamarck suggests, Sub-Saharan Africa may be divided into three distinct tropical climatic zones.[25] A belt of wet tropical climates extends across the coastal states of the Gulf of Guinea through Zaire to the highlands of Uganda and Kenya; it also includes parts of the coasts of Kenya, Mozambique, and Tanzania. These areas usually have annual rainfalls of between 75 and 120 inches (187 and 300 cm) per year; rain typically falls in all months. Constant heat and extreme humidity are common. In contrast, a dry tropical climatic belt stretches across the continent from Mauritania to northern Sudan. Here, rainfall is irregular at best and insufficient to support agriculture. Between these two belts is a zone (from Gambia through Somalia) characterized by alternate wet and dry climates: There is considerable variation within this zone, not only between different areas, but also from one year to the next. Unpredictability, in fact, is one of the principal characteristics of all tropical climates and one of their major constraining features. Rainfall from one year to the next frequently varies by as much as 300 percent and typically falls in torrents in concentrated periods; occasionally, no rain comes at all.

No place in these three zones of Sub-Saharan Africa, except the highest mountain ranges, experiences frost—nature's great executioner. In consequence, pests and diseases proliferate. Fungi are a particularly acute agricultural problem given the humid climate. African countries are frequently victims of locust plagues. Tsetse flies not only have prevented the introduction of cattle and of animal traction in many parts of the continent but also carry the deadly disease trypanosomiasis (a principal form of which is sleeping sickness). This illness debilitates victims, prevents individuals from engaging in sustained strenuous activity, and eventually results in early death. Other diseases to which African populations are particularly vulnerable include malaria, schistosomiasis (a parasitic infestation with approximately 200 million sufferers), onchocerciasis (river blindness, from which approximately 20 million suffer), leprosy (which affects 4 million people in Africa), and, most recently, AIDS, especially in East and Central Africa. In all these cases, attempts at eradication have made few inroads into the incidence of the diseases, all of which considerably reduce the human productive potential of the continent.

A further ecological constraint on Africa's development is poor tropical soils. Rich soil is dependent upon living organisms to provide humus. In tropical climates the heat of the sun tends to kill these organisms. Heavy tropical rains destroy the particle structure of the topsoil, which is then eroded by strong winds. As a result, the main plant foods in the soil are removed, leaving a clay (laterite) that hardens on exposure to air and sun. In many parts of Africa the soil is inadequate to sustain permanent agriculture.

Proliferation of pests and diseases has inhibited attempts to improve African livestock and plants through crossbreeding with imports from overseas (which have proved to be especially vulnerable to local disease). The multitude of species and of climatic zones has also made agricultural research more difficult than has been the case in temperate areas, which enjoy greater uniformity of soils and climates. Africans, then, are faced by ecological constraints that are far more severe than those in most Western countries.

Africa has traditionally been a continent of sparse population. This has had a profound impact on its economic evolution. Most economic historians are agreed that population pressure has been an enormously important factor in stimulating invention and new modes of productive activity. In most parts of Africa until the last quarter of this century land has been plentiful, and population pressure provided little stimulus toward an agricultural revolution. This demographic pattern has also had a profound impact on economic and political structures. Many African countries remain—by Western European and Asian standards—underpopulated. Distances between settlements are great, which increases the costs of delivery of government services and communications. Underpopulation also means that domestic markets in most countries are small (the principal exception is Nigeria, with its population of approximately 100 million; only five other black African countries—Ethiopia, Kenya, Sudan, Tanzania, and Zaire—have populations in excess of 15 million).

Yet, although the continent's total population is relatively low, the population growth rate is the highest in the world. Improved health care has greatly reduced infant mortality, but families have failed to respond by reducing the number of children that they desire. The average African woman will bear seven children. Population grew in black Africa in the period from 1970 to 1982 by 2.8 percent per year; in the period since then, the average population growth has risen to 3.3 percent per year, a figure that the World Bank projects will be maintained for the remainder of this century. Aggregate figures obscure significant differences across the continent: Some countries are already experiencing dramatically higher rates of growth. In Kenya, for instance, the population is growing at more than 4 percent annually, with the consequence that the country's total population will double every fifteen years. In order merely to sustain existing levels of per capita incomes, African economies will have to achieve exceptionally high rates of economic growth.

☐ Historical Inheritance

The constraints of the environment have been compounded by those of history. The newly independent states of Africa, despite their many differences, shared a common and troubled inheritance at the point of transition from colonial rule. The first, most obvious, and profound characteristic of Africa on the eve of independence was the artificiality of its political boundaries. The political map of present-day Africa was carved out by European countries during the scramble for Africa in the late nineteenth and early twentieth centuries. Since the European powers assembled at the Congress of Berlin in 1884–1885 to delineate spheres of influence and lay down the ground rules for imperial expansion, the political frontiers of Africa have undergone only minor adjustments. The African state system is hence a product of external logic, and it reflects the ambitions and capabilities of European powers rather than any geographical or social realities of the African continent.

African countries vary drastically in terms of their economic resource base, demographic composition, and potential for development. Chad and Mali, for example, are sparsely populated, landlocked states containing large stretches of desert; they do not have the access to the sea, the strong population concentrations, or the vibrant local economies of Angola or Côte d'Ivoire. Tiny Gambia cannot but be affected by the shadow of its larger neighbor, Senegal. In Burkina Faso, poverty prevails, whereas mineral-rich Gabon boasts the highest per capita income in the Sub-Sahara. These units are the uneasy products of arbitrary foreign considerations.

The second shared legacy of Africa on the eve of independence is associated with the first: The new states of Africa contain a multiplicity of societies whose institutions predate the colonial intrusion. The indigenous African inheritance is a rich one. The great empires of Ghana, Mali, and Songhai in the western Sudan flourished during the medieval period and controlled the trans-Saharan trade routes for many centuries. At the same time, in southern Africa political authority was sufficiently centralized to oversee the construction of the magnificent stone edifices of Zimbabwe. Migrants from the Nile Valley established the early lacustrine kingdoms in East Africa, and the Hausa city-states of northern Nigeria were already well in place before Europeans first reached the African coast. More centralized entities proliferated in the sixteenth and seventeenth centuries: the forest states of West Africa (most notably Asante,

Dahomey, Oyo, and Benin), the Kongo empire, the Lozi and Barotse states in Central Africa, and the Mwenomutapa in present-day Mozambique.

When the Europeans arrived in Africa, they encountered indigenous states alongside well-organized segmentary societies with no overarching leadership structures (for example the Kikuyu and the Igbo). These groups had long-established patterns of interaction within their own cultural settings and with their more elaborately structured neighbors. The colonial conquest disrupted these flows. The new boundaries not only divided existing political entities but, more significant, compelled groups that frequently had no history of ongoing ties to relate to each other. The very plural composition of the colonial units was, in many instances, subsequently nurtured by the administration. As a result, African states at independence were socially amorphous; the structures of the colonial state superseded but did not displace the complex social, cultural, and political institutions of indigenous Africa.

The continuity of African institutions need not, however, obscure certain important influences of the colonial presence. The third historical constraint on African countries on the eve of independence was the burden of economic weakness. Colonial rule was accompanied by the systematic introduction of economic changes. Cash cropping altered the agricultural base of African economies. Although most rural dwellers continued to produce for subsistence needs and local markets, farmers began to grow for export as well. Groundnuts in Senegal, cotton in northern Nigeria, sisal in Tanganyika, cocoa in the Gold Coast and western Nigeria, tea and coffee in Kenya and Uganda brought African producers into the cash economy. The transformation of rural Africa came together with the growth of urban services, transportation facilities, and petty manufacturing. The colonial economies were, however, malintegrated. Heavy investments in the small export sector came at the expense of the under-developed and largely ignored indigenous economies in which most Africans operated. Taxation, forced labor, and a variety of levies affected virtually everyone. Those outside the money economy felt the economic strain of colonial rule but did not always share in its benefits. At the termination of the colonial era, economic resources—human, capital, technological—were still scarce. These constraints were accompanied, at the end of the phase of direct foreign administration, by the additional onus of severe structural inequalities.

African economies at the end of the colonial period were not only weak, they were also exposed. The fourth legacy for Africa at this conjuncture was a history of external dependence. The conquest of Africa in the nineteenth century underlined the continent's global vulnerability. Its uneven development in the early part of the twentieth century reflected the concerns of external economic interests and colonial administrators. During the brief period of colonial domination, African territories were first brought into the world economy and then systematically subordinated to the needs of the industrialized north. The colonial experience rendered African economies particularly open to external shocks. Political independence did not alleviate this external reliance. Decolonization marked the termination of responsibility for the day-to-day affairs of African territories; it by no means implied the cessation of foreign influence. The new states of Africa were, and in most instances still are, internationally weak. They have little room to maneuver in the global arena. Like all weak states, they suffered, to one degree or another, from an inability to design their futures independent of foreign considerations.

This external dependence was compounded by a fifth inheritance: the creation within African states of a small, Western-educated elite quite distinct from the bulk of the population. Colonialism came to Africa together with Christianity and formal education. Each colonial power, in its own way, developed a local stratum that could provide the personnel necessary to carry out the imperatives of rule. Educational institutions helped to transmit much-needed skills and to lay the foundations for the development of human resources capable of managing the multiple needs of societies in the process of rapid change. Colonial education, although introducing new criteria for social mobility, was highly selective. In French West Africa, postprimary education was the domain of a select few. In Ghana, which boasted some of the finest educational institutions in Africa, over 70 percent of the population was illiterate on the eve of independence. The Belgian Congo (today Zaire) barely had any university graduates when Belgian authorities withdrew hastily in 1960.

Those Africans fortunate enough to acquire a Western education were drawn to the colonial center and subsisted on its margins. Many became the core of the postcolonial civil service. Others established positions in business and the professions. They enjoyed European salaries and life-styles. It is not insignificant that they were disproportionately represented in the anticolonial movements that proliferated after World War II. The new elites were the direct inheritors of the colonial mantle. They were, however, too few to have a forceful impact on their surroundings, too different to have strong roots in their society, and too bound to Western institutions to undertake a significant transformation of their environment. In the social realm, much as in the economic, the colonial experience offered new opportunities while simultaneously curtailing the prospects for their realization.

This pattern was especially pronounced in the political and administrative spheres. The sixth historical legacy for African countries at independence was the fragility of their state institutions. The colonial framework was not only alien, it was also underdeveloped. The administrative apparatus of the colonial state was the minimum necessary to ensure a semblance of control. The British, French, Belgian, and Portuguese authorities, in very different ways, encouraged an institutional dualism that has in many cases survived to the present day. Mechanisms for the extraction of resources were refined, those for distribution rudimentary. Military and police forces were everywhere carefully elaborated as instruments of rule; participation in political life was actively discouraged. Thus, although the colonial state was highly centralized, its apparatus was not necessarily suited to the needs of independence.

At independence, African countries also shared a seventh, and particularly burdensome, inheritance: the absence of a constructive political culture.[26] Colonial rule, although it varied in intensity, severity, and intrusiveness from one part of Africa to another, was fundamentally authoritarian. Government was imposed but not shared, hortatory rather than consultative. In French-speaking West Africa and throughout most of English-speaking Africa, where the transition to independence was relatively smooth, Western-styled democratic constitutions were designed on the eve of the transfer of power. These efforts to democratize Africa stood in stark contrast to the authoritarian patterns of government laid down under colonial rule. They were also made just as protest against foreign domination peaked. Many of the leaders of the anticolonial movements were not allowed the time to guide their followers through the complex move from defiance to construction.

The task of these leaders was further complicated by the fact that they stood at the head of relatively weak parties that had only recently been established. Not one major governing party at independence had been formed prior to World War II. If the colonial administrative apparatus evoked resistance, the new parties provided quite feeble alternative rallying points. Only in those areas where the struggle against colonialism had been prolonged and violent—Algeria, Kenya and later Guinea-Bissau, Mozambique, Angola, and Rhodesia (Zimbabwe)—did the anticolonial movements strike deeper roots in their societies. In many of these cases, however, the attainment of independence was abrupt and unplanned; it took place in countries deeply divided in the course of the decolonization process. Thus, the national and institutional bonds that linked people together on the eve of independence were tenuous at best.

The final aspect of the continent's historical legacy lies in the psychological realm. The collective memory of colonialism was one of humiliation: political, cultural, moral, economic, social, and physical.[27] This sentiment gave rise to the organized backlash against foreign rule; it also captured the hopes associated with the achievement of sovereignty.

The inheritance of the past left the new entities on the continent with severe constraints. It is within this context that the options available to African governments, social groups, regional organizations, and international agencies must be understood. It is also within this framework that the selection of strategies must be examined and their implications assessed. On this basis, it is possible to identify diverse processes and to venture explanations for these differences.

☐ The Selection of Strategies

At independence, individual Africans, social groups, and government agencies had to deal simultaneously with the need to define their identities, consolidate their positions, assure their access to resources, interact with each other, delimit the parameters of their autonomy, augment their productive capacities, and confront the outside world. Although communities and institutions, leaders and citizens, producers and managers brought different tools to bear on these nearly overwhelming tasks and often had contradictory objectives in mind, they all shared in the ongoing effort to find ways to adjust to changing and uncertain circumstances. How did they meet these separate challenges, with what results, and with what implications? How did social and political actors organize to grapple with these issues? What rules did they devise to regulate their interaction? How, in fact, did they interrelate? How have these patterns affected economic production and distribution? What have been the consequences for Africa's position in the global arena?

In order to elucidate the choices that Africans have made, it is necessary to look at both the frameworks and the activities of governance. We shall detail the precise social constellations that exist in particular settings (ethnic, geographic, religious, cultural, occupational, and voluntary), the prevalent modes of economic production and exchange, political and ideological predilections embedded in concrete social configurations, prevailing attitudes and norms, and linkages. Likewise, we examine the main features of political institutions, their inner workings, and their relations with concrete social groups and economic forces. On this basis, the impediments placed on political action are specified, as are the areas for political manipulation and choice.

Using this approach, we then examine ongoing processes. Key questions include: What resources are obtained, produced, by whom and why? How are they distributed? What are the rules that govern these decisions? What are the resulting structures of power? What type of social organization is associated with specific patterns? How do culture and ideology reflect and influence these political processes? What is the nature of conflict and cooperation? What is the direction of flow between the activities of groups, institutions, and societies, both formally and informally?[28]

Answers to these questions help to illuminate policy directions and consequences. The selection of development strategies, survival mechanisms, and the connections between domestic production and the global economy can be explored. So, too, can the links between African countries and their shifting positions in the international arena.

By refocusing analysis on state-society ties in terms of ongoing and shifting relations, this approach is avowedly inductive (in contrast to the top-down propensities of existing theories). By utilizing various levels of analysis, it incorporates the local community, the state, and the international arena within a single framework. By shifting the object of analysis to the organization and modes of interchange, it may help to shed further light on the content of political processes. And by disaggregating the forces involved, it may add to the understanding of the variety contained in present-day Africa.

The political choice method thus represents a mixture of the modernizers' stress on the challenges to the political system posed by economic and social change; of the emphasis placed by writers within the underdevelopment and dependency schools on the constraints that the world economy places on African governments and on the effects of particular development strategies on social inequalities; and, finally, of the statists' concern with the importance of the state's political and economic role in contemporary African politics. It also relies unabashedly on insights furnished by historical studies of modern Africa, by anthropological analyses of social organization and cultural meaning, and by economic research on resource availability, distribution, and utilization. This perspective is therefore multidisciplinary in conception and multilayered in design.

In this book, we explore the diversity of present-day Africa in terms of constraints, possibilities, and alternatives, recognizing the fact that the parameters of choice since independence have been limited. Economic scarcity, fragile institutions, ambiguous power networks, structural dependency, and gross inequalities have severely circumscribed the range of maneuverability within the African political domain. Nevertheless, political occurrences reflect what people chose to do in a world not of their own making. They also shed light on the persistent search for relevant and effective ways of preserving human dignity and forwarding the quest for meaningful development. Political choice thus highlights the challenges inherent in the African world of the 1980s: the need to exercise imagination and ingenuity in unraveling priorities and designing options for societies under pressure. The dynamics of power in Africa have been recalcitrant to existing conceptual approaches. The new synthetic perspective offered in these pages is built on substantial research; with it, we seek to extend the understanding of Africa since independence.

The attempt to come to terms with the constraints and diversity of African political processes is at the heart of this undertaking. Heterogeneity and complexity in conditions of uncertainty have marked the recent history of the continent. This theme underlies key events and patterns and provides the critical framework within which ongoing processes are unfolding. The difficult and compelling realities of Africa furnish the subject matter and the challenge facing the continent and its inhabitants on the eve of the twenty-first century.

■ NOTES

1. An excellent overview may be found in Richard Sandbrook, *The Politics of Africa's Economic Stagnation* (Cambridge: Cambridge University Press, 1985), esp. pp. 1–62.

2. Robert H. Jackson and Carl G. Rosberg, "Why Africa's Weak States Persist: The Empirical and the Judicial in Statehood," *World Politics* 35, no. 1 (1982): 1–25, offer external explanations for this durability. More recently, other interpretations have been suggested. See Donald Rothchild and Naomi Chazan, eds., *The Precarious Balance: State and Society in Africa* (Boulder, Colo.: Westview Press, 1988).

3. Roger Charlton, "Dehomogenising the Study of African Politics—The Case of Inter-State Influence on Regime Formation and Change," *Plural Societies* 14, no. 1/2 (1983): 32–48.

4. Richard Hodder-Williams, *An Introduction to the Politics of Tropical Africa* (London: George Allen and Unwin, 1984), is insistent on this point.

5. For some overviews of this literature, see Richard A. Higgott, *Political Development Theory: The Contemporary Debate* (London: Croom Helm, 1983), and Samuel P. Huntington, "The Change to Change: Modernization, Development and Politics," *Comparative Politics* 4, no. 3 (1971): 55–79. For a critical discussion, see Irene L. Gendzier, *Managing Political Change: Social Scientists and the Third World* (Boulder, Colo.: Westview Press, 1985).

6. Leonard Binder et al., *Crises and Sequences in Political Development* (Princeton, N.J.: Princeton University Press, 1971). In this text, the term "challenges" is preferred to "crises."

7. For two examples, see Ronald Cohen and John Middleton, eds., *From Tribe to Nation in Africa: Studies in Incorporation Processes* (Scranton, Pa.: Chandler Publishing, 1970), and Leo Kuper and M. G. Smith, eds., *Pluralism in Africa* (Berkeley: University of California Press, 1971).

8. For a good summary of this literature, see Aristide Zolberg, *Creating Political Order: The Party States of West Africa* (Chicago: Rand McNally, 1966).

9. For one example, see Roger Genoud, *Nationalism and Economic Development in Ghana* (New York: Praeger, 1969).

10. This term was promulgated by Samuel Huntington. See his *Political Order in Changing Societies* (New Haven: Yale University Press, 1968) and "Political Development and Political Decay," *World Politics* 17, no. 3 (1965): 386–430.

11. See Huntington, *Political Order in Changing Societies,* for one example.

12. Richard Sandbrook, "The Crisis in Political Development Theory," *The Journal of Development Studies* 12, no. 2 (1976): 165–185.

13. Some of the most notable examples of these early studies include: Aristide Zolberg, *One Party Government in the Ivory Coast* (Princeton, N.J.: Princeton University Press, 1964); James S. Coleman, *Nigeria: Background to Nationalism* (Berkeley: University of California Press, 1958); Ruth Schachter Morgenthau, *Political Parties in French-Speaking Africa* (London: Oxford University Press, 1964); Crawford Young, *Politics in the Congo* (Princeton, N.J.: Princeton University Press, 1965).

14. Theotonio Dos Santos, "The Structure of Dependence," in Charles K. Wilbert, ed., *The Political Economy of Development and Underdevelopment* (New York: Random House, 1973), p. 109 and passim.

15. Immanuel Wallerstein, "Dependence in an Interdependent World," *African Studies Review* 17, no. 1 (1974): 7. Also see Walter Rodney, *How Europe Underdeveloped Africa* (Washington, D.C.: Howard University Press, 1974).

16. For a good collection of such essays, see Dennis L. Cohen and John Daniel, eds., *Political Economy of Africa: Selected Readings* (London: Longman, 1981).

17. For a good critique, see Tony Smith, "The Underdevelopment of Development Literature," *World Politics* 31, no. 2 (1979).

18. See, for some examples, Nicola Swainson, *The Development of Corporate Capitalism in Kenya 1918–1977* (Berkeley: University of California Press, 1980): Colin Leys, *Underdevelopment in Kenya* (Berkeley: University of California Press, 1974); and John Saul, *The State and Revolution in Eastern Africa* (New York: Monthly Review Press, 1979).

19. This more careful revision of existing approaches is apparent, for example, in such works as Crawford Young, *Ideology and Development in Africa* (New Haven: Yale University Press, 1982) and Sara Berry, *Fathers Work for Their Sons: Accumulation, Mobility and Class Formation in an Extended Yoruba Community* (Berkeley: University of California Press, 1985). Also see Frederick Cooper, "Africa and the World Economy," *African Studies Review* 24, no. 2/3 (1981): 1–86.

20. Ali A. Mazrui and Michael Tidy, *Nationalism and New States in Africa* (London: Heinemann, 1984).

21. The most sophisticated analysis in this approach may be found in Thomas M. Callaghy, *The State-Society Struggle: Zaire in Comparative Perspective* (New York: Columbia University Press, 1984). Also see Christopher Clapham, *Third World Politics: An Introduction* (Madison: University of Wisconsin Press, 1985), and Sandbrook, *The Politics of Africa's Economic Stagnation*. For a general collection see Peter B. Evans, Dietrich Reuschemeyer, and Theda Skocpol, eds., *Bringing the State Back In* (New York: Cambridge University Press, 1985). Also, for a more patrimonial view, see Robert H. Jackson and Carl G. Rosberg, *Personal Rule in Black Africa: Prince, Autocrat, Prophet, Tyrant* (Berkeley: University of California Press, 1984).

22. For some general examples, see Ken C. Koteka and Robert W. Adams, *The Corruption of Power: African Politics* (Washington, D.C.: University Press of America, 1981), and Henry Bretton, *Power and Politics in Africa* (Chicago: Aldine Publishing, 1973). Also see Patrick Chabal, ed., *Political Domination in Africa* (London: Cambridge University Press, 1986).

23. Donald Rothchild and Robert L. Curry, *Scarcity, Choice and Public Policy in Middle Africa* (Berkeley: University of California Press, 1978). See also Robert Bates, "Agrarian Politics," in Myron Weiner and Samuel P. Huntington, eds., *Understanding Political Development* (Boston: Little, Brown, 1987), pp. 160–195, for a collective choice approach, which is based on somewhat different premises.

24. Myron Weiner "Introduction" in Weiner and Huntington *Understanding Political Development*, p. xxviii.

25. Andrew M. Kamarck, *The Tropics and Economic Development* (Baltimore: Johns Hopkins University Press, 1976), Chapter 2.

26. This point is highlighted in William Tordoff, *Government and Politics in Africa* (Bloomington: Indiana University Press, 1984), pp. 2–3.

27. Ali A. Mazrui, *The African Condition: A Political Diagnosis* (London: Cambridge University Press, 1980).

28. Adrian Leftwich, *Redefining Politics* (London: Routledge and Kegan Paul, 1983), pp. 26–27. Also see Richard A. Higgott, "From Modernization Theory to Public Policy: Continuity and Change in the Political Science of Political Development," *Studies in Cooperative International Development* 5, no. 4 (1980): pp. 26–57.

Part 1

THE STRUCTURES OF POLITICS

2

State Institutions and the Organization of the Public Arena

In the first part of this book we examine the types of organizations devised by Africans at various levels to mobilize themselves, their allies, and their resources to deal with their constantly changing surroundings, and we introduce the basic concepts of contemporary African politics: state, social groups, ethnicity, and class. Who are the main political actors in Africa today? What interests do they have and what resources do they control? How are they structured? In what ways are they connected? And what are their capabilities and their weaknesses? In Chapter 2 we focus on the consolidation and alteration of formal government institutions and in Chapter 3 deal with the structures of social and economic life. Because state and society are analytical categories that intersect and frequently overlap, Chapter 4 is devoted specifically to the investigation of the many forms of state-society relations that have evolved in Africa in the postcolonial period. These relationships provide the basis for understanding how choices are made, why certain policies are adopted, and with what results.

Politics in Africa take place most obviously, though hardly exclusively, in and around the associations and agencies that make up the state. The organization of the public domain has an important bearing on political, social, and economic processes and is itself affected and molded by these forces. The discussion of political structures in contemporary Africa begins, therefore, with an analysis of formal institutions and the changes they have undergone in recent years.

In this chapter we explore the ways in which the institutional frameworks of governance have been shaped and used since independence. First, we briefly examine different approaches to the study of the state and state institutions; second, we survey the institutional legacy of the colonial period; third, we look at the various constructions of the public arena immediately after the transfer of power and trace the changes that have been introduced since then; fourth, we assess some emerging patterns of state organization and offer explanations for these configurations; and, finally, we discuss some of the implications of these processes for political interactions and policymaking in various parts of the continent.

Almost all African countries followed a course of centralization and bureaucratic expansion in the first few years of independence, effectively excluding most social groups from participation in public affairs. Why did this authoritarian thrust develop? What impact has it had on the ability of formal agencies to penetrate society and to carry out policy successfully? Who has benefited from these arrangements? What are the prospects for their alteration?

Despite the overwhelming propensity toward statism (the concentration of political, economic, and social activity around the state), various leaders chose to structure the public domain in different ways. The pattern of state organization that developed in Côte d'Ivoire and Kenya, for example, has not been identical to that favored by the Tanzanian government since independence. The type of patrimonial politics (authority placed in a leader, rather than in legally backed structures) devised by Mobutu Sese Seko differs substantially from the party-centric national organizations developed in the Afro-Marxist states of Angola and Mozambique. The varieties of states that have evolved have had important repercussions on the capacities of public institutions: The nature and extent of state consolidation (stateness) on the continent vary markedly from Cameroon and Côte d'Ivoire, on the one hand, to Chad and Uganda, on the other. Understanding the forms of official organization provides essential insights into the channels of and possibilities for political and socioeconomic interchange.

■ THE CONCEPT OF THE STATE IN AFRICA

The concept of the state is inevitably elusive. Although most observers of Africa have employed the term freely, they have differed considerably in their interpretation of its significance and its main characteristics. Although state structures and agencies have deep roots in African society in the precolonial and the colonial periods, and although central state institutions were the object of conflict and struggle during decolonization, observers paid little attention during the first years of independence to the state or to state organs. Indeed, during most of the 1960s, the African state was virtually ignored. The state was perceived as an arena of sovereignty, of territoriality, and perhaps of nation-building, but it was not seen as an interconnected set of institutions with an existence of its own. Studies of parties, ideologies, and even of the civil service were carried out separately, and little effort was made to grasp the state as an actor in the public domain.[1]

In the 1970s, the importance of the state was recognized, at least in part, by those who viewed these institutions as agents in the global arena. At this juncture, the state was conceptualized (and rarified) as an instrument of capitalist exploitation.[2] The close connections between class formation, capitalism, and the character of the state in Africa generated a variety of social definitions of African states. Because the state, from this perspective, was seen as synonymous with the ruling class, special emphasis was placed on understanding the process of class formation, its characteristics, and its implications.[3]

Neo-Marxist scholars pioneered the effort, in the late 1970s, to dissociate the state from the ruling class by pointing out that although there is an affinity between the state and dominant groups, the two terms are hardly coterminous.[4] Thus, state institutions may reflect and in fact even produce social forces and conflicts; they are, however, quite clearly distinct empirically. This shift in emphasis occurred at the same time as other scholars began to take a renewed interest in public structures, their functions, and their capacities.

Throughout the recent literature there is substantial agreement on the definition of the state as "the organized aggregate of relatively permanent institutions of governance."[5] The state is seen as a set of associations and agencies claiming control over defined territories and their populations.[6] The main components of the state are, consequently, decision-making structures (executives, parties, parliaments), decision-enforcing institutions (bureaucracies, parastatal organizations, and security forces), and decision-mediating bodies (primarily courts, tribunals, and investigatory commissions). The character of the state in any particular country is determined by the pattern of organization of these institutions at specific points in time.

The definition of the state as an institutionalized legal order separates this notion, conceptually, from those of regime and government. The structures of the *state,* through the organization of people and resources and the establishment of policy outlines and priorities, are essentially institutions of power. From Max Weber on, the state has been viewed as a set of instruments of domination. *Regime,* in contrast, refers to the rules, principles, norms, and modes of interaction between social groups and state organs.[7] The concept of regime is, therefore, concerned with the form of rule. It deals with how political relations are carried out, with the procedures and mechanisms of political exchange. If the idea of the state is associated primarily with the organization of power, regime focuses on how state power is exercised and legitimated. *Government,* in turn, relates to the specific occupants of public office who are in a position to make binding decisions at any given time.[8] State, regime, and government may or may not overlap empirically. In concept, however, they are quite distinct.

States are located at the intersection of domestic and international processes. Viewed in global terms, states are fundamental components of the international system. They vie with other states and transnational actors for survival and advantage in the external arena. Domestically, states are "sprawling organizations within society that coexist with many other formal and informal social organizations, from families to tribes to large industrial enterprises. What distinguishes the state, at least in the modern era, is that state officials seek predominance over these myriad other organizations."[9] This goal is achieved through the making and implementation of binding rules. State institutions are neither neutral nor aloof; they are organizations with interests of their own.

The precondition for the effective functioning of state organs is military control of a given territory (security) and some recognition of sovereignty (international and/or domestic legitimation). The operational capabilities of the organizations in the public domain rely, in fact, on the skill and loyalty of officials (expertise) and on the revenue at their disposal.[10] The authority of states is measured, then, in terms of the supremacy of their laws over those of other groups in the population.

By the early 1980s, there was substantial agreement among analysts regarding the importance of the state in Africa as the focus for the institutionalization of central power. There has been no consensus, however, on the meaning of the growing salience of state agencies. Indeed, the postcolonial state in Africa has been depicted, alternately, as weak and powerful, as repressive and feeble, as fragile and absolutist, as dependent and autonomous, as expanding and as collapsing.

At this juncture, three main approaches to the understanding of the state in Africa have emerged. Proponents of one approach, the organic one, view the state as the critical actor in the public arena, directly influencing social and economic processes and affecting outcomes. The interpretations associated with this perspective have several themes in common. First is the notion of the state as a structure of domination; second is the idea of the state as a unitary actor separated (autonomous) from society; and third is the concept of the state as fulfilling certain functions.[11] Underlying these shared themes is an assumption regarding the centrality of the state in the independence period. In this view of the state extraordinary weight is placed on statist explanations for socioeconomic phenomena. Adherents of this view posit that major occurrences (and calamities) are directly attributable to state actions and the behavior of its officials. Events and activities taking place beyond this rubric (on the societal or external planes) are consequently difficult to explore. However important the contributions of the organic approach, this view of the state is incomplete and somewhat mechanistic.

Proponents of a second conceptual approach to the state in Africa, the configurational one, suggest that the state apparatus provides the main framework in which social groups form and in which certain types of political action are made possible and others are circumscribed. The organization of state institutions thus affects the types of political issues raised and the way they are played out.[12] The impact of the state is, however, no longer direct; political activities resonate from the options presented by the institutional configuration of any given state. The configurational approach, therefore, differs from the organic approach not in its insistence on the predominance of the state but in the way it views the state's impact.[13] In the organic perspective, the state assumes anthropomorphic qualities; in the configurational view, state structures determine the substantive parameters of social action.

, Proponents of a third, interactive, approach build on the insights of these predecessors but suggest that social structures, especially in complex settings like those found in Africa, must be taken as seriously as those of the state. From this conceptual vantage point, specific groups have evolved their own rules and survival strategies, which may compete or even conflict with those presented by the state. In order to understand the character of states, it is necessary to look at how transactions between social groups and state institutions are carried out and how these, in turn, alter the nature of public institutions as well as of social formations.[14] The manner and the extent to which public institutions actually synthesize the interests of civil society is thus a critical subject of inquiry that can help to shed light on the very divergent frameworks of political life in African countries in recent years.[15]

This view of the state is less assertive of the centrality of postcolonial governmental bodies in Africa than the organic or configurational approaches. It therefore also leaves open the question of what activities these agencies engage in, according to what guidelines, and with what consequences. The capacity of states to exercise control over resources and people—to govern—is thus dependent on the concrete interests they reflect and manage. There are many possibilities that emerge from such a nuanced approach: the prospect of a continuous gap between state agencies and social groups; the option of total absorption of social interests by institutions in the public domain; or, more probably, different forms of unequal integrations corresponding to different patterns of organization and aggregation of interests.[16] By stressing the significance of coalitions, transactions, and exchanges in historical perspective, the interactive approach is more open to societal as well as statist explanations. Because they recognize the importance of the state as an independent actor but do not insist on the exclusivity of its role, adherents of this conceptualization seek to explore the capacities of the state more empirically. In a precarious period such an attitude is justified: It does not imply that the state is the repository of all power and public activity at precisely the point when its institutions are visibly strained.[17]

The three approaches to the study of the state in Africa reflect different premises, orientations, concerns, and explanatory dispositions. The political choice method adopted in this book builds on the insights of organic and configurational approaches to the state but stresses interactive perspectives. We take into account the role of state structures as direct actors and as organizations influencing social, economic, and political institutions but go on to examine social responses and their effects on state capacities as well. We investigate the types of connections between institutions in the public domain and assess their differing capabilities and implicit operating rules. On this basis, it is possible to trace changes in state organization and to highlight the varying characteristics of the state in specific African countries. In the following pages, we examine these processes in greater detail and expound upon their ramifications.

■ THE STRUCTURAL FOUNDATIONS OF AFRICAN STATES: THE COLONIAL LEGACY

The basis of the postcolonial state in Africa is the colonial state. Although colonial governments retained many indigenous social institutions and brought about the redefinition of others, colonial rule superimposed a new administrative structure on these social and political orders. This colonial apparatus of power operated within newly delineated boundaries. Even the French federal structures of Afrique Occidentale Française (AOF, French West Africa) and Afrique Equatoriale Française (AEF, French Equatorial Africa) clearly distinguished between component territories (later to become the independent French-speaking states of Africa) on a geographic basis, thus superimposing physical definitions of frontiers on indigenous (and still ensconced) African perceptions of boundaries as belts of separation between social units.[18]

Colonial states all created an administrative hierarchy through the concentration of political and administrative functions in the hands of the colonial civil service. The British in their colonies and mandated territories, the French in their grand federations, and the Belgians and Portuguese in their overseas possessions went about the task of governance by establishing a bureaucratic network staffed by officers who had charge of specific duties (such as revenue collection, public order, medicine, education, infrastructural organization, adjudication, social services, and even, in the later colonial period, development projects). In some cases, broad policies were made in the metropole (this was especially true in French-speaking areas), and in others colonial administrators were granted a great deal of power on the spot (in principle the norm in British colonies). Nevertheless, the essential feature of colonial rule throughout the continent was a functional notion of government that did not distinguish between decision-making and implementation roles.

The functional pattern of organization during the colonial period was backed by a well-developed coercive apparatus. Police forces were established in each territory ostensibly to maintain order but also to ensure compliance with specific dictates. When necessary, colonial troops were brought in to quell expressions of dissatisfaction, and behind every colonial government stood a strong security service. The colonial state was essentially a military-administrative unit. "The political culture bequeathed by colonialism contained the notions that authoritarianism was an appropriate mode of rule and that political activity was merely a disguised form of self-interest, subversive of the public welfare."[19] The administration undertook activities that it deemed appropriate without widespread consultation and without questioning its superior knowledge. In general, therefore, the power apparatus inherited at independence was aloof and also surprisingly weak. It penetrated and directly (often repressively) affected only portions of daily life and succeeded in bringing about changes in a very limited number of spheres. It did, however, provide a new referent for social and economic activities.

The formal agencies transferred to African hands were thus alien in derivation, functionally conceived, bureaucratically designed, authoritarian in nature, and primarily concerned with issues of domination rather than legitimacy. During decolonization these patterns were, in most cases, elaborated rather than transformed. In the postwar period, development concerns and social welfare questions were brought directly into the purview of formal government agencies. This bureaucratic expansion was not, however, always accompanied by the careful preparation of the transfer of power. In the 1940s and the early 1950s, Britain attempted to Africanize large portions of the civil service in the Gold Coast (Ghana), Nigeria, and Sierra Leone. In these areas of West Africa, over 50 percent of civil service posts were held by Africans at independence. In East Africa, the British turned their attention to these matters rather late, and in Kenya and Tanganyika only about 10 percent of the administration had been localized at independence.[20] In the French territories, Africans had gained a good deal of experience during the course of the colonial period in the upper echelons of the administration, but their numbers were limited. In both cases, technical (as opposed to bureaucratic) skills were less developed. With few exceptions, however—perhaps Zimbabwe, because of its very late independence in 1980—colonial educational systems had not produced a sufficient number of qualified people to staff the rapidly growing bureaucracies at the time.

The preparation for independence, from the administrative point of view, was even in the best of circumstances rather hasty and incomplete. Given that in 1945 there was virtually no expectation that events would move so quickly, the skills of the new civil servants were too few and their experience all too often too limited to master the many tasks of governance. The colonial administrative structure was, nevertheless, the institutional mainstay of the power apparatus inherited on the eve of independence. To a large extent, these administrative agencies retained a remarkable continuity during the transition from imperial rule to self-government. African administrators received from colonial rulers a structure of control—however flawed—that was largely untouched by the political currents of decolonization.

Indeed, if significant change did occur at this juncture, it was evident in the political, rather than the bureaucratic, organization of the public domain. Decolonization was essentially about the rearrangement of the political structure of African states. The transfer of power, ipso facto, implied a shift in the location of control and in the composition of decision-making structures.

The main vehicles for these alterations in the political realm were the nationalist movements and parties that sprung up on very different social foundations throughout the continent virtually from the beginnings of colonial rule.

Anticolonialism was articulated in many ways. Urban discontent, rural revolt, religious heterodoxies, and literary dissent were all distinct, and often unconnected, expressions of disaffection with the colonial order. Political parties flourished after World War II, and where extra-parliamentary action failed, the parties were followed by liberation movements and armies. Parties differed from each other in derivation, in social composition, ideological predilection, and, of course, in recruitment patterns, strategies, and tactics. The leadership that emerged from these frameworks also varied: The skills, personality, and concerns of Kwame Nkrumah of Ghana were quite different from those of his contemporary and political ally, Sekou Touré of Guinea. Hastings Kamuzu Banda pursued a highly pragmatic course that set him and Habib Bourguiba in Tunisia apart—ideologically and temperamentally—from Kenneth Kaunda in Zambia or Robert Mugabe in Zimbabwe. Political styles and patterns, techniques and support bases thus took on the character of local social forces and tensions, circumstances and opportunities. Parties provided the medium for the organization of these vastly differing concerns in each territory.[21]

Competition and even open conflict came in two different forms. The first consisted of a confrontation with the colonial power; the second of a local struggle over control of the political system-in-formation. In most cases in British and French Africa, the demand for political autonomy was recognized in principle before there was a need to engage in a prolonged struggle for independence. In these countries, decolonization included a period in which competing groups vied with each other for domination internally and negotiated with the colonial rulers for favorable arrangements in the process of political devolution. Where the notion of African self-rule was contested (lusophone Africa, the settler societies of Kenya, Zimbabwe, Namibia, and Algeria), the quest for liberation took on violent forms that were usually accompanied by fragmentation within the national liberation movements. In these instances, the internal struggle for power coincided with the continued contestation with recalcitrant imperialist powers. With very few exceptions, however (Angola, Mozambique, Guinea-Bissau, Western Sahara), elections were held on the eve of independence to determine the precise composition of the new governments.

The number, the type, and the ideological leanings of the parties that stood for office in the preindependence elections varied significantly. Participation rates ranged from relatively high proportions in Côte d'Ivoire and Senegal to lower levels in Ghana, Nigeria, and Tanganyika. The winners, however, emerged in a strengthened position: They not only held the reins of power at this crucial historical conjuncture; they also could claim the halo of success in ridding their countries of the stigma of foreign rule.

The precise political arrangements for the future were ironed out in a series of negotiations between the presumptive heirs and the colonial government. Broadly speaking (again with the notable exception of the Portuguese areas), the political frameworks devised at the time followed either variations on the British Westminster model of parliamentary democracy or the more centralist model of the Fifth Republic in France. In each case, special pacts were made with the inheritors, and peculiarities were introduced to take local conditions and specific colonial interests into account. Political arrangements were, throughout most of Africa, a combination of nationalist demands and ongoing colonial concerns.

In most of the continent, the transition to independence was smooth and uneventful. If nationalist leaders did not always succeed in obtaining all that they demanded, colonial powers were also unable to impose their preferred models in their entirety. Thus, independence did not constitute a total break with colonial political values and interests. It did, however, mean that the location of political power altered and that the rules of the political game were no longer unassailable.

The process of decolonization, therefore, involved a change in regime. The political legacy bequeathed at independence was at best unformed and uncertain. The new leaders of political parties had earned their positions as a result of their ability to organize and capitalize upon anticolonial protest. They had little, if any, experience in actually governing a small area, let alone an entire country. When they took over the reins of office, they were confronted with the paradoxical situation of having to operate with newly conceived pluralist institutions of alien derivation (including parties and parliaments), whereas the bulk of their own political understanding had been molded in a centralized and authoritarian colonial context. The contradictions they faced were therefore real and not easily reconcilable.

The two aspects of decolonization—devolution of the administrative apparatus and the transfer of the political apparatus—were not always integrally linked. The bureaucratic structures, and the concepts that guided their creation and operations, reflected the concerns of their colonial designers. These institutions, together with their underlying assumptions, were handed over virtually intact and constituted the organizational legacy of African states at independence. The political inheritance, however, was far more ambiguous. New rules had been devised—although hardly tested—just prior to the African takeover of decision-making roles. The political arena was, virtually by definition, in flux. Economic conditions were hardly favorable to smooth government, and anticolonialism was not necessarily accompanied by the formation of a national consciousness in countries that encompassed an ensemble of different groups with many diverse interests.[22]

African leaders received a structure of control but lacked a power base from which they could effectively establish priorities and pursue policies. It was within this context of power impoverishment and political fluidity, buttressed by inherited institutions of control, that they operated during the first years of independence. It was this mixed inheritance that also defined the central problem of African governments at that time: They all had to deal, in one way or another, with the issue of power consolidation in a situation where their own legitimacy was tenuous, demands were exacerbated, resources were meager, expectations were high, external vulnerability was pronounced, and allegiances were uncertain.

■ CONSTRUCTIONS OF THE PUBLIC ARENA SINCE INDEPENDENCE

□ Phase 1: The Concentration of State Power

The first few years of independence were accompanied by systematic efforts on the part of the new state leaders to overcome the constraints of the colonial legacy by reorganizing public institutions and by concentrating power at the center. In an almost uniform manner in Gabon, Mali, Sierra Leone, Kenya, Tanganyika, Zambia, Algeria, Tunisia, Uganda, Senegal, to name but a few, political competition was curtailed, dominant political parties were fortified, administrative structures were expanded, and decision making was heavily centralized around the head of state and his cohorts. A process of power consolidation with strong authoritarian and even repressive overtones occurred throughout the continent.

During the initial postcolonial phase, new governments were subjected to additional pressures from several directions. As state structures occupied a gatekeeper position between external resources and domestic processes, their economic role was magnified greatly upon the achievement of independence.[23] They were also expected to provide social services on a grand scale. A series of strikes, demonstrations, and spontaneous actions kept many leaders preoccupied with the task of maintaining order. Moreover, anticolonial activists and militants demanded some tangible returns for their political support during the crucial years of decolonization.

In this situation, the choices confronting the political elites were very limited indeed: They could either use their positions to fortify themselves politically, or they could maintain existing arrangements and run the risk of alienating their supporters. Almost without exception the new leaders opted to concentrate power in their own hands.

Several factors contributed to this choice. First, most ruling coalitions at independence enjoyed a certain amount of leeway as a result of their successful role in the achievement of independence.[24] Second, these leaders had little commitment to uphold the precepts of the independence constitutions. These legal arrangements were frequently viewed as pragmatic compromises agreed upon in order to hasten the transfer of power. Once independence was acquired, the complicated provisions they entailed could easily be discarded, especially as they often constituted an apparent impediment to efficient government. Third, the Westminster-style model or the more presidential francophone counterpart offered precious few answers to the very real dilemmas of the time. As insufficient experience had been gained in adapting general rules to the particular situation of given countries, other options were explored with greater vigor. Fourth, most countries had not evolved a strong independent middle class during the colonial period. The social foundations for effective political competition or for capital accumulation away from the state were not in place. The state was seen by ruling elites as an avenue for the attainment of wealth as well as status. Above all, however, the trend toward power consolidation was eased by a search for a legitimating formula. If existing arrangements sowed confusion, the centralization of power could be justified as a more direct way to achieve rapid development and hence advance the general public welfare. This utilitarian argument rationalized the quest for control by suggesting that curtailment of personal liberties was a necessary sacrifice to fulfill a broader notion of the public good.[25] African leaders could also claim that by discarding alien institutions they were continuing the process of Africanization. The combination of these considerations determined, to a large extent, the path of the reordering of government institutions in most parts of Africa in the immediate postcolonial period.

The purpose, then, of the changes introduced in the early years of independence was to increase the concentration of power around the state and reduce social and intraelite competition. This goal could be achieved in two ways: either by weakening or eliminating participatory institutions inherited from the colonial period (the process of *impedance*) or by strengthening and enlarging upon existing bureaucratic structures (the process of *facilitation*). These alterations did not imply a total transformation of public structures. Indeed, in no African state was an entirely new set of government bodies constructed at independence. Rather, those institutions perpetuating formalized rivalry with the ruling coalition were reshaped or eradicated, whereas those that enhanced central leadership were sustained and elaborated.

The first step in this process revolved around limiting the opportunities for opposition. Shortly after securing political power, the new rulers moved in a determined way to dismantle many of the constitutional protections put in place at the time of independence. One way to curb opposition was to emasculate quasi-federal provisions in preindependence constitutions. In Kenya, Uganda, and Ghana the new leaders denounced regionalism and regional structures, claiming that these not only hindered national unity but also that their acceptance prior to independence was an expedient that was no longer necessary. Thus, the Nkrumah government reduced the regional (middle) tier of government to a purely advisory position.

It would be wasteful, cumbersome and altogether unsound administratively [argued government spokesmen] to have in the proposed local government structure another tier, in the form of Regional Assemblies, where would be exercised powers and functions which have normally been exercised by local authorities. This would mean taking a retrograde step and departing from the principle which the Government has always observed of permitting Local Authorities to develop more and more into responsible bodies with extensive functions.[26]

The effect of such moves was twofold: the placement of local government directly under the aegis of central institutions (with the notable exception of Nigeria, which has always maintained a federal-type structure); and the elimination of regional political bases that could enhance the power and autonomy of local leaders in competition with ruling coalitions at the national level.

Another way to reduce opposition was to outlaw rival political organizations based on particularistic, sectarian, or ethnic interests. Ghana, once again, together with Guinea, paved the way for such actions by declaring local political parties illegal and contrary to national interests. In Kenya, Jomo Kenyatta hounded opposition leaders and accused them of fueling regional and separatist tendencies. In Senegal, Muslim religious authorities were either coopted or discredited; in Sierra Leone, traditional institutions were manipulated; and in Guinea, chieftaincy was declared illegal. With alternate power constellations enfeebled, reconstructed opposition parties were on tenuous ground when they sought to mobilize support or criticize government actions.

The opportunities to voice discontent were also substantially reduced. The notion of a loyal opposition was alien to the colonial and decolonization experiences of most African leaders; once in power, they assumed that hesitations and reservations threatened the essential unity of their endeavor. Steps were taken to enforce newly formulated sedition laws. Vocal opponents of ruling parties and of their methods of government were either incarcerated or exiled. By the early 1960s, for example, in Kenya, Algeria, Ghana, and Guinea, most leaders of contending parties during decolonization were either in jail or had left the country to carry out their political struggles from abroad. Where the insecurity of the new regimes was especially apparent, the notion of opposition itself was considered to be immoral. Unity was equated with uniformity, disagreement with treason.

The enfeeblement of opposition in many cases also involved the actual dismantling of the multiparty system. The trend toward the creation of one-party states is perhaps the best known and the most noted of the political changes introduced at independence.[27] In the quest for consolidation, political competition, it was suggested, had to be controlled and some monopoly of the governing political apparatus assured. African leaders throughout the continent, arguing from different perspectives, thus supported the transition to single-party dominance. Felix Houphouët-Boigny in Côte d'Ivoire claimed that the elimination of opposition merely sanctioned the unity that actually existed. Kwame Nkrumah defended the move to one-party rule by suggesting that the multiparty system was divisive and antithetical to the needs of economic development and national integration. Sekou Touré in Guinea, by correlating the proposed nation with the party, thought that alternative political poles undermined the national purpose. And in Tanzania, Julius Nyerere saw the one-party concept as essentially democratic and reflective of African culture and deep-rooted norms of consensus.[28]

Many methods were employed to bring about the consolidation of one-party dominance. In some cases, persuasion was used to encourage the fusion of opposition and ruling parties, as in Senegal and in Kenya during the first years of independence. In other instances, legal means were employed to make it essentially impossible for opposition parties to subsist. Kwame Nkrumah employed such techniques in Ghana, as did Ahmadou Ahidjo in Cameroon. In other countries, coercion was the key: Opposition leaders were harassed in Guinea and Uganda, and attempts to voice discontent were put down forcefully in Angola and Mozambique. In many places, the leaders did not have to do much of anything: They could, as in Côte d'Ivoire, assume that the electorate would not find it beneficial to support weak parties with no access to state resources and, by astute collaboration, would allow the single-party monopoly to evolve. In all cases, the process of impedance of multiparty competition resulted in the creation of palpably monopolistic formal political institutions.

These moves were reinforced by purposeful changes in the laws guiding political activities and possibilities. In Ghana, for example, the British, determined to forestall rash actions on the part of a majoritarian-backed chief executive or central legislature, provided a highly inflexible amendment in the 1957 constitution. Two-thirds approval of all members of the national and regional assemblies was required to alter clauses in the constitution. The government of the Convention People's party (CPP), describing this limitation as unnecessary, made use of its overwhelming support in parliament to allow for amendment by a simple majority. In a similar fashion, the Kenyan and Zambian leaderships, faced with amendment procedures that seemed to inhibit government-sponsored political and economic change, moved to alter amendment procedures.

The message, in these and other instances, was quite clear. Those legal safeguards standing in the way of firm central control were regarded as unacceptable. To drive home this point, many governments undertook to rewrite preindependence constitutions to reflect the shifts in the political sphere and ostensibly to provide themselves with greater power. Kenya, Uganda, Malawi, Zambia, Ghana, and Sierra Leone stand out in this respect.

These very elaborate means of impeding opposition also had the effect of profoundly altering the function of participatory and representative institutions. National assemblies and parliaments, packed with ruling party supporters, were downgraded in many cases from legislative bodies to decree-sanctioning organs. Although careful efforts were made to maintain some notion of representation, parliamentary debates mostly offered opportunities to express support or to allow for a certain measure of bargaining. They rarely permitted real engagement in policy formulation or even constructive commentary on the direction of government policies.[29]

The process of impedance, in all its various forms, was one that concentrated directly (if not exclusively) on the fragile and fluid political apparatus inherited at independence. The limitation or outright elimination of competition, coupled with the assertion of single-party dominance, had the effect of circumscribing access to the central government and reducing formal pressure on its resources.

The other side of the institutional readjustment process focused on measures designed to augment the power apparatus. These reinforcement procedures centered on three main structures: the administration, the coercive apparatus, and the executive. The administrative institutions of Africa at independence possessed the main reservoir of skilled personnel in every single African country. The knowledge concentrated in these bodies was essential to devise and implement economic policies and to maintain order. In these circumstances, rulers sought not to undermine the administrative infrastructure but to remold these functional bodies so that they would promote their interests.

With independence, therefore, the process of Africanization was expedited and the size and functions of the administrative agencies were augmented dramatically. Young graduates were rapidly absorbed into the civil service, endowed with broad responsibilities, and in the name of parity, granted the same terms of service and perquisites previously accorded to colonial administrators. Service ministries, such as education, health, and community welfare, were greatly expanded. Every country developed a foreign service and established economic planning bureaus and state-owned parastatal corporations. With independence came the need for currency changes and new fiscal arrangements and consequently also for enlarged finance ministries. It seemed that at every turn, administrative bodies multiplied.

This process also encompassed the military and police services. The new rulers in Sudan, Zimbabwe, Zaire, Kenya, Uganda, Mauritania, and elsewhere were keenly aware of the fact that various ethnoregional elements did not accept their legitimacy. These political leaders came to rely heavily on the army and security forces inherited from the colonial period in order to maintain order in their countries. The perceived threat of disruption or secession was a serious one that demanded the Africanization, the enlargement, and the modernization of the new armies. With very few exceptions, therefore, the coercive apparatus grew alongside the bureaucratic.

The expansion of the administrative apparatus also proved to be a crucial means for personal advancement. The facilitation of bureaucratic institutions allowed select individuals to gain direct access to state resources and to enjoy the not inconsiderable privileges associated with administrative office. In Tanzania, Zimbabwe, Côte d'Ivoire, Kenya, Senegal, Mali, Cameroon, and Zaire, the increase in the number of state personnel also involved an increase in administrative costs. As David Abernathy notes,

> At the time of independence, top-level salary scales set initially with European conditions in mind were accepted by the incoming African regimes as appropriate scales for those Africans fortunate enough to occupy the most responsible administrative posts. When there was talk in Africa of "reforming" the civil

service, the issue was how to move local citizens more rapidly and effectively into the existing hierarchical structure, or how to expand the structure laterally to assume new developmental functions. What was never seriously addressed . . . was the appropriateness of a situation in which the top civil servant earned at least 40 and sometimes over 100 times more than the per capita GDP of the country.[30]

The requirements of governance, it appeared, dovetailed quite well with the personal interests of technocrats, educated groups, and party militants. Association with the state complex began to emerge as one, if not the, key avenue to social advancement and class differentiation.

The bureaucratic growth that accompanied the consolidation of power had important implications for the organization of the state. The downgrading of political opportunities and the vast opening of administrative and coercive ones made for an institutional imbalance not dissimilar to the one that existed throughout the colonial period. It also created a different type of problem for political leaders. As the bureaucratic apparatus was growing rapidly, as its members held privileged positions, and as their political loyalties were not always clear, governments approached the proliferating administration with some measure of suspicion. In order to keep an eye on the administration (in some instances to take over key offices), the party was often used as a means of bureaucratic supervision. The process of politicization, therefore, followed upon that of bureaucratic facilitation. Party functionaries were injected into the civil service, the police, the army, and local government. It was inevitable that party and government tended to overlap in many different ways.

In some places, real efforts were made to maintain a separation between the party and the administration. Thus, although Tanzanian leaders went so far as to proclaim the party (then the Tanzanian African National Union, TANU) as the preeminent public institution in the country, in reality the division between party and state was not always so clear-cut. The administrative apparatus was always central in policy implementation, even though the party had some role in policy formulation.[31] Such an uneasy separation also characterized Nkrumah's Ghana in the early 1960s.

In other countries, the party actually absorbed state structures. This was the case with the transformation-minded regimes of Mozambique, Guinea, and Angola. In Angola, the ruling Popular Movement for the Liberation of Angola (MPLA) has played a central role in setting out basic principles for governmental and societal action and for mobilizing popular support behind a regime under military attack from the National Union for the Total Independence of Angola (UNITA) and South African forces. The MPLA Politburo and Central Committee have placed themselves as the key policymaking bodies. Matters of implementation are dealt with in the National Assembly and the ministries, where MPLA party members are very prominent.

In still other states, the growth of the administrative apparatus resulted in a contrary trend: the subordination of the party to government institutions. In

Côte d'Ivoire, for one, emphasis was placed on building up bureaucratic mechanisms, whereas the party was relegated to more symbolic tasks. In Kenya during the 1960s, membership in the Kenya African National Union (KANU) became an important vehicle for the attainment of bureaucratic position. In Algeria, too, though officially supreme, the ruling party has been less central as a regulatory institution. "Since independence the FLN has possessed neither the authority nor the technical competence to orient and supervise the administrative apparatus of the state. . . . Neither armed forces nor bureaucracy have been subject to its authority. In a sense, therefore, the Party and its ramifications could be regarded as part of the bureaucracy, performing essentially a public relations function on its behalf. . . . Its job was to explain and justify decisions taken elsewhere, not to reason why."[32]

Whatever the precise pattern of party-state relations, a clear feature of governmental reorganization during the early years of independence was the intrusion of party political elements into the decision-enforcing institutions of government. This had two significant implications. First, although the political role of the party as a means of participation and competition was downplayed, the party became a channel to the administration, thus making the administrative apparatus subject to particular political pressures. Second, in this situation the location of decision making was unclear. To be sure, administrative units could make decisions on technical matters or in specific areas, but they were dependent on government decision makers. On the other hand, as the lines of distinction between party and bureaucracy were nebulous, the party could not function on a regular basis as the center of policy formulation. Under these conditions, the executive took on particular significance in the decision making sphere.

The final element in the process of strengthening already existing administrative institutions at the expense of participatory ones centered on the concentration of the state power apparatus in the hands of individual leaders. The personalization of decision making was a concomitant of the overall trend toward centralization. Leadership became a substitute for regularized channels of policymaking. This was the case in Guinea, Senegal, Ghana, Kenya, Tanzania, and Uganda—indeed, throughout the continent. Even when, because of the complex nature of decision making, other agencies were naturally involved in making key policy decisions, it usually was the president (endowed with increased executive powers) who had the final say.[33]

These executive presidents were undoubtedly informed by the opinions of party officials, personal advisors, technical experts, senior bureaucrats, friends, and specific local and at times foreign interests. But unlike their counterparts in the West or, for that matter, in portions of Asia and Latin America, African leaders during the first generation of independence were not institutionally constrained in their decision-making capacities, nor were they necessarily subject (at least at the outset) to organized pressures from below. The centrality of leaders in decision making did not, however, imply that they possessed total power. Rather, it suggested that under the new institutional arrangements they became the hub that connected the party with the army and the civil service with the politicians.

The process of facilitation, geared almost exclusively toward augmenting the power apparatus, had the effect of strengthening the extractive machinery of the new states at independence. State-linked structures were reinforced, whereas political institutions rooted in society were stymied. A system of domination came to replace the inherently fluid and dispersed institutional networks prevalent at the close of the colonial period.

The reorganization of public structures during the first years of independence, regardless of political philosophies and the personal inclinations of particular leaders, therefore assumed the characteristics of what has been termed the typical postcolonial state. This state is characterized by the limitation of pluralism to very small enclaves, the strong emphasis on statism and bureaucratic structures, the politicization of administrative institutions, and personalistic forms of decision making.[34] It has frequently been referred to as a *neopatrimonial* state, one in which relationships to a person (rather than an officeholder) thrive within a purportedly legal-rational administrative system.[35] Although monopolistic, the postcolonial state had only tenuous power and legitimacy and very little authority. Centralization became a means for consolidation but did not necessarily imply full control. In fact, the highly concentrated system of rule created at this time was as noted for what it excluded as for what it sought to encompass. Social groups, local communities, and even party diehards were often kept outside the official domain. The consolidation of state institutions in the first postcolonial phase, therefore, implied a combination of power concentration and power weakness. It was this broad pattern of distancing the state from societal constraints, of pushing society out, that constituted the initial response of African governments to the problems of control that they faced when they took office; it was also within this general framework that specific adjustments were made in individual countries in the ensuing years.

☐ Phase 2: The Elaboration of State Power

The reorganization of government structures at independence laid the groundwork for the amplification of the institutional order in different African states since the early postcolonial years. During the 1960s and the 1970s, African leaders further molded the various components of government—the public administration, the coercive apparatus, the legal order, and political institutions.[36] These actions had the paradoxical dual effect of expanding state structures while at the same time frequently limiting the effectiveness of these agencies.

Administration.   The growth of the public bureaucracy in African states has been one of the most notable formal features of African politics in the past three decades. The nature of this expansion, and its significance for politics and development, have been the subject of not inconsiderable controversy. Some have seen the proliferation of the administration as evidence of the emergence of a monopolistic class that has preyed on society and systematically extracted its resources. Some have viewed this process as a sign of inefficiency: as a further indication of the absence of rational norms of public behavior. Other observers bemoan the lack of experience and skills that continues to plague the public sector, pointing to the dearth of qualifications as the immediate cause of poor implementation. And many commentators have highlighted the unclear connection between administrative and political institutions as a reason for grave problems of governability. A common thread runs through these debates: a comprehension both of the extensiveness and the inadequacy of administrative structures in the postcolonial period.[37]

The 1960s were marked by rapid bureaucratic expansion. This trend began with heavy demands for the Africanization of the civil service on the eve of independence. Very few African governments were able to stem these demands. Hastings Kamuzu Banda in Malawi and Felix Houphouët-Boigny in Côte d'Ivoire did, in fact, moderate Africanization procedures until suitably trained candidates could be found to fill professional positions. In most cases, however, local cadres were given intensive courses to enable them to take over positions held by departing expatriates, and younger civil servants were promoted rapidly in administrative, if not always in technical and professional, posts. Higher education and vocational training institutions were strengthened. Graduates were quickly assimilated into the civil service and granted relatively senior positions.

The results, in quantitative terms, were startling. In each year during the 1960s, the civil service in Africa grew on an average of 7 percent. By 1970, 60 percent of wage earners were government employees. A decade later, at least 50 percent of government expenditures were allocated to paying salaries. In some countries, a full 80 percent of government revenues were spent on supporting the civil service.[38] Tanzania provides one illustration of this immense growth. The total number of established state posts increased from 65,708 in 1966 to 191,046 in 1976 and to an estimated 295,352 in 1980. Rwekaza Mukandala puts this growth in perspective: "While the GDP expanded at an annual rate of 3.88 percent between 1966 and 1976 . . . and total wage employment increased at an average annual rate of around 2.84 percent between 1966 and 1976, the civil service expanded at an average annual rate of 13.3 percent, a rate more than treble that of GDP and total wage employment."[39]

The outcome of this spurt was not only to skew expenditure patterns, but also, almost inevitably, to create a privileged group that gradually developed corporate interests of its own. Civil servants stood out in comparison to other groups in African countries; they were also well placed to advance themselves financially. The manner of bureaucratic expansion enhanced their status and opened opportunities for the personal aggrandizement of state officials at the expense of other groups.

Civil servants and government employees consequently emerged as the core of a new dominant class in the postcolonial period. This state managerial stratum—often called a bureaucratic bourgeoisie—derived its strength (and its wealth) from its proximity to state resources.[40] The shift toward statism made politics a main avenue to material advancement and hence a key criterion for social differentiation. With bureaucratic growth came more pronounced inequalities and new lines of social cleavage and tension. The dilemmas of administrative expansion were, therefore, quite severe: If development requirements demanded the concentration of rare skills around the civil service, this process also engendered new social problems whose ramifications could be particularly unsettling.

The difficulties that accompanied the Africanization and spread of the bureaucratic apparatus were compounded by the tendency of governments to strengthen existing public corporations inherited from the colonial period and to establish state enterprises of their own (parastatals). Colonial governments had created some such organizations, most notably utility companies (for the supply of electricity and water) and export commodity marketing boards (cocoa and coffee marketing boards were the most notable in the British colonies). At independence, these institutions were transferred as part of the colonial legacy. The weakness of indigenous enterprises and the paucity of domestic capital at this time also led many leaders to set up their own corporations to deal with particular areas: for example, the Ghana Industrial Holding Corporation or the State Import-Export Organization in Mali. And, in many countries, a desire to reduce the extent of foreign participation and even control of the economy led governments to nationalize certain foreign concerns. The correlation of local control over the economy with government enterprises induced, regardless of the ideological leanings of any particular regime, a proliferation of state-owned companies.

The expansion of parastatals throughout Africa in the first decades of independence has bordered on the phenomenal. Some deal specifically with the extraction and sale of agricultural produce, others with industry, mining, and manufacturing. Public companies control telecommunications, transportation, and infrastructural growth. Others handle distribution of goods, banking, and even health and housing. In Tanzania, there were 142 parastatals in 1976; in Côte d'Ivoire the number of state-owned enterprises reached over 80 by the early 1980s. During the Nkrumah era in Ghana, parastatals coexisted with privately owned companies but dominated every major sphere of macroeconomic activity in the country. Nigeria, which experienced a comparatively slow growth in state corporations in the 1960s, had over 250 state-owned companies by the mid-1970s.

The use of state corporations as a key economic instrument has thus been quite common. These enterprises have been established as semiautonomous or statutory bodies with a fair amount of independence, both financially and institutionally, from the more established bureaucracy. This relative freedom has allowed managers of public enterprises to act with only limited supervision and has enabled political leaders to use state corporations for a variety of political and social, as well as economic, purposes. For these reasons, the performance of state corporations, has been, consequently, at best, uneven. Some banking and financial institutions have been relatively successful in Tanzania and Côte d'Ivoire. East African public enterprises, on the whole, have a better record than West African ones. But, in many instances, publicly owned corporations have incurred large debts that have proven to be a major drain on already strained treasuries (for more information see Chapter 9).

The reasons for the equivocal achievements of parastatals are many. Indifferent recruitment procedures, financial mishandling, lack of accountability, political appointments, and at times gross corruption and mismanagement have plagued public enterprises in socialist Mozambique and capitalist Gabon, in Nigeria as well as Uganda, Tanzania, Ghana, Algeria, and Cameroon.[41] In Ghana, after the fall of the First Republic and again after the demise of Kofi Busia's short-lived Progress party government (1969–1972), investigative commissions delved into the affairs of parastatals, revealed multiple instances of financial abuse, and punished officials who had used public companies as private banks. In Zambia in 1978, a parliamentary commission established to review the functioning of state companies revealed theft, mismanagement, and inefficiency on a grand scale. Côte d'Ivoire was wracked in the early 1980s by a major scandal surrounding the state-owned housing corporation. The inefficiency of many parastatals has thus overshadowed the successful work carried out by others.

The public sector in many African states had a history in the 1960s and 1970s of immense growth and equivocal accomplishments. By the 1980s many governments decided to either reorganize inefficient corporations, reduce the number of state corporations, or establish more stringent controls over the public sector.[42] The precise position of parastatal organizations within the public domain is consequently currently in flux.

When taken together, bureaucratic expansion and the proliferation of state-owned enterprises vastly augmented the network of administrative institutions in African countries. Yet this sprawling and often unwieldly administrative apparatus has not assured efficiency or responsiveness. Bureaucratic roles have often been ill defined,[43] and the pressures upon public servants for personal favors have been especially intense.[44] Corrupt practices have permeated the civil service in most African states,[45] and the relations between government officials and civil servants have frequently been strained. As one peasant explained to a civil servant, "I can't hear what you're saying because who you are thunders in my ears."[46] Thus, structures intended as institutional vehicles for development have, by their inefficiency, become obstacles to effective growth. The first two decades of independence witnessed administrative expansion and, concomitantly, highlighted the extent of institutional frailty in most African states.[47]

The coercive apparatus. The fortification of administrative institutions in the 1960s and 1970s came hand in hand with the growth of enforcement agencies and, most significantly, the army and the police. Armed forces were retained at first as a symbol of sovereignty and national independence; then they were sustained and expanded to quell disturbances, ensure compliance, and provide necessary props for frail regimes. With few exceptions (Botswana, Lesotho, Gambia, Swaziland), African leaders engaged in the construction and expansion of the military during the first two decades of independence.

The small military forces of the mid-1960s (Nigeria's army, for example, numbered 11,500; Côte d'Ivoire's, 4,000; Togo's, 1,450; Zambia's, 3,000; Kenya's, 4,755; Tanzania's, 1,800; Uganda's, 5,960) and relatively low financial outlays for these units (defense as a percentage of GNP ranged from Tanzania's .3 percent and Nigeria's .9 to Côte d'Ivoire's 2.4 percent and Kenya's rather high 9.8 percent) reflected the limited and ceremonial roles of the earlier colonial armies.[48] By the late 1970s, however, military size and expenditures had risen significantly. In 1978, the Nigerian armed forces stood at 231,000, mirroring the rapid expansion that took place during the civil war and the problems attendant upon demobilization. The armed forces in Côte d'Ivoire increased to approximately 9,000; in Togo, to 4,800; in Zambia to 20,000; in Kenya to 13,700; and in Tanzania to 26,700 (further expanded in 1980-1981 to 44,850, as additional troops were mobilized to aid the Tanzanian incursion into Uganda and to maintain order in that country after the ouster of Idi Amin Dada).[49]

A rise in military expenditures naturally accompanied these increases in troops. For Africa as a whole, military expenditures as a proportion of GNP rose from 1.8 percent in 1963 to 2.6 percent in 1968 and then to 3.4 percent in 1971, decreasing slightly to 2.9 percent in 1980.[50] As military power grew, Africa's share of world arms imports climbed from 4.6 percent in 1971 to 18.8 percent in 1980, indicating an annual growth rate in arms expenditures of 33.4 percent. The effects of this heavy burden of military expenditures have been distributed quite unevenly among African states. As indicated in Table 2.1, approximately 50 percent of the countries on the continent had military outlays of more than 2 percent of GNP during this period. A large number of poor countries, usually coinciding with areas of internal insurrection and major political instability, carried especially heavy military burdens.

It is possible to point to an overall process of militarization in the phase of the elaboration of state power. This trend was visible also in the expansion of paramilitary structures.[51] In the early years of independence, new rulers, uneasy about the loyalty of their British- or French-trained officer corps or the remnants of national liberation armies, bolstered the police force and sometimes even es-

TABLE 2.1
Relative Burden of Military Expenditures in Sub-Saharan Africa, 1984

Military Expenditure as Percent of GNP	GNP Per Capita (1983 dollars)	
10% and over		
5–9.99%	under $200	Ethiopia
	$200–499	Cape Verde; Zambia; Somalia
	$500–999	Angola; Lesotho; Zimbabwe
2–4.99%	under $200	Burkina Faso; Equatorial Guinea; Guinea-Bissau; Mali
	$200–499	Mauritania; Mozambique; Burundi; Kenya; Tanzania; Guinea; Senegal; Madagascar; Benin; Togo; Liberia; Rwanda; Sudan
	$500–999	Botswana
	$1,000–2,999	South Africa; Congo
1–1.99%	under $200	Malawi; Chad
	$200–499	Central African Republic; Sao Tomé and Principe; Zaire; Uganda
	$500–999	Cameroon; Nigeria; Swaziland; Côte d'Ivoire
Under 1%	$200–499	Niger; Sierra Leone; Gambia
	$1,000–2,999	Mauritius

Source: Adapted from United States Arms Control and Disarmament Agency, *World Military Expenditures and Arms Transfers 1986* (Washington, D.C.: U.S. Government Printing Office, 1987), p. 5.

tablished their own armed guard alongside the military establishment. In many parts of francophone Africa the gendarmerie was used to maintain order, and throughout the continent border guards and elite presidential units were created.

The growth of the coercive branch of government resulted in the formation of highly organized groups with distinct professional and corporate interests. The definition of new tasks generated demands for higher salaries, improved living conditions, an expanded array of consumer goods, and expensive military equipment. This trend first became evident in 1963 and 1964, when soldiers in Togo, Tanzania, Kenya, and Uganda mutinied to support their demands for improved service conditions. Leaders in these countries, despite some embarrassment, called in troops from the ex-colonial metropole to quell these military insurrections. Salaries were consequently increased and conditions in the armed forces improved. The coercive apparatus thereby became a potential political force not only in these but in most African countries. Indeed, the mutinies of the early 1960s presaged a series of military interventions that have been part and parcel of African political history in the postcolonial era (military coups will be discussed fully in Chapter 8).

The growth of the coercive instruments of rule generated an additional set of issues of coordination and control. The first problem that developed around the military related, as in the administration, to questions of internal cohesion and specialization. In some countries, where the size of the military was relatively small, external military support available, and economic conditions relatively stable, it was possible to retain a high degree of professionalism and discipline. Côte d'Ivoire and Senegal are two cases in point. But in most countries, the growth of military institutions, coupled with their politicization, led to friction between the senior officer corps and the lower ranks and between various branches of the armed services. This tendency was especially apparent in countries like Ghana, Benin, and Nigeria, which had undergone several military interventions. It was further exacerbated by interethnic and interregional strife within the military, especially in countries where recruitment patterns were ethnically slanted (Zaire, 1960; Nigeria, 1966; Uganda, 1972).

The question of military cohesion was closely tied to patterns of civil-military relations. The dilemma of rulers in this regard was pronounced. They had to learn how to navigate between their need for coercive enforcement and the dangers attendant upon the threat of military politicization. Some leaders—Houphouët-Boigny in Côte d'Ivoire, Kenneth Kaunda in Zambia, and Leopold Sedar Senghor in Senegal—were able to balance prudently these countervailing pressures and remain in office. Others, such as Hilla Limann in Ghana or Shehu Shagari in Nigeria, were less successful in this regard and were compelled to suffer the consequences (both were overthrown in military coups).[52]

The relations between decision makers and the armed forces also had an impact on the links between these agencies and their social environment. Well-disciplined military personnel not prone to preying on innocent citizens to supplement their incomes have succeeded in gaining respect in some African states. On the other hand, faulty lines of command, inadequate salaries, and raw ambition have allowed soldiers in other countries to become, themselves, the cause of indiscriminate lawlessness. This was the case in many parts of Nigeria in 1966, in Zaire in the 1970s, and in Uganda during the 1970s and early 1980s. "Such is the anarchy," wrote one observer, "that even the very notion of a Ugandan army is blurred." The army, described as divided, disorganized, and frightened, "came to undermine the very state which built it up and relied upon it."[53]

Patterns of military growth and of civil-military relations vary substantially from one country to another. In certain places—most notably, Côte d'Ivoire, Botswana, Senegal, and Tunisia—the military has not been an important political factor. In other countries, the political scene has almost continuously been integrally linked to the status and orientation of soldiers (Ghana and Nigeria stand out in this regard). In almost all countries, the coercive apparatus emerged as an essential branch of formal governmental structures. This trend was less a statement on the centrality of the armed forces to the conduct of state affairs than a commentary on the fragility of civilian institutions and the insecurity of many leaders on the continent.[54]

The legal order.   Administrative and military expansion and entrenchment in the 1960s and 1970s was part of the process of strengthening the power apparatus at the expense of broadly based political institutions. Judicial structures, in contrast, although developing at a steady pace, remained somewhat separate from the rapid growth that took place in the decision-enforcing spheres. The legal systems of African countries at independence were generally constructed on two foundations evolved during the colonial period. The first was customary law, which varied from locale to locale. Long-standing rules developed by local communities regarding land tenure, marriage, divorce, and petty offenses were codified and continued to govern many aspects of daily life. In Muslim areas, the Shari'a law prevailed. On top of this preexisting legal system, colonial rulers superimposed a second set of judicial institutions to serve as courts of appeal and to adjudicate disputes resulting from infringements on colonial decrees. These structures were modeled faithfully on the lines of metropolitan judicial institutions.

On the eve of independence, these courts, much as the civil service and the military, underwent a process of Africanization. The judicial system in each country was charged with upholding customary law as well as provisions in the new independence constitutions. Inevitably, therefore, the courts became the focus of a great deal of activity. At the local level, litigation increased as land claims were disputed and inheritance laws were altered. In English-speaking countries in particular, access to resources also involved an ability to work through the court system. Here the courts became a crucial vehicle for contesting decisions of traditional authorities and gaining control of desired assets. In Zaire, the nationalization of land also increased activity around the courts. The judicial system also attempted to act as the watchdog of decision makers. This implied that the courts had a say in evaluating the behavior of politicians and civil servants. The tension between the courts and the politicians was not inconsiderable.

In Ghana, for example, Kwame Nkrumah sought on several occasions to ignore unfavorable court decisions. When these actions aroused indignation, first specific laws and then the constitution in its entirety were changed. Kofi Busia defied a court order overturning his dismissal of over five hundred civil servants, thereby laying himself open to charges of interfering with the judicial process. In Uganda, both Idi Amin and Milton Obote bypassed the courts and directly attacked the authority of judges. In Nigeria, the courts were seen as a means, albeit indirect, of supervising politicians and attaining some measure of redress from unbridled bureaucrats. The centralizing efforts of Robert Mugabe in Zimbabwe have involved a confrontation between the regime and the courts over civil rights issues. In all these cases the judicial system became the object of a great deal of manipulation.

The court system has not, moreover, been entirely free of political favoritism or, for that matter, a measure of elitism. Although local courts and religious judicial authorities have, over the years, remained relatively accessible, dealings with the complex legal systems inherited from the colonial period have required more skills and expertise. Rural dwellers or impoverished urban populations have either avoided the national court systems or found themselves outclassed in intricate court cases. When feelings of exclusion ran high (Ghana and Uganda during the late 1970s are two examples), judges were denounced alongside politicians. Even in these cases, however, it was rarely the judiciary in its entirety that was repudiated but rather the individual actions of specific justices and lawyers.

Changes in judicial structures per se have, in general, been few and far between. Only on rare occasions did the judicial structure itself become the object of a major revamping. This was the case in Ghana in 1979 and again in 1982, when public tribunals and popular commissions were set up to bypass the formal judicial system and dispense justice quickly.[55] The assault on the courts did not, however, succeed in displacing existing institutions, nor did it undermine the essential faith of citizens in Ghana and elsewhere in the established judicial system.

At issue in many African states, therefore, was not the judicial system specifically, but the notion of the rule of law in general. Authoritarianism was frequently accompanied by repression. If rulers such as Idi Amin in Uganda, Jean-Bedel Bokassa in the Central African Republic, and Macias Nguema in Equatorial Guinea became notorious for their flagrant violations of the law, human rights violations were not unknown in other parts of the continent in the 1960s and the 1970s. Political detainees were held without trial in Kenya, Malawi, Guinea, Liberia, Gabon, Zambia, Tanzania, Zaire, and Ethiopia, to name but a few. Government officials and policymakers openly flaunted import restrictions, foreign currency controls, and even curfew laws that they themselves had imposed. The resiliency of judicial structures was maintained, but the system of public accountability in many countries did become frayed. The growth of administrative and coercive structures therefore adversely affected the separation of powers and judicial autonomy in most parts of Africa.[56]

The political machinery.   The heavy emphasis on administrative and coercive institutions during the phase of power elaboration had its effects on the organization and functions of the political machinery as well. The history of African politics during the first two decades of independence (and beyond) was one of the systematic subordination of the political apparatus in the bulk of the continent to the executive. The margin for political maneuvering at the national level was severely constrained.

The single-party systems that were created in the early period of independence gradually took on distinct forms in subsequent years. Some parties were quickly changed into auxiliaries of the administration and their representative functions undermined. This was the case in Côte d'Ivoire throughout the 1960s and the 1970s and in Cameroon during the same period. In these cases, the party was viewed as a channel for the dispensation of patronage, as a medium for political communication, and, above all, as a legitimating device. Here single-party politics became machine politics, and the regime a one-party plebiscite. The legislatures in these countries became forums for discussion but had little, if any, voice in decision making.

In other instances, more stress was placed on finding ways for permitting political participation within a single-party setup. Tanzania, Kenya, and Algeria pioneered a system of limited competition within the one-party framework, enabling a rotation of members of parliament in regularly scheduled elections. In these African states, the single parties did assume at least a linkage role between local constituents and the central government.[57] Parliamentary debates in these countries, inevitably, have been more lively. Consideration of constituency concerns has become part of the legislative scene. Nevertheless, decision-making functions were still severely constricted.

In still other cases—Ghana under Nkrumah, Uganda under Obote, Guinea under Sekou Touré, Sierra Leone under Siaka Stevens—the party deteriorated into a hollow shell whose functions were unclear and whose utility was uncertain. In these instances, the single party was used primarily as an instrument of control and, again, patronage, frequently under the guise of ideological innovation. Parliamentary activity virtually ground to a halt. Eventually, the combination of low party dominance and decreased participation transformed these countries into what has been termed no-party states.

To be sure, a few countries in Africa succeeded in establishing and sustaining a multiparty system since independence. In Gambia and Botswana, one party has remained in power throughout this period, but opposition parties were able to organize, compete in elections, and have their voices heard in parliaments possessing some real legislative role. In Mauritius, a vibrant multiparty system developed that allowed for a change in governing parties at the ballot box. In these instances, the single party was eschewed in favor of a more penetrating competitive system. Executive government was also attenuated by checks imposed by parliaments.

During the course of the 1970s, with the creation of Afro-Marxist regimes in Angola, Mozambique, Guinea-Bissau, and Ethiopia, another, revolutionary-mobilizing, pattern was laid down. In these cases, the party became the focal point of policymaking efforts. In Angola, party initiatives made a significant contribution to regime performance and perhaps survival. In 1981, for example, the party proclaimed a year of "discipline and control," thereby asserting itself as a key monitoring agency in the country. In Ethiopia, a formal Soviet-styled communist party was proclaimed on 10 September 1984 in an effort by the country's leader, Lieutenant Colonel Mengistu Haile Mariam, to consolidate his rule and to strengthen his control over society. The party was meant to provide a vehicle for the ruling clique's drive to transform Ethiopian society from a "feudal-bourgeois" regime to a genuinely communist one. In these countries, the party supplanted the legislature as a forum for voicing opinions on significant issues.

The party framework, and, by extension, legislative structures in Africa, therefore evolved in many different ways and exhibited varying degrees of stability. During the phase of power elaboration, the party apparatus became an auxiliary of the administrative coercive institutions, and parliaments forfeited many of their policymaking and supervisory roles. At best, the political machinery was subordinated to executive structures; in at least 50 percent of African states, parties and parliaments were dissolved in the aftermath of a military coup.

The fact that power elaboration under military rule further deemphasized the political apparatus drives home the extreme vulnerability of political institutions in Africa during the 1960s and 1970s. These were the first to be monopolized by insecure leaders and the first to be abandoned by incoming military rulers. The organization of the political realm was thus the most arbitrary, haphazard, and unpredictable component of power elaboration during the first two decades after independence.

This trend accentuated what had become obvious during the initial reorganization of government institutions after the transfer of power: that in most of Africa government institutions lacked a well-defined popular foundation. Authoritarian structures evolved and were refined by personal rulers who became substitutes for regularized organizations and decision-making procedures. The bases of power were still not clearly laid out even when the parameters of the unacceptable had been tested and delineated. As one observer stated at the end of the second postcolonial decade, "the state still faces a crisis of legitimacy before the tribunal of African pluralism."[58]

The entrenchment of administrative institutions at the expense of regularized channels of political involvement left many African leaders in a situation in which their control was uncertain, their reach arbitrary, and their reliance on force greater than at the time of independence.[59] The process of administrative proliferation and political enfeeblement had rendered many African institutions weak and others insufficiently effective.

☐ Phase 3: The Reconsideration of State Power

By the late 1970s and early 1980s most, if not all, African states were undergoing an organizational crisis. The first, and most widely noted, characteristic of this crisis was the fraying character of state-society relations. Many govern- ① ments, particularly in those countries that had experienced numerous regime changes since independence, had not been able to gain the trust of large portions of their populations. Government directives were seen as intrusive and even destructive; distrust of officials abounded. Decrees were frequently skirted, laws flaunted, and although bureaucrats were courted, they were also regarded as oppressors.[60] A second feature of the dilemma of African states at this juncture was the extensive nature of the administrative and coercive apparatus. Govern- ② ment structures were overmanned and costly (large portions of wage labor were employed in the public sector).[61] The propensity of unwieldy institutions to overconsume inevitably taxed already scarce resources and further reduced the capacity of state institutions. A third dimension of the crisis of government institutions related to the widespread use of public funds and positions for the personal enrichment of civil servants and politicians. In many African states, the distinction between the private and the public realms was not sufficiently clear-cut.[62]

Fourth, the abuse of public office had a debilitating effect on the support accorded to state leaders and officeholders. Authoritarianism was a poor substitute for legitimacy and authority; consent and consensus were undermined. In the absence of state supremacy, politics came to involve competition among a small and fractured elite for control over a dwindling state pie.[63] The lack of power and authority fostered a counterproductive elitism that perpetuated gross inequality and induced divisions among those social groups that had achieved privileged positions around the state.

The final, and most pernicious, dimension of the state crisis was the inability of many formal institutions to fulfill even the most basic tasks. To be sure, most African governments recorded impressive gains in education, health, and social welfare during the first two decades of independence. But by the late 1970s anemic rates of development and a relative reduction in social services and infrastructural maintenance indicated a diminution in administrative capabilities.[64]

Not all African countries experienced the crisis of state institutions to the same degree and in the same ways. Some countries, like Ghana, Chad, Uganda, and Tanzania in the early 1980s, appeared to be on the verge of disintegration. Others, such as Zaire and Nigeria, were stagnating. But even states with relatively strong records, such as Côte d'Ivoire, Zambia, and Kenya, felt the adverse effects of dwindling resources, growing violence, and decreased capabilities. In the first two decades of independence, state institutions had become more salient: Their capacities had rarely increased accordingly.

What explains the relative weakness of governmental structures in the first decades of independence? The answer would appear to include at least six critical elements: scarcity of resources, politicized patterns of social differentiation, overexpanded state structures, insufficient state legitimacy, inadequate state power, and the lack of adaptation of alien institutions to local conditions.[65] The challenge of state organization was therefore particularly pronounced as the postcolonial phase of African independence began to come to an end.

The heavily centralized statism that marked the first decades of independence has been subjected to close scrutiny in recent years. And although many of the authoritarian and repressive tendencies of the first independence generation persist into the 1980s, most countries have undertaken some reviews of the structure of the public sphere and others have proceeded to make institutional adjustments as well.

The first, and most obvious, target of this reordering has been the administrative apparatus. Foreign donors and international monetary agencies (especially the IMF and the World Bank) have tied capital support to plans for the contraction of the administrative and public sector. In line with these programs of structural adjustment, the size of ministries has been purposely cut, and in some countries governments have systematically divested themselves of unprofitable or costly state enterprises. The quantitative reduction of the administrative apparatus was undertaken in Côte d'Ivoire, Zaire, Ghana, Zambia, Senegal, and Guinea, and in 1986 in Nigeria and Cameroon, to mention but a few.

This process has been accompanied by a concomitant trend toward increased reliance on market mechanisms. Although government structures still act as entrepreneurs, more economic activity has been fostered in the private sector, and state economic controls have been relaxed. The dismantling of marketing boards in many West African states is a case in point. The governmental arena has cut back on its economic involvement in many places without totally relinquishing its regulatory roles. The reduction of bureaucratic involvement in the economy frequently has come hand in hand with plans for the devolution of central authority to local agencies. Decentralization schemes have been devised in countries like Zaire and Ghana, and similar plans are being drawn up in other countries. They have yet to be fully implemented in practice.

The political side of this process has involved some opening of participatory opportunities. Certain single-party systems allowed for greater competition in the early 1980s (Côte d'Ivoire, for one) and others actually permitted multiparty competition (Senegal). Some military governments, especially in anglophone Africa, withdrew in favor of (short-lived) multiparty regimes, as in Ghana and Nigeria in the late 1970s and early 1980s. Others, particularly in francophone countries (Mali, Togo, Niger, Benin), underwent a process of civilization in the dominant party mode. Populist governments—Ghana and Burkina Faso—experimented with new types of direct participation and related populist institutional arrangements. And in countries where the founding fathers survived the first decades of independence and military coups, the initial generation gave way, at times voluntarily, to a new crop of rulers (Cameroon, Senegal, Tanzania, Sierra Leone, and Kenya).[66] If political patterns were no more regularized toward the end of the 1980s than at the beginning of the decade, they were at least more heterogeneous and innovative than in the preceding years.

The rethinking that began to take place at this juncture has also included a reassessment of the size and role of the armed forces in a select number of African states. Nigeria, for example, grappled, especially after the 1983 coup, with trimming down its military establishment and with reorganizing the internal chain of command. Ghana in 1984 and 1985 also reduced the size of its army and began to deal more systematically with the growing problem of military indiscipline. And although many leaders, still heavily dependent on coercive devices and wary of antagonizing the armed forces, have been reluctant to interfere in this sphere, the issue of the military, and of military participation in politics, has become a topic of serious political discussion. This observation has also held true for questions related to the judicial process. The rise of populist leaders has accentuated the concern with questions of public accountability and problems of severe social inequality. The underlying principles that guided, or misdirected, public affairs during the first postcolonial generation were at least aired more thoroughly in African capitals.

The experimentation of the 1980s varied in intensity and direction. Although many past patterns persisted and were even highlighted, the notion of exclusive state domination was gradually undergoing reconsideration. There appeared to be a movement in many countries toward "renewed yet partial liberalism at the level of politics and . . . capitalism at the level of economics, indicating a greater openness at both levels as inherited institutions decay."[67]

The question of viable constructions of the public arena was, perhaps, more urgent at the outset of the second twenty-five years of African independence than at the beginning of the postcolonial era. From this ongoing evaluation may yet emerge a formula for the decolonization of the state.[68] As past experiences mesh with present possibilities and future prospects, the question of institutional remolding remains a pressing and ongoing issue on the African political agenda. The process of introspection and reevaluation which followed the realization of the crisis of public structures in the 1980s constituted an important step in the sober confrontation with this fundamental challenge.

■ STATES AND STATE VARIETY IN AFRICA: SOME IMPLICATIONS

The task of molding public institutions in Africa has been a fundamental and ongoing concern of African governments over the years. Different countries and ruling coalitions have approached this challenge in a variety of ways. By the mid-1980s, some African countries had succeeded in establishing a workable set of structures that has endured over time. These stronger states (Kenya, Côte d'Ivoire, Cameroon, Algeria), contrasted sharply with a small group of countries (Chad, Uganda) that had failed to coalesce viable institutions of governance. And most countries were still, nearly thirty years after independence, grappling with the complex problems of shaping public organizations that would accommodate the resources and needs of societies constrained by scarcity and external dependency.[69] Authoritarianism has been a common theme in these efforts.

The main question raised at the outset of this chapter dealt with the connection between statism and governmental capacities. During the first postindependence phase, as this analysis has shown, the range and scope of public institutions expanded palpably. The growth of state agencies should not, however, be confused with a concomitant increase in their effectiveness or their penetrative capacities. Indeed, current analyses have highlighted the frailties of many public institutions in recent years. This tendency has led certain observers to write off the state entity as an important factor in African political life and to predict the decomposition of the public structures inherited from the colonial period.[70] Despite the vicissitudes of administrative organs, coercive agencies, political parties, and judicial structures, state institutions (even when enfeebled) have survived, as has the idea of stateness. "The African state's resilience is remarkable and its relative influence on society is still greater than that of any other organization."[71] Indeed, "at a minimum we have seen that the threat of anarchy . . . is unfounded."[72] Public institutions are significant as funnels of resources (both domestic and international), as repositories of expertise, and as coordinators of a variety of activities. For all their weaknesses, the state institutions imposed during the colonial period and subsequently redesigned since independence have become an inseparable part of life on the continent. The question facing the current generation of African leaders is, thus, not so much one of averting state collapse as one of adjusting public organizations in a way that previous mistakes will not be repeated and that institutional devices will be more in tune with local conditions and needs.[73]

African elites, those who have benefited the most from statism, have, in light of the recent crisis of control, begun to reassess some of their methods. They have examined ways of fortifying the state or, conversely, decentralizing power or reducing the size of state institutions. The overall thrust of these suggestions has been away from overconcentration and toward a reaggregation that takes into account not only the extent of public resources but also social and economic realities. If the dynamic of statism prevailed through the heady years immediately after independence, the pendulum in the 1980s has begun to shift in the direction of less direct control and perhaps more supervision and regulation.

The question of the amount of government, in the final analysis, may therefore be giving way to a more careful consideration of the varieties of organization in the public domain. Just as formal structures provide frameworks within which social and economic processes take place, their organizational abilities, in turn, are molded by these forces. Different economic resources, historical legacies, foreign attachments and interests, social composition, types of stratification, and political skills have affected the capacity and prospects of public institutions.[74]

The experiences of the first decades of independence have underlined the danger inherent in the lopsided development of the power apparatus at the expense of political mechanisms. They have also given stress to the pitfalls of power elaboration divorced from social currents, economic conditions, and existing concepts of authority.[75] The initial frameworks of public life in Africa suffered perhaps from too great a detachment from local processes and societal concerns. In the coming decades, imposed models and forms may continue to yield, as in recent years, to institutional reformulations more attuned to changing circumstances within the continent. The shape of public institutions, nevertheless, and the nature of their activities, will continue to define the central reference point of economic, social, and external processes.

■ NOTES

1. For a review of the concept of the state, see J. P. Nettl, "The State as a Conceptual Variable," *World Politics* 20, no. 4 (1968): 559–592. See also Stephen D. Krasner, "Approaches to the State: Alternative Conceptions and Historical Dynamics," *Comparative Politics* 16, no. 2 (1984): 223–245.

2. Peter Anyang' Nyongo, "The Economic Foundations of the State in Contemporary Africa: Stratification and Social Classes," *Présence Africaine* no. 127/128 (1983): 195. Also see Andre Gunder Frank, *Crisis: In the Third World* (London: Heinemann, 1981), pp. 245–249.

3. Joel Samoff, "Class, Class Conflict, and the State in Africa," *Political Science Quarterly* 97, no. 1 (1982): 105–128; Issa Shivji, "The State in the Dominated Social Formations of Africa: Some Theoretical Issues," *Social Sciences Journal* 32, no. 4 (1980): 730–742.

4. Claude Ake, *A Political Economy of Africa* (London: Longman, 1981): pp. 126–127.

5. Raymond Duvall and John R. Freeman, "The State and Dependent Capitalism," *International Studies Quarterly* 25, no. 1 (1981): 106.

6. This is essentially a paraphrase of the definition suggested by Max Weber. See Theda Skocpol, *Bringing the State Back In: Current Research,* in Peter B. Evans, Dietrich Rueschmeyer, and Theda Skocpol, eds., *Bringing the State Back In* (Cambridge: Cambridge University Press, 1985): pp. 7–8.

7. Stephen D. Krasner, *Structural Conflict: The Third World Against Global Liberalism* (Berkeley: University of California Press, 1985), p. 4. The concept of regime may be applied both on the domestic and the international levels.

8. Ruth Berins Collier, *Regimes in Tropical Africa* (Berkeley: University of California Press, 1982), pp. 7–10, views states as pacts of domination and regimes as modes of domination.

9. Joel S. Migdal, "Strong States, Weak States: Power and Accommodation," in Myron Weiner and Samuel P. Huntington, eds., *Understanding Political Development* (Boston: Little, Brown, 1987), pp. 396–397.

10. See Crawford Young, "Africa's Colonial Legacy," in Robert J. Berg and Jennifer Seymour Whitaker, eds., *Strategies for African Development* (Berkeley: University of California Press, 1985), esp. pp. 26–27.

11. Otwin Marenin, "The Managerial State in Africa: A Conflict Coalition Perspective," in Zaki Ergas, ed., *The African State in Transition* (London: Macmillan, 1987).

12. Skocpol, *Bringing the State Back In,* p. 21. Much of this type of analysis may be found in Theda Skocpol, *The State and Social Revolutions* (London: Cambridge University Press, 1980), esp. pp. 24–33.

13. David P. Laitin, "Hegemony and Religious Conflict: British Imperial Control and Political Cleavages in Yorubaland," in Evans, Rueschmeyer, and Skocpol, *Bringing the State Back In,* p. 287.

14. See Victor Azarya and Naomi Chazan, "Disengagement from the State in Africa: Reflections on the Experience of Ghana and Guinea," *Comparative Studies in Soci-*

ety and History 19, no. 1 (1987): 106–131.

15. Guillermo O'Donnell, "Comparative Historical Formations of the State Apparatus and Socio-Economic Change in the Third World," *International Social Sciences Journal* 32, no. 4 (1980): 7–8.

16. G. van Benthem van den Berghe, *The Interconnection Between Processes of State and Class Formation: Problems of Conceptualization* (The Hague: Institute of Social Studies Occasional Papers no. 52, August 1975), p. 15.

17. Victor Azarya, "Reordering State-Society Relations: Incorporation and Disengagement," in Donald Rothchild and Naomi Chazan, eds., *The Precarious Balance: State and Society in Africa* (Boulder, Colo.: Westview Press, 1987).

18. A. I. Asiwaju, "The Concept of Frontier in the Setting of States in Pre-Colonial Africa," *Présence Africaine* 127/128 (1983): 44–45, and Adekunle Ajake, "The Nature of African Boundaries," *Afrika Spectrum* 18, no. 2 (1982/1983): 177–190.

19. Nelson Kasfir, "Designs and Dilemmas: An Overview," in Phillip Mahwood, ed., *Local Government in the Third World: The Experience of Tropical Africa* (New York: John Wiley, 1983), p. 34.

20. Richard Hodder-Williams, *An Introduction to the Politics of Tropical Africa* (London: George Allen and Unwin, 1984), p. 86.

21. The discussion of this period is necessarily brief in this context. For an overview, see Thomas Hodgkin, *Nationalism in Colonial Africa* (New York: New York University Press, 1957) and *African Political Parties* (Harmondsworth: Penguin, 1961).

22. Yves Person, "L'état nation en Afrique," *Le Mois en Afrique* 190/191 (1981): 27–35; Bakary Traoré, "De la genèse de la nation et de l'état en Afrique noire," *Présence Africaine* no. 127/128 (1983): 149–160.

23. Robert Price, "Neo-Colonialism and Ghana's Economic Decline: A Critical Assessment," *Canadian Journal of African Studies* 18, no. 1 (1984): 188–190.

24. I. William Zartman, "Issues of African Diplomacy in the 1980s," *Orbis* 25, no. 4 (1982): 1026.

25. Thomas M. Callaghy, "Politics and Vision in Africa: The Interplay of Domination, Equality and Liberty," in Patrick Chabal, ed., *Political Domination in Africa* (London: Cambridge University Press, 1986), pp. 30–51.

26. Quoted in Donald Rothchild, "On the Application of the Westminster Model to Ghana," *Centennial Review* 4, no. 4 (Fall 1960): 478. On this, also see his "Majimbo Schemes in Kenya and Uganda," in Jefferey Butler and A. A. Castagno, eds., *Boston University Papers on Africa* (New York: Praeger, 1967), pp. 291–318.

27. Aristide Zolberg, *Creating Political Order: The Party States of West Africa* (Chicago: Rand McNally, 1966).

28. Julius K. Nyerere, "Democracy and the Party System," in Julius K. Nyerere, *Freedom and Unity* (Dar es Salaam: Oxford University Press, 1966), pp. 196–197. Also see Ahmed Sekou Touré, *The Doctrine and Methods of the Democratic Party of Guinea*, Part 1 (Conakry: Democratic Party of Guinea, n.d.), p. 52.

29. Michael F. Lofchie, "Representative Government, Bureaucracy and Political Development: The African Case," in Marion Doro and Newell Stultz, eds., *Governing in Black Africa* (Englewood Cliffs, N.J.: Prentice Hall, 1970), pp. 278–294.

30. David B. Abernathy, "Bureaucratic Growth and Economic Decline in Sub-Saharan Africa," (Paper presented at the African Studies Association, Boston, December 1983), p. 11.

31. Dean E. McHenry, *Tanzania's Ujamaa Villages* (Berkeley, Calif.: Institute of International Studies, 1979), p. 68.

32. Hugh Roberts, "The Algerian Bureaucracy," *Review of African Political Economy,* no. 24 (1982), p. 53, as quoted in William Tordoff, *Government and Politics in Africa* (Bloomington: Indiana University Press, 1984), p. 108.

33. Highlighted in Tordoff, *Government and Politics in Africa,* pp. 105–106.

34. For a full exposition of this notion, see Thomas M. Callaghy, *The State-Society Struggle: Zaire in Comparative Perspective* (New York: Columbia University Press, 1984).

35. Christopher Clapham, *Third World Politics: An Introduction* (Madison: University of Wisconsin Press, 1985), pp. 47–48.

36. Collier, *Regimes in Tropical Africa*, p. 9.

37. Gatian F. Lungi and John O. Oni, "Administrative Weakness in Contemporary Africa," *African Quarterly* 24, no. 4 (1979): 3–16.

38. See Irving Leonard Markovitz, "Bureaucratic Development and Economic Growth," *Journal of Modern African Studies* 14, no. 2 (1970): 183–200, and Lungi and Oni, "Administrative Weakness."

39. Rwekaza Mukandala, "Trends in Civil Service Size and Income in Tanzania, 1967–1982," *Canadian Journal of African Studies* 2 (1983): 254.

40. For a full discussion, see Richard Sklar, "The Nature of Class Domination in Africa," *Journal of Modern African Studies* 17, no. 4 (1979): 531–552.

41. A good summary may be found in Tordoff, *Government and Politics in Africa*, pp. 139–144.

42. Paul Collins, "The State and Industrial Capitalism in West Africa," *Development and Change* 14, no. 3 (1983): 403–430; J. O. Udoji, "Reforming the Public Enterprises in Africa," *Quarterly Journal of Administration* 4, no. 3 (1970): 217–234; David B. Jones, "State Structure in New Nations: The Case of Primary Agricultural Marketing in Africa," *Journal of Modern African Studies* 20, no. 4 (1982): 553–570.

43. See, especially, Richard Crook, "Bureaucracy and Politics in Ghana: A Comparative Perspective," in Peter Lyon and James Manor, eds., *Transfer and Transformation: Political Institutions in the New Commonwealth* (Leicester: Leicester University Press, 1983). See also J. R. Nellis, "Is the Kenyan Bureaucracy Developmental? Political Considerations in Development Administration," *African Studies Review* 14, no. 3 (1971): 389–401.

44. John Ayoade, "States Without Citizens: An Emerging African Phenomenon," in Rothchild and Chazan, *The Precarious Balance*, p. 115. Also see Robert Price, *Society and Bureaucracy in Contemporary Ghana* (Berkeley: University of California Press, 1975), and Goran Hyden, "Social Structure, Bureaucracy and Development Administration in Kenya," *The African Review* 1, no. 3 (1972): 118–129.

45. For one example, see Victor Le Vine, *Political Corruption: The Ghana Case* (Stanford, Calif.: Hoover Institution, 1975).

46. David Abernathy, "Bureaucracy and Economic Development in Africa," *African Review* 1, no. 1 (1974): 93–107.

47. Goran Hyden, *No Shortcuts to Progress* (Berkeley: University of California Press, 1983), pp. 60–63, and A.H.M. Kirk-Greene, "The New African Administration," *Journal of Modern African Studies* 10, no. 1 (1972): 93–108.

48. Statistics from Claude E. Welch, ed., *Soldier and State in Africa* (Evanston, Ill.: Northwestern University Press, 1970), pp. 268–269.

49. Calculated from Colin Legum, ed., *African Contemporary Record 1981–82* (New York: Africana Publishing Co., 1981), B279, B309, C62–65, and *Africa Contemporary Record 1978–79* (New York: Africana Publishing Co., 1980), B736.

50. U.S. Arms Control and Disarmament Agency, *World Military Expenditures and Arms Trade 1963–73* (Washington, D.C.: U.S. Government Printing Office, 1975), p. 16; *World Military Expenditures and Arms Transfers 1968–1977* (Washington, D.C.: U.S. Government Printing Office, 1979), p. 27; and *World Military Expenditures and Arms Transfers 1971–1980* (Washington, D.C.: U.S. Government Printing Office, 1983), p. 33.

51. A general overview may be found in Eboe Hutchful, "Trends in Africa," *Alternatives* 10 (1985): 115–137.

52. For a good overview, see Olatunde Odetola, *Military Regimes and Development: A Comparative Analysis in African Societies* (London: George Allen and Unwin, 1982).

53. Jacques de Barrin, "Behind the Facade of Uganda's Democracy," *Manchester Guardian Weekly* 131, no. 4 (22 July 1984): 12.

54. Dennis Austin, "The Ghana Armed Forces and Ghanaian Society," *Third World Quarterly* 7, no. 1 (1985): 99.

55. E. Gyimah-Boadi and Donald Rothchild, "Rawlings, Populism and the Civil Liberties Tradition in Ghana," *Issue* 12, no. 3/4 (1982): 64–69.

56. Richard L. Sklar, "Developmental Democracy" (Paper presented at the American Political Science Association Meeting, Washington, D.C., September 1985), esp. pp. 8–25.

57. Ruth Berins Collier, "Parties, Coups and Authoritarian Rule: Patterns of Political Change in Tropical Africa," *Comparative Political Studies* 11, no. 1 (1978): 62–94; Joel D. Barkan and John J. Okumu, "Linkage Without Parties: Legislators and Constituents in Kenya," in Kay Lawson, ed., *Political Parties and Linkage,* (New Haven: Yale University Press, 1980), pp. 289–324.

58. Ali A. Mazrui, "Political Engineering in Africa," *International Social Science Journal* 25, no. 2 (1983): 244. Also see Robert H. Jackson and Carl G. Rosberg, *Personal Rule in Black Africa: Prince, Autocrat, Prophet, Tyrant* (Berkeley: University of California Press, 1982), p. 23.

59. Aristide Zolberg, "The Structure of Political Conflict in the New States of Tropical Africa," *American Political Science Review* 62, no. 1 (1968): 70–87.

60. Hyden, *No Shortcuts to Progress,* p. 19. Also see Donald Rothchild and Victor A. Olorunsola, eds., *State Versus Ethnic Claims: African Policy Dilemmas* (Boulder, Colo.: Westview Press, 1983), esp. p. 7.

61. Donald Rothchild and E. Gyimah-Boadi, "Ghana's Economic Decline and Development Strategies," in John Ravenhill, ed., *Africa in Economic Crisis* (London: Macmillan, 1986). For a fuller, though earlier, discussion see Michael Lofchie, ed., *The State of the Nations* (Berkeley: University of California Press, 1971).

62. Nelson Kasfir, "Introduction: State and Class in Africa," *Journal of Commonwealth and Comparative Politics* 21, no. 3 (1983): 4.

63. Richard Sandbrook, *The Politics of Africa's Economic Stagnation* (London: Cambridge University Press, 1985): pp. 112–113.

64. See John S. Saul, *The State and Revolution in Eastern Africa* (New York: Monthly Review Press, 1979). See also Marenin, "The Managerial State," pp. 6–10.

65. For an earlier and fuller discussion of these points, see Donald Rothchild and Michael Foley, "The Implications of Scarcity for Governance in Africa," *International Political Science Review* 4, no. 3 (1983): 311–326.

66. For a discussion of populism, see Henry Bienen, "Populist Military Regimes in West Africa," *Armed Forces and Society* 11, no. 3 (1985): 357–377.

67. Timothy M. Shaw, "The State of Crisis: African and International Capitalism in the Late Twentieth Century," in Rothchild and Chazan, *The Precarious Balance,* p. 307.

68. Crawford Young, "The African Colonial State and its Political Legacy," in Rothchild and Chazan, *The Precarious Balance,* p. 60.

69. Sandbrook, *The Politics of Africa's Economic Stagnation,* pp. 35–36.

70. Hyden, *No Shortcuts to Progress,* pp. 45–47 and passim.

71. Azarya, "Reordering State-Society Relations," p. 18.

72. Irving Leonard Markovitz, *Power and Class in Africa* (Englewood Cliffs, N.J.: Prentice Hall, 1977), pp. 3–12.

73. Bernard Schaffer, "Organization Is Not Equity: Theories of Political Integration," *Development and Change* 8, no. 1 (1977): 19–44.

74. Philip Lemaitre, "Who Will Rule Africa in the Year 2000?" in Helen Kitchen, ed., *Africa: Mystery or Maze* (New York: Council on Foreign Relations, 1979).

75. Peter Skalnik, "Questioning the Concept of the State in Indigenous Africa," *Social Dynamics* 9, no. 2 (1983): 11–28; Jean-François Bayart, "Les sociétés africaines face à l'etat," *Pouvoirs* 25 (1983): 23–39.

3

Social Groupings

Political life in Africa is conducted through a complex web of social forces, institutional settings, and interpersonal relationships. If government structures furnish the context for official interactions in the public domain, social groups constitute the fundamental building blocks of political action and interchange. In Chapter 2, we demonstrated that it is difficult to understand the state in Africa, and consequently to assess its capacity to formulate and implement policy, without probing its social underpinnings. Most studies of contemporary Africa, cast either in the modernization, dependency, or statist molds, have emphasized the importance of class and ethnicity in determining the social roots of public institutions. African social and material life, however, revolves, in the first instance, around a medley of more compact organizations, groupings, associations, and around movements that have evolved over the centuries in response to changing circumstances. Although they frequently serve disparate interests, vary widely in composition, operate in many different ways, and have altered substantially over time, these groups have consistently formed a broad tapestry of social, political, and economic communication. The political choice approach suggests that it is vital to begin with a closer look at these arenas of social interaction.

Our purpose in this chapter is to examine the cultural, social, and material frameworks of African political life and the manner and extent of their transformation in the postcolonial era. First, we introduce basic concepts of societal organization in Africa and identify the factors that affect group autonomy and cohesion. Then we portray, in some detail, the various primary and associational organizations that exist in different parts of the continent and the changes they have undergone in the past two decades. On this basis, various patterns of

71

differentiation emerging at independence are identified and major trends analyzed.

The discussion is organized around several key questions: What are the main concerns of various groups? How do they organize to pursue these goals? How do they deal with each other? What is their connection with formal government institutions? And what are the implications of their activities for politics and policy?

Virtually no corner of Africa has been left untouched by broader economic influences. As Africans have undergone a process of commercialization and as new problems and opportunities have arisen, existing structures have been re-shaped or new groups formed to promote interests, obtain access to resources, and enhance cultural meaning. There is much of the old in the new, and although the social bases of African life have been altered, their capitalist roots remain fragile.[1] Civil society in African countries may thus lack uniformity; it does, however, possess an underlying coherence.[2]

Social constructions in Africa, because of the intricate kinds of interpenetration on which they are built, usually cover an area that is broader than the official, the public, the formal. These groups have accumulated varying amounts and types of resources, and consequently power, independent of government institutions. Thus, state agencies may, in many cases, exercise a degree of direct or indirect control in the social realm. But because of the complex social structures in African countries, governments do not have a monopoly over power, let alone authority or legitimacy. The location of power concentrations and the extent of power dispersion depends, to a great extent, on the nature and degree of interactions between social groups and public institutions. The way these relationships are organized lies at the foundation of the dynamics of politics on the continent.

By examining the intricacies of social reality, choice, and action, it is possible not only to delve into important aspects of group behavior but also to obtain a better grasp of the persistent elements of the African experience that have been achieved during periods of extraordinary instability and structural change.[3] Such a study also helps to delineate the location and effects of power vectors in given African countries. To focus on the structure of socioeconomic organization is therefore to gain an important glimpse of the main features of the African political landscape.

■ SOCIAL GROUPS AND SOCIAL PROCESS

The main basis of political and socioeconomic activity in Africa is the group, rather than the individual or broader social constellation. Membership in groups has been an outgrowth of perceived or real common bonds. These ties may be ones of blood, affinity, identity, utility, or worship. People join organizations not only because they were born into them but also because a certain association or community can advance their interests and concerns and aid them in coping with their surroundings. As more groups have sprung up on the African scene, individuals have tended to attach themselves to a number of organizations simultaneously. Group frameworks are therefore at the core of the African social fabric: Although some social action may be conducted by classes or ethnic groups writ large, the reality of social organization consists of participation in smaller groupings limited in membership and/or geographic scope.

The group-based concepts of African social structures have their roots in traditional forms of social organization. The political culture of group action was deeply embedded in precolonial Africa. Both status and prestige at that time were dependent on group affiliation and on the relative position of each group in the social hierarchy. In the colonial period, the associational basis of social life continued and often intensified. Colonial administrations in most parts of the continent viewed coherent groups as desirable precisely because they facilitated control. This orientation encouraged the persistence of existing social structures and, frequently, traditional political units. In some cases these frameworks were allowed to maintain their separate identity, as in the past, but were incorporated simultaneously into the colonial structures. In other instances, people who were engaged in wage labor or in the colonial economy used their proceeds to invest in kin groups or in local polities. New means were therefore used to enhance status in existing groups.[4]

Colonial attitudes also guided the ways in which Africans could organize to take advantage of opportunities presented by the penetration of Western education and different modes of economic production. In the rural areas, the introduction of cash crops fueled the growth of farmer organizations and migrant associations. The expansion of commerce nurtured trader groups, whereas gender differences took on organizational shape in the form of women's associations and market women's cooperatives.[5] From the urban perspective, group life allowed Africans to control fragments of daily life. It constituted a significant channel for individual mobility and a psychological cushion against the dislocations of a changing environment.[6] Trade unions, secret societies, savings clubs, ethnic and religious associations, literary societies, sports clubs, and old-boys' networks sprung up in virtually every African city.

The constrictions placed on formal political activity by the colonial authorities meant that voluntary organizations and social and economic groups also became political frameworks in which anticolonial ideas were articulated and leaders schooled, and upon which political support was drawn. Almost every nationalist leader started his political career in a voluntary or economic organization: Felix Houphouët-Boigny in the Syndicat Agricole Africain, Nnamdi Azikiwe in the Ibo State Union, and Julius Nyerere in the Tanganyika Teachers' Association are just some examples. These early organizations also became the cornerstones of party structures and political movements.[7]

In the postcolonial period, this pattern has not only been maintained but has actually flourished. The range of groups in any political context in the 1980s varies widely. In Ghana, literally hundreds of separate associations have been recorded in the 1980s alone. Nigeria, too, has witnessed a plethora of social and economic groupings under military rule. A steep rise in the formation of such groups has been traced in Côte d'Ivoire; similar levels have been visible in Zaire, Zambia, Kenya, and Senegal (to mention but a few).[8] Even in Mozambique and Angola, new local associations have begun to emerge. By the beginning of the third decade of independence, vibrant organizations at the grassroots and intermediary levels had become a central vehicle of social interaction.

The aims of these groups reflect the mixture of interest, identity, and consciousness that motivate their members and define their roles.[9] Their primary purpose is to cater to the needs of their members. Ability to dispense goods and services is a decided asset. The strength of these networks grows in direct relationship to the resources they can obtain, control, and distribute.[10] A second objective of these organizations centers on group maintenance. They provide small-scale settings for meaningful participation in a context frequently devoid of possibilities for popular involvement. Most groups have clearly defined codes and norms of behavior. Leaders are subject to scrutiny. Regulations for access to office and for the rotation of persons in positions of responsibility exist. Tools of enforcement and the dispensation of justice have been developed. Decision making is often consultative. Many groups, therefore, have evolved their own concepts of power and authority and devised the means to put them into action.

A third, and related, set of goals focuses on group interaction with broader economic, social, and political frameworks. Specific associations actively pursue formal power or access to those in such positions. They cooperate or conflict with other associations over their place in the market and the social hierarchy. They seek to affect policy, the composition of power holders, and the content of the system itself. They act, therefore, not only as channels of information and communication and barometers of popular feeling, but also, to no mean degree, as contenders for power and molders of the determinants of the political process.[11]

The ability of groups to pursue their interests is linked to general contextual factors, such as prevailing economic conditions, transnational links and influences, and above all, existing official power constellations.[12] Their capacities are also determined by factors internal to their organization, such as historical continuity, access to or control of autonomous resources (particularly land or labor), location, size, and social organizing principles. For these reasons, social entities vary drastically in scope, ability to act, intensity of operations, internal structure, and impact on others.

The socioeconomic scene in African countries is composed of a multiplicity of interlocking yet distinct social organizations. In any given African country, it is possible to discern three main layers of social structures. The first consists of groups based on identity and affinity. Kinship associations, hometown organizations, and cultural units fall into this category. The second, or associational, level of social organization revolves around principles of affiliation. Here it is possible to place professional and occupational groups, such as lawyer associations, medical societies, trade unions, and farmer cooperatives, as well as religious communities, student groups, and neighborhood or village development groups. The third level of social organization is of an intermediary sort: It links specific groups and organizations to each other and to the state. Ethnicity and class are the main categories at this level of social organization (see Chapter 4). Individuals move between the various levels of social organization in the course of a lifetime. Their security, well-being, and development are tied to the nature of the groups to which they belong and how they interrelate.

■ THE ORGANIZATION OF SOCIAL LIFE

In the following pages the main primary and associational structures prevalent on the African scene will be examined in greater detail. The origins of each type of grouping will be traced, its main characteristics examined, the changes it has undergone in recent years explored, and its relations with other social and political entities elaborated.

□ Primary Groups

The first broad category of social structures in Africa consists of indigenous institutions that have deep historical roots, such as clans, lineages, cultural associations, and village communities. As many of these organizations are ascriptive—one is born into them—they are frequently referred to as primary groups. These divisions distinguish African societies along vertical lines: They highlight the differences between groups but do not order them hierarchically. Four main subtypes fall into this rubric: groups based on kinship; territoriality or location; traditional political affiliation; and cultural affinity.

The most continuously significant ascriptive structures throughout Africa have remained those based on *kinship*. Kinship is the bedrock of African social relationships. The extended family, the lineage, and in some cases the more inclusive clan define a person's immediate social network and obligations. In most cases, descent and inheritance are calculated through the male line: Patrilineality has delineated the shape of kinship links. In some parts of Africa, matrilineal descent arrangements still prevail. Among the Akan of Ghana, for example, inheritance procedures and kin group connections have been determined for centuries through the female line. The mother's brother has been the important person in a child's life; the uncle-nephew relationship has evolved as the most significant. In other instances, mixed descent patterns have developed, in which both female and male ties are salient. Marriage bonds, which are still in many places polygynous, further broaden the social network of kin ties.

Kinship not only defines a person's identity but also a set of values, norms, responsibilities, and life-styles. The kin group is an individual's initial community. Relations with other members of the group are governed by rules deeply embedded in local cultures. Nevertheless, two normative referents appear to be common to most kin connections: the notion of kinship solidarity and the reverence for age and seniority.

Kinship ties are also economic ties. In the past, access to land was granted to lineages and extended families. In many places this pattern has continued to the present. Through kinship, one also gained control of labor, perhaps the single most important determinant of survival prospects and possibilities for well-being. The kin bond was, and continues to be, the cornerstone upon which other economic relations are constructed.[13]

Despite many changes during the colonial period and the first years of independence—including a move toward a more nuclear family in the urban areas and the development of inequalities based on education and income within the extended family—kin ties have rarely been consciously severed or kin obligations easily ignored. It is commonplace, for example, to see agricultural cultivation carried out in rural areas according to principles of household division of labor practiced for years. In areas where a rural exodus has been the norm, if only on a seasonal basis, the rural household still acts as a refuge into which wage laborers withdraw and to which they retire to live out their old age. Kinship responsibilities, moreover, extend to new settings and to new occupations. Illiterate fathers educate their sons, who in turn are expected to provide material support and channels of access for their families in later years. There is rarely a bureaucrat, university lecturer, or migrant worker who does not feel the need to meet the expectations of his or her relatives.

The flexibility of kin groups means that uncertainty and insecurity may be met by adherence to age-old patterns redefined to meet the exigencies of new circumstances and constantly changing surroundings. Although not all kin have equal recourse to group resources (women, in particular, may encounter ongoing discrimination), the adhesive of kinship gives meaning when other institutions are being transformed or fail.

Kinship has frequently been linked to ties of *locality*. The local community is delineated in geographical or territorial terms (even though many residents are kin). Place of origin—whether it is a village, town, or a ward of a city—is an inherited bond of not insignificant consequence. If the kinship unit is by definition exclusive, the geographical community tends to be more all-inclusive.[14] The local collectivity was associated, historically, with the framework of production and interchange, with the sources of livelihood. Here different kin groups interacted, social positions were established and at times sanctified, needs met, and interests pursued. If the kin group was the hub of identity, the community was the foundation of material life and exchange.

Homogeneous communities are, in many parts of Africa, a thing of the past. Nevertheless, the notion of locality and local identification is still very strong. In the rural areas, the sense of community has been maintained in the twentieth century through the town association, the local improvement society, or the village development committee. Local government, whether formalized or not, is the business of the indigenous inhabitants. Thus, even in major metropolises such as Lagos or Accra, the affairs of the community are managed by families that can trace their roots back to the original inhabitants of the area.[15]

Migrants, in turn, maintain strong ties to their places of origins. Hometown organizations in English-speaking Africa, and *associations des originaires* in francophone countries, are among the most prominent frameworks in the urban areas. Members aid in the absorption of newcomers, provide them with shelter and food, and help them find jobs in the city. Hometown groupings also raise funds for village improvement, initiate projects, and support local festivals. Although the demands of cohabitation in new settings do foster specific interests, these usually do not dispel ties to one's place of origin. The territorial bond provides a psychological and practical anchor for those who continue to live in the local community as well as for those millions of Africans who have left their place of origin over the years.

Kinship and territoriality were in the past, and in many cases still are today, closely connected to *traditional political institutions* and authority structures. The village community or the extended family were either themselves the framework of political affiliation or were component units of wider political entities, such as states or empires. In precolonial Africa, a variety of political forms were established, ranging from local village headmen and councils, through chiefdoms that included a number of villages, to elaborate state entities such as Asante and Benin in West Africa or Buganda and Zulu in East and southern Africa. These political institutions incorporated fragments of clans or lineages, entire social groups, or a wide array of unrelated peoples loosely connected by bonds of territoriality. In each political unit specific concepts of authority and methods of acquiring and using power were developed.

These indigenous structures evolved their own notions of status, prestige, social privilege, and patterns of leadership. The pastoral polities of northeastern Africa therefore differed in organization and guiding rules from the more egalitarian and age-based political structures of the Kikuyu in East Africa or the Igbo of present-day Nigeria. The foundations of legitimacy, authority, and power varied; so did processes of political participation, leadership succession, and decision making.[16]

When the Europeans first reached the shores of Africa, they encountered a multiplicity of rulers and institutions with which they had to come to terms. The political structures and practices of indigenous Africa were frequently coopted, manipulated, distorted, or at times even dismantled. In very few instances, however, was the authority of local leaders so undermined or their access to economic resources so circumscribed that they did not survive the processes of colonization and decolonization. Traditional political structures, though often greatly altered or transformed, remain in place in most parts of the continent.

Chiefs, paramounts, or other traditional officeholders still control much land and have access to communal labor. These authorities allocate shares of jointly owned lands to kin groups and define community holdings. They may still levy taxes, collect other forms of revenue, and serve as judges and arbiters of local disputes.

The position of the chief varies from country to country. In the Akan areas of Côte d'Ivoire, for example, those traditional leaders who are still in place are often state functionaries or local civil servants. In neighboring Ghana, in contrast, the importance of local authorities, many of whom are highly educated, actually increased during the 1960s and 1970s, when political turmoil at the national level enhanced the appeal of indigenous institutions and augmented their power. Traditional political structures flourish in Nigeria and regions of Senegal; their role is still debated in Sierra Leone; in Guinea their formal position was abolished at the time of independence.[17]

Although chiefs collectively may constitute a pressure group and pursue their own interests at the state level, they stand accountable to their local communities and must abide by accepted rules and practices. Affiliation with traditional yet altered political structures is still a part of daily life in contemporary Africa. In situations of political fluctuation or opportunity, these structures offer the security of familiarity and control and may also furnish channels for mobility and growth.

The final type of primary grouping is one that has developed around notions of *cultural identity.* Language groups and cultural associations are, in contrast to the other types of primary groups, very much twentieth-century constructs. Organizations such as the Egba Omo Oduduwa among the Yoruba, the Asante Kotoko Society, or other cultural clubs were created as a response to growing contacts between different groups in the colonial period. They have provided a focus of linguistic assertion and historical grounding as well as another vehicle for group action. These culturally based organizations have often evolved into ethnic associations, as they highlight the subjective perception of cultural belonging and, by extension, also distinctiveness. Around these groupings, which blossomed among urban migrants during the colonial period and have continued to thrive ever since, there developed political forms of ethnic action and agitation in the postcolonial period. Usually fueled by members of the elite vying for position among themselves, sectarian-based political mobilization has become an important tool for competing for positions of power or wealth within the formal domain. The ethnic patron, or "big man," has been able to manipulate sentiments of cultural identity and local interests to fulfill personal ambitions. At the same time, however, this framework has provided an important vehicle for group mobility and differentiation.

In some cases, cultural identity has taken on a regional dimension as well. During the colonial period, the imperial powers divided up their colonies for administrative purposes. The French set up *cercles* and *sous-divisions;* the British, districts and provinces; the Belgians, large administrative regions. At independence, many of these administrative regions were geographically re-defined and others were deprived of resources or official political roles. Never-theless, in several countries administrative regions have been retained and, in fact, institutionalized. Liberia is still divided into counties. In Nigeria, the three regions of the independence constitution have been transformed by stages into nineteen states that have fairly significant administrative responsibilities. Ghana's unitary governments have maintained and even further subdivided the colonial regions. In Zaire, provincial governments are still significant funnels of official resource allocation, as are the *wilayas* in Algeria. In some areas, espe-cially where regional divisions overlap cultural identities, a sense of regionality has developed. In Ethiopia, Sudan, Zaire, Mozambique, Angola, Senegal, Côte d'Ivoire, and Chad, the regional unit per se has assumed a special position as a focus for both affiliation and action.

The kin, territorial, political, and cultural vertical structures evident on the African scene have in common an ascriptive and/or delimited geographic defi-nition of membership. Particular, subnational, symbolic schemes bind mem-bers together. These groups adhere to patterns of authority established by tradi-tional or revised custom, and members have a clear notion of belonging to a community linked together around common norms and values. The locations of these groups span, and at times transcend, the boundaries of a given country. The commitment to the primary tie has promoted some perception of a com-monality of goals and interests. In political terms, demands have been raised, votes given, and support withdrawn depending on government responses to these concerns.

Together, primary groupings lay the foundation for an understanding of the nature of social pluralism in given African countries. The degree of heterogeneity evident in any country (or, conversely, the degree of homogeneity) defines the social connection among various groups and deter-mines many of the types of social conflict. This ascriptive pole, therefore, out-lines the national structure and the predominant lines of cleavage in a particular country.

Vertical boundaries are based on intricate and constantly changing notions of inclusion and exclusion. Asantes in Ghana may see themselves as Akan in relation to the Ewe (another broad linguistic group), as Asante in relation to the Fante (an Akan ethnic group), or as Mampong in relation to people from Offinsu (two political and geographical units). Each of these identities evokes situa-tional considerations, material aspirations, and symbolic concerns. Without question, lines of cooperation and conflict do refer back to historical patterns of interaction and social memory. But what is more emphatic in recent years is that the self-perceptions and interest delineation of vertical groups are significantly molded by government composition, policies, and performance.[18] How people view themselves is thus often a mixture of objective criteria as well as some reflection of how others categorize and behave toward them.

The web of relations around interlocking vertical frameworks varies substantially from place to place. During the colonial and postcolonial periods, kin connections have endured and frequently been transformed. They have not, however, been discarded.[19] Similarly, the bond of the local community has been retained and, in many cases, has increased in periods of grave economic uncertainty. Cultural links, on the other hand, have vacillated according to circumstances. And traditional political institutions have persisted when these authorities have succeeded in retaining access to resources and/or when formal government structures have been incapacitated. The significance of each of these entities, however, has increased when ties of kinship and territoriality have overlapped. This was the case, for example, among the Igbo of Nigeria in the late 1960s and the Oromo in Ethiopia or the Ovimbundu in Angola in the 1980s.

Primary groupings and group identity in Africa, despite alterations in definition and relative position, have ongoing meaning for their participants. These frameworks are highly institutionalized, and within their confines presumptive rules of behavior—well-known to members—do prevail. They are also flexible. Ascriptive structures have consequently usually maintained a high degree of cohesion.[20] In the wider setting, these groups offer channels for lateral interaction and for engagement with central government authorities. With very few exceptions, however, they do not preclude other forms of association. Groupings of this sort, precisely because they are particularistic, are not by definition all-embracing: They may stand alone, but more often than not they comprise the source of basic identities without impeding other forms of affiliation and action.

☐ Social and Economic Organizations

Social and economic organizations, unlike primary groups, have emerged explicitly around associational interests. This horizontal constellation of basic social structures covers a diversity of groups established to serve occupational, social, ideological, leisure, self-improvement, and service goals. Membership in these associations is frequently on a voluntary basis. These structures have usually, though by no means exclusively, sprung up initially around urban centers and have been connected with the growth of state institutions and official markets. For this reason, these associations have generally operated within broader geographic frameworks than primary groups and have helped to determine the organization of social and economic life in individual countries.

Occupational groups.   The most visible of these horizontal groupings developed around occupational concerns and include various associations of workers, farmers, teachers, lawyers, engineers, police, soldiers, entrepreneurs, and traders. *Professional associations* bring together educated people to pursue joint substantive concerns and to vie for benefits as a group. Prominent among these organizations are the bar associations (which incorporate lawyers within each country and also on regional and continental bases) and the medical, nurses', teachers', journalists', architects', engineers', chartered accountants', insurance agents', and university lecturers' groups. Of the many occupational organizations, the professional ones tend to be among the best organized and most cohesive.

The origins of the professional associations of contemporary Africa lie in the colonial period, when the first educated Africans banded together to exchange professional information and to promote their interests within the frameworks created by colonial rule. By definition, professional organizations have been limited to a select group of people who have had Western education and possess superior skills. The approximately one hundred fifty thousand professionally qualified people in Africa constitute a small fraction of the population of the continent.[21] Although there is internal equality among members of these groups, there is also a fair amount of distance between them and other social organizations in each country. The resources of these groups are a function of their bargaining power—of the perquisites they can gain, the salaries they can negotiate, and the fees that they can demand for their services.

As more Africans entered the ranks of the highly educated and as their qualifications became more specialized, the size and diversity of these organizations increased. The growth of these associations also augmented their capacity to lobby for more benefits. Professional organizations provide basic social services and thereby help to mold urban life-styles. They have consequently secured both special access to official resources and privileged positions in many countries.

Because professional status has been linked to government activities in many cases, and because many professionals are government employees, professional associations have been heavily represented in the formal political arena. Some of these groups were active in the initial phases of decolonization and, indeed, spearheaded anticolonial movements.[22] Others defined the terms of decolonization. Since independence, these groups have been constantly involved in public affairs. They are salient and forceful pressure groups on any African government and have been at the forefront, not only of support for particular regimes, but also of opposition, protest, and dissent.[23] They constitute, therefore, a highly visible barometer of public opinion in and around the state. When they have come together under an umbrella organization, such as the Association of Recognized Professional Bodies in Ghana, they have been transformed into a formidable political force capable of toppling unpopular governments or inducing significant change in policy orientations.

Closely related to these professional groupings, yet nevertheless distinct, are organizations of people employed, in one way or another, by the state. The most important associations of this sort are those of *civil servants*. Similar organizations exist for the police, and in almost every African country the military also acts as an interest group, even where the armed forces are in power. Membership in these groups—whether institutionalized or loosely organized—is defined by place of work. Although state employees have in common direct access to and even control over state resources, the interests of these subgroups do not always coincide. Bureaucrats may be viewed as a cohesive social segment united by long-range security interests that are frequently at odds with those of more transitory political cadres. Each of these groups, therefore, is separable analytically, and each is distinct from the state apparatus that it purports to serve.[24]

Associations of civil servants, military, and loosely knit groupings of politicians have proliferated as state institutions have expanded and parastatal corporations have grown. These organizations are highly instrumental in nature: They attempt to preserve the status of their members and forward their corporate self-interest. As this group does not itself engage in economic production but in the control of formal resources, it has built up a culture of power. "The power cult is everywhere embedded in the total culture of elite groups."[25] Power, in the view of members of these groups, is integrally linked to the state nexus; its location, conceptually and physically, is at the center of government institutions. This group has become the embodiment of the formal sector.

In the 1980s, with the depletion of state resources, stringent adherence to programs of bureaucratic streamlining, and wage constraints, public salaried employees have witnessed a reduction in their standards of living and a diminution of their incomes. They have suffered palpably from food shortages in the urban areas and have, in countries such as Ghana, Nigeria, Côte d'Ivoire, and Zaire, begun to move into the private sector. The civil service may no longer be the only major repository of skills in many African states.

A third, government-linked, occupational group is that of *chiefs,* or traditional authorities. In various parts of the continent, the position of chiefs has been formalized, and in some cases they have enjoyed income from the state. In Sierra Leone, for example, "the office of paramount chief, although used as an instrument of social control by the central government, has nevertheless been ardently sought because it has represented an important avenue to wealth and social prestige."[26] In Nigeria, most traditional authorities, known as natural rulers, have been organized in houses of chiefs and receive government sanction and salaries (but the role of the great emirs of northern Nigeria has been curtailed). In Ghana, despite attempts by Kwame Nkrumah to downplay the chieftancy, chiefs as a group have been protected by subsequent constitutions and have been able to wield power as a group through formal and informal organizations.

Entrepreneurs, particularly owners of industrial enterprises, have also established organizations to forward their common concerns and to forge avenues of access to official agencies. Many entrepreneurs, a fairly new social category on the continent, come from the ranks of politicians or government employees. Others began as petty traders and small businesspeople and succeeded in establishing vast manufacturing concerns. The opportunity for entrepreneurial expansion has been heavily dependent on government policy. In countries that have stressed state ownership of industries, such as Guinea, Ethiopia, Algeria,

Somalia, Mozambique, and Angola, businesspeople as a group have not risen to the fore. In states that have relied on foreign firms and capital, such as Côte d'Ivoire and Zaire, local industrialists were few and far between until the beginning of the 1980s. On the other hand, in mixed enterprise or systems of nurture capitalism, as in Kenya, Nigeria, Ghana, Morocco, and Senegal, private entrepreneurs have blossomed. In Ghana, they account for at least 50 percent of industrial ownership; in Nigeria, with the indigenization decrees of the late 1970s, they constitute even higher proportions of ownership of large-scale businesses.[27] These industrialists have come together in chambers of commerce and employers' associations to protect the private sector and to lobby government for favorable credit terms, flexible trade policies, import provisions, and licensing arrangements. Thus, especially since the 1970s, an indigenous monied bourgeoisie of not insignificant proportions has emerged. This closely knit group has transnational links, often bypasses state frontiers, and possesses many of its own sources of capital.

When taken together, associations of professionals, government employees, chiefs, and entrepreneurs constitute elite groupings that are bound to each other by interlocking membership, income, status, and life-style. These elite organizations are composed of individuals who have had access to education, the state apparatus, and concomitant wealth. Members of these groups are frequently closely related personally. They live in the better parts of each capital city, send their children to the best schools at home or in Europe, and enjoy the most modern amenities of the Western world.[28] Their children are disproportionately represented in institutions of higher education. They themselves move easily from public to private enterprises, and their standard of living is scrupulously maintained through astute political action.[29] This system has been sustained because elite groups have not been totally exclusionary: They continuously held forth the promise of membership to young people who have followed the path of education or government service. Because of the close interpenetration of these groups and their reliance on government resources, they have come to constitute, despite internal factionalization and cleavage, what may best be described as the dominant class or the managerial bourgeoisie. Their interests are heavily represented in the formal apparatus; public institutions, in turn, provide an opportunity for them to further pursue their objectives, and policies frequently reflect their concerns.

Elite culture during the first decades of independence revolved around the close connection between education, state power, and personal wealth. Informed by kinship and ethnic affinity—although hardly confined to these links—elites nurtured an extractive view of politics that dominated the national scene in these countries during the first postcolonial years. Norms of public behavior and social interactions were initially laid down by these groups, which in the name of development and social progress frequently enhanced their own status and position. They molded patterns of domination, social stratification, and separation.[30] Without these groups, it would have been impossible to maintain basic services or to administer a country; their corporate interests also made them a drain on public resources. In recent years, however, much of the attention of professional groups and even state employees shifted from the political domain, where opportunities had been constricted, to that of the market. At this juncture, the beginnings of a new definition of interests, and perhaps identity, began to surface among these groups, possibly paving the way for different forms of interaction.

Unlike elite occupational groups, other occupational associations have usually been more amorphous organizationally, and only segments have been consolidated in discrete groupings. *Trade unions* were among the first nonelite groups to coalesce during the colonial period. Workers' groups were formed around sources of wage labor: in the mining regions of the Zambian copperbelt and Katanga, the ports and the railways in East and West Africa, and major urban concentrations. Although trade unions were banned in many parts of the continent in the prewar period, since 1945 labor unions have multiplied.

During early independence these unions were consolidated, and frequently trade union congresses, or *associations des syndicats,* were established. The experience of organized labor since independence has been one of increased government control and periodic dissension.[31] Officials have attempted to standardize criteria for membership, control wages, and exact loyalty from labor leaders. Despite concerted efforts to subordinate trade unions to state policies and to coopt leaders, as more people have entered the labor force, and as individual unions have pressed for better conditions for their members, unions have persisted and have been reorganized and in many cases reinvigorated.

The social organizing principles of workers' organizations, which still encompass only a small proportion of African laborers, center on the pragmatic struggle for improved work conditions, salaries, and at times prices and subsidies. Because trade unions have sprung up in economic centers and at crucial economic conjunctures, their visibility has been particularly high. Around trade unions and workers' organizations there have developed new forms of consciousness and radical subcultures. In contrast to the avowed nationalism of Nigerian elites, for example, laborers in Nigeria's cities have evolved a form of urban populism heavily imbued with ethnicity and religion.[32] In Ghana, the railway workers of Sekondi-Takoradi stood at the forefront of opposition to elite privilege and bureaucratic domination. Through strikes and demonstrations, song and dance, in popular literature and the theater, workers have expressed contempt for patterns of public power abuse and corruption and have backed, if only implicitly, movements for radical transformation.[33] They have frequently not only created a mood of discontent but also found their own methods of protest. These range from community withdrawal, desertion, and target working to time bargaining, sabotage, and theft.[34] Trade unions, consequently, have been in a position to make government officials more accountable; they have not, however, been able to bring about substantial political transformation.

Trade union organization and worker action in various parts of Africa has, indeed, been marked by a great deal of ambiguity. Union organizers have continuously been caught between their dependence on those in power at the state level and the demands and needs of their members. Worker reliance on elite social groups and on the state as the major wage employer has therefore constrained their options and fostered an uneasy alliance with public officials.

One cushion of wage laborers in these circumstances has been to engage in petty commerce or trade in conjunction with their salaried employment. *Trade networks* have a long history in most parts of Africa. Along the West African coast, women have monopolized petty trade throughout the twentieth century, controlling the markets in Lagos, Ibadan, Accra, Kumasi, Abidjan, and Monrovia, to name but a few. Hausa and Dioula traders (mostly male) have operated in the savannah regions, frequently roaming down to the coast to sell their wares. In Central and East Africa, women traders have been joined by Asians and Swahilis along the coast and by other male traders in the interior.[35]

Trader organizations have multiplied as commerce has grown. In many cases, they possess a well-defined internal structure. Market women groups, for example, elect their own leaders and employ elaborate sanctions to discipline members. Leaders of the Kumasi marketing pools, to illustrate from one case, "settle disputes, primarily over credit and commercial procedure, and represent traders in external negotiations and at ceremonies such as funerals. Leaders of the predominantly female foodstuffs group represent the market as a whole."[36] Through their organizations, traders divide routes, commodities, market stalls, and even entire transportation systems. The marketplace is thus an important hub of social as well as economic life in many parts of Africa. The vibrancy of particular markets is an excellent indicator of social conditions and productive capacities in particular countries.

Traders, and especially market women, have been the object of public debate and, at times, of official scapegoating, especially when commodities are scarce and food prices skyrocket. In Ghana in 1979, the main Accra market, Makola, was razed in an effort to eradicate trade malpractices. Goods quickly became unavailable and prices rose even more. In 1983, when the markets were deregulated, the supply of goods became more predictable. In Ghana, therefore, "if the chief liability for traders has been government interference, their chief asset has been the creation of, and participation in, a distribution system suited to Ghana's needs."[37] As most salaried people take part directly or through their families in some form of trade or petty manufacturing, they were able to survive and even thrive during the economic crisis of the early 1980s. These associations, together with *artisan groups,* therefore constitute the core of contemporary nonstate yet market-oriented processes of social reconstruction. Although they are affected by government policies, they are not dependent on the state. Within this rubric there have also developed small craft guilds, rotating credit associations, apprenticeship systems, and organizations of small manufacturers. Microindustrial units are, like their commercial counterparts, tied to market processes and reinforce the significance of this form of social organization.

Trading networks link local producers with the market and often with the state. At least 70 percent of Africa's population is engaged, in one form or another, in agricultural production. Most agricultural activity takes place in *peasant households,* where a small-scale, family economy prevails. Each group of agricultural producers has rights to land and labor but is, at the same time, also involved in a wider system of production that defines its status and options.[38]

The evolution of African rural production patterns has been dictated by ecological possibilities and local traditions and customs as well as by official orientations. For this reason, the molding of farming cultures has differed quite significantly from place to place. Thus, in southern Rhodesia (present-day Zimbabwe) there emerged a group of small-scale cash farmers who were gradually stripped of their access to land and labor and thereby proletarianized during the course of the twentieth century. In Ghana, capitalist cocoa farmers developed export production at the household level with the assistance of seasonal workers provided by labor-exporting groups on the fringe of the forest zones. In Tanzania, a stratified pattern of development was evident, with various farmers coexisting on an unequal basis in the countryside. In Rwanda, an independent form of labor consciousness coalesced around *ubureetwa,* a method of labor clientship used widely during the colonial period. In each African country, then, and in each subregion, different types of rural differentiation emerged.[39]

In any given rural area it was possible to identify, by the beginning of the postcolonial period, groups of petty bourgeois farmers who expropriated large tracts of land and brought in seasonal migrant laborers; a middle peasantry, usually with one farm and its own family labor; an indebted peasantry—which borrowed money and engaged in sharecropping; and landless migrant laborers.[40] Rural variety and rural inequalities, therefore, defy the tendency to aggregate agriculturalists into an overarching category of "peasant." The culture of peasants is marked, in most parts of the continent, by local, particularistic orientations and specific semiautonomous interest structures.[41]

The degree of institutionalization of farmer groups varies. Some governments have sought to control rural inhabitants by establishing large producer organizations, such as the United Ghana Farmers Council during the Nkrumah period. Although many similar efforts have been made to force the diversity of rural life into some uniform grid controlled by governments, many of these efforts have not been particularly successful.[42] Farmers have often organized their own self-help groups. Such producer and marketing cooperatives have blossomed in many parts of the continent since independence, with the dual effect of politicizing farmer groups and creating spheres of independent activity autonomous of state control.

Small farmers are poorly represented in central government. Nevertheless, they hold the key to development prospects. They may totally oppose government measures and bypass or ignore official channels. They may bargain with officials. They may receive some support from particular regimes, or they may even enjoy substantial encouragement, as in the case, at various junctures, of Niger, Kenya, and Tanzania.[43] Networks of peasant producers usually do not interact laterally with each other, but deal, separately, with other social groups and local and state bureaucrats. Peasants, because of their proximity to vital resources, do have power; in most parts of Africa, however, they are only marginally represented in the formal sector, thus diminishing their immediate impact on policy, although hardly their long-range political influence.

The processes of capitalist penetration and state aggrandizement have fostered fragmentation and growing inequalities in the rural areas. The political cultures of these groups reveal their diffuse world views. Exclusion from activities at the state level, coupled with the capacity to evade formal control, have generated many combinations of fatalism and defiance throughout rural Africa.[44] As an unformed, usually unmobilized group, farmers have continued to maintain their own spheres of activity while nevertheless interacting more regularly with official institutions. Their networks, like those of traders and petty manufacturers, extend beyond the reach of government agencies.

Occupational structures (of professionals, state employees, workers, traders, entrepreneurs, and farmers) cover a wide range of interests and concerns, although they differ from one another in the extent of their organizational coherence, the degree of their access to and the kinds of resources they control, the cultures they have elaborated, their historical legacies, and hence their capacities. By the outset of the third decade of independence, these interlocking networks had been commercialized, thus emerging as the most readily apparent of the essential frameworks of daily economic life.

Women's and students' associations.   A second major horizontal constellation has evolved around the universal sociobiological distinctions of age and sex. *Women's organizations* have played a prominent role in African political history in the twentieth century, especially in the western part of the continent. The roots of gender-based social groups lie in the development of a sexual division of labor in many African societies in the precolonial period. The colonial intrusion added new dimensions to the differentiation between the sexes. During this period, wage labor and export production came to be considered men's work. Women continued to produce food and to market their goods locally. Some women's organizations did provide support and even financial backing for anticolonial movements. Since independence, however, as a group women have generally been neglected and underrepresented in central institutions. The public (state) and private (household) distinctions have assumed gender overtones as well.[45] Development policies have frequently excluded women, and when specific projects were designed for their benefit, these projects often resulted in women's further marginalization.[46]

Some facts regarding the condition of African women in the postcolonial period are pertinent here. Women predominate in the subsistence sector in most parts of the continent. It is estimated that their activities account for 78 percent of food production, 80 percent of food processing, 80 percent of fuel preparation, 80 percent of water supplies, 90 percent of brewing, and 50 percent of animal husbandry.[47] Between 60 and 80 percent of field hands in black Africa are women, as are 50 percent of cattle tenders.[48]

Women also play an important role in petty trade. Sixty percent of internal trade in Africa is conducted by women. Despite their centrality in the local economy, women are grossly underrepresented in wage labor. They make up only 15 percent of workers in the wage sector. Even where women do take part in modern wage employment, they tend to congregate in the lower income categories. The incomes of 50 percent of female wage earners in Kenya are below the poverty line.[49] Specific efforts to improve women's access to and status in wage employment have been slow.

The lopsided participation of African women in economic life reveals a picture of growing gender disparities. This divergence has increased the dependence of women on men for cash income. Many women find themselves more burdened, more impoverished, and more on their own economically than in the past. This trend is reflected in figures on literacy and school enrollment, two vital indicators of the current and potential status of women in Africa. Female literacy is 67 percent in Lesotho and only 6 percent in Chad. With the exception of Botswana and Lesotho, females are less literate than males throughout the continent. When coupled with higher mortality rates and inferior health facilities, it appears that the process of impoverishment falls disproportionately on females.

The position of women in various parts of Africa is determined to a large extent by cultural norms and traditional practices. Although African women frequently share common concerns, specific forms of inequality vary from country to country and from one group to another. New problems have cropped up since independence. Incidences of rape, prostitution, and child-dumping have increased alarmingly in recent years. The image of women has suffered tremendously from scapegoating in the media. Working women have been particularly exposed to derision in the press.

Matters of personal and social status have inevitably led to a call for greater gender equality. In Muslim societies of the Sahel this has taken on the form of a demand for the liberation of women from certain conditions imposed by religion. In the agrarian countries of West Africa it has been expressed in a call for greater property rights in general and access to land in particular. There is a growing recognition in women's quarters that women's depressed status in society is closely related to the ambiguity of their place in the public realm. Although they still possess spheres of autonomy (especially financial), they have witnessed a reduction in their political positions in comparison to their status in traditional society. The symbolic features of women's existence, therefore, capture many of the anomalies of contemporary life in Africa. Women, like some farmers, workers, and local communities, resist subordination to official institutions. Still, the "reality that African women have constructed lingers and remains a vision for a world without the state leviathan."[50]

The many different views of African women on their condition have been given expression in a myriad of women's organizations that fall into several distinct categories. First are the official women's associations. Each African country has its own umbrella organization (the All Women's Association of Ghana, the Organization of Mozambican Women, etc.). At times, there is a women's branch of the ruling party that either fills this role or exists side by side with the general association. Official women's groups tend to reflect the position of their regimes on women's matters.

A second type of women's association is based on employment. Every major trade union in Africa has a women's branch (which usually follows government guidelines). Professions that have a high representation of women (nurses, teachers) also have an allied women's organization. Traders have established their own institutions to meet their needs, as have female farmers in recent years.

Voluntary associations constitute the third form of women's organization. These groups provide services for women, extend nonformal training, operate child-care facilities, and furnish support networks. Many of these organizations (the YWCA and the Ahmaddiyah, for example) are tied to international women's associations or to religious institutions (churches, mosques).

A fourth kind of women's organization is of a grass-roots sort. These local associations have sprung up in rural and urban areas to meet specific needs of working women. They differ from the voluntary groups in their more spontaneous origins, their localized roots, their self-help orientation, and their avowed (nonestablishment) activism. A fifth type of group, to be found in some major cities, falls into the radical feminist category. Highly educated women have banded together to militate for basic changes in social attitudes toward their sex. These notions are evident in relations between decisionmakers and parliamentarians, as well as in the interactions between social groups and government institutions. The underlying value of a measure of reciprocity is central to the continued operation of these socially dependent constructs. Once again, competition has generally taken on elite and factional forms, although in Senegal religiously based opposition has also been in evidence.

The split between mass-based and government-backed groups has become more apparent. So, too, has the disparity between elite and nonelite women. With the crystallization of African women's organizations, a growing understanding of the profundity of the implications of the gender division of labor in many portions of Africa has emerged. Their experiences and their responses to their condition highlight a crucial, and all too often neglected, theme in African social organization.

Much in the same mold as women's organizations, although quite different in its political implications, is the *youth sector,* which consists of a series of associations that have frequently bisected other types of horizontal formations and primary groups. The notion of differentiation by age has deep roots in African cultures. Seniority has, traditionally, been closely associated with political office and positions of responsibility. Norms of deference, as well as rights and obligations, were defined in many societies in terms of age and status associated with elders. Youth, therefore, was conceived of as rebellious and critical; in many places its role as a limited watchdog was institutionalized (the *asafo* companies in West Africa, made up of "brigades of youngmen," are a case in point).[51]

Youth groups spearheaded the formation of protest movements in the colonial period (the Gold Coast Youth Conference and the Nigerian Youth Movement, for example) and constituted the preliminary frameworks around which many anticolonial movements were constructed in the postwar era. In the initial years of independence, these youth wings were incorporated into the ruling parties, and official youth organizations were established. At the same time the creation of national universities witnessed the establishment of student unions at all major universities.

Over the years, organizations such as the National Association of Nigerian Students (NANS) or the National Union of Ghanaian Students (NUGS) have engaged in highly visible political activity. They have lobbied to protect student disbursements and the unusually luxurious conditions of student life in many portions of Africa; they have also set themselves up as units to monitor the quality of public life in most African countries. Students have therefore emerged as a vital barometer of the status of particular regimes, being among the first groups to voice discontent and to indicate levels of dissatisfaction with government policies.[52] Although not an economic force, student groups have played an important role in molding popular attitudes.[53]

Youth organizations have not been confined to student activity. In many local communities small youth associations—often the successors of traditional constructs—have resurfaced in recent years. Some youth groups are attached to church groups and Muslim communities. Separate youth organizations have also been established to cater to the interests of elite youth in the cities (the Boy Scouts and Girl Guides are major examples). These associations, much like their student counterparts, represent certain interests and worldviews and help to define the individual member's social position and standing.

Women's and youth associations differ from other forms of social and economic organization in that they cut across conventional structures of affiliation and identity and establish settings for linking otherwise disparate groups. Their numbers, cohesion, and modes of activism reflect the content of many broader societal concerns in particular African states and establish patterns of lateral transaction. For these reasons they mirror, perhaps better than many of their counterparts, some fundamental societal values, norms, and practices.

Other voluntary organizations. During the twentieth century, Africans have also created a variety of associations that provide outlets for leisure and service activities. In the urban areas, many sports clubs, improvement associations, literary societies, alumni associations (generally known as old boys' and old girls' networks), debating groups, credit clubs, and neighborhood development institutions have developed. These organizations furnish frameworks for discussion, debate, support, and interaction. Recreation groups help to structure leisure activities, just as credit associations (known as *esusu* in Nigeria) offer loans and provide some financial security.[54] Cities have also been the setting for the formation of street gangs, drug rings, gambling groups, and organized crime networks, which are a rarely studied byproduct of rapid urbanization. In the past two decades, some of these voluntary associations have also spread to the rural areas. Small towns and villages now boast stadiums or athletic fields where soccer has become a favorite activity. Many local communities have their own reading societies and self-help organizations. Thus, many voluntary groups fill in the spaces that other institutions have not been able to bridge.

When taken together, social and economic groups of various sorts have emerged to deal with virtually every aspect of human existence in Africa. Although they vary widely in size, scope, and degree of institutionalization, they do furnish a resilient and pliant network that supports social, material, and cultural life throughout the continent. These associations, based on interest articulation and affiliation, have several features in common. First, their expansion and growth have been closely linked to the creation of colonial and ex-colonial centers and to the spread of market mechanisms. They are, therefore, more salient in and around administrative and economic centers (in contrast with the local focus of primary groupings). Second, many of these groups, although by no means all, are marked by the ethnically crosscutting composition of their membership. And third, these horizontal groups have quite different political connections and, hence, impact on state policies. Elite groups tend to be better organized, their membership more cohesive, and their representation in state institutions more pronounced than other forms of horizontal organization. The web of relations between various groups mirrors patterns of subordination and social cleavage even when it is not possible to point to coherent class formations. Indeed, these institutions emerge both as vehicles for joint activity and as manifestations of social and political differentiation.

☐ Religious Communities

The symbolic sphere is best articulated by a medley of religious structures that have been shaped around historical experiences and contacts and have provided mechanisms for dealing with the exigencies of daily life for centuries. Participation in religious organizations is the most prevalent form of associational life in Africa today.[55] Africans belong to religious frameworks ranging from organized churches, Muslim brotherhoods, secret sects, messianic movements, and prayer gatherings to antiwitchcraft groups and animistic cults.

Traditional African religions, which are still followed in many parts of the continent, are based on particularistic worldviews and involve worship of ancestors and natural objects. Each African society evolved its own set of deities; around these gods there developed explanations for natural and social phenomena and well-defined concepts of power and legitimacy. Muslim invaders and traders who came in contact with Africans through the trans-Saharan trade and East African trading routes introduced their great tradition into Africa at an early date. The diffusion of Islam was accomplished either by conquest, by the Islamization of African rulers (first in ancient Ghana and Mali and then in other areas), and most notably, by the gradual adaptation of Islamic practices in many African societies, usually as a result of economic contacts. In this process of the piecemeal spread of Islam, the religion became Africanized, undergoing modifications to suit local conditions.[56]

By the time Europeans began to arrive on the shores of the continent, the Islamic presence had been established in the Sahel, along the East African coast, in the Sudan, and throughout most of West Africa. The nineteenth-century *jihads* (holy wars) in West Africa led to the formation of large Islamic states and entrenched the position of some Muslim orders at the apex of politico-religious entities (such as the Fulani empire in northern Nigeria, Massina in Senegal, Kong in Côte d'Ivoire).

Christianity has existed in Africa for some time (most notably in Ethiopia), but its spread is related to the white encounter. The religious expression of colonialism came in the form of Christian missionaries and proselytizing societies. The Portuguese, and then the Dutch, the British, the Germans, the French, and the Belgians, were accompanied in their initial intrusions into Africa by clerics and religious leaders. Christianity, with the backing of the colonial powers, spread rapidly through non-Muslim areas of Africa at the same time as Islam continued to expand as a barrier against cultural and religious imperialism.[57] Even in Muslim areas, however, religious leaders sometimes cooperated with colonial authorities and benefited economically from the association (as in the case of the Mourides of Senegal) or resisted colonial penetration and stood apart from the colonial world view.[58] The "role of religion as a symbolic medium of contact and conflict is striking in the colonial history of Africa."[59]

Anticolonialism and religious activity were intertwined, although the two processes did not always intersect. Each may be viewed "as a combined cultural/ideological/social/political response to the situation."[60] Thus, although religious activity in the later colonial period was intrinsically political, as it is in South Africa in the 1980s, it was not necessarily anticolonial. Indeed, nationalism in Africa, in contrast to Asia, for example, was fundamentally secular. When the colonial rulers departed the continent, however, they left behind a religious legacy whose impact in terms of cultural change and conflict was immeasurable.

The early years of independence seemingly reflected the secular spirit of anticolonialism. Religious commitment was a fact of life for individual Africans, but it rarely emerged as a major factor in national affairs during the 1960s. At this time, religious institutions, like many of their socioeconomic and political counterparts, underwent a process of Africanization. Umbrella religious organizations, such as National Christian Councils, African branches of the World Council of Churches, national Catholic organizations, and Muslim councils, were set up in many African capitals. Also, separate religious communities proliferated. Orthodox churches and spiritual movements continued to grow. Mosque construction increased, and progressive Muslim orders, such as the Ahmaddiyah, expanded.

In the 1970s, as secular political structures were enfeebled and economic conditions worsened, a widespread religious renaissance began to take place. Although periods of religious fervor and revivalism are not new in African history, this most recent demonstration of religious activity reaffirms the close connection between religious identity, power, and politics on the continent. Religious institutions became important vehicles for the expression of popular discontent and for the elaboration of alternative survival strategies.[61]

The assertion of religious consciousness has been most noticeable in the Islamic portions of the continent. In some countries—such as Senegal, Mauritania, Sudan, Somalia, and, most notably, Libya—state institutions have assumed religious trappings and explicitly shed many of their secular characteristics.[62] Islamic frameworks have also supplied important channels for the expression of discontent with secular authorities. In northern Nigeria, Islam has become a crucial vehicle for voicing dissatisfaction with the government. In Senegal, the Mouride marabouts (holy men) became self-appointed spokesmen for peasant political dissent; they transformed themselves into trade union leaders of a new sort. Some Muslim communities have withheld allegiance from official bodies and created alternative constructs of a totally independent order. In West Africa and the Sahel, fundamentalist Islamic sects have sprouted up. The Arab societies of North Africa have likewise seen the rise of fundamentalist movements in protest against ruling elites. In these areas, an Islamic network may be basically reordering political allegiances.[63]

Christian activism has also become more apparent during the past decade. Fundamentalist denominations have enjoyed a new resurgence. Millenarian sects and spiritual movements, such as the Watchtower Society, have flourished. Traditional secret societies are still operative. In some countries, such as Tanzania and Zaire, established churches have provided employment and food at times of scarcity. These have also been vocal in opposing the violations of the rule of law by government officials, actively denouncing administrative conduct in countries such as Ghana and Kenya.[64] In extreme cases, such as in portions of southern and South Africa, churches have furnished settings for the grouping of the devout in communities consciously withdrawn from broader political currents.

Africa in the 1980s is thus also divided along religious lines. Relations between Muslims and Christians within and across international boundaries are affected by their external associations as well as by their differing symbolic orientations. The increasingly close connections between African Muslims and the central lands of Islam, especially through the *haj* (pilgrimage) to Mecca, have influenced their attitudes toward the Western world.[65] Christian affiliations with international ecumenical bodies have also had an impact on political orientations. Religious ties, therefore, add new dimensions to both inter- and intra-African relations. The proliferation of religious organizations reflects the uncertainty inherent in political and economic trends on the continent. It also provides compelling evidence of the ongoing significance of religious life in African culture and history.

■ SOCIAL NETWORKS AND SOCIAL TRENDS

African civil society has responded to the challenges of external dependence, economic uncertainty, and political change by the activation of existing organizations and the formation of new groups to deal with the many facets of material, cultural, and political existence. African social orders are marked by the fact that their component units are related to, yet also distinct from, each other. Each group or association occupies a particular social space yet, at the same time, interlocks with other groups both hierarchically and laterally. Economic, cultural, material, and social fields are made up of these organizational spaces, which tend to come together mostly at the apex, much less so at the base. The picture that emerges is one of social richness but rarely of societal uniformity.

The diversity yet interconnectedness of African social systems is a function of many factors. In a continent of many little traditions, specific social groups developed their own mechanisms of dealing with their environments. Colonial conquest, and with it new forms of economic production and of state consolidation, not only evoked responses and adjustments from existing groups but also sparked the creation of new associations and networks. During decolonization further contacts were made and alliances forged. And the period of independence has reinforced this pattern of autonomy and interpenetration. African societies are, indeed, an intricate mosaic.

The composition of civil society and the shape of social structures vary substantially from place to place and country to country on the continent. Cultural legacies and differing manners of social and economic organization have yielded quite distinct patterns. Thus, in Senegal, for example, Islamic brotherhoods control major facets of daily existence, as they do in northern Nigeria. In southern Nigeria, Ghana, and Sierra Leone, professional and voluntary organizations proliferate. These are much weaker and more amorphous in countries like Zaire, Tanzania, and Malawi, where church groups play a more significant role. African states vary culturally, too, from the relatively homogeneous Somalia and Swaziland to the extremely diffuse situation in Tanzania. In some instances (Ghana, Botswana, Zimbabwe) one ethnolinguistic group has a clear plurality; in others (Nigeria, Ethiopia, Zaire), there are several relatively large groups, often in competition with each other.

The structure of social relations in each African country has differed in light of group composition and possibilities for action. These vary quite distinctly from one country to another. In Ghana, for example, the horizontal axis of social and economic organizations has provided the dynamic framework within which mobility has occurred. A great many social and economic structures have developed at the interface between the local community, market, and formal institutions. In Tanzania, hierarchical structures have been less salient and intermediate levels of social organization less cohesive and elaborate. Here transactions are more limited. Nigeria, in turn, presents a different picture: A highly differentiated system of interactions has emerged, which has been sustained by a multiplicity of unequal flows. In Zaire, this pattern has solidified even more: A minute group of public officials has been able to penetrate the countryside, perpetuating the position of a small political "aristocracy."[66] Weak intermediary organizations (with the exception, perhaps, of some churches and newly formed cooperatives) and extreme vulnerability has increased the dependency of most social groups on state officials. In Côte d'Ivoire a more gradiated structure of civil society has developed, with a strong group of dominant professionals and bureaucrats at the core and numerous associations spanning the urban and extending to the rural areas. By way of contrast, social structures in Uganda and Chad in the 1980s have been based on intense primary-group identities but on much fewer social and economic networks.

Official institutions have in the past, and continue today, to try to mold social allegiances and reshape social groupings. Even when formal agencies do not engage directly in social engineering, the organizational configuration of public structures opens opportunities for certain kinds of action and forecloses other possibilities. Specific groups, however, have access to their own resources and constituencies and may at times provide alternative services as well. In some cases, therefore, they seek representation in the formal realm; in some they stand in opposition to existing officeholders, and in others they may develop avenues of exchange that either evade or subvert official channels. Social groups have positioned themselves as both vehicles of interaction with official bodies and as substitutes or alternatives to formal networks.[67] The degree and nature of these exchanges may range from one extreme of total separation, mutual mistrust, and lack of cooperation (Uganda in the early 1980s) to intricate patterns of power diffusion (Tanzania), intermittent power networks (Ghana), and varying degrees of power concentration (Botswana, Nigeria, Zambia, or Malawi).

In every country, however, the span of social networks is far broader than the reach of formal institutions. Indeed, state structures have tended to reflect the interests and concerns of a small, elite minority (professionals, bureaucrats, some ethnic groups) whose vertical hold remains rather tenuous. At the same time, social and economic contacts have proliferated. More significant, the rates and types of exchanges between rural and urban areas are constantly growing. With communication expanding, the stark separation between the city and the countryside is giving way to a more complex picture of multiple inter-actions. There has been a gradual, yet palpable, transition from purely hier-archical to lateral transactions in the past few decades. In political terms, this trend means that state power is not unlimited. Although individuals and social groups cannot easily detach themselves from their national environments, gov-ernments, in turn, may not be able to skirt demands from well-organized social forces without losing access to the vital resources controlled by these associa-tions. As the outlines of civil societies are emerging in many African countries, previous patterns of state-society relations may also be undergoing change.

Specific groups have molded a variety of means to mobilize their resources and to fulfill their aspirations. These associations are the bedrock of political life on the continent. Their activities do not always intersect with those of state institutions. Class and ethnicity have been the main vehicles for linking these groups to formal structures. In Chapter 4 we look more closely at how these overarching formations have evolved and at the kinds of relations they have fostered.

■ NOTES

1. Many thanks are due to Frank Holmquist, who suggested this formulation.

2. Jean-François Bayart, "La revanche des sociétés africaines," *Politique Africaine* 11 (1983): 95–127. Also see Margaret Peil, *Consensus and Conflict in African Society: An Introduction to Sociology* (London: Longman, 1977).

3. Jane I. Guyer, "Comparative Epilogue," in Jane I. Guyer, ed., *Feeding Africa's Cities* (Manchester: Manchester University Press, 1987), p. 27.

4. Peter C. W. Gutkind and Peter Waterman, eds., *African Social Studies: A Radical Reader* (London: Heinemann, 1977). Also see Sara Berry, *Fathers Work for Their Sons: Accumulation, Mobility and Class Formation in an Extended Yoruba Community* (Berkeley: University of California Press, 1985), p. 7 and elsewhere.

5. For a good overview, see Chris Allen and Gavin Williams, eds., *Sociology of "Developing Societies": Sub-Saharan Africa* (New York: Monthly Review Press, 1982).

6. Immanuel Wallerstein, "Voluntary Associations," in James Coleman and Carl Rosberg, eds., *Political Parties and National Integration in Tropical Africa* (Berkeley: University of California Press, 1966), pp. 318–339; Kenneth Little, *West African Urbanization: A Study of Voluntary Associations in Social Change* (Cambridge: Cambridge University Press, 1967); John M. Hamer, "Preconditions and Limits in the Formation of Associations: The Self-Help and Cooperative Movement in Subsaharan Africa," *African Studies Review* 24, no. 1 (1981): 113–128. In contrast, Sandra T. Barnes and Margaret Peil, "Voluntary Association Membership in Five West African Cities," *Urban Anthropology* 6, no. 1 (1977): 83–106, do not see voluntary associations as necessarily integrative.

7. Roger Tangri, *Politics in Sub-Saharan Africa* (London: James Currey, 1985): pp. 1–27. For an excellent case study see Yaw Twumasi, "Prelude to the Rise of Nationalism in Ghana, 1920–1949: Nationalists and Voluntary Associations," *Ghana Social Science Journal* 3, no. 1 (1976): 35–46.

8. Margaret Peil, *Nigerian Politics: The People's View* (London: Cassel, 1976): p. 162; John Hanna, ed., *Students and Politics in Africa* (New York: Africana Publishing Co., 1975). For an overview, see Naomi Chazan, "The New Politics of Participation in Tropical Africa," *Comparative Politics* 14, no. 2 (1982): 169–189.

9. Otwin Marenin, "Essence and Empiricism in African Politics," in Yolamu Barongo, ed., *Political Science in Africa* (London: Zed Press, 1985), p. 230 and passim.

10. M. K. Schutz, "Observations on the Functions of Voluntary Associations with Special Reference to West African Cities," *Human Relations* 30, no. 9 (1977): 803–816.

11. This definition goes beyond that of Richard Hodder-Williams, *An Introduction to the Politics of Tropical Africa* (London: George Allen and Unwin, 1984), p. 164.

12. Barnes and Peil, "Voluntary Association Membership," p. 91. Also see Crawford Young, *The Politics of Cultural Pluralism* (Madison: University of Wisconsin Press, 1976).

13. Peil, *Consensus and Conflict in African Society.*

14. Maxwell Owusu, "Policy Studies, Development and Political Anthropology," *Journal of Modern African Studies* 13, no. 3 (1975): 367–382.

15. Margaret Peil, "The Common Man's Reaction to Nigerian Urban Government," *African Affairs* 74, no. 296 (1975): 300.

16. For an excellent typology, see Paula Brown, "Patterns of Authority in West Africa," in Irving Leonard Markovitz, *Politics and Society in Africa* (New York: Free Press, 1970).

17. René Lemarchand, ed., *African Kingships in Perspective* (London: Frank Cass, 1977); Roger Tangri, "Paramount Chiefs and Central Governments in Sierra Leone," *African Studies Review* 39, no. 2 (1980): 183–196; Harry Silver, "Going for Brokers: Political Innovations and Structural Integration in a Changing Ashanti Community," *Comparative Political Studies* 14, no. 2 (1981): 233–263; and Maxwell Owusu, "Chieftancy and Constitutionalism in Ghana: The Case of the Third Republic," *Studies in Third World Societies* 24 (1983): 29–53.

18. For a case study, see Naomi Chazan, "Ethnicity and Politics in Ghana," *Political Science Quarterly* 47, no. 3 (1982): 461–485.

19. Berry, *Fathers Work for Their Sons,* p. 193.

20. Peter Ekeh, "Colonialism and the Two Publics in Africa: A Theoretical Statement," *Comparative Studies in Society and History* 17, no. 1 (1975): 91–112.

21. *Afriscope* 7, no. 4 (1977): 24–25.

22. Immanuel Wallerstein, *The Road to Independence: Ghana and the Ivory Coast* (The Hague: Mouton, 1964).

23. For one case study, see Naomi Chazan and Victor Le Vine, "Politics in a 'Non-Political' System: The March 30, 1978 Referendum in Ghana," *African Studies Review* 22, no. 1 (1979): 177–208.

24. The literature is somewhat divided on this point. See, for an excellent discussion of the nomenclature, Richard L. Sklar, "The Nature of Class Domination in Africa," *Journal of Modern African Studies* 17, no. 4 (1979): 544–547.

25. Abner Cohen, *The Politics of Elite Culture: Exploration in the Dramaturgy of Power in a Modern African Society* (Berkeley: University of California Press, 1981): p. 9.

26. Tangri, "Paramount Chiefs and Central Government," p. 183.

27. Paul Bennell, "Industrial Class Formation in Ghana: Some Empirical Observations," *Development and Change* 15 (1985): 593–612; Richard Rathbone, "Businessmen

in Politics: Party Struggle in Ghana, 1949–1957," *Journal of Development Studies* 9, no. 3 (1973): 391–402; Sayre P. Schatz, "Government Lending to African Businessmen: Inept Incentives," *Journal of Modern African Studies* 6, no. 4 (1968): 519–529; Paul Kennedy, "Capitalism in Ghana," *Review of African Political Economy* 8 (1977): 21–38.

28. See P. C. Lloyd, ed., *The New Elites of Tropical Africa* (London: Oxford University Press, 1966).

29. Philip Foster, "Education and Social Inequality in Sub-Saharan Africa," *Journal of Modern African Studies* 18, no. 2 (1980): 201–236; Remi Clignet, "Education and Elite Formation," in John Paden and Edward Soja, eds., *The African Experience,* vol. 1 (Evanston, Ill.: Northwestern University Press, 1970), pp. 304-330.

30. Ali A. Mazrui, *Political Values and the Educated Class in Africa* (London: Heinemann, 1978).

31. Yves Person, "Les syndicats en Afrique noire," *Le mois en Afrique* 172/173 (1980): 22–46; Richard Sandbrook and Robin Cohen, eds., *The Development of an African Working Class: Studies in Class Formation and Action* (London: Longman, 1975).

32. Lawrence P. Frank, "Ideological Competition in Nigeria: Urban Populism Versus Elite Nationalism," *Journal of Modern African Studies* 17, no. 3 (1979): 433–452; Bernard Magubane and Nzongola-Ntalaja, eds., "Proletarianization and Class Struggle in Africa," *Contemporary Marxism,* no. 6 (1983).

33. Richard Jeffries, *Class, Power and Ideology in Africa: The Railwaymen of Sekondi* (Cambridge: Cambridge University Press, 1978). Also see Peter C. W. Gutkind, "Change and Consciousness in Urban Africa: African Workers in Transition," *Cahiers d'études Africaines* 81–83 (1981): 299–346.

34. Robin Cohen, "Resistance and Hidden Forms of Consciousness Amongst African Workers," *Review of African Political Economy* 19 (1980): 8–22.

35. Guyer, "Comparative Epilogue," p. 21 and elsewhere.

36. Gracia Clark, "Pools, Clients and Markets" (Paper presented at the Twenty-sixth Annual Meeting of the African Studies Association, Los Angeles, October 1984), p. 7.

37. Claire Robertson, "The Death of Makola and Other Tragedies," *Canadian Journal of African Studies* 17, no. 3 (1983): 477.

38. For background, see Martin A. Klein, ed., *Peasants in Africa: Historical and Contemporary Perspectives* (Beverly Hills: Sage Publications, 1980); John C. Saul and Roger Woods, "African Peasantries," in Dennis L. Cohen and John Daniel, eds., *Political Economy of Africa* (London: Longman, 1981), pp. 112–118; and Claude E. Welch, "Peasants as a Focus in African Studies," *African Studies Review* 20, no. 3 (1977): 2–5.

39. M. Catharine Newbury, "*Ubureetwa* and *Thangata:* Catalysts to Peasant Political Consciousness in Rwanda and Malawi," *Canadian Journal of African Studies* 14, no. 1 (1980): 97–111; Szymon Chodak, "Birth of an African Peasantry," *Canadian Journal of African Studies* 12, no. 3 (1971): 327–349.

40. Rhoda Howard, *Colonialism and Underdevelopment in Ghana* (London: Croom Helm, 1978). Also see Sharon Stichter, *Migrant Laborers* (London: Cambridge University Press, 1985).

41. Contrast with Goran Hyden, *Beyond Ujamaa in Tanzania: Underdevelopment and an Uncaptured Peasantry* (London: Heinemann, 1980). Also see Joshua B. Forrest, "Defining African Peasants," *Peasant Studies* 9, no. 4 (1982): 242–249.

42. Keith Hart, *The Political Economy of West African Agriculture* (London: Cambridge University Press, 1982), p. 105.

43. Jonathan Barker, "Political Space and the Quality of Participation in Rural Africa: A Case from Senegal" (University of Toronto, Development Studies Programme, Working Paper no. C4, July 1984), and his, "Can the Poor in Africa Fight Poverty?" *Journal of African Studies* 7, no. 3 (1980): 161–166.

44. See Michael Watts, *Silent Violence* (Berkeley: University of California Press, 1983).

45. Kathleen Staudt, "Women's Politics and Capitalist Transformation in Subsaharan Africa," *Women in Development Working Paper 54* (1984), p. 2.

46. Achola O. Pala, "La femme africaine dans le développement rurale," *Cahiers économiques et sociaux* 16, no. 3 (1978): 306–333; *Review of African Political Economy* 27/28 (1983), Special Issue on Women in Africa.

47. Margaret Snyder, "The African Woman in Economic Development: A Regional Perspective," in *The African Women in Economic Development Conference Proceedings* (Washington, D.C.: African-American Scholars Council, 1975), p. 11.

48. "Masculin-féminin: L'autre apartheid," *Jeune Afrique plus* 2 (September-October 1983): 57–58.

49. Ibid., p. 57.

50. Staudt, "Women's Politics," p. 21; Jette Bukh, *The Village Woman in Ghana* (Uppsala: Scandinavian Institute of African Studies, 1979).

51. Naomi Chazan, "The Manipulation of Youth Politics in Ghana and the Ivory Coast," *Geneva-Africa* 15, no. 2 (1976): 38–63.

52. "Student Power: The Credit and Debit Side," *New African* 154 (1980): 11–18; Nono Lutula Piame-Ololo, "La jeunesse et la politique en Afrique noire," *Le mois en Afrique* 215/216 (1983–1984): 11–17.

53. William John Hanna, *University Students and African Politics* (New York: Africana Publishing Co., 1975).

54. For one case study, see Claude Meillassoux, *Urbanization of an African Community: Voluntary Associations in Bamako* (Seattle: University of Washington Press, 1968).

55. Sandra T. Barnes, "Voluntary Associations in a Metropolis: The Case of Lagos, Nigeria," *African Studies Review* 18, no. 2 (1975): 75–88.

56. O. K. Finagnon, "Notes sur les forces religieuses dans les états africains," *Le mois en Afrique* 213/214 (1983): 110–114; Kofi Asare Opoku, *West African Traditional Religion* (Accra: University of Ghana Press, 1978).

57. D. C. O'Brien, "La filière musulmane: Confréries soufies et politique en Afrique noire," *Politique africaine* 1, no. 4 (1981): 7–30.

58. D. C. O'Brien, "A Veritable Charisma: The Mouride Brotherhood 1967–1975," *Archives européenes de sociologie* 18 (1977): 84–106.

59. Johannes Fabian, "Religion and Change," in Paden and Soja, *The African Experience*, vol. 1, p. 383. Also see Raymond F. Hopkins, "Christianity in Sub-Saharan Africa," *Social Forces* 44, no. 4 (1966): 555–562.

60. Terence O. Ranger, "Religious Movements and Politics in Sub-Saharan Africa" (Paper presented at the Twenty-eighth Annual Meeting of the African Studies Association, New Orleans, November 1985), p. 39.

61. Paul Lubeck, "Conscience de classe et nationalisme islamique à Kano," *Politique africaine* 4 (1981): 40. Also see Martial Sinda, "L'état africain postcolonial: Les forces sociales et les communautés religieuses dans l'état postcolonial en Afrique," *Présence africaine* 127/128 (1983): 240–260.

62. Mar Fall, "L'état sénégalais et le renouveau récent de l'islam: Une introduction," *Le mois en Afrique* 219/220 (1984): 154–159. Also see John N. Paden, *Religion and Political Culture in Kano* (Berkeley: University of California Press, 1973).

63. Christian Coulon, "Le réseau islamique," *Politique africaine* 9 (1983): 68–83. Also see Guy Nicholas, "Islam et 'constructions nationales' au sud du Sahara," *Revue francaise d'études politiques africaines* 165/166 (1979): 86–107. *Politique africaine* no. 4 (1981), features a special issue on Islam in Africa.

64. For some examples, see Peil, *Consensus and Conflict in African Society,* p.

239; and Allen and Williams, *Sociology of "Developing Societies" : Sub-Saharan Africa*, pp. 93–120.

65. Guy Nicholas, "Societés africaines, monde arabe et culture islamique," *Le mois en Afrique* no. 173/174 (1980): 47–64; Babiatu Amman, "New Light on Muslim Statistics for Africa," *Bulletin on Islam and Christian-Muslim Relations in Africa* 2, no. 1 (1984): 11–20.

66. This term is taken from Thomas M. Callaghy, *The State-Society Struggle: Zaire in Comparative Perspective* (New York: Columbia University Press, 1984).

67. Berry, *Fathers Work for Their Sons*, pp. 16–17, 194; Szymon Chodak, "Social Stratification in Sub-Saharan Africa," *Canadian Journal of African Studies* 7, no. 3 (1973): 401–417. Also see Immanuel Wallerstein, "Class and Status in Contemporary Africa," in Gutkind and Waterman, *African Social Studies*, pp. 277–283.

4

Ethnicity, Class, and the State

Our political choice approach emphasizes the complexity of the group demands that the African state faces. It assumes a constant engagement of rival interests in the contemporary political arena, an interaction among various groups mobilized to secure public resources from those in authority. These groups—based on ethnicity, region, race, religion, generation, class, and so forth—may be distinct in terms of origins and appeals, but they share common features in the way they organize to engage in a dynamic interplay of interest-inspired conflict and collaboration. In some instances cultural communities succeed in uniting people for some of the primary purposes of existence—cultural fulfillment, belongingness, psychological security, and social intercourse; where this occurs, such communities can play an important role in gathering group members around an intermediary for the purpose of making collective demands on state decision makers. The range of these demands varies considerably. Not only do group representatives lay claim to a full share of public political power, protections, economic resources, administrative positions, contracts, awards, and scholarships, but they make appeals, sometimes more conflict-laden in their effects, for broad grants of political autonomy and independence.

It is this accent upon organized group action in the political arena and upon expressed collective claims to resources, participation, and security that makes a political choice approach so appropriate to the study of the many political identities on the African scene. It is in this vein that Joel Samoff's remark that "all people have multiple identities—which identity is salient depends on the situation" has significance for our purposes.[1] Our objective here will be to differentiate these multiple identities, attempting thereby to understand the nature of the struggle that each one engages in for various public benefits. In particular, we will concentrate upon the most effective identities for demands on the state—ethnicity and socioeconomic class—noting their special appeals as well as their intertwining natures. With this as background, we will turn to the interactions of identities with each other and with the state, examining the conflicting demands that these mobilized identities make upon the state, the state's role in responding to and mediating between these claims, and the state's role in molding these identities. Then, in Chapter 9, we will examine the policy preferences formulated and implemented by state decision makers.

■ ETHNICITY AND ETHNIC GROUP

As used in this context, *ethnicity* refers to a subjective perception of common origins, historical memories, ties, and aspirations; ethnic group pertains to organized activities by persons, linked by a consciousness of a special identity, who jointly seek to maximize their corporate political, economic, and social interests. Ethnicity, or a sense of peoplehood, has its foundations in combined remembrances of past experience and in common inspirations, values, norms, and expectations. The validity of these beliefs and remembrances is of less significance to an overarching sense of affinity than is their ability to symbolize a people's closeness to one another. Ethnicity as a subjective basis for collective consciousness gains relevance to the political process when it spurs group formation and underpins political organization. In its capacity to stimulate awareness and a sense of belonging among the potential membership of a group, the psychological dimension of ethnicity complements and buttresses the political dimension of interest-oriented social action. Thus, a sense of peoplehood may be instrumental to group formation and participation in the political process; nevertheless, initiative on the part of an elite remains indispensable to the promotion and defense of group interests.

Hence, as discussed in Chapter 3, *ethnic groups* may engage in social interactions with other organized units in the society. The ethnic group—defined here as a distinct group in society self-consciously united around shared histories, traditions, beliefs, cultures, and values, which mobilizes its membership for common political, economic, and social purposes—is in essence a culturally based social organization.[2] The ethnic group joins the subjective dimension of peoplehood with the objective dimension of economic and social interests. It operates socially in a relationship governed, in certain instances, by informal and formal rules of interaction that may be both recurrent and predictable. Provided that agreed-upon rules of encounter effectively define intergroup competition and conflict, the social relations of these groups may prove constructive.

At this point, several aspects of the ethnic group's political role need to be examined: its fluidity; its lack of homogeneity and cohesiveness; and its espousal of the common (indivisible) interests of its membership as a whole. On the first point, it is less than accurate to characterize the ethnic groups on the African continent as having a fixed, centuries-old, primordial consciousness.

Among such peoples as the Sukuma in what is now Tanzania, the Sara of Chad, the Yoruba and Igbo of Nigeria, the Kikuyu and Luhya of Kenya, the Ngoni and Plateau Tonga of Zambia, and the Karamojong of Uganda, there were affinities based upon coresidence in a region and upon similarities of culture, traditions, and legal and economic practices. However, an awareness of the group as a distinct entity in relationship to other cultural groups remains a relatively recent phenomenon. In fact, the process of ethnic self-definition occurred in the short time span that it did because of the impact of colonial interventions and the intense competition over power, status, economic resources, and social services happening during the late colonial and postcolonial periods. For purposes of administrative convenience, colonial governments encouraged the integration of autonomous sections living side by side in order to consolidate territory and identity groups. In other cases, colonial officials went beyond this to create modern ethnic entities. Aidan Southall, writing about the Luhya, notes that this group is a striking example of a named entity that was first identified as a "tribe" during the colonial era "and must in this sense necessarily be considered a product" of colonial rule.[3] Crawford Young describes how Belgian officials first made use of the term Ngala in the nineteenth century to distinguish the people dwelling alongside the Zaire River and later extended the term to include those from the riverine area who migrated to urban Kinshasa. In this instance, the colonial outsider succeeded, unwittingly, in establishing a new ethnic identity. A grouping never before aware of its existence now "remained as a meaningful identity in everyday sociological vocabulary."[4] Still another case, which points up the modernity of many ethnic group identities, is that of the Hutu in Burundi. There it took the Tutsi repressions of 1972 to forge a sense of shared fate among the organizationally distinct Hutu of the north-center and those of the south-Imbo, a process that one observer describes as "enforced ethnicity."[5]

The relatively recent origin and flexibility of many African ethnic groups points to another characteristic—their tendency to lack homogeneity and cohesiveness. Although the ethnic group differs from other contemporary economic and social interest groups in the diffuseness of the obligations it places upon the membership, it nonetheless allows for the emergence of multiple identities and interests. In fact, group control over individual conduct frequently is insufficient to prevent the emergence of diverse interests, values, and commitments. The individual member, variously involved in economic roles such as worker, professional, businessperson, or administrator, develops crosscutting ties of socioeconomic class, religion, region, and so forth, that modify the exclusivity of primary group obligations. Insofar as the ethnic group, as a culturally based social organization, interacts with other ethnic, economic, and social interest groups, it promotes the salient interests—political power, economic resources, public positions, status, protection—of the dominant coalition among the membership at a particular time. The membership must negotiate a common position within the group and continually act so as to maintain the unity and strength of the heterogeneous unit before it can engage in meaningful bargaining encounters at the top of the system. No matter how successful these coalition-building efforts may prove, intragroup differences are likely to persist, allowing rivals the option to interact with factions on separate bases rather than to deal with the ethnic collectivity as a whole.

In addition to class differences, the postindependence political behavior of African ethnic groups reveals a persistence of internal or subethnic schisms along the lines of clan, age-set, and areal differences. Thus, an understanding of intra-Shona conflicts among the Karanga, Zezuru, Manica, and other clans for power and patronage in Zimbabwe is critical to gaining a comprehensive insight into the complicated politics of that country. And clan politics is highly significant in Somalia where, since Mohammed Siad Barre's ascendancy, the powerful Mijerteyn clan feels dissatisfied in relation to the president's own Marehan clan and his mother's clan, the Ogaden. Similarly, Kenya's interethnic conflicts are not as straightforward as is sometimes assumed; not only is predominantly Kikuyu Central Province divided by the three rival districts of Muranga, Nyeri, and Kiambu, but clan and generational differences remain as intense as ever.[6] Moreover, Kenya's other major ethnic groups—the Luo, Kamba, Kalenjin, and Luhya—are also torn by divided interests and leadership and are not, as is so frequently assumed, united internally.[7]

To be sure, the existence of such internal divisions must not blind us to the fact that ethnic identities, which may vary under different circumstances, can be highly effective politically, even with only a limited attachment on the part of their members to their goals and values. Thus, for example, in the early 1960s, various groups among the Yorubas contested power in the then Western Region of Nigeria. Each faction (in particular, the Oyo Yoruba around Chief Samuel Ladoke Akintola and the Ijebu Yoruba who looked to Chief Obafemi Awolowo) vied for political power in the region. It was to build linkages between these competing interests within the larger Yoruba community that Chief Awolowo played an instrumental role in organizing a pan-Yoruba cultural organization, the Society of the Descendants of Oduduwa, which subsequently led to the founding of a Yoruba-led political party, the Action Group. However, the "divisive rivalry between traditional Yoruba groups"[8] continued into the 1960s and, combined with ideological differences and competing alliance politics, culminated in the 1962 proclamation of a state of emergency in the Western Region and the subsequent trial and imprisonment of Chief Awolowo for possessing arms and ammunition illegally. Some fifteen years later, commenting on Chief Obafemi Awolowo's consolidation of various Yoruba ethnic subgroups for electoral purposes in 1979, Richard Joseph asserts: "By sweeping Yorubaland so convincingly, Chief Awolowo became leader of the Yorubas with a completeness whose significance can be fully comprehended only when placed in the context of the historical rivalries among the Yoruba subgroups."[9]

The impact of this internal diversity upon intergroup exchange is also noteworthy. Rather than a simple dichotomized relationship between bargaining partners, internal differences require a more complicated two-level process of negotiations, within the heterogeneous ethnic group at the regional and central levels and among the ethnic bloc intermediaries and central leaders at the top. A Kalenjin leader in Kenya must forge a united position among diverse representatives for Kipsigis, Marakwet, Nandi, Pokot, Elgeyo, Tugen, and other interests prior to dealing with the leaders of other important ethnic peoples in public forums (the Kikuyu, Luo, Embu, Meru, Masai, Luhya, Mijikenda, etc.). It is the two-level aspect of this political process that so often frustrates state leaders as they seek to negotiate with ethnoregional go-betweens who may or may not be able to keep their constituents in line and deliver on the terms of bargains.

Yet another characteristic of the ethnic group germane to our analysis is its role in promoting the common, as opposed to the like, interests of its members. Like interests may be said to be in evidence where individuals "severally or distributively pursue a like object, each for himself"; common interests may be said to exist where individuals "seek a goal or objective which is one and indivisible for them all, which unites them with one another in a quest that cannot be resolved merely into an aggregate of individual quests."[10] In this sense, the interest group whose members seek to improve their economic conditions must be distinguished from the ethnically based social organization whose members join forces to advance the unspecialized goals of the community "for itself." Thus, if railway or construction workers organize to promote the occupational or class interests of individuals similarly situated in society, the members of an ethnic group combine to protect and improve what they broadly define as communal concerns—in particular, the security, identity, and well-being of a people as a whole. Although the ethnic group strives to fulfill its own potentialities in relationship to other sociocultural organizations, its commitment to common interests is not to be taken as indicating a denial of the like interests of its members. The existence of a common interest does not preclude a limit on an individual member's commitment to group purposes. The group finds its meaning through interaction with other such social organizations, but the common interests of its members by no means preclude the emergence of crosscutting class or other interests, creating a diversity of identities that may have the effect of reducing group cohesiveness.

■ THE ETHNIC INTERMEDIARY'S CRITICAL ROLE

So far we have described the ethnic group in Africa as a phenomenon that has grown in significance in the twentieth century. What colonial administrators previously grouped together as "tribal" identities for administrative purposes became the basis for urban-led demands in the postindependence period. As such, the ethnic group has become a useful instrument for mobilizing and aggregating interests in competition with other ethnic, occupational, and business interest groups for state-controlled political and economic resources. Thus, ethnicity, like socioeconomic class, has proved to be a state-linked category that places claims upon the state and to which the state normally responds. Ethnic group participation in this dynamic struggle over scarce state resources is a continuing element in contemporary African political life. It reflects the political impera- tives of the times and cannot be wished away by the exhortations of rulers; on the contrary, it is part and parcel of today's political process. African ethnicity, as Abner Cohen observes, is "basically a political and not a cultural phenome- non, and it operates within contemporary political contexts and is not an archaic survival arrangement carried over into the present by conservative people."[11]

The task of promoting collective political and economic interests at the center naturally requires leadership, and in this instance authority positions are assumed by what we will call ethnic intermediaries. An intermediary's role on the contemporary African scene exists within a broader category of relation- ships characterized as political clientelism (discussed also in Chapter 6). "Un- like 'class' and 'ethnicity,' both of which are group phenomena," René Lemarchand and Keith Legg remark, "clientelism refers to a personalized and reciprocal relationship between an inferior [client] and a superior [patron] com- manding unequal resources."[12] If patron-client ties often prove coextensive with ethnic cleavages in society, it is also important to keep in mind that local patron/ leaders can also engage in reciprocal relations with subordinates outside the ethnic community, extending protection, services, and material benefits to members of other identity groups in exchange for support and assistance. Here, however, we will emphasize the overlaps between ethnicity and clientelism at the system level. Such a focus will allow us to concentrate upon the process utilized by the ethnic intermediary when articulating communal interests to decision-making elites at the political center.

Because state institutions in Africa are fragile and command only limited public acceptance, informal networks of personal relationships emerge in soci- ety to link a relatively powerful and well-placed patron with a less powerful client or clients for the purpose of advancing their mutual interests. Political clientelism, which involves ties of reciprocity between actors controlling un- equal political, economic, or social resources, takes various forms; we can therefore distinguish traditional clientelist structures bringing together actors of unequal status at the local level from what René Lemarchand and others call "machine-like clientelism," political exchange patterns at the top of the politi- cal system that link powerful and partially autonomous state and ethnoregional leaders for the purposes of governance and resource distribution. Certainly a range of interconnecting clientelist relations exists between the local and sys- temwide levels. As Lemarchand notes, "clientelism can lead to a *pyramiding of client-patron ties,* and, through the recruitment of new brokers, to an expansion of local or regional reciprocities on a more inclusive scale."[13] Hence, a focus upon clientelism at the system level embraces local level clientelist relations within it.

In terms of the nature of the relationship, the patron is linked vertically to his or her subordinates on a basis of unequal status and exchange, distributing limited political and economic benefits to clients largely dependent on his or her protection in a scarcity-prone and sometimes hazardous environment. Moreover, the patron is linked horizontally to other patrons and state officials on a more or less equal basis to assure access to a share of the public resources controlled by the state. In his or her negotiations at the center, the patron/intermediary's influence and bargaining power is dependent in no small part on that person's ability to maintain stable, informal ties with clients at the periphery. If his or her local constituency base is successfully challenged by a new patron—an ever-present possibility where material resources are generally scarce and opportunities limited—the informal ties of reciprocity may unravel and rivals may take over the leadership role. Yet, as James Scott cautions, based on an extended experience with patron-client relationships in Southeast Asia, the probability that structures will prove resilient is not to be discounted.[14] In fact, black Africa's experience with political clientelism both at the local and system-wide levels bears out Scott's contentions on the likely durability of such linkages.

It is quite clear, then, that the patron/ethnic intermediary plays a leading role in promoting the interests of his or her ethnic constituents at the system level. Even within the context of the African one-party or no-party system, ethnic intermediaries remain active, engaging state leaders at the political center in a continual process of informal political exchanges. Ethnic intermediaries, themselves members of the dominant political class, must strive to maintain a loyal following within their ethnic constituencies if they are to be able to negotiate effectively at the top with other ethnic and state leaders, whether in the legislature, the cabinet, or the party executive committee. The styles and preferences of these dominant political class members are critical to the regularity and persistence of these interactional relationships. Where the state leadership makes effective use of the political exchange process to facilitate mutual accommodations, constructive state-ethnoregional relations may materialize. Partially autonomous state and ethnoregional leaders will then encounter one another in accordance with prevailing state norms and values, especially those on conflict management.

To be sure, something of a gap exists between the felt dissatisfactions of the general public and the ethnic intermediary's selection and shaping of public demands prior to channeling these into the political process.[15] Not only are African peasants essentially unorganized and dependent upon their representatives for articulating their claims, but the ethnic intermediaries, who maintain close ties with the dominant political class living mostly in urban areas, have interests and life-styles that diverge from those of their constituents. Nevertheless, it is these ethnic intermediaries, the go-betweens for the rural constituencies at the political center, who are in a position to manipulate symbols and thereby to communicate collective claims to those in authority. Consequently, what the various ethnic intermediaries determine as their primary objectives and the effectiveness with which they make their claims are critical to the demand process and the manner in which scarce economic and political resources are distributed. The ethnic intermediary's appeals, both for specific goods and services and for general developmental assistance, often prove an effective catalyst for increased governmental attention and support. It is inevitable that the intermediary will be selective in how demands are organized and presented to those in control at the political center. The intermediary cannot possibly convey all of the public's wishes at the same time and expect to have a significant impact; hence, task effectiveness necessitates setting priorities, requiring that the ethnic intermediary structure collective claims in a generalized, coherent, and sophisticated manner. As a result, political judgment on what demands to present, as well as ability to cope with local factional dissent and the counterclaims of state and other ethnic leaders at the political center, become critical to the intermediary's performance as an ethnic champion. If the intermediary's choice of demands masks class privilege without taking account of his or her constituents' concerns, that person is likely to find it difficult to maintain support in his or her home area over time (as became evident in many electoral contests in one-party Kenya and Tanzania).

Ethnic intermediaries make use of the classic tactics of interest group delegates the world over in pressing their claims upon public authorities at the political center. Varying enormously in terms of influence, access, and types of relationships with both state elites and other ethnic intermediaries, these group representatives operate in all kinds of political contexts: authoritarian and constitutional Marxist, neo-Marxist and liberal pluralist, military and civilian. In highly authoritarian or military-led regimes, the provincial commissioner or military governor quite commonly acts as the main official point of contact with the central executive leader or his ministerial heads. Thus, during Nigeria's 1966 military regime, military commanders carefully reconciled a central perspective with the advocacy of subregional interests at the center.[16] Similarly, in the Sudan, the man who served as president of the High Executive Council for the Southern Region during part of the 1981–1982 period, Major General Gasmallah Rassas, behaved in a manner similar to that of his civilian predecessor, traveling to Khartoum and negotiating with President Gaafar Nimeiri or the appropriate ministers for increased public allocations for his region.[17] Civilian provincial commissioners have acted in a very similar manner. The four civilian presidents or acting presidents of the High Executive Council of Sudan's southern region from 1972, when the Addis Ababa agreement was signed, to 1983 all acted to represent ethnoregional interests at the political center. And in post-revolutionary Ethiopia, provincial commissioners appointed by the *derg*, more often than not originally hailing from the area over which they had come to exercise authority, acted as ethnoregional intermediaries, making demands on the state for an increased share of public resources and services.[18]

In a somewhat more systematic fashion, a more broadly embracing, two-directional process of state-ethnoregional linkages emerged during post-independence times in such countries as Uganda, Zambia, Cameroon, Côte d'Ivoire, and Kenya. Although Uganda's President Milton Obote and Zambia's President Kenneth Kaunda both denied the legitimacy of reciprocity in the relations between state elites and ethnoregional intermediaries, they nonetheless accepted the reality of this informal relationship and acted to apply a principle of proportionality in such areas as fiscal allocations, elite recruitment, and coalition formation in the upper levels of the party and government. Thus, Obote declared that a "National Assembly . . . as an assembly of peace conference delegates and tribal diplomatic and legislative functionaries"[19] was unacceptable, but he went on engaging in political exchange relationships with these ethnoregional ambassadors nonetheless. Similarly, Kaunda expressed distaste for the idea of provincial "champions"; yet he was careful, in forming his cabinets, to "delicately [balance] between the tribal poles of the Bemba in the north and Barotse (Lozi) in the south."[20] Also, true to his commitments to equitable allocations between subregions, his government pursued a principled policy of redistribution, aimed at securing an equalization of rural and urban services and more equal incomes within a relatively short time span.[21] State-ethnoregional relations remained informal and without official recognition or sanction in these two cases, but the outcomes reflected a pragmatic adjustment to the reality of soft state conditions.

Finally, in the cases of Côte d'Ivoire and Kenya, and to some extent also Cameroon, a system akin to a cartel of state and ethnoregional elites may be said to have developed under Felix Houphouët-Boigny and Jomo Kenyatta. In such political coalitions, all major ethnic groups are assured some minimal participation in the governing process—whether by formal rules (for example, the provisions in Nigeria's 1979 constitution on the "federal character" of federal decision-making bodies) or by informal rules (in hegemonic Côte d'Ivoire, Kenya, and Cameroon). This participation is encouraged by the inclusion of major ethnoregional intermediaries in the cabinet and/or the party national executive committee. Such inclusion encourages bargaining by prominent communal representatives over major issues within the key centers of power, thereby promoting collaboration rather than group competition. Other informal rules on the maintenance of an elite cartel of state and ethnoregional intermediaries appear with some regularity: the decision not to drop a minister who has been reelected to parliament; the replacement of retiring ministers and high party officials with others from the same subregion; and the preservation, when succession occurs, of a balance in high government and party appointments.

In both Côte d'Ivoire and Kenya, the founding fathers were careful to consolidate their rule through practices of ethnic inclusion and hegemonic exchange. Especially in the 1960s and early 1970s, where the rules of the political game in Côte d'Ivoire involved an "acknowledge[ment]," but not a public display of ethnic politics, President Houphouët-Boigny "tried to achieve some ethnic balance in his cabinets in order to mollify the resentment of Baoule dominance."[22] Rather than challenging the validity of ethnic appeals, Houphouët-Boigny prudently provided for their incorporation in what Aristide Zolberg describes as a "one-party coalition, a heterogeneous monolith."[23] All major ethnic groups were represented in the cabinet and on a basis roughly proportional to their position in the National Assembly. In doing this, Houphouët-Boigny was careful to demobilize potential ethnoregional challengers by coopting these intermediaries into the ruling coalition at the center. Playing a key role by dominating and, if necessary, mediating between the different factions in the cabinet, Houphouët-Boigny built a political structure that ensured his survival as president over a relatively long period of time.

In a similar way, Kenya's Jomo Kenyatta ensured considerable stability for his regime by establishing a one-party cabinet coalition of ethnoregional notables. With the central party organization of the ruling Kenya African National Union exercising only loose control over affairs at the branch level, ethnoregional party notables were able to build strong bases of power in their constituencies and then, as in the case of such prominent ethnoregional champions as Ronald Ngala and Paul Ngei, to negotiate over the nature of their participation in the central cabinet.[24] Kenyatta's system of competitive bargaining underwent significant change under his successor, Daniel arap Moi, who appointed a number of his protégés to high party and cabinet positions. It is quite possible that this change in leadership style had adverse political and economic consequences, for Kenya in the 1980s has not known the same level of stability and development that marked the earlier period.

Operating for the most part out of the public view, the ethnic intermediaries use a variety of formal and informal channels—contacts with politicians and bureaucrats, support for sympathetic parties or candidates, pressures on legislators, logrolling, threats of noncooperation and noncompliance, etc.—to influence decision makers to act positively on their demands for jobs, services, and public resources. In Ghana, for example, ethnoregional spokespeople, especially those hailing from the less-advantaged subregions, made extensive use of parliamentary forums in the years immediately after independence to push the government to accelerate development of their home areas. However, with the demise of party competition under President Kwame Nkrumah, the ethnic power brokers found face-to-face contacts as advisors to "the Redeemer" to be the surest means of securing a full share of state patronage for their constituents. Then, with the advent of President Kofi Busia and the return to parliamentary government, the power brokers became, in the early years of the Busia administration at least, "largely synonymous with cabinet members."[25] With the eclipse of party government following Colonel I. K. Acheampong's military intervention in 1972, the opportunities for an open articulation of demands largely disappeared, and the style of putting forth group claims became concealed. However, ethnoregional intermediaries—often traditional leaders, civil servants, or highly placed military officers—continued to communicate their constituents' wishes (as they interpreted them) to those in authority positions, though in a less dramatic fashion. Thus, the Upper Regional House of Chiefs openly appealed in 1976 for the establishment of a university and a brewery in that relatively disadvantaged area.

Further confirmation of this relation between changing political structures and the process of ethnic interest articulation became evident as Ghana passed through subsequent cycles of parliamentary government (the Hilla Limann administration) and military rule (the second Jerry Rawlings administration). What proved constant through all these switches was the critical role played by the ethnic broker, even if the means used to advance the interests of rural constituents at the political center changed noticeably with each switch in authority system. By dint of their political skill, knowledge, initiative, contacts, and resources, the ethnic intermediaries are the ones who inevitably give direction to the diffuse claims of their constituents for state resources. Should the dominant political elite at the center become inattentive to the intermediary's appeals, the precariousness of his or her personal position is likely to become apparent. Nevertheless, the role itself may be expected to survive, and another ethnic intermediary will more than likely seize the patron/intermediary mantle on behalf of those same constituents.

The African ethnic intermediary must forge unity to promote the collective interests of his/her group at the political center. Similarly, the representative for occupational and other economic interests competes in the political marketplace for a full share of status, political power, and publicly controlled resources. In the case of class and occupational leaders, a distinction may usefully be made between the open political and economic action of union leaders and some representatives of opposition organizations (for example, the outspoken criticism by the president of the Ghana Bar Association with respect to alleged abuses of civil liberties under the regimes of I. K. Acheampong and Jerry Rawlings; or the critical role of doctors and other professional people in agitating against the regime of President Gaafar Nimeiri in the Sudan in 1985) and the behind-the-scenes lobbying and interest-influencing by manufacturing and commercial interests. In Kenya and Zimbabwe, for example, the move from colonialism to formal independence brought with it a change of tactics on the part of business leaders, who avoided open political action in postindependence times in favor of quiet contacts with parliamentarians and bureaucrats. This raises an important question: If the ethnic intermediary resembles the class spokesperson in participating in the struggle for benefits, how is the ethnic intermediary and the interests that that person represents distinguishable from a class leader and his or her interests? It is clear that ethnicity and crosscutting class identities overlap and become intermeshed, and it is essential for us to point to the kinds of situations in which each of these state-linked categories appears to be primary. But first it is necessary to examine the emergent class cleavages in African societies.

■ AFRICAN CLASS CLEAVAGES AND SOCIAL CONFLICTS

The analysis of African political conflicts in class terms is relatively recent and often represents a reaction to what is perceived as the ethnocentrism and determinism implicit in modernization theory. Social scientists as well as political leaders in the 1950s and early 1960s frequently denied that conflicts based on class identities were occurring and spoke instead of mass-elite divisions or cultural pluralism. A Kenya government paper on African socialism declared, not atypically, in 1965: "The sharp class divisions that once existed in Europe have no place in African Socialism and no parallel in African society. No class problem arose in the traditional African society and none exists today among Africans."[26] Such denials of class relations in African societies did not go unchallenged, however. Scholars from the Marxist, neo-Marxist, and structural dependency schools argued that both colonialism and the incorporation of African societies into a world capitalist system (and the class divisions this entailed) contributed to the formation of modern classes based on their relationship to the means of production and their conflicts with other classes on issues of private and public policy.

Although such a process of class formation remains "incomplete" and, because of underdevelopment and the penetration of external capitalism, involves "weak class differentiation," class relations, as viewed by these schools, are nonetheless the critical element in determining objective reality.[27] Consciously thinking in class rather than ethnic terms, Marxist regimes are inclined to dismiss references to ethnic domination as irrelevant and counterrevolutionary. Hence, where conservative, capitalist-oriented regime analysts often tend to downplay the significance of class affinities, their radical, Marxist-oriented counterparts frequently tend to reduce ethnic attachments to relative unimportance.[28] A more comprehensive political choice orientation must, for the sake of effectiveness, give heed simultaneously to the impact of each variable or combination of variables in different time and place contexts.

It is certain that much of the responsibility for current class cleavages in the typical contemporary African country arises from colonial policies and programs, particularly the colonial administration's emphasis upon attracting European civil servants, professionals, farmers, and businesspeople to Africa and giving a higher priority to the modernization of the core area within the country. Colonial developmental efforts largely concentrated upon the relatively high-income urban enclaves, leaving the majority of people in the rural areas neglected and with limited opportunity for advancement in the modern sector. This differentiated rate of modernization, reinforced by subsequent policy decisions in many of the newly independent African countries, became the basis for contemporary uneven development—both between the various racial identity groups and the subregions of a country. Such a process had important implications for class relations, as these disparities were related to income, occupation, and status. Subregional interests entered differently into the productive process, not only in terms of the goods they produced and the distribution of benefits and services that took place, but also in their linkages outward to the industrial centers of the West. Precapitalist and capitalist features of the production process, therefore, tended to exist side by side in the same state.[29] As Robert Bates observes, modernization helped to shape a new stratification system that produced competition for scarce state-controlled resources between traditional and modern classes.[30]

Given the constraints that colonial development priorities placed upon subsequent African leaders, it is important to examine the challenge these leaders encountered in uniting their countries around the time of independence. For this purpose, we will look at interregional disparities in Zambia, surveying the inequalities of opportunity between the relatively advantaged line-of-rail provinces (Copperbelt, Central, and Southern) and the five relatively disadvantaged off-line-of-rail provinces (Northern, Luapula, North-Western, Eastern, and Western).[31] Inequality of opportunity between residents of the line-of-rail provinces and the rest was evident with respect to both economic and social variables. Not only were the greatest number of employment opportunities found near the railway strip (which could carry the products to domestic and international markets), but the average wages for such African employees tended to be higher. In 1969, the line-of-rail accounted for 84 percent of the total number of employees in Zambia (more than half of them in the Copperbelt alone). Manufacturing activity was heavily concentrated along the rail line, with 98 percent of the 31,938 employees in manufacturing-related activities finding work in Copperbelt, Central, or Southern provinces. This imbalance was reflected as well with regard to average African earnings in the public and private sectors. Average earnings of K935 ($2,618) in Copperbelt Province was well above the national average of K789 ($2,209); furthermore, annual earnings in North-Western Province (K404, $1,131), Northern Province (K430, $1,204), and Western Province (K483, $1,352) were well below the average.[32]

Disparities with respect to amenities and social services between the line-of-rail and off-line-of-rail provinces were also striking. For example, with respect to the availability of electricity, 94 percent of all dwellings equipped with electricity were found in the three line-of-rail provinces. Moreover, rural deprivation, as a holdover from colonial times, was apparent, from available data, in such social services as health and education. Unlike the urban dweller, who is often relatively close to adequate medical assistance, the average villager, and particularly those in the off-line-of-rail areas, traveled some 9 or 10 miles (16 km) to the most rudimentary dispensary and considerably further to a modern, well-equipped hospital. As a member of parliament depicted the plight of the rural villager, "Looking, Sir, at our health in the rural areas, Sir, our dispensaries are very far apart. You have got to walk about 70 miles [112 km] to reach the nearest dispensary in the rural areas where there is no public transport. And most of the rural health centres, Sir, are manned by untrained people."[33] If urban hospitals were unable to cope with the pressure of a heavy patient load from all over the country, rural clinics and dispensaries lacked the staff and facilities to give any but the most elementary kind of medicine.

Finally, in the face of what Dr. Kaunda described as "a revolutionary urge for education among all our people," hopes for universal primary education remained unfulfilled, and rural opportunities, particularly in the off-line-of-rail provinces, continued to be more circumscribed than in the more-advantaged areas.[34] Ministry of Education data for 1966 showed that enrollment in the high-quality fee-paying government primary schools heavily favored pupils from the line-of-rail provinces, as 94 percent of the student body in these schools came from these relatively advantaged subregions.[35] Moreover, data on all fee- and non-fee-paying schools showed that the population-teacher ratios in the three line-of-rail provinces were roughly half those of the rest of the country. Whereas the ratios for Copperbelt, Central, and Southern were 212, 255, and 246, respectively, those for North-Western and Eastern were 383 and 384, respectively, and that for Luapula ran to a high of 493.[36]

The implications for Zambia, and many other African countries, are clear. Colonial efforts to modernize affected various parts of the country differently, resulting in a stratification of opportunities that could not be altered easily by African policymakers, even where they were determined to balance the imbalances of the past. The consequence was to perpetuate grave disparities in production, distribution, and social welfare. Urban enclaves, as well as some advantaged rural areas, gained an access to scarce resources, which set them apart from the majority of rural dwellers. As Kaunda himself warned, Zambia faced the danger of creating two nations within one. It is quite evident, then, that class stratification in Africa is complicated by its historical origins. A stratification between center and periphery overlaps with the more standard types of socioeconomic class divisions found within the modern sector. And because of the extent of these various kinds of inequalities, the possibilities for conflict abound.

If class and ethnic relations are both fluid and overlapping, they may nonetheless be described as resting on different attributes and types of behavior.[37] Birth-ascribed systems, which frequently have a basis of existence external to the societies they are united with politically, make comprehensive claims on the loyalties and activities of their memberships. More often than not, status is assigned and mobility across ranks is difficult. In a class (or non-birth-ascribed) system, group membership is determined largely by relationship to the productive process and the relations of classes to one another. The claims of the members in a class-stratified system tend to be less total, and movement up ranks, although infrequent, is possible. Such variables as income, occupation, and education are indicators of separate and possibly conflicting interests and life-styles around which class identities might develop; however, no connection necessarily exists between the presence of acquired attributes and the actual formation of class groups. Hence, the emergence of a full-blown class system requires a conscious recognition of membership on the part of individuals with similar backgrounds and experiences who share common economic and political objectives.

In the most general terms, class analysts, despite their many differences, do tend to make similar distinctions among broad classes and class fractions (that is, the elements within a class). The bourgeoisie, who own and control the means of production, rank at the top of the class continuum. The bourgeoisie includes the various dominant elements of the new African emerging order: the political elite and leading bureaucratic and parastatal officials; the local auxiliaries of multinational companies; businesspeople, landlords, large plantation and cash-crop farmers; high-ranking service personnel (corporate lawyers and accountants). Not only is it useful to distinguish the state bourgeoisie from the private bourgeoisie with respect to their exercise of political power and their access to political decision makers, but the state bourgeoisie itself may be classified in terms of the special roles played by its various fractions (making, executing, and interpreting public rules). And if an "auxiliary bourgeoisie" facilitates multinational investment activities in African countries, these so-called compradors may be distinguished from the emergent national capitalists. Despite government "ambivalence" in a number of countries, the national capitalists nonetheless have gained considerable success on their own in establishing successful trading, retailing, and even some manufacturing businesses.[38] In the rural areas, nascent bourgeois interests are increasingly apparent, reflecting the penetration of capitalism into the countryside. Thus, large capitalist farmers maintain a privileged relationship with state officialdom and privileged access to state-controlled financial credit and farm inputs and to civil service personnel, resulting in social conflict with the less-advantaged classes in their midst.

Normally lower in terms of social and economic status than the bourgeoisie, the petty bourgeoisie, proletariat, and peasant classes are heterogeneous identities. The market women of West Africa, a diversified identity group most fittingly described as petty bourgeois, are something of an exception to this generalization about their status, for they may amass considerable wealth over the years. The petty bourgeois class, one of the least studied in the African context, is clearly a very diverse grouping of people in terms of income, education, and occupation. Their class interests may clash with the dominant bourgeoisie or mesh in various ways, allowing them, in a number of cases, to play an important, if not an indispensable, role in the productive process. They typically engage in smaller retailing and trading activities and perform a variety of middle-level functions in the areas of finance, construction, transportation, communication, and education. The petty bourgeoisie frequently aspire to higher class levels than do the peasants or workers, seizing whatever opportunities avail to improve the quality of their lives. Elementary school teachers, for example, may rise quickly to high positions in central or local government or, indicative of the transient character of their station, fall largely from sight and resign themselves to a modest retirement on a small farm.

But if petty bourgeois class interests intermittently clash with those of the bourgeoisie, it is those of the proletariat and the peasants that are most likely to appear in open conflict with those of the dominant African bourgeoisie. As Claude Ake notes,

> The subordinate classes exercise considerable influence on the character of African socio-economic formations by their latent radicalism. In most of Africa the class contradictions are all too visible in the different lifestyles and living conditions of the bourgeoisie and the subordinate classes. And the bourgeoisie is constantly reminded of the potential danger of the contradiction by occasional outbursts of violence, crimes against property, workers' militancy, and the subversion by workers and peasants of some "development" policies.[39]

Worker and peasant resistance takes a variety of forms, ranging from violent resistance to sabotage, theft, and organized protest. Fully cognizant of the repressive power of the African state and the bourgeois interests identified with it, the subordinate classes adjust to their relative weakness by adopting tactics that they regard as appropriate to the situation at hand.

Like their bourgeois counterparts, the African peasants and the working class are incompletely formed and internally differentiated in terms of status and power.[40] As seen in Chapter 3, such incomplete class formation may result, in African circumstances, in the emergence of weakly integrated interests. With respect to the proletariat, this incomplete formation is partly attributable to the low level of industrial activity in most of contemporary Africa. And because the number of urban job openings in the formal sector has fallen short of the pressing need for employment, a rapid increase in employment in the informal sector, with its labor intensive, small-scale activities, has occurred.[41] This has had the effect of creating a fast-growing unemployed or underemployed labor force—described by some as a lumpenproletariat "class"—which lives precariously at the margins of the urban wage-labor system. It is not surprising that the interests of those living off the informal sector clash with those holding down secure and relatively better paying positions in the formal sector, especially where those receiving wages have only minimal education and skill levels.

The African proletariat, then, is just becoming aware of its separate class interests. Consciousness of what unites the working class is held back by the socioeconomic conditions of underdevelopment. Moreover, the strike weapon and other modes of resistance are less easily employed against a nationalist government, which controls many of the levers of political power and manipulates many of the symbols of community consensus. A number of urban wage laborers are careful to preserve their ties with their kin in their home villages, returning frequently for celebrations and funerals and sending part of their earnings back to their relatives at home. They also save a portion of their meager salaries to purchase land in their home areas for retirement purposes.

Nevertheless, to note the nascent character of the African proletariat is not to blind us to the African trade unionists' capacity for effective collective action. To attend union rallies is to gain an appreciation of relatively effective organization and popular consensus under difficult circumstances. A weak ruling class has at times made significant concessions to organized union demands, seeking to blunt the dynamics of class action by accommodations on issues of wages, transportation, and working conditions. As Richard Jeffries maintains, there certainly are reasons to doubt whether such concessions have resulted in the creation of a "privileged" working class, as is sometimes contended, but skilled union labor has gained a limited advantage as compared to unskilled workers in Ghana's informal sector as a consequence of organization.[42] It is clear, then, that the African subordinate working class is increasingly conscious of its unequal circumstances vis-à-vis the bourgeoisie. However, the combined conditions of narrow industrialization, abundant manual and semiskilled labor competing for scarce positions, and state-corporate resistance to collective demands make it difficult for trade union leaders to translate their legitimate claims into public or private policies.

The other subordinate class or social stratum, the peasants, includes the vast number of citizens in the new African state who, as small farmers, "have similar economic motivation because they have similar economic opportunities."[43] Scattered throughout the rural areas, these small farmers (who produce either for their own consumption or for the wider national or international market) are identifiable in terms of such variables as occupation, income, and education. They inevitably represent a class-in-themselves, even if they lack the collective consciousness and organization to be a class-for-themselves. This low level of group consciousness results in a lack of political power vis-à-vis other classes and interests on the national scene. Moreover, small farmers are virtually powerless to influence pricing policies at the regional and international levels.

The tendency to remain politically unmobilized, except on specific occasions, has other consequences for the peasants as well. In their competition with large-scale individual or corporate farmers or urban interests for state support, the often politically ineffective small farmers are clearly at a disadvantage in terms of pricing, credit, and support policies and programs. Food prices are frequently held down, to the advantage of urban consumers, and currency and import policies work to the benefit of large, mechanized agricultural producers.[44]

Moreover, the state in Africa, influenced by dominant class interests in the vicinity of the capital city, has all too often tended to skew its resource allocation policies in such a way as to favor other classes, to the disadvantage of the small farmers. Priorities on roadbuilding, hospitals, piped water, and social services have frequently emphasized the needs of the relatively advantaged, precisely because these classes and class fragments are the most mobilized and have the best access to decision makers. As the relatively disadvantaged peasants and subregions show lower expectations and make less far-reaching demands, they allow central state authorities greater latitude in expenditure policies than do other classes and subregional interests.[45] It remains to be seen, however, whether a policy of providing the peasants and other relatively disadvantaged groups with minimal allocations will frustrate the achievement of longer-term system goals of stability, equity, and increasing state capacity. The rural small farmers, who largely underwrite the expansion of industry, parastatals, state farms, bureaucracy, military, and urban life-styles, will be allowed to flounder at everyone's peril.

Although the peasants are at a political disadvantage in organizing for effective class action, this is not to say that they are always powerless to influence policy. Governments, recognizing the potential power of the peasants, have striven to gain their cooperation. Peasant representatives have been coopted by governments that are seeking rural support. Thus, as these representatives are included in party ranks or selected to district- or national-level positions, they are well suited to bring influence to bear upon public officials.[46] But state neglect of the rural farmers has persisted despite this cooptation process. It is not surprising, therefore, that peasants have responded to what they regard as an overburdensome state by resisting state regulations in a variety of subtle but damaging ways: refusing to plant cash crops; avoiding regulations on soil erosion; evading tax payments; illegally chopping out firewood; burning cash crops; and absenting themselves from required chores on state farms. Ugandan smallholders, resentful of government mismanagement and mistreatment during the period of Idi Amin's rule, moved steadily away from participation in the official market for monetary agriculture and toward the sale of their cash crops through informal channels or, as an alternative, retreated into subsistence farming.[47] Although it is perhaps too much to contend that peasants can or want to cut themselves off fully from market incentives or state regulations, it is certainly the case that smallholders have a limited autonomy that they can use to distance themselves from external control.[48]

Resistance by peasants is most manifest when expressed in the form of open rebellion. At times, such revolutionary proclivities came into view in the anticolonial struggles where educated elites were able to mobilize the countryside against the colonial state and its supporters in the urban administrative centers. However, in postcolonial times similar rebellions by peasantries lacking in consciousness and solidarity may be difficult to organize. Arguing against any inherent revolutionary potential upon the part of the peasants, Claude Welch writes:

> African governments may not be perceived by substantial portions of their populaces as holding legitimate authority. Such weaknesses, however, cannot be directly translated into strength for insurgent efforts. The syncretic nature of African societies imposes serious limits on the extent to which any government, or any peasant movement, can achieve significant alteration. Social divisions afflict both. Would-be guerrillas confront significantly greater organizational and logistical problems than do the incumbents. Unless serious rifts open in the armed forces of the particular state, prospects for peasant success appear to be low.[49]

"Peasant success" is clearly different from "peasant movements" of resistance, and where the interests of peasants coincide with ethnicity, as in Sudan and Burundi, the result is likely to be powerful demands, if not successful revolts. Even so, it seems possible to contend that the peasants' lack of class consciousness limits successful class action, whether it be influencing political decision makers as to appropriate public policies and programs or actively resisting state manipulation and exploitation.

Because of the peasants' low level of class development and consciousness, a number of analysts have raised questions about the applicability of the classical Marxist model under African conditions. This questioning has led in due course to a search for alternative classifications more relevant to the African experience. For example, Richard Sklar, emphasizing the dominant political class' capacity for autonomous action, describes class relations as "determined by relations of power." "Class formation," he writes, "is a consequence of determinants that are specifically political as well as economic. However 'dependent' . . . the economy of an underdeveloped country may be, the autonomy of its bourgeoisie may yet be firmly established upon a foundation of indigenous political organization."[50] Sklar is consciously taking note of the political dimension of African class relations, stressing the basic conflicts of interest between the rulers and the ruled. And Michael Cohen, specifically rejecting a stratification system along traditional Marxist lines as ignoring the "political origins of social mobility," concludes, on the basis of his work in Côte d'Ivoire, that "classes are categories of people sharing common political and economic interests arising from their access to public authorities and the public resources and opportunities which they control."[51] It is clear that a process of redefinition is taking place here, one that tries to take account of the fluid and undetermined nature of class relations evident in the current context. Because this fluidity parallels the malleable nature of ethnic relations, it is important for us to examine the interrelationship of these variables and the implication of these overlaps for political choice.

■ CLASS AND ETHNICITY AS SITUATIONAL VARIABLES

Class and ethnicity are by no means hard and fast identities, unchanging in new circumstances. Both are products of the state, which must respond, to some extent, to their various demands for public resources. They certainly rest upon somewhat different attributes and types of behavior; yet, in practice, they often overlap and become intertwined with one another. Patron-client ties, interest articulation, language, and occupation patterns are not static but respond to the impact of new political and economic developments in the postindependence environment. The effect of these realignments is to shape and give meaning to both class and ethnic attachments. Hence, rather than being interpreted as fixed, rigid, and exclusive categories, class and ethnicity seem more accurately viewed situationally—in terms of the social, economic, and political contexts in which the various groups interact and attempt to achieve their collective purposes.

In light of these overlaps, determining which, if any, of these variables is salient at any particular time is largely a matter of the context in which they operate. As Nelson Kasfir observes, "Class and ethnicity, as well as regionalism or religion, are organising principles of social action that may act alone, may reinforce, or may work against each other, depending on the social situation."[52] Ethnoregional leaders, often members of the dominant class themselves, may make different uses of class and ethnic appeals to gain support for their claims upon the state. As they mobilize these identities for their political purposes, they help to shape which particular identity, or mix of identities, comes to the fore.

Because these elites mobilize identities to secure political and economic resources from the state, they inevitably vest the state with considerable power to influence the nature of class and ethnic identities. The state's capacity to allocate resources and to mediate societal conflicts makes it a central link in the political process. It is able to use the coercive powers at its disposal to set informal guidelines as to relations between interest groups and the state and among the interests themselves. The state's ability to determine the rules for competition and conflict gives the state elites a vantage from which to legitimate the organizations of collective interests and allow them access to decision makers. Will the state define the basis of organization along class or ethnic lines? Will it identify individuals primarily in terms of class or ethnic affiliations? The answers to these questions are critical in terms of the way individuals align themselves and participate as social actors. As Henry Bienen points out, "The fluidity, heterogeneity, and complexity of processes of identity and group formation suggest that state interventions may be very important for outcomes."[53]

Not the least of these outcomes is the impact of state action in distinguishing between class and ethnicity or, as an alternative, blurring the distinction between these two forms of attachment. As we have already noted distinctions between class and ethnic action, we will concentrate here upon patterns of overlapping identities. In a situation of horizontal stratification, where parallel structures exist and there is a presumption of equality among these groupings,[54] powerful ethnoregional patrons organize their home-base constituents, ethnic compatriots, and others alike to make demands at the political center for a wide range of benefits. Whether in a one-party, no-party, or mixed type of system, they engage within their hierarchically organized system in a process of informal and quiet exchanges with state elites and intermediaries for other ethnoregional interests. The relatively advantaged frequently concede limited material benefits to ensure political stability and the acceptance of state regulations; the relatively disadvantaged, seeking increased material resources to enable them to gain greater equality with the more advantaged areas, may be prepared to trade compliance with state rules for improved material distributions.

But either way, this is a transactional process that sees the subjective principle of social action, ethnicity, reinforcing the objective one of class. Describing one extreme process of hegemonial exchange, Richard Joseph asserts: "The grid of Nigerian political society is an intricate and expanding network of patron-client ties, which serve to link communities in a pyramidal manner. At the summit of such networks can be found individual office-holders in the federal and state capitals."[55] The same point may be made about other systems, such as in Kenya and Cameroon, where the cabinet at the political center traditionally brings together a coalition of various ethnoregional and other interest group leaders, on a roughly proportional basis. In doing so, the class and ethnic principles of social action are combined under the rubric of "ethnoregional" and then used by the unit's intermediary at the center to advance the collective interests of the people living in the territory as a whole.

In a situation of vertical stratification, however, the ethnic groups are ranked in terms of power, status, and wealth, and mobility between strata is normally difficult. In the extreme cases of Rwanda, Burundi, and Zanzibar around the time of decolonization, privileged minorities, in control of state institutions and determined to preserve colonially inherited patterns of social stratification, perceived themselves as pitted against an underprivileged ethnic-class majority determined to restructure opportunities in a fundamental manner. In Rwanda, the rather unstructured Hutu uprising of November 1959 and the dominant Tutsi minority's reprisals that followed revealed a reciprocity of fear and aggressive behavior of terrifying dimensions. Quoting Grégoire Kayibanda's remark that between these peoples "there is no intercourse and no sympathy, [they] are ignorant of each other's habits, thoughts and feelings," René Lemarchand stresses the polarization of expectations in the period after the uprising and "the all-pervasive climate of fear and suspicion which gripped the country at the approach of the [1960] elections."[56] These events in Rwanda also exacerbated latent fears in neighboring Burundi where, according to a former U.S. ambassador, an "either-or mentality of dominating or being eliminated" became prevalent in the Hutu and Tutsi mind-sets.[57] In a similar vein, Michael Lofchie describes Zanzibar's African nationalism as a reaction to the perceived "threat of [minority] Arab domination posed by the ZNP [Zanzibar Nationalist Party]."[58]

It is important to reiterate that these are extreme examples of totalist perceptions in the period around the time of decolonization and by no means typical of the pragmatic perceptions that generally prevail in middle Africa, but they do point up the possibility that worst-case scenarios can surface in Africa, as elsewhere. In such a context, political exchange relationships are inevitably irregular. Because interactions tend to be seen in more threatening or totalist terms, the proportionality principle is a less-ready guide to political coalition formation, elite recruitment, or resource allocation. The dominant elite is even more reliant, than is the case in horizontally stratified societies, upon the coercive capacity of the state to maintain political order. It often shuns explicit redistributive policies, preferring instead to opt for market actions in the form of a trickling down of benefits to the relatively disadvantaged classes and ethnoregional units. Quite frequently, socioeconomic class coincides with ethnic identity in these vertically stratified societies. Hence, the dominance of an ethnic-class elite over the state and its institutions is regarded by the dominant strata as essential to its general strategy of control: for example, the institutionalization of grand apartheid in South Africa.

In such racially stratified colonial societies as Kenya, Northern Rhodesia (Zambia), and Southern Rhodesia (Zimbabwe), a small racial-class cluster of white Europeans predominated in the top ranks of the economy and administrative services of the society, with the Asians and/or "Coloreds" (people of mixed racial background) performing indispensable roles as adjuncts of the colonial system, assuming a variety of tasks as artisans, clerks, professionals, and shopkeepers. The pyramid of power and privilege was filled out by the African masses, who acted as laborers on the farms and in the mines.[59] Moreover, in Rwanda, as Catharine Newbury emphasizes, the role of colonialism in facilitating Tutsi use of the state apparatus to refine and increase their exploitation over the majority Hutus resulted in a heightened racial-class consciousness on the part of both groups. The Hutu, an exploited class in terms of weakened land rights, increasing demands on Hutu labor, and reduced access to dramatically altered structures of power, acted to seize control of the state as independence approached. As Newbury concludes, elements of both class and ethnicity were in evidence during the 1950s: "For the majority of the population, ethnic status and class overlapped—that is, most of the people who were poor and exploited were categorized as Hutu."[60]

In brief, then, representatives for group interests can mobilize their constituents by appeals to class or ethnic identity, or they can take account of the overlaps between these organizing principles of social action. The grounds upon which a support base is built are largely dependent upon the social situation prevailing in each specific context. Hence, effective policymaking requires sensitivity to the social dynamics at work and the forces giving rise to constituency demands. It is clear that there is no overriding need to disentangle class and ethnic identifications in all instances. An effective political choice approach requires a recognition of all politically mobilized identities—whether single or multiple—and the different parts they may play in the articulation and processing of demands and the implementation of policy. In Chapter 9, we will look more closely at the role of the state in processing demands and determining policies.

■ NOTES

1. Joel Samoff, "Pluralism and Conflict in Africa: Ethnicity, Interests, and Class in Africa" (Paper presented to the International Political Science Association, Rio de Janeiro, 9–14 August 1982, p. 19.

2. Introduction, in Fredrick Barth, ed., *Ethnic Groups and Boundaries* (Boston: Little, Brown, 1969), pp. 13–14.

3. Aidan W. Southall, "The Illusion of Tribe," *Journal of Asian and African Studies* 5, no. 1/2 (January-April 1970): 33.

4. Crawford Young, *The Politics of Cultural Pluralism* (Madison: University of Wisconsin Press, 1976), pp. 171–173.

5. Warren Weinstein, "Conflict and Confrontation in Central Africa: The Revolt in Burundi 1972," *Africa Today* 19, no. 4 (Fall 1972): 27.

6. On the frustrations the younger generation of educated Africans feel over lack of opportunity, see Aristide Zolberg, "The Structure of Conflict in the New States of Tropical Africa," *American Political Science Review* 62, no. 1 (March 1968): 75–76. Expressions of such frustration have been vented in student demonstrations against political authorities. See *West Africa*, 18 April 1983, pp. 933–934.

7. Cherry Gertzel, *The Politics of Independent Kenya 1963–68* (London: Heinemann, 1970), p. 17.

8. See Richard L. Sklar, "Nigerian Politics: The Ordeal of Chief Awolowo, 1960–65," in Gwendolen M. Carter, ed., *Politics in Africa: 7 Cases* (New York: Harcourt, Brace and World, 1966), p. 128.

9. Richard A. Joseph, "Democratization Under Military Tutelage," *Comparative Politics* 14, no. 1 (October 1981): 92.

10. Robert MacIver, *On Community, Society and Power* (Chicago: University of Chicago Press, 1970), p. 48.

11. Abner Cohen, *Custom and Politics in Urban Africa* (Berkeley: University of California Press, 1969), p. 190.

12. René Lemarchand and Keith Legg, "Political Clientelism and Development: A Preliminary Analysis," *Comparative Politics* 4, no. 2 (January 1972): 151. Also see René Lemarchand, "Political Clientelism and Ethnicity in Tropical Africa: Competing Solidarities in Nation-Building," *American Political Science Review* 64, no. 1 (March 1972): 86, and Henry Bienen, "Political Parties and Political Machines in Africa," in Michael F. Lofchie, ed., *The State of the Nations* (Berkeley: University of California Press, 1971), Chapter 9.

13. Lemarchand, "Political Clientelism and Ethnicity," p. 76 (italics in the text). See also John Duncan Powell, "Peasant Society and Clientelist Politics," *American Political Science Review* 54, no. 2 (June 1970): 413.

14. James C. Scott, "Patron-Client Politics and Political Change in Southeast Asia," *American Political Science Review* 64, no. 1 (March 1972): 100.

15. On this divergence, see Donald Rothchild, "Collective Demands for Improved Distributions," in Donald Rothchild and Victor A. Olorunsola, eds., *State Versus Ethnic Claims* (Boulder, Colo.: Westview Press, 1983), pp. 172–193.

16. Robin Luckham, *The Nigerian Military* (Cambridge: Cambridge University Press, 1971), p. 296.

17. See his comments in *Sudanow* 6, no. 11 (November 1981): 15.

18. For a fuller discussion, see Donald Rothchild, "State-Ethnic Relations in Middle Africa," in Gwendolen M. Carter and Patrick O'Meara, eds., *African Independence: The First Twenty-Five Years* (Bloomington: Indiana University Press, 1985), pp. 74–82.

19. A. Milton Obote, *Proposals for New Methods of Election of Representatives of the People to Parliament* (Kampala: Milton Obote Foundation, 1970), pp. 6–7.

20. Richard Hall, *The High Price of Principles* (New York: Africana Publishing Co., 1969), p. 195.

21. See Donald Rothchild, "Rural-Urban Inequities and Resource Allocation in Zambia," *Journal of Commonwealth Political Studies,* 10, no. 3 (November 1972): 234–239.

22. Robert A. Mortimer, "Ivory Coast: Succession and Recession," *Africa Report* 28, no. 1 (January-February 1983): 5,7.

23. Aristide R. Zolberg, "Politics in the Ivory Coast: 2," *West Africa,* 6 August 1960, p. 833; also see his *One-Party Government in the Ivory Coast* (Princeton, N.J.: Princeton University Press, 1964), p. 283.

24. Robert H. Jackson, "Planning, Politics, and Administration," in Goran Hyden, Robert Jackson, and John Okumu, eds., *Development Administration: The Kenyan Experience* (Nairobi: Oxford University Press, 1970), pp. 177–178. On the Moi period, see Victoria Brittain, "Five Months That Took Kenya to the Brink," *Manchester Guardian Weekly* 127, no. 6 (8 April 1982).

25. Naomi Chazan, *An Anatomy of Ghanaian Politics* (Boulder, Colo.: Westview Press, 1983), p. 96.

26. Republic of Kenya, *African Socialism and Its Application to Planning in Kenya* (Nairobi: Government Printer, 1965), p. 12. Also see remarks made by President Houphouët-Boigny of Côte d'Ivoire in Michael Cohen, *Urban Policy and Political Conflict in Africa: A Study of the Ivory Coast* (Chicago: University of Chicago Press, 1974), p. 192.

27. R. N. Ismagilova, *Ethnic Problems of the Tropical Africa* (Moscow: Progress Publishers, 1978), pp. 44, 96.

28. This tendency leads John S. Saul "to suggest that marxist scientists and African revolutionaries can only make progress when they take ethnicity . . . seriously as a real rather than ephemeral and/or vaguely illegitimate variable in Africa." "The Dialectic of Race and Class," *Race and Class* 20, no. 4 (1979): 371.

29. Ibid., p. 358.

30. Robert H. Bates, "Modernization, Ethnic Competition, and the Rationality of Politics in Contemporary Africa," in Rothchild and Olorunsola, *State Versus Ethnic Claims,* p. 154.

31. Some of the material on Zambia in this section is drawn from Rothchild, "Rural-Urban Inequities and Resource Allocation in Zambia," pp. 222–224.

32. Colin Legum and John Drysdale, eds., *Africa Contemporary Record 1968–1969* (London: Africa Research, 1969), p. 252.

33. Republic of Zambia, Official Report, *Debates of the Second National Assembly* 25, no. 3 (25 February 1971): 1549. Statement by Mr. Noyoo. (Lusaka: Government Printer, 1971).

34. Republic of Zambia, *His Excellency the President's Address to Parliament on the Opening of the Third Session of the Second National Assembly,* 8 January 1971 (Lusaka: Government Printer, 1971), p. 4.

35. Calculated from Republic of Zambia, Ministry of Education, "Digest of Statistical Information for School Year, 1966" (mimeo.). Fee-paying requirements were terminated for schools in January 1971.

36. *Population and Housing Census in Zambia in 1969,* report on a mission to Zambia from 16 September to 23 October 1967, by Vaino Kannisto (Lusaka: United Nations, October 1967), p. 15.

37. Gerald D. Berreman, "Race, Caste, and Other Invidious Distinctions in Social Stratification," *Race* 13, no. 4 (April 1972): 398–399.

38. Andrew A. Beveridge and Anthony R. Oberschall, *African Businessmen and Development in Zambia* (Princeton, N.J.: Princeton University Press, 1979), Chapter 7;

Peter Marris and Anthony Somerset, *African Businessmen* (London: Routledge & Kegan Paul, 1971); and Nicola Swainson, *The Development of Corporate Capitalism in Kenya, 1918–1977* (Berkeley: University of California Press, 1980), pp. 288–290.

39. Claude Ake, *A Political Economy of Africa* (Essex: Longman, 1981), p. 186.

40. Henry Bienen, "The State and Ethnicity: Integrative Formulas in Africa," in Rothchild and Olorunsola, *State Versus Ethnic Claims*, p. 104.

41. International Labour Office, *Employment, Incomes and Equality: A Strategy for Increasing Productive Employment in Kenya* (Geneva: ILO, 1972), pp. 93–94.

42. Richard Jeffries, *Class, Power and Ideology in Ghana: The Railwaymen of Sekondi* (Cambridge: Cambridge University Press, 1978), pp. 172–173.

43. Nelson Kasfir, "Relating Class to State in Africa," *Journal of Commonwealth and Comparative Politics* 21, no. 3 (November 1983): 5.

44. Robert H. Bates, *Markets and States in Tropical Africa* (Berkeley: University of California Press, 1981), p. 55.

45. Donald Rothchild, "Collective Demands for Improved Distributions," in Rothchild and Orlorunsola, *State Versus Ethnic Claims,* pp. 192–193.

46. On the possibilities for peasant-bourgeois collaboration under populist, bourgeois-dominated regimes, see Richard Sklar, "The Nature of Class Domination in Africa," *Journal of Modern African Studies* 17, no. 4 (December 1979): 549.

47. The effects of this retreat in terms of aggregate productivity are discussed in Donald Rothchild and John W. Harbeson, "Rehabitation in Uganda," *Current History* 80, no. 463 (March 1981): 135.

48. See Jonathan Barker, "Politics and Production," in Jonathan Barker, ed., *The Politics of Agriculture in Tropical Africa* (Beverly Hills, Calif.: Sage Publications, 1984), p. 18.

49. Claude E. Welch, Jr., "Obstacles to 'Peasant War' in Africa," *African Studies Review* 20, no. 3 (December 1977): 129. Also see his introduction to this special issue, p. 4.

50. Sklar, "The Nature of Class Domination," p. 550.

51. Michael A. Cohen, *Urban Policy and Political Conflict in Africa* (Chicago: University of Chicago Press, 1974), p. 194.

52. Kasfir, "Relating Class to State in Africa," p. 6.

53. Bienen, "The State and Ethnicity," p. 106.

54. Donald Horowitz, "Three Dimensions of Ethnic Politics," *World Politics* 23, no. 2 (January 1971): 232.

55. Richard A. Joseph, "Class, State, and Prebendel Politics in Nigeria," *Journal of Commonwealth and Comparative Politics* 21, no. 3 (November 1983): 28.

56. René Lemarchand, *Rwanda and Burundi* (London: Pall Mall Press, 1970), pp. 169, 179. Also see Leo Kuper, *The Pity of It All* (Minneapolis: University of Minnesota Press, 1977).

57. Thomas P. Melady, *Burundi: The Tragic Years* (Maryknoll, New York: Orbus Books, 1974), p. 72.

58. Michael Lofchie, "The Plural Society in Zanzibar," in Leo Kuper and M. G. Smith, eds., *Pluralism in Africa* (Berkeley: University of California Press, 1969), p. 312.

59. Donald Rothchild, *Racial Bargaining in Independent Kenya* (London: Oxford University Press, 1973), Chapters 2, 3.

60. M. Catherine Newbury, *The Cohesion of Oppression: Clientship and Ethnicity in Rwanda (1860-1960)* (New York: Columbia University Press, 1988), Chapter 10. Also see her article, "Colonialism, Ethnicity and Rural Political Protest," *Comparative Politics* 15, no. 3 (April 1983): 253–280.

Part 2

POLITICAL PROCESS AND POLITICAL CHANGE

5

Regimes in Independent Africa

Political processes—the ways in which political rules, norms, methods, and modes of interaction are established, maintained and change—have evolved in Africa in an historical environment of economic adversity and external dependency and in a structural context of fragility and diffusion. Patterns of political conduct determine priorities, preoccupations, and possibilities. Development strategies and foreign policies (the substance of politics) are therefore the concrete outcome of how politics are conceived, practiced, and transformed. The dynamics of politics in Africa is about the procedures and mechanisms by which state agencies and social groups cooperate, conflict, intertwine, and consequently act.

Leaders have had to devise strategies of legitimation and find appropriate means of maintaining social control, frequently without the benefit of viable domestic structures supported by widespread sentiments of national loyalty and without the ability to avert the adverse influence of global forces. Individuals and social groups, in turn, have sought to protect their security, assure their access to resources, improve their well-being, and strive for a semblance of order and perhaps even justice in the absence of political predictability. How have politics worked in these circumstances? Assuming that rulers have neither resorted exclusively to the use of force nor been entirely ineffective, how have they balanced their quest for power with their need for support?[1] What methods have citizens used to voice demands, increase government responsiveness, and curb excesses? What rules have guided the political game, how have they operated, and what have been their consequences? What efforts have been made to alter the conduct of political life and what has been their effect? What political trends emerge, and what are their implications for understanding the content of policies and their consequences?

Our purpose in Part II of this textbook is to explore political processes in contemporary Africa, to understand how politics works. The treatment of African political dynamics has suffered from many attempts to generalize from approaches designed to deal with one aspect of politics into overarching frameworks for understanding politics in general. Some scholars have sought to study political patterns through the lens of ideology, some have found the concepts of patronage to be effective guides to overall political trends. It has been suggested, alternatively, that leadership styles, corporatist arrangements, party systems, or even the distinction between civilian and military governments capture the main flow of politics on the continent. Although each of these emphases makes an important contribution to comprehending the practice of politics (and is, consequently, incorporated into the ensuing discussion), not one of these methods can, by itself, illuminate all of the many complex facets of the African political dynamic. In this book, therefore, we focus squarely on the search for viable formulae for the conduct of politics. We look at the kinds of regimes that have developed in Africa and then explore how their modes of institutionalization have affected the various dimensions of the political process—decision making, policy application, societal reactions, and consequent change. Such a strategy highlights options and choices and enables a better comparison of political processes both within Africa and between Africa and other parts of the world.

The starting point for this discussion is the presentation of regime forms. In this chapter, we lay out the characteristics of the main types of regimes that have emerged on the continent and analyze their different norms, patterns, and behavioral manifestations. In Chapter 6, we look at the high politics of the political center—at the ways in which various regimes make decisions and the means they have devised to carry them out. In Chapter 7, we delve into the deep politics of society, examining social responses to regime policies and performance through an analysis of the major forms of conflict, the strategies and tactics of dissent and insurrection, and official reactions to challenges from below. In Chapter 8, we deal with political change: we trace the methods by which continuity has been maintained or regimes altered and assess both the degree and direction of political transformation since independence.

The overriding themes of the first phase of postcolonial politics in Africa have been personal rule, political domination, and resistance to such hegemonic impulses.[2] The generally weak structures linking social groups and government agencies have highlighted the role of individual leaders as the pivot of official political thought and action. In this rather ambiguous political world, different regimes have set down their own guidelines and identifiable norms have prevailed. Choices have been made by both rulers and their constituencies, leading in some cases to chronic turmoil and in others to a measure of continuity and order. The path of African politics has consequently been far from inexorable "as the courage, the determination, the humor and often the political wisdom of anonymous populaces demonstrate."[3]

The key political problem has, therefore, revolved around the type of institutionalization that has prevailed (rather than the absence of any regularized patterns). Many African regimes have been unable to establish political procedures that could be simultaneously efficient and representative. In fact, political processes have been marked by varying amounts of repression, inequality, instability, dishonesty, ineffectiveness, and disorder. Many governments have lacked legitimacy and have consequently been assailed by discontented groups unwilling to extend support to often corrupt rulers. Laws have been subverted by officials and ignored by irate citizens, and in many instances politics have been not only uncertain but also grimly brutal.

Even if the conduct of politics has followed tortuous paths in the decades since independence, the parameters of the politically permissible have, implicitly and informally, been laid down. Limits have been placed on the ability of leaders to act with impunity, just as recalcitrant populations have found their quest for autonomy firmly curtailed. The crux of the political conundrum in independent Africa—the issue of good government—has consequently emerged with renewed force on the eve of the twenty-first century. The lesson gleaned from the past political record is that "power is always tied to legitimacy," that the effective conduct of public affairs requires some measure of political accountability (of rulers responsible to citizens who hold them to account).[4] How some governments have instituted steps to ensure accountability and why others have been woefully lacking in this regard is the common thread that unites our discussion of African political processes.

■ REGIME EVOLUTION IN POSTCOLONIAL AFRICA

Political processes in Africa have been complex, heterogeneous, and frequently both perplexing and uncertain. The political procedures and patterns of change combine to draw a diverse picture of politics. These images portray cases of mismanagement and gross inhumanity, of irresponsibility and official pillaging, alongside those of experimentation, disappointment, vacillation, and ongoing confrontation. They also convey instances of efficient management and responsiveness, of the creation of widely accepted notions of political behavior, and sometimes of allied organizations for their maintenance. In each of these many instances, political processes have assumed definite shapes and possessed recognizable dynamics.

The criteria for the classification of regime types have varied widely.[5] The crudest distinction and the least helpful has been based on the division between civilian and military regimes, highlighting a confusion between means of regime change and their outcomes. Employing a similar conceptual foundation, some typologies have relied on the differentiation of leadership styles: mobilizing, conciliatory, coercive, autocratic. Others have favored categories derived from ideology or policy orientations: Marxist, socialist, capitalist, and the like. More sophisticated distinctions have been drawn on the basis of degrees of competition, participation, and control.[6] We propose to distinguish between regimes by reference to the dynamic interactions between rulers and ruled and the norms governing these exchanges.

If the concept of regime indeed refers to the rules of the political game and its concomitant institutions, to the ways in which society is linked to the apparatus of the state, then regime types should be defined in these terms. The intent of rulers is far less important than the latent principles that have guided their exercise of power. Regimes in Africa may vary according to seven main criteria: the structure of the relationship between the administrative, the political, the coercive, and the legal apparatus; the degree of elite cohesion; the extent of societal exclusion and/or inclusion; rules and modes of social-governmental interaction; spheres of operation; longevity of institutional arrangements; and workability. On this basis, it is possible to identify seven distinct kinds of regime constructions that have emerged in Africa since independence (with the exception of South Africa, which is discussed in Chapter 13).

The first part of the 1960s was marked by the rise of single-party governments and the consolidation of authoritarian patterns of rule, some of which have persisted to the present day, either in *administrative-hegemonial* or *party-mobilizing* forms.[7] The latter part of the 1960s witnessed the introduction of the military component and, with it, both the entrenchment of administrative regimes and the injection of instability into the progression of political change. The 1970s began with the rise of African tyrants and *personal-coercive* modes of rule (and ended with the demise of many of them). The middle part of this decade was characterized by the addition of an Afro-Marxist, *party-centralist* dimension to the African political map; and the latter years were accompanied by the brief resurrection of *pluralist* experiments. The transition to the 1980s was unquestionably the most turbulent. Putsches, abdications, elections, repeated military takeovers, and populist uprisings seemed to take place in rapid succession throughout the continent, magnifying the heterogeneity of political conflicts and further accentuating the growing economic malaise. In some cases where regimes broke down, *populist* forms of government were created. If by the mid-1980s some brakes had been placed on these gyrations, the varieties of authoritarianism had multiplied, its limitations accentuated, and the search for alternatives intensified (see Table 5.1).

The general thrust of African politics in postindependence times has been in an authoritarian direction. Within this broad path, however, no uniformity is evident. This is a reflection of different definitions of the responsibilities of rulers to ruled, of the regularization of alternative courses of action and norms of political conduct, and, it is clear, of variations in stability and continuity. The examination of each of these regime types lays the foundation for a better understanding of political process.

TABLE 5.1
Typology of Regimes

Regime Type	Examples
Administrative-hegemonial	Kenya, Zaire, Togo, Côte d'Ivoire, Cameroon, Zambia, Malawi, Morocco, Nigeria
Pluralist	Botswana, Gambia, Mauritius, Senegal
Party-mobilizing	Ghana (Nkrumah), Mali (Keita), Guinea (Sekou Touré), Zambia, Algeria (Boumedienne), Tanzania, Zimbabwe
Party-centralist	Angola, Mozambique, Ethiopia, Guinea-Bissau, Congo, Benin
Personal-coercive	Uganda (Amin), Central African Republic (Bokassa), Equatorial Guinea (Nguema)
Populist	Ghana (Rawlings), Libya (Qaddafi), Burkina Faso (Sankara)
Ambiguous	Contemporary Uganda and Chad

■ REGIME TYPES AND THEIR VARIATIONS

The regime forms that have emerged in independent Africa have multiplied as various experiments were attempted and lessons gleaned from past experience. The conduct of politics has also undergone a process of localization, accounting for further heterogeneity. The seven major kinds of regimes outlined in the following pages have themselves, therefore, been quite fluid.

□ Administrative-Hegemonial Regimes

Kenya, Zaire, Togo, Côte d'Ivoire, Cameroon, Zambia, Malawi, Morocco, and Nigeria at various junctures fall into this category. These regimes were first established in the early 1960s and later sometimes adopted by military leaders. In this type of regime, the three key institutions are the executive, the administration, and the coercive apparatus (at times with a one-party dominant auxiliary organ subordinated to the presidency). Main policy decisions are centralized around the leader and his close advisors. Specific technical and professional decision making is carried out in the bureaucracy (sometimes with foreign advice), and the military is generally controlled. More significant, the bureaucratic structures and the judiciary maintain a certain autonomy vis-à-vis each other. Political operations, however, are strictly guided by the executive. This type of bureaucratic-personal organization has encompassed both military and civilian governments. Thus, pragmatic one-party states in which the position of the party has been marginalized (Kenya and Côte d'Ivoire); firmly entrenched one-party states permitting a plurality of presidential candidates (Paul Biya's Cameroon); one-party dominant systems allowing for some form of legitimate party competition (Senegal during the late 1960s and 1970s); and military governments attendant to certain social interests (Nigeria, Niger, Zaire at certain points) all fall within this rubric.

The administrative-hegemonial regimes, however exclusionary on the surface, nevertheless involve major actors in the decision-making process. Policymakers have assumed that to the extent to which key interest group (ethnic, regional, class, occupational) leaders are part of the policymaking process, they will be more likely to cooperate with government institutions and their regulations. A number of African rulers certainly have shown themselves to be highly alert to the need for broad inclusiveness in the deliberations of state. In the Cameroon Republic, former President Ahmadou Ahidjo, despite his heavy-handed and secretive authoritarian tendencies, was careful to use his ministerial appointments as a means of balancing ethnoregional, linguistic, religious, and economic interests. Deeply concerned to preserve national unity, this northern Muslim took steps to preserve an "equilibrium" by appointing Paul Biya, a Catholic from the south-central region, as prime minister, and to maintain a rough ethnoregional balance in ministerial, bureaucratic, and parastatal appointments.

When Ahidjo retired in 1982, Biya succeeded him as president, and the policy of ethnic balancing became, if anything, more pronounced. Biya appointed Bello Bouga Malgari, a northerner, as his prime minister; this upheld the north-south balance at the top and assured that another northern Muslim would eventually succeed to the presidency. But the presidential transition was not destined to be an entirely smooth one. In 1983, this coalition received a jolt as a deepening Biya-Ahidjo quarrel led to growing north-south schisms and then to an attempted coup d'état against the Biya government in April 1984. Although the coup was crushed and the main plotters (the great majority of whom were northerners, according to the armed forces minister)[8] were executed, Biya took special pains to preserve his national coalition by insisting that people from both the south as well as the north were involved in the attempt to topple his regime.

Similarly, in Kenya, the late President Jomo Kenyatta consolidated power by incorporating leaders not only from his Kikuyu ethnic group but also from other ethnoregional units. And although Kenyatta ruled largely through the bureaucracy, he allowed for a measured pluralism in the cabinet and high party organs. Robert H. Jackson writes,

> The art of statecraft in Kenya is largely a careful exercise in maintaining the support of key ethnic and other interests through the judicious allocation of scarce public resources, while at the same time preventing overt opposition or hostility to government from those less favored through the skillful threat or application of coercion. Government itself is highly plural, with bargaining and competition occurring among Cabinet members acting on behalf of supporting groups and between the ministries themselves.[9]

This strategy was passed on intact to Kenyatta's successor, <u>Daniel arap Moi, a Kalenjin</u> from the Rift Valley. At the outset, Moi appeared careful to preserve the networks of reciprocity carefully built up by his predecessor. Later, however, he made adjustments to secure his control, preferring to work closely with his own protégés rather than to perpetuate a broad-based working relationship with key social groups. Major figures such as Kamba leader Paul Ngei, Luo strongman Oginga Odinga, Kikuyu influential Charles Njonjo, and leading Rift Valley intermediaries Masinde Muliro and Jean Marie Seroney were soon distanced from power, and, in 1983, the influence of the Kalenjin group in the cabinet was significantly increased. Nevertheless, the cabinet remained geographically balanced, indicating an adherence to some notion, however skewed, of geographic representation.

The <u>administrative-hegemonial regimes in Africa have therefore developed some type of ordered relationship with key social interests.</u> This phenomenon however, has been predicated, not only in Kenya and Cameroon but also in Côte d'Ivoire and Malawi, on the <u>concomitant nurturing of elite cohesion.</u> Strategies of social control have been avowedly elitist in orientation. Leaders have <u>used state resources and state offices as a means of constructing a state managerial class with a common interest in bolstering the public apparatus.</u> The conscious promotion of elite interests was visible in the selective training and recruitment of civil servants in Côte d'Ivoire, Malawi, and Kenya, as well as in the effort made to enable parliamentarians in Nigeria and Cameroon to maintain their status locally through the careful allocation of resources. These regimes have therefore been <u>marked by the relative solidity of their dominant class, even if instability has been apparent as a result of growing competition</u> (especially in Nigeria and Kenya in the 1980s).

Certain rules of social-governmental exchange have flowed from these arrangements. The <u>underlying norm</u> in these regimes has been a <u>willingness</u> to enter into <u>bargaining</u> relations with domestic and international interests. In Kenya, Côte d'Ivoire, Malawi, and Nigeria, leaders have retained strong notions of power concentration while acquiescing to the <u>need to make concessions to well-placed interests.</u> On the domestic side, this organizing principle has involved the <u>careful construction of networks of patrons and clients.</u> In international matters, <u>foreign concerns have been encouraged to invest</u> in these countries, and the government has attempted to impose some controls or enhance its revenue through the utilization of external bargaining techniques. In this framework, there has been a notion of <u>some, however reluctant, redistribution of resources to powerful local groups as well as foreign interests. Conflicts</u> have tended to be conducted <u>primarily within the elite</u> or among factions organized by members of the ruling circle. Bargaining, however, has its limits: It is carried out to preserve elite interests and <u>rarely includes significant concessions to workers or small farmers. Policy outcomes consequently have a built-in class bias.</u> The notion of centralization through reciprocity has meant that the governmental domain has not attempted to attain a total monopoly over all spheres of activity.

The administrative-hegemonial regimes, through flexibility and sensitivity to predominant class and ethnic forces, have established a certain degree of stability. The workability of this form of state construction has, however, not always been clear-cut. In Nigeria and Kenya, Zaire, Niger, and Cameroon, some limited pluralism has been entertained, but the cost of hegemonial exchange has been high in terms of efficiency and equity. As one observer remarked about Cameroon, "The very nature of the coalition, with its tendency to favor ethnic, regional and economic interests at the expense of competence, operates to bring mediocrity to the top of the political heap."[10] More to the point, at times gross inequalities have been tolerated and certain social groups purposefully marginalized (as in Zaire, for example) in order to maintain the grasp of the ruling coalition.[11] More concerted efforts at inclusion have, nevertheless, enabled the achievement of some continuity in this select group of relatively resilient regimes in Africa. A differentiation between more stable administrative-hegemonial and more strife-ridden *administrative-competitive* regimes, on the one hand (Nigeria, for one), and *patrimonial-administrative* regimes, on the other hand (Togo, Zaire), may be emerging.

☐ Pluralist Regimes

The pluralist regime type in Africa has had a far more precarious history to date. This category includes Botswana, Gambia, and Mauritius and, increasingly, Senegal in the mid-1980s. Experiments of this sort were first attempted in most countries at independence and have since been tried and faltered in Ghana, Nigeria, and Uganda. The relationship of public bodies to each other in this construct has been based on a notion of the separation of powers, with multiparty political institutions and fairly vibrant representative structures. In these few countries an effort has been made not only to pursue interest-group involvement but also to allow for a fair amount of autonomous nongovernmental activity. At least some notion of checks and balances has been retained, and therefore the very centralized political structures apparent in administrative regimes are not present in this more loosely organized context.

Nevertheless, in the more resilient pluralist countries, regimes have possessed a strong elitist strain. Although internal disagreement between civil servants and parliamentarians has been noted, the position of the dominant group has been protected through the judicious use of resource allocation. "Big men" in government have been dependent on their constituencies and, hence, subjected to some popular scrutiny at regular intervals. In Senegal and Mauritius, turnover of parliamentarians has been fairly frequent, but mechanisms for overseeing bureaucratic behavior have been far less well developed. The sphere of political inclusion is broader in this arrangement and tends to be more clearly concerned with local issues; actual involvement in the administrative decision-making process has been, evidently, contained.

The principles guiding pluralist regime activities have been a mixture of bargaining, compromise, and reciprocity. Many of these women are aggregated in the continent-wide Association of African Women for Research and Development. A final, and quite distinct, kind of women's group is that connected to liberation movements. The best organized are the women's sections of the African National Congress (ANC) in South Africa and of the South-West African People's Organization (SWAPO) in Namibia.

There are literally thousands of women's associations in Africa today (many individuals hold multiple membership in several groups). Each women's organization reflects the social composition, age, geographical location, occupational constellation, and ideological predilection of its participants. Over time, the spheres of activity of government and social institutions in pluralist systems are less well defined than in their administrative-hegemonial counterparts. In Nigeria and Ghana in the early 1980s, for example, the strong emphasis on freedom of expression and the fortification of social autonomy left the role of government institutions, especially in economic matters, somewhat nebulous. The stress on supervisory mechanisms highlighted questions of process but left the substantive division of labor between the executive, the legislative, private entrepreneurs, and local communities rather hazy. Overlapping spheres of activity made decision making cumbersome and permitted excesses. This situation has not been the case in Botswana, where pluralism has been more controlled, or in Senegal, where the privileged position of the bureaucracy has been carefully safeguarded.[12]

Pluralist regimes in Africa have not succeeded in most instances in maintaining themselves for a reasonable period of time. Efforts at instituting political arrangements that incorporate large segments of the population have been repeatedly tried and, in most cases, failed. In Ghana, Uganda, and Nigeria these attempts have not altered the predominance of the administrative machinery, contained factional disputes, or resolved dilemmas of decision making. Moreover, leaders operating within these frameworks have faced problems of elite control, even if their social composition has been ostensibly broader. The workability of pluralist constructions, therefore, has proven itself, to date, only in relatively small and homogeneous countries (Botswana), in systems that have essentially retained one-party dominance (Gambia), and/or in countries in which bureaucratic privilege has not been threatened by autonomous and well-organized social groups, especially at the intermediate level. Thus, pluralist regimes, with their attention to the political as well as the administrative apparatus, have not fared well in many parts of the continent, sometimes changing to administrative-competitive forms. Experimentations with variations on this kind of arrangement have, however, resurfaced regularly and continue to be discussed in virtually every African country.

The difficulties encountered by pluralist experiments should not be taken to imply the inapplicability of democratic modes of rule to Africa. In many parts of the continent, pluralism has been associated with elite privilege. Ongoing efforts to break the connection between elitism and pluralism (as in the Nigerian plan for a return to civilian rule in 1992) may yield other, more equitable and workable forms of pluralist regimes.[13]

☐ Party-Mobilizing Regimes

The *party-mobilizing* type of regime bears the imprint of some of the participatory elements of regimes in the pluralist category together with the monopolistic tendencies of administrative-hegemonial regimes.[14] Within this category, it is possible to place Ghana under Nkrumah, Mali under Modibo Keita, Guinea under Sekou Touré, Zambia under Kenneth Kaunda, Algeria under Houari Boumedienne, Tanzania under Julius Nyerere, and Zimbabwe under Robert Mugabe. In all these instances, regimes in this category reflect the organizational preferences of founding fathers with strong socialist predispositions.

The ordering of public institutions in these regimes has rested on a combination of strong one-party domination coupled with bureaucratic expansion firmly under the control of an executive president. Unlike administrative-hegemonial regimes, the center of gravity in these regimes is an ideological party. The politico-administrative pattern of institutionalization fostered in these countries has encouraged the centralization of power around the leader and the party. Thus the Politburo of Guinea's Parti Democratique de Guineé (PDG), operating on the basis of democratic centralism, retained a decisive capacity to shape public policies, discipline party members, and process appointments to high executive and civil service positions. Similarly, in Tanzania the party (TANU, subsequently renamed Chama Cha Mapinduzi—CCM) and particularly its National Executive Committee, have gained a preeminent position in the country's decision-making process. Nevertheless, in Tanzania, the CCM's formal supremacy in the articulation of public policy did not obviate the growth of a powerful bureaucratic apparatus, primarily charged with the implementation of policy.[15]

In these and other cases, coercive devices have been used to consolidate party-state control. In Guinea and in Ghana during the First Republic, political opponents were jailed regularly and supervisory legal structures subordinated to party interests. In this way, power concentration enhanced the position and the cohesion of a dominant party elite. This group itself was closely knit, but it frequently was in conflict with other powerful interests with ethnic or economic bases beyond governmental control.

Strategies of social control in mobilizing regimes have relied heavily on national and party identification and affiliation. Although these regimes have shared a concern with mobilizing common people into politics, certain groups or factions were purposely excluded from the party's central organs, and non-party-linked social groups, especially in elite occupational categories, were undermined and even eliminated. In Guinea, the quest for uniformity precluded the legal maintenance of separate social institutions (even market women were not allowed to operate), and in Tanzania middle-level social groups were discouraged. Mobilization, therefore, was politically selective, if not ethnically or regionally partial.

The principles underlying this regime type highlight notions not only of unity but also of uniformity. For this reason, party-mobilizing regimes have placed a great deal of emphasis on ideology—usually socialist—as a means of appealing to their populations and fostering support for monopolistic policies. The identification between the leader, the party, the nation, and the administrative apparatus has been asserted strongly, if not always convincingly. Elite and factional conflicts have persisted; in some countries passivity and indifference have set in.

These regimes consequently have been less inclined to bargain openly with external and domestic interests. President Nyerere and his party supporters have taken strong measures to present a unified face to the world and to downplay local discontent. Similarly, Nkrumah and Sekou Touré strove to achieve a measure of autonomy globally and to curb dissidence domestically. In fact, party-mobilizing regimes have been relatively successful in curtailing most kinds of immediate political dissent but have been susceptible to more widespread disaffection that could lead to profound domestic conflict.[16]

Although the principles of socialist unity have been guarded fairly systematically internally, they have been bent, however reluctantly, internationally. Both Guinea and Tanzania made their own accommodations with international capitalism. Thus, Sekou Touré agreed in 1973 that Guinea would own only 49 percent of the shares in the Fria bauxite interests (and was to receive 65 percent of profits), and Tanzanian parastatals and National Development Corporation subsidiaries have accommodated transnational economic concerns, even though Tanzania in the 1980s initially refused to comply with IMF preconditions for the extension of its international credit.[17]

In this situation, the spheres of activity of government institutions have been fairly all-embracing. The public arena has intruded into the daily lives of citizens and attempted to affect directly social organizations and institutions. Moreover, these regimes have assumed well-defined economic roles, both as regulators and entrepreneurs. In Guinea, pursuing a policy of "total decolonization," the PDG increased the state's economic role by expanding public ownership, exerting greater control over industrial and commercial activities, and promoting collective farms and cooperative organizations. In Tanzania, by the mid-1970s, government agencies or government-sponsored parastatals accounted for an estimated 80 percent of the medium- and large-scale economic activities and 44 percent of the monetary GDP.[18] In Ghana, Mali, Zambia, and Uganda in the 1960s, not dissimilar trends were identifiable. In party-mobilizing regimes the public domain has been broadly defined.

These regimes have had a mixed history since independence. In some cases, especially where strong social (both primary and horizontal) organizations were present (Uganda, Ghana), it proved difficult to sustain a monopolistic ruling coalition. In Guinea, coercion was used as a substitute for acquiescence, and while Sekou Touré was alive this framework endured. With his death, however, his successors were unable to perpetuate the institutional arrangements that he had devised. Algeria underwent a process of bureaucratization. Tanzania in 1985 experienced a voluntary change in leadership as Julius Nyerere retired in favor of then–prime minister Ali Hassan Mwinyi. The Tanzanian example has differed from the other cases, however, not only in the extent of competition afforded within the one-party structure, but also in the flexibility demonstrated by the first generation leadership.

The workability of mobilizing regimes has therefore been closely tied to the skills of a particular leader and to the absence of intermediary organizations rather than to the viability of such regimes' institutional arrangements. This construct has exhibited virtually all of the difficulties associated with the crisis of African governance at the close of the second decade of independence: overextended administrative structures, societal detachment, structural dualism, inefficiency, and poor performance. Perhaps for this reason, too, this regime form has become much less prevalent in the 1980s than it was in the early years of independence.

☐ Party-Centralist Regimes

A quite distinct regime type is of the party-centralist sort. Its proponents have insisted on virtually absolute central control and direction and have generally been less tolerant of accommodation with local social forces or with most external actors. This category includes the Afro-Marxist states of Angola, Mozambique, Ethiopia, Guinea-Bissau, Congo, and Benin. The institutional arrangements in this kind of regime put the unitary (and usually vanguard) party apparatus above the administrative structures and in some countries (Ethiopia, Benin) the role of the military is also pronounced. Although the executive remains important, this pattern of institutionalization subordinates all other structures to the party mechanism.[19] Ethiopia, for example, in 1984 became Africa's first formal communist state. Over time, the ruling military clique, the *derg,* systematically suppressed all of the original movements that made up the joint civilian front established in 1977. What emerged from the struggle among these movements was the triumph of Mengistu Haile Mariam's view on the need for a centralized model of party organization. The outcome of Mengistu's approach has been to confirm the *derg*'s control over the administrative apparatus by inserting a tightly organized monopolistic party structure, the Workers' Party of Ethiopia, at its helm.

In Angola, as in Ethiopia, Angolan President José Eduardo dos Santos confirmed the commitment of his predecessor, Agostino Neto, both to Marxist-Leninist principles and to the construction of strong state institutions under firm party control. Influence over the bureaucracy by the MPLA's Politburo and Central Committee has been enhanced. Moreover, dos Santos has attempted, with Soviet-Cuban support, to establish an army powerful enough to insure regime stability and to resolve any challenge to the party's position. In Angola, as in Mozambique and Ethiopia, the pattern of party-based organization has relied most heavily on the support and control of the military.

The monopolistic party-rooted arrangements in this type of regime have encouraged a process of <u>exclusion of those social groups calling for local autonomy or insistent on the maintenance of local cultural identities</u> (usually organized by elites antagonistic to the rulers and supported by external forces). The MPLA government in Angola has been severely challenged for over a decade by Jonas Savimbi's South African–backed UNITA. Ethiopia, too, has encountered resistance from major nationality groups and has been unable to avert demands for local autonomy. Thus, the Ethiopian government dismissed Eritrean claims to nationhood:

> Eritrea does not constitute a nation. This is because, she does not satisfy the Marxists principles that characterize a nation: common territory, common language, integrated economic set-up, common culture and a common psychological make up. . . . In short, while such are the realities of the Eritrean peoples, the secessionist movement parades from one world capital to another propagating the false theory that the Eritrean peoples constitute a nation. This kind of false propaganda is nothing but [a] cheap method of obtaining arms and money from international imperialism and the reactionary Arab ruling classes.[20]

<u>One major basis for the linkage of various social groups to government in this type of regime, therefore, is ideological.</u> The party-centralist type of regime in theory rejects state-society relations constructed on a pluralist foundation, although some accommodations, of necessity, have been entertained. Patronage systems have existed in these settings but have not been, as in administrative regimes, the mainstay of political exchange. Elite cohesion derives, in this instance, from solidarity among an ideological party vanguard, many of whom shared in long anticolonial struggles. In these cases, as in Mozambique, a relatively small group has held sway over public affairs.

The guiding principles of interaction have been formulated in terms of adherence to the basic premises of the binding ideology of the party. As a rule, <u>compromise and bargaining have been seen as forms of capitulation</u> that go against the grain of the regime's centralizing thrust. These regimes have consequently had to deal with <u>violent rebellions</u>, most often supported by inimical external forces. In Angola and Ethiopia, as in Mozambique's struggle against the South African–backed Mozambique National Resistance Movement (RENAMO), direct military confrontation between the formal government and dissident movements has been the norm for over a decade. The <u>use of the army to quell social discontent has further accentuated the military component</u> of the centralized party structures. It is in these regimes that conflict has often taken on violent and generalized forms.

Of course, the centralist inclination to resist entering into bargaining relations with opposing interests has been counterbalanced by expedient adaptations to reality. But these have never come together with a relinquishment of principles. Thus, the late President Samora Machel in Mozambique insisted that the Nkomati accords with South Africa did not signal the beginning of any sort of "ideological coexistence" with that country.[21] In Angola, too, the grave post-independence economic crisis required a tempering of the pledge to achieve collectivist goals and to nationalize private industries. Economic difficulties compelled dos Santos to negotiate a series of special arrangements with such multinational companies as Gulf Oil, Texaco, de Beers, and Fiat. In these and other instances, accommodations did take place, even if they were viewed as temporary and necessary to the coalescence of strong public institutions.

As reconciliation between conflicting interests is resisted, and as bargaining with international capital has taken place reluctantly, party-centralist regimes initially engaged in establishing alternate, state-owned institutions, especially in the economic sphere. The public arena has been perceived as the alternative to existing retrogressive social organizations (viewed as anathema because they are controlled by antagonistic classes), and emphasis has been placed on the fortification of those bodies and organs that would support party domination. Ethiopia, Mozambique, and Angola, as well as Benin and Congo, therefore sought to impose a uniformity on public institutions and to constrict the latitude allowed to social, cultural, religious, or economic associations that might threaten the hold of the central structures. The absence of a large group of indigenous entrepreneurs in these countries has facilitated this task. Collective farms, party cells, or nationalized industries were given preference, at least initially, over other forms of social organization.

The persistence of party-centralist regimes has been remarkably high in comparison with other forms. Indeed, Afro-communist regimes in Africa have not been overthrown since they were first set in place in the mid-1970s. But if the party-centralist machinery has been relatively stable, governability has not always been enhanced during this period. Indeed, each of these countries has been noted for the volatility of its internal affairs, for civil wars, and for excruciatingly poor economic performance records. The party-centralist regime form may combine a perplexing admixture of regime durability and state fragility.

☐ Personal-Coercive Regimes

Idi Amin's Uganda, Jean-Bedel Bokassa's Central African Republic, and Macias Nguema's Equatorial Guinea provide the best examples of this type, although Liberia under Samuel Doe may also fall into this category. In these cases, the entrenchment of the regime has been predicated on the connection between a strong leader and the coercive apparatus. All other structures—the bureaucracy, the political machinery where it existed, the court system—have been subjugated to the whims of the leader backed by military force. Unlike the party-centralist countries, where a ruling clique dominates, in dictatorial regimes the predominance of the leader has precluded any firm pattern of regularized exchanges.

Personally based, coercive regime constructs have limited access to public institutions to those individuals or social groups loyal to the leader. Samuel Doe in Liberia, for example, has systematically practiced a strategy of absolutist control, and in Uganda even Amin's cohorts were powerless in the face of the rapid changes in his personal likes and dislikes. The ruling clique in this situation is fundamentally variable and incohesive. Rules of political behavior have consequently also tended to be haphazard. Under these conditions, resistance to the regime, and outright repression of these efforts, has been marked.

The involvement of the executive in other spheres of activity has also been unpredictable. In Uganda, at first Amin evinced a concern with the control of petty commerce and certain foreign holdings (the Asian and the British, most notably). Then he intruded into the domain of the judiciary; later he tampered with local institutions; and, in general, the areas of regime action changed with each change of mind. In Equatorial Guinea, similarly, idiosyncratic behavior became a substitute for any measured program of formal involvement in areas of economic and social activity. The underlying theme was not only one of personal variability but also of widespread exploitation and brutality. The rules of interaction in these cases were based on the threat of the use of force rather than on any visible principle of negotiation, reciprocity, or ideological preference.

Contrary to conventional wisdom, personal-coercive regimes, unless routinized through the creation of a group of loyal followers (as in the extremely patrimonial system established in Zaire),[22] have not fared well in postindependence Africa. Consistent abuse of public institutions has evoked vocal and organized dissent and, frequently, the armed ouster of excessive leaders. This was the case with Acheampong in Ghana, Bokassa in the Central African Republic, and Amin in Uganda, all of whom personalized the public arena to such an extent that they threatened its very existence.

The ephemerality of dictatorial regimes does not mean that elements of personalization and privatization of the public arena have not intruded in other countries as well. This pattern, however, has been unworkable and over the years has provided perhaps the single most important indicator of civil discontent and subsequent repression. Personal-coercive rule, unlike other forms of authoritarian government, may be understood as a sign of the absence of any clear concept of institutionalization or of recognized norms of political behavior.

☐ Populist Regimes

A form of regime that emerged in the 1980s was in part a response to unpredictable dictatorial trends. Populist regimes in Ghana under Jerry Rawlings, Libya under Qaddafi, Burkina Faso under Thomas Sankara, and perhaps for a brief period in the early 1980s in Liberia under Samuel Doe (who later exhibited personal-coercive tendencies), marked a departure from previous patterns in that they sought to reconstruct public structures by rearranging their inter-relationship with social groups and with each other. The cornerstone of the populist mold, best exemplified by Ghana during the first phase of the Provisional National Defense Council (PNDC), has been the subordination of the administrative apparatus to direct public scrutiny. In Ghana during the 1980s, senior civil servants and public employees were either dismissed or were monitored by people's defense committees or workers' defense committees (later called Committees for the Defense of the Revolution). Thus, although the civil service, certain public corporations and the judiciary continued to function, their activities were circumscribed for a time by the establishment of an alternate set of institutions, including public tribunals, citizens' vetting committees, and national investigative commissions.

The effect of the reformulation of public organizations was twofold: to introduce a direct popular voice in policymaking; and to limit the independence of the sprawling bureaucracy, not by politicization or personalization, but by pressure to adhere to certain declared norms. Because this arrangement in 1981 and 1982 led to an institutional dualism and to the flight of trained personnel, after 1983 the PNDC proceeded to establish some safeguards against undue interference in the professional and technical roles of the administrative apparatus, while at the same time sustaining notions of public vigilance (thereby coming more to resemble administrative regime forms). Emphasis shifted to improving efficiency, to streamlining the public sector, and to downplaying direct participation through a promise to reexamine and rebuild the political machinery. Throughout this period, nevertheless, the crucial link has been between the head of state, a small group of close advisors, and popular organizations in a combined effort to reorganize the administration and to curb its excesses.[23]

A not dissimilar pattern was attempted at first in Liberia, but rapidly gave way to a personal-coercive form of government. In Burkina Faso, however, the administration of former president Thomas Sankara, looking closely at the Ghanaian experience, also altered the relationship between the executive, the administration, and its mass constituency with a view toward eliminating waste and undermining the bureaucracy as a bastion of privilege. In all these instances, the objective has been to depart from the familiar modes of yesteryear in the hope of effecting a more thoroughgoing revision of the public arena.

An essential tenet of the populist regime form has been, therefore, a concept of social inclusion defined in nonelite terms. In the 1980s, there has been a growing attempt to incorporate professionals and technocrats. Therefore, populist regimes have questioned elite cohesion without evincing a capacity to entrench other social organizations in the center. Indeed, rhetoric aside, prevailing patron-client networks and factional alliances have persisted. Popular calls for greater accountability have been as vocal in these regimes as in many of their predecessors. The principles underlying populist regimes have consequently differed from those guiding other types. Instead of highlighting either accommodation, compromise, or nationalist ideological rules, the main concern of these regimes has been with assailing pockets of elite privilege. However, by gaining control of the state apparatus, nonestablishment groups have not necessarily taken measures to change channels of political interaction.

The spheres of activity of the public arena in populist arrangements have been broadly defined. Although the key concern has been the regulation of state economic enterprises (and sometimes their dismantling), much activity has focused on marketing and distribution mechanisms as well. Legal, organizational, and administrative life has been closely controlled and autonomous political opportunities circumscribed.

The governments established along populist lines have proven, as in the examples of Ghana and Burkina Faso, to possess a certain degree of persistence, although this mode is still fragile. Durable political structures have not been put in place, and therefore it is too early to assess the long-term workability of these experiments. Without significant resources to redistribute, these regimes may prove to be transitory.[24] It is not improbable that leaders of these governments may initiate regime changes to stay in power.

Ambiguous Regimes

By the late 1970s and early 1980s, a handful of countries were in a situation in which the institutions in the public arena had either collapsed or ceased to function in any familiar or identifiable manner. Chad until 1987, Uganda from 1981 to 1986, and perhaps, episodically, Sudan in the early 1980s, would fall into this category. The ambiguous regime is the end result of the inability to meet and overcome the crisis that afflicted public agencies at the close of the second decade of independence and to establish a modicum of sociopolitical exchange. In these grim cases, chaos, as opposed to order, prevails. "A fictitious state of armed men detaches itself from society and preys upon a dying economy. The picture is a grim one, but not without hope."[25] With no organized public arena, with little or no social links, without a recognizable governing elite, and hence with no rules of interaction and defined spheres of activity, it is difficult to speak of specific regime principles, let alone examine their activities. In this worst-case scenario, then, the challenge of power organization and consolidation has been posed anew thirty years after independence.

■ REGIME TYPES AND POLITICAL PROCESS

In brief, regimes and the political processes they reflect, may be arranged along a continuum according to different degrees of structural autonomy and channels of political interchange. At one pole stand those regimes that have no clear organizing principles and hence possess highly erratic and conflictual relations with their constituent social constellations (ambiguous and personal-coercive types). At the other pole, it is possible to place those countries in which the practice of government and the management of conflict rest on some shared notions of obligation and in which mechanisms for the operationalization of such transactions do exist (pluralist and various administrative-hegemonial forms). In between these two extremes lie those regimes that have operated on monopolistic principles and where social tensions are high (party-mobilizing and party-centralist kinds); those in which participatory exchanges exist, but structures are weak (populist governments); and those regimes where competition is either pronounced or purposely circumscribed (administrative-competitive and patrimonial-administrative models). As time has progressed, the more administrative modes have become more prevalent, achieving a modicum of salience in the late 1980s.

The various regime types that have emerged on the continent have reflected both the many constraints and the variegated options open to African citizens and leaders since independence. Close analysis of regime forms and of their mutation assists in linking the practice of government with its purpose; the political process with the state and the dominant modes of social organization; and the theory of politics with the African setting in which it unfolds. Indeed, the study of political processes in Africa through the lens of these fluid regime forms requires not only the unraveling of the ways decisions are made and implemented and what responses these actions evoke (although this is an essential part of such an undertaking); it also draws attention to the fundamentals of politics: to how centers are constructed and legitimated; how their political visions are crystallized and authority conceived; how civil societies form and break down; how transformations take root and why. It is to an examination of these facets of the political process that we now turn.

■ NOTES

1. This may be the most fundamental problem facing Third World leaders. See Christopher Clapham, *Third World Politics: An Introduction* (Madison: University of Wisconsin Press, 1985), pp. 43–44.

2. Robert H. Jackson and Carl G. Rosberg, *Personal Rule in Black Africa* (Berkeley: University of California Press, 1982).

3. Jean-François Bayart, "Civil Society in Africa," in Patrick Chabal, ed., *Political Domination in Africa: Reflections on the Limits of Power* (London: Cambridge University Press, 1986), p. 124.

4. Patrick Chabal, "Introduction: Thinking About Politics in Africa," in ibid., p. 12.

5. Roger Charlton, "Dehomogenising the Study of African Politics—The Case of Inter-State Influence on Regime Formation and Change," *Plural Societies* 14, no. 1/2 (1983): 32–48.

6. Roger Tangri, *Politics in Sub-Saharan Africa* (London: James Curry, 1985); Ruth Berins Collier, *Regimes in Tropical Africa* (Berkeley: University of California Press, 1982); and Dirk Berg-Schlosser, "African Political Systems: Typology and Performance," *Comparative Political Studies,* 17 no. 1 (1984): 121–151, are some examples of these various approaches.

7. Richard Hodder-Williams, *An Introduction to the Politics of Tropical Africa* (London: George Allen and Unwin, 1984), pp. 113–146, suggests such a line of analysis.

8. *West Africa,* April 23, 1984, p. 865.

9. Robert H. Jackson, "Planning, Politics and Administration," in Goran Hyden, Robert Jackson, and John Okumu, eds., *Development Administration: The Kenyan Experience* (Nairobi: Oxford University Press, 1970), pp. 177–178.

10. Victor T. Le Vine, Cameroonian Politics: Scholarship and Partisanship," *Africa Today* 29, no. 4 (1982): 58. Also see Mordechai Tamarkin, "The Roots of Political Stability in Kenya," *African Affairs* 77, no. 308 (1978): 297–320.

11. Richard A. Joseph, "Class, State and Prebendal Politics in Nigeria," *Journal of Commonwealth and Comparative Politics* 21, no. 3 (1983): 21–38.

12. Richard Sklar, "Democracy in Africa" (UCLA: Special Publication of the African Studies Center, 1982), and Ali A. Mazrui, "The Cultural Fate of African Legislatures: Rise, Decline and Prospects for Revival," *Présence Africaine* 112 (1979): 26–47.

13. See Larry Diamond, Juan Linz, and Seymour Martin Lipset, eds., *Democracy in Developing Countries: Africa* (Boulder, Colo.: Lynne Rienner Publishers, 1988).

14. Robert H. Jackson and Carl G. Rosberg, "Personal Rule: Theory and Practice in Africa," *Comparative Politics* 16, no. 4 (1984): 421–442.

15. John J. Okumu, "Party and Party-State Relations," in Joel D. Barkan with John J. Okumu, eds., *Politics and Public Policy in Kenya and Tanzania* (New York: Praeger, 1979), pp. 52–53.

16. Ekkart Zimmerman, "Macro-Comparative Research on Political Protest," in Ted Robert Gurr, ed., *Handbook of Political Conflict* (New York: Free Press, 1980), p. 210.

17. Lapido Adamolekun, *Sekou Touré's Guinea: An Experiment in Nation-Building* (London: Methuen, 1976), p. 77, and Issa Shivji, "Tanzania—The Silent Class Struggle," in Lionel Cliffe and John Saul, eds., *Socialism in Tanzania II* (Nairobi: EAPH, 1973), p. 327.

18. Aguibou Y. Yansane, *Decolonization in West African States with French Colonial Legacy* (Cambridge, Mass.: Schenkman Publishing Co., 1984), pp. 140–141. These estimates were made by Reginald Green and referred to in Crawford Young, *Ideology and Development in Africa* (New Haven: Yale University Press, 1982), p. 106.

19. For a good overview, see David and Marina Ottaway, *Afrocommunism* (New York: Africana Publishing Co., 1981).

20. Provisional Military Government of Ethiopia, *The Ethiopian Revolution and the Problem in Eritrea* (Addis Ababa: Ethiopian Revolutionary Information Center, n.d.), pp. 11–12.

21. *Africa Research Bulletin* 21, 3 (15 April 1984), pp. 7167–7168.

22. Thomas Callaghy, *The State-Society Struggle: Zaire in Comparative Perspective* (New York: Columbia University Press, 1984), gives full details.

23. Zaya Yeebo, "Ghana Defence Committees and the Class Struggle," *Review of African Political Economy* 32 (1985): 64–72; Adotey Bing, "Popular Participation Versus People's Power: Notes on Politics and Power Struggles in Ghana," *Review of African Political Economy* 31 (1984): 91–104.

24. Frank Holmquist pointed out these characteristics.

25. Richard Sandbrook, *The Politics of Africa's Economic Stagnation* (London: Cambridge University Press, 1985), p. 41.

# 6

High Politics: The Procedures and Practices of Government

The analysis of the political process commences with the study of high politics, with regime efforts to lay down procedures for decision making and to create the mechanisms for their enforcement.[1] From the perspective of rulers, two core concerns guide this undertaking. First, how do rulers consolidate and entrench their position in the center: What rules do they establish and what patterns of decision making do they encourage to increase their power? Second, how do they gain the compliance of their constituencies: What support bases do they construct and what means do they devise to maintain these alliances?

The various regimes that have emerged in Africa during the past three decades have provided different answers to these questions. Since independence, a wide variety of political centers, propelled by quite distinct principles and operating in diverse ways, have emerged. Despite the common constraints they faced, individual leaders have put their imprint on the manner in which politics is conducted. In some instances, their thoughts, rhetoric, and actions yielded uncertainty and in extreme cases even brought about the collapse of the core (Uganda, Chad). In other countries, rules and procedures survived their originators, furnishing presumptive principles of political behavior (Kenya, Senegal, Algeria, Cameroon, Tanzania). In many parts of the continent, however, experimentation and trial and error became the norm. As one leader succeeded another, different visions were expounded and diverse instruments devised to carry them out. Throughout, the connection between the rules of the political game and the institutions of government have been filtered through the ambitions, interests, limitations, and capabilities of the political elite. Nevertheless, the fact that in most cases state leadership is less salient in 1987 than it was immediately after independence is indicative of the entrenchment of

148

some procedures and norms—indeed, perhaps of an attenuation, however slight, of state fragility.

■ THE POLITICS OF THE CENTER: DECISION MAKING AND THE RULES OF THE POLITICAL GAME

The consolidation and entrenchment of the political center—the source of political decisions—is the critical first step in the practice of politics. There are three main elements of this aspect of the political process: the articulation of a political vision, frequently an ideology, which sets forth the goals of the rulers and their plans for governing (principles for decision making); the refinement of leadership styles and modes of operation (locus of decision making); and the establishment of the rules of the political game (manner of decision making). These facets are integrally linked: Together they define the essential features of the daily workings of various governments throughout the continent.

□ The Ideologies of Independent Africa

The crystallization of political centers relies on, and inevitably mirrors, the premises outlined by their founders. The considerations guiding political action—whether explicitly stated or implicitly understood—constitute the political worldview within which decisions are made and initiatives launched. Political ideologies, as distinct from policies, are systems "of beliefs that serve as a standard of evaluation and a guide to action."[2] They give an indication of the preferences of rulers, of their reasons for acting. In a very real sense, ideologies attempt to grapple with tangible problems, describe and explain existing conditions, and prescribe desired courses of behavior. In this respect, they encompass the conceptual, and hence the subjective, principles of political action.

In the aftermath of decolonization, most African regimes attempted to set out the framework of a political vision that would capture the exigencies of their circumstances and also provide a referent for policymaking. The transition to independence, in many cases, left a normative political vacuum. The ideas and propositions that upheld the colonial apparatus had been rejected, and substitute organizing notions had to be formulated. The ideologies of independent Africa have tried to offer answers to three interrelated problems: how to organize the psychological mobilization of identities around a concept of the new political entity; how to provide theoretical legitimation for the incoming regimes and their leaders; and how to design a blueprint for political and economic action in the future. The manner in which these issues have been addressed has varied markedly, both geographically and temporally. Regardless of precise contents, however, throughout the postcolonial phase the ideological component has set forth the charter of the rulers: the foundations for the rationalization and justification of prevailing modes of government.

The first official wave of ideological construction occurred immediately after independence and bore a self-proclaimed *African socialist* label.[3] Pioneered by the leaders of party-mobilizing regimes (Kwame Nkrumah in Ghana, Ahmed Sekou Touré in Guinea, Modibo Keita in Mali, Gamal Abdel Nasser in Egypt, Ahmed Ben Bella in Algeria, and Julius Nyerere in Tanzania), African socialism had its origins in anticolonial movements and was propagated most forcefully by select members of the first generation of African leaders.[4] The founding fathers espousing notions of African socialism shared an aversion to colonialism and themselves held a somewhat marginal position in the existing social order. They viewed independence as an opportunity to build a new society: to shed the intellectual and cultural as well as the material and political shackles of the colonial inheritance.[5]

The African socialism of the 1960s was nationalist in orientation and evolutionary in thrust. Although encompassing quite divergent strands, all early socialists, from Nyerere to Sekou Touré, proclaimed a commitment to the creation of an egalitarian, just, and self-sufficient polity. The mechanism for the attainment of these goals was the state, which would furnish the pivot of critical identities, organize the economy, and supervise the second, societal, phase of decolonization. Although differing substantially in the degree to which they relied on precolonial values and traditional institutions to promote these goals, African socialist worldviews extolled political centralization and mobilization as the vehicles for real transformation. Socialism at this juncture was hence both Afrocentric and nonaligned: It shunned the unselective transfer of socialist terminology (such as the class struggle) to Africa and at the same time laid claim to a universality of political ideals.

The early socialist stirrings in Africa were, in many respects, the intellectual counterpart to the quest for political autonomy. They were avowedly all-encompassing, they contained a strong programmatic dimension, they evinced a real preoccupation with defining the basis of a national interest, they were concerned with retaining a populist aura, and they provided the rationalization for the imposition of political uniformity (via the single party) under the guise of forwarding national unity. In Mali and Guinea, Ghana and Tanzania, and to some extent in Zambia and Senegal, notions of socialism were carefully explicated to highlight the idea of the primacy of politics.

The orientation toward change implicit in the political thought of African socialist leaders was, therefore, accompanied by the firm belief that officials and party activists were best positioned to interpret the general will and hence to define the interests of the collectivity. Even when this stance was adopted with the best intentions in mind, it furnished a justification for authoritarian rule.

African socialism came to be regarded, as a consequence, as indelibly intertwined with the careers of its formulators. And, indeed, as a philosophy of rule it barely survived the first decade of independence. By the beginning of the 1970s Kwame Nkrumah, Ahmed Ben Bella, and Modibo Keita had been deposed, Nasser had died, and Nyerere and Sekou Touré had parted political paths.[6] Nevertheless, the impact of these first ideological experiments has outlasted their initiators. The sense of national pride and African dignity instilled by party mobilizing regimes via the principles of African socialism still has widespread appeal. The commitment to pan-Africanism may be traced back to these leaders. Most significant, because they were the first to attempt the exposition of a coherent (if also inconsistent) system of political ideas, their concepts have become a signpost against which subsequent political ideologies have been measured and evaluated.

While notions of African socialism gained currency during the course of the 1960s, another series of organizing principles were more quietly, though perhaps more firmly, implanted on the African scene. Dominant elites in the administrative-hegemonial regimes of Côte d'Ivoire, Nigeria, Gabon, Sierra Leone, Morocco, Cameroon, and Malawi opted for an ideology of *political pragmatism*. The first leaders who supported a more cautious approach to the articulation of binding values were also, like their socialist counterparts, part of the initial crop of African leaders. In contrast, however, to their peers, they tended to draw their support from more established groups in colonial society, to possess channels of access to nonstate resources within their countries, and to confine their anticolonialism to the elimination of the colonial political presence but hardly the colonial influence in other spheres.

The pragmatism of Felix Houphouët-Boigny, Abubakar Tafawa Balewa, and Hastings Banda set economic growth and prosperity squarely at the center of the preferred order. For this reason, emphasis was placed on continuity rather than change, on the emulation of the Western model of development, and on the nurturing of private initiative in the capitalist mode. Although declaring themselves nonideological (and in some instances, such as Ahidjo in Cameroon and Banda in Malawi, openly antiideological), these leaders did propound precepts that coalesced into an alternative to the more strident socialist ideologies of mobilizing regimes. Tolerance toward traditional and colonial institutions and practices was stressed, and the state was endowed with the task of facilitating entrepreneurship, attracting foreign investments, and establishing a climate conducive to material advancement. For the articulators of this approach, the meaning of independence was defined in economic terms; the refinement of the market economy to suit African conditions was encouraged.

Pragmatic worldviews were no less statist than the more populist-socialist theories; they were, however, advanced for different reasons and with other goals in mind (related, also, to the preservation of elite privilege). No pretense to a cohesive, holistic, political orientation exists in these notions of government. Neither, in most instances, is it possible to point to strong liberal underpinnings. Existing conditions rather than ideal-values were deemed to dictate the range of options and choice, and economic concerns furnished the rationalization for the demand for political conformity. Centralization, therefore, was delineated not in a social or political but in an administrative sense; it nevertheless was as deeply ensconced in the political attitudes of pragmatists as in those of self-proclaimed socialists.[7]

African pragmatism has fared better over the years than African socialism, if only because the upholders of these views have exhibited a greater capacity for endurance. To be sure, Balewa in Nigeria, Sylvanus Olympio in Togo, and Foulbert Youlou in the Congo were among the first leaders to fall in military coups d'état. But Houphouët-Boigny, Ahidjo, Bourguiba, Banda, and Kenyatta combined ideological pragmatism with political skills to achieve remarkable longevity. And, as important, the orientations of these leaders were attractive to incoming military leaders, such as Yakubu Gowon and A. A. Afrifa, who were impressed by notions of administrative order and organizational efficiency and were concerned with gaining support of existing elites. African pragmatism and state capitalism, therefore, have furnished guidance to successive generations of African leaders. They thus constituted a second, more resilient, ideological pole devised during the first years of independence.

The late 1960s and early 1970s coincided with the rise of military leaders with a notable dictatorial bent: Idi Amin in Uganda, Jean-Bedel Bokassa in the Central African Republic, Mobutu in Zaire in his early years, and possibly Gnassingbe Eyadema in Togo. These rulers were not central in the political struggle for independence. In these countries, political concepts were most evidently promulgated as rhetorical props for precarious heads of personal-coercive regimes who almost uniformly chose to forward crude *military-nationalist* precepts as a substitute for coherent political ideologies. They justified their actions as genuinely African and independent—as the first steps in the formation of a truly autonomous national existence.

Military-nationalist ideologies in Africa have in common a conscious xenophobia coupled with the glorification of African prowess (and by extension, of the warrior tradition in African history).[8] The emphasis in these thought patterns was most evident in purportedly cultural matters, especially the Africanization of names (Mobutu Sese Seko, Kutu Acheampong) and places (Zaire, Ndjaména). National dress codes were designed, indigenous music was aired, and certain traditional practices were revived. In economic terms, the idea of full control over national resources was underlined not only to deflect pressures from external creditors but also to account for statist monopolies. In the name of "authenticity" or "national redemption," all opposition was deemed treasonous and dissent forcibly quashed.[9]

Military nationalism in Africa developed a rhetorical terminology to exalt problematic leaders and to compel obedience. In many respects these notions lack even the minimal markings of ideologies: They are by and large bereft of intellectual content, they are replete with contradictions, they address key issues haphazardly. These orientations, at best, may be viewed as feeble attempts to legitimate their purveyors; in most instances, they have provided a cover for the exercise of brute force. Manifestations of this sort of military-nationalism resurface periodically as insecure leaders with dwindling support bases find refuge in cultural symbols in a desperate effort to gain some loyalty and legitimacy. In the last days of his rule in Chad, François Tombalbaye encouraged the revival of traditional cults. Acheampong in Ghana invoked culture and religion as an explanation for his unwillingness to leave office. The resort to such devices has become one of the first (and quite accurate) signals of the breakdown of regularized patterns and hence of instability and ruler vulnerability.

In the mid-1970s, a concerted ideological regeneration in the form of *Afro-Marxism* came to the fore. Pioneered by military leaders in Somalia, Congo, Madagascar, and Benin, the place of Marxism-Leninism in Africa was accentuated with the independence of the lusophone states of Angola, Mozambique, and Guinea-Bissau and with the overthrow of the traditional monarchy of Haile Selassie in Ethiopia. The turn to a more scientific socialism, the mark of party-centralist regimes, was partly a result of protracted wars of national liberation; partly a reflection of the disillusionment of segments of the urban intellegentsia and rural dwellers with feeble and ineffective elites; partly an indication of the growth of Soviet influence on the continent; and partly a consequence of the appeal of a pure, universal, and change-bearing ideological framework heretofore untested on African soil.

Afro-Marxists negate the precolonial and colonial past in their quest for societal transformation. They uniformly attribute the maladies of the African experience to the lingering effects of imperialism and the ongoing perniciousness of neocolonial influences both within and outside Africa. In this approach, a totally new social order is required to abolish private ownership of the means of production and, with the help of a revolutionary vanguard, to alter drastically the distribution of power in society. Unlike African socialism, Afro-Marxism has integrated class theory into domestic politics.[10] In this worldview, the Leninist principles of democratic centralism and state-directed economic institutions are seen as the crucial vehicles for the alteration of the social order. Scientific socialism as articulated in Angola, Mozambique, Ethiopia, and the Congo, has therefore set forth a revolutionary vision based on political unity, economic prosperity, and the elimination of a long legacy of inequality.

The introduction of Marxism-Leninism to Africa was, in many respects, a departure from the more eclectic ideological experiments of the preceding years. Professing a commitment to the application of universal truths to alter the African condition, scientific socialists transferred an entire, well-formulated, cohesive, and all-embracing political philosophy to the continent. They regarded the conceptual framework not only as a means of justifying their exercise of power but, and this is more telling, as a true guide to political action.[11] This second official wave of ideological construction sought theoretical understanding and practical direction in the philosophy and prescriptions of Marxism-Leninism.

African Marxism has remained a conceptual force on the continent as the regimes established on its foundations have continued to entrench themselves despite economic upheavals and continuing internal wars. Close contacts with the Eastern bloc have been established, whereas economic links with the West have either been sustained or actually strengthened of necessity: Adaptations in perceptions have been made, but the general conceptual framework still defines the thrust of political life in this group of African states.

In the late 1970s, another ideological strain of the period of the transition to independence was revived as official dogma, albeit only temporarily. The ideas of *liberal democracy* were resurrected with the efforts of certain one-party states, such as Senegal, and briefly Kenya, and Côte d'Ivoire to open channels for greater competition and participation; these ideas were reinforced as tyrannies were abolished in the Central African Republic and Uganda and as military regimes were terminated in Nigeria, Ghana, and Burkina Faso (then Upper Volta). Indigenous educated elites concerned with civil liberties, human rights, and the protection of opportunities for free enterprise promoted liberal ideology.

Democratic precepts in Africa in 1980 rested on the lifting of prohibitions on political competition, on the nurturing of private enterprise, and on the protection of personal freedoms. New constitutions were written to reflect the move away from the concentration of power in the hands of personal leaders and to expound on the need for greater representation. The guidelines for the reinstatement of democratic rule nevertheless highlighted nationalist orientations and generally evinced (Ghana, Nigeria, Senegal) a preference for presidential as opposed to parliamentary models.[12] The appearance of liberalism in Africa was the political correlate of the more-economic notions inherent in earlier pragmatic concepts. These ideas, however, could not strike deep roots in the conditions of economic recession and social inequality that prevailed at the time.

The rise of a young, postindependence generation of military leaders (Jerry Rawlings in Ghana, Muammar Qaddafi in Libya, Thomas Sankara in Burkina Faso) gave formal expression to the thoughts and aspirations of the have-nots of the continent. *Populism* in Africa, bred on resentment of the privileged establishment, arose in periods of sharp economic decline and growing scarcity and, at least at the outset, conveyed an African brand of radicalism aimed at restructuring the power apparatus to suit the needs of the common person.

Although Libya's Qaddafi set in motion the populist strain in Africa, Jerry Rawlings is, perhaps, the most vocal exponent of African populism to emerge to date.[13] Unlike Afro-Marxists, Rawlings has pressed for revolution from within through the reassertion of moral rectitude, probity, and accountability in ruling circles. The key element of the populist ideal in Africa is the need to restructure political institutions and to dismantle the elite establishment that has dominated public affairs since independence. This goal will be achieved through mass participation in decision making, decentralization of economic control, and the establishment of mechanisms for popular scrutiny of governmental affairs. The vehicles for this transformation, in populist thinking, are twofold: new inclusive organizations based on notions of direct mobilization; and the reformulation of values underlying behavior in the public domain. Corruption, exploitation, and abuse of office were proclaimed to be antisocial; industriousness, cooperation, and productivity were accentuated as virtues. The key, then, to economic recovery and social cohesion was to be found within Africa—in the mores, practices, and capabilities of its workers and farmers.

African populism contains strong moralistic and messianic overtones. It promises personal salvation and national redemption through hard work and cooperation. Populist thought is fiercely nationalist and antiimperialist, and its basis is deeply entrenched in frustration, anguish, negation, and protest. In this worldview, the objects of change have shifted from the colonial legacy in general to the domestic purveyors of neocolonialism, from external exploiters to corrupt elites. Although containing traces of socialist and Marxist terminology, African populism advocates radical change from below. As such, it constitutes a set of ideas directly linked in time and place to local exigencies.

Populist notions have proliferated during the course of the 1980s as an emotional antidote to economic dislocation and political disintegration. The psychological force of these ideas, as well as their future (sometimes millenarian) thrust, has enhanced their appeal. Although frequently incohesive and unquestionably fraught with logical inconsistencies, populism proffers very simple and controllable solutions to complex problems: In this respect, its basic precepts can be sustained as long as poverty prevails and abuses of power are widespread.

The 1980s have also proven to be a breeding ground for the insertion of *religious,* primarily Islamic, thought patterns into the realm of official African political discourse. Some of the prescriptions of Shari'a law were adopted by Gaafar Nimeiri in Sudan in an attempt to redefine the foundations of his rule; the constitution of the Second Republic of Nigeria made provisions for Islamic courts of appeal. References to the Koran as justifications for policy have been cited repeatedly in Senegal and Somalia, Mauritania and Libya, even in Cameroon and Gabon.[14] This recourse to religious or particularistic arguments is another manifestation of the retreat from secularism that has characterized this third and latest wave of ideological experimentation in independent Africa.

African socialist, pragmatic, military-nationalist, Afro-Marxist, liberal, and populist ideological constructs have exhibited a broad range of ideas and a diversity of perceptions of reality and desired goals. Some regimes have enunciated fairly cohesive principles, whereas others have forwarded more haphazard political notions (military-nationalism, for one). Over the years, too, there have been sharp gyrations in the intensity of political rhetoric and in the relative significance of the ideological dimension of politics. Since independence, anticolonial ideologies were first adapted to local conditions and then universalized. The thought patterns of the 1980s have been marked by the predominance of more parochial worldviews.

During the course of the first three decades of African independence, nevertheless, the broad outlines of African political ideologies have been defined and some of their key features have been consolidated. Several themes transcend these different political thought frameworks. All official ideologies are avowedly nationalistic and seek to carve out an independent African position in the global arena. All, too, contain the terminology, if not the conceptual tools, of anticolonialism and dependency theories.[15] They share a primary concern with overcoming poverty and underdevelopment. In the political realm, the vindication of state power, with very few exceptions, has been a major preoccupation.

Ideology is not always a sure guide to unraveling decision-making procedures, especially in Africa where few regimes have been able to assert a symbolic distinctiveness; it does, however, provide irreplaceable clues to the motives, desires, penetrative capacities, and underlying principles of various regimes. By capturing the language of official political discussion and debate (although hardly of all political discourse), the ideologies of independent Africa are a significant part of the political process. They are as important for what they preclude as for what they encompass, for what they obfuscate as for what they illuminate. These notions, regardless of relative salience or logical coherence, do consequently have a direct bearing on the conduct of political life in African capitals.

☐ Leadership Styles and Modes of Operation

If ideologies establish some of the organizing principles of African political centers, the behavior of rulers furnishes the axis around which decision making takes place. The prominence of political personalities in postcolonial Africa is largely an outgrowth of the fragility of many state structures. The emergent leaders of African countries on the eve of independence lacked many of the institutional bases of legitimate authority. Although a leader's standing rested to some extent on consensus or popular approval, his status resulted largely from his position within the new political structure. Not limited by constitutional restraints, and usually supported only by fragments of their diffuse societies, these men gained salience initially as the embodiment of the nascent political center and subsequently as the personification of its modes of operation. In this situation latter-day forms of patrimonialism became commonplace.[16] Most African political centers have exhibited varying degrees of neopatrimonial rule.[17] Thus, although top leadership in all political systems tends to be highly individualized, in Africa political leaders, most notably in the early years of independence, have been especially instrumental in defining the rules of the political game.

Center construction, therefore, bore the personal stamp of particular leaders. However, although all such centers are by nature authoritarian, only some have evolved into full-fledged networks of individual, or personal, rule.[18] Other leaders have succeeded in laying down more regularized channels of access and decision making. Under these circumstances, the salience of leaders diminishes. For this reason, the way that the role of leaders has been interpreted in different regimes has had a special impact on the nature of the political process in their polities.

The first distinctive style of leadership to surface in postindependence Africa was of a *charismatic* sort.[19] It has usually been associated with socialist leaders of the first generation of independence (Kwame Nkrumah, Julius Nyerere, Sekou Touré, Houari Boumedienne, Ahmed Ben Bella, and, to a lesser extent, Modibo Keita, Kenneth Kaunda, and Robert Mugabe; Hastings Kamuzu Banda of Malawi, a distinctly nonsocialist leader, also falls into this category). Common to the background of these leaders was their schooling in the colonial system and their central role in the anticolonial struggle. Some of these leaders did not enjoy a strong position either within their societies in general or specifically within the elite. Their support was based largely on the popular appeal of their message and their successes during decolonization. Their institutional backing was, as a result, frequently fragile. Charismatic personalities tended to emerge in situations of political uncertainty and social fluidity.

Charismatic leadership in Africa has been tied to a commitment to the implementation of ideological concepts. The political style it has fostered is consequently autocratic: Leaders of this sort chose to dominate rather than compromise, to dictate rather than to reconcile. Charismatic leadership in Africa therefore bore the external trappings, whether consciously or by attribution, of omnipotence. In the case of Kwame Nkrumah, it was exaggerated to the point of endowing the leader with godlike attributes. With the notable exception of Julius Nyerere, who subordinated personal ambitions to the prophecy of the political vision he sought to bring about, charismatic leaders nurtured an image of themselves as the embodiment of the nation, the state, power, and the future. They took on honorific titles, engaged in ostentatious practices, allowed (and even promoted) leadership cults, and methodically centralized political control.

The charismatic mode of operation was predicated on the creation of a coterie of followers with personal loyalty to the head of state and to the ideology he espoused. Rivals were systematically crushed, imprisoned, or exiled. Advisors were subordinated to the leaders and frequently dismissed or replaced when the need or the whim arose. In this mode of operation decision making was politicized: The test of inclusion was fealty to the leader and his precepts. The single party became the repository of the faithful as well as the critical avenue to elite status. The politics of court intrigue flourish in such settings: Conspiracies, plots, purges, and reshufflings are the political order of the day.

The charismatic style, therefore, is invariably a high-risk one. "It tends to restrict choice, in the same way that it restricts the political groups actively involved in government, and it leads easily to the creation of an embittered opposition whose leaders are in prison or in exile."[20] It can therefore be effectively maintained only by those leaders who have sustained broad public support or who have not confronted organized groups with alternate worldviews. Although Nyerere, Kaunda, Banda, Nasser, and Sekou Touré stand out in this regard, Nkrumah, Ben Bella, and Modibo Keita were unable to perpetuate their position for a protracted period. Because charisma acted as a substitute for institutionalization, it was also susceptible to abuse: It could be misused to repress as well as to promote, as opponents in Guinea, Malawi, Ghana, and Egypt quickly discovered. The charismatic choice and the practices it engendered continued to possess some appeal because when it succeeded—as in the case of Nyerere—it could bring about far-reaching changes that could not otherwise have been achieved. Charismatic leadership, however, has been particularly vulnerable to crises of succession. Such leaders cannot afford to designate their inheritors, as such an act might tarnish their purported invincibility. When the leader was not overthrown by the military, charismatic leadership patterns inevitably underwent a process of routinization.

The second style of political leadership to appear on the African scene, the *patriarchal* one, has provided one prototype for such routinization, usually found in administrative-hegemonial regimes. Patriarchical leaders have best been represented by Jomo Kenyatta, Leopold Sedar Senghor, Habib Bourguiba, and Felix Houphouët-Boigny among the civilians or by Yakubu Gowon, Olusegun Obasanjo, and J. A. Ankrah among military rulers. These leaders, much like their charismatic counterparts, rose to the top of the educational ladder during the colonial period and usually led successful coalitions at the time of decolonization. They differed from charismatic leaders, however, in several important respects. Both civilian and military leaders of this sort sprung up from preexisting elites, and, not surprisingly, they evinced a personal preference for pragmatism as a guiding conceptual framework.

The style developed by Africa's "princes"[21] has been manipulatory in essence. The role adopted by these leaders has been that of adjudicator and maneuverer, of instigator and peacemaker. By placing themselves above the conspiracies of daily political maneuvering, Houphouët, Kenyatta, Ahidjo, and Senghor, for example, were in a position to juggle vying factions, coopt opposition groups, and to enhance dependence on their persons. Patriarchal leaders in Africa projected a carefully nurtured father image: Kenyatta liked to be called *Mzee* (the elder), Houphouët forwarded the image of a wise man and a chief, and Ahidjo held himself purposely aloof and reserved.[22] At the same time, aristocratic life-styles were practiced, monarchical residences constructed, and patriarchal leaders glorified as the "fathers of the nation."

The patriarchal mode of operation has rested on a mixture of clientelism between the head of state and powerful patrons, on the one hand, and the creation of similar bonds with bureaucratic elites, on the other. Rival groups in this type of pattern are usually pitted against each other to enhance the position of the father figure. Although key decisions are still made by the leader and a handful of trusted advisors (who themselves may change from time to time), they are usually promulgated through subordinates. Decision making is therefore centralized yet indirect. Personal relations have counted, but so have administrative skills and the political (usually electoral) power of mediators and brokers. Patriarchal modes of operation have thus rewarded favoritism and nepotism and fueled factionalism and corruption at the same time as they have generated a modicum of institutionalization, at least in an administrative sense.

Authoritarian rule of the patriarchal type has proven in Africa to be less fraught with dangers than charismatic-autocratic forms. Patriarchal leaders have options of when to intervene or not, of when to use the carrot and when to employ the stick. Mistakes can be more easily covered up and credit claimed for wise decisions of underlings. Felix Houphouët-Boigny exemplifies this pattern. In most instances he allows subordinates to manage daily political affairs. By purposely inducing competition between rival ministers, he has succeeded in placing emphasis on tangible outcomes. Recalcitrant officials, on the other hand, are removed with alacrity. The astute manipulation of party members, opponents, and civil servants has maintained Houphouët indisputably at the helm while at the same time laying the foundation for some measure of structural growth. Thus, this mode, because of the looser controls it imposes (frequently of necessity) does have the merit of greater elasticity. On the other hand, patriarchal rule tends to be conservative: It props up the existing order and does little to promote change. It requires the exertion of a great deal of energy simply to maintain control; in many cases, it has bred inequalities and consequently social resentment. The key to successful patriarchal rule in Africa has been the skill of those who have adopted this style. Houphouët, Kenyatta, Kaunda, Banda, and Senghor, each in his own way, has proved with the benefit of hindsight to be a master politician. When this style was adopted by less astute leaders, it tended to fail as its wielders (Balewa, Gowon) lost their autonomy or resorted to coercion (Omar Bongo, Acheampong).

The practices generated by patriarchal leaders have, nevertheless, often survived the demise of their originators. Patriarchal leaders have been able to put in place a dominant administrative-bureaucratic elite whose interest lies in perpetuating this system. These leaders have also frequently been able to appoint their successors. Whether they died in office (Kenyatta) or voluntarily retired (Senghor, Ahidjo, perhaps Siaka Stevens), the network these successful patriarchal leaders had established and manipulated had assumed more institutional trappings.[23]

Successors to patriarchal leaders, because they could not lay claim to the birthright enjoyed by the founding fathers, and because they usually were selected from the ranks, adjusted their style, if not their mode, of operation. Paul Biya in Cameroon and Daniel arap Moi in Kenya evinced more autocratic tendencies, whereas Abdou Diouf in Senegal and Olusegun Obasanjo in Nigeria tended to stress more *technocratic* and conciliatory patterns of rule. This was also the disposition of the second wave of democratically elected leaders: Shehu Shagari in Nigeria, Hilla Limann in Ghana, David Dacko in the Central African Republic. These men, usually highly educated administrators as well as successful politicians, had amassed a great deal of professional experience since independence. They have preferred to view themselves as implementers rather than molders, as efficient rather than innovative. In this way, they have come to reflect the altered position of leaders in the more resilient pluralist and administrative hegemonial regimes: Their lower profile is in line with the changed relations between leadership and government institutions in these countries.

In the same vein, the 1980s version of the charismatic leader, the *populist prophetic* one, replicates many of the features of the early autocrats. Rawlings and ex-President Sankara, like Nkrumah and Sekou Touré, came to power amid great social unrest. They also had to confront severe poverty, having taken over the political mantle after years of economic mismanagement. Rawlings and Sankara were both educated primarily within their own country; they assumed office at a young age. Each has exhibited a great deal of flair and developed his own unique style. Rawlings, for example, made it a point to travel freely in the country, deliver impromptu speeches, and dress in pilot fatigues during his early years in office. He tried, at that point, to embody the notion of a man of the people. Like their earlier models, populist leaders have brought with them a set of political objectives that they have propounded with messianic vigor.

The authority of these populist leaders is, indeed, autocratic, although they pride themselves on a down-to-earth life-style more attuned to their populist rhetoric. Rawlings and Sankara in many respects resurrected the mode of operation of their predecessors. The creation of participatory institutions (Committees for the Defense of the Revolution and public tribunals) did not change the location of decision making, which still rested with the head of state and a small group of loyal advisors. Status and position depended on ideological purity and/or on total personal allegiance to the prophet. Expressions of opposition were quelled, possibly more violently than in the past. Order was thus maintained through personal friendships and constant reshufflings in the composition of ruling organs. As populist leaders in the 1980s, as military men, were not able to rely on political parties to regulate access, purges became more haphazard, and the turnover in auxiliary personnel was particularly noticeable.

Prophets, perhaps even more than charismatic leaders, have therefore been especially aware of the absence of adequate decision-making structures. They have attempted to overcome this weakness not only through decentralization and local-level mobilization and through the invitation of discussion on desired modes of government but also through the projection of religious images (in Ghana: the second coming of Jerry Rawlings, the reference to Rawlings as J. J.—"Junior Jesus"). By the mid-1980s, both Rawlings and Sankara, however, although still personally popular, were finding it difficult to maintain their style because they were unable to consolidate their social support base. They condoned abuses by their cohorts, tended to retreat regularly from the public view, and were clearly aware of the tenuousness attendant upon their incapacity to routinize their charisma.

Autocratic and patriarchal styles of leadership (and their prophetic and technocratic variants) have evinced recognizable—if deeply problematic—modes of operation. *Tyrannical leadership,* the hallmark of personal-coercive regimes, in contrast, has been noted for its capriciousness and unpredictability. The rule of Idi Amin Dada, Emperor Bokassa I, and Macias Nguema (of Equatorial Guinea) exemplifies the distortions that can accompany autocratic modes of government. Africa's tyrants—Samuel Doe being an example in the mid-1980s—most frequently came to power via the barrel of a gun. Their backgrounds differed from those of most African leaders: Possessing a rudimentary education, they joined the regular army and slowly rose through the ranks, often achieving officer status only after their rise to power. Little in their childhood or early adulthood indicated particular leadership skills or organizational capacities. In many cases, they hailed from minority ethnic groups and had few, if any, connections with major social constellations in their countries.[24]

Africa's dictators chose a domineering, sometimes described as sultanic, style of rule. They saw the state as their private domain; its resources and people were to be exploited and used for personal gain. In this leadership type the distinction between private ambitions and public goods was completely erased. Potential sources of opposition were eliminated; repression and violence came to replace entreaties, cajolery, or emotional fervor. These leaders projected, and took pride in, a strongman image: warriorlike, defiant, and, supposedly, also invincible. Idi Amin, for example, highlighted his personal prowess and reveled in surrounding himself with sophisticated military hardware. He not only sported many uniforms and medals but tried to carve out a place for himself as a modern African military hero.

The dictatorial mode of operation in postcolonial Africa was characterized by its coercive, idiosyncratic, and whimsical nature. Leaders like Amin and Bokassa sought to tower above officials, bureaucrats, other officers. If the army itself could no longer be counted on, private mercenaries were hired to protect the leaders and partake in their spoils. It is difficult to exaggerate the severity of the abuses carried out within this framework: State coffers were emptied, human rights regularly violated, and fear instilled to maintain domination. Autocracy gone bad in Africa led to the individualization of politics—to the disengagement of government from any normative or institutional constraints and, consequently, to the hinging of political procedures on a single person.

Sultanic strains have surfaced in patriarchal and charismatic, prophetic and conciliatory leadership styles. Nevertheless, authority based purely on such procedures has been much more confined than usually imagined. Africa's most grotesque dictators have been forcibly ousted from office, usually with the assistance of sympathetic external actors. Not one has been able to arrange for his own succession. In a very real sense, African patrimonialism has not been accompanied by the acceptance of tyrants or their methods.

The resilience of leadership patterns in centers of Afro-Marxist persuasion, in contrast, has been quite striking. Mengistu Haile Mariam, Mathieu Kerekou, Samora Machel (and his successor Joaquim Chissano), Agostinho Neto, and, later, Eduardo dos Santos were all selected for their leadership positions from a pool of activists at the vanguard of movements, cliques, or militant groups. Prior to their accession to office they had taken part, in the case of the civilians in this group, in the struggle for national liberation or, in the case of the military men, in the preparations for the overthrow of the previous government. From the outset, therefore, they were bound by the rules of the structures that nurtured them and guided by the ideologies they sought to apply.[25]

In style, Afro-Marxists have usually combined domination with some collective leadership. The role of the leader was defined, therefore, as the bearer and implementor of the message designed by his peers. Personal ambitions have usually been subordinated to broader objectives. Management skills, in this situation, were frequently as important as ideological zeal. In many respects, therefore, Afro-Marxist leaders resemble both technocrats and prophets; they seek conciliation and agreement in governing circles but still convey, as forcefully as they can, a message of change.

The mode of operation of ideological leadership in postcolonial Africa has shifted some of the location of policymaking from the individual to the group. In these party-centralist regimes, major decisions are ironed out in the institutions of the ruling circle: the *derg* in Ethiopia, ruling councils in Congo and Benin, the party in Angola and Mozambique. Because of their limited membership, these decision-making bodies, mostly in the form of ruling parties, are monopolistic without being personalized. They emphasize bureaucratization as opposed to mobilization. In this setting, high politics revolves around purges, clandestine machinations, rehabilitations, internal conflict, and in extreme cases, incarcerations and even assassinations. The degree of repression that is part of these patterns of rule depends, to a large extent, on the amount of insecurity felt by the top leadership. The Provisional Military Administrative Council (PMAC) in Ethiopia was far more overtly coercive than its counterpart in Benin, whereas the MPLA in Angola has tended to be more oppressive than the much more benign and cohesive Front for the Liberation of Mozambique (FRELIMO).[26]

The measure of institutionalization of ideological leadership in Africa has been its ability to provide for peaceful succession. Eduardo Mondlane was replaced by Samora Machel, who, after his untimely death in the fall of 1986, was quickly and efficiently succeeded by Chissano, not the ranking member of the ruling hierarchy at the time. The transition from Agostinho Neto to Eduardo dos Santos was also relatively smooth. These patterns of rule, when not distorted by personal greed, have, quite significantly, been able to assure their own reproduction.

Several notable trends emerge from this discussion of leadership styles. First, since the early years of independence, during which the leader was for all intents and purposes synonymous with the political center, styles of rule have been refined and amplified, largely in light of institutional developments. Thus, although tyrants still dictate the course of politics in some countries, we are unhappy to say, the leaders of Africa in the 1980s are less well known and their individual traits are more separable from the regimes they oversee. Second, then, leadership trends evince a shift, however muted, from personalization to routinization, in some cases from individual to more collective modes of rule. This pattern is indicative of the emergence of some constraints on authority. In countries like Senegal and Côte d'Ivoire, Mozambique, Botswana, and perhaps Cameroon, these constraints are institutional. In other instances—Uganda and Ghana, Nigeria and Zaire—they are normative and popular.[27] In all cases, they have evolved on the basis of precedent and experience. If the first decade of African leadership was marked by the appearance of salient and innovative leaders, the second was characterized by a mixture of unpredictability and reliability, and the third by the injection in some countries of managerial traits. The current crop of leaders reflects its environment more than it affects its surroundings.[28] As a result, leadership is only one of many guides to the intricacies of political processes on the continent.

Authoritarian modes of operation still prevail throughout Sub-Saharan Africa. The patterns of interaction they foster are not, however, uniformly repressive, intolerant, uncompetitive, or capricious (although they contain many of these elements). Through their behavior and conduct, varieties of regimes have formulated distinctive rules of the political game. Africa's first generation of rulers established procedures for policy formulation that, where not negated, have come (with all the problems they entail) to define the organizational distinctiveness of the centers they created. The weight of political processes has, therefore, slowly shifted from the leaders themselves to the procedures they have put in place.

☐ Decision-making Patterns

The conduct of daily political life in African capitals has derived from the diverse principles guiding ruling elites as well as from the patterns of interaction among their leaders. Each of these, in turn, has been molded in light of both external and domestic constraints. Variations in core political practices are noticeable, first, in the number of people involved in policy formulation. In highly personalized systems, Liberia for example, the head of state has a hand, directly or indirectly, in minute as well as fundamental policy choices. In administrative-hegemonial regimes, professional issues are discussed by bureaucrats and experts; only basic political matters are handled regularly by, say, Houphouët-Boigny or Abdou Diouf. Alternatively, in places such as populist Ghana or Burkina Faso, the distribution of decision-making powers does not follow clear lines.[29]

The quantity of people involved in policy formulation and the spheres of their influence dictate, to a large extent, how decisions are made. In Marxist

Mozambique as in pluralist Botswana, consultation is practiced on a regular basis. In most countries, leaders rely on the advice and ideas of friends and trusted lieutenants. The degree of discussion permitted also varies. In parliamentary systems, major issues are publicly aired; in many military governments, although debates are circumscribed at times, some controlled commentary is allowed.[30]

In these quite heterogeneous circumstances, the role of formal agencies does differ substantially from place to place. Administrative-hegemonial regimes rely heavily on the bureaucracy and civil service both to design and carry out decisions. Party regimes use the party as an instrument to enforce, if not to suggest, preferred paths. Each of these centers does resort to the armed forces, but hardly as consistently and as exclusively as do personal-coercive autocrats.

Avenues of approach to politicians and decision makers therefore differ. In most countries, understanding who makes decisions and what networks are activated is critical to gaining access and even, at times, attention. The durability of particular centers is a crucial guide in this regard: The longer certain arrangements have been in place, the easier it is to unravel personal and structural relationships, to know where pressure can be applied, and to use this knowledge as leverage to gain results. Foreign concerns engage in such analysis as much as local citizens. In more ambiguous regimes—Chad or Uganda—patterns are not always clear, and citizen involvement is more often shunned (foreign interests usually seek direct access to the head of state). It is important to note that identification of decision-making procedures should not be confused with the power of any center to make binding rules. The power of centers is closely connected to the resilience of the state apparatus and to its penetrative capacity. External agencies and local social groups may attenuate the decision-making powers of many African countries.[31]

The centers that have developed in Africa since independence, for all their variation, possess certain features in common: Their workings have been unduly influenced by the personalities and preferences of the elites who constructed them; the rules of the political game that these elites have devised usually attained a modicum of coherence, even if they have generally diverged from rational-legal organizational precepts; and the decision-making procedures of these elites have tended to be restrictive if not insular. Political centers in Africa have, therefore, coalesced around differently designed pacts of domination established by relatively small elite groups of people. The fact that they became the domestic sources of public policy does not, therefore, imply that they are necessarily strong foci of activity. Their record in this regard has depended on how they have managed social relations and dealt with protest and dissent. It is to these aspects of the political process that we now turn.

■ THE POLITICS OF SOCIAL RELATIONS

The maintenance of political centers is an outgrowth not just of the establishment of political procedures but also of the manner of their application. The practice of politics focuses on the exercise of power: on the mechanisms of decision enforcement and the means of social control. The crux of the political process relates to the structures and methods of interaction between leaders and followers. These interchanges revolve around channels of participation and control and forms of political exchange.

Regimes in independent Africa have experimented with a variety of techniques to ensure compliance and to maintain order. By a mixture of enticement and coercion, some have built up firm coalitions, whereas others have faltered in this task. The workability, and hence the viability, of regimes has rested to no mean degree on the internal supports they have constructed and on the kinds of methods they have used to sustain their social bases. The attempt to achieve effective hegemony unites the efforts of African rulers, as it does of political leaders in other parts of the globe. The outcomes of these efforts have varied because the possibilities, dimensions, and dynamics of political transactions have differed.[32]

□ Strategies of Coalition Construction

Confronted with social diversity expressed in cultural, ethnic, linguistic, geographic, religious and racial terms, and with growing social differentiation based on location, income, occupation, education, and life-styles, specific regimes have sought ways to mold and regulate social relations. This has involved making arrangements for the representation of key interests whose support was necessary to keep them in power, as well as deflecting demands for full participation from groups and forces either inimical to the government or too demanding of its resources. Most regimes have sought to carry out this task through a variety of corporatist schemes—the limitation of competition through the definition of permissable bases of social organization, the delineation of their functions and roles in the political and economic process, and the nurturing of their allegiance to the center.[33]

These experiments in social ordering have been undertaken to consolidate the power of rulers, to promote their legitimacy, to enhance their penetrative capacity, and to assist in overcoming external constraints. Such endeavors have proven to be most effective when alliances have been cemented with a network of already existing social groups. In the many instances where social foundations have been tampered with, new groups formed, and major constellations excluded from ruling coalitions, social control has been curtailed by the very forces it has sought to dominate. Attempts to impose monolithic structures have usually been greeted by the realignment of interests or the withdrawal of support.[34]

The majority of African states achieved independence after a brief but intense period of party formation and electoral competition. Their first constitutions provided for multiparty structures, for political representation, and for participation via the ballot box. The liberal-democratic origins of these instruments presumed that existing social groups could be allowed to vie freely without undermining the power structure or its ability to implement decisions. The competitive option created at this time has survived in only a fraction of pluralist African countries: Mauritius, Morocco, Gambia, Botswana. It has been revived in the 1980s in Senegal. Here the lack of control of the center by a particular social group or alliance has not implied an inability to gain access to its decision makers or to enjoy its benefits. Participation, in these few cases, is direct and instrumental; continuity stems from the belief of all groups that they can garner enough electoral support to gain office and that the existence of rival centers of power does not irrevocably threaten their own political prospects.[35] Most leaders of nationalist movements were neither secure enough in their position nor firm enough in their commitment to liberal ideologies to maintain these arrangements. Each of the major regime types has since developed its own formulae for the construction of social support.

The first, and perhaps one of the most problematic, attempts to reformulate the bases of representation and participation and to enhance social control was carried out by party-mobilizing regimes.[36] Traditional institutions were downgraded, ethnically based associations prohibited, and independent economic organizations and trade unions curbed. These were replaced, in most instances, by center-designed and functionally conceived monolithic interest groups closely tied to the ruling party: national associations of farmers, workers, students, women. The imposition of a uniform associational structure was intended to reshape social and economic relations, eradicate the competing coalitions that had begun to form during decolonization, and lay the foundation for other, broader channels of representation and mobilization.

This policy was justified by an appeal to notions of the common good, the national interest, and the new society. The focus of social ties in, for example, Guinea, Tanzania, and Ghana during the 1960s was shifted to the state and its leaders. This strategy was not, however, exclusionary. Participation was open to all those who accepted the government's ideology and identified with its goals. As these notions tended to appeal to young, mostly urban, partially educated, upwardly mobile, or ethnically peripheral segments of the population, the ruling coalitions constructed at this juncture possessed a progressive, usually change-oriented, aura.

The main instrument of participation and control was the single party. In Tanzania, Guinea, Uganda, as well as Ghana and Mali, the ruling party was reconstructed to serve as an umbrella for the new organizations and as a funnel for the distribution of goods and services. Even though elections were held at regular intervals, they tended to be more symbolic than real. Elections provided ritual occasions for sanctioning the existing power constellation but allowed precious few opportunities for affecting the composition of ruling circles or policy outcomes. The Tanzanian innovation that permitted several candidates to compete for office within the single-party rubric offered a partial solution to some of the problems of alienation in such systems.

Mobilizing-regime experiments at social control usually resulted in an institutional dualism (party versus bureaucracy), which permeated the public sector and extended to the lowest levels of government. Tensions between the party and the civil service were exacerbated and at times actually reduced the hold of the leadership on the apparatus of government. More to the point, in these examples (Ghana stands out in this regard), the party itself was consequently enfeebled, and the political arena contracted.[37] These strategies, consequently, were neither particularly representative nor necessarily conducive to the effective management of social demands.

A second, more enduring, formula for social control was devised in administrative-hegemonial regimes. Introduced first by Houphouët-Boigny in Côte d'Ivoire, Kenyatta in Kenya, Banda in Malawi, and Ahidjo in Cameroon, it was also implemented by military leaders in Nigeria and Ghana and is still widely practiced in many parts of the continent. This strategy has generally been used by rulers who have a strong standing in the elite establishment, whose opposition is fairly weak or fragmented, and who are wary of popular movements.[38]

This scheme of social regulation is predicated on the idea of curbing or deflecting popular participation through the granting of a representational monopoly to powerful existing social formations and scrupulously monitoring their activities. Each of these groups is accorded limited autonomy to pursue its own interests within the parameters laid down by the rulers. The key bases of group definition in this method of social organization have been central ethnic units and elite professional and occupational associations. Chiefs, businesspeople, church leaders, large commercial interests, and religious communities have been recognized; regional affiliations have been accorded official sanction by governments in Cameroon, Gabon, Senegal, Nigeria, and Malawi.

This strategy was defended as efficient and hence beneficial for the fulfillment of development objectives. Competition was constricted and the superior knowledge of elites accentuated as the foundation for progress. This system was therefore, almost by definition, both statist and exclusionary. Departicipation and depoliticization of the bulk of the population were extolled. Administrative-hegemonial modes of social control unabashedly upheld elite interests and concerns. Needless to say, this approach appealed to middle- class groups and to major ethnic associations. Kenyatta, Houphouët, Balewa, and Banda, by espousing clear class and ethnic preferences, thus propped up existing institutions of social domination and sought to coopt them for their own purposes. Those included in privileged categories were allowed to enjoy the benefits of their station; those not part of this classification were clearly disadvantaged in this system.[39] The ruling coalitions here conserved the interests of the already powerful in the cities and the countryside.

This type of social regulation relied heavily, although not exclusively, on fortifying the administrative apparatus at the expense of political institutions, most notably the party. In civilian regimes such as Kenya, Malawi, or Côte d'Ivoire, the significance of the party was downgraded and the bureaucracy reinforced. Elections were held, but as their outcomes were foregone conclusions, they became a perfunctory legitimation device except (as periodically in Kenya and lately in Côte d'Ivoire) when they could be used to bring about a circulation of elites.[40] Political participation, if it took place at all, was, in both civilian and military settings, far more indirect: It was routed through a complex network of patrons, or locally entrenched "big men," who became the main intermediaries between the citizen and the political center.

Administrative strategies have usually bred a good deal of centralization, although still suggesting the possibility that diverse interests could be pursued as long as they did not impinge on the hold of the center. Thus, in Abidjan and Nairobi, for example, traders and businesspeople have been given a measure of independence; attitudes toward the press, students, and intellectuals have vacillated depending on specific circumstances. Perhaps less overtly coercive than other forms of social control, these techniques have hardly been indulgent of pluralism or individual liberties. Indeed, in most instances these practices have led to (at times even indulged in) social inequalities.

The administrative-hegemonial strategy, nevertheless, has passed the test of durability (although hardly of equity) far better than its mobilizational counterpart. Ruling groups in Malawi and Cameroon as well as in countless other countries found this formula useful in consolidating their holds over the periphery. In these centers, the ability to coopt key opponents, to attract foreign support, and to maintain elite cohesion assisted in establishing an ongoing rhythm of interaction between rulers and subjects.[41] These techniques have, however, relied heavily on the success of the center in generating resources to sustain its attractiveness to major social groups and their supporters. Where economic performance has faltered (as in Nigeria in the late 1970s and early 1980s, Togo in the 1960s, and Upper Volta/Burkina Faso) not only has the specific government been undermined; so, too, has the basis of its system of control. What is more fundamental is that this approach has exhibited a tendency to evoke class as well as ethnic resentments: Social tensions are both more evident and more pronounced. As a result, leaders in some centers employing these measures have conceded the need to allow limited competition and to open up access to the center. This may help to explain the shift to multipartyism in several countries (Senegal, for one), the lifting of restrictions on the press in others (Nigeria), and measures for the civilianization of military governments in certain places (in 1987 in the Sudan).

Neotraditional strategies of social control are a variant of these more hegemonial administrative modes. They have been instituted mostly by military leaders ensconced in particularly weak centers (Niger) or by traditional elites in power in new states (Swaziland). The neotraditionalist form relies more heavily on attracting the support of already established leaders and, most especially, of chiefs, traders, civil servants, army officers, and sometimes even key foreign entrepreneurs. It is, in concept and implementation, far more decentralized than the administrative strategy. By channeling participation through these groups, leaders of the center entrench notions of political involvement by proxy. This system does have some attraction to local interests, but especially so when the center also has something to offer. The coalition on which neotraditional patterns rest is necessarily loose. Younger people, without traditional status and position, find difficulty in accommodating to these structures. In any event, direct participation is confined to the local level; it is rarely able to reach up to, let alone influence, national decisions.

Neotraditional strategies help the center maintain some networks of communication, although they do limit mobilization. If they are much less unequal than their exclusionary administrative counterparts, they are also less vigorous. These are more in the order of strategies of social transaction than of social control. They have proven useful in the few areas where they have been attempted, although they have not been put into widespread use as they offer few possibilities for social or economic change.[42]

Africa's tyrants have had to search for quite different mechanisms of establishing social order since they usually could rely only on a very narrow social support base and have headed political centers that are poorly institutionalized. They have generally turned to personal and coercive techniques.[43] This approach was employed by Bokassa in the Central African Republic, Amin in Uganda, and also by Samuel Doe in Liberia. Personal modes of social control purposely deny the representational legitimacy of most existing groups and do not try in any systematic way to create new ones. Notions of national self-reliance, common objectives, and obedience are propagated in an effort to link citizens directly to the rulers. The dangers of politicization and competition have been used as excuses for the exercise of direct, and frequently arbitrary, control. The possibilities for access to the decision-making apparatus are severely circumscribed and require personal contact with the leader or his intimate circle (usually friends, family members, or army cohorts). The alliance of power in this type of regime has been purposefully narrow. What such a regime lacked in legitimate power it tried to achieve by force. In these situations, restrictions abounded: Curbs were placed on political activities, on public liberties, on middle-level interest groupings, on all forms of expression, on the judiciary, and eventually on the military as well. No critical monitoring of government policy was entertained, and few institutional brakes were in evidence.[44] In general, control was exercised most notably through intimidation:

tax raids, incarcerations, disappearances, public executions, forced labor. No meaningful participation in center activities, however indirect, was possible in these conditions. Some individuals went into self-imposed exile; more often, withdrawal into informal organizations, passive resistance, and detachment from state-related activities became the norm.

Personal modes of control in independent Africa have been particularly cruel. They have generated protest, exacerbated violence, and, what is somewhat ironical, terminated in the constriction of the spheres of official control. These methods are more difficult to counteract than they are to avoid. They expand the distance between the political center and its social environment, restrict the capacity to govern, and most insidiously, violate human dignity.

The party-centralist approach to social ordering, although rooted in quite different ideas, has not fared much better than many personal-coercive schemes. This method, adopted by Afro-Marxist centers such as Mozambique, Angola, and Ethiopia, has been devised to deal with conditions of economic and social uncertainty and to promote a more fundamental societal reordering. The concept underlying party-centralist techniques of coalition construction in Africa is the reorganization of representation in line with ideological precepts. Existing class-based or ethnically defined associations were discredited (with the exception of the church in Ethiopia), and new institutions—farmer cooperatives, collective villages, worker-controlled enterprises—were put in their stead. The test of inclusion has been ideological commitment, and the vanguard party—MPLA, FRELIMO, the Workers' Party of Ethiopia (WPE)—has become the main instrument of societal monitoring.

The justification for the social control strategy of Afro-Marxist regimes is presented, as expected, in scientific socialist terms. But mass mobilization, as has already been pointed out, has not been actively encouraged in either Angola or Congo, let alone Ethiopia or Benin. This strategy has, therefore, tended to be most attractive to precisely those elements who already benefited from the new system: party activists and portions of the urban population or the army who supported its rise to power. It has been resisted, often vigorously, by existing social groups and especially by well-organized ethnic, regional, or professional organizations. The ruling coalitions in Afro-Marxist countries have, therefore, tended to rely on a narrow social base and to be confined spatially to the capital cities and their immediate environs (with the exception, possibly, of Mozambique).[45] These governments, much like those led by dictators, have been confronted by problems of penetration and have therefore frequently had to resort to force to achieve compliance. They have engaged not only in direct military operations but also, increasingly, in population relocation, resettlement schemes, and conscription. In these settings, the ability to influence government policy has been the privilege of a select few; informal and insurrectionist modes of political activity have been more commonplace.

The party-based centralist strategy of social control has not worked well either in Sub-Saharan Africa or in the Maghreb. Although the regimes that have tried to mold social relations in this way have remained intact, they have not been able to find a viable formula for interacting with their constituencies. In many cases, they exemplify the pitfalls of revolution from above impeded by poor networks of representation and mobilization. In Mozambique, Angola, and Ethiopia, ruling coalitions have had to admit the loss of control of some of their territories to resistance movements.

In the 1980s, populist governments in Ghana and Burkina Faso, following on the Libyan example, tried to design other means of gaining social backing. The basis of acceptable representation was defined by way of elimination: Those tainted by association with prior governments or those part of the establishment were excluded from the network. This approach enabled the formation, at least initially, of a ruling coalition composed mostly of the young, the disadvantaged in the rural areas, and the discontent. The task of societal reorganization was carried out not by dismantling existing structures but by establishing alternative ones, such as people's defense committees and citizens' vetting committees.[46] The PNDC in Ghana and the Sankara government in Burkina Faso used these groups both as foundations for the creation of support for the regime as well as organizations to monitor the population at large: Members were to report any evidence of opposition or expressions of disaffection. Individuals and groups that did not take part in these efforts at mass mobilization either voiced their dissatisfaction through informal group activity or simply opted out of the system.

Because this form of social organization has proven less than efficient in maintaining social order, it has undergone some revisions in both Ghana and Burkina Faso. Representative possibilities have been expanded within the organs established by the center (the defense committees in Ghana are no longer restricted to certain nonelite groups). At the same time, a variety of regime-sanctioned organizations have been established (including women's and student groups), and the stress on direct participation in all decision making has been downplayed. Although the Rawlings regime has remained in power, instead of assuring order and curtailing wasteful competition, its populist strategy has sown confusion and fomented discord, leaving a great deal of room for haphazard actions and unpredictable (also repressive) behavior.

African regimes have thus experimented widely with schemes aimed at realizing state control, social cooperation, and efficiency. The basis of representation proposed by each of these strategies has varied from total reliance on existing social structures or the manipulation of these social groups to various attempts to redefine the acceptable foundations of social organization. Most of these approaches, even those purportedly committed to mobilization, involved ways to limit participation. The size of coalitions has, therefore, varied from fairly broad networks of established interests to the most narrow alliances. The instruments of social control have also differed: Besides the single party and the administration, various regimes in independent Africa have tried to supervise their populations through patrons, vanguard parties, committees, and tribunals and, most ubiquitously, via coercive mechanisms.

Each of these strategies, therefore, has revealed a particular Achilles heel. Mobilizational efforts have faltered in the face of resilient social constructions; administrative-hegemonial experiments have accentuated class cleavages; neo-traditional schemes have proven exceptionally static; personal ventures have been brutal and exploitative; party-centralist attempts have hampered the exercise of control; populist measures have proven to be too diffuse, and in extreme instances, some centers have simply been unable to establish any meaningful ties with their constituencies. It has gradually become apparent that those social control strategies that attempted to undermine existing foundations of social organization were those that backfired most resoundingly.

In every instance, however, the coalition of groups with access to power in a particular country has usually found that other groups have coalesced into an elaborate faction in opposition to their alliance. Despite their ongoing quest for uniformity, official efforts at social control have therefore succumbed, in one way or another, to the heterogeneous social reality of contemporary Africa because they could not find adequate means to allow for the representation and participation of diverse localities in the political process.[47] There are several reasons for this pattern: Elites in most countries have been too fragmented to agree on rules of access and participation; political centers have not been sufficiently strong to exercise authority consistently in their territories; most rulers have not been willing to take into account the existence of alternative social institutions capable of disposing benefits and mobilizing support. These rulers have overestimated the willingness of social constellations to relinquish their autonomy, and ultimately all have fallen victim, in different degrees, to monopolistic fallacies. Nevertheless, the different networks of representation and participation they established became the pathways for policy implementation and political transactions.

☐ Means of Center Maintenance: Patrons, Clients, and Linkages

Regardless of the specific strategies used to construct alliances and to insure a modicum of supervision over social relations, African regimes had to find ways to carry out their decisions, to extract resources, and to maintain their support bases, however fragile or incoherent. In a similar vein, citizens have needed to devise means to obtain desired goods and services and to assure their security. Within the channels of participation and control designed by each regime, mechanisms of political interchange were put in operation and means of enforcement instituted. Throughout the postcolonial period in Africa, patron-client and patron-patron relations became the most common form of political exchange (as discussed in Chapter 4). Despite the tendency to view all political transactions in patronage terms, other instruments of interchange have evolved in the 1980s to counteract the instability inherent in these kinds of political ties.

The patronage method of postcolonial political interaction may be in the process of reformulation.

The initial foundation of political exchange in independent Africa was rooted in the symbols of nationalism. Support was garnered by successful anti-colonial leaders, who in turn vowed to distribute the benefits of independence. Once delivery had to be made on these promises, it became apparent that more tangible means of exchange had to be designed. Ideological principles helped to define distributional preferences, but as class formations were too ambiguous to coalesce around common interests, and cultural symbols could not galvanize strong joint solidarity attachments, other forms of linkage had to be explored. In a few countries, participatory mechanisms were cemented (Botswana is a notable example). Even in competitive party systems, however, these were of themselves inadequate to guarantee ongoing penetration and support.[48] What was palpably missing in most countries were organized structures of exchange backed by legally sanctioned rules for interaction between government officials and citizens. These structural linkages had not been developed during the colonial period and were given little time to solidify and become part of everyday practice during decolonization. When pressures on governments from different quarters mounted immediately after independence, other means of achieving support and responding to demands had to be established. The answer was found in most countries through the more personal mechanism of clientelistic ties.[49]

Specifically political modes of patronage have been organized along several quite distinct lines.[50] The first to emerge, and perhaps the most resilient, has sought to connect decision makers at the political center with many local communities through direct links with local leaders. During the anticolonial phase, organizers of nationalist movements identified local authority figures—frequently chiefs or prosperous farmers—who commanded respect in their communities. By giving these local leaders a role in the movement (as local representatives or functionaries) organizers garnered their support and that of their followers. "Big men" in various constituencies were courted with promises either of personal gain, public office, or local improvements; rival parties took advantage of local factionalism to wean electoral support away from these patrons.

National-local patronage ties have endured, especially in countries where elections still take place or where parties have survived (Tanzania, Zambia, Algeria, Senegal, Kenya) and in countries where these networks have been used by successive military and civilian regimes (Nigeria). These geographically defined patrons have become *mediators* in the full sense of the word: They represent the locale to the government and the political center to the community.

A second, more administrative, form of clientelistic exchange has emerged in countries where party systems are either unimportant or no longer operative. It is in widespread use in administrative-hegemonial regimes. This type of patronage uses the various rungs of the civil service to bind officeholders in the central apparatus with lower echelons of the bureaucracy both in the capital city and in the rural areas. Patronage standing is, therefore, defined by position in the decision-making apparatus, by proximity to the head of state and his courtiers in more coercive centers. At the bottom of the administrative rung, appointed officials implement government directives at the local level and become the funnel for communication between the citizen and the administration. This kind of political clientage is more centrally controlled than its electorally rooted counterpart. Each patron in this hierarchy depends more on approval from above than on support from below. Entire series of patrons and clients range the vertical length of the administrative ladder.[51] Administrative patronage may, therefore, become highly personalized. These intermediaries are power *brokers* more than mediators: They represent the higher rungs vis-à-vis the lower ones; although they enforce decisions, they do not always transmit demands from their constituents.

A third way clientelistic ties have been organized has been on the basis of solidarity ties (ethnicity, religion, racial group). Such social modes of patronage have surfaced in areas where cultural forms of social organization and differentiation are particularly pronounced: Rwanda, Burundi, Sudan, South Africa, for example. In these countries, the ruling coalition depends heavily on the approval of the racial or ethnic group that brought it to office. Patrons at the political center direct funds and resources to members of their social constituency. In return, they hope to ensure these members' ongoing support. This type of patronage reverses the political weight apparent in administrative forms: In these instances, patrons are more beholden to their clients than the clients are to any individual patron. If the ethnic or religious clientele is dissatisfied with the services rendered and with the way their interests are maintained, they can take steps to replace their patrons. These types of patrons are hence more in the order of *emissaries* than brokers or mediators.

A fourth type of patron-client linkage, associated mostly with populist regimes that have struck out against existing patronage structures, has been of an associational sort. Even though the leaders of these centers have consistently denounced the patronage system in its entirety, as Jerry Rawlings's proclamations exemplify, they have not dismantled its underlying structures so much as substituted one form of clientelism for another. The popular organizations established by these centers have become a key vehicle for the disbursement of benefits, just as membership in government-approved worker or village cooperatives has become one of the main means of access to government resources. Patronage position here, as in administrative patterns, derives from above. It is, however, far more haphazard than its bureaucratic counterpart.

The final kind of political patronage is of an individual sort. In situations of severe vulnerability and lack of institutionalization, as in Uganda and Chad during most of the last two decades, people have tied themselves to personal strongmen or warlords capable of providing some security. These highly personalistic forms of patronage delineate the role of this intermediary as that of *protector*. Protectionism also appears in urban settings—Lagos or Durban are cases in point—where migrants have few contacts and are vulnerable to the vicissitudes of unfamiliar surroundings. Individualized patron-client structures are thus reflective of situations where more formal and encompassing clientelistic networks have broken down.

The various types of political patronage that have developed in twentieth-century Africa form intricate networks of communication and enforcement. The view of politics generated by such ties is essentially extractive. The political arena is seen as a source of benefits with wealth, in the broadest sense, the reward for successful engagement.[52] This kind of thinking has, in many places, encouraged a vicious cycle of competition for access to and control over national resources. It has also frequently nurtured a zero-sum approach to politics. Winners take all to appease their backers and to make use of their position before other patrons take control and divert resources to their own ends. Patron-client modes of exchange do not draw sharp distinctions between the public and private domains.

Several problems are endemic to patron-client linkage arrangements. In the first place, because of their instrumental underpinnings, such arrangements are especially open to misuse through corruption. Political corruption encompasses a series of practices aimed at achieving personal gain from public office.[53] Bribery, embezzlement, and theft—sometimes on a grand scale—divert resources from public coffers to private hands.[54] Corruption is commonplace in Africa, as in many parts of the globe. Its degree and extensiveness have varied, however, from one setting to another.

In most African countries, petty corruption on a small scale is a daily phenomenon: Police extract bribes from hawkers and lorry drivers; clerks demand payment for issuing licenses, permits, or passports; chiefs receive presents from their communities; and politicians use official cars to go shopping and national airlines to relax on the Riviera. Institutionalized corruption is evident in places where geographical, ethnic, and administrative forms of clientage prevail. In these countries, corruption is systemic, and informal rules govern the amounts that may be skimmed by officials off public transactions. In Nigeria during the course of the 1970s, the expected kickback on contracts rose from 15 to 50 percent; in Ghana the figures fluctuated between 10 and 25 percent in the mid-1980s. Because institutionalized corruption permeates every facet of public life, its effects are corrosive to the moral fiber of the society. By far the most pernicious form of corruption has been kleptocracy, a system in which the wealth of the state has been systematically plundered by a leader and his entourage.[55] The Swiss bank accounts of Mobutu Sese Seko, I. K. Acheampong, Jean-Bedel Bokassa, and Omaru Dikko (the wealthy Nigerian finance minister during the Second Republic) attest to the existence of such phenomena. Kleptocracy is usually propped up by officially sanctioned networks of smuggling, hoarding, and black-marketeering (*kalabule* in Ghana, *magendo* in Uganda and Zaire).

In many instances, the norms of reciprocity inherent in patron-client ties control against excessive corruption. When the gap between the standard of living of patrons and clients has gone beyond acceptable limits, popular resentment has been aroused (Nigeria, Zaire, Gabon) and demands made to hold politicians to account. Where public criticism is allowed, intellectuals have consistently decried corrupt practices.[56] By these methods, corruption has rarely been eliminated; it has, however, usually been contained within a predictable range.

A second common problem associated with clientelistic modes of exchange is inefficiency. As transactions based on patronage are concerned with garnering support, allocations are not always made according to considerations of cost efficiency or productivity. Patronage methods of political exchange are directly responsible for the rapid expansion of the public sector in many countries. Bureaucratic office is a valued prize for consistent support. Clientelistic alliances, although they may promote some integration, may also seriously hinder development.[57]

What is more profound, patronage linkages encourage passivity. They foster a concept of government that is based on the private consumption of purportedly public goods, but they do very little to suggest how these public goods may be expanded.[58] Nevertheless, patron-client ties have been a key method of political exchange in the postcolonial period. The norms underlying these linkages have exhibited a great deal of durability. This persistence is partly a result of the fact that, whatever their drawbacks, at least for the first two decades of independence these networks gave some assurances to both patrons and their clients. It is partly a result of the fact that patronage connections furnished many leaders with a measure of backing beyond the center, reducing demands for participation, offering some possibilities for representation, and guaranteeing some support.

These mechanisms could not, however, have been set in motion if African states had not monopolized so many desired resources and controlled so directly essential goods and services. These modes of exchange seemed to work better than other alternatives. If coercion and intimidation were employed instead of such personal links, the costs, both materially and politically, became too high. If force could not be used effectively and patronage was not in operation, no other means of exchange were readily available, with the result that decisions could not be enforced and relations between governments and their societies broke down (again, the situation in Chad was symptomatic of this dilemma).

Several occurrences in the late 1970s and early 1980s have, however, forced a reevaluation of the efficacy of these methods of maintaining support. The economic crisis of the third decade of independence meant that government patrons had less and less to offer their constituents. The imposition of structural adjustment policies by the World Bank and IMF either froze government recruitment or streamlined the number of public-sector positions. Appointments to the bureaucracy—a key instrument of patronage—were consequently blocked. The appeal of many patrons waned. On the other hand, local leaders with control over nonstate resources offered alternative poles of allegiance. Informal systems of patronage continued in some locations, but these were not always connected with the state.[59] Where conditions deteriorated drastically and poverty became widespread, patrons were frequently blamed. More people were willing to take political risks in order to survive.

Above all, however, rulers themselves began to reassess the benefits of clientelistic exchanges. The experience accumulated since independence seemed to show that although patronage ties did help engender political support, they also increased competition within the elite, frequently creating internal divisions among patrons and eventually fomenting instability. Put simply, it appeared as if "with clientelism no stability, without it no support."[60] This realization has led to a renewed quest for substitutes to patron-client ties. One direction has been to contain competition through decentralization and the funneling of resources to the local level. This option, however, has had limited effects, altering the form of patronage and enhancing the status of local administrators (Zaire is one example). Another method has been to reinforce bureaucratic structures and redefine procedures in an attempt to promote rational-legal modes of exchange. And in some countries, more effort has been devoted to finding ways of reviving transactions based on participatory linkages, either through parties or through other structures of representation. In all of these instances, the thrust of this rethinking has focused on the need to replace the instrumental foundations and the extractive norms that have sustained patronage schemes in the past. Thus, although it is much too early to comment on the outcome of these experiments, the centrality of personalistic means of exchange may diminish as more organizational mechanisms of implementation and support maintenance are established.

■ CENTER CONSOLIDATION AND MAINTENANCE: SOME TRENDS

The multiple forms of center construction and political practice discussed in these pages capture only some of the variety of sociopolitical relations in Africa. Each regime possesses its own rhythm of interaction. In most cases, regularized patterns of decision making and known methods of enforcement (via patrons more often than government agencies) have evolved. These have tended, with few exceptions, to be based on different combinations of ruling elite interests and personalized clientelistic ties. But in some countries hegemony and domination may be giving way to various types of more sophisticated reciprocity and interdependence, to a quest for appropriate structures that would replace personal types of linkage.[61]

These trends highlight the complexities inherent in establishing rules of the political game and the means for their implementation. The ambitions, interests, and impulses of ruling elites (high politics) cannot be understood independently of the parallel concerns of social groups and local institutions (deep politics). The experience of the decades since independence has shown that although elites may establish decision-making procedures, define strategies of social control, and delimit the forms of political exchange—and in the process sometimes wreak considerable havoc and generate incredible human misery—they cannot always determine the outcomes of their designs. Although some regimes in Africa have been cruel and suppressive and most have been not only inequitable but also fragile, several have become more efficient and tolerant. Center consolidation and maintenance has depended more on the competence of leaders in forging alliances via adequate representation, participation, and regularized transactions than on their capacity to indiscriminately employ force. Effective power utilization has relied on subtle political practices. From the standpoint of the regimes that have emerged since independence, therefore, specific norms, procedures, and methods have been created and regularized; the results of these, however, have depended, to no mean degree, on the nature of social responses.

■ NOTES

1. The distinction between high politics and deep politics is based on John Lonsdale, "Political Accountability in African History," in Patrick Chabal, ed., *Political Domination in Africa: Reflections on the Limits of Power* (London: Cambridge University Press, 1986), p. 130.

2. Crawford Young, *Ideology and Development in Africa* (New Haven: Yale University Press, 1982), p. 184. The definition of ideology is a complex issue. This definition is used for working purposes but implies neither the invalidity of other approaches nor the exclusion of possibilities for refinement and amplification.

3. For a good overview of the various ideological "waves" since independence, see Carl G. Rosberg and Thomas M. Callaghy, eds., *Socialism in Sub-Saharan Africa: A New Assessment* (Berkeley: University of California, Institute of International Studies, 1979).

4. Although Leopold Senghor and Jomo Kenyatta also labeled themselves socialists, in most respects they do not fall into this category. See William Friedland and Carl G. Rosberg, eds., *African Socialism* (Stanford, Calif.: Stanford University Press, 1964).

5. For some examples, consult Kwame Nkrumah, *Africa Must Unite* (London: Heinemann, 1963), and Julius Nyerere, *Uhuru na Umoja: Freedom and Unity* (London: Oxford University Press, 1964).

6. Erich Leistner, "Socialism on the Wane in Africa," *Africa Insight* 14, no. 1 (1984): 2–3.

7. The best discussion of pragmatism as ideology may be found in Young, *Ideology and Development in Africa*.

8. See Ali A. Mazrui, "The Resurrection of the Warrior Tradition in African Political Culture," *Journal of Modern African Studies* 13, no. 1 (1975): 67–84.

9. For a good exposition, see Ladipo Adamolekun, "Mobutu's Authenticity: Rhetoric or Revolution?" *Afriscope* 5, no. 2 (1975): 29–30.

10. David Ottaway and Marina Ottaway, *Afrocommunism* (New York: Praeger, 1980), and Edmond J. Keller and Donald Rothchild, eds., *Afro-Marxist Regimes* (Boulder, Colo.: Lynne Rienner Publishers, 1987), provide good summaries of these concepts.

11. Michael Radu, "Ideology, Parties and Foreign Policy in Sub-Saharan Africa," *Orbis* 15, no. 4 (1982): 967–992.

12. Ali A. Mazrui, "The Liberal Revival in Black Africa," *Africa Report* 25, no. 4 (1980): 45–47. The discussion of one case study may be found in Richard Sklar, "Democracy for the Second Republic," *Issue* 11, no. 1 (1981): 14–16.

13. Richard Jeffries, "Ghana: Jerry Rawlings ou un populisme à deux coups," *Politique africaine* 2, no. 8 (1982): 8–20. Also Donald I. Ray, *Ghana: Politics, Economics and Society* (London: Frances Pinter, 1986).

14. Christian Coulon, "Le réseau islamique," *Politique africaine* 9 (1983): 68–83; Guy Nicholas, "Islam et 'constructions nationales' au sud du Sahara," *Revue française d'études politiques africaines* 165/166 (1979): 86–107.

15. Roger Charlton and Roy May, "African Politics and World System Theory" (Paper presented to the annual conference of the Political Studies Conference, University of Manchester, 16–18 April 1985).

16. Christopher Clapham, *Third World Politics: An Introduction* (Madison: University of Wisconsin Press, 1985), pp. 47–49.

17. S. N. Eisenstadt, *Traditionalism, Patrimonialism and Modern Neopatrimonialism* (Beverly Hills, Calif.: Sage Publications, 1975).

18. Contrast with Robert H. Jackson and Carl G. Rosberg, *Personal Rule in Black Africa* (Berkeley: University of California Press, 1982), p. 19 and elsewhere, who view personal rule as any kind of patrimonial regime.

19. Ali A. Mazrui, "Leadership in Africa," *New Guinea* 5, no. 1 (1971): 33–50. Also see his "The Monarchical Tendency in African Political Culture," in Marion Doro and Newell E. Stultz, eds., *Governing in Black Africa* (Englewood Cliffs, N.J.: Prentice Hall, 1970), pp. 18–38.

20. Clapham, *Third World Politics,* p. 74.

21. This term is used extensively in Jackson and Rosberg, *Personal Rule in Black Africa,* although the style of leadership suggested by this term dates back to Machiavelli.

22. Victor T. Le Vine, "Leadership Styles and Political Images: Some Preliminary Notes," *Journal of Modern African Studies* 15, no. 4 (1977): 631–638. For one example, see Brigitte Masquet, "Côte d'Ivoire: Pouvoir présidentiel, palabre et démocratie," *Afrique contemporaine* 114 (1981): 10–12.

23. Lancine Sylla, "Succession of the Charismatic Leader: The Gordian Knot of African Politics," *Daedalus* 111, no. 2 (1982): 11–28. For an earlier treatment of the subject, see Victor T. Le Vine, "Leadership Transition in Black Africa: Elite Generations and Political Succession," *Munger Africana Library Notes* 30 (1975).

24. For one example, see Peter Woodward, "Ambiguous Amin," *African Affairs* 77, no. 307 (1978): 153–164.

25. Richard Sandbrook, *The Politics of Africa's Economic Stagnation* (London: Cambridge University Press, 1986), p. 89, highlights this point.

26. See John Markakis, "Garrison Socialism: The Case of Ethiopia," *Middle East Research and Information Program Report* no. 79 (1979): 3–17.

27. See Thomas M. Callaghy, "State-Subject Communication in Zaire: Domination and the Concept of Domain Consensus," *Journal of Modern African Studies* 17, no. 3 (1980): 469–492.

28. Timothy M. Shaw and Naomi Chazan, "The Limits of Leadership: Africa in Contemporary World Politics," *International Journal* 37, no. 4 (1982): 543–554.

29. The entire issue of decision making has been woefully neglected in studies of African politics. For one excellent case study, see Robert Price, *Society and Bureau-*

cracy in Contemporary Ghana (Berkeley: University of California Press, 1975).

30. Joel D. Barkan with John J. Okumu, eds., *Politics and Public Policy in Kenya and Tanzania* (New York: Praeger, 1979).

31. Sara Berry of Boston University deserves credit for the distinction between decision-making procedures and decision-making power.

32. For an exposition of the need to map out the dimensions and features of state analysis in this respect, see Roger Charlton and Roy May, "The State of Africa: Evaluating Contemporary Challenges to Authority and Legitimacy" (Paper presented at the African Studies Association of the United Kingdom and the Centre of Commonwealth Studies Symposium on Legitimacy and Authority in Africa, University of Stirling, 23 May 1986).

33. These ideas are the basis for the analysis of corporatism. For background, see Phillippe Schmitter and Gerhard Lehmbruch, eds., *Trends Toward Corporatist Intermediation* (Beverly Hills, Calif.: Sage Publications, 1979); Howard J. Wiarda, *Corporatism and National Development in Latin America* (Athens, Ohio: Center for International Studies, Ohio University, 1981); and Julius E. Nyang'oro, "On the Concept of Corporatism and the African State" (University of North Carolina, draft manuscript, 1985).

34. Kiflé Selassie Béseat, "Convaincre, contrôler ou contraindre? Systèmes et mécanismes de contrôle du pouvoir en Afrique," *Présence africaine* 127/128 (1983): 79–113.

35. For background on regime types, see Ruth Berins Collier, *Regimes in Tropical Africa: Changing Forms of Supremacy, 1945–1975* (Berkeley: University of California Press, 1982).

36. Much of the following analysis is based on Naomi Chazan and Donald Rothchild, "Corporatism and Political Transactions: Some Ruminations on the Ghanaian Experience" (Paper presented at the Twenty-ninth Annual Meeting of the African Studies Association, Madison, Wisconsin, 30 October–2 November 1986).

37. For a case study, see Ben Amonoo, *Ghana 1957–1966: The Politics of Institutional Dualism* (London: George Allen and Unwin, 1981). Also see Nelson Kasfir, *The Shrinking Political Arena* (Berkeley: University of California Press, 1976), as well as his "Departicipation and Political Development in Black African Politics," *Studies in Comparative International Development* 9, no. 3 (1975): 3–26.

38. Samuel P. Huntington, *Political Order in Changing Societies* (New Haven: Yale University Press, 1968), p. 7.

39. See Richard L. Sklar, "Political Science and National Integration—A Radical Approach," *Journal of Modern African Studies* 6, no. 1 (1967): 1–11. Also, for some cases, see Larry Diamond, "Class, Ethnicity and the Democratic State: Nigeria, 1950–1966," *Comparative Studies in Society and History* 25, no. 3 (1983): 457–489, and David Brown, "Who Are the Tribalists? Social Pluralism and Political Ideology in Ghana," *African Affairs* 322 (1982): 37–70.

40. Dirk Berg-Schlosser, "Modes and Meaning of Political Participation in Kenya," *Comparative Politics* 14, no. 4 (1982): 397–416, gives one example.

41. Ali A. Mazrui, "Political Engineering in Africa," *International Social Science Journal* 35, no. 2 (1983): 279–284.

42. For one discussion, see Pearl Robinson, "Neotraditional Corporatism" (Discussion paper presented at the Walter Rodney Seminar, Boston University, October 1985).

43. For a case study, see Mike Oquaye, *Politics in Ghana, 1972–1979* (Accra: Tornado Press, 1980).

44. Some of these methods have been monitored by Amnesty International. For example, see the annual reports of Amnesty International during the course of the 1980s.

Amnesty International, *Amnesty International Report 1987* (London: Amnesty International Publications, 1987).

45. Personal communication with Marina Ottaway. Also see Allen Isaacman and Barbara Isaacman, *Mozambique: From Colonialism to Revolution, 1900–1982* (Boulder, Colo.: Westview Press, 1983).

46. A description of the PNDC policies in Ghana may be found in Donald I. Ray, *Ghana: Politics, Economics, Society* (Boulder, Colo.: Lynne Rienner Publishers, 1986), and in Deborah Pellow and Naomi Chazan, *Ghana: Coping with Uncertainty* (Boulder, Colo.: Westview Press, 1986).

47. Fred M. Hayward, "Political Participation and its Role in Development: Some Observations Drawn from the African Context," *Journal of Developing Areas* 7, no. 4 (1973): 591–612; also see Naomi Chazan, "The New Politics of Participation in Tropical Africa," *Comparative Politics* 14, no. 2 (1982): 169–189.

48. Kay Lawson, ed., *Political Parties and Linkage: A Comparative Perspective* (New Haven: Yale University Press, 1980).

49. Clapham, *Third World Politics*. Also see: S. N. Eisenstadt and René Lemarchand, eds., *Political Clientelism, Patronage and Development* (Beverly Hills, Calif.: Sage Publications, 1981), and J. C. Scott, *The Moral Economy of the Peasant: Rebellion and Subsistence in Southeast Asia* (New Haven: Yale University Press, 1976).

50. René Lemarchand, "Political Exchange, Clientelism and Development in Tropical Africa," *Cultures et développement* 4, no. 3 (1972): 484–516.

51. The outlines of this type of patronage are discussed in Artistide Zolberg, *One-Party Government in the Ivory Coast* (Princeton, N.J.: Princeton University Press, 1964).

52. Richard Hodder-Williams, *An Introduction to the Politics of Tropical Africa* (London: George Allen and Unwin, 1984): pp. 95–100.

53. Monday V. Ekpo, ed., *Bureaucratic Corruption in Sub-Saharan Africa: Toward a Search for Causes and Consequences* (Washington, D.C.: University Press of America, 1979). For an excellent case study, see Victor T. Le Vine, *Political Corruption: The Ghana Case* (Stanford, Calif.: Hoover Institution Press, 1975).

54. Nathaniel H. Leff, "Economic Development Through Bureaucratic Corruption," *American Behavioral Scientist* 7 (1964): 8–14.

55. Stanislav Andreski, *The African Predicament: A Study in the Pathology of Modernization* (London: Michael Joseph, 1968), pp. 92–109, first outlined the features of such a system.

56. For an excellent example, see Ayi Kwei Armah, *The Beautyful Ones Are Not Yet Born* (London: Heinemann, 1971).

57. Walter L. Barrows, "Comparative Grassroots Politics in Africa," *World Politics* 24, no. 2 (1974), esp. p. 232.

58. Thomas M. Callaghy, "Politics and Vision in Africa: The Interplay of Domination, Equality and Liberty," in Patrick Chabal, ed., *Political Domination in Africa: Reflections on the Limits of Power* (London: Cambridge University Press, 1986), pp. 30–51.

59. René Lemarchand, "The State, the Parallel Economy and the Changing Structure of Patronage Systems in Africa," in Donald Rothchild and Naomi Chazan, eds., *The Precarious Balance: State and Society in Africa* (Boulder, Colo.: Westview Press, 1988), pp. 149–170; also see J. C. Scott and B. Kerkvliet, "How Traditional Patrons Lose their Legitimacy: A Theory with Special Reference to Southeast Asia," *Cultures et développement* 5, no. 3 (1978): 502–540.

60. Chris Allen, "Staying Put: Handy Hints for Heads of State" (Paper presented at the Symposium on Authority and Legitimacy in Africa organized by the African Studies Association of the United Kingdom and the Centre for Commonwealth Studies,

University of Stirling, 23 May 1986).
    61. Frank Holmquist, "Correspondent's Report: Tanzania's Retreat from Statism in the Countryside," *Africa Today* 30, no. 4 (1983): 35.

7

Deep Politics:
Political Response, Protest,
and Conflict

Formal decision-making procedures and practices, high politics, are only one (albeit key) component of the political process. These formal procedures may be part of, subsist alongside, or stand in opposition to the deep politics of society. Deep politics are concerned not only with the way power is exercised but also with the purposes of governance; they may present challenges to policy, to the incumbents of public office, or to the dominant political vision.[1] At issue, hence, are questions of authority and power as well as legitimacy. Participation, collaboration, cooperation, cynicism, dissatisfaction, rebellion, insurrection, revolt, civil war, disengagement, and withdrawal are all ways of reacting to specific regimes; they may also be profound responses to reigning political doctrines.[2] Patterns of political conflict, therefore, have a direct bearing on policy decisions and on the dynamics of civil order and disorder in African countries. They also touch upon the fundamentals of political organization, on the creation of a civic public.

What do social groups complain about? How are their demands organized? How are they expressed? With what results? Societal responses to formal political actions in postcolonial Africa have varied in degree of organization, in scale of activities, in the amounts and types of resources utilized, in the reactions they have evoked, and invariably, in outcomes and implications. Five main types of domestic political conflict, which frequently take place concurrently in the same context, have developed during this period: elite, factional, communal, mass, and popular.[3]

No government has escaped the effects of one of these forms of social response. Some countries have experienced prolonged cycles of instability and violence, whereas others have been more successful in maintaining order and establishing viable means to handle protest. The history of political conflict in most African countries has been punctuated by constant efforts to curtail unrest and refine the premises of political interaction. Gradually, though quite methodically, the focus of conflict has consequently shifted from disputes over political boundaries to disagreements over political values. As the center of political concern has shifted, however violent and dislocating this move, most countries in Africa have begun to develop coherent politics.

■ ELITE CONFLICTS

Conflicts within the political center are the most common form of political strife in Africa. They have occurred in every African country throughout the postindependence period. Elites of different backgrounds, favoring diverging policy positions, and often pursuing a multiplicity of interests, have contended with each other to promote their separate concerns and to protest against measures perceived as detrimental to their well-being.

In Côte d'Ivoire, for example, during the past three decades, politicians of the old guard have competed with younger technocrats for party positions and for cabinet posts. In Tanzania, with its established party-mobilizing regime, one of the most persistent lines of division has been between ideologues and bureaucrats, between party functionaries and senior civil servants. Even in Jerry Rawlings's populist government, not to mention Mobutu's Zaire, machinations between individuals seeking the ear of the leader and between civil and military groups provide the fodder for the rumor mills of Accra and Kinshasa.

Elite conflict is, virtually by definition, extremely confined: It takes place in the capital cities and among the upper echelons of the government apparatus. It is so prevalent precisely because it relates directly to the everyday activities of the political leadership—to bureaucratic appointments, policy directions, governmental allocations. The aim of vying elites is to affect political decisions—to strengthen their position in the hierarchy, to have a say in the molding of policy, and, as a result, to increase their share of the political pie. The objective of these demands, often cast in class, ethnic, or ideological terms, is to alter the uses of state power.

The protagonists in these struggles are mostly urban elites whose social positions are defined by the political center and whose circumstances are most directly affected by government: professionals, big businesspeople, students, intellectuals, and in some cases chiefs and religious leaders. Elite conflict, though small in scale and limited in scope, involves the actual or potentially powerful strata in African states. This form of conflict is frequently represented as espousing some concept of the way government should act and for what ends. It is usually, however, not terribly well organized: Sometimes individuals act alone or form temporary alliances with other people in order to bring about specific changes; sometimes such coalitions have endured for a long period of time as interests of key groups have coalesced (and, in these cases, elite conflicts have assumed factional dimensions as well).

Strategies and tactics in these kinds of conflict are indicative of the selective nature of demands and the narrow social foundations of their purveyors. Many of the activities of competing groups take place behind the scenes: Allies are wooed through lavish entertainment, gifts, and promises of appointments or other benefits. Lobbying is commonplace as deals are struck between key personalities. Pork-barrel techniques, backroom manipulations, pacts, and negotiations are an important aspect of juggling for position and enhancing influence in African capitals. A good indication of the prevalence of these tactics is the degree of interest aroused in Yaoundé, Abidjan, Nairobi, Addis Ababa, Algiers, or Maputo by such issues as why the president's secretary was seen in the company of the party chairman; who was not invited to someone's reception; what a prominent intellectual was doing in deep conversation with a certain cabinet minister; the circumstances behind the cancellation of the director-general's trip to Washington; and the meaning of that all-night meeting at the castle.

In party systems, elite conflict also takes place in the parliament and the central organs of the party. In Senegal, Zambia, Angola, and Gabon, statements made in budget debates are indicative of political currents. The outcome of votes provides more tangible evidence of alliances as well as of agreements arrived at behind closed doors. These explicit and implicit modes of elite conflict are sometimes accompanied by more demonstrative manifestations as well: speeches criticizing government actions, grumblings in the market about particular decisions, and most notably, where the tradition of free journalism still exists despite formal constraints (Ghana, Nigeria, Kenya, Senegal), through newspaper editorials, the dissemination of pamphlets, the growth of an underground press.[4]

Elite conflicts, especially where government performance has been unimpressive, have sometimes assumed more active expressions. In Ghana and Nigeria since independence, in Kenya and Zambia with increased regularity, sometimes in Côte d'Ivoire, Zaire, and Togo, when elites have not been able to gain concessions they have used petitions, demonstrations, and even strikes to press their claims. Some groups—usually students—have marched to voice their discontent, and these organizations (at the margins of the elite structure) have also taken strike action. In general, however, this kind of conflict (with the notable exception of some palace coups), remains within the bounds of the legal and the nonviolent. Because the tactics of elite conflict are concerned more with gaining benefits within the system rather than undermining its foundations, such tactics evince a great deal of self-restraint.

Elite strife is normally of a low intensity. It usually does evoke some official reaction, as leaders can rarely afford to alienate key elite groups. Felix Houphouët-Boigny and Jomo Kenyatta proved to be masters in the management of elite discontent. Both used a mixture of cooptation and repression, compromise and contempt, to mollify competing factions and to maintain control. When students in Côte d'Ivoire denounced government orientations and criticized what they considered to be inequitable practices, some of their leaders were dispatched abroad on government grants, some were incarcerated, and others given high positions in the administration. The key means of dealing with elite demands has been through the manipulation of appointments and policy shifts. The careful disposition of bureaucratic posts is used as a means of appeasement (and partly accounts for the rapid growth of the state machinery). In relatively stable administrative regimes, such as those of Kenya, Cameroon, and Côte d'Ivoire, where issues of succession are a pivot of intraelite strife, cabinet reshuffling and constitutional changes have been used to keep pretenders in check. When discontent was rife in elite circles in these countries at the end of the 1970s, some policy concessions were made: Salaries were raised in the public service, certain state corporations were closed down, and steps were taken to offer new opportunities for the accumulation of wealth.

Leaders confronted by elite demands have, when all else fails, a final, most effective, tool at their disposal: political excommunication. This measure is employed when the position of the leader is seriously threatened by elite machinations. Kwame Nkrumah imprisoned J. B. Danquah in Ghana and forced Kofi Busia into exile; Houphouët-Boigny has regularly sacrificed the careers of some of his most trusted lieutenants to hold other politicians at bay; Daniel arap Moi engineered the political demise of Charles Njonjo; Kenyatta stood by as J. M. Kariuki was assassinated, and Mengistu Haile Mariam physically eliminated major portions of the urban intelligentsia.

It is inevitable that accommodation of elite demands has also involved some overtures toward the external partners of domestic elites. Leaders have periodically met the claims of local business interests (and by extension their foreign counterparts) by lowering taxes, giving preferred access to foreign exchange, providing credit facilities, or granting immigration permits. However costly such actions are, every government has had to make some gestures to elite groups in order to insure its own survival.

The dynamic of elite conflicts has subsequently tended to fluctuate: The more personalized are elite demands, the lower the level of confrontation; the more generalized and contradictory, the higher the level of tension and the more varied the techniques employed to stem them. Most governments have gone to great lengths to avoid the consolidation of permanent elite factions either through purposely narrowing the size of elite groups (Côte d'Ivoire, Malawi) or through engineering the constant circulation of elites (Zaire, Ghana under Rawlings). The outcomes of these efforts have a direct bearing on government stability. Where elites have been successfully manipulated, leaders have enjoyed remarkable continuity (Sekou Touré, Kenneth Kaunda, Mathieu Kerekou, H. Kamuzu Banda, Samora Machel). Where elite conflicts have been continuously mishandled and internal factions have coalesced (Uganda, Nigeria, Burkina Faso), the conflicts have resulted in palace coups or have spread beyond the confines of the center and constituted a more serious challenge to its stability. The meaning of elite conflicts, therefore, lies in their implications for the resilience of officeholders and, at times, of their governments.

■ FACTIONAL CONFLICTS

Factional conflicts, in many respects elite conflicts writ large, are nevertheless distinct: They assume different dimensions, possess their own unique dynamic, and carry quite separate implications. Factional strife, organized by elites, nevertheless reaches out to a variety of social groups and down to the local level. This mobilization takes place to further access to the center, increase participation and even control of the government, and influence political outlooks as well as specific policies.

Factional conflict, unlike elite competition, has not appeared in all African states. It has been most noticeable in those pluralist and administrative-hegemonial regimes where either intermediate social organizations have flourished and/or where elaborate patronage networks have thrived (Nigeria, Ghana, Senegal, Zambia, Sierra Leone, Kenya).[5] Factionalism has become the most visible and consistent form of formal confrontation in countries that experienced a great deal of party competition on the eve of independence and in which elite cohesion has been relatively low.

Factional disputes tend to be wider in scope than their counterparts among the elite. The purpose of factional politics is to influence the composition of the official power apparatus, to determine who rules in a given political center. The minimum demand raised is for a place in the decision-making apparatus—for a say in the direction of government affairs and in the disbursement of government benefits. At times, factions aim at gaining control, at possibly bringing about a more basic change in regime. Factional strife, therefore, is a dispute over access to and/or control over the reins of government.

Factional conflicts in contemporary Africa commence as contending elites mobilize their constituents to vie with other groups for scarce state-controlled resources. This competition is sharpened by the makeup of the political coalition controlling the offices of state, the different access that urban and rural patrons have to decision-making elites at the center, and the varying rates of subregional development. In Nigeria, Cameroon, Sudan, Zaire, and elsewhere, ethnoregional inequalities have intensified competition and conflict among various interests. It is precisely because socioeconomic change differentially affects ethnoregional interests that it raises the consciousness of the people living in the less-advantaged areas about their relative lack of services, amenities, and economic opportunities.[6]

Where leaders of the relatively disadvantaged have reason to hope that demands for proportional or extraproportional (redistributive) treatment will lead to more balanced development policies, they may mobilize constituent support for a change of priorities. However, such a call for proportional, and especially extraproportional, allocations is never put forward in a political vacuum. The relatively advantaged, who often have better access to state decision makers, can be expected to respond vigorously, basing their counterdemands upon what they contend is a common imperative for rapid economic growth. These appeals are frequently received positively by bureaucratic officials at the political center, who shrink from the heavy expenditures involved in meaningful social transformation and who are protective of their own interests. In Zambia, for example, the former governor of the Bank of Zambia, raising questions about President Kenneth Kaunda's call for a decisive effort to reverse colonially determined rural-urban disparities, asserted bluntly that "the rural areas have the human material neither to [pursue] nor sustain a development effort, and such development as is created has only temporary effect as it depends largely on urban manpower and materials."[7]

Factional conflicts are organized by elite groups and, therefore, have a decidedly elitist flavor. In Ghana, chiefs, lawyers, and businesspeople have banded together against progressive intellectuals, trade union leaders, middle-level clerks, and independent farmers. In Senegal, Muslim marabouts have competed with bureaucrats; in Nigeria, ethnoregional leaders have struggled against each other for political power. But factionalism requires mobilization of support beyond the confines of the urban areas: It breeds on local conflicts and strikes deep roots in the countryside. Limited in political scope, it is quite broad in scale.

Mobilization takes place through conscious appeals on the basis of ethnicity and class. In Nigeria, political elites have unabashedly played on ethnic, religious, and sectional identities and tensions. In Ghana, Zaire, Sierra Leone, and Liberia, similar calls have been made. At the level of the village, too, local leaders have been coopted. The particularistic basis of recruitment concluded by factional leaders feeds on the competition and inequality wrought by processes of social and economic change and takes advantage of cultural cleavages to advance the goals and ambitions of big patrons.[8] Factional alliances (however elitist in derivation) are therefore represented as cutting across different class distinctions.

The recruitment of factional support, however, is generally also conducted along interest lines, resting on the backing of key horizontal groups (professional organizations, women's associations, trade unions, students, religious communities, youth, and farmers). Leaders try to delineate common concerns: free enterprise or equality, competition or justice, equitable distribution or increased opportunities. The maintenance of viable factions relies heavily on ideological rhetoric, if not on deep ideological conviction. The differences among parties in Nigeria during the Second Republic or in Senegal since the early 1980s are cases in point. Factional networks thus have a vertical structure (they divide the society from the top down) but are heavily weighted in favor of elite interest.

As the social bases of factions may cut across ethnic and class distinctions (while still drawing on these cleavages), factional strength depends on the capacity of elite leaders to meet the demands of constituent units. Factional demands, in most instances, are low in intensity and negotiable: access to jobs for supporters, expanded educational opportunities, funds for local development, salary hikes, higher producer prices, and improved roads, clinics, marketing facilities, and sanitation. Stress is placed on benefits; efforts are therefore directed, at least in the first instance, to attaining distributional gains. Factional leaders have consequently employed a variety of political tactics. They devote a great deal of time and energy to establishing close ties with decision makers. In the best patronage tradition, marabouts in Senegal and trade unionists in Nigeria offer political support in exchange for goods and services. Negotiations, backslapping, and trade-offs are the stuff of factional politics: Such activities can be seen in the streets of Lagos and the government complexes of Dakar. Lobbying, rallying public opinion (especially in the urban areas), petitions, strikes, and demonstrations are also commonplace.

Factional conflict galvanizes at the time of elections, which in many places have come to embody and accentuate factional disputes. At these times, gains are assessed, scores settled, and alliances reformed. Factionalism doesn't require regular electoral opportunities to function; but this mode of political confrontation has thrived in countries where elections have been held periodically or where some circulation of elites is possible via the ballot box (Kenya to some extent, Senegal in the 1980s, Ghana and Nigeria in the late 1960s and late 1970s).[9]

Government responses to initial factional demands generally consist of well-placed handouts to factional leaders and their constituencies, hence the class bias of so many policies. Allocations are the main instrument of conflict management at this level and consequently depend on the availability of resources as well as adherence to some distributional principles. In a number of situations where the state apparatus is controlled by a particular ethnic group or cluster of groups (white domination in South Africa, Amharic leadership in Ethiopia, Northern/Arab influence in the Sudan), the allocation of public resources is likely to be skewed in favor of those groups in control of the center. In many cases, however, leaders have utilized some measure of proportionality to guide disbursements. In Nigeria and Ghana in the 1970s, for example, attempts were made to distribute resources as equitably as possible.[10] When the resource supply diminishes or is in any event scarce (as happened in Nigeria in the early 1980s or Ghana during the same time period), government leaders may attempt to ignore factional demands, increase their requests for foreign aid, justify their actions by appeals for understanding, devise and publicize new criteria for disbursement, or conduct an all-out campaign to discredit their opponents.[11] These techniques are familiar to politicians and citizens in all countries where factional politics prevail.

If initial requests are not satisfied, usually a second set of demands is raised by dissatisfied factional leaders: for greater participation or for the displacement of existing officeholders. Calls for a change in government—inevitably forwarded most emphatically by those who benefit the least from the current system—require different strategies. Assemblies, strikes, and demonstrations, the fundamentals of protest politics, have been used regularly in factionalized countries throughout the period of independence. These techniques frequently cross the frontiers of the legal and the nonviolent; calls are made for civil disobedience and noncooperation. Direct clashes between government supporters (especially when these belong to one particular faction) and opponents take place; at times, sporadic violence occurs. The opposition to Acheampong in Ghana during the mid-1970s and to Shehu Shagari in Nigeria several years later illustrates the multiplicity of methods used by spurned factional leaders and their allies.

As these higher-intensity pressures directly affect the position and the influence of those in power, governments can ignore them only at their peril. Several sorts of responses have been used. First, many governments have attempted to reduce such demands by incorporating vocal opposition leaders into their ranks and by negotiating with them within the cabinet or party executive committee (this is sometimes referred to as hegemonial exchange). In Kenya, Zambia, and Niger, in very different ways, factional leaders have been brought into the policymaking process. If these gestures do not suffice, or if a government ignores demands for inclusion (on ideological or other grounds), the conflict might escalate even further. Second, political changes have been launched to alleviate demands. These have often involved opportunities for greater participation. Military governments have sometimes capitulated to demands by agreeing to transfer power to civilians, as happened in Nigeria in 1979 and in Ghana in 1969 and in 1979.

Third, and usually in tandem, the government has cracked down on its main detractors: Opposition leaders are cautioned or imprisoned, in some cases driven into exile; their supporters are hounded and election results manipulated should the opportunity arise. If pressures continue to mount, emergency measures have been brought to bear: Competition has been circumscribed, channels for the articulation of criticism foreclosed. At times, more administrative methods have also been employed: Governments faced with acute factional demands have tried to decentralize the bureaucratic apparatus and place certain allocational decisions in local hands. These methods, when effectively implemented, may buy time and set in motion factional realignments that maintain center stability. When they fail, military interventions may occur or secessionist movements form.

Factional conflicts have a distinctive rhythm and dynamic. They proceed in several waves of action and response, receding if demands are met or proceeding either to the overthrow of the incumbents and their replacement by competing factional leaders or by the intensification of strife. When they are prolonged and unresolved, they may embrace broader segments of the population and involve greater amounts of violence. Because they bind (albeit in conflict) different levels of social organization and heterogeneous groups, they play, not inconsequentially, an important role in consolidating national identities and norms.

The outcomes of factional disputes are, nevertheless, consistently skewed in favor of segments of the elite. For this reason, it is difficult to contain factionalism without major modifications. The skills required are subtle, the resources needed are great, and as factions also have external allies and backers, the techniques demanded are intricate. Moreover, even if individual leaders and governments succumb to their rivals, this form of conflict may endure as long as there is reason to believe that power may be regained by similar means. The displacement of one faction by another perpetuates this sort of competition and the patronage networks that prop them up. Factionalism may induce regime changes; it also delineates a pattern of political engagement over time. This kind of conflict may consequently foster protracted instability. It can, as has happened in certain countries, be controlled, although at great cost to state coffers. But if regime changes are frequent and living conditions decline, this kind of conflict can deteriorate into more severe, and violent, conflagrations.

■ COMMUNAL CONFLICTS

Communal and mass conflicts, in contrast to elite and factional disputes, call into question, in quite different ways, not only the legitimacy of specific regimes but also the essentials of state power. Communal conflicts challenge the state's territorial integrity, and mass confrontations protest the existing distribution of power. Communal demands, by far the more prevalent in postcolonial Africa, seek to forward the political expression of subnational identities. This goal can be achieved either through adequate representation (including the protection of minority rights), the granting of autonomy, or through secession, the creation of an independent political entity. Communal conflicts, therefore, pose a threat by a portion of the state to its territorial sovereignty.

Ostensibly, most African countries should be subject to communal disturbances, because, with the rare exceptions of Swaziland, Somalia, Lesotho, and some of the Maghreb countries (most notably Tunisia) all of them have internal subdivisions and do not qualify as nation-states. The fact that only a handful of serious secessionist movements have emerged on the continent, and that not one has been successful, is an important measure of the durability of colonial frontiers, if not of the independent political entities that came into being within their boundaries.

Nevertheless, several important communal confrontations have taken place: the Katanga secession in Congo (1960–1963); the Biafran secession from Nigeria (1967–1970); the Sudanese civil wars (1955 and 1962–1972); and the ongoing communal conflicts in Chad and Ethiopia.[12] In several places, serious ethnic tensions persist: Zaire, Zimbabwe, Angola, and Uganda. Unlike most African countries, which either encompass many small and disparate ethnic groups or contain a dominant configuration and many smaller agglomerations, the national structure in communally unstable cases has been characterized by the existence of several large, geographically distinct ethnoregional groups (Nigeria, Sudan, Zaire) or by a dominant group and an extremely cohesive, culturally distinct, and usually economically more advanced minority (Ethiopia, Uganda, Zimbabwe).

The basis for the organization of sectional demands and secessionist movements is the ethnic community located in a regional stronghold, usually at some distance from the capital. The definition of the group (the potential nation) rests on a combination of several criteria: a territorial base, history, language, religion, kinship, cultural norms, traditional institutions, colonial experience, race, economic circumstances, and/or colonial experience. The more these aspects of ethnicity overlap in any instance, the greater the likelihood of political organization along sectional lines.

The evolution of ethnic conflict also has a strong subjective component. The differential diffusion of economic change during the colonial period and the administrative divisions of the colonial state activated local identities and underlined the differences between major groups (Katanga in the Belgian Congo; the Yoruba, the Igbo, and the Hausa-Fulani in Nigeria; the Sara and the Toubou in Chad). Electoral competition during the transition to independence politicized these distinctions. Because democratic competition gives an undue advantage to numerically superior constellations, the underrepresentation of smaller, although frequently more educationally and economically advanced groups, exacerbated a feeling of inequality.[13]

The sense of exploitation, discrimination, and neglect (of the annexed Eritreans by the Ethiopians, of the Ndebele by the Shona, of the Ovimbundu by the Mbundu) intensified after independence, when factional leaders of rival groups in power pursued policies that were perceived as favoring other ethnic communities and their elites. Interethnic animosity grew, especially when religion and custom clearly distinguished between groups. As inimical or ostensibly inequitable decisions were implemented, ethnoregional leaders began to reassess the profitability of continued participation in the center. In all these cases, leaders first demanded greater representation; only when these demands were not met to their satisfaction did they proceed to conceive of autonomy or separate independence as a way of assuring their physical survival and development. As tensions escalated, ruling coalitions took specific actions that served to fuel the crystallization of a full-fledged secessionist movement. In Nigeria, the overthrow of the Johnson Aguiyi Ironsi regime, pogroms against Igbo in the north, and the discovery of oil in commercial quantities in the east provided the necessary catalysts. The departure of the Belgians from the Congo and the annexation of Eritrea in 1960 were triggering devices in these two countries. These formal actions were evidence of the fragility of the political center. Indeed, "only the extraordinary conjuncture of a virtual decomposition of the state really opens the way for successful separation."[14]

Demands for territory or for guarantees of group identity and survival are not easily negotiable. The call for ethnic autonomy is usually presented in zero-sum terms: The intentions of secessionists cannot but be viewed as irredeemably detrimental to those in power at the center. This is particularly noticeable in vertically stratified countries such as Rwanda, Burundi, and Zanzibar before their revolutions. It is also evident, however, in horizontally stratified countries (Nigeria, Ethiopia, Sudan) where cohesive social linkages did not develop and the claims of rulers to central political control clashed with the demands of strong ethnoregional leaders for autonomous power. Seen in this light, Biafra's, Eritrea's, and the southern Sudan's secessionist actions were not surprising. Recognizing the central state's general fragility and receiving what they considered to be inadequate responses to their claims for self-determination, these groups took matters into their own hands and resorted to violence. These acts, invariably, were justified in terms of a higher law of collective survival.

Communal conflicts in their secessionist form are broad in scale. Their organization has rested, first, on the careful preparation of the community, the mobilization of political support, and the methodical accumulation of resources through contributions in the countryside and appeals for outside assistance. In Katanga this meant the coalescence of popular support behind Moise Tshombe and the procurement of the financial backing of the Union Miniere du Haute Katanga (and perhaps sections of the Belgian government). In Biafra, C. Odumegwu Ojukwu and his peers capitalized on Igbo fears and aspirations, consolidating local opinion behind their movement. Goukouni Oueddei in northern Chad engaged in a mobilization effort based on appeals to kin and locale in the early 1970s, while simultaneously garnering Libyan backing for his undertaking. The early Eritrean stirrings involved discussions with Muslim countries as well as calls for the revival of Eritrean nationalism. In the southern Sudan, black African (often Christian) leaders sought the support of ethnic cohorts in Uganda and Ethiopia. At the outset, therefore, secessionist leaders utilized political strategies to build up their movements. They also publicized their demands and attempted to negotiate for their realization. When these techniques did not yield desired results, proclamations of independence were promulgated and violent strategies were brought into play.

Communal conflicts, at their zenith, are expressed in the form of civil war and direct military confrontations.[15] Secessionists created armed branches of their movements, usually led by former officers and soldiers in the national army. These militias recruited local conscripts, organized logistical support in the villages, and externalized their conflict by acquiring arms (and sometimes training and mercenaries) from abroad. They generally employed the tactics of guerrilla warfare, mixing attacks on government installations with limited skirmishes with government forces. Where the military confrontation was protracted, as has been the case in Eritrea, Chad, and the Sudan, tactics of people's war (based on the Chinese and Latin American examples) have also been utilized. Despite these measures, however, the military balance of power has rarely been in favor of the secessionist groups.

Consistently, the organization of communally based secessionist claims has evoked an immediate, and aggressive, military response on the part of governments. Nigeria, Zaire, Ethiopia, Sudan, Angola, and Chad expanded their armies and imported military hardware from abroad. For African leaders, resistance to secession was axiomatic: These demands threatened the basis of the postcolonial state system in Africa, they set a totally unacceptable precedent for communal claims in neighboring countries, and they constituted a direct challenge to leaders' authority. This official position has found widespread support in African capitals and, more significant, in the international community. Armed with superior might, therefore, governments set out to quell communal uprisings forcibly.

The outcome of these efforts has always resulted in the coercive reduction, if not the termination, of violent ethnic insurrections. The Katangan and Biafran independence movements were militarily defeated. The Oromo and Tigre uprisings in Ethiopia are being curbed. Sudan negotiated an accord with the Anya Nya in 1972 that lasted for over a decade. The Ethiopian-Eritrean, Chadian, and Angolan communal confrontations still persist, but with a lower level of intensity.

Two dynamic patterns of violent communal conflicts have consequently emerged. The first, evident in Nigeria and Congo, is one of escalation and military resolution. The second, one of protracted conflict, has a vacillating rhythm: Periods of political negotiation are followed by short violent spurts, which subside and then are revived at periodic intervals. The ongoing civil wars in Chad, Sudan, and Eritrea (all on the boundary between the Maghreb and the Sub-Sahara) fall into this latter category. The discrepancies between these two types may be attributed partly to the different ethnic structures prevailing in these countries (prolonged communal conflicts are usually conducted by disaffected minorities); partly to the continued involvement of competing external actors (usually both on the side of the government and of the rebels based in neighboring countries); and partly to the relative strength of the political center. In Nigeria and Zaire, military engagement served to fortify the state and augment its apparatus of control. In Ethiopia and Sudan, initial military successes temporarily had the same effect, but these gains were not cemented for other reasons. Chad is still in the process of center construction. Thus, the containment of continued communal violence has also depended on the measures introduced immediately after the end of the military phase of the conflict.

All governments in Africa have had to contend with the possibility of communal insurrection. They have, therefore, enacted policies to deal with ethnic strife.[16] Three main strategies have been devised and applied. The first is essentially structural: The reorganization of the federal system in Nigeria after the civil war and the granting of administrative autonomy to the southern Sudan in the 1970s are two cases in point. The second is normative: the introduction of national symbols, values, and cultural orientations through education, indoctrination, and language policies, in the hope of implanting national identities to supplant or coexist with ethnic ones (Tanzania provides a good example). The third technique has been political: the application of provisions for carefully balanced representation of all ethnic groups or, conversely, the replacement of ethnic with other (usually class) bases of representation.

The careful ethnic arithmetic practiced in Côte d'Ivoire is an instance of the first political method. The attempted redefinition of criteria for participation in Angola is an example of the latter political strategy. The MPLA, after its rise to power, expressed its "longstanding . . . disdain for racial and ethnic loyalties" by banning all organizations established on that basis.[17] This method of dealing with ethnic friction has not, however, been particularly successful. Ignoring ethnic divisions has not helped them disappear, as the Angolan government's ongoing battle with Jonas Savimbi's Ovimbundu-based UNITA so aptly demonstrates. Indeed, in recent years the MPLA regime has taken pains to insure a good degree of ethnic representation in their recruitment of members for Angola's Political Bureau. Social foundations of political action do not necessarily have to be ethnically conceived; it is doubtful, however, whether ethnic affinities can be achieved by government fiat.

Although the motivation behind these approaches to the containment of communal conflict may vary (in some countries the aim of integration policies is to displace existing ties through the amalgamation of a new set of identities; in some it is to assimilate smaller ethnic groups into the culture of the dominant constellation; in others it is to aggregate existing links in a pluralistic community), African leaders have exhibited a great deal of sensitivity in analyzing the roots of communal conflicts and an equal sophistication in designing policies to handle such disputes.

The record of African governments in the management of communal conflicts has been, on the whole, quite impressive. Violent insurrections have generally been firmly put down (with rare exceptions that may spill over international boundaries),[18] and communal confrontations have either been diverted through provisions for adequate representation or channeled into more familiar factional paths. The fact that the territorial integrity of the African state has not been assailed through successful separation does not mean that its viability has not been questioned in other ways. These challenges, however, have been of a different order.

■ MASS CONFLICTS

Political movements with the purpose of inducing a rapid, complete, and permanent alteration of the power structure have been a rarity in independent Africa. By definition, revolutionary conflicts of this sort pose a basic threat to the validity of state power as currently constituted and offer an alternative political vision guided by a clearly defined set of organizing principles. The continent has known only a single transformation of the social order, the Ethiopian revolution (which brought about the irreversible demise of the feudal structures that had existed in that country for centuries). Ethiopia was one of the few African states not subjected to colonial rule. The 1974 revolution, even though it has not yet achieved its proclaimed Marxist-Leninist objectives, nevertheless did achieve a fundamental shift in social structures and in the distribution of power in society. Africa has also witnessed two revolutionary experiments, in Mozambique and Angola. The stirrings of mass discontent, however, are evident in several places and deserve some, albeit abbreviated, attention.

The social basis of mass conflict of a revolutionary sort is the crystallization of class distinctions and class consciousness and, consequently, the creation of a class foundation for political action. In most independent African countries, politics intensified social differentiation and underscored inequalities, instead of generating political organization along class lines. The entrenchment of factional alliances acted as a brake to the emergence of such ties. Links between farmers and their local or national patrons have provided a substitute for class action in most instances. The slow emergence of an indigenous and independent middle class has also impeded class formation. Revolutionary ideologues, usually comfortably ensconced in capital cities, have not been able to capitalize on peasant or worker discontent, as in many parts of Latin America.[19] Where mass protest does occur, it is usually a result of the development of a gap between factional leaders as a group and their followers.

Radical political change has taken place in Africa only in the very specific circumstances of the decaying traditional monarchy of Ethiopia and the prolonged struggles for national liberation in lusophone countries, which may also be occurring in South Africa (see Chapter 13). In the first case, an oligarchic regime failed to maintain strong links with the rural areas, to furnish opportunities for urban intellectuals, to protect an apparatus of control even with the assistance of an external power, and to begin to confront the effects of the drought and subsequent widespread famine of the early 1970s. The strong sense of Ethiopian nationalism and the equally embedded tradition of central government, coupled with the absence of viable alternative social institutions to those of the state, combined to focus dissent on the imperial authority structure. In Ethiopia, the revolution was carried out from above. In the second set of examples, the lusophone countries, violent and protracted anticolonial wars provided opportunities for the forging of strong bonds between nationalist leaders and the population at the local level. Although such links were established in Zimbabwe and Guinea-Bissau as well as in Angola and Mozambique, only the latter two chose to follow a revolutionary course, and leaders there have been engaged in an ongoing battle to consolidate their authority (challenged by UNITA and RENAMO, respectively).

Despite the absence of revolutionary situations in most parts of Africa, some indications of mass (although not revolutionary) forms of conflict have surfaced, most notably in Ghana and Burkina Faso. Behind these appearances of mass-based political protest is the distinction between the establishment and the loosely defined "have-nots," those who did not benefit from existing patterns of distribution. As vertical patronage networks were weakened and their leaders discredited, some alliances were formed between the cities and the rural areas (a shadow, perhaps, of established factional coalitions), thereby creating urban-based movements with some claim to a nationwide constituency. The aim of mass conflicts in these settings was defined essentially in negative terms as the displacement of the dominant elites and the institution of direct popular supervision over public officials; no firm alternative political doctrine was proffered or elaborated.

The quasi-mass political movements in Ghana and Burkina Faso, although initially embracing large segments of the population, possessed only a rudimentary organization. They relied heavily on the emergence of a leader (usually in uniform) who would give voice to the movement's sentiments and act upon them. The tactics employed by groups organized along these lines have been purposefully confrontational: Not only in these two cases, but also in Nigeria, Kenya, Zambia, and Zaire in the 1980s, these movements have openly condemned regime policies and denounced the corruption and insensitivity of public officials. They have advocated noncompliance with official policies and engaged in illegal practices. They have not, however, been able to carry out the more violent strategies that they so vociferously espouse. Indeed, governments have generally responded to these outbursts by jailing movement leaders and by closing opportunities for the expression of such forms of dissent (in Kenya protest leaders have been jailed or exiled, in Nigeria they have been muzzled; in the Ghanaian case, Hilla Limann allowed Jerry Rawlings to state his opinions publicly, thus laying the foundation for his own subsequent ouster).

What these governments have been unable to accomplish—unless they could engineer a massive internal reform and bring about rapid improvements in living conditions—is the suppression of mass rumblings. Potentially, if not in actuality, mass conflicts contain the ingredients of intense, widespread, and particularly violent conflict. Thus, although the possibility of revolutionary change may be greater in the stronger states on the continent (Nigeria, Kenya, Côte d'Ivoire), where center consolidation has taken place and class distinctions have begun to appear as a consequence of factional disputes, implicit in the history of mass conflicts in Africa is the possibility of another, fifth and most recent, form of political confrontation.

■ POPULAR CONFLICTS

Popular political protest chips away at the foundations of state power from below, thereby undermining its viability without altering its form. It constitutes a quiet rebellion against state authority, a way of responding to exclusion and lack of access by limiting the reach of existing central institutions. Popular conflict of this kind emerges most emphatically in conditions where state structures are especially weak and leaders capricious, where patronage networks have broken down, where alternate avenues for power accumulation exist, and where economic conditions have wrought widespread misery.[20] Popular conflict has come to the surface in most parts of the continent in the third decade of independence.

Incidences of popular protest reflect a desire to minimize vulnerability to official interventions and to reduce exposure to the vicissitudes of government actions, regardless of regime type. They are expressions, on a micro level, of a quest by the officially disempowered for protection from uncertainty and economic hardship through some form of self-encapsulation. Popular protest is thus a series of attempts to assert autonomy in a multiplicity of locations and ways. It differs from all the previous forms of conflict in that it is not directly concerned with gaining access to the center (elite or factional disputes) or with changing the political center or altering its forms (communal and mass conflicts) but is concerned with creating a distance between the formal domain and individual citizens, local communities, and specific social groups.[21]

Popular modes of political confrontation have emerged in countries where certain social groups have been systematically excluded from the center and have been unable to partake in its benefits. The growing divergence between the life-styles of patrons and their clients created fissures in patronage structures and intensified the gnawing resentment that had been brewing within factional alliances. The exploitation felt by individuals and groups had come to outweigh the gains they gleaned from such associations.

The social basis of these activities, therefore, rests on formations not inextricably bound with the construction of the formal power structures. Ethnicity and class in Africa have been shaped and defined in important ways by the state, which has served as the primary arena for their articulation (as demonstrated not only in mass and communal conflicts but, most significantly, in factional cleavages).[22] Popular protest commences, then, with the disorganization of ethnicity and with class fragility.[23] The most obvious framework for such activities has been the rural collectivity. Territorially defined and physically removed from official power centers, local communities do control some resources and usually have evolved their own political institutions based on shared norms. Although they cannot exercise a full exit option, they carve out their own independent niches in certain spheres. In urban areas, local neighborhood groups have sometimes been able to fulfill similar roles.

In many countries, however, as evidence from the 1980s in Ghana,

Nigeria, Somalia, Zaire, Kenya, Angola, and Ethiopia corroborates, new bases of social organization have surfaced. Islamic networks throughout the western Sudan, trading alliances around domestic and transnational markets, craft guilds, women's associations at the interstices of local and state power, and mafia-type bands are all cases in point. In many respects, kin groups possess several crucial features of these new forms of affiliation: They are based on strong personal bonds, advocate clearly defined joint interests, revolve around shared symbolic schemes, and may have a broad geographic scope.[24] Whatever the precise social foundation of specific manifestations of popular resistance, popular conflict in general is characterized by a variety of activities conducted by separate, sometimes overlapping, small-scale groups and social agglomerations that maintain lateral ties with each other and that, although not cohering in any umbrellalike frameworks, do comprise time-spaces in the African social web.[25]

Popular acts of protest are thus defined emphatically by their lack of overarching organization, although they carry concrete meaning mostly for the particular individuals involved. They remain sporadic and informal but together yield a general pattern of disengagement.[26] Techniques of dissent vary: In economic terms, local microeconomies have been fortified and elaborated, self-help schemes initiated, new commercial ventures launched, artisan collectives formed, black markets expanded, and smuggling techniques refined. Job absenteeism, petty theft, industrial sabotage, embezzlements, work stoppages, and periodic strikes are some tactics used to whittle away at manufacturing capacity. The informal economy, in its many manifestations, has proliferated. On the cultural plane, "songs and anecdotes may be the principal channel of communication for people who are denied access to the official media."[27] Popular arts —music, film, dance, theater, street performances, market literature, underground presses, graphic art, sculpture, painting—are freed from the constraints of the official traditions of the state and indigenous political institutions. They act as cultural brokers of an informal sort. Religious revivals, antiwitchcraft movements, and messianic sects may serve as expressions of popular protest as well, as do migrations on a more individual level.

Popular strategies all contain a political dimension: Some are more distinctly political in fact. Antisocial political acts have spread in recent years; armed robbers, bandits, and thugs roam the highways of Nigeria and the streets of Lagos. Small acts of sabotage (cutting of phone wires to obtain copper) may wreak havoc in communication systems. Gangs threaten social order in the cities of Zaire and have taken over the rural areas in Uganda. Their activities are felt in many African countries. They have had the effect of undermining security, as have activities such as distributing anonymous political circulars and spontaneous rioting in the workplace and the countryside (in quite different ways). Most political acts of popular protest are more nuanced: engagement in constant and acrimonious political debates, cynicism, indifference to government dictates, regular noncompliance with laws, systematic tax evasion, avoidance of participation in elections and plebiscites, and increasingly, political withdrawal through the revitalization of traditional, or the creation of alternate, decision-making institutions and networks of adjudication.

Popular protest, then, is mostly about coping mechanisms. It is expressed not only through confrontation but also through quiet alienation and passivity. These seemingly disparate undertakings do tend to gravitate around the unofficial and the informal: They are clear indications of the prevalence of straddling (between state and society, between the formal economy and the unofficial market) in everyday life on the continent.[28]

African governments have found it difficult to control, let alone curtail, popular political protest measures, as these are disorganized and their eruption is usually unpredictable. Because actions undermine the existing political fabric by limiting its reach, even promises of better economic management and large-scale political reforms have only gone a short way toward reducing the threat to central authority inherent in this form of conflict. Unlike factional demands, it is difficult to appease popular complaints by buying off local leaders and thereby mitigating calls for greater accountability. Unable to govern exclusively through coercion precisely because of the weaknesses that engendered this kind of protest, some governments have consciously reconciled themselves to their reduced circumstances, divesting themselves of responsibility in critical spheres or regions of the country (the policies of Ghana and Guinea in the mid-1980s pointed in this direction). Others have combined such approaches with the intensification of repression and officially sanctioned violence (Uganda, Nigeria, Zaire). Ironically, in many cases, localized rebellions, at root an attempt to escape the vise of state brutality, have in actuality invited its institutionalization.

In the short term, therefore, popular protest has underscored disintegrative and autocratic trends in many African political environments. But its deeper political meaning may lie elsewhere. When taken together, acts of popular confrontation may reveal the outlines of a hidden deep politics in situations where official political organization is not endowed with a vision based on an integrative set of values other than a commitment to domination. Implicit in many of the strategies adopted in this mode of conflict are "customary notions of political obligation such as trusteeship, probity and public accountability in the public institutions of the state."[29] Thus, some essential tenets have been formulated; they cohere around a notion of a civic public. What they lack at this juncture is a more precise institutional expression, a concrete formula for power-sharing. Whether this will take the shape of a rehabilitation of existing authoritarian state structures or require a broader process of democratization is unclear. In the meantime, popular types of political expression highlight civil unrest and magnify the predicament of governance on the continent.

■ THE INTERPLAY OF POLITICAL CONFLICTS

The five main kinds of political conflict in independent Africa reflect an absence of consensus on questions of policy, participation, representation, equality, justice, and accountability. In distinct ways, they have challenged either the decisions or composition of the particular regimes or the integrity, validity, or viability of state authority. None of these categories is mutually exclusive: Different forms of conflict appear in different combinations in Sub-Saharan Africa. Each African country and each regime type has invited its own structure of political conflict.

If issues of elite competition or communal strife preoccupied leaders at the outset of independence, in the third decade leaders have been forced to confront the consequences of their rule. The role and position of patrons provide a fairly accurate guide to the nature of conflict in any given setting. A cohesive set of patrons points to elite conflict; divided leadership indicates factionalism; strong local patrons excluded from state power circles suggest communal conflict; the breakdown of communication in clientelistic networks may yield mass conflict when control of state resources is desired and appears feasible. When it is not, popular protest might ensue under similar circumstances.

Political instability and civilian insurrection have been the order of the day in quite a few African countries. Although no single political entity has collapsed entirely, neither has any one country totally escaped periods of militant or subversive strife. "At a minimum we have seen that the threat of anarchy is unfounded."[30] Political cohesion has been equally elusive. Violence, however, need not be politically dysfunctional, just as fundamental political change does not have to be contingent on an organized opposition.[31] Out of some of these confrontations new types of coalitions are forming and new rules for the management of conflict may be emerging. In due course these might yet compel the formulation of some principles of power-sharing and their translation into more workable political practices. The ways in which such changes have been carried out and what patterns they may yield is the subject of the final chapter in this section on political processes.

■ NOTES

1. John Lonsdale, "Political Accountability in African History", in Patrick Chabal, ed., *Political Domination in Africa: Reflections on the Limits of Power* (London: Cambridge University Press, 1986), p. 130.

2. A much more straightforward view is suggested by Robert H. Jackson and Carl. G. Rosberg, "Popular Legitimacy in African Multi-Ethnic States," *Journal of Modern African Studies* 22, no. 2 (1984): 177–198.

3. This classification expands substantially on a scheme originally presented in Donald G. Morrison and Hugh Michael Stevenson, "Integration and Instability: Patterns

of African Political Development," *American Political Science Review* 76, no. 2 (1972): 902–927.

4. Alhaji Babatunde Joseph, "Press Freedom in Africa," *African Affairs* 74, no. 296 (1975): 255–262.

5. Many works recognize the significance of factional conflicts but do not analyze them in detail. For one notable exception, see Jonathan S. Barker, "Political Factionalism in Senegal," *Canadian Journal of African Studies* 7, no. 2 (1975): 287–315.

6. Karl W. Deutsch, "Social Mobilization and Political Development," *American Political Science Review* 55, no. 3 (September 1961): 493–514; Robert Melson and Howard Wolpe, "Modernization and the Politics of Communalism," *American Political Science Review* 64, no. 4 (December 1970): 1114–1117; and James R. Scarritt and William Safran, "The Relationship of Ethnicity to Modernization and Democracy," *International Studies Notes* 10, no. 2 (Summer 1983): 17.

7. Quoted in Donald Rothchild, "Rural-Urban Inequities and Resource Allocations in Zambia," *Journal of Commonwealth Political Studies* 10, no. 3 (1972): 233.

8. Robert H. Bates, "Ethnic Competition and Modernization in Contemporary Africa," *Comparative Political Studies* 6, no. 4 (1974): 457–484. Also see Nelson Kasfir, "Explaining Ethnic Political Participation," *World Politics* 31, 3 (1979): 365–388.

9. For an excellent discussion of elections in Africa, see Fred M. Hayward, ed., *Elections in Independent Africa* (Boulder, Colo.: Westview Press, 1986).

10. Donald Rothchild, "Middle Africa: Hegemonial Exchange and Resource Allocation," in Alexander J. Groth and Larry L. Wade, eds., *Comparative Resource Allocation* (Beverly Hills, Calif.: Sage Publications, 1984), pp. 172–175.

11. Donald Rothchild, "Comparative Public Demand and Expectation Patterns: The Ghana Experience," *African Studies Review* 22, no. 1 (1979): 127–149. Also see Donald Rothchild and Victor Olorunsola, "Managing Competing State and Ethnic Claims," in Donald Rothchild and Victor Olorunsola, eds., *State Versus Ethnic Claims: African Policy Dilemmas* (Boulder, Colo.: Westview, 1983), pp. 1–25.

12. Not included are irredentist schemes, which spill across boundaries. For a superb analysis of these ethnic conflicts, see Benyamin Neuberger, *National Self-Determination in Postcolonial Africa* (Boulder, Colo.: Lynne Rienner Publishers, 1986).

13. Crawford Young, *The Politics of Cultural Pluralism* (New Haven: Yale University Press, 1978).

14. Crawford Young, "Comparative Claims to Political Sovereignty: Biafra, Katanga and Eritrea," in Rothchild and Olorunsola, *State Versus Ethnic Claims,* pp. 199–232.

15. Samuel Decalo, "Chad: The Roots of Centre-Periphery Strife," *African Affairs* 79, no. 317 (1980): 491–509; Samuel Decalo, "Regionalism, Political Decay and Civil Strife in Chad," *Journal of Modern African Studies* 18, no. 1 (1980): 23–56.

16. Donald Rothchild, "Inter-Ethnic Conflict and Policy Analysis in Africa," *Ethnic and Racial Studies* 9, no. 1 (1986): 66–86; Henry Bienen, "The State and Ethnicity: Integrative Formulas in Africa," in Rothchild and Olorunsola, *State Versus Ethnic Claims,* pp. 100–124; and David R. Smock and Kwamena Bentsi-Enchill, eds., *The Search for National Integration in Africa* (New York: Free Press, 1975).

17. John A. Marcum, "Angola: A Quarter Century of War," *CSIS Africa Notes,* no. 37 (21 December 1984), p. 3.

18. John Ravenhill, "Redrawing the Map of Africa," in Donald Rothchild and Naomi Chazan, eds., *The Precarious Balance: State and Society in Africa* (Boulder, Colo.: Westview Press, 1988).

19. Much of the following discussion is based on Christopher Clapham, *Third World Politics: An Introduction* (Madison: University of Wisconsin Press, 1985), pp. 160–168.

20. Jean-François Bayart, "Civil Society in Africa," in Chabal, *Political Domination in Africa,* pp. 114–115.

21. This type of conflict is not limited to Africa. See D. L. Steth, "Grassroots Stirrings and the Future of Politics," *Alternatives* 9 (1983): 1–24.

22. Crawford Young, "Patterns of Social Conflict: State, Class, and Ethnicity," *Daedalus* 111, no. 2 (1982): 71–99. This sentence is a paraphrase of p. 72.

23. Nelson Kasfir, "Class, Political Domination and the African State," in Zaki Ergas, ed., *The African State in Transition* (London: Macmillan, 1987).

24. This notion was suggested by Sara Berry in a series of discussions: Thanks are due to her for her assistance in clarifying this matter.

25. Bayart, "Civil Society in Africa," p. 118.

26. This analysis is based on Naomi Chazan, "Patterns of State-Society Incorporation and Disengagement," in Rothchild and Chazan, *The Precarious Balance,* and on Victor Azarya and Naomi Chazan, "Disengagement from the State in Africa: Reflections on the Experience of Ghana and Guinea," *Comparative Studies in Society and History* 19, no. 1 (1987). For a more general discussion, see Albert O. Hirschman, *Exit, Voice and Loyalty* (London: Oxford University Press, 1970), pp. 106–131.

27. Karin Barber, "The Popular Arts in Africa," (ACLS/SSRC Paper presented at the Twenty-ninth Annual Meeting of the African Studies Association in Madison, Wisconsin, 29 October–2 November 1986), p. 6. This is a superb discussion of politics and popular arts in Africa.

28. See Irving Leonard Markovitz, ed., *Studies in Power and Class in Africa* (London: Oxford University Press, 1987), esp. pp. 27–66. Also see Sara Berry, *Fathers Work for Their Sons: Accumulation, Mobility and Class Formation in an Extended Yoruba Community* (Berkeley: University of California Press, 1985).

29. Maxwell Owusu, "Custom and Coups: A Juridical Interpretation of Civil Order and Disorder in Ghana," *Journal of Modern African Studies* 24, no. 1 (1986): 72.

30. Irving Leonard Markovitz, *Power and Class in Africa* (Englewood Cliffs, N.J.: Prentice Hall, 1977), p. 346.

31. Roger Charlton and Roy May, "The State of Africa: Evaluating Contemporary Challenges to Authority and Legitimacy" (Paper presented at the African Studies Association of the United Kingdom and the Centre of Commonwealth Studies Symposium on Legitimacy and Authority in Africa, University of Stirling, 23 May 1986). Also see, for one example, Thomas M. Callaghy, "State-Subject Communication in Zaire: Domination and the Concept of Domain Consensus, *Journal of Modern African Studies* 18, no. 3 (1980): 469–492.

 8

Political Transitions and Patterns of Change

The political history of Africa since independence, so diverse in its details, has been marked not only by the establishment of identifiable norms and procedures but also by its fluidity and movement. No one set of rules, practices, or processes has remained unaltered—as the concept of politics infers—by the dynamic of state action and social response. The question of political change is therefore central to understanding the course of political processes over time. Political transitions have been set in motion either from within, through the initiative of incumbents themselves, or by individuals and groups outside the circle of officeholders, frequently employing violent political means. Each of these methods has involved some dislocation: Whether they have also brought about more significant changes in the organization of the public arena or in its practices is still open to question.

In this chapter, we examine how political changes have taken place and what effects these shifts have had on the course of contemporary African politics. At issue are the nature of representation and participation and the mechanisms of political accountability. The study of regime dynamics makes it possible to analyze emerging patterns of state-society interactions and to determine their significance for policy formulation and effective implementation.

Although preemptive actions by civilian leaders and military coups continue to determine the manner in which formal transitions take place, the impetus for change as well as its direction are an outgrowth of the many interactions between governments and social groups, between rulers and citizens. Periodic reevaluations, negotiations, and confrontations have yielded different formulae for political conduct. The nature of political processes has had a direct impact on the extent of state-society exchanges and, therefore, on the capacity of formal institutions to carry out their programs. As political relations have solidified and more Africanized patterns have begun to emerge, attention has shifted from the outward forms of governments to a greater preoccupation with defining governments' underlying norms and creating structures to monitor their behavior.

■ MODES OF POLITICAL CHANGE

□ Managed Political Transitions

Some of the shifting currents of politics in Africa may be attributed to measures introduced by those in power. Three main methods of supervised transition, excluding decolonization, have been in constant use over the years: reform, succession, and change through elections. The purpose of *reform* by fiat is to alter the procedures or the practices of the political center. Most changes of this sort have been of a substantive order: the launching of a new economic program, expanding external alliances, drawing up or modifying an official ideology, designing new techniques of social control or clamping down on dissent. These decisions are made by the head of state or select advisors, frequently under pressure from international financial agencies and donor institutions, and may require different allocations of resources or even institutional adjustments on a broad scale. In almost all instances, such shifts herald a self-imposed policy reorientation.

Policy reform may stand alone or come together with changes in personnel. Reshuffles and purges may be used to apportion blame for failure, justify a change in policy direction, eradicate corruption, improve efficiency, or, as is most common, assure continued control over key operations. When major policy changes are instituted, as in accordance with World Bank and IMF proposals, these generally involve more massive changes in the size of the public sector and in its capabilities.

Guided shifts of this kind have been most significant when they have involved a restructuring of government agencies. The decision to create new states in Nigeria or to decentralize decision making in Ghana are two examples of important modifications in the frameworks of political action. The reorganization of political institutions has been of particular significance. The transition to a one-party system was usually implemented on the initiative of the leaders of the day, as has the process of civilianization of military coalitions in Togo, Mali, Niger, and Zaire. Indeed, in retrospect, many changes in the delineation of political centers or in the structures of political interchange have been the result of executive command. The meaning of these moves lies, therefore, in their implications for the conduct of the political center. They do not influence the composition of its leadership and, therefore, even when progressive in orientation and design, tend to entrench the positions of its ruling elite.

Succession and inheritance, in contrast, are mechanisms for bringing

about a change in the top leadership without also causing a subsequent alteration in regime.[1] Inheritance entails the designation of an heir apparent (usually
by the president himself) and the formalization of this choice through proclamation or appropriate constitutional amendment. Provisions of this sort have been
made in almost every African capital, although they are of particular interest in
countries where the founding father is still in office: Kenneth Kaunda in Zambia, Felix Houphouët-Boigny in Côte d'Ivoire, Hastings Banda in Malawi,
Habib Bourguiba in Tunisia. Such provisions assured continuity after the death
of William Tubman in Liberia, Lebua Jonathan in Botswana, Houari
Boumedienne in Algeria, Abdel Nasser in Egypt, Jomo Kenyatta in Kenya,
Agostino Neto in Angola, and Samora Machel in Mozambique (they faltered
after the passing away of Sekou Touré in Guinea). Succession involves not only
the appointment of a new head of state but also the voluntary abdication of the
incumbent. Peaceful succession took place in Senegal, Tanzania, Cameroon,
and Sierra Leone in the first part of the 1980s. Despite ongoing strains between
ex-leaders and present incumbents, the importance of such transitions through
succession cannot be exaggerated: What has been shattered is the axiom prevalent during the first two decades of independence that no rotation of civilian
leaders could occur without a concomitant regime change.

Managed political change has also been launched through the ballot box.
Myths aside, *elections* in most parts of the continent have been neither infrequent nor totally manipulated. Five main types of postcolonial elections may
be identified.[2] The first are symbolic elections—mostly the hallmark of rigid
one-party governments—in which a single slate of candidates for parliament
and the presidency is presented to the voters and receives a near unanimous (engineered) mandate. In symbolic elections no significant change of any sort
transpires. The second kind of elections permits competition for office within a
single-party system. Kenya and Tanzania pioneered this form of elections,
which has since been adopted in Mali, Côte d'Ivoire, Zambia, and Cameroon.[3]
In this way, it has been possible to allow for some monitoring of politicians (indeed, frequently cabinet members have not secured reelection and the composition of national assemblies has been altered) and to tie parliamentarians to local
constituencies. A third form of elections, held regularly in the pluralist regimes
of Gambia, Botswana, Mauritius, and Senegal throughout the 1970s and 1980s,
entertains limited multiparty competition. In these countries, the scope of political debate has been expanded, although with the sole exception of Mauritius
the position of the dominant party has not been called into question. These three
electoral modes are essentially minimalist: They allow for some political activity but do not constitute a means of altering either the top leadership, the administration, or the regime.

The last two types of elections are maximalist in thrust. Plebescites seek
popular approval for constitutional changes or proposed adjustments in the organization of the political center. In Ghana, the 1960 plebescite on the republi-
can constitution and the Union government referendum are two examples of the

widespread practice of seeking to bring about a regime change without a shift in the composition of the government. A fifth kind of elections, however, has provided a mechanism for the simultaneous turnover of both leaders and regimes. These elections (held primarily in administrative regimes) are a concomitant of a military withdrawal from the political arena. The 1978 elections in Upper Volta and the 1979 elections in Ghana and Nigeria are cases in point.[4] The pattern of these elections is fairly clear. Following the drafting of a new civilian constitution and its approval by a constituent assembly, the ban on party politics is lifted, and open elections are held. The military then hands over the reins of government and returns (if only temporarily) to the barracks. The newly installed leaders, at the head of pluralist and often factionalized systems, usually pursue many of the policies of their military predecessors. Although decision-making procedures, modes of operation, and practices may change dramatically after transfer elections, such elections have proven to be a critical instrument for the maintenance of the continuity of ruling elites.

Elections in Africa have offered greater scope for political change than other modes of supervised transition. Although some have merely endorsed decisions already made in policymaking circles, most elections have been a mechanism for some political movement. They differ from other managed transition measures in that they institutionalize means of supervising change and shift part of the responsibility of determining future directions from the top leadership to the electorate. In no case have they implied, to date, a fundamental alteration in the organization or distribution of power in society.

Supervised methods of political change, including elections, all insert a dynamism into the public domain without undermining the continuity of the political order. The joint thread underlying these techniques is the preservation of the position of already dominant groups in the society. Nevertheless, transitions initiated from above, especially when institutionalized through regularized procedures, have proven to be an important tool for the self-regulation of the political center (even under duress) and for compelling periodic reevaluations. Indeed, these guided mechanisms, where firmly in place, have nurtured a climate of predictability vital to the constructive formulation and realization of tangible goals.

☐ Forced Political Transitions

Political changes in Africa have come as often in a violent as in a peaceful wrapping. The *military coup d'état* has been the most prevalent way of inducing change against the will of those in office. The incidence of coup attempts and successful military takeovers in Africa is exceedingly high: Virtually every country on the continent has experienced at least one threat of a military intervention; over half the states in Africa were governed by soldiers in 1987.

The recurrence of military coups highlights the pervasiveness of generalized conditions for armed incursions into the political realm. Theories on the underlying causes of military intervention, however, differ in the relative weight they have placed on environmental, external, organizational, idiosyncratic, and systemic factors.[5] Although this is not the place to delve into the vast literature on the subject, the militarization of politics in Africa may be explained by reference to a configuration of several variables. First, economic stagnation, and especially rapid decreases in standards of living, foster political uncertainty and intensify demands for change.[6] Second, military takeovers are, therefore, frequently tied to the loss of political legitimacy of the incumbent government, to the shrinkage of its ruling coalition. In these circumstances, there are few popular constraints to prevent armed intervention. Third, military coups are integrally linked to low levels of institutionalization and relatively high levels of factional competition.[7] Direct military action is probable under these conditions. Fourth, access to most African regimes (and the rewards they offer) is circumscribed. Military intervention is one way of allowing factions excluded from the governing alliance to gain control of the state and its resources. Fifth, then, there must be some military predisposition to articulate its corporate interest and to act on these perceptions.[8] Sixth, personal ambitions of individual soldiers also play a role. Many studies seeking to uncover why a specific coup took place fall back on idiosyncratic explications.[9] Seventh, precedents do matter: Successful coups in neighboring countries may spur a rash of attempted takeovers. Over time, therefore, African armies have been integrated into the political arena.[10] Thus, in many respects, military coups are an outgrowth of and contribute to the ineffectiveness, inefficiency, and, most significant, the fragility of the power apparatus in many African countries.

It is, perhaps, as important to point to reasons why coups have not taken place as to analyze the elements conducive to their occurrence. Malawi, Zambia, Tanzania, Kenya, Angola, Mozambique, Zimbabwe, Gabon, Côte d'Ivoire, Cameroon, Botswana, Swaziland, Senegal, Tunisia, and Morocco have not experienced successful military takeovers in the first three decades of African independence. In some of these countries external military support was instrumental in putting down attempted coups (Kenya, Gabon, Gambia); the location of foreign military bases in these countries has served as an ongoing deterrent. Some countries simply did not establish an army at independence (although in the Gambia the tiny National Guard almost took over). In a few places the lack of a military takeover may be attributable to sheer luck. Usually, however, the skillful management of civil-military relations and the gradual legitimation of civilian institutions provide the key for the successful deflection of military takeovers.[11] Political skill, in the sense of astute responsiveness to demands and the initiation of reforms, plays an important role. Indeed, the subordination of the military to civilian institutions through the use of a variety of techniques, such as indigenization, reorganization, professionalization, adequate finance, and appropriate training, has gone a long way toward averting coups. When these measures have been accompanied by the implantation of acceptable methods for changes in government within existing regimes, takeovers have perhaps been attempted but have rarely succeeded.

The proliferation of coups in Africa does not, however, imply that all military takeovers have been similar or that the immediate motivations underlying them have always been identical.[12] The history of military interventions reveals important shifts in the objectives of soldiers turned politicians and in the types of political changes their actions have generated. Initial uprisings in the armed forces, dating back to the 1963 mutinies in Kenya, Tanzania, and Uganda, were spurred by internal military concerns: low salaries, slow rates of Africanization in the officer corps, poor service conditions. Though primarily in the mode of a trade union dispute, these first stirrings were a precursor of broader army political action.

The early 1960s also furnished evidence of a more abrupt type of transition brought about by violent means: *political assassination*. The murder of Togo's Sylvanus Olympio in 1963 was the first instance of such an occurrence; the death of Colonel E. K. Kotoka in Ghana in 1967, and of Murtala Mohammed in Nigeria in 1976 at the hands of army officers are other examples of this phenomenon. In these cases, the effective head of state or a key political personality was eliminated; his regime (as in cases of civilian succession) endured.

By the end of the 1960s, quite a few civilian regimes had been ousted by the armed forces in full-scale military takeovers. The common purpose of all these interventions was to depose ruling coalitions and their leaders and to establish other dominant alliances in their stead. First coups, therefore, in the 1980s as well as in the preceeding decades, have always signaled a regime change, in the sense that the principles, rules, and behavioral patterns of incoming rulers differed from those of their predecessors. Other than that, however, initial coups did not indicate a shift in political orientations or in decision-making procedures or practices in any one common direction. The only certainty was that the new leaders would adopt approaches that differed from those of their discredited precursors. The Ghanaian and Nigerian coups of 1966 and the Mobutu takeover in Zaire in 1965 provided ample substantiation for the observation that the meaning of initial military interventions (and many subsequent ones as well) lay mostly in the circulation of ruling elites.

Frequently, countercoups (the Gowon intervention in Nigeria in 1966, a series of military takeovers in Dahomey—now Benin—in the 1960s) revealed deep divisions within the military hierarchy. Although first coups were carried out either by senior, middle-level, or junior officers (in some cases by noncommissioned officers, such as Samuel Doe in Liberia), countercoups have almost always been initiated by soldiers of a rank lower than the initial military incumbents.

By the end of the 1970s, repeated military interventions in some countries (Benin, Ghana, Nigeria, Uganda) exposed a more complex pattern of military-induced political change. First, the *putsch* technique had come into use: the impeachment of the ruling military leader to protect the interests of the military clique in power. The forced abdication of Acheampong in Ghana and of Gowon and later Mohammed Buhari in Nigeria highlighted a growing tendency of senior military officers to preempt more radical change by regulating what they perceived to be unacceptable behavior by incumbents. The putsch, therefore, has become a method for bringing about a change in leadership without a change in government. Second, some coups had become instruments of political reform, as in the populist-inspired interventions of Jerry Rawlings and Thomas Sankara. In these cases, fragments of the military, usually led by young officers joined by rank-and-file soldiers, have challenged not only the previous ruling coalition but also, more fundamentally, the hegemony of dominant elites in general.[13] The possible degree of change wrought by such coups has been more extensive than in any managed modes of political transition.

This trend, third, has been particularly apparent in the handful of instances where military leaders sought, through recurrent coups or internal reordering within the army, to lay the foundation for a more comprehensive redistribution of power in the society. The emergence of Mengistu in Ethiopia, or second or third coups in Congo, Madagascar, and Benin, points to the fact that the possibility of revolutionary change in postcolonial situations, however rare, has usually been set in motion by military men. Fourth, at least in two cases—the ouster of Idi Amin in Uganda and of Jean-Bedel Bokassa in the Central African Republic—a countercoup has involved the direct intervention of external forces. In these instances, the political center was weakened and social order could not easily be maintained. Finally, in 1986, Yoweri Museveni, at the head of an armed movement, defeated the military in power in Uganda. This latest Ugandan takeover is an example of a privately organized army assuming control of the center.

The political implications of the involvement of the military in African politics have, therefore, appeared to diverge over the years. Although, in general, transition by coercion has implied little more than the rotation of factions in the political center, during the past decade the coup has been a tool, on the one hand, to obviate any political change or, on the other hand, to set the stage for a more basic political transformation. These latter patterns are especially significant as, with the sole exception of Guinea, no first military takeover has occurred since 1980. These variations may be more a reflection of the diversification of political and social conditions on the continent in the 1980s than of drastic changes in the impact of military interventions on political change. "As society changes, so does the role of the military. In the world of the oligarchy, the soldier is a radical; in the middle-class world he is a participant and arbiter; as the mass society looms on the horizon, he becomes the conservative guardian of the existing order."[14]

Military regimes, once in power, have generally not diverged markedly from their civilian counterparts. Some have been more efficient, others more corrupt; in some countries their rulers have been technocrats, in others they have developed into tyrants; some have constructed viable social alliances, others have failed.[15] Any attempt to go beyond the specific case in drawing conclusions on the performance of soldiers as governors would be missing the central point that in the vast majority of African countries, the means by which formal power has been achieved, whether violent or not, are less significant than how that power has been used and for what ends. Thus, although later military interventions may have opened the door for widening the opportunities for political participation, it is the conduct of the new regime and its leadership that, ultimately, has been the key to such political transformations.

This is especially true of military governments, as they confront, more directly than civilian regimes, continuous problems of legitimation. Within a few years of their rise to power, they face a choice between attempting to routinize their rule or handing over power to civilians.[16] Military governments are consequently inherently transitory: If they do not reform themselves, they will be replaced. Many leaders have opted for undergoing a process of civilianization: The general becomes a president, a party is formed, symbolic elections are held (Zaire, Togo, Mali). In the late 1970s and early 1980s more subtle techniques have been employed. Acheampong in Ghana suggested a representative no-party Union government with ongoing military involvement as a way of staying in power. The merits of a military-civilian dyarchy have been debated in Nigeria since the beginning of the 1980s. The most stable governments actually retaining a military label in Africa—and several have consolidated their positions in the past decade—have coopted civilians into decision-making circles or engaged in mass mobilization (Ghana, Benin, Congo). In some cases, the military has disengaged from politics, usually to return within several years either because the successor civilian government duplicates problems of previous administrations or because civil-military relations in such circumstances are severely strained.[17] In many instances, therefore, one military regime is replaced with another, and, unless halted, a cycle of unplanned and unstable transition ensues.

The military has not proven to be essential to the conduct of politics in Africa, even though it has gradually become an integral part of that process. Military engagements in political affairs have led to political fluctuation, although not necessarily to political movement. In some cases, military coups have been the only way to depose oppressive regimes; these acts have not, however, provided any guarantee that the incoming military leaders would behave any differently (Uganda in the late 1970s and early 1980s). All Africa's tyrants have been military men; so have some of its more enlightened rulers. The African experience with the military coup as a mechanism of political change has been, at best, equivocal; the fascination with military politics has all too often diverted analyses away from the careful scrutiny of political process and obfuscated the centrality of other instruments of transition and change.

Violence, nevertheless, in potential if not in actual fact, may be a central catalyst for political transformation. Countries that have undergone civil wars have frequently emerged from these confrontations not only intact but also with well-defined political centers. The possibility of revolutionary change, which inevitably involves violence, cannot be summarily dismissed, as the situation in South Africa so forcefully demonstrates. Localized rebellions and disturbances may be transforming African politics from below. Even if external powers impose change from outside, this may involve some recourse to force. In the meantime, however, violent transitions have generally constituted more of a manifestation of chronic political uncertainty than an instrument for its elimination. Like their nonviolent counterparts, they may be conceived of as different attempts by those in the political center to alter aspects of its operations.

☐ The Course of Postcolonial Political Change

How political transitions have been effected in Africa in the past provides only a crude guide to the degree and direction of political change on the continent. Managed political transitions do not generally offer opportunities for the radical redefinition of the political process; violent mechanisms may slightly enlarge the options in this regard, but usually prevent the regularization of political practices and foster a climate of unpredictability. What these methods do not reflect is the possibility of the existence of other sources of transformation outside the dominant power constellation. It is not inconceivable that as the state cannot change itself, society, through its interaction with government agencies over time, might impose its wishes on the state. For the most part, therefore, these formal mechanisms reveal the forms in which change will take place. Supervised modes are usually evolutionary and continuous; violent ones may be disruptive and disjointed. Political processes have shifted, however, largely as a result of varying patterns of interchange set in motion by global economic trends, material circumstances, and the exercise of choice by actors of all levels of social organization.

■ PATTERNS OF POLITICAL INTERACTION

The political experiences of African countries since independence have yielded differing modes of interchange between specific regimes and their local constituencies. The frequency and the nature of these relationships are reflective not only of the relative success or failure of governmental efforts to penetrate the dense social matrix in their countries; they also mirror the willingness of individuals and groups to collaborate with official agencies and to involve themselves in their activities. The resilience of indigenous social institutions and practices has meant that the effectiveness of official designs has been filtered through local interests, needs, values, and concerns. The exercise of political power has, therefore, been a function both of the resources, capacities, objectives, techniques, and political conduct of ruling elites and of the vulnerability, organization, and priorities of specific communities.[18]

Forms of political interaction have varied substantially in different countries since independence. In some instances, center domination has been achieved; in others, increasingly larger portions of the population have sought to detach themselves from the reach of government agents. In most instances, however, intricate combinations of autonomy and reciprocity have prevailed. South Africa, Rhodesia until the independence of Zimbabwe, and Burundi during the 1960s lie at one extreme on this continuum. In these countries the regime is particularly repressive and has few structural linkages with the bulk of the population. Local communities have few autonomous resources at their disposal and are extremely vulnerable to outside interferences. The other extreme on the continuum is best illustrated by the recurrent cases of Chad and Uganda during the 1970s and early 1980s. In these countries the political center, for much of the postcolonial period, could barely muster control of the capital city. Local communities devised ways of disengaging from the center and its vagaries: They mobilized their own resources, established autonomous systems of justice, sought protection behind warlords, and reduced their exposure (although not always their vulnerability) to the center. Political life was unpredictable and haphazard.

In between these two extremes, various dynamic patterns of political interaction have emerged, including those of individual domination, (as in Liberia and Equatorial Guinea), state-society confrontation (the mark of many Afro-Marxist countries), and subtle forms of vertical interchange (Malawi, Algeria, Côte d'Ivoire, Cameroon, and Gabon).[19] In Nigeria, Kenya, and Zambia, competition, often of an unproductive sort, has intruded.[20] On the other hand, Senegal and Botswana have permitted relatively participatory patterns to evolve, and reciprocity (albeit unequal) is in evidence.[21] Ghana and Sierra Leone exhibit intermittent rhythms of state-society transactions, whereas in Tanzania local communities have been able to detach themselves from the formal arena.[22]

As the 1980s draw to a close it has become clear that certain countries, as presently constituted, could hardly expect more than continued unrest, decline, or stagnation. In others, the severity of the crisis of the early part of the decade evoked certain adjustments: more responsible financial management, cutbacks in the public sector, a relaxation of repression, decentralization. Most significant, the realization that the monopolization of official power by authoritarian means had limited its uses and hence that political problems required political solutions had been grimly drawn to the attention of many of the continent's leaders. Through a process of forced reckoning, introspection, and consultation, some have not only assumed fuller responsibility for their predicament but have also begun to seek ways to break away from the deleterious consequences of authoritarian rule.

The quest for a stable and more effective form of government has elicited a growing distaste for military interventions and a search, even in centers led by soldiers, for the establishment or institutionalization of political procedures and practices based not on patrimonial principles but on some constitutional notions of power-sharing and reciprocity between rulers and ruled. Although these efforts have generally not yet yielded concrete results, they do indicate a willingness to raise questions that had heretofore been considered to be taboo and, more important, to go beyond the formal domain to find some answers. Intrinsic to these processes is an understanding that if the political center is to be consolidated, the method for its entrenchment may have to commence with the creation of organized mechanisms of interchange between it and its social environments, especially in light of shifts in social organization and in the direction of social and economic transactions. Such a process involves the localization of political change—in all probability, an even greater diversity in political practices and dynamics. In some, although surely not all, countries these increasingly verbalized reflections may signify the end of the beginning phase of African political processes. Whatever their outcome, the scope of choice has been expanded and with it the range of change mechanisms and the possible directions of political transformation.[23]

The outlines of African political dynamics—despite their vagaries and marked fluctuations—have coalesced substantially during the few short years since independence. Political centers have established themselves and devised means to extend their reach, not always resourcefully, to the countryside. Although dependence on government has become inescapable, lateral transactions among formerly separate individuals and groups have increased and been given expression through new social networks pressing for a modicum of reciprocity in the conduct of political life. These demands are not the preserve of any one ideal regime type; they do, however, require the normalization of effective, and stable, checks on power. Indeed, workable government structures buttressed by norms of regime conduct may be a precondition for fortifying state capacities. The political challenge, therefore, in the years ahead, focuses squarely on the delineation of firm criteria for accountability and the construction of structures to guarantee their enforcement.[24]

Good government is inextricably tied to economic prospects. Probity curbs the dissipation of resources; obligations and responsibilities may engender greater efficiency. Stability is surely a precondition for development. Economic policies cannot be effective if their political prerequisites are not in place.

Political processes have to do with modes of decision making, not with their substance. "The problem is not where you should be trying to go, but how you should get there."[25] The procedures, practices, and underlying premises of political conduct have had a direct bearing on the selection of domestic and foreign policies and on the manner in which they have been carried out. Indeed, the content of African politics cannot usefully be separated from the ways politics work on the continent.

■ NOTES

1. Victor T. Le Vine, "The Politics of Presidential Succession," *Africa Report* 28, no. 3 (1983): 22–26.

2. Naomi Chazan, "African Voters at the Polls: A Reexamination of the Role of Elections in African Politics," *Journal of Commonwealth and Comparative Politics* 17, no. 2 (1979): 135–158. Also see Dennis L. Cohen, "Elections and Election Studies in Africa," in Yolamu Barongo, ed., *Political Science in Africa: A Critical Review* (London: Zed Press, 1983), pp. 72–93, and Fred M. Hayward, ed., *Elections in Independent Africa* (Boulder, Colo.: Westview Press, 1986).

3. It is interesting that such limited competition was being considered by Mikhail Gorbachev in the Soviet Union in 1987.

4. For a good discussion of these issues and of the Nigerian case, see Richard A. Joseph, "Democratization Under Military Tutelage: Crisis and Consensus in the Nigerian 1979 Elections," *Comparative Politics* 14, no. 1 (1981): 75–100.

5. These debates are summarized well in Roger Charlton, "Plus Ça Change? A Review of Two Decades of Theoretical Analyses of African Coups d'État," *Cultures et développement* 13, no. 1/2 (1981): 26–62. Also see L. Adele Jinadu, "Why the Guns are Never Silent: Military Coups in Africa," *Afriscope* (July 1979), pp. 13–19.

6. Pat McGowan and Thomas H. Johnson, "African Military Coups d'État and Underdevelopment: A Quantitative Historical Analysis," *Journal of Modern African Studies* 22, no. 4 (1984): 633–66, and their "Forecasting African Military Coups" (Paper presented at the American Political Science Association Meeting, New Orleans, 29 August–1 September 1985).

7. Robert Jackman, "The Predictability of Coups d'État: A Model with African Data," *American Political Science Review* 72, no. 4 (1978): 1262–1275.

8. William Gutteridge, *The Military in African Politics* (London: Methuen, 1968).

9. Samuel Decalo, *Coups and Army Rule in Africa* (New Haven: Yale University Press, 1975). Also see his "Praetorianism, Corporate Grievances and Idiosyncratic Factors in African Military Hierarchies," *Journal of African Studies* 2, no. 2 (1975): 247–273, and "The Colonel in the Command Car: Towards a Reexamination of Motives for Military Invention in Africa," *Cultures et développement* 5, no. 4 (1973): 765–778.

10. David L. Huff and James M. Lutz, "The Contagion of Political Unrest in Independent Africa," *Economic Geography* 50 (1974): 352–367; J. I. Eliagwu, "Military Intervention in Politics: An African Perspective," *Genève-Afrique* 19, no. 1 (1981): 17–38.

11. David Goldsworthy, "Civilian Control of the Military in Black Africa," *African Affairs* 318 (1981): 49–71; Elise Forbes Pachter, "Contra-Coup: Civilian Control of the Military in Guinea, Tanzania and Mozambique," *Journal of Modern African Studies* 20, no. 4 (1982): 595–612; and Agola Auma-Osolo, "Objective African Military Control: A New Paradigm in Civil Military Relations," *Journal of Peace Research* 17, no. 1 (1980): 29–46.

12. Roger Charlton, "Predicting African Military Coups," *Futures* (August 1983), pp. 281–291.

13. Maxwell Owusu, "Custom and Coups: A Juridical Interpretation of Civil Order and Disorder," *Journal of Modern African Studies* 24, no. 1 (1986): 72.

14. Samuel Huntington, *Political Order in Changing Societies* (New Haven: Yale University Press, 1968), p. 221.

15. Isaac James Mowoe, ed., *The Performance of Soldiers as Governors: African Politics and the African Military* (Washington, D.C.: University Press of America, 1980): William Gutteridge, *Military Regimes in Africa* (London: Methuen, 1975); R. D.

McKinlay and D. D. Cohan, "A Comparative Analysis of the Political and Economic Performance of Military and Civilian Regimes," *Comparative Politics* 8, no. 1 (1975): 1–30; Eric A. Nordlinger, "Soldiers in Mufti: The Impact of Military Rule Upon Economic and Social Change in Non-Western Society," *American Political Science Review* 64, no. 4 (1970): 1131–1149; and John Ravenhill, "Comparing Regime Performance in Africa: The Limits of Cross-National Aggregate Analysis," *Journal of Modern African Studies* 18, no. 1 (1980): 99–126.

16. Claude E. Welch, "Military Disengagement from Politics," *Armed Forces and Society* 9, no. 4 (1983): esp. 539–540. Also see William Gutteridge, "Undoing Military Coups in Africa," *Third World Quarterly* 7, no. 1 (1985): 78–89.

17. Christopher Clapham, *Third World Politics: An Introduction* (Madison: University of Wisconsin Press, 1985), p. 156.

18. Jonathan Barker, "Local-Central Relations: A Perspective on the Politics of Development in Africa," *Canadian Journal of African Studies* 4, no. 1 (1970): 3–16.

19. Michael Cohen, "The Myth of the Expanding Center: Politics in the Ivory Coast," *Journal of Modern African Studies* 11, no. 2 (1973): 227–246; and Martin Staniland, "The Rhetoric of Centre-Periphery Relations," *Journal of Modern African Studies* 8, no. 4 (1970): 617–636.

20. Frank Holmquist, "Toward a Political Theory of Rural Self-Help Development in Africa," *Rural Africana* 18 (1972): 60–80 and esp. 76. For a superb case study, see Sara Berry, *Fathers Work for Their Sons: Accumulation, Mobility and Class Formation in an Extended Yoruba Community* (Berkeley: University of California Press, 1985).

21. Donal Cruise O'Brien, "Des bienfaits de l'inégalité: L'état et l'économie rurale au Sénégal," *Politique africaine* 14 (1984): 34–38; Jonathan Barker, ed., *The Politics of Agriculture in Tropical Africa* (Beverly Hills, Calif.: Sage Publications, 1984).

22. Walter Barrows, *Grassroots Politics in an African State: Integration and Development in Sierra Leone* (New York: Africana Publishing Co., 1976). Also see Roger Tangri, *Politics in Sub-Saharan Africa* (London: James Currey, 1985), pp. 39–42. On Tanzania, see Zaki Ergas, "Why Did the Ujamaa Village Policy Fail? Towards a Global Analysis," *Journal of Modern African Studies* 18, no. 3 (1980): 387–410, and Goran Hyden, *Beyond Ujamaa in Tanzania: Underdevelopment and the Uncaptured Peasantry* (Berkeley: University of California Press, 1980).

23. There is much more discussion around the idea of democracy, partly motivated by Richard L. Sklar's challenging presidential address, "Democracy in Africa" (Presented at the Twenty-fifth Annual Meeting of the African Studies Association, Boston, December 1983), published in the *African Studies Review* 26, no. 3/4 (1983). Also see Robert H. Jackson and Carl G. Rosberg's more sober analysis, "Democracy in Tropical Africa: Democracy Versus Autocracy in African Politics," *Journal of International Affairs* 38, no. 2 (1985): 293–305.

24. John Dunn, "The Politics of Representation and Good Government in Post-Colonial Africa," in Patrick Chabal, ed., *Political Domination in Africa: Reflections on the Limits of Power* (London: Cambridge University Press, 1986), p. 177.

25. Clapham, *Third World Politics*, p. 186.

Part 3

POLITICAL ECONOMY

 **9**

Political Economy: Policy Choices in a Constraining Environment

African governments are severely constrained in the viable policy choices available to them. Resources—human, capital, technological—are all scarce. Ecological conditions are often unfavorable and limit the productive potential of African agriculture. Africa's role in the world economy, conditioned by the colonial experience, renders countries particularly vulnerable to external shocks. As latecomers to industrial production, African exporters often face markets that have been saturated by more advanced developing countries and confront consequent protectionist tendencies toward their exports on the part of industrialized countries. Heavily dependent on international finance for their capital formation, African countries have frequently been subject to pressure by international agencies to modify their preferred development paths.

This is not to argue, however, as has been done by some writers using the underdevelopment approach, that African governments enjoy no autonomy when it comes to decision making and choices on development strategy. Our political choice approach emphasizes that although choices may be constrained, they do exist. And, as we will see, there has been considerable variation among the development paths that African governments have chosen, with concomitant variations in results. Policy choices are often a concrete manifestation of a regime's ideology. Thus, it is not surprising to find that regimes that have adopted a Marxist-Leninist or African socialist ideology (such as Algeria, Angola, Ethiopia, Mozambique, and Tanzania) have pursued markedly different policies in many spheres from those regimes (such as Kenya, Côte d'Ivoire, Morocco, and Nigeria) that profess a capitalist orientation. Simplistic assumptions on the relationship between ideology and policies can be dangerous, however. Angola, for instance, which is often categorized as an Afro-Marxist regime, welcomes foreign investment; the terms and conditions that it offers

but not totaly determinstc

219

have been praised by managers of U.S. oil companies. Before the contemporary development strategies pursued by African governments are reviewed, we will examine the evolution of Africa's role in the world economy up until independence.

■ AFRICAN ECONOMIES IN HISTORICAL PERSPECTIVE

As we noted in Chapter 1, many writers on Africa since the 1970s have borrowed from the underdevelopment literature, which had its origins in the writings of the U.S. economist Paul Baran and which came to be used widely in the late 1960s by some specialists on Latin America. Unfortunately, many of the applications of the approach to Africa relied heavily on one of the least-sophisticated approaches, the development of underdevelopment hypothesis associated with Andre Gunder Frank. Frank follows Baran in arguing that an essential feature of the capitalist world economy is the extraction of surplus from nonindustrialized countries. Rather than being in an original state—that is, undeveloped—they are actually worse off because of their contacts with Western capitalism: They have been "underdeveloped." Economic surplus has been expropriated, depriving underdeveloped countries of the capital necessary for economic growth. Underdevelopment is perceived as being implemented through an alliance between elites in the industrialized countries (the metropole or center) and elites in the underdeveloped countries (the periphery), who it is assumed have been "bought off" by international monopoly capitalism and will always act in its interests.

The attractiveness of the hypothesis is evident. The enthusiasm with which it was taken up by some African scholars in the years after independence may be seen as a reaction to the racist literature of the early colonial period, which, in justifying the "civilizing mission" of European imperialism, portrayed African societies as primitive and the population as lazy, etc. Against the argument that Africa's economic backwardness was a result of some character deficiency on the part of its inhabitants or of economic mismanagement by governments, the underdevelopment approach places the blame primarily on factors external to Africa. Its pessimistic evaluation of Africa's economic prospects stands in marked contrast to the optimism that characterizes much of the modernization literature.

Debate on the causes of Africa's economic backwardness has often been highly emotionally charged; participants have seldom attempted to present a balanced approach. Merely to suggest that colonialism had some positive as well as negative features has been interpreted as an attempt to whitewash the activities of the colonial powers. Similarly, critics of the performance of African governments have been accused of a new paternalism and of ignoring the constraints imposed by the international economic system. It is fortunate that the last decade has seen a new realism among many African leaders, a willingness to be self-critical and to accept responsibility for their policy decisions. In a similar way, external donors have become more willing to admit that some of their past policy advice has been faulty and projects that they have financed poorly conceptualized and executed. This has opened the way for a more rational discussion of Africa's economic problems.

☐ Precolonial Economies

Any serious discussion of the impact of colonialism needs to pose the counterfactual—that is, what would have been the situation today if Africa had not been subject to colonial rule? Of course, the problem with most counterfactuals in the social sciences is that they cannot be answered with any degree of certainty. One of the weaknesses of many underdevelopment approaches is that they share an implicit counterfactual scenario that suggests that in the absence of colonial exploitation, African countries would have entered on a path of self-sustaining economic growth. In reaction to the often racist presentation of traditional society in imperial literature, precolonial Africa has frequently been portrayed by underdevelopment theorists in a very romantic manner. Any attempt to answer the counterfactual has to begin with a realistic assessment of the economic potential of precolonial African societies.

Contrary to the stereotype of precolonial Africa as being populated solely by hunter-gatherers like the Pygmies of Zaire or the !Kung Bushmen, there was a tremendous variety of political and economic forms in Africa prior to colonization. Small hunter-gatherer groups were very much the exception, confined to the fringes of desert areas or to the very heart of the tropical forest swamps of the Congo basin. Elsewhere, political systems ranged from the stateless systems typical of much of East Africa, in which political activity occurred primarily within age-set associations (although even here, there were exceptions where richer soils favored permanent settlement, such as the kingdom of Buganda), to the centralized kingdoms of the savannah of West Africa. There were very few villages that produced only for local subsistence; patterns of long-distance trade to the coast and across the Sahara were long-established. Control over trade was often a major element of political power; it was particularly important in determining access to imported firearms, whose possession in turn reinforced the ability of rulers to exert political domination.

Precolonial Africa was far from static. Kingdoms and, indeed, vast empires encompassing many different peoples waxed and waned. Ethnic identities emerged and were redefined as a result of conquest and assimilation. But there was little fundamental change in the mode of production in precolonial Africa; in particular, the types of technological innovation that occurred in Europe in the period from the sixteenth century onward lacked an African counterpart. African societies at the time of the colonial conquest had not harnessed water, wind, or animal power for human uses; production was almost entirely dependent upon human muscle. Neither the plow nor the wheel, crucial technological breakthroughs in Europe, had been adopted in most parts of Sub-Saharan Africa. Part of the explanation for this is provided by the ecological and population factors that we have already noted. In the areas south of the savannah belt, the presence of the tsetse fly prevented the use of draught animals. And the sparse population combined with poor transport routes made investments in wheeled vehicles a dubious proposition.[1]

Relative abundance of land in most areas of the continent had the consequence that little pressure was exerted for technological innovation in order to enable more intensive agriculture to occur. The slash-and-burn technique was an entirely "appropriate" technology given Africa's factor endowments. As a result, however, there was no agricultural revolution similar to that in Europe to generate the economic surplus essential for industrialization. Although new crops had been adopted over the centuries from as far afield as Asia, there was no effort at improving seed quality and no systematic application of organic fertilizers. Because transport and storage facilities remained rudimentary, there was little encouragement to produce an agricultural surplus. Apart from the areas of permanent settlement where agricultural markets were more developed, trade was concentrated in high-value goods of small bulk.

The absence of major technological breakthroughs also constrained the development of manufacturing. Although some African societies had great skills in metalworking, Africans did not develop the furnaces capable of generating high temperatures that were to play a significant role in the European industrial revolution. Mining technology was extremely rudimentary—no pumps, no explosives, little knowledge of geology—such that the vast mineral riches of the African continent remained virtually untouched before European colonization. And, of course, the small surplus generated by traditional agriculture limited the potential market for manufactures.[2]

There is little reason to believe, then, that African countries were on the verge of an indigenous agricultural or industrial revolution at the time of European conquest following the Congress of Berlin. For some writers in the dependency tradition, however, Africa's role in the world economy had already been indelibly conditioned by contact with Europe prior to the formal colonial period. Most notorious, of course, is the Atlantic slave trade. European traders had originally come to West Africa in the fifteenth and sixteenth centuries interested in goods other than slaves—principally gold, ivory, and timber. Slave trading did not become important until the seventeenth century, with the rise of the West Indian sugar industry. Over the four centuries from 1450 to 1870, Philip Curtin estimates, approximately 9.5 million slaves were imported by the Americas and Europe from Africa.[3] Given the appalling treatment of the captives, the number of people removed from Africa was certainly higher: Curtin's figures do not reflect deaths during slave raiding, captivity, and transportation.

It is undoubtedly true that the Atlantic slave trade had a profound effect on Africa's political economy from the seventeenth through the nineteenth centuries. As Anthony Hopkins notes, the "remarkable expansion of the slave trade in the eighteenth century provides a horrific illustration of the rapid response of producers in an underdeveloped economy to price incentives."[4] Slave trading became a major source of wealth for African entrepreneurs who were able to supply the significant capital necessary to mount sustained slave raiding. Slave trading gave rise to coastal trading towns such as Lagos and Old Calabar, which not only were the embarkation point for slaves but also supplied the slaving ships with provisions for the Atlantic voyage and became distribution points for the goods received in exchange. A class of middlemen emerged in the coastal cities whose function it was to act as intermediaries between European buyers and African suppliers. Involvement in the slave trade played a significant role in the emergence of some of the more powerful kingdoms in West Africa such as Dahomey. And, in exchange for slaves, African traders received a variety of imported goods—cloth, guns and ammunition, and utensils and tools.

The trade in humans has aroused justifiable moral indignation. That the trade integrated Africa into the world economy is indisputable. Whether it had a decisive negative impact on Africa's economic development is much more debatable. Hopkins provides one of the most carefully reasoned accounts.[5] He notes that there is little evidence to support the notion of unequal exchange during this period: African slave traders were well placed to bargain effectively with European purchasers; given the high demand for slaves, it was very much a suppliers' market. Involvement in slave trading gave rise to considerable personal fortunes, such as on the part of the king of Dahomey, while the growth of entrepôts provided new employment opportunities. There is also little evidence to support the argument that indigenous handicraft industries were destroyed as a result of competition from imported manufactures received in exchange for slaves; rather, the increase in incomes and the growth of coastal towns appeared to enlarge the market for local as well as imported manufactures.

There are two dimensions of the slave trade whose assessment remains more problematic. The first is the impact of slave raiding on everyday life and ① commerce. Frequent raids increased the uncertainty of life in inland areas and thus undermined the stability necessary for domestic commerce. It is almost impossible to judge how serious this effect was in that there is little evidence on the extent of disruption, and, of course, we have no idea of whether similar disruption would have occurred in the absence of the Atlantic slave trade. Second, the removal of people in such large numbers undoubtedly had an impact ② on the prospects for economic growth. We have already noted that one factor that held back Africa's economic development was sparseness of population. How significant a contribution slavery made to this sparseness is difficult to estimate, given our lack of knowledge of the size of the total population of Africa at this time. Rather than slavery, the inhospitable environmental conditions of Africa's interior may have been the principal factor constraining population growth. Hopkins estimates that the rate of loss of population through slave trading was roughly equivalent to the rate of natural increase in the eighteenth century. He concludes:

> For the external slave trade to have been an economic disaster, it is necessary to postulate that West Africa would have achieved a major economic break-through before the nineteenth century if the supply of manpower had not been diminished by the amount specified. The evidence does not support this hypothesis, and it is hard to see how the retention of those slaves sent abroad would have caused the economy to develop along significantly different lines.[6]

Contrary to what might have been expected, the ending of the slave trade, at the insistence of the European powers, did not diminish Africa's integration into the world economy. Rather, this integration was accelerated by the rapid expansion of African production of groundnuts and palm nuts and oils in the first half of the nineteenth century, an indigenous response to expanded commercial opportunities. Groundnuts and palm nuts were already cultivated in West Africa as foodstuffs; exports of these products were greatly expanded to cater to the demands of newly industrialized Europe for lubricants. Production continued to be undertaken primarily by African households; considerable African entrepreneurial skills were in evidence in organizing the marketing of the production. Expanding the production of an existing crop appeared to be an entirely rational economic strategy, perhaps the only one available for economies at the levels of development of those of Africa. And, until the 1860s, when new sources of oils were opened up with the construction of the Suez Canal and the increased settlement by Europeans of temperate colonial areas, the strategy paid handsome dividends: African economies benefited from a sustained improvement in their terms of trade as the unit price of palm oil rose while that of imported manufactures fell. But the gap between the undiversified African economies and the economies of Europe was widening rapidly; neither political nor economic systems in Africa were strong enough to prevent European colonization.

☐ The Colonial Impact

An assessment of the colonial impact on African political economy must begin with an explicit recognition of the diversity of the colonial experience. Among the factors that shaped this diversity were the natural resources of the colony, whether or not significant numbers of European settlers were present, the nationality of the colonial power, and even the philosophy and influence of individual colonial administrations. A succinct summary of the differential impact of colonial rule is provided by Samir Amin.

Amin identifies three macroregions in black Africa. He labels these "Africa of the labor reserves," "Africa of the colonial trade economy," and "Africa of the concession-owning companies." The regions, he argues, were differentiated on the basis of the resources that could be exploited by the colonial powers.

The economic development of "Africa of the labor reserves" (Kenya,

Uganda, Tanzania, Rwanda, Burundi, Malawi, Angola, Mozambique, Zimbabwe, Botswana, Lesotho, Swaziland, and South Africa) was conditioned by the need for large amounts of labor for the mines of Central and southern Africa and the settler agricultural plantations of Kenya, Zimbabwe, and German Tanganyika. As a result, many of the traditional social systems of this region were "distorted and impoverished."

In contrast, in West Africa—Amin's "Africa of the colonial trade economy" —there was no large-scale mineral wealth known during most of the colonial period. Here, the slave trade had provided the sociopolitical foundation for the emergence of large-scale production and trade in tropical agricultural products.

In the third macroregion, "Africa of the concession-owning companies" (Central African Republic, Congo, Gabon, and Zaire), the relatively low density of population coupled with the difficult ecological conditions cast doubt on the prospects for West African–style peasant agriculture. Instead, the colonial authorities gave over these territories to concessionary companies, whose objective was to exploit the territories while providing a minimum of investment. This proved to be one of the most brutal forms of colonial exploitation.[7]

Despite the diversity of colonial experiences, a number of common principles may be identified in the approach by the European powers to their colonies' economies. First, all of the colonial authorities conceived of the relationship as one of complementarity in which Africa would have a subordinate role. James Mill, the nineteenth-century political economist, defined a colony as a place where the colonizing power found it convenient to carry out some of its business. The objective of the imperial powers was to construct an integrated economy in which the principal role of the colonies was to service metropolitan needs. This, of course, is the foundation for the external orientation that continues to characterize African economies today. Complementarity and integration were conceived of in terms of the metropole rather than of neighboring countries; as a consequence, infrastructure—railways, ports, and roads—was directed primarily toward the facilitation of overseas rather than internal or regional trade and communications. Integration of colonial and metropolitan economies was intensified in the economic slump of the 1930s, when colonial powers attempted to conserve scarce foreign exchange by constructing closed trading blocs on the basis of imperial preferences. Hopkins estimates, for example, that whereas French West Africa directed 40 percent of its total trade toward France in 1898, and this had increased to only 50 percent by 1930, the construction of imperial preferences caused this figure to jump to 75 percent for the years from 1935 to 1960.[8]

Complementarity was also conceived of in terms of an exchange of African raw materials and markets, on the one hand, and European industrial goods, on the other. The attitude of colonial powers toward African industrialization can probably best be characterized as indifference rather than pronounced hostility: Until the period after World War II, neither European colonial powers nor their trading companies perceived African markets as sufficiently significant to en-

courage import-substituting industrialization. And, again, Africa's "specialization" in the production of primary products did not always work against its immediate economic interests: The terms of trade moved in favor of Africa in most
of the period between colonization and World War I, throughout the 1920s until
the stockmarket crash of 1929, and throughout most of the post–World War II
period until decolonization.

Although the colonial authorities placed restrictions on the type and location of economic activities that Africans could engage in—particularly in countries like Kenya, where there were large numbers of European settlers[9]—it is a
caricature to suggest that African enterprise was always discouraged. Although
large colonial trading companies played a dominant role in most African
economies, opportunities still existed for African traders. Significant indigenous capital accumulation occurred in the more-developed economies such as
Kenya and Nigeria—which, as Michael Cowen, Gavin Kitching, and others
demonstrate, was to have a substantial impact on the postindependence political
economy.[10]

A second key principle for most of the period of colonial rule was that the
colonies should be financially self-sufficient. Colonies were to pay not only for
the cost of any development expenditure but also for the not insubstantial expenses of colonial administration: In Crawford Young's piercing terminology,
"the newly subordinated African societies were called upon to finance their own
conquest."[11] Revenue was derived primarily from customs duties, although
head taxes played an important role in countries where foreign trade was of little
significance and in times when trade was depressed. Hopkins estimates that 50
percent of the revenue of the colonial authorities was expended on the payment
of salaries and pensions of expatriate administrators; as much as a third of the
remainder was devoted to servicing loans undertaken for capital expenditure—
often on projects such as railways that were undertaken as much for their
strategic as their economic value to some colonies.[12] As a consequence, few
resources were available to government departments such as education and agriculture to promote economic development. Colonial miserliness ensured that
public and private investment lagged behind such investment in independent
countries.

"Development" as a means of legitimizing colonialism gradually gained
acceptance during the 1920s. It was only in the period after World War II, however, as a new emphasis on human equality and on the obligations of colonial
powers was enshrined in the United Nations Charter, that the major metropolitan powers fully abandoned the principle of financial self-sufficiency in the colonies. As a result of both international pressure and demands from the growing
nationalist movements, expenditure on colonial development was significantly
increased. French public investment in its West African colonies, for instance,
in the ten-year period 1947–1956 was more than double the total amount for the
years 1903–1946. In the Belgian Congo, which had long lagged behind most
French and British colonies in terms of welfare expenditure—government out-

lays increased eleven times between 1939 and 1950 and tripled again in the decade before independence in 1960. Similarly, in the Gold Coast (Ghana), state expenditure increased ten-fold in the decade before independence.

There was a substantial difference between French West Africa and the relatively wealthy British colonies—more than 75 percent of investment in the latter was internally generated in the years 1946–1958 whereas in the French colonies in the same years 70–75 percent was derived from France.[13] In all cases, however, public and private investment increased substantially. Multiyear plans were drawn up for the colonies' development, with considerable emphasis given to health and education and to the improvement of internal transport. For the first time, tariff policy was used as a means of encouraging local manufacturing industry as well as for raising revenue. Tariffs, together with the enlarged local market that resulted from improved earnings from commodity exports, enticed investment in import-substituting industries from metropole-based transnationals.

Although substantial gains were made both in terms of economic growth and human development in the post-1945 period, the economies inherited by African leaders at independence imposed considerable constraints on their policy choices. Not only had the gap between Africa and the industrialized economies continued to widen during the colonial period, but African economies lagged substantially behind those of most other developing countries. Manufacturing constituted a tiny percentage of overall economic activities in most African countries. For Sub-Saharan Africa as a whole, industry accounted for a weighted mean of 9 percent of GDP in 1965 compared to 14 percent in other low-income economies and 20 percent in middle-income economies.[14] Manufacturing for export, except within regional schemes such as the East African Community, was rare: Manufactures contributed a weighted mean of only 7 percent of Sub-Saharan Africa's exports in 1962.

Exports were overwhelmingly of raw materials and agricultural products; most economies depended on one to three products for over 75 percent of their export earnings. Compared to those of other developing countries, African exports typically had undergone substantially less domestic processing. African economies thus were particularly vulnerable to fluctuations in world commodity markets. Despite the dismantling of imperial preferences, the trade of most countries remained overwhelmingly concentrated with the colonial metropole, offering the latter considerable potential leverage over the former colonies. Although benefits had been gained from the grants and loans received from the colonial power in the years preceding its departure, one consequence of these was that many African countries were unable to finance their current levels of development expenditure from internal funds: Dependence on (often unpredictable) foreign sources of finance was a further constraint faced by the new leaders.

Skilled human resources were also scarce. In 1960, less than one adult in six was literate, a figure that contrasted with one adult in four in other low-income countries and every other adult in middle-income developing countries. For Sub-Saharan Africa as a whole, 36 percent of children of primary-school age were enrolled in school, again contrasting unfavorably with the 75 percent that was the mean figure for school enrollment in other developing countries. Secondary schools in Sub-Saharan Africa enrolled only 3 percent of their age group in contrast to a 15 percent enrollment in other developing countries. University enrollment was negligible. In all of French Equatorial Africa—which, at independence, became Gabon, Chad, Central African Republic, and Congo—there were only five university graduates at independence in 1960. Other countries—with the partial exceptions of Ghana and Nigeria—were similarly lacking in university-educated personnel. In many countries, the colonial authorities had relied on missionary societies to provide education to Africans.

In countries with substantial numbers of white settlers—Algeria, Kenya, Zambia, and the former Portuguese colonies of Angola and Mozambique—whites had occupied most of the middle-level as well as executive positions in administration. Even in the years immediately before independence, a color-bar in most colonies effectively excluded qualified Africans from appointment to administrative positions in the civil service. Low levels of investment in education were reflected in the large percentage of positions held by expatriates even in colonies without large settler populations.

The precipitous withdrawal of Portugal from Africa in 1974 left enormous gaps in administrative expertise. But many other countries at independence had not been substantially better placed than the former Portugese colonies in that there were few Africans with the education and experience to take over from the civil servants of the departing colonial power. Tanzania's first personnel survey, conducted in 1962/63, documented that 80 percent of all positions that required a university education were occupied by non-Africans. In the country at this time there were only twelve African civil engineers, eight African telecommunication engineers, nine African veterinarians, and five African chemists. No Africans had been trained as geologists or mechanical or electrical engineers. Only 38 of the 600 secondary-school teachers holding university degrees were African. Similarly, in Zambia at independence, there were only 1,200 Africans with secondary schooling and 108 who had received higher education.[15] As a result, many African countries had to rely on expatriates in key administrative roles for the first decade after independence; a few, most noticeably Côte d'Ivoire, have continued to do so, but this has now become largely a matter of choice in terms of development priorities rather than of necessity.

African countries reached independence poorly equipped to tackle the enormous development tasks that they faced. The continent as a whole was less advantageously placed than most other developing countries on such dimensions as the possession of an industrial base or of skilled personnel. Although living standards for many groups had risen during the colonial period, there was little margin above absolute poverty and starvation. The export trade of most countries was dependent on one or two agricultural crops or minerals; it remained highly concentrated with the metropole economy. The late commitment of the colonial powers to providing "development," coupled with the more rapid than anticipated movement toward independence, provided African governments with a very fragile foundation on which to build in the postindependence period.

Colonization had undoubtedly integrated African economies into the capitalist world system. Almost all Africans were now part of the cash economy—they had to earn cash either to pay taxes or to purchase essential goods. On the other hand, colonialism did not dramatically transform African economies nor the economic lives of many of its inhabitants. African economies at independence were characterized by what John Lonsdale terms "syncretic articulation"—the uneven and combined development of both capitalist and precapitalist modes of production. The ready availability of land in most countries afforded peasants the opportunity to retreat into subsistence production—in Goran Hyden's terminology, the peasantry remained "uncaptured."[16] Rather than promoting the complete transformation of precapitalist modes of production, colonial governments usually preferred to allow indigenous structures to coexist with the capitalist framework that they introduced.

■ SECTORAL POLICIES IN THE POSTINDEPENDENCE PERIOD

In the remainder of this chapter, we first review the policies pursued by African states since independence in four sectors: education; health and population; industry; and agriculture. We then examine the strategies that Africans have adopted to cope with the economic crisis that has afflicted most countries in the 1980s.

□ Educational Policies

African leaders inherited educational systems that had effectively excluded the vast majority of Africans from schooling, systems whose structure and curricula were typically modeled on those of the metropole and which were often divided on racial lines—with separate schools for Europeans, Africans, and for minority groups such as Asians and Lebanese. There is widespread evidence that colonial powers feared the effects of creating an educated class of Africans, realizing, correctly, that such a class would mount an effective challenge to their continued rule. Although educational enrollments had increased rapidly in the post–World War II years, there were only nine countries—Cameroon, Congo, Gabon, Lesotho, Madagascar, Mauritius, Swaziland, Zaire, and Zimbabwe—in 1960 where more than 50 percent of children of primary-school age were actually enrolled. And, although the departing colonial powers, especially the British, attempted to "Africanize" education through curriculum reform, in particular, by teaching more African history and "practical" subjects, such moves were quickly terminated in the face of opposition from parents and African nationalist leaders. The reaction of parents and leaders was against what they perceived to be an inferior education; their objective was to ensure that their children acquired through book-learning the paper qualifications that were held by Europeans and which were perceived to be a passport to higher status.[17]

African families have given a very high priority to obtaining education for their children. In this context, the concept of family should be understood not in the sense of the Western nuclear family but of an extended family that includes nephews, nieces, cousins, and other kin. The reason for the emphasis on education is that it is regarded as a passport to a better life—not just for the person who receives the education but for the family as a whole. The expectation is that educated members will enable the family to more effectively stake a claim to resources in the system, especially those provided by the state. Not just parents but extended families and even whole villages are willing to make financial sacrifices to enable a "son" (much less frequently, a "daughter") of the village to obtain education.[18]

Popular aspirations for improved access to education coincided in the years immediately following independence with the desire of most governments to Africanize their administrations. The result was a rapid expansion of both primary and secondary education. Most countries also established their own universities in this period. Subsequently, faced both by budgetary pressures and, once Africanization was completed, by a limited demand for personnel with secondary-school qualifications, there has been a marked divergence in the approach to educational policy. Some countries have attempted to curtail secondary-school enrollments and have laid substantial emphasis in the primary-school curriculum on skills relevant to the life that most adults will lead as peasant agricultural producers. Other countries have continued with the inherited educational structure with emphasis placed on achievement in traditional academic subjects. Before we examine these divergent approaches in more detail, some commonalities of policy may be identified.

All African states have devoted considerable resources to education: As Young notes, regardless of ideological preference, there has been "no discernible difference in the priority accorded to educational expenditures."[19] In Sub-Saharan Africa as a whole, education expenditures accounted for an average of 16 percent of all central government expenditures in 1983; for middle-income African countries the average was 17 percent. This was substantially higher than the percentage spent on education in other developing countries: an average of 4.7 percent of total government expenditure in low-income countries and 12.1 percent in middle-income countries.[20] In many African countries, education expenditure amounts to 4 percent of GDP.

Throughout the continent, considerable emphasis has been placed on primary education as a means of providing basic literacy to the mass of the population. This emphasis has obvious relevance to economic development and to the government's ability, in the term used by modernization theorists, to "penetrate" society—that is, to ensure that the policies decided at the center reach those at the periphery of the society. In many countries, primary-school fees were abolished in an attempt to increase access to primary education; countries as diverse as Nigeria and Tanzania have proclaimed their commitment to universal primary education. The financial implications of such policies are immense: It has been estimated, for instance, that over $1 billion would need to be invested in the construction of new school buildings in Nigeria to realize the goal of primary education for all.

Massive investments in the educational sector have paid dividends. Substantial achievements have been made in the period since independence. Literacy rates have more than doubled throughout the continent. In some countries, the increase has been even more spectacular: In Tanzania, rural adult literacy rose from 10 percent to 65 percent in the years 1961–1981. By 1982, primary-school enrollments throughout Sub-Saharan Africa averaged 77 percent of the total population of primary-school age. There were very few countries—primarily those with low per capita incomes, such as Chad, Mali, Burkina Faso, Somalia, Niger, Burundi, and Mauritania—where the enrollments were less than 50 percent of the age group. In some countries, such as Congo and Gabon, the figure for enrollments was more than 130 percent, reflecting the enrollment in primary education of large numbers of people beyond the normal primary-school age group. Although female enrollments lagged behind those of males— a weighted mean of 60 percent of the female primary-school age population in 1982—there was widespread evidence that traditional prejudice against the education of females is being overcome.

Although governments of all political hues have rapidly expanded primary education enrollments, there have been significant differences between them in relation to policies on secondary and postsecondary education and in other areas such as curriculum reform. Governments have faced a number of constraints on their actions. A first constraint has been the financial problem. With education expenditures consuming a large proportion of revenues, governments have been forced to make hard choices regarding the areas to which they wish to accord priority. Second, governments have had to contend with popular expectations of improved access to all levels of schooling. Against these popular expectations is a third constraint: the lack of employment opportunities for secondary-school leavers and for some university graduates (mainly those with a liberal arts education). Realizing the discontent that would be bred by frustrated expectations, and the demands that large numbers of school leavers would make for employment in what are often already-bloated state agencies, some governments have been reluctant to increase the output of secondary-school and university-educated students beyond the short-term personnel needs of their economies.

Government response to these dilemmas has differed markedly. States espousing variants of Afro-Marxist and socialist ideologies have often given priority to mass adult literacy campaigns, perceiving these as a means through which equality may be enhanced. The principal examples are Ethiopia, Somalia, and Tanzania; Mozambique has also embarked on a similar scheme. Ethiopia's campaign, begun in the late 1970s, was estimated by 1981 to have reached 7 million people, over 70 percent of them women. Over a quarter of a million part-time instructors—students, civil servants, army personnel, teachers—were mobilized. Most of those reached by the campaign attained basic literacy and numeracy despite the formidable obstacles of language diversity and the limited administrative and financial resources available to the scheme. Ethiopia's scheme was acclaimed by UNESCO's International Reading Association in 1980 when it was given the association's annual literacy award. Similar success was enjoyed in Tanzania, where an estimated 5 million adults were reached by a mass literacy campaign; over 3 million of these succeeded in a competency examination.

In contrast, Afro-Marxist and socialist countries have typically not accorded high priority to the expansion of secondary education. Governments have asserted that there are greater benefits to be derived from the massive expansion of adult literacy than from more years of education for a relatively small percentage of the population. Tanzania, for instance, had only 3 percent of the secondary-school age group actually enrolled in secondary education in 1981, only a marginal increase on the figure during the colonial period. The government has argued that secondary education is a luxury that the country cannot afford other than to produce qualified personnel to meet the needs of the economy.

As the educational system in Tanzania is often cited as a model for other developing countries, we will examine it in more detail. The blueprint for Tanzania's system was laid down in ex-President Nyerere's pamphlet *Education for Self-Reliance,* issued in 1967 following the Arusha Declaration. Nyerere rejected the "academic" emphasis in education that had been inherited from the colonial power and practiced in the early postindependence years. Education was to be reoriented to meeting the practical needs of the mass of the people, which meant, in effect, the needs of life in an agricultural and rural society. Egalitarian values were to be fostered, the distinction between mental and manual work abolished, and cooperative attitudes and loyalty to the party and government encouraged. Primary-school education was to be considered "complete in itself" and not a route to secondary and higher education. To facilitate this, the entry age for primary schools was to be raised to seven years in order that primary-school leavers would be old enough to enter the work force directly. Schools were to become productive units, maintaining their own mini-farms so that students could learn practical agricultural skills.[21]

Although this strategy has enabled the Tanzanian government to economize on expenditure on postprimary education, it generates its own constraints and contradictions. The policy of limiting secondary-school enrollments has had two consequences. First, it alienates parents and children who aspire to additional qualifications. Second, it ensures that those who receive secondary schooling, and even more so those who proceed to higher education, constitute a small elite that will enjoy guaranteed access to prestige and relatively well paid employment. In David Court's terminology, the limitation on secondary-school numbers tends to delegitimize the reward structure in society.[22] The reorientation of education in Tanzania cannot, of course, be viewed outside of the context of other government efforts to restructure society. Factors taken into account in deciding admission to the university have been widened to include work record and employee and party recommendations. Restrictions on government salaries and the emphasis on the unity of manual and mental work were intended to reduce both the prestige and the material rewards enjoyed by those who completed secondary and/or higher education to become government employees. Nevertheless, there continue to be very large disparities (albeit lower than those in many other African countries) between the salaries of government employees and the income of workers and peasants.

The government's dilemma is that the bulk of the population, not unreasonably, still view secondary and higher education as a passport to an improved life-style. One response has been the growth of private secondary schools in the country. Parents who can afford school fees have sent their children to private schools when their performance has been inadequate for them to gain entry to the government system. The obvious problem is of the possible emergence of a self-perpetuating elite: The wealthy have unequal access to secondary schools, which in turn provide a greatly improved opportunity for higher-paid employment in the country. Other observers have reported resistance among parents and children to the teaching of basic agricultural skills; meanwhile, many teachers simply have not had the training to perform this task effectively, whereas some have been reluctant to engage in manual tasks alongside students as the government's policy originally intended.[23] Another problem is that educators remain uncertain as to what is essential by way of school-taught knowledge for agricultural productivity or productive self-employment.[24] Also, a strategy of this type is heavily dependent on the ability of the government to estimate accurately the economy's need for personnel educated at the secondary and university levels. There is evidence in Tanzania of a severe shortage of skilled personnel at all levels, in part because graduates have been attracted to higher salaries in neighboring countries and international organizations.

Tanzania's Education for Self-Reliance represents an experiment whose results are as yet uncertain. Other countries, most notably those that have adopted a capitalist ideology and many francophone states, have continued to place considerable emphasis upon secondary and tertiary education. In many of these countries, the secondary-school enrollment is between 20 and 30 percent of the secondary-school age group. One country that fits this pattern is Kenya. Here, the population has been encouraged to contribute toward formal primary and secondary education through the *harambee,* or self-help, movement through which local groups finance and build schools. The government then accepts the responsibility for providing teachers and teaching materials, etc. Unlike the situation in neighboring Tanzania, in Kenya there has been little break with the inherited pattern of academic credentials. Indeed, as Court points out, the legitimacy of the system has rested on academic achievement both as the means of advancement in the system and of subsequently obtaining employment. To attempt to increase the education system's legitimacy by encouraging popular perceptions of its impartiality, the government has relied extensively on external examinations.

Kenya's educational programs have their own internal inconsistencies and contradictions. Although equality of *opportunity* has been stressed, in reality the wealthier and politically more influential parts of the country have been able to retain advantages through the establishment of self-help *harambee* schools. These inequalities in access to educational facilities have often reflected ethnic divisions and thus reinforced ethnic tensions. The educational system itself reflects the three-tier colonial system, in which separate educational systems had been established, with different educational emphases and widely divergent resources, for Africans, Asians, and Europeans. Although racial divisions have been abolished, the schools remain differentiated in terms of teachers and resources. Again, this differentiation serves primarily to benefit the children of the political and economic elite. Examinations in English again tend to favor students from privileged backgrounds. Two further tensions are apparent. First, the proliferation of *harambee* schools has added to the strain on government resources; if the promise of the *harambee* system is to be fulfilled, the government must respond through accepting most of the responsibility for recurrent costs, such as teacher salaries. Second, the government has had to find employment for increasing numbers of students graduating with secondary and higher education or face the frustration of those whose hopes have been built up. The result has been the expansion of public-sector employment with concomitant reductions in efficiency.

A more general weakness of some educational systems that have continued to follow the colonial model is their neglect of agriculture and applied sciences. In some countries, too many liberal arts graduates have been produced while desperate shortages of agricultural experts and engineers continue to be experienced. An educational system built on the basis of individual choice and the tradition of a classical education is ill equipped to direct resources to those areas where they are most needed.

Whichever educational model governments follow, it is clear that they face major constraints in the form both of raised popular expectations and of growing budgetary problems. The latter are exacerbated by the relatively high salaries paid to teachers (teacher salaries constitute between 75 and 90 percent of total recurrent costs in education). Reflecting their relative scarcity at independence, and often the maintenance of colonial salary structures, primary-school teachers in Sub-Saharan Africa are paid, on average, six to seven times the average per capita GDP; in Asia and Latin America, their counterparts receive about

2.5 times per capita GDP. The costs of maintaining students in secondary and higher education in Africa are also high relative to Asia and Latin America—in part, the consequence of the high cost of elaborate university buildings constructed by foreign donors. Each student in secondary schooling each year in West Africa costs the equivalent of 140 percent of an average person's income; a year of university education costs more than ten times the average per capita income. The equivalent figures for Asia are 27 percent and 205 percent.[25]

Faced with increasing budgetary problems, some governments have found it necessary to curtail expenditure on education. In Togo, budget cuts led to a reduction in the number of teachers and the closure of some schools: Primary-school enrollments fell from 72 percent of the age group in 1980/81 to 63 percent in 1982/83.[26] Throughout the continent, educational systems are under severe strain as expansion of enrollments and budgetary problems threaten the quality of existing programs. Unless some means are found to reduce the costs of education, the major achievements made by African countries in this field since independence will be in danger of being reversed. Agencies such as the World Bank have advised some countries to reintroduce primary-school fees. This will inevitably have a negative impact on enrollments from poorer groups in society.

☐ Health and Population Policies

The health care services inherited by most African governments at independence typically provided a fairly high standard of curative medicine for European expatriates and senior civil servants and minimal service for the vast majority of the population. Colonial authorities depended heavily on missionary societies for the provision of services to Africans: Those few hospitals and medical centers that existed outside the major urban areas were often run by missionary organizations. African governments have faced a situation in which a wide gap exists between the scarce financial resources at their disposal and the enormous health care needs of the population. In many African countries, diseases such as bilharzia, schistosomiasis, malaria, tuberculosis, cholera, typhoid, polio, AIDS, and measles are epidemic. Susceptibility to these diseases is exacerbated by malnutrition; for instance, measles, which in industrialized countries used to be a common and usually easily-overcome childhood illness even before immunization was available, is a major killer in African countries as a result of malnourishment. Malnourishment and illness severely affect the ability of many members of the population to work effectively; a very close relationship exists, therefore, between health and development.[27]

The very magnitude of the problem has prevented progress in the health care field equivalent to that made in education. In addition, governments have devoted a considerably smaller portion of their expenditure to health care than to education: an average of 5.5 percent for Sub-Saharan Africa as a whole in 1981 (compared to 16 percent on education). A plausible argument may be made that most African governments have not employed their health care budgets in an optimal manner in that they have largely maintained the pattern of health care inherited from the colonial period. Concentration has been on Western-style curative medicine practiced in large hospitals in urban areas by doctors that have undergone a full Western-style educational training. Rural areas have continued to be largely neglected in many countries. Only a few countries have adopted an alternative approach, in part modeled on the Chinese experience of "barefoot" doctors. In this approach, the emphasis has been placed on providing preventative health care for most of the population largely through paramedical staff, who have undergone a more limited training than that of conventional doctors, and through the provision of rural dispensaries and clinics. This strategy of alternative medicine has been pursued almost exclusively by states that have adopted some variant of socialist ideology. Young's tentative conclusion is a correct one: "While levels of health expenditures do not appear to vary by ideological type, it is possible that market-economy states are more prone to follow the Western medical model of high cost, high quality, and, for a country of meager means, limited access health care."[28]

Again, the Tanzanian case has attracted considerable interest. Tanzania followed the inherited colonial health care model for the first decade after independence. By 1971/72, hospitals consumed 87 percent of the recurrent expenditure of the Ministry of Health. One hospital in the capital, Dar es Salaam, was allocated 41 percent of the ministry's annual budget for drugs and equipment—and then exceeded its allocation by more than 100 percent. Yet, like the other major hospitals, this one drew patients predominantly from the local neighborhood and reached, at most, 5 percent of the country's total population. In 1972 the government decided to switch its emphasis to the provision of preventative medicine for the majority of the population, who continued to live in rural areas. From 1972, no new large hospitals were built; emphasis was placed instead on the construction of health centers and dispensaries. By the end of 1975, over one hundred sixty health centers had been established and close to eighteen hundred dispensaries; these were located so that 90 percent of the population was no more than 10 kilometers (6 miles) from some health facility. The health care centers were staffed by medical assistants who had completed a three-year course after secondary school and rural medical aides whose training comprised a three-year postprimary-school course. By the mid-1970s, the proportion of the health budget allocated to hospitals had dropped to under 50 percent.[29]

Tanzania's scheme initially appeared to function successfully despite opposition from entrenched interests in existing hospitals and severe shortages of funds and medical supplies. However, unanticipated situations arose. New concentrations of people as a result of villagization schemes led to unprecedented epidemics of typhoid and cholera. In the 1980s, the overall decline of the Tanzanian economy has led to dislocations in the rural health care system: breakdown of communications, a decay of rural buildings, and, at times, a complete lack of drugs. Despite its current problems, the Tanzanian model appears to hold out better prospects for improving overall health care than do those systems adopted elsewhere on the continent. In the World Bank's judgment, "most African countries have chosen systems of health care that do not meet the needs of their people."[30]

The entrenched interests faced by governments attempting to reorient their health care systems should not be underestimated. Urban hospitals with highly trained medical staff are often perceived as symbols of modernity. Large-scale hospitals have also often been favored by aid donors, who view them not only as monuments to their generosity but also as a means whereby construction and equipment contracts will be channeled to their transnational corporations. International drug companies have also played a major role in promoting the inherited curative approach to medicine: Andrew Coulson notes, for example, that in Tanzania in the mid-1970s there were 147 drug company representatives compared with only 600 doctors. Drug companies had attracted medical assistants from the medical service by offering higher salaries and commissions on sales.[31]

There is also widespread evidence that transnational pharmaceutical companies in Africa, as well as in other Third World areas, have abused their market power in various ways. African countries have been charged prices for brand-name drugs far in excess of the world market prices for their generic equivalents. Drugs that have either not been fully tested or have been banned in the West have also been promoted through such means as free samples, kick-back commissions, and gifts to hospitals. Coulson cites the examples of aminopyrine and dipyrone. These were promoted in Tanzania in the mid-1970s as alternatives to aspirin and were estimated to have killed 630 of the 117,000 people to whom they were administered. In the United States, these drugs could only be used as a last resort for patients with terminal illnesses.[32]

Another notorious abuse by transnational corporations (TNCs) of their market power in the health care field was the promotion of milk powder, primarily in West Africa. Medical experts have long warned that bottle feeding of infants is a health risk unless there is access to safe water supplies, bottles can be sterilized, and the appropriate concentration of milk solution employed. It is quite clear that such conditions do not prevail for the great majority of Africans. Yet, TNCs continued to market their products and attempted to increase consumption by advertising bottle-feeding as a modern method in contrast to traditional breastfeeding. Only after a worldwide protest and boycott in the early 1980s of the products of the principal transnational company involved, and the establishment of an international code of conduct, was company practice changed.

The milk-powder issue illustrates the importance of access to clean water as a major prerequisite for improving health care in Africa, serving also to emphasize the interrelation of health care with other basic human needs such as adequate shelter and, of course, education. To meet these needs requires significant financial effort sustained over a long period. Yet, relatively low-cost measures can be taken to improve health care for the mass of the population—for example, vaccination against such common diseases as measles, tetanus, whooping cough, polio, and tuberculosis, largely ignored as emphasis continues to be placed on curative medicine.

The delivery of medical services is but one dimension of improving the health of Africans. Also of great importance is the achievement of a significant improvement in general living conditions, such as through the provision of improved sanitation and access to clean water supplies. These were the central focus of the "basic human needs" approach that was popular in aid circles in the late 1970s. Many donors at this time gave priority to "site and service" schemes in which sites with sanitation and water facilities were provided on which people could construct their own low-cost housing. Only about one-sixth of the aid provided by industrialized countries, however, has been directed toward health and welfare. Despite the continuing needs in this sector, the trend in most bilateral aid (although not in that provided by nongovernmental voluntary organizations) has been away from the provision of basic human needs and toward the rehabilitation of agricultural production.

Africa's progress in the health field thus must be considered as very limited since independence. Advances have occurred on some conventional Western indicators, such as number of people per physician and per nurse. There were, for example, an average of over 53,000 people per physician in Sub-Saharan Africa in 1960; by 1980 this figure had fallen to 21,000 (still approximately four times the average for other developing countries). The equivalent figures for people per nurse were 5,900 and 3,000. Although child mortality rates fell by 40 percent in the period 1950–1980, this drop contrasted with a higher reduction in other developing countries from a lower base. As a result, the gap between Africa and other developing countries widened in this period so that by 1980, child mortality (at an average of 27.5 per thousand) in Africa was almost twice the rate in other developing countries. Childhood immunization rates in Africa are the lowest in the world. The gap between the average life expectancy of 47.5 years in Africa and average life expectancy in the rest of the world continues to grow.[33]

The failure of agricultural productivity to keep pace with population growth has contributed to malnutrition. We discuss agricultural failures later in this chapter. The other component in the equation has been population growth. The population of Sub-Saharan Africa is growing at a faster rate than that of any other area of the world. The growth rate in the second half of the 1980s is estimated to be 3.1 percent per annum, a marked acceleration from the 2.3 percent per annum rate that prevailed at independence. For some countries the rate is substantially higher: 4.4 percent per annum in Kenya and Zimbabwe; 3.9 percent in Ghana and Swaziland; 3.7 percent in Côte d'Ivoire.[34] Higher growth rates, ironically, reflect improvements in health care, most notably reductions in infant mortality rates. Popular expectations have yet to adjust to the new realities, however, with people continuing to want large families. The World

Bank estimates that the population of Nigeria will not stabilize until it reaches 550 million (five times the present level); that of Ghana, until it reaches 53 million; Uganda, 74 million; and Zaire, 130 million.

Some African countries are still relatively sparsely populated. But the rapid rate of increase in population that is occurring places severe strains on all aspects of the economy including government services and contributes to the problem of malnutrition. Very few African governments have shown any inclination whatsoever to tackle the birthrate problem. Some countries—for example, Sudan—actually provide incentives to families to have more children. Birth-control services are very limited in most countries and seldom extend beyond the middle class in urban areas. Sometimes they are opposed by religious groups. Widespread education on birth-control methods and a political commitment on the part of governments to reduce birthrates is called for. Without them few African countries have a realistic possibility of sustaining any significant growth in per capita incomes: With the present rates of population growth, unprecedented in world history, African economies are having to grow at high rates merely to maintain existing levels of income.

Food production growth in the 1970s was barely half the rate of population growth; by 1981, the average daily calorie supply throughout Sub-Saharan Africa was only 90 percent of the calculated minimum requirement. In only eleven of the thirty-nine countries for which the World Bank reported data—Benin, Cameroon, Côte d'Ivoire, Lesotho, Liberia, Madagascar, Mauritius, Niger, Senegal, Sierra Leone, and Somalia—was average daily calorie intake above the estimated minimum requirement. Continued drought almost certainly has reduced these figures further. These rates of malnutrition expose the destructive interconnection between poverty, population growth, hunger, and disease. The complexity of this relationship is a significant constraint on the ability of governments to tackle these problems effectively. Unless African governments are able to mount a systematic attack on several dimensions simultaneously—and they will obviously need significant external assistance—the African future will be as bleak as the pessimists' most dire predictions.

In the 1980s, Africa has faced another health tragedy in the form of Acquired Immune Deficiency Syndrome (AIDS). This disease, which in Africa, unlike the West, has spread primarily through heterosexual contact, is epidemic in parts of Central and eastern Africa. Even if health agencies are successful in encouraging "safe sex" in the future, the disease already appears to be sufficiently entrenched that an enormous number of casualties will result.

☐ Industrial Policies

African leaders inherited economies at independence that possessed only small industrial sectors, a reflection of the colonial conception of economic complementarity. Throughout Sub-Saharan Africa, the industrial sector contributed on average only 16 percent of GDP at independence. This figure probably even overestimates the share of industry, given the difficulties of calculating the contribution of the subsistence agricultural sector to GDP. And it is important to note that "industry" is defined in national accounts statistics to include mining, construction, manufacturing, and utilities, such as electricity, gas, and water. The share of manufacturing in African economies thus was substantially smaller than the figure for "industry"—on average, less than 10 percent of GDP. Of course, the *average* for the whole of Sub-Saharan Africa conceals tremendous variations between countries. The industrial sector contributed 63 percent of the GDP of Zambia in 1960, a reflection of the importance of that country's copper mines, whereas it constituted less than 10 percent of the GDP of Benin, Mozambique, Niger, Rwanda, Somalia, and the Sudan.

All African governments at independence were determined to increase the share of industry in their economies. Industrialization was regarded as the cornerstone of economic development and modernization. This belief has had substantial theoretical support over the last two hundred years, first from writers in the mercantilist tradition, such as Alexander Hamilton and Friedrich List, and subsequently by most development economists. Hamilton had warned his fellows among the founding fathers of the United States of the dangers to the new republic of reliance on the export of primary goods at a time when its competitors reaped the benefits of industrialization. Similarly, List, a German economist writing in the middle of the nineteenth century, argued that production according to "comparative advantage" and a policy of laissez-faire favored those countries that had already industrialized and was a means of preserving their domination over other countries.

These arguments have been echoed and refined in the post-1945 period by development economists and dependency theorists. The latter have detailed the mechanisms of "unequal exchange," whereby high-cost manufactured products from industrialized countries are traded for low-cost primary products from less-developed countries (LDCs). They allege that, as a result, surplus is extracted from the periphery toward the industrialized center of the world economy. Unequal exchange is also perceived by some writers as leading to an inevitable decline in the terms of trade for primary-product-exporting countries —that is, over a period of time the volume of primary products that such countries must export in order to be able to purchase a given volume of manufactured goods from industrialized countries will inevitably increase. Whether the experience of the postwar years justifies these arguments is still a matter of considerable controversy among economists.

As we have already noted, there were periods, such as in the 1950s and in the mid-1970s, when the terms of trade appeared to move quite markedly in Africa's favor. It is misleading, however, to discuss aggregate terms of trade, as these disguise the marked differences between various commodities—for example, the temporary success of oil producers in the period 1974–1982 in substantially improving their terms of trade, the marked decline in the price of copper in the period after 1973. Two conclusions may, however, be drawn with reasonable confidence. First, although there may not have been a long-term decline in aggregate terms of trade for Africa in the years since 1945, there is certainly no evidence to support the contrary idea of a sustained improvement throughout this period. Second, most economists are in agreement that Africa as a whole has suffered a marked deterioration in its terms of trade from the late 1970s through the mid-1980s.

Whereas the early mercantilist writers such as List and Hamilton emphasized the importance of industrialization to national security, contemporary development economists have provided a sophisticated argument on the importance of industrialization for sustained economic growth in developing countries. Manufacturing industry, they assert, inevitably grows more rapidly than primary production, given people's propensity to spend a larger portion of their income on manufactured goods as income rises. Manufacturing industry is seen as providing a stimulus to overall economic growth, as it achieves dynamic economies of scale as the internal market grows. Manufacturing, alone, it is argued, has dynamic effects on restructuring the economy through the learning of skills and the development of technology. The growth of manufacturing industry also increases productivity in the agricultural sector by absorbing surplus labor and through the provision of new inputs and technology for agricultural producers.[35]

For most developing countries, the obvious initial pathway toward industrialization is through local production of goods currently being imported, particularly consumer goods, as these generally require less-sophisticated manufacturing methods than do machinery and other capital goods. This process is known as import-substituting industrialization (ISI). Development economists are well aware of the fact that ISI will initially impose additional costs on the local economy, as the new industries established ("infant" industries) typically will not be able to produce as efficiently as the companies currently exporting to the local market. This results from a variety of factors, such as the initial costs of establishment and the limited size of the domestic market, which precludes economies of scale. New industries almost inevitably will have to be protected from competition from lower-cost imports through such means as tariffs. Local consumers will, therefore, initially have to pay more for these locally-manufactured goods than they would if imports continued. Development economists argue, however, that these increased costs will be more than offset by the dynamic gains to the economy that local manufacturing generates; scarce foreign exchange should be saved; and, eventually, it should be possible to remove the protection given to local industry as it becomes more competitive with imports as the local market expands.

Since the early 1970s, some developing countries have increased local manufacturing on the basis of producing consumer goods to be exported to the markets of developed countries, often in association with TNCs, which typically provide the components for assembly in the developing country. Again, this is an area in which there is considerable disagreement among economists.

Those writing in the dependency tradition perceive this offshore assembly as merely another dimension of the underdevelopment of LDCs, typically at the expense of the exploitation of low-cost labor, often young women. Other development economists argue, however, that over a period of years the TNC often purchases an increasing proportion of its inputs from local suppliers and thus generates linkages with the local economy, thereby promoting economic growth. They also argue that skills are learned by both the labor force and by local management: The latter are then able to establish their own companies that can challenge the TNCs.[36] As we will see, few African countries have yet been able to follow this strategy.

African governments at independence faced formidable constraints in their efforts to promote local manufacturing industry. In many countries, the local market for manufactured goods was extremely small, a reflection of both the relatively small population of many countries and low per capita income. Production runs inevitably were short, thereby preventing local industry from reaping economies of scale. A possible solution was to produce for a regional market created through the establishment of customs unions and common markets. As we will see in Chapter 10, although this strategy has enjoyed considerable nominal support from African leaders over the years, the structural factors that impede regional integration have prevented most customs unions and common markets from operating effectively. A second constraint faced by most governments was the extremely low level of infrastructure in their economies and the fact that most of it was directed toward facilitating foreign trade rather than the manufacture and distribution of locally produced goods. In consequence, the establishment costs for new industries in Africa tend to be much higher than those in other countries—the World Bank estimated that the paucity of infrastructure in African countries necessitates initial investments that are 25 to 60 percent higher than for similar industries in developed countries.[37] Poor infrastructure often causes delays, such as where necessary imports are held up in congested ports, or causes inefficiencies in production, when, for instance, electricity or water supplies break down.

A shortage of skilled personnel again had a negative effect. Most African countries lacked a labor force that had experience in industry; probably even more important was the paucity of personnel with management skills. Many African countries had to rely on expatriate management—a factor that inevitably increased the costs incurred by the industry compared to its equivalent in many other developing countries. According to World Bank data, management salaries paid to expatriates working in Africa are typically two to three times those paid to their counterparts in home countries. A survey of textile mills showed that expatriate salaries added 25 to 50 percent to the payroll of African companies in comparison with payrolls for firms operating in Latin America.[38]

Another constraint faced by most African governments at independence was the absence of indigenous entrepreneurs with sufficient accumulated capital with which to initiate an industrial enterprise. The lack of entrepreneurs had two repercussions: It led inevitably to a large role for the state in industrializa- tion in Africa, reinforcing a tendency that economic historians have noted as common to all "late-industrializing" countries;[39] it also inevitably increased the reliance of African governments upon transnational corporations. Industrializa- tion in the postindependence period in Africa thus cannot be considered without reference to the activities of TNCs. As we discuss the relationship of African governments with transnational companies in detail in Chapter 10, we will only briefly mention here a number of ways in which reliance on TNCs has affected the course of industrialization in Africa.

First, as part of the agreement on the licensing of technology to their Afri- can subsidiaries, many TNCs (sometimes at the insistence of trade unions in their home countries) have insisted on a clause preventing this technology from being used to produce goods for export to other countries. The transnational was attempting to protect either a subsidiary in the third country or, alterna- tively, its exports to that market from another company subsidiary. The net result was that many African subsidiaries were limited to producing for the small domestic market, thereby condemning them to short, relatively high-cost pro- duction runs. Second, TNCs typically tend to employ production methods that have been devised for their home countries in which the relative costs of various factors of production, most notably labor and capital, may be very different from those prevailing in Africa. In short, TNCs tend to favor capital-intensive and automated production techniques that generate relatively few employment opportunities. But in Africa, it is labor that is the relatively abundant factor. Third, TNCs typically manufacture products developed for the high-income consumer societies in which they have their home bases. Critics of TNC ac- tivities argue that these goods are often not "appropriate" for developing coun- tries; a misallocation of resources occurs when a large proportion of low incomes is devoted to purchasing "luxury" goods and other items, such as cigarettes and soft drinks, that are perceived as health hazards.

Through their economic power, critics argue, TNCs are able both to influ- ence government decision makers to pursue irrational industrialization strategies and, through advertising, to persuade consumers to purchase prod- ucts that are largely irrelevant to their development needs. Unless one accepts the extreme dependency argument that all government elites are essentially "compradors"—that is, agents or auxiliaries of transnational capital—it is evi- dent that governments enjoy some autonomy in negotiations with TNCs. They may, therefore, be able to affect the type of technique utilized. We will discuss the factors that affect the balance of bargaining power between the parties in Chapter 10.

Following independence, a variety of measures were taken to promote local industrialization. Virtually all countries initially encouraged foreign in- vestment through incentives such as tax holidays, preferential foreign- exchange arrangements, and guarantees of a domestic market not subject to competition from imports. By the late 1960s, attitudes toward foreign investment had changed. Many countries (particularly, though not exclusively nor always, those proclaiming their allegiance to a socialist path) insisted that a substantial shareholding in the local subsidiaries of TNCs be made available to the government. And, as we will see in Chapter 10, in the 1970s other governments required that TNC subsidiaries sell a portion of their shares to local citizens. At the same time, most governments were directly promoting local industry through the establishment of parastatal organizations—state-owned corporations that enjoyed some degree of budgetary autonomy. Again, their activities were often protected from foreign competition through the use of tariff and nontariff barriers (such as import licensing); priority in the allocation of scarce foreign exchange was usually given to the purchase of capital and intermediary goods needed by industry.

Africa's experience with import substitution has not, on the whole, been a particularly happy one. By the early 1970s, substantial evidence had been accumulated from other Third World countries that ISI had often not brought the benefits expected from it. Rather than conserving scarce foreign exchange, as proponents had argued, ISI had frequently proved to be import-intensive, as capital goods and many of the components used in manufacturing had to be imported. The foreign-exchange problem was often made worse where ISI was being conducted by a subsidiary of a transnational company (as it repatriated profits, interest, and dividends to its parent overseas). Rather than reducing external dependence, ISI had merely led to a change in the nature of that dependence—for example, on foreign technology.

Neoclassical economists also attacked ISI on the grounds that it led to a misallocation of resources. One of the problems was that infant industries failed to grow up; they continued to rely on high levels of protection from potential competitors. Import-substituting industries thus frequently enjoyed a quasi-monopolistic position in the supply of various goods and services. With high levels of protection, however, there was little incentive for industry to become more efficient. Inefficient ISI caused local consumers to pay unnecessarily high prices; ISI, therefore, discriminated directly against other sectors of the economy, especially agriculture, that were dependent on inputs from import-substituting industries. And, because the industries operated so inefficiently, there was little prospect of their being able to sell on the world market and thus to reap economies of scale.

Other policies associated with ISI were also seen as causing distortions. Governments typically maintained an overvalued exchange rate in order to reduce the relative cost of inputs needed by industry. This policy, however, directly discriminated against the export sectors of the economy—agriculture and mining—as it made their products relatively more expensive for foreigners to purchase. State corporations were judged to be particularly inefficient, often because governments insisted that they take on a variety of functions, such as giving employment to secondary-school leavers and providing below-cost services to other sectors of the economy, functions that directly undermined economic rationality. Loss-making industries were a drain on the national budget, leading to higher taxes for other sectors, particularly agriculture. As the World Bank asserts, although industrialization has a crucial role to play in economic development, its benefits "do not justify the promotion of industry at any cost."[40]

A number of serious policy errors were undoubtedly also made, particularly in opting for the latest high-technology processes rather than those more suitable for local conditions. Again, the prestige of the latest equipment (the "big and modern are beautiful" syndrome), and the pressure of foreign donors, often played a role. Among the more notorious examples was the creation of six vehicle assembly plants in Nigeria that were largely dependent on imported materials. The range of models produced was so wide that production runs were extremely short; the multiplication of plants also ensured that all operated at very low levels in capacity. As a result, some recorded a negative value added in manufacturing: Just the costs of assembly in Nigeria were in excess of the cost of importing a fully built vehicle from overseas. Another classic mistake was the building of a large automated bakery in Tanzania that was allegedly more capital-intensive than the country's oil refinery, was highly dependent on imported wheat, and displaced a number of local, more efficient manufacturers. Industries have often been established without sufficient consideration being given to the availability of necessary inputs, the development of the necessary infrastructure, and potential alternative sources of supply for machinery, etc. As Coulson notes in the context of the Tanzanian bakery, decision making on industrial policy has often been made in an ad hoc manner by overworked bureaucrats under extreme pressure from donor agencies. Although policy mistakes are understandable, the unfortunate consequence of a series of ad hoc errors for some countries was an industrial strategy that not only was self-defeating but that also had a negative impact on other areas of the economy.[41]

Not only was the industrial strategy promoted by most African states inefficient, but it also appears to have largely failed in bringing about a dramatic increase in local manufacturing. Although UNIDO (United Nations Industrial Development Organization) data show that Sub-Saharan Africa recorded a growth of 7 percent in manufacturing value added in the period 1963–1973, this growth was reduced to 5.7 percent in the period 1973–1981. Subsequently, there has been stagnation. In the period 1973–1981, fourteen countries actually recorded a decrease in manufacturing value added. And, in the same period, the contribution of manufacturing to total GDP fell in twenty Sub-Saharan countries. By 1983, the share of manufacturing in GDP in low-income countries throughout the region was lower than it had been in 1965 (down from 9 to 7 percent), whereas it had remained constant in non-African low-income developing countries. Similarly, although the share of manufactures in the exports of low-income countries in Africa had risen from 5 to 9 percent in the same period, the figure for other low-income developing countries had moved from 24 to 50 percent. Africa's share of world manufactured exports fell by almost half over the years 1970 to 1976 to a miserable .6 percent.[42]

Africa's industrialization experience cannot be divorced from developments in the international economic system. Two factors are particularly important. The first is the global recession of the 1970s and 1980s. The demand for and prices of Africa's refined minerals (classified as manufactured goods in many surveys) has fallen substantially as a result of recession. Faced by huge increases in the price that they had to pay for fuel, substantial increases in the prices of imported manufactured goods, and a growing debt-servicing burden, while simultaneously experiencing a drop in the prices that they received for many of their principal exports, African countries faced severe balance-of-payments constraints. As a result, they have often not been able to afford to import the necessary spare parts to keep some of their manufacturing industry in operation. Shortage of spare parts has similarly affected the operation of key utilities, whose failures in turn have caused declines in manufactured output. The recession has also exacerbated the trend toward protectionism in industrialized countries, which has had a particularly adverse effect on newcomers to industrial production.[43]

The second constraining influence has been the evolution of a new international division of labor. Although there is a danger that this concept is given an unduly deterministic status, rather than being perceived in large part as a reflection of a multitude of domestic and international factors that influence decision making on industrial location, there is little doubt that few international companies perceive Africa as a desirable location for their offshore assembly. Some of the reasons for this are the perceived instability of the political and economic environment, the poor infrastructure, the allegedly low level of worker and management skills, relatively high transport costs from Africa to industrialized countries, and the high cost of labor in Africa relative to that in Asia.[44] As a result, Africa has largely been left out of the massive relocation of manufacturing industry that occurred in the 1970s. Most African states have not attempted to industrialize on the basis of exported manufactures. Two states that have at least partially pursued this strategy, Côte d'Ivoire and Kenya, have found that their access to their "natural" market, the European Economic Community (EEC), with which they have long-established and well-developed trading links, has been curtailed by protective measures despite the free access they supposedly enjoy as a result of their participation in the Lomé Conventions.[45] As Steven Langdon shows, however, manufacturing for export in Kenya has also been constrained by a number of internal factors, such as the high cost of inputs from other protected industries and the small production runs that characterize most companies' output.[46]

Africa remains the least industrialized of the continents. In a survey conducted by UNIDO of 100 commodities in forty African countries, the organization found "a truly alarming picture of the extent of Africa's import dependence as far as manufacturing industry is concerned." For 55 percent of the commodities surveyed, all countries imported close to 100 percent of domestic consumption. For another 20 percent of commodities, a majority imported close to 100 percent of their needs. These two groups included virtually all the intermediate industrial inputs necessary to establish a viable industrial base. Only for food products and textiles is the import to consumption ratio below 25 percent for the majority of countries. Only a handful of countries manufacture the inputs required by their agricultural sectors.[47]

Most analysts are extremely pessimistic regarding Africa's future industrial prospects. Although some countries have achieved limited success with manufactured exports—most notably Mauritius, Zimbabwe, and Côte d'Ivoire—prevailing conditions in the world economy appear unfavorable to a significant expansion of exports of manufactured goods. As latecomers to industrialization, African countries face world markets that are subject to protectionism in response to the success of the newly industrializing countries (NICs), and where increased investment by industrialized countries in robotization has shifted comparative advantage in some production processes away from developing countries. African governments will have to achieve a major improvement in their domestic industrial policies if the decline in industrial production experienced in many countries since 1975 is to be reversed. In particular, there is a need to force protected industries to be more efficient through reducing levels of protection, to devalue exchange rates, to promote an integrated industrial policy that ensures that adequate infrastructure is available, and to foster the use of local raw materials and, especially, linkages with the agricultural sector.

□ Policies Toward Agriculture

It is appropriate that the last sector to be examined in this survey of government strategies is agriculture—as this is the position that it has been accorded far too often by African governments. Agriculture has often been perceived as a "traditional" sector; governments consequently have tended to give priority to industry. Their inclinations in this direction have been reinforced by the writings of many economists and dependency theorists, who argued that industrial development provided the only viable basis for the creation of a dynamic economy. What has often been overlooked, however, is the emphasis that many development economists have placed on the necessity of an agricultural revolution accompanying industrialization if successful economic transformation is to take place. The capital necessary to promote industrialization has to be generated from somewhere—for most countries, the only viable option is to obtain it from the agricultural sector.

The recent history of African agricultural production has been little short of disastrous. Africa is the only continent where per capita agricultural production has fallen since the early 1970s. The predominance of agriculture in African economies—it contributes approximately one-third of Africa's GDP (50 percent in low-income countries), over 70 percent of employment, and over 40 percent of all exports—ensures that failure in the agricultural sector critically weakens overall growth prospects.

Africa's agriculture at independence was relatively healthy. During the colonial period, cash-crop production had been introduced throughout the continent or, in those areas where cash crops had replaced slaves as the principal basis for trade with the West, significantly extended. There is considerable controversy among economists on the issue of whether cash-crop production inevitably occurred at the expense of food crops and whether it thereby placed the subsistence of African households at risk. This certainly was the case in some countries, particularly those in which forced labor was widespread, such as Mozambique. As a general rule, however, the picture is less clear-cut. In most countries, there was considerable underemployment of resources in agriculture at the time of colonization; it was possible to grow new crops for sale on the world market while maintaining food crop production. At independence, Africa was actually a net exporter of staple foods. But the slow rates of growth in agricultural production coupled with the rapid rise in population turned this food surplus into a deficit within fifteen years. By the mid-1970s, Africa was a net importer of staple foods; domestic production fell short of total food needs by 4 percent. By the 1980–1982 period, Africa was importing 11.2 million metric tons (12.5 million short tons) of foodstuffs each year with an annual value of over $6.8 billion (one-seventh of the total value of African imports in 1982). The volume of cereals imports was such that the World Bank estimated that one in five people in Africa in 1982 (equivalent to the continent's entire urban population) depended on them.

The causes of Africa's agricultural crisis are multidimensional. Drought has played a role, particularly in the Sahel and throughout the savannah belt in the years from 1982 to 1985. But Africa's agricultural crisis has been of such a duration and so widespread that it cannot be explained by reference to drought alone. Environmental constraints have also been evident in the rapid erosion of surface soils following deforestation. Unpredictable rainfall and the large variety of soils on the continent have made agricultural research difficult. Food aid has also had a disincentive effect for African farmers because it tends to drive the prices for their production down. But most observers are agreed that a considerable portion of the blame must be laid at the foot of African governments, which, they argue, have shown a consistently antiagricultural bias through such policies as offering low prices to farmers, reliance on food imports, especially food aid, and maintaining overvalued exchange rates. The crisis has affected not only food production but also production of export crops. Africa's share of the world market for its principal agricultural exports declined significantly in the period from 1970 to 1982.

One of the legacies of the colonial era is a system of government-controlled crop marketing boards. These often have a monopsony role—that is, they are the sole buyer for the export crops produced by African farmers. The marketing boards fix a price to be paid to domestic producers that often bears little resemblance to the prevailing world market price. One objective of the boards was to provide relatively stable income for farmers by shielding them from fluctuating world market prices. Another principal objective, however, was to extract a surplus from agriculture that could then be used to promote economic diversification. This was—and continues to be—achieved by paying farmers less than the board receives when it sells the crop on the world market. Through this means, the colonial administrations extracted resources not only to pay for the costs of government but also to finance development projects, many of which benefited urban dwellers. This practice has been continued since independence in part because governments have found it difficult to tax other sectors of the economy.

If the argument that diversification into industry is crucial for economic development is accepted, then the extraction of some resources from agriculture is essential. The problem is to achieve a fine balance between gaining the resources needed for diversification, on the one hand, and providing a disincentive to continued agricultural production, on the other—killing the goose that lays the golden egg. Many commentators believe that one of the reasons for Africa's poor agricultural performance is that African governments have overstepped this line and created a situation in which production of crops for the market is no longer perceived as worthwhile by many farmers.

Robert Bates provides a convincing explanation for the antiagricultural bias on the part of many African governments. Farmers in many countries—especially peasant producers—have been a relatively ineffective political constituency compared with urban and industrial groups, whose interests in cheap food coincide with those of the government. Because peasant farmers are dispersed throughout the country and have relatively low incomes, they are difficult to organize. Peasant producers thus fail to make their voice heard in government policymaking circles; it is easier for them to protest against government policy simply by terminating production for the market than to attempt to change policy through lobbying. Food prices thus have been kept low not only as a means of extracting surplus from agriculture but also in order to placate urban dwellers, whose strategic location enables them to exert more political pressure on incumbent governments than rural producers can. Governments may also prefer to rely on food imports, Bates argues, rather than raise domestic prices, as scarcity and the management of the importing system provide opportunities for political patronage. Similarly, the often noted inefficiencies of crop marketing boards may be partly explained by their use by governments as instruments of patronage—primarily as a means of providing employment.[48]

Antiagricultural bias is thus a classic instance of the divergence of short-term political rationality from long-term economic rationality. During the 1970s the problems caused by government policies became very apparent. Africa's aggregate annual increase in food production of 1.7 percent in the years 1970–1982 was only one-half of the rate of population growth. In this period, only seven of thirty-nine countries (Benin, Cameroon, Central African Republic,

Côte d'Ivoire, Mauritius, Rwanda, and Swaziland) for which the World Bank reported data maintained or improved on their index of food production per capita recorded for the 1969–1971 period. That so many countries have recorded poor performances in the agricultural sector suggests that the operation of anti-agricultural bias has not been restricted to any particular type of regime. African governments have, however, diverged quite markedly in their policies toward agriculture; we will now briefly consider some of the alternative strategies that have been pursued.

Almost certainly, the least successful of all approaches has been the large-scale, mechanized state farm. There were already several notable failures of this method in the preindependence period, the most notorious of which was the attempt to set up mechanized production of peanuts—the so-called Groundnuts Scheme—in Tanganyika in the years immediately following World War II. This project proved totally inappropriate to the local conditions and, over a ten-year period, cost a total of more than £35 million sterling ($100 million). Similar failures were experienced in northern Nigeria. In the years after independence, countries espousing a socialist ideology have been tempted most frequently to experiment with the state farm model. State farms have been seen as a means of transcending the low productivity of traditional peasant production without encouraging capitalist differentiation in the countryside.

The first significant postindependence experiment with mechanized state farms was undertaken by Ghana during the last years of the Nkrumah period. Government expenditure on agriculture was focused on the state farm sector, in which large-scale mechanized production was encouraged. Some of the resources for this were to be extracted from cocoa producers, whom Nkrumah perceived as the principal manifestation of rural capitalism and a significant threat to his regime. By 1965 there were 105 state farms, nominally controlling 1 million acres (400,000 hectares), but only one-tenth of this area was actually cultivated. More than four thousand tractors were purchased for the farms, which also were allocated the bulk of the government's agricultural extension services. But the farms proved to be extremely inefficient. Tractors were poorly maintained and frequently out of service. Productivity was substantially below that of the peasant farm sector. Tony Killick estimates, for instance, that yields per acre were less than one-quarter of those of peasant farms, whereas labor productivity on the state farms was only one-sixth of that of peasant agriculture.[49] During the years 1963–1965 alone, Ghana's State Farm Corporation lost $19.8 million.[50] Perhaps even more devastating for the long-term development of Ghana's agriculture was the effect on the cocoa sector. Failure to provide services to this sector during this period and the low prices paid by the government to cocoa producers (to extract resources not only for state farms but also for Nkrumah's ambitious industrialization program) dealt the cocoa sector—Ghana's principal source of exports—a blow from which it is only now recovering. The world's most important cocoa exporter in the early 1960s, Ghana sank to third place by the end of the 1970s, when Ghanaian cocoa exports were less than half those of its long-standing rival, Côte d'Ivoire.

Apparently failing to heed the lessons of these earlier experiments with large-scale mechanized state farms, Mozambique adopted a similar policy in the years immediately following its independence. Many of the large farms and plantations abandoned by Portuguese settlers when Mozambique gained its independence were converted into state farms. As Barry Munslow points out, a major reason for the failure of the state farms was an "over-estimation of the managerial, technical, and financial resources" available for such ambitious projects, a reflection, he argues, of the government's "over-zealous desire to socialise the countryside."[51] Once again, maintenance of tractors proved to be a formidable problem; centralized planning proved to be too rigid a straitjacket; and the government found it difficult to attract labor to work on the farms. Despite the bulk of government expenditure on agriculture that was devoted to state farms in the late 1970s, the results were disappointing. In consequence, the FRELIMO government decided in 1982 to reorient its agricultural policies toward supporting cooperatives and peasant production.

A second agricultural strategy pursued by some socialist governments has been to encourage collectivized or communal, agriculture. This strategy appears to have enjoyed more popularity with political elites than with peasants themselves. One of the aims behind collectivization has been to encourage peasants to live in villages as a means of facilitating the delivery of services to the population. Yet, although villagization has enjoyed some success, albeit sometimes under coercion, communal production has not. In Tanzania, as much as 90 percent of all peasants are organized in villages, yet under 5 percent of agricultural output is derived from communal production. Similarly, more than 20 percent of the peasant population in Mozambique lives in communal villages, but only 1.5 percent of them were producing crops communally. As Reginald Green argues, the principal reason for this low level of communal production is that there is an inability on the part of governments to demonstrate that communal production is inherently more effective than traditional household production. As peasants cannot be shown the value of communal production by pointing to successful experiences—indeed, the contrary is often the case, especially where mechanization has been introduced—they have no incentive to adopt it. Rather than a demonstration of the alleged inherent conservatism of the peasantry, this should be perceived as a rational choice—why place your survival at risk when the advantages of the alternative have not been clearly demonstrated?[52]

An approach adopted by some governments pursuing a capitalist development strategy has been the promotion of plantation agriculture. The most notable examples of this are to be found in Côte d'Ivoire and Malawi, although plantation agriculture has also been significant in parts of Ghana and Nigeria. Once again, a principal rationale for this mode of production is its perceived advantages over traditional peasant agriculture—a belief that mechanization is necessary to increase productivity. Services, it is argued, can be delivered more efficiently to plantations than to small farms. As plantations are usually owned by members of the political elite, they have often fared far better than peasant agriculture in terms of the allocation of resources, such as extension services, disease prevention, and access to inputs, and have as well received more favorable prices for their products. For instance, in Côte d'Ivoire, the state has not taxed the production of pineapples—which occurs largely on plantations—in the same way that it has extracted resources from the production of other export crops.

One of the problems faced by plantation agriculture has been a shortage of labor. To be profitable, plantations must pay low wages. But, in most African countries, farm laborers usually have the option—not available in most other Third World areas—of returning to their home villages and undertaking their own production. In Malawi this problem has been addressed by deliberately lowering the returns to peasant agriculture and by reducing the labor migration to South Africa, thereby creating additional population pressure on the available land. Côte d'Ivoire attempted to resolve the problem by recruiting large numbers of migrants from neighboring countries, particularly Burkina Faso.

Although there is some evidence to support the view that plantation agriculture has been relatively successful in expanding production of certain cash crops for export, it is difficult to perceive it as an answer to Africa's agricultural problems. First, the sector has been very heavily favored in terms of government expenditure; the cost of hidden subsidies is difficult to estimate. Second, plantation agriculture has often relied on a coercive labor environment. Third, and perhaps somewhat paradoxically, plantation agriculture creates little overall employment—if introduced on a countrywide basis it would rob a large number of peasants of their livelihoods without providing employment for them. The natural result would be a huge increase in rural-urban migration, with the urban areas being unable to provide employment for the newcomers. Fourth, plantation agriculture, given its heavy reliance on machinery and fertilizers, is highly import-intensive and places additional strains on Africa's already difficult balance of trade. Finally, plantation agriculture, with its mechanized mode of production, may well be ecologically unsound in many parts of Africa, given the fragility of the soils.[53] This has been suggested to be the case, for example, for rice production in northern Ghana.

Most agricultural production in Africa in the past and in the forseeable future will be conducted by households. It is in relation to household production that government policies have failed so badly since the early 1970s. One part of the reason has undoubtedly been the decline in the prices received for many of Africa's agricultural exports. This decline, however, cannot explain all of the policy failure. A starting point in reviving agricultural production would be to pay higher prices to peasant farmers. But higher prices are particularly costly. Other incentives to rural producers—such as improved availability of agricultural inputs; educational, health, and water facilities; roads and transport—may provide an equally effective but lower-cost method of encouraging production.

Evidence from countries as diverse as Burkina Faso, Mali, and Kenya suggests that farmers are more concerned with their incomes than with prices alone. Production can be increased, without having to pay higher prices, by offering farmers higher-yielding varieties.[54]

In addition, governments simply have not given enough attention to the agricultural sector in their allocation of expenditure. The median share of government expenditure in Africa devoted to agriculture for the 1963 to 1973 period was only 7.6 percent. In Tanzania, despite the government's commitment to agricultural self-reliance, the share of agriculture in development expenditure declined from over 20 percent in the mid-1960s to 10 percent in 1978/79. Many governments reportedly devote as little as 3 to 5 percent of their budgets to agriculture. This contrasts with the record of other developing countries with successful agricultural sectors, which typically devote 10 to 15 percent of government investment to agriculture.[55]

Research and development has been virtually ignored in some countries. In Sierra Leone, for instance, agricultural research expenditure was only .21 percent of GDP in 1980; there were only thirty-five scientists in Sierra Leone working on agricultural research in that year. Some countries are even worse off in terms of skilled personnel—Benin had only nineteen agricultural researchers in 1980.[56] In large part, this neglect reflects the lack of priority given to training agricultural economists and engineers, again a product of the emphasis given to traditional liberal arts education at many universities; it also reflects undergraduates' perceptions of the relative unattractiveness of agriculture as a career. Not only have relatively few resources been devoted to agricultural research and development, but those invested often appear not to have been productively utilized. Michael Lipton asserts that twenty years have been wasted in agricultural research in many (not all) Sub-Saharan African countries. This reflects, in part, poorly conceived priorities: The colonial emphasis on research on export crops has been maintained and food crops relatively neglected. Aid donors share the blame because they have tended to emphasize export agriculture and, therefore, favor cash crops. Present researchers are characterized as underqualified, underproductive, and overpaid. Too often, research has not been tested in on-farm conditions.[57]

Even if the current trend toward increased research and development expenditure is accelerated, however, there are few reasons to believe that a breakthrough in African crop production comparable to that achieved by the Green Revolution in Asia will be forthcoming. Although some success has been achieved in some countries with hybrid varieties of maize, there have been few breakthroughs. In large part, this situation results from the nature of African agriculture, which unlike that of Asia is primarily rainfed rather than irrigated, and from the variability of climate and soils throughout the African continent.[58]

In the first half of the 1980s, however, African governments gained a greater appreciation of the importance of the agricultural sector for their future economic growth. In part, this was forced upon them by the food shortages that afflicted many countries. Efforts to hold down food prices in order to placate urban interests proved impossible in the context of food shortages. Rather than sell their products to the government at low official prices, farmers sold their crops on "parallel" (unofficial) markets; in a context of scarcity, urban consumers had no choice but to pay the higher prices that prevailed in the parallel markets. These markets are estimated to handle as much as 70 percent of the food supplies in some countries. African governments also found that an increasing share of their scarce foreign exchange was being devoted to food imports and that, contrary to their professed goal of self-reliance, they were becoming increasingly dependent on the whims of food-aid donors.

At the July 1985 summit of the Organization of African Unity, the first to be devoted to economic issues, member states pledged to raise the share of agriculture in public expenditure to 25 percent over the following five years. In its submission to the UN General Assembly's June 1986 Special Session on Africa's Economic and Social Crisis, the OAU pledged $57.4 billion, or 44.8 percent of the total investment projected under Africa's Priority Programme for Economic Recovery 1986–90 to the agricultural sector. Whether these sums will be realized remains to be seen—the lukewarm response of foreign donors certainly places them at risk. Increasing interest by members of the political elite in engaging in agricultural production suggests, however, that the sector may receive more favorable treatment than it has in the past.

Agriculture presents the single most important policy challenge faced by African governments in the remaining years of this century. Aggregate performance since 1970 has been little short of disastrous. Declining per capita output has not only had a negative impact on social development through increased malnutrition but has also undermined the whole economic development strategy of many governments. Enormous sums of scarce foreign exchange are being spent on food imports; even so, these alone cannot meet the food gap. African states have become increasingly reliant on food aid, which can fluctuate according to the level of agricultural surpluses in industrialized countries. Together with the growing debt crisis to which the failure of agricultural exports has contributed, reliance on food aid makes African states more dependent than at any time since their independence.

■ POPULAR STRATEGIES
FOR ECONOMIC SURVIVAL

So far in this chapter we have examined the ways in which government policies have both contributed to and attempted to cope with the economic crisis that has beset Africa since the late 1970s. As the economic crisis has deepened, however, many states have lost their control over resources; their capacity for penetrating societies has been substantially diminished. As the state became less effective—and, indeed, in some extreme cases, became a predator on society—

the mass of the population has had to devise its own strategies to ensure its economic survival. Four of these strategies have been identified.[59]

1.   *Belt-tightening strategies* represent an attempt to cope with scarcities without departing from conventional codes of conduct. As goods have become increasingly expensive or disappeared from circulation altogether, people have had to adjust their tastes to match their reduced purchasing power. Less-expensive (and often less-fashionable) foods have been substituted for the previous diet. As spare parts for cars and consumer durables have disappeared from the market, innovative local repairs have been carried out; where this has not been possible, items have had to be left in their broken state. Those with access to transport and foreign exchange have sometimes been able to purchase foodstuffs and other goods in short supply from neighboring countries.

There are a variety of costs involved with this strategy. Standards of living, already low, may decline below the absolute poverty line. Malnourishment may accompany an inferior diet. Enormous quantities of time and energy are wasted in locating and queuing for basic necessities.

2.   *Black market strategies* have come into play as goods have become scarce; the temptation to hoard goods and force prices even higher has grown. Similarly, a popular response to the low prices that some governments have offered agricultural (and some precious metal) producers has been to sell the goods outside official channels and/or smuggle them into adjacent countries. In most African countries, an enormous "informal" economy has grown up parallel to the countries' official markets. Often the black market has become the only source of scarce goods—but at a price.

The obvious problem with this strategy is that it encourages corruption and ultimately destroys the moral fabric of society. Officials have to be paid off to induce them to turn a blind eye to illicit dealings; those with access to scarce foreign exchange and import licenses can make enormous profits. Corruption can rapidly become a way of life; it has often (as in Uganda) been accompanied by a breakdown of law and order as soldiers seize what they cannot afford or are unwilling to buy.

3.   *Back-to-the-farm strategies* are possible because most Africans retain a right of access to land in the villages of their families. Unlike urban dwellers in most Latin American and Asian countries, therefore, Africans have the option of responding to economic crisis by returning to agricultural production. This has happened on a significant scale in countries such as Ghana, Nigeria, and Tanzania. For many, this is a retreat into subsistence production. Some urban professionals, however, responding to the economic crisis and especially agricultural shortages, have been encouraged to establish plantations, where they hope to capitalize on the higher prices for agricultural products prevailing both on official and black markets.

4.   *Migration strategies* have been another response to economic crisis. Hundreds of thousands of Africans have sought their economic fortunes outside

their native lands. The unskilled typically looked for employment in adjacent countries where the economies were somewhat more healthy. Large-scale migration was especially prominent in West Africa, where people were attracted to the relatively-prosperous Côte d'Ivoire and Nigeria. As economies even in these countries encountered severe problems in the 1980s, migration became less feasible. Existing migrants became the subject of personal abuse and sometimes of physical assaults. The Nigerian government twice responded to popular pressure by forcing mass expulsions of migrants from neighboring countries. Deteriorating economic conditions have provided a further incentive to those possessing professional skills to migrate. The shortage of skilled personnel in African countries has been severely exacerbated by the recent exodus from the professions, government departments, and universities. The damage to African economies will take many years to reverse.

Although the strategies that Africans have adopted to cope with economic crisis have shown their adaptability and creativity, they do not in themselves provide the foundation for a viable long-term strategy for the rehabilitation of African economies. Indeed, many of them tend in the opposite direction. Migration and black market strategies further weaken the fragile economic base, reduce the control of the state over resources, and further threaten its legitimacy. Belt-tightening and a return to subsistence are at best short-term strategies for survival at the margin. For a longer-term strategy to reverse the continent's economic decline, one has to look to governments—if only to create the conditions in which legitimate markets can operate effectively.

■ CONCLUSION: AN OVEREXTENDED STATE?

This chapter has focused mainly upon state policies in various sectors of the economy and reflects the primacy of the state in African political economy. Governments not only set the conditions under which individuals and corporations must operate but in many African countries are themselves the principal employers. Public consumption (government expenditure) in Africa is a higher percentage of GDP than in all other developing countries and is increasing. The weighted mean for public consumption as a percentage of GDP for Sub-Saharan Africa grew from 10 percent in 1960 to 14 percent in 1982. For some countries, the figure is more than double this—in both Zambia and Mauritania, for instance, public consumption in 1982 accounted for over 30 percent of GDP (compared to 18 percent in industrial market economies where government expenditure on welfare is much larger).

Although African governments have brought about major advances in the educational field and, in some cases, in the health field, their records in other sectors have been disappointing. Many critics suggest that the state in most African countries is overextended. Suffering from a shortage of capabilities, African governments, it is argued, have taken on too many tasks. In particular, they have entered into unnecessary burdensome functions, such as retailing and agricultural production, that might easily be performed by the private sector. Far too often, the extension of state activities has been accompanied by inefficiencies, which result, for example, from the desire of governments to create additional political patronage. Government organizations have been asked to undertake production and provide services that undermine their ability to perform their proper organizational tasks effectively. Parastatal organizations have been a frequent target of criticism. These state-owned corporations enjoy (in theory if not always in practice) some degree of financial and managerial autonomy from the government. Typically, the parastatal form was used by African governments to handle agricultural marketing boards they inherited from the colonial power and as instruments to manage industries taken under state control. In many countries, parastatals have had an appalling financial record. Rather than contributing to government revenues, they have been a major drain on them. Part of the problem has arisen from inefficient management. Also of significance, however, has been government interference, which has prevented parastatals from being managed on commercial lines. This has taken the form, for example, of insistence that parastatals offer jobs to unemployed secondary-school leavers or that they provide subsidized services to other sectors of the economy.

Much of the criticism of the economic role of the state has come from the World Bank, whose influence in Africa has increased dramatically in the 1980s as a result of the poor performances recorded by many countries. Although many observers do not share the faith of the World Bank in the inevitable efficiency of the private sector or agree that the best strategy for African development is to open up African economies to greater influence from international market forces, there is now a growing consensus among commentators and many African heads of government alike that the state has indeed become overextended. A complete withdrawal of the state from the economy is not required; rather it should play a more committed and realistic role. A "retreat from statism" has been noted in many countries,[60] even in those that have espoused a socialist ideology. Samora Machel, the former president of Mozambique, is reported to have remarked that there is nothing in socialist ideology that compels the state to sell tomatoes. Given the important role that state intervention in the economy plays in generating political patronage and thus sustaining governments in office, an obvious tension is created by any retreat from statism. There is a general realization, however, that governments and their parastatal corporations in the 1970s in many countries became more of a burden than a stimulus to economic development. Unless action is taken to turn around the contemporary trends in African economies dramatically, the very impressive welfare gains that some states have made since independence will be jeopardized.

■ NOTES

1. Anthony Hopkins, *An Economic History of West Africa* (New York: Columbia University Press, 1973), Chapter 2.

2. Peter Duignan and L. H. Gann, "The Pre-Colonial Economies of Sub-Saharan Africa," in Duignan and Gann, eds., *Colonialism in Africa* (Cambridge: Cambridge University Press, 1975), vol. 4, pp. 35–67, is a useful introduction to the subject.

3. Philip D. Curtin, *The Atlantic Slave Trade* (Madison: University of Wisconsin Press, 1969), p. 87.

4. Hopkins, *An Economic History of West Africa*, p. 105.

5. Ibid., Chapter 3.

6. Ibid., p. 122.

7. Samir Amin, "Underdevelopment and Dependence in Black Africa: Origins and Contemporary Forms," *Journal of Modern African Studies* 10, no. 4 (1972): 503–524.

8. Hopkins, *An Economic History of West Africa*, p. 174.

9. E. A. Brett, *Colonialism and Underdevelopment in East Africa* (London: Heinemann, 1973).

10. Michael P. Cowen, "The Commercialization of Food Production in Kenya after 1945," in Robert I. Rotberg, ed., *Imperialism, Colonialism, and Hunger: East and Central Africa* (Lexington, Mass.: D.C. Heath & Co., 1983), pp. 199–224; Gavin Kitching, *Class and Economic Change in Kenya* (New Haven: Yale University Press, 1980).

11. Crawford Young, "The African Colonial State and Its Political Legacy," in Donald Rothchild and Naomi Chazan, eds., *The Precarious Balance: State and Society in Africa* (Boulder, Colo.: Westview Press, 1988), p. 45.

12. Hopkins, *An Economic History of West Africa*, pp. 190–191; and Young, "The Colonial State."

13. Hopkins, *An Economic History of West Africa*, p. 282.

14. World Bank, *World Development Report 1986* (New York: Oxford University Press, 1986), p. 184. Other data in this section are derived from World Bank, *Financing Adjustment with Growth* (Washington, D.C.: World Bank, 1986), Statistical Appendix.

15. Ajit Singh, "Industrialization in Africa: A Structuralist View," in Martin Fransman, ed., *Industry and Accumulation in Africa* (London: Heinemann, 1982).

16. John Lonsdale, "States and Social Processes in Africa: A Historiographical Survey," *African Studies Review* 24, no. 2/3 (June-September 1981): 139–225; Goran Hyden, *Beyond Ujamaa in Tanzania: Underdevelopment and an Uncaptured Peasantry* (Berkeley: University of California Press, 1980). See also Frederick Cooper, "Africa and the World Economy," *African Studies Review* 24, no. 2/3 (June-September 1981): 1–86.

17. Andrew Coulson, *Tanzania: A Political Economy* (Oxford: Oxford University Press, 1982); Philip Foster, *Education and Social Change in Ghana* (Chicago: University of Chicago Press, 1965).

18. Sara S. Berry, *Fathers Work for Their Sons: Accumulation, Mobility and Class Formation in an Extended Yoruba Community* (Berkeley: University of California Press, 1985).

19. Crawford Young, *Ideology and Development in Africa* (New Haven: Yale University Press, 1982), p. 186.

20. World Bank, *World Development Report 1986*, p. 222.

21. Julius K. Nyerere, "Education for Self-Reliance," in *Freedom and Socialism* (New York: Oxford University Press, 1968), pp. 267–290; Marjorie Mbilinyi, "Contradictions in Tanzanian Educational Reform," in Andrew Coulson, ed., *African Socialism in Practice: The Tanzanian Experience* (Nottingham: Spokesman, 1979), Chapter 17.

22. David Court, "The Education System as a Response to Inequality," in Joel D. Barkan with John J. Okumu, eds., *Politics and Public Policy in Kenya and Tanzania* (New York: Praeger, 1979), p. 227.

23. Ibid., p. 224, citing the work of Ruth Beska.

24. David Court and Kabiru Kinyanjui, "African Education: Problems in a High Growth Sector," in Robert J. Berg and Jennifer Seymour Whitaker, eds., *Strategies for African Development* (Berkeley: University of California Press, 1986), p. 374.

25. World Bank, *Accelerated Development in Sub-Saharan Africa* (Washington, D.C.: World Bank, 1981), pp. 82–83.

26. World Bank, *Toward Sustained Development in Sub-Saharan Africa* (Washington, D.C.: World Bank, 1984), p. 30.

27. See, for example, Stanley Scheyer and David Dunlop, "Health Services and Development in Uganda," *Rural Africana* 11 (Fall 1981): 37–57.

28. Young, *Ideology and Development in Africa,* p. 307.

29. Coulson, *Tanzania,* pp. 208–209; Young, *Ideology and Development in Africa.*

30. World Bank, *Toward Sustained Development,* p. 28.

31. Coulson, *Tanzania,* p. 209.

32. Ibid.

33. Reginald Herbold Green and Hans Singer, " Sub-Saharan Africa in Depression: The Impact on the Welfare of Children," *World Development* 12, no. 3 (March 1984): 283–284.

34. World Bank, *Financing Adjustment with Growth,* Statistical Appendix.

35. For a succinct summary of these arguments, see Singh, "Industrialization in Africa: A Structuralist View," pp. 24–37.

36. For contrasting views compare, for example, Folker Frobel, Jurgen Heinrichs, and Otto Kreye, *The New International Division of Labour* (Cambridge: Cambridge University Press), and Gerald K. Helleiner, *Intra-Firm Trade and Developing Countries* (London: Macmillan, 1981).

37. World Bank, *Accelerated Development,* p. 93.

38. Ibid.

39. Alexander Gerschenkron, *Economic Backwardness in Historical Perspective* (Cambridge: Harvard University Press, 1962).

40. World Bank, *Accelerated Development,* p. 91. For an early criticism of ISI, see I. Little, T. Scitovsky and M. Scott, *Industry and Trade in Some Developing Countries* (London: Oxford University Press, 1970). The World Bank's annual *World Development Report,* as well as *Accelerated Development,* have frequently criticized inefficient ISI strategies.

41. Andrew Coulson, "The Automated Bread Factory," in Coulson, *African Socialism in Practice,* Chapter 13. See also Overseas Development Institute (ODI) (London), "Industrialization in Sub-Saharan Africa," *Briefing Paper* (January 1986).

42. Data from ODI, *Briefing Paper;* Martin Fransman, Introduction to Fransman, *Industry and Accumulation in Africa,* p. 1; and UNIDO, *Africa in Figures* [UNIDO/LS.517] (6 February 1985).

43. John Ravenhill, "Aid Through Trade: Reforming the International Trade Regime in the Interests of Least Developed Countries," *Third World Quarterly* 8, no. 2 (April 1986).

44. According to the International Labour Organization, the median wage for textile workers in ten African countries was fifty percent higher than in Pakistan and more than twice as high as in Bangladesh. Quoted in World Bank, *Accelerated Development,* p. 93. On Africa's role in the evolving world economy, see Richard Higgott, "Africa and the New International Division of Labor," in John Ravenhill, ed., *Africa in Economic*

Crisis (New York: Columbia University Press, 1986).

45. John Ravenhill, *Collective Clientelism: The Lomé Conventions and North-South Relations* (New York: Columbia University Press, 1985), Chapter 4. For more details of the Lomé relationship, see our next chapter in this book.

46. Steven Langdon, "Industrial Dependence and Export Manufacturing in Kenya," in Ravenhill, ed., *Africa in Economic Crisis*.

47. UNIDO, *Africa in Figures*.

48. Robert H. Bates, *Markets and States in Tropical Africa* (Berkeley: University of California Press, 1981), and his *Essays on the Political Economy of Africa* (Cambridge: Cambridge University Press, 1983).

49. Tony Killick, *Development Economics in Action* (London: Heinemann, 1978).

50. Young, *Ideology and Development in Africa*, p. 158.

51. Barry Munslow, "State Intervention in Agriculture: The Mozambican Experience," *Journal of Modern African Studies* 22, no. 2 (1984): 211 and 216.

52. Reginald Herbold Green, "Agricultural Crises in Sub-Saharan Africa: Capitalism and Transitions to Socialism," *Bulletin of the Institute of Development Studies at the University of Sussex* 13, no. 4 (September 1982): 77.

53. The alternative case is well argued by Keith Hart, *The Political Economy of West African Agriculture* (Cambridge: Cambridge University Press, 1980).

54. Cathy L. Jabara, "Agricultural Pricing Policy in Kenya," *World Development* 13, no. 5 (May 1985): 611–626; Jean-Jacques Faucher and Hartmut Schneider, "Agricultural Crisis: Structural Constraints, Prices and Other Policy Issues," and Christian Morrisson, "Agricultural Production and Government Policy in Burkina Faso and Mali," both in Tore Rose, ed., *Crisis and Recovery in Sub-Saharan Africa* (Paris: OECD, 1985), pp. 50–65 and 66–77, respectively.

55. Data cited in Carl K. Eicher, "West Africa's Agrarian Crisis" (Paper presented to the Fifth Biannual Conference of the West African Association of Agricultural Economists, Abidjan, Côte d'Ivoire, December 1983), p. 29.

56. Ibid, p. 45.

57. Michael Lipton, "The Place of Agricultural Research in the Development of Sub-Saharan Africa," *Bulletin of the Institute of Development Studies at the University of Sussex* 16, no. 3 (1985), and his "Research and the Design of a Policy Frame for Agriculture," in Rose, ed., *Crisis and Recovery in Sub-Saharan Africa*.

58. Carl K. Eicher, "Facing Up to Africa's Food Crisis," in Ravenhill, ed., *Africa in Economic Crisis*, Chapter 6.

59. This section relies heavily on Deborah Pellow and Naomi Chazan, *Ghana: Coping with Uncertainty* (Boulder, Colo.: Westview Press, 1986), pp. 167–172. See also Victor Azarya and Naomi Chazan, "Disengagement from the State in Africa: Reflections on the Experience of Ghana and Guinea," *Comparative Studies in Society and History* 29, no. 1 (January 1987): 106–131.

60. Frank Holmquist, "Correspondent's Report: Tanzania's Retreat from Statism in the Countryside," *Africa Today* 30, no. 4 (1983): 23–35.

10

Africa and the World Economy

When African countries received their independence, most had economies that were closely tied to those of the former colonial power. At least one-third of the trade of most countries occurred with the former metropole; in many cases, particularly the francophone states, the concentration was much higher. France, for instance, accounted for three-quarters of the external trade of Benin, Chad, Niger, and Senegal at independence. Most countries had given preferential tariff treatment to imports from the metropole during the colonial period; similarly, most countries tied their domestic currency to the value of that of the metropole. Colonial powers had typically monopolized foreign investment in their colonies: A similar concentration was found in aid receipts. Decolonization offered the opportunity to African governments to diversify their economic links and to reduce their economic dependence on the former colonial power.

In this chapter, we examine a number of strategies that African governments have pursued in attempting to restructure their external economic relations. We focus on efforts to promote self-reliance; on relations with transnational corporations (TNCs); on Africa and the New International Economic Order (NIEO); and on Africa's relations with the former colonial powers of the EEC through the Yaoundé and Lomé Conventions. Finally, we examine how developments in the international economy have affected Africa's economic development in recent years.

■ SELF-RELIANCE

Although there is little contemporary support for the crude dependency argument that development in the industrialized world has come at the expense of underdevelopment in the periphery, economists ranging across the spectrum from Marxist to liberal democrat agree that the asymmetry in economic power between the industrialized and the poorer developing countries has at times adversely affected the economic development of the latter. Although there is considerable debate as to whether any long-term decline in the overall terms of trade of developing countries has occurred, there is now substantial evidence that the real values of many of Africa's important exports, such as copper, cotton, iron, and cocoa, have not risen as rapidly as those of the manufactured goods that Africa imports from industrialized countries. The dependence of most African countries on the export of a limited number of primary commodities renders them vulnerable to extreme fluctuations in export earnings as a result both of local crop failures and changes in the world market price for their exports. For many African economies, in fact, only one export provides the largest part by far of the country's foreign-exchange earnings: copper for Zambia, oil for Nigeria, uranium for Niger, tobacco for Malawi, iron ore for Mauritania. Fluctuations in foreign-exchange earnings have an obvious adverse impact on development planning and government budgeting. With the onset of economic recession in the West, following the first round of oil price rises in 1973/74, developing countries have also faced increased barriers to their exports of manufactured goods to industrialized countries.

In response to these negative aspects of the external economic relations faced by developing countries, some economists and political scientists have advocated that a conscious policy of "de-linking" from the world economy be pursued through the means of collective and individual self-reliance.[1] Disappointment with the results of economic development in the two decades since independence has made self-reliant strategies more attractive to African leaders: The OAU in 1980 adopted the Lagos Plan of Action, which had self-reliance as the centerpiece of its strategy. De-linking does not imply autarky—a severance of all economic relations with the outside world—but a deliberate partial disengagement of a country from the dominant relationships prevailing in the international economic system. Collective self-reliance refers to measures taken by developing countries to cooperate in reducing their economic dependence on industrialized countries. Such measures include the promotion of trade between developing countries (referred to as South-South trade) and joint ventures in manufacturing, mining, and the provision of services. National self-reliance similarly refers to measures taken to reduce the dependence of economies on international linkages but through such *domestic* policy measures as increasing food self-sufficiency, the generation of a larger proportion of investment funds domestically, and local production of a higher percentage of essential manufactured goods.[2]

☐ Collective Self-Reliance

Given their small populations and limited economic resources, economic co-operation with their neighbors is, in principle, an eminently sensible strategy for African states. Many cannot provide a domestic market of sufficient size to permit manufacturing plants to reap economies of scale through long production runs. Besides production for a regional market, scale economies can also be realized through the joint financing of services such as agricultural research, meteorology, telecommunications, and transport. For example, some African countries, such as Ghana, have considerable potential for hydroelectric generation; this potential can only be realized economically, however (as in the Volta River project), if the power is sold to neighboring countries—in this case, Togo and Benin. Africa's thirteen landlocked countries have no option but to cooperate with neighbors on whom they are dependent for transport links to move their imports and exports.

Colonial powers found it convenient to administer a number of services on a regional basis. Indeed, for a long period, France governed its twelve African colonies as two administrative units: French West Africa and French Equatorial Africa. In East Africa, Britain administered a variety of common services for the colonies of Kenya and Uganda and for the UN trust territory of Tanganyika through the East African High Commission, established in January 1948. Similarly, in 1953 a federation was created between the self-governing colony of Southern Rhodesia (Zimbabwe) and the protectorates of Northern Rhodesia (Zambia) and Nyasaland (Malawi). A solid foundation not only for collective self-reliance but for the integration of various countries into a supranational grouping might appear to have been laid prior to independence. This proved not to be the case.

There were two principal reasons for subsequent fragmentation. First, although some of the colonies may have been administered jointly, each had its own governor and ultimately its own elected assembly: The local territorial unit inevitably came to be the focal point for African political ambitions in the period leading up to independence. A continuation of federal or other forms of regional arrangement after independence would have limited the powers exercised by national administrations. African governments have jealously guarded their newly acquired sovereignty, a major reason why regional integration—which requires the transfer of some powers to regional institutions—has been so difficult to achieve. Second, the administrative units embraced states of widely differing resource bases and levels of development. Some states clearly benefited more than others from the joint services and facilities; in all cases the colonial authorities used the administrative arrangements as a means of transferring resources between colonies. In the East African High Commission and in the Central African Federation, white settlers in the relatively more developed countries in the organizations (Kenya and Southern Rhodesia, respectively) were successful in ensuring that they gained disproportionately from the arrangements (for example, through subsidized rail charges in Kenya and, in the Central African Federation, through the redistribution of tax revenue contributed predominantly by Northern Rhodesia's copper mines).

Only the cooperative arrangements in East Africa survived the period of decolonization. When leaders of the French African colonies were offered the choice of national or federal links with France in 1959, the majority opted for the first of these alternatives. The voice of Houphouët-Boigny, the leading nationalist politician in Côte d'Ivoire, was particularly influential. His opposition to maintaining a federal arrangement stemmed in large part from fears that the relatively prosperous Côte d'Ivoire would inevitably end up subsidizing other members of the federation. Eventually, only two states—Senegal and Soudan (Mali)—chose independence as a federation. This arrangement, however, survived only three months after independence was received, its demise resulting from disputes over economic development and fears on the part of politicians (largely from the Senegalese leadership) that the federal arrangements would undermine their national political constituencies.[3] As was to be the case with other failed integrative efforts, the breakup of the Mali Federation led to a period of bitter relations between the previous partners. In the Central African Federation, the favored position of the settlers of Southern Rhodesia—and their unwillingness to allow for black majority rule—ensured that a continuation of the cooperative arrangements would be unacceptable to the leaders of Zambia and Malawi once their independence was achieved.

In East Africa, however, the regional arrangements survived until 1977, albeit in a situation of almost perpetual crisis once Kenya, Uganda, and Tanganyika (Tanzania after the union with Zanzibar in 1964) achieved their independence. As the experience of regional cooperation in East Africa was the longest-lived and most extensive of the various integrative schemes attempted in Africa, its demise is instructive regarding the problems faced in efforts to undertake collective self-reliance in Africa.

The east african community.   Cooperative arrangements in East Africa included jointly financed railways, posts and telecommunications, harbors, an airline (East African Airways), meteorological services, and medical and veterinary research services. More than twenty thousand people were employed in the various services. The three states were also linked in a common market (a common tariff was applied by the three countries to imports from outside the region; trade within the region was nominally free from tariff and nontariff barriers). Trade within the common market was a higher percentage of the countries' total trade than has been true for any other African regional scheme. In the colonial period, there was also a joint currency administered by the East African Currency Board, as well as an East African Navy. As independence for the three countries became imminent, responsibility for the cooperative arrangements was transferred from the East African High Commission to the East African Common Services Organization, which was governed by the principal ministers from the three countries. Plans to create an East African Federation when the last of the three territories, Kenya, gained its independence in 1964 came to naught, again largely because of the unwillingness of national politicians to cede power to a supranational organization.

With independence, the cooperative arrangements came under increasing strain. The primary problem was not so much with the various services—although disputes occurred over which country was benefiting the most from the employment generated by them—but with distribution of gains from the common market. We have already noted that, in principle, the construction of a larger regional market through the abolition of tariff barriers is eminently rational in terms of economic theory for small economies like those of Africa. In practice, however, free trade within regional customs unions or common markets has an inherent tendency to undermine the political rationality of such cooperation. This tendency occurs as a result of what have been termed "backwash" or "polarization" effects—that is, the benefits of free trade tend to accrue overwhelmingly to the more developed areas within a region.

The reason is quite straightforward: Companies are attracted to the better infrastructure (roads, ports, power supplies) that are found in the more-developed areas and by the possibilities of trading with low transport costs with other companies already established. Once a free trade area is created, companies attempt to service the whole region from plants sited in the most developed area. One exception to this process might be noted: Chaos occurs when infrastructure in the most developed region fails to keep pace with the demands placed on it by rapid economic growth. A notable instance of this generation of "external diseconomies" has been evident in Lagos. In most regional schemes, however, inequalities in levels of development become self-perpetuating. Although all states in a grouping may ultimately enjoy gains from regional integration, the distribution of the benefits, inevitably a matter of great political sensitivity, will, in the absence of effective corrective measures, be unequal.

Within East Africa, Kenya was the most developed of the three states. It enjoyed a number of advantages—a good port at Mombasa, which was the "natural" outlet for Uganda's exports, a pleasant climate in Nairobi, and good infrastructure constructed during the colonial period primarily to aid white settler farmers. The presence of the white settlers had provided a market for local manufacturing industry. These historical advantages were reinforced after independence when Kenya offered incentives to attract foreign investment, whereas Tanzania and Uganda (under the first Obote administration after 1967) both pursued socialist development strategies that were often perceived to be hostile to foreign capital and created an uncertain investment climate. It is not surprising that TNCs overwhelmingly chose Kenya as the location for their subsidiaries and attempted to supply the regional market from there.

In the years after independence, various attempts were made to address the issue of unequal benefits from integration. The common services were decentralized, leading to employment gains for Tanzania and Uganda. A number of measures were introduced in an effort to provide a more equal sharing of the gains from free trade, including a system of compensatory tax payments from Kenya to its partners. Regional industrial planning—directing industries to locate in particular countries—would have been the most effective means of countering the polarization of benefits that occurred under a system of free trade. Although an agreement was reached in 1964–1965 (the Kampala Agreement) on the allocation of new industrial investment in the region, Kenya failed to implement it. After a period of crisis, during which the East African Currency Board was dissolved and replaced with national central banks and currencies, a new treaty was drawn up in 1967 establishing an East African Community. Its major innovation was the establishment of an East African Development Bank, which was intended to channel investment toward the less-favored areas of the region. But the problem of unequal gains from trade was left largely unresolved; the principal measure in the treaty to combat this problem provided for Uganda and Tanzania to protect infant industries by erecting tariffs against imports from Kenya, a recipe for the duplication of inefficient manufacturing plants.

Although the community survived for ten years before its eventual dissolution, it was racked by almost perpetual crisis during this period. Cooperation proved to be extremely difficult as the ideologies of the three states took increasingly divergent paths, a matter made much worse by the coming to power of the erratic dictatorship of Idi Amin in Uganda. An accumulation of crises precipitated the collapse of the community. The underlying cause was the continued failure to effectively counteract the uneven gains from free trade within the region. Again, the failure of the community created considerable bitterness: The border between Tanzania and Kenya was closed for six years. The demise of Africa's oldest and most sophisticated regional scheme illustrates a number of problems that face efforts at collective self-reliance on the continent:[4]

1.   Schemes based on free trade will be undermined by the backwash effect of uneven gains. African countries have relatively few goods to trade with each other: Their economies for the most part are competitive rather than complementary. Much of the trade generated within regional schemes thus will derive from newly established import-substituting industries. These are able to survive because of the protection provided by the common external tariff. Because many of these plants are infant industries facing significant startup costs, consumers often have to pay more for goods produced within the region than if they were purchased on the world market. This is particularly irksome for the governments of countries other than the one in which the industry is located, especially if they have to pay for the imports with scarce foreign exchange. The experience of the East African Community and that of other Third World free trade areas suggests that the relatively disadvantaged countries within a region will not regard a redistribution of tax revenue as adequate compensation for the perceived "loss" of industry to their neighbors. Other measures, such as permitting the less-favored countries to protect their infant industries against competi-

tion from within the region (as permitted, for example, in the Customs and Economic Union of Central Africa) undermine the rationale for free trade and encourage the duplication of inefficient plants.[5] Industrial planning, where all countries receive an equitable share of new industrial investment within a region, appears to be the only viable solution to the problem, but one that is unacceptable to many governments in that it impinges on their policymaking autonomy.

Given that African economies compete with one another for investment and markets, and African governments are reluctant to cede any of their authority to a supranational regional organization, integration on the basis of free trade does not appear to be a particularly propitious means of pursuing collective self-reliance. The implementation of free trade requires that governments give up significant powers, (such as those over tariffs, import licensing, etc.) for benefits that will at best be achieved over the long term. Organized trade—possibly on the basis of barter—offers the prospect of generating benefits without the costs associated with the laissez-faire arrangements of free trade within customs unions or common markets. Other forms of cooperation, such as the joint provision of services, similarly hold forth the prospects of increasing collective self-reliance without inevitably increasing the possibility of intraregional conflicts.

2. The difficulties of persuading governments to give up any of their powers to a supranational authority suggests that it may be futile to attempt to construct elaborate regional arrangements such as customs unions and common markets that inevitably require such a transfer of power. A more realistic method of forging collective self-reliance may be a form of limited intergovernmental cooperation. This could avoid the nominal automaticity inherent in the timetables for the trade liberalization necessary to construct customs unions. Rather perversely, by consciously affording national governments center place in the arrangements, intergovernmental cooperation may reduce the potential for conflict.

Despite the difficulties of successful implementation, there has been no diminution in African governments' support (at least in nominal terms) for the concept of collective self-reliance over the years. Regional cooperation draws on the considerable emotional commitment that African heads of state have shown to the idea of African unity. Far too often, however, it seems that they have ignored the warning that those who fail to heed the lessons of history are condemned to repeat its mistakes. Despite the accumulation of evidence that regional integration in the Third World on the basis of free trade will not work, the Economic Commission for Africa (ECA) continues to enshrine free trade as the basis for African collective self-reliance. The OAU's Lagos Plan contained only one firm commitment by the heads of state toward realizing the goal of increasing self-reliance: the establishment by the year 2000 of an African Common Market.

Although the ECA has constructed a series of regional groupings—

ECOWAS (the Economic Community of West African States), the Preferential Trade Area (PTA) for East and Southern Africa, and the Economic Community of Central Africa—many of these remain little more than paper arrangements. Although states have been willing to sign and ratify these agreements (often under considerable pressure not to be seen as obstructing ECA's and OAU's designs), they have been reluctant to implement the policy measures and commit the financial resources necessary for the schemes to succeed. Some of the difficulties that they face may be seen from an examination of the longest-established of the groupings, ECOWAS.

ECOWAS.   The signing of the Treaty of Lagos, which established ECOWAS in May 1975, marked a major breakthrough in long-standing efforts to overcome the anglophone-francophone divide in West Africa. The francophone states—often encouraged by France, which feared any threat to its influence in the region—had long been wary of the potential influence of Nigeria, by far the dominant economic power in the area. Nigeria alone accounts for over 70 percent of West Africa's GDP. Anglophone states, on the other hand, harbored long-standing suspicions of what were perceived to be neocolonial links between the francophone states and the EEC in general and France in particular. The unprecedented cooperation of francophone and anglophone states in negotiating the Lomé Convention with the EEC facilitated the reconciliation between the groups that led to the Treaty of Lagos.

ECOWAS has as its principal goal the construction of a common market over a fifteen-year period between its sixteen member states (Benin, Burkina Faso, Cape Verde, Gambia, Ghana, Guinea, Guinea-Bissau, Côte d'Ivoire, Liberia, Mali, Mauritania, Niger, Nigeria, Senegal, Sierra Leone, and Togo). A gradual liberalization of internal trade is to be followed by a harmonization of member states' external tariffs and of their agricultural, industrial, investment, and monetary policies. Obstacles to the free movement of capital, services, and people within the community are to be abolished. ECOWAS attempted to counteract the problem of unequal gains from trade liberalization through the creation of a Fund for Compensation, Co-operation and Development. Member states are to contribute to the fund according to a complex formula based on GDP and per capita income. Nigeria is to provide 32 percent and Ghana and Côte d'Ivoire 13 percent each to the total capital. The fund is intended to compensate member states for the revenue loss suffered as a result of the dismantling of tariff barriers and to promote industrialization in the less-developed members of the community. Particular attention was given to providing a balance of the various nationalities in the composition of the community's senior executive corps. The secretariat of the community is located in Lagos; the headquarters of the fund in Lomé. But even if the fund's subscriptions are paid in full, which has not been the case up to now, its resources appear inadequate to deal with the question of unequal gains: As Peter Robson notes, "Despite the emphasis on protecting the interests of the less advanced member states, the

Treaty [of Lagos] cannot be regarded as adequately doing so."[6]

The community has failed to meet its deadlines for progress toward the construction of a common market. ECOWAS has hovered on the verge of disintegration for several years, and various factors have contributed to its failure to achieve its timetable for scheduled liberalization. Its workings have certainly been hampered by unfavorable developments in the international economy. With all member states encountering severe balance-of-payments problems, there has been a temptation to economize on scarce foreign exchange by not making the required contributions to the fund and to the secretariat's operating expenses. The decline in oil prices in the mid-1980s severely weakened the economy of Nigeria, whose strength had earlier been expected to sustain the community through difficult times. Conflict between key officials and continuing suspicions between francophone and anglophone states have also impeded progress (Côte d'Ivoire and Senegal at one time delayed implementation of the treaty by insisting that Zaire be invited to participate, a transparent attempt to reduce the influence of Nigeria within the community).

Another problem besetting the community has been the imbalance between the immediate costs and benefits of implementing the treaty. Again, this problem is typical of customs unions—their establishment requires governments to immediately give up substantial control over important areas of economic decision making, yet the benefits of free trade are realized only in the long term. The reluctance of ECOWAS members to apply the provisions of the treaty is a clear signal that many have doubts regarding the long-term viability of the community. Meanwhile, by choosing the Protocol on the Free Movement of Peoples as one of the first projects to be implemented, the community's secretariat created unnecessary difficulties for itself. Given the latent hostility between ethnic communities and discontent over "foreigners" occupying scarce jobs, it was inevitable that migration within the community would generate considerable hostility. As has so often been the case throughout history, aliens became a convenient target for governments attempting to divert attention from their domestic difficulties: Nigeria's mass expulsions of aliens in 1983 and 1985 soured relations with its community neighbors.

Difficulties were also created by the predominance given in the treaty to national politicians as the chief executives of the community. Like the East African Community, the supreme decision-making organ of ECOWAS is the Authority of Heads of State and Government. Inevitably, as in the East African Community, disputes between heads of state have spilled over to affect community activities. West African politics have been so volatile in the 1980s—both Ghana and Nigeria, for instance, have closed their borders for long periods, and war occurred between Burkina Faso and Mali—that the prospects for any meaningful cooperative scheme, however well designed, appear dim.

One other factor, common to other ECA-inspired regional groupings, that has handicapped ECOWAS is the overlap between it and other existing regional arrangements. In West Africa, the principal conflict has been between

ECOWAS and the Economic Community of West Africa (CEAO), whose members are Burkina Faso, Côte d'Ivoire, Mali, Mauritania, Niger, and Senegal. CEAO has its origins in the Customs Union of West Africa (UDAO), which was created in Paris when it became obvious that the colonies of French West Africa would decide against independence as a federation. Both UDAO and its successor, the Customs Union of West African States (UDEAO), proved short-lived. In Robson's words, "The principal reason for failure undoubtedly lay in the inherent defectiveness of an orthodox customs union as an effectual policy instrument for African regional cooperation."[7]

The revival of the arrangements in 1970 and the treaty of Abidjan establishing CEAO in 1973 owe much to the fears of the francophone countries of Nigerian dominance of the region. Although emphasizing a more positive approach to integration than its ill-fated predecessors, CEAO is also committed to the ultimate establishment of a unified regional market. Unlike other arrangements, however, tariff-free treatment for local trade is to be accorded automatically only to nonindustrial products. Provision exists, however, for the negotiation of a rate of duty lower than that of the external tariff to be applied to locally produced manufactures; in such cases, the importing states are to be compensated for two-thirds of the estimated loss of tariff revenue. This provides CEAO with a certain flexibility that is lacking in arrangements like ECOWAS that prescribe movement toward a complete elimination of internal tariffs. CEAO has also established a Solidarity Fund designed to promote the economic development of the region, with priority to be given to the least-developed member states.

Although CEAO officials have on a number of occasions pledged to cooperate fully with ECOWAS, there are serious incompatibilities between the two organizations, not least the desire of CEAO member states to obtain a derogation from their obligations under ECOWAS in order to continue to offer preferential treatment to exports originating within CEAO. Although CEAO has not met its own timetable for the implementation of a common external tariff, it has made more progress than ECOWAS in reducing internal trade barriers and enjoys certain advantages—the historical ties of the countries and their francophone heritage and the existence of a common currency in the African Financial Community's (CFA) franc.[8]

The Southern African Development Coordination Conference.   A similar conflict between an ECA-designated region and an existing cooperative scheme occurs in eastern and southern Africa between the ECA's Preferential Trade Area (PTA) and the Southern African Development Coordination Conference (SADCC). SADCC, which grew out of the grouping of Front Line States created to promote the transition to majority rule in Zimbabwe, is the most innovative of Africa's attempts to translate aspirations for collective self-reliance into reality.[9] Unlike the ECA, OAU, and regional groupings such as ECOWAS and CEAO, SADCC's member states (Angola, Botswana, Lesotho, Malawi,

Mozambique, Tanzania, Swaziland, Zambia, and Zimbabwe) have self-consciously eschewed free trade and centralized bureaucratic institutions as the basis for regional cooperation.

Launched in April 1980, SADCC's principal objective as declared at its first summit meeting is "the reduction of economic dependence, particularly, but not only, on the Republic of South Africa." SADCC is a direct counter to South African ambitions of creating a "constellation" of states that would have further integrated its black African neighbors into the South African economy. Leaders of SADCC member states recognized that the disparities between economies in the region—Zimbabwe and Zambia are significantly larger and more sophisticated than their neighbors—would inevitably lead to gross inequalities in the distribution of benefits if a regional common market were established. At its first summit meeting, each participating state was given responsibility for drawing up plans for cooperation in key sectors: agriculture, development finance, energy, industrialization, mining, personnel development, and transport. The division of labor reflected the interests and resources of the states so that, for example, Angola (the region's only oil exporter) assumed responsibility for energy and Zambia for mining.

The aim was to identify projects in each area where immediate gains from cooperation could be realized and which could be presented to foreign donors for financing. Unlike the ECA-inspired regional groupings, there was no grandiose master plan. SADCC's name reflects its mode of operation: as a series of conferences rather than a centralized bureaucracy. Commissions (such as the Southern African Transport and Communications Commission established in 1980) created to coordinate activities in the various fields are based in the state with particular responsibility for that area of cooperation. SADCC headquarters in Botswana was to have only four professional and four support staff.

SADCC has enjoyed moderate success in its first years of operation. In particular, it has attracted finance for a number of projects in the transport and communications fields. Trade between some of the member states—often on the basis of barter or paid for in local currencies—has increased. Perhaps most significant, projects pursued under SADCC auspices appear to have contributed to the maintenance of friendly relations between the states in the region, rather than being a major source of tension as has been the case with many of the more elaborate regional schemes in Africa. SADCC does, however, have two major vulnerabilities. First, it is very heavily dependent on support from foreign donors for its projects. Although its annual donors' conferences have succeeded in attracting support for some projects, the total assistance provided has fallen far short of expectations; in most cases, assistance has actually represented the redirection of existing aid pledges rather than additional finance. Donors have shown a marked reluctance to finance SADCC agricultural and industrial projects. This reliance on foreign assistance is, of course, somewhat paradoxical for an organization whose stated goal is to reduce external dependence; the costs involved in restoring regional infrastructure are such, however, that it is unlikely that they could be met from the domestic resources of the participant states.

SADCC's second source of vulnerability is South Africa. Because the organization directly challenges South Africa's role within the region, it is scarcely surprising, if regrettable, that South Africa has attempted to undermine it. The member states, particularly those that share a border with South Africa, have little ability to resist South African attempts at sabotage—whether these take the form of invasion by South African military forces, the sponsoring of guerrilla movements hostile to the established governments (such as RENAMO in Mozambique and UNITA in Angola), or the destruction of transport and communications links. Indeed, SADCC has expended considerable effort at rehabilitating transport and communication links in the region only to see them destroyed again by South Africa or its proxies. RENAMO, for instance, has blown up the power lines from the Cabora Bassa Dam. SADCC officials estimated in 1985 that South African aggression cost its nine members states about $10 billion in the years 1980–1984, a figure well above total resource inflows during this period.

A second form of sabotage has been somewhat more subtle—attempts to undermine the economic viability of some of the region's transport facilities. These have taken various forms: South African refusal to provide railroad locomotives to head trains originating in Zimbabwe; the redirection of South African trade away from the Mozambique port of Maputo; and the offering of reduced tariffs on rail transport through the Republic of South Africa for Zimbabwe's main exports of tobacco and cotton to encourage traders not to switch to SADCC routes.

Despite its vulnerabilities, SADCC points to a more promising road for African efforts at collective self-reliance in the future. There are few cases where the liberalization of trade within a region will generate significant benefits given the poor infrastructure and low levels of industrialization that characterize African economies. With most African states suffering severe foreign-exchange shortages, barter appears to be the most realistic basis for trade. Emphasis on production, such as through jointly owned facilities, rather than on trade appears more appropriate. Similarly, joint services and research facilities offer considerable potential for realizing gains. Various functional organizations throughout the continent—such as the Organisation pour la Mise en Valeur du Fleuve Sénégal (OMVS, Organization for the Development of the Senegal River), the West African Rice Development Association, the Niger Basin Authority—have received less attention than the more-grandiose schemes aimed at trade liberalization but have probably contributed more to inter-African cooperation.[10] To be sure, there is potential for interstate conflict over the distribution of benefits from jointly owned services, as has been seen, for example, in the disputes over Air Afrique, the airline owned jointly by Benin, Burkina Faso, Central African Republic, Chad, Congo, Côte d'Ivoire, Mauritania, Niger, Senegal, and Togo. But there appears to be greater potential for containing such disputes in functional organizations than in customs unions or common markets.

Unfortunately, the lessons of failed integrative efforts in Africa over the last three decades appear not to have been learned by either of the continent's principal organizations, the ECA and the OAU. They continue to insist on the construction of common markets as the optimal means of pursuing collective self-reliance. This insistence flies in the face of reality. African states have shown their lack of faith in trade liberalization in their failure to comply with the timetables established by the various integration schemes and by the Lagos Plan itself. As the OAU itself has admitted, the Lagos Plan has been largely ignored by its member states when they have drawn up their national development plans. Rather than helping to realize the goal of collective self-reliance, the continuing worship at the altar of free trade by the OAU and ECA is likely to exacerbate tensions between states and undermine the bases for cooperation.[11]

☐ National Self-Reliance

There is a certain paradox in the concept of collective self-reliance. To realize greater self-reliance in this context inevitably involves depending on cooperation from others. As we have seen, this imposes constraints on national autonomy that many governments have found unacceptable. Indeed, at times governments have found that their obligations under regional schemes have conflicted with policies designed to further their national self-reliance. National self-reliance thus might appear as a more attractive alternative, as it allows governments another important element of self-reliance: complete control over policymaking.

Self-reliance itself has many dimensions and a multitude of interpretations. Self-reliance strategies came to the fore in the early 1970s, in part a reflection of the disillusionment with the policy performances of the initial postindependence years. This was also the period in which southern countries were vociferous in their demands in international organizations for the introduction of a New International Economic Order. Self-reliance became a prominent theme of the Mobutu government in Zaire in the early 1970s (where it was accompanied by an emphasis on "authenticity"—the Africanization of names). It also received a strong emphasis in the rhetoric of the Acheampong government in Ghana in 1972–1975. Although generally less prominent throughout the continent in the years after 1975, it has enjoyed a revival in the rhetoric of the populist regimes of Burkina Faso and Ghana in the mid-1980s. Most writers on Africa would agree, however, that the countries that have pursued a policy of national self-reliance most consistently have been Tanzania and Algeria.

Tanzania.   Tanzania's commitment to self-reliance has its foundations in the Arusha Declaration drawn up by Julius Nyerere in February 1967. The starting point for the declaration was a frank appraisal of Tanzania's economic problems and prospects. Nyerere was concerned at the demands being made on the government for the provision of social services. Popular expectations had been heightened with the achievement of independence and demands were now being made that far exceeded anything the government might feasibly provide—even with substantial foreign assistance. But Tanzania's experience over the previous few years had demonstrated how unreliable foreign aid could be. Relations with the three largest donors of its aid had deteriorated dramatically: with West Germany, over Tanzania's establishment of diplomatic relations with East Germany; with the United States, over accusations that the CIA was attempting to overthrow the Tanzanian government; and with Britain, over what Tanzania regarded as an inadequate British response to the Unilateral Declaration of Independence by the white minority in Rhodesia. Both Britain and West Germany froze their aid to Tanzania, thereby removing any possibility that the government might meet the development targets outlined in the First Five-Year Plan it had adopted in 1964.

In the absence of any significant offers of aid from the Eastern bloc, the government had little option but to adopt a policy of self-reliance at this time if it wished to continue its independent foreign policy stance. The Arusha Declaration pointed to the dangers of relying on foreign aid and how this dependence could prevent Tanzania from pursuing its nonaligned foreign policy. Rather than looking to the government to provide the desired social services, the people would have to finance them from their own efforts. If individuals were self-reliant, the declaration asserted, then districts, regions, and the whole nation would be self-reliant. The declaration placed emphasis on rural development (the provision of education, health care, and a clean water supply) and agriculture because, Nyerere argued, the vast majority of the Tanzanian population lived and would continue to live in rural areas. Priority in industrialization should, therefore, be given to industries that could service the needs of the rural population. Greater self-reliance would necessitate acceptance by the population of (sometimes lower-quality) locally produced goods rather than imported luxuries. Emphasis was placed not only on reducing imports but on diversifying Tanzanian trade links so that the country's dependence on existing markets and suppliers would be reduced.

Because Tanzania's policies of self-reliance and of socialist development are so closely intertwined, the success or failure of one inevitably impinges on the other. The performance of Tanzania's agricultural policies has been particularly critical, given the overwhelming role of agriculture in the Tanzanian economy. Nyerere's objective was to group people into villages so as to reduce the costs to the government of providing essential services, such as clean water supplies. Earlier movements toward villagization had taken two forms: capital-intensive village settlement projects established under the First Five-Year Plan and spontaneous settlement schemes that were founded in response to Nyerere's emphasis on rural development. The capital-intensive villages—with modern housing for settlers, water supply, and tractors—proved to be a disaster, with almost no returns on the large sums invested. Of the spontaneous settlement schemes, about one-half were established by the TANU Youth League with the objective of providing a livelihood for young people on the land. Many were poorly organized, lacked access to good land and to credit, and failed quite quickly. There were a few success stories, such as the Ruvuma Development Association, but, ironically, these were regarded as a threat by some elements of the party and were subsequently dissolved.

Nyerere elaborated on the implications for rural production of the Arusha Declaration in a publication also issued in 1967, *Socialism and Rural Development*. Self-reliance would be realized through living and working together in rural communities; land would be *collectively* worked. Some degree of specialization and the acquisition of necessary modern tools would be possible. Although only limited gains in wealth might be anticipated, the important factor was that these would be locally generated. Responsibility for the establishment of villages was left to committed individuals; coercion was ruled out. But the government soon lost patience with the slow pace of progress in the establishment of new villages. It first attempted to induce people into villages by proclaiming that they would receive priority in the allocation of development expenditures; eventually (in 1973), it ordered that all people should live in villages. Large numbers of people were forcibly moved in the following year to rural sites that were then declared to be *Ujamaa* (socialist) villages. In many cases, it appeared that little research had gone into choosing the sites. Elsewhere, existing settlements were simply declared to be villages without any significant change in the organization of production. Villagization had been transformed from a voluntary process into one of coercion, from a grass-roots movement to a bureaucratized and centrally directed process.

Although large numbers of *Ujamaa* villages now existed on paper, very few were being farmed on a collective basis as originally intended. Indeed, by 1975, the government had largely backed down from the idea of communal production. The crash program of villagization inevitably disrupted agricultural production; this disruption was compounded in 1974 by drought. Rather than becoming more self-sufficient in agriculture, Tanzania had to import foodstuffs in large quantities. In subsequent years, food imports have grown further, placing a major burden on the country's scarce foreign exchange. A number of factors have caused this agricultural decline: the resistance of peasants to the villagization program; inadequate incentives for peasant producers (low prices for their crops, lack of availability of consumer goods, etc.); long periods of drought; and loss of crops caused by poor transport and storage arrangements. It is impossible to give any exact weight to the relative importance of these factors. What is most evident, however, is that the policy of encouraging self-reliance in the most critical sector of the Tanzanian economy—agriculture—has not succeeded. Surveys reported that very few villagers had any conception of what self-reliance meant in practice: The government had clearly failed to convey to the population the philosophical underpinnings of its development strategy.[12] Since 1981, in an attempt to encourage food self-sufficiency, the government has raised the prices it pays to peasant producers and dramatically reversed its policy by allowing the resumption of private, large-scale farming.

Tanzania has enjoyed somewhat more success in reorienting its external economic relations.[13] The ratio of exports to GDP has declined, pointing to a declining significance of foreign trade in the domestic economy. The State Trading Corporation and the Bank of Tanzania used their import licensing powers to effect a significant decline in the imports of luxury goods, such as motor vehicles and television sets. Similar success was achieved in diversifying export markets. Whereas at the time of the Arusha Declaration between 30 and 35 percent of Tanzanian exports went to Britain, by 1979 the British share had declined to under 17 percent. Although part of the reason for this change has been the decline of the British economy relative to that of other industrialized countries, no other market has assumed the same dominance that Britain once enjoyed. West Germany is now Tanzania's principal export market but accounts for less than 20 percent of total exports. A similar diversification has occurred in sources of imports, although this in part reflects the rise in oil prices during the 1970s, which significantly increased the share of Organization of Petroleum Exporting Countries (OPEC) in Tanzania's imports.

Despite the success in diversifying trade between the markets of Western industrialized economies. Tanzania has not been successful in significantly reducing its dependence on this group of countries as a whole. Western countries accounted for 63 percent of total Tanzanian exports in 1967 and 57 percent in 1982. Exports to the Second World—Eastern bloc countries—have stagnated, as have exports to other developing countries. The reasons for this lie in large part beyond Tanzania's control. Trade with Eastern bloc countries has proved difficult; as a result of Eastern bloc shortages of foreign exchange, trade has had to be conducted primarily on a barter basis. As regards trade with other developing countries, a number of formidable problems are faced. As a primary commodities exporter (these constitute more than 85 percent of the total value of Tanzanian exports), Tanzania produces items that are competitive with those of other developing countries and, thus, are not in demand by them—with the exception of a few of the more developed NICs (such as Taiwan and South Korea). Tanzanian manufactures are not competitive on world or, in most cases, on regional markets. Efforts to redirect trade thus encounter the same problems as does collective self-reliance. In the Tanzanian case, these have been particularly pertinent: Whereas at the time of the Arusha Declaration more than 10 percent of Tanzania's total trade was with Kenya and Uganda, its partners in the East African community, trade with these countries is now negligible following the community's disintegration. Some success has been achieved in arranging trade on the basis of barter with Mozambique, one of Tanzania's partners in SADCC, but this trade remains very small in relation to total imports and exports.

The Tanzanian experience demonstrates how difficult it is for weak, dependent economies to effect a major change in their international economic relations. Tanzanian efforts at self-reliance have been disrupted by factors beyond the government's control and by the structural constraints of the world economy. The oil price shocks and recession in Western industrialized countries (which have contributed to a dramatic deterioration in the country's terms of trade since the 1970s) subjected the economy to severe balance-of-payments constraints. Foreign exchange has not been available to purchase crucial capital goods nor, as the situation has deteriorated, for the spare parts vital for keeping Tanzanian manufacturing plants in production. But the Tanzanian experience also emphasizes once again the importance of the agricultural sector. Any serious attempts at national self-reliance must begin with agriculture, given the importance of this sector to all African economies. Food self-sufficiency is the foundation for a policy of self-reliance. In relation to food self-sufficiency, it must be admitted, the policies of the Tanzanian government have contributed to the undermining of the achievement of the goal of national self-reliance.

Algeria.   As in Tanzania, self-reliance and socialist development have been intertwined in Algeria. Algeria, however, had the advantage of being on the opposite side of the oil shocks. Well endowed with energy resources, Algeria has promoted a conception of self-reliance that emphasizes national control over natural resources as the prerequisite for being "master in one's own house."[14]

Algerian policy has expressed a passion for national autonomy that was a reaction to the dispossession of the colonial period. Because of the scale of colonization (a million Europeans were settled in Algeria in 1960) and foreign ownership of land, Algerian society was profoundly disrupted by the colonial order. During the war for independence (1954–1962), Algerian intellectuals articulated a critique of the colonialist/capitalist political economy that dictated an agenda of recovering natural resources and developing them through centralized planning.

The principal features of Algeria's quest for "mastery" were: nationalization of foreign-owned means of production; creation of an array of state-owned enterprises; insistence upon Algerian rather than expatriate managers; reinvestment of energy revenues so as to minimize recourse to foreign capital; and a policy of leadership in Third World affairs, especially concerning the concept of a New International Economic Order. For Algeria, self-reliance essentially meant national control.

At independence, the government of Ahmed Ben Bella nationalized a large amount of agricultural land, a task facilitated by the mass exodus of the French landowners. The National Liberation Front's program also stipulated the nationalization of credit, trade, and the relatively small mining and industrial sectors. The longer-term task was to gain control over the emergent energy sector (oil having been discovered in the Sahara only in 1956). In 1963, the government initiated this process by creating the first new state enterprise, an oil pipeline company called SONATRACH (Société Nationale de Transports et de

Commercialisation des Hydrocarbures), which proved to be but the first of a large number of *sociétés nationales* or state firms. From its modest beginning as a transport facility, SONATRACH grew into a huge company controlling the entirety of Algeria's burgeoning energy industry.

In the 1962 negotiations that led to Algerian independence, Algeria had accepted a privileged position for the French oil companies operating in the Sahara. In 1965, the Boumedienne government renegotiated this accord to make SONATRACH an equal partner in a new Franco-Algerian Cooperative Association. The new agreement also increased the royalties paid to the Algerian government, revenues that the Algerians promptly invested in a host of auxiliary enterprises—drilling, engineering, geological research, additional pipelines, and eventually refineries. By 1969, having acquired greater expertise in the technology of the petroleum industry, Algeria called for talks to revise the 1965 agreement. When these dragged on into February 1971 without satisfaction, Boumedienne nationalized all foreign energy holdings, making the Algerian state master in its own house in this critical sector. Over the ensuing decade, the state invested massively in further energy projects, most important of which were the technologically sophisticated gas liquefaction complexes necessary to exploit its natural gas resources.

The 1976 National Charter, which is the Algerian counterpart to the Arusha Declaration, states that economic liberation requires "the recovery of natural riches, appropriation by the collectivity of the major means of production, equilibrium in foreign trade, the financial independence of the State, the creation of a national market, and the mastery of technology. . . . In sum it is a matter of . . . the nation counting first upon itself."[15] Self-reliance thus stressed national accumulation of capital for investment rather than recourse to foreign investors. Algeria has shunned multinational corporations and has urged other developing countries to do likewise. While counting first upon itself, it has urged fellow Third World states to form producers' associations like OPEC in order to be able to exert influence on the prices of raw materials.

Algerians liked to say that they were sowing their oil in order to reap industry. The petrochemical sector was seen as the foundation for forward and backward linkages. Under a series of three- and four-year plans, state firms were planted in such sectors as iron and steel, machinery, vehicles, building materials, and agricultural equipment; likewise, numerous consumer goods industries, including textiles, leather, plastics, and electronics, sprung up, all under the auspices of the state. The surge of national investment was impressive, but it was also a strain on Algeria's managerial capacities; and it was uneven insofar as a balance between industrial and agricultural investment was concerned. By the early 1980s, the post-Boumedienne leadership began to worry particularly about what was being reaped in the rural sector.

Agricultural production slackened over the period of concentrated investment in industrialization. In the face of a rapidly growing population, this meant a slide from agricultural self-sufficiency into a dependence upon food imports.

In fact, Algeria had always imported food (grains, dairy products, sugar, tea), but during the colonial period imports were balanced by the export of wine, citrus, and dates. Production has simply not kept up with growing consumption; whereas Algeria imported about half a million tons of cereals in 1961–1965, by the 1980s, import needs were above 2 million tons per year. Lack of rural investment and a policy of low prices (to feed the urban population cheaply) undermined the incentives for agricultural production. The Chadli Benjedid government's Second Five-Year Plan (1985–1989) increased the sum allocated to rural development and liberalized the pricing and marketing structures. In effect, the government recognized that food import bills were causing Algeria to eat rather than to sow its oil and gas revenues.

Failure to increase production in the agricultural sector has struck a serious blow to Algeria's model of self-reliance, just as it has in Tanzania. Moreover, there have been shortcomings in the management of the industrial sector that have necessitated decentralization policies since Benjedid assumed power in 1978. Yet, it remains the case that Algeria has achieved significant diversification of its national economy without recourse to foreign private investment. Mastery in one's own house has never implied autarky to the Algerian planners. Algeria must engage in trade; the real issue is the terms of that trade, and Algeria has consistently bargained for fair terms of trade for its energy exports.

During 1985–1986, Benjedid carried out a revision of the National Charter adopted during the Boumedienne era. Charter '86 authorized a somewhat greater role for private Algerian capital than did the 1976 version, but it did not alter the basic commitment to a predominantly public-sector economy. It also sanctioned Benjedid's decentralization policies, which allow local managers greater autonomy over their enterprises. The theme of self-reliance was fully retained, however; if anything, Charter '86 devoted even more emphasis to the principle of counting on oneself (*"le 'compter sur soi'"*).[16] What self-reliance means to the Benjedid government is not merely national ownership of the means of production but more efficient management of the state sector and greater attention to the needs of rural producers. The decline of oil prices in the mid-1980s required the Algerians to revise their investment projections and tighten their belts, but it did not dim their ardor for achieving mastery in their own house.

■ BARGAINING WITH TRANSNATIONAL CORPORATIONS

When African states received their independence, few areas of their economies beyond traditional agriculture were under African control. Mining and manufacturing were dominated by transnational corporations, which also played a significant role in export agriculture in some countries through the ownership of plantations. Domestic commerce was often in the hands of Lebanese and Indian traders whose settlement had been encouraged during the colonial period. This gave rise on the part of African governments to a perception of powerlessness, most forcefully expressed by Kwame Nkrumah, who wrote that colonialism had been replaced by a neocolonialism that undermined Africa's nominal political independence. Even those governments that did not subscribe to Nkrumah's rhetoric were concerned that their lack of control over their economies would render them politically impotent. A renegotiation of the terms under which foreign capital operated was inevitable.

In absolute terms, the total foreign investment in African countries has always been small. In 1967, investment from Organization for Economic Cooperation and Development (OECD) countries in black Africa amounted to $4.3 billion, 12.3 percent of total investment in developing countries. Mining and petroleum accounted for over 50 percent of this total; manufacturing accounted for only 20 percent—a much smaller percentage than in other developing countries. Countries such as Burkina Faso, Mali, Togo, Gabon, and Malawi had a total foreign investment in manufacturing in 1967 of less than $5 million.[17] These figures attest not to the lack of importance of foreign investment in African economies but rather to low levels of economic development. Many of the foreign corporations with investments in Africa had annual turnovers far in excess of the GDP of the states in which they invested: In most cases the relative economic size of states and multinationals were very unequal.

The activities of multinational corporations in Third World countries are a matter of considerable controversy. How they are viewed depends on the ideological perspective of the commentator. Some dependency theorists have a negative attitude, believing TNCs inevitably have an adverse effect on the economies in which they operate; some proponents of the free market believe that TNCs always contribute to global efficiency and that their activities inevitably benefit Third World countries. Most development economists adopt an intermediate position: that TNCs have considerable oligopolistic and/or oligopsonistic power, which can be and has been abused at times. On the other hand, they assert that it is possible, although not necessarily easy, for governments to curb the abuse by TNCs of their economic power through successful bargaining with them—that is, by setting the terms under which TNCs are allowed to participate in the domestic economy.[18]

On the positive side, TNCs are able to supply capital, technology, management, and marketing networks—factors that have been in short supply in all African economies. The costs of mineral exploitation (exploration, construction of mines and the necessary infrastructure, etc.) are enormous and clearly beyond the investment capacity of indigenous entrepreneurs or most African governments. Until the development of the Eurodollar market, which enabled African governments to borrow substantial sums from consortia of private banks, there was little choice but to rely on TNCs for the capital needed in this field. Similarly, until the mid-1970s, there were few alternatives to TNCs for obtaining technology, management, and the means of marketing output.

It is inevitable that there are costs in dependence on TNCs.[19] Subsidiaries of TNCs are part of a global network of companies. Invariably, the interests of the corporation as a global entity are placed before those of the country in which the subsidiary is operating. Technology transferred by TNCs is usually designed for the economies of their home countries and thus tends to be capital-intensive. Often, constraints are placed on the use of such technology—most commonly, a prohibition on the recipient firm exporting to third markets. Also, the products that TNCs manufacture in Third World countries are typically those sold in their home countries—sophisticated consumer items that are often promoted through advertising. Allegations have frequently been made, therefore, that TNCs are responsible for "taste transfer" in Third World countries, a process that leads to a reliance on relatively expensive imported products and to the destruction of traditional manufacturing industries.[20]

Studies have shown that TNCs seldom import large quantities of capital but instead raise most of their investment funds from the host country. This has been perceived as having a negative effect on the capital and investment opportunities available to local entrepreneurs. As little capital is imported (with the possible exception of minerals investments), the activities of TNCs, particularly in the establishment of import-substituting industries, have often been found to have a negative effect on a country's balance of payments: Costs are incurred for the import of capital goods and intermediate inputs, while the high costs of local production and/or restrictions attached to the licensed technology preclude exporting.

Two other matters have been particularly important to host country governments. The first is the ability of TNCs to avoid government foreign-exchange controls by engaging in "transfer pricing,"—that is, overinvoicing their subsidiaries in Third World countries for inputs supplied by other branches of the corporation. Prices that subsidiaries pay for their supplies from other branches may bear no relation to the world markets prices for these inputs. Second, TNCs can obviously use their economic power to attempt to change government policy. In the most notorious examples, such as the activities of the International Telephone and Telegraph Company in Allende's Chile, TNCs have allegedly attempted to undermine the government of a country whose actions appeared to threaten the interests of a local subsidiary.

African governments have pursued a number of policies designed to reduce the dominant role of TNCs in their economies. Local entrepreneurs have been promoted through the establishment of development banks and similar institutions, such as the Office for the Promotion of Ivorian Enterprise in Côte d'Ivoire. In all African countries, the state itself has become a major investor in sectors such as utilities (in Côte d'Ivoire, which has encouraged foreign investment, the public sector is responsible for over 60 percent of total investment). And governments have attempted to shape the role of foreign investment through indicative planning. But the most direct attempts to control the activities of TNCs have come through nationalization and indigenization moves.

Nationalization may be defined as the process whereby a government acquires a majority shareholding in an enterprise. This does not necessarily imply total government ownership—a 51 percent holding of stock would constitute a majority shareholding. Nor is nationalization necessarily the same as expropriation. Although the terms are sometimes used interchangably, expropriation is often used in a pejorative sense to refer to nationalization without paying compensation to the previous owner of the assets. Indigenization, on the other hand, refers to the transfer of ownership into national hands. This transfer may include private actors as well as the state.

An aggregate study of nationalizations that took place in the period 1960–1977 shows that more occurred in black Africa than anywhere else—47 percent of all nationalizations.[21] These occurred during a period when black Africa accounted for only 10 percent of foreign direct investment in LDCs. The reason is straightforward. African countries were latecomers to independence; most gained it during the years covered by this study, whereas governments in other developing regions of the world had achieved independence earlier and thus had the opportunity in an earlier period to take action to limit the role of foreign corporations. Although some form of nationalization has occurred in most African states, the form and timing of such moves has varied considerably from country to country, largely a product of the ideology of the regime in power.

States that have pursued an avowedly socialist development strategy have generally tended to take a larger shareholding in foreign enterprises and have attempted to impose stricter conditions on their operations. Ghana under Nkrumah and Acheampong, as well as Tanzania, are excellent examples. In Reginald Green's words, "Tanzania has not viewed it as practical to have African capitalism even if it wanted to."[22] In the years from 1967 to 1971, most productive enterprises in Tanzania were nationalized: banking and other commercial services such as insurance; manufacturing; mining; tourism; agricultural marketing; and even urban real estate—a move aimed primarily at Asian capitalists. Nationalization moves were supplemented by the establishment of new state enterprises. In most cases, the state did not assume 100 percent control, but established joint ventures with foreign capital in which the state maintained a majority shareholding.

Similar moves were planned by Milton Obote in Uganda in 1970, initially reversed and subsequently erratically pursued by Idi Amin; in Mozambique; in Ethiopia under the *derg;* and in Zambia. In non Afro-Marxist or nonsocialist, regimes, the nationalizations have been less extensive and, in many cases, the role of the state sector somewhat less. Even in Côte d'Ivoire, however, which has probably offered more of an open door policy to foreign capital than any other African state, the Ivorian state has pursued a policy of establishing joint ventures with foreign capital (with the state typically holding 12–25 percent of the shares) while also creating wholly state-owned parastatal corporations.

In countries not committed to a socialist approach, indigenization has offered an alternative method of attempting to increase national control over the economy. Policies of indigenization have been most clearly articulated since the early 1970s by the governments of Ghana and Nigeria. The Nigerian Enterprises Decree of 1972 established a Nigerian Enterprises Promotion Board and classified all industrial enterprises into two schedules. The first schedule identified enterprises that were to be reserved exclusively for Nigerians. The second listed industries open to foreign investment provided that Nigerians held at least 40 percent of the equity capital. In 1977, industries were reclassified into three groupings: those (forty categories) that required limited capital and operated with low technology and which were to be reserved exclusively for Nigerians; a second grouping of fifty-seven categories of enterprise in which foreign participation was permissible, providing Nigerians held at least 60 percent of the equity; and a third grouping of thirty-nine relatively capital-intensive sectors, such as vehicle assembly and shipbuilding, in which a minimum Nigerian-held equity of 40 percent was required. Similarly, the Investment Policy Decree proclaimed in Ghana in 1975 required the indigenization of all or some of the equity of commercial and manufacturing enterprises. In Ghana also, a group of industries were listed that could only be wholly owned by citizens. These included bakery products, tire retreading, and garment manufacture.

Underlying the various nationalization moves has been the idea that equity ownership and the resulting seats on the Boards of Directors will provide greater control over the activities of affected companies. It soon became clear, however, that ownership does not necessarily equate with control. There are multiple reasons for this. At the heart of all of them is the problem that even with a local capital contribution, a considerable dependence on the TNC remains. There are a number of dimensions to this situation that vary according to the type of enterprise. Companies that manufacture for import substitution usually produce brand-name products—Coca Cola, Volkswagen, National Panasonic, etc. Licenses to use the patents of these corporations have to be negotiated in order for the firms to continue in operation. In many cases in Africa, manufacturing consists primarily of the assembly of parts provided by the parent corporation and is dependent on the parent for the inputs. In the mining sector, equity ownership in itself does not provide access to the advanced technology that is often required. Dependence on the TNC for refining, manufacturing, and distributing the product often continues. Both in manufacturing and mining, the severe shortage of skilled personnel ensures that there has often been a continuing dependence on the TNC for management. Although it has been possible for governments to insist, as a prerequisite for a company's continuing its local operation, that local personnel be trained, this does not necessarily produce a local manager whose sympathies lie with the government rather than with the corporation.

If state equity ownership does not bring control, indigenization is even less likely to do so. Indigenization moves have often been accompanied by limits on the number of shares that any individual may hold. The parent company, therefore, remains the largest single shareholder. To compound matters, a survey of the effects of indigenization in Nigeria found that it was often the case that none of the Nigerian equity holders with the largest individual shareholdings had been appointed to the Board of Directors, again tending to strengthen the control of the parent company.[23] And, of course, indigenous board members cannot necessarily be counted on to side with the government in any dispute between it and the company: Financial interests often conflict with national loyalties. Various investigations have shown that companies have been adept at circumventing the legislation through such means as subsidizing the purchase of shares by "front men."[24] The principal effects of the indigenization measures appear to have been to enrich a relatively small number of Ghanaians and Nigerians who were able to purchase shares and to benefit some small businesspeople whose principal competition—noncitizen Indian and Lebanese traders—were driven out of sectors reserved for the indigenous population.

Since the mid-1970s, TNCs have often appeared at least resigned to, if not always welcoming, partial nationalization and indigenization. A new legitimacy is obtained by securing local participation in the ownership of the subsidiary; local equity participation may lead perversely to reduced competition for TNCs, as capital that might otherwise be employed to establish competitive enterprises is instead diverted to the purchase of shares in the TNC subsidiary. TNCs have, however, reacted negatively to situations where an uncertain business climate has been created either by capricious government action toward foreign capital or by general economic crisis.

The first of these situations is best illustrated by events in the mining industry. There is now a general recognition that bargaining between TNCs and governments over minerals investments goes through a series of stages. In the initial instance, when the government is hoping to attract TNC participation and is dependent on the corporation both for exploration and for capital, the TNC is in a particularly strong bargaining position and can extract generous terms for its participation. Once, however, the corporation has undertaken extensive investments in the host country, these are "hostage" to the host state and may be used as leverage in order to force a renegotiation of the terms of its operations.[25] Such a pattern has occurred in mining ventures throughout all parts of the world, including, for instance, British and Norwegian renegotiation of the terms under which TNCs operate in the North Sea oilfields. As host countries acquired a more sophisticated understanding of the operation of minerals industries, so renegotiation of the terms of operation of TNCs became commonplace. Governments have had to attempt to forge a contractual relationship that enables them to tax some of the rents generated by a resource project yet provides a sufficiently remunerative and stable environment to induce continued TNC investment in the venture. In the 1970s, few African states managed to achieve this balance.

Two of the most important examples, given their predominance in Africa's minerals exports, involve Zambia and Zaire. In 1968, President Kaunda of Zambia announced a sweeping series of economic reforms that appeared to be inspired by Tanzania's Arusha Declaration of the previous year. Among the measures adopted was the nationalization of the country's copper mines, the chief source of exports. The government agreed to purchase 51 percent of the shares in the principal mining companies at an enormous cost to state finances. The mining companies were to remain as minority shareholders and were given generous five-year management contracts. The government soon expressed dissatisfaction with the terms of the agreement and sought, in 1973, to renegotiate the tax and foreign-exchange concessions previously given to the mining companies. Several attempts were also made to renegotiate the management contracts; some companies found themselves ejected. The result was to create considerable uncertainty. Zambia did not at this time have sufficient skilled personnel to manage the copper mines itself; the termination of contracts caused a severe shortage of management personnel to the detriment of the efficient operation of the mines. Similar uncertainty was created in Zaire, where the government of General Mobutu adopted a policy of Zairianization in 1973 for the copper mines, only to be forced, in 1975, following massive dislocations in production, to invite the Belgian mining companies back.

One of the reasons for the repeated renegotiation by some governments of the terms of operation of foreign capital was their lack of bargaining expertise. In many cases, overworked state officials did not have adequate knowledge, such as of the financial operations of TNCs and the structure of the industry. This was particularly the case in the mining industry. Such knowledge is a prerequisite for effective bargaining. Its absence was seen in experiences such as that of the copper mines in Zambia, where the government quickly became dissatisfied with the terms of the original bargain that it had struck. Negotiators were also often anxious to achieve a quick success: Their desire for agreement led to the acceptance of terms that were inferior to those that might have been obtained if they had been more patient.

A significant problem in bargaining with TNCs has been that too much attention was given to the question of ownership and insufficient consideration of whether ownership would necessarily provide the control over company operations that governments sought. Again the Zambia case is an excellent example: The nationalization of the copper mines was an enormous financial burden to the Zambian government and generated a substantial foreign debt. Yet, Zambia's majority shareholdings in itself had a negligible impact on the companies' operations. With hindsight, it appeared that the government's objectives might have been more effectively obtained by negotiating specific agreements in the areas in which it was interested, such as management, training of personnel, repatriation of profits, and tax concessions. TNCs have often been happy to sell a majority of the shares in their subsidiaries to host governments, as this raises capital for them (and thus reduces the risk to the company), provides the subsidiary with a new legitimacy, and yet has little impact on their operations.

African governments have gradually acquired more bargaining expertise and have more options available in choosing foreign partners than was the case when they first achieved their independence. The growth of African universities and the training overseas of African students has produced substantially more graduates—although, in some countries, educated personnel remain in desperately short supply. Governments have been able to learn from the experience of others in bargaining with TNCs—a significant example of effective South-South cooperation. More information has become available—about, for example, the operations of TNCs, the structure and profitability of various industries, and the contracts that TNCs have negotiated elsewhere—through such agencies as the UN Centre on Transnational Corporations.

With the advent of increasing numbers of TNCs from countries such as Germany and Japan, host countries are placed in a better bargaining position, enjoying the potential to play TNCs from various countries off against each other. Since the 1970s, one of the most significant developments has been the growth of TNCs based in Third World countries, particularly Brazil, India, and South Korea. These firms often are able to offer a package that is better suited to the factor endowments of African states—for example, more labor-intensive technology. Some companies, such as the giant U.S. Bechtel Corporation, now specialize in "turnkey" projects—building and equipping an industrial plant, oil refinery, etc., and then handing control over to the purchasing government with no strings (such as future management contracts and licensing arrangements) necessarily attached. Other companies offer, on a commercial basis, an assessment of the real market worth of services and inputs supplied by one branch of a TNC to another, which offers governments the opportunity to maintain a stricter control of the use of transfer pricing by TNCs. And, with the emergence of the Eurodollar market, governments deemed to be credit-worthy have been able to raise capital for large-scale projects whose finance in the past would almost certainly have to be sought from TNCs.

African governments, then, now have more information and opportunities available to them in bargaining with foreign capital. This, of course, does not imply that the bargaining relationship will always be an equal one nor that governments will always achieve their objectives. As Donald Rothchild and Robert Curry point out, one of the weaknesses of African governments in their bargaining with TNCs has been their impatience to conclude transactions.[26] The economic crisis that has beset many African economies in the last decade has made it more difficult for many governments to exercise patience. In general, the bargaining position of African governments will be maximized the more that alternatives are available to them and the fewer that are available to TNCs.

African governments, therefore, undermine their bargaining strength when they compete with one another for TNC investment. One of the intentions behind regional integration schemes has been to create a common regime for foreign investment to prevent TNCs from playing one potential African host country off against another. Ultimately, such a common regime would be expected to bring benefits to all countries in the region as a whole. It is clear, however, that governments in some of the more developed and capitalist-oriented countries, most notably Côte d'Ivoire and Kenya, perceive that *national* gains will be maximized by offering generous terms to attempt to attract TNCs. This disjunction between short-term national rationality and what is rational for the whole region in the longer term is one of the classic problems that have beset regional integration attempts.

At a time when African governments are better placed than ever before to bargain with TNCs, there has been a marked trend toward the withdrawal of TNCs from African economies. From the perspective of TNCs, an uncertain investment climate created by sometimes capricious government behavior has been compounded by the general economic decline that has afflicted Africa in the past ten years. Foreign exchange has not been available to purchase the necessary spare parts; manufacturing plants and mining machinery have suffered directly not only from lack of parts but also from breakdowns in essential infrastructure such as power and water supplies. It has been estimated, for example, that manufacturing production in Ghana was only 20 percent, approximately, of maximum capacity throughout the 1970s.[27] Foreign-exchange shortages have led to governments restricting the amount of royalties and profits that TNCs can repatriate.

Uncertainties have led to a policy of *withdrawal* by foreign capital from African states. In the mining industry, for instance, the EEC estimated that there had been no new investment, except in uranium extraction, in black Africa in the years from 1975 to 1984.[28] Following the first round of decisive action by OPEC producers in 1973–1974, mining companies have preferred to invest in countries regarded as providing a more hospitable investment climate. Investments have been redirected away from Africa toward Australia, Canada, and, in the Third World, the relatively more politically stable countries of Latin America, such as Brazil, Mexico, and Venezuela.

A similar withdrawal of foreign capital has been evident in manufacturing industries. Economic crisis has not only made the production process difficult but has reduced the market for goods provided by import-substituting industries. Africa has also not become a preferred location for TNCs that manufacture labor-intensive products for export back to the industrialized countries. Among the factors that contribute to this situation are uncertain investment climates; poor infrastructure; undeveloped and relatively costly transport links with industrialized countries; and a relatively unskilled, poorly disciplined, and expensive labor force. As Frederick Cooper notes, Africa lacks the "disciplined battalions of South Korea, Taiwan and Hong Kong."[29] Withdrawal by foreign capital thus may force Africa into a path of involuntary self-reliance just at a time when the skills to bargain more effectively with TNCs are being acquired.

■ AFRICA AND THE NORTH-SOUTH DIALOGUE

OPEC's success in dramatically raising the price of oil in 1973 enabled developing countries to raise North-South economic issues to the top of the international agenda. Although the Group of 77 (the grouping of Third World countries
in international organizations) had been in existence since the foundation of the
UN Conference on Trade and Development (UNCTAD) in 1964, it had previously been unable to persuade industrialized countries to give serious attention
to its demands for global reform. New concerns in industrialized countries regarding the future security of supply of raw materials changed this situation—at
least temporarily. With the proclamation of the Charter of Economic Rights and
Duties of States, and the Declaration on the Establishment of a New International Economic Order in the mid-1970s, African governments believed that
their joint action with other developing countries in the United Nations had established the basis for a radical restructuring of their external economic
relations.

African states acting individually have little power in the overall international economic system. The largest African economy, Nigeria, accounts for
less than 1 percent of the world's imports and exports—a lower volume than
that of Hong Kong or such small industrial countries as Australia and Switzer-
land. The trade of the next largest black African economy, Côte d'Ivoire, is only
one-tenth that of Nigeria. Nor, individually, do any African countries have a
dominant position as producers of any commodity: Nigeria accounts for only 2
percent of the world's total oil output; Zambia and Zaire for approximately 6
percent each of the world's copper production; Guinea for 15 percent of international bauxite production. A similar situation prevails in the production of major
agricultural commodities: The largest single-country market share is Côte
d'Ivoire's 22 percent of total world cocoa output. Although it is the case that
African countries' shares of world *trade* in commodities are higher, these shares
are insufficient to enable them to unilaterally exercise power over international
markets.

Given their economic weakness, a logical strategy for African regimes to
adopt is to act in concert with other developing countries. African governments
have perceived joint action in such forums as the United Nations as the best
means through which they may compensate for the structural asymmetries that
characterize their external economic relations. These forums provide opportunities to attempt to change the rules of the game, which African governments
perceive as having been against their interests.[30] The success of OPEC in 1973
was also seen as a model that might be emulated by groups of other commodity-
producing countries. The Algerian government was one of the most active
promoters of joint action. Algeria hosted the first major conference of the Group
of 77 in 1967, during which the developing countries drafted a common position for the 1968 session of UNCTAD. Subsequent meetings of the Nonaligned
Movement (NAM), including the Algiers nonaligned summit in 1973, pro-

moted such ideas as commodities producers' associations fashioned on the OPEC model. A year later, Algeria initiated the process that led to adoption of the NIEO proposals. Unfortunately, from the perspective of African governments, neither strategy has brought results commensurate with aspirations.

Within a few years it became obvious that OPEC's success would not be replicated by other commodity producers. Oil has a number of uncommon attributes that explain the ability of OPEC to achieve short-run success: its central place in the economies of industrialized countries; the predominance of a relatively small number of developing countries as its principal exporters, including some whose income was so high that they could afford to limit production in order to force up prices; the absence in the short term of readily available substitutes; and the high costs of generating alternative sources of supply. These characteristics were absent for many of the commodities of most interest to Africa: copper, for instance, can be substituted for by other metals, particularly aluminum, or replaced by synthetics, such as fiberoptics, or can be recycled from scrap. In addition, a number of industrialized countries, notably Australia and Canada, that have been unwilling to participate in Third World–dominated commodity groupings are among the major exporters. Demand for many of Africa's agricultural exports is responsive to price changes; substitutes are readily available for most products; and it is also relatively inexpensive to establish new sources of supply.

Although a number of groupings of commodity producers have been promoted under UNCTAD auspices, they have recorded little success. In large part, this has been a result of an inability on the part of the groups to agree on arrangements to limit output and of the need to establish national production quotas. Again, in this instance short-term national rationality has conflicted with the long-term interests of the group. For an individual country, it is rational in the short term to attempt to "cheat" by expanding production while other countries limit their own. An increase in national revenue may be obtained in the short term. In the longer run, however, such expansion inevitably undermines the producers' agreement, and all countries may end up worse off: Output increases but prices decline. Such disputes have undermined one of the commodity agreements of most interest to West African states: the International Cocoa Agreement. This agreement was largely moribund over the first half of the 1980s, a major cause being the refusal of the world's second largest producer, Côte d'Ivoire, to accept its production quota. Côte d'Ivoire attempted to maximize national revenue by initially withholding its cocoa from the market in an effort to force prices upward. In the end, it had no option but to sell its production at a lower price and incurred a substantial loss (estimated at $100 million) in the process. Although a new cocoa agreement was negotiated in 1986, producing countries had to accept prices below the levels of those established by previous agreements.

Oil power has largely rebounded against African interests as a whole, although the states that have become oil exporters—Nigeria, Libya, Algeria,

Gabon, Angola, Cameroon, and the Congo—enjoyed significant windfall gains in the period from 1973 to 1985. With the world economy experiencing two major recessions largely induced by the increases in oil prices in 1973/74 and again in 1979, other commodity producers certainly have experienced lower prices for their exports than would have been the case if the world economy had continued to grow at the rates prevailing in the 1960s. The IMF's composite index of commodity prices reached its lowest level ever in the early 1980s. Africa's copper producers—Zambia, Zaire, and, on a smaller scale, Zimbabwe and Botswana—have been most severely hit, as copper prices fell below even the nominal levels achieved before 1973.

Many African states cut their diplomatic relations with Israel after 1973 in the hope of obtaining substantial aid from the Arab members of OPEC. Although some considerable quantity of aid has been forthcoming, particularly to Islamic countries, the amounts have fallen far short of African expectations and have done little to compensate governments for the higher prices they have had to pay for their imported fuel and the lower prices received for their commodity exports. Meanwhile, by 1985 it was apparent that OPEC's power was waning. Non-OPEC producers had expanded production; consumption had been reduced; oil users had switched to alternative sources of energy, such as coal and natural gas. With gluts in the oil market, OPEC would have had to reduce its production significantly if its market control was to be maintained. This proved to be impossible, as the poorest producers, most notably Nigeria, had embarked on ambitious development plans that were based on projections of rising revenues. In a situation that was similar to the case Côte d'Ivoire in the International Cocoa Agreement, Nigeria's inability to accept a lower production quota was a factor in OPEC's enfeeblement.

The global North-South dialogue has proved equally disappointing for African states. In the mid-1970s there was optimism that the NIEO would bring a major restructuring of the international economy in such areas as international monetary arrangements and aid, trade, industrialization, technology transfer, the activities of TNCs, and the Law of the Sea. The international recession and the advent of more conservative regimes in the United States, Britain, and West Germany dashed these hopes. As the initial fears regarding future supplies of raw materials passed, developing countries found that they had little leverage over industrialized countries. Stalemate ensued in many of the forums in which North-South issues were discussed. Furthermore, the governments of the industrialized countries sought to move the discussion on many of the important issues away from organizations where the principle of one state–one vote gave the South a numerical majority to institutions such as the IMF and World Bank, where voting rights are weighted according to countries' shareholdings, and thus the views of the industrialized countries prevail.

Although Southern countries have made a number of incremental gains in many areas of international economic relations, these have fallen far short of the basic restructuring that they sought. Even if the NIEO had been implemented, there is some doubt as to whether the proposals would have benefited African countries as much as some other members of the Third World. The more-developed members of the Group of 77 were dominant in framing the NIEO proposals, which, it is not surprising, reflect their interests. These do not necessarily always coincide with those of most African states. For instance, proposals to stabilize and raise commodity prices through the establishment of international commodity agreements financed by a Common Fund would have been of principal benefit to countries that exported a variety of commodities amenable to being stockpiled. This is rarely the case for African countries. Although gains would have been made from a stabilization of their export prices, many countries depend overwhelmingly on only one or two exports. These countries would thus have to pay more for their imports of other commodities as well as for their imports of goods manufactured from these commodities. Some significant African agricultural exports, such as bananas and cocoa, are impossible to store for a sustained period and are, therefore, not amenable to the buffer-stocking proposals. Similar divergence of interest between middle-income LDCs and Africa was obvious in areas such as trade (where most African countries need special advantages not only over industrialized but also over more-advanced developing countries in order to compete in world markets) and debt relief. One area in which some African countries have traditionally enjoyed such special advantages is in relations with the EEC.

■ AFRICA AND THE EEC

As we noted in our discussion of collective self-reliance, a division between anglophone and francophone countries has hampered economic cooperation in Africa. One of the principal reasons for this division was the links that most francophone countries had with the European Community. When the EEC was founded in 1957 with the signature of the Treaty of Rome, France was determined that special trade arrangements should be made for its colonies. Despite the reluctance of the other members of the community, France succeeded in adding a section to the Treaty of Rome that provided for the eventual establishment of a free trade area between the six founding members of the EEC (Belgium, France, Italy, Luxembourg, Netherlands, and West Germany) and their colonies in Africa. When most French colonies received their independence in 1960, these arrangements were renegotiated, leading to the eventual conclusion of the first Yaoundé Convention in 1963. Under its terms, exports from the eighteen associated African countries, with the important exception of agricultural products included within the EEC's Common Agricultural Policy, were granted free access to the European market. A European Development Fund (EDF) was established to provide aid from the six member states to the African associates. In return, the African associates were obliged to offer tariff preferences to the six member states of the community

Anglophone countries were deeply suspicious of the arrangements, perceiving the "reverse" preferences demanded of the associates as a means of perpetuating neocolonialism. Relations with the community, therefore, reinforced the anglophone-francophone divide and were a stumbling bloc for intra-African cooperation. It soon became clear, however, that Britain was determined to seek admission to the EEC regardless of the views of Commonwealth countries and that, in any case, the EEC market was growing more rapidly and offered more opportunities to Commonwealth African countries than did the British market. As a result, Nigeria and the three member states of the East African community —Kenya, Uganda, and Tanzania—sought special arrangements for their exports to the EEC in the mid-1960s to enable them to compete on an equal basis with francophone countries. Treaties were signed (although that with Nigeria was never implemented because of the Biafran war) that allowed for duty-free treatment to be accorded specified quantities of exports to the community; again, however, reverse preferences were demanded of the four African countries.[31]

With British entry into the EEC in 1973, Commonwealth countries were in danger not only of being excluded from the expanded European market but also of losing their traditional preferences in Britain. This urgent need to reach a satisfactory arrangement with the EEC offered an opportunity to overcome the traditional divisions with francophone states and forge a joint negotiating position. This task was by no means easy, given the desire of some francophone countries to maintain the advantages that they enjoyed. Eventually, however, a negotiating group was formed that included not only the existing associates but all developing Commonwealth countries (from the Caribbean and Pacific as well as Africa) and African countries of "comparable economic structure" not previously associated with Britain or the EEC (Ethiopia, Guinea, and Liberia— later to be joined by the former Portuguese colonies). These forty-six countries became known as the ACP (African, Caribbean, and Pacific) Group and successfully negotiated the first of the Lomé Conventions in 1975.[32]

Signature of the first convention was greeted with a great deal of euphoria by the participants. Not only did it mark unprecedented cooperation between anglophone and francophone countries (laying the way, it has been argued, for the signature of the ECOWAS treaty), but the unity of the ACP Group (coupled with the relatively favorable environment induced by the concern over the future supply of raw materials following OPEC's success in raising oil prices in 1973–1974) had enabled it to extract a number of concessions from the EEC. ACP countries now were offered free access to the European market without having to provide reverse preferences to the EEC; a fund called STABEX (Stabilization of Export Earnings Scheme) was established to compensate ACP countries for fluctuations in their earnings from primary commodity exports to the EEC; a protocol on sugar maintained advantages for ACP sugar producers similar to those previously given through the Commonwealth Sugar Agreement; at the request of the ACP, a Centre for Industrial Development was created with the objective of promoting industrialization in ACP states; and the EDF was expanded.

The Lomé Convention has subsequently been renewed twice (1980 and 1984), and the ACP Group has now expanded to sixty-six members, including all of the countries of black Africa (the countries of North Africa have separate, less comprehensive agreements with the EEC).[33] The euphoria that accompanied the signature of the first convention has, however, long since disappeared. Not long after it had been implemented, it became apparent that the parties to the convention had widely different views of the obligations that the EEC had entered into. ACP leaders believed that the EEC had given a commitment to preserve the position of their countries in the European market. EEC representatives indicated, however, that their understanding of the convention was that ACP countries were to be provided with favorable treatment but not necessarily more advantageous treatment than that given other developing countries; they asserted that no guarantee had been given that ACP market shares would be preserved. Although the convention maintains the rhetoric of a partnership between equals, the EEC alone has the ultimate responsibility for interpreting the treaty; it is not surprising, therefore, that the narrow interpretation of EEC obligations has prevailed.

ACP states have voiced their dissatisfaction at various times over almost all of the chapters of the convention. In the trade field, they have argued that the preferences enjoyed by the ACP Group have been eroded and that this has contributed to the group's loss of its share of the EEC market. The EEC has refused to grant free access to ACP agricultural products that compete with its own domestic production; ACP producers of goods regarded as "sensitive" by the European Community, most notably clothing, have been forced to restrict exports to the EEC market. Despite the absence of reverse preferences, a study showed that the EEC had been more successful in maintaining its share of ACP markets than the ACP had been in EEC markets.[34]

Although generally welcomed by ACP governments, the STABEX scheme has been widely criticized for its restrictive product and market coverage, its failure to calculate compensation in terms of real rather than nominal export earnings, and the arbitrary way in which it has been administered by the EEC. In 1981 and 1982, STABEX funds were exhausted, largely as a result of precipitous falls in the price of coffee and cocoa: ACP states were not fully compensated even when their right to a transfer had been established.[35] The provisions for industrial cooperation have had little impact, in part the product of inadequate financial support for them. Aid under the conventions has been disbursed very slowly, and, although the EDF has increased substantially to the figure of 8.5 billion European Currency Units (approximately $6.8 billion) for the five years covered by the third convention, this figure fails to preserve the aid at the real level obtained in the first convention. All of these factors have contributed to a widespread disappointment on the part of African countries with this "special relationship" with their former colonial powers.

Radical critics have argued that the Lomé Conventions are merely neocolonial devices that maintain European influence in the ACP countries in general and in Africa in particular. There is little doubt that it is at Africa that the convention is largely directed—to the extent that EEC representatives have been embarrassed on occasion when they have failed to refer to the Caribbean and Pacific dimensions of the relationship. And there are dimensions to the convention that give some support to the radical critique: STABEX covers only raw materials or products that have undergone very limited processing and may thus be perceived as discouraging states from promoting economic diversification through further processing or manufacturing of their exports; the mineral scheme, SYSMIN, which provides loans to mineral-exporting countries, had as its stated objective the preservation of exports to the European market; and EEC-based multinational companies are offered preferential treatment under the trade rules of the convention. It is doubtful whether these provisions have a significant impact in practice. But it is abundantly clear that Lomé has fallen far short of the claim made in 1975 in the preamble to the convention: that the convention had established a model for a New International Economic Order. The convention appears, rather, to be a remnant of the days of imperial preference and to have an uncertain future.

■ AFRICA, ECONOMIC CRISIS, AND INTERNATIONAL ORGANIZATIONS

Africa's economic fragility was exposed when the international economy went into recession following the 1973 oil price rises. Many countries had achieved quite respectable rates of economic growth in the years between independence and 1979—the weighted mean for black Africa as a whole was 3.8 percent per annum in the years 1960–1970 and 3 percent per annum in the 1970s. This average, however, conceals marked variations in individual countries' records. Some economies performed very well: Botswana, Cameroon, Congo, Côte d'Ivoire, Lesotho, Malawi, Mauritius, and Sudan all grew at over 5 percent each year in the 1970s. In contrast, those of Angola, Burkina Faso, Chad, Ghana, Mozambique, Uganda, and Zaire actually contracted during this period, whereas those of Liberia and Zambia grew by less than 1 percent each year. When Africa's high rates of population growth are taken into account, the record of other countries becomes less impressive—Africa's oil-importing countries recorded per capita rates of economic growth of less than 1 percent each year over the 1960–1979 period. Problems were also becoming evident in Africa's foreign trade. Exports grew in volume by only 1.5 percent per year in the years 1969–1978 (a decline on a per capita basis); this was a period when import volumes were growing each year by over 4 percent. As Africa's barter terms of trade (the volume of exports necessary to purchase one unit of imports) were fairly constant in this period, many African countries were inevitably heading toward a balance-of-trade crisis.[36]

This situation erupted following the enormous increases in the price of oil imports in 1979. Not only did African states have to pay much more for their oil, but the international recession that followed OPEC's action also caused a significant decline in the prices for many of Africa's commodity exports. Governments attempted to borrow from international institutions to finance the crisis but were compelled by the magnitude of the problem to reduce nonoil imports. In many instances, essential imports had to be curtailed; the result was a shortage of spare parts for manufacturing industries and utilities and a consequent decline in their outputs. Since 1979, the continent has been in a state of deep economic crisis. Most economies contracted in this period—even the relatively prosperous Côte d'Ivoire experienced a decline in GDP of over 1.5 percent each year during the first half of the 1980s. Nigeria, which made large windfall gains from the oil price rises, squandered its increased revenue, borrowed heavily, and found itself with enormous debt problems when oil prices collapsed in the mid-1980s. The net result for many African countries, once the high rates of population growth are taken into account, is that a quarter of a century after independence their per capita incomes are no higher than they were when decolonization took place.

One of the most obvious manifestations of the contemporary crisis is Africa's burgeoning debt problem. Low-income Africa's debt-service ratio (the ratio of debt payments to exports) rose from 6.1 percent in 1970 to 19.9 percent in 1984. For some countries, the figure is substantially higher: For every dollar that Morocco, Niger, Côte d'Ivoire, and Nigeria earn in exports, more than 30 cents has to be given over to debt servicing. Sub-Saharan Africa has the highest ratio of debt to GNP of any world region. Another indicator of the seriousness of the situation is a comparison of total debt with exports: Sudan, for instance, in 1980–1982 had the highest ratio (437 percent) of total debts to exports of any developing country; Tanzania was next highest with 324 percent.

Africa's total debt was estimated by the IMF in 1987 to be close to $175 billion, of which approximately 60 percent is owed to foreign governments and international agencies. Although the *total* debt of individual African countries is much lower than that of some of their Latin American counterparts (which makes it easier for the international financial system to ignore their problems), the debts of some African countries have been rescheduled more times than those of any other developing countries. The World Bank, in its *World Development Report 1985*, comments that debt relief had been extended "more or less continuously" during the past decade to Liberia, Senegal, Sudan, Togo, and Zaire.[37]

Whichever way the debt problem is examined, by the mid-1980s Africa faced a crisis of horrific proportions—the future of many countries was mortgaged to international lenders. Contrary to aspirations for greater self-reliance, many countries had also become more dependent on foreign aid. Africa's share of the aid given by members of the OECD's Development Assistance Committee (DAC) rose from 24 percent in 1975 to 31 percent in 1983. In 1983, Africa received a total of over $6.4 billion from DAC countries and approximately an additional 10 percent of this figure from OPEC sources. Although most development economists accept the idea that aid, if properly used, can contribute to growth and development, there are clear drawbacks in depending so heavily on it.[38] In 1982, for instance, the World Bank estimated that aid contributed 13 percent of all gross domestic investment in black Africa. The figure for oil-importing countries was close to double this; for low-income semiarid countries the proportion was as high as 80 percent. Aid seldom comes with no strings attached. Aid donors have increasingly coordinated their activities and presented a united front toward recipients; accordingly, their potential leverage over African governments' choice of policies has increased.

Although many commentators believe that the economic crisis in Africa has been more severe than it need have been as a result of the failure of the international community to provide additional finance on concessional terms for Africa,[39] there is now a widespread consensus that the crisis has also revealed fundamental problems with African governments' economic strategies and performance since independence (some of which we have reviewed in Chapter 9). Although African governments committed themselves to policy change in the submission that the OAU made to the UN General Assembly's Special Session on Africa's Economic and Social Crisis, they have found that to a considerable extent matters have been taken out of their hands. Continuing trade imbalances, the ongoing debt problem, and the reliance on overseas donors for investment finance have give international creditors, particularly the World Bank and the IMF, unprecedented leverage over the choices available to African governments.[40]

To some extent, a fragile consensus has emerged between the views of many African governments and those of the international agencies. These views include:

1. Priority must be given to the rehabilitation of the agricultural sector.
2. "Getting the prices right"—including higher returns for farmers and the establishment of realistic exchange rates—is a necessary first step toward the creation of appropriate incentives for domestic producers.
3. However, domestic policy reforms will not succeed unless they are supported by a massive flow of resources on concessional terms. Many African economies are now suffering "import strangulation," and, in the words of the former president of the World Bank, "adjustment through further economic contraction is not a feasible alternative."[41]
4. In particular, Africa's debt burden is now "unmanageable." To preclude widespread defaults, significant rescheduling will have to occur.

Among nonofficial commentators, at least, the consensus appears to go further in asserting that a cancellation of some debts is necessary.

5.   African states are overextended: There is a need for states to establish clearer priorities for their activities. The public-sector deficit, often arising in large part from the inefficient operation of parastatals, must be significantly reduced.

6.   Aid policies toward the continent have been far from optimal, excessive emphasis having been given, in the words of Edgard Pisani, a former development commissioner of the EEC, to the construction of "cathedrals in the sand." A change in priorities toward rehabilitation of existing infrastructure, greater financing of recurrent costs, and more program and sector rather than project aid is required. There is also a growing recognition that the proliferation of donors has placed a severe burden on the administrations of many African countries and that greater coordination among donors is necessary.

7.   Africa's rate of population growth will severely hamper efforts at raising standards of living. There is now a widespread, although not universal, consensus among African governments that greater efforts must be made to curb the birthrate.

Beyond these general themes, however, there is widespread disagreement on instrumentalities, on timing, and on how policy reforms might best be implemented. Agreement between African countries and their creditors has been easier to reach on what measures are appropriate for the short term rather than on long-term principles, largely because African countries have so few policy alternatives available to them in the immediate future. To move beyond short-term adjustment to a discussion of the measures necessary to promote long-term economic growth is to become entangled in a much wider debate, which may impinge on policies that are at the heart of a regime's ideology and development strategy.

Even on short-term measures—for instance, exchange-rate changes and the necessity of reducing consumer subsidies—substantial disagreement has occurred between some governments and the World Bank/IMF. One reason is the different opinions that are held on the likely impact of policy changes. Many economists acknowledge that we simply do not know how African economies will respond to some of the proposed changes. The international agencies have tended to attempt to impose a standard package of policy reforms, which some critics argue pays insufficient attention to the uncertainties involved and to the differing characteristics of individual economies.

Another reason for disagreement is more directly political: Many of the allegedly irrational economic policies of African governments were pursued because they were perceived to be entirely politically rational in that they generated political patronage or reduced the prospects for unrest by significant political groups. A major reversal of policies inevitably will impose political costs.

One of the best illustrations of this is the insistence by international agencies on the removal of food price subsidies to urban consumers. Fear of the political consequences of an action of this type led the Zambian government in May 1987 to reject the conditions attached to IMF loans.

As yet, it is too early to judge the effectiveness of the policy reforms that were undertaken in the mid-1980s. Some short-term positive effects are evident. One of the most remarkable performances has been that of the Ghanaian economy after the Rawlings government negotiated a structural adjustment program with the IMF and World Bank. Government expenditure was cut and prices to agricultural producers raised. The cedi was devalued dramatically. The result has been a marked improvement in Ghana's agricultural production and exports and a large drop in the rate of inflation.

As the World Bank has acknowledged, however, such processes of painful adjustment can only be sustained if donors substantially increase their foreign assistance to African countries. Aid is needed to rehabilitate infrastructure and production facilities and to ease the foreign-exchange constraint until the policies succeed in substantially boosting export earnings. The special session of the UN General Assembly held in May 1986 to consider the policy changes and financing needed for coping with Africa's economic crisis was particularly disappointing for African leaders. Although many Western representatives were happy to offer advice to African governments, pledges of financial assistance were far less forthcoming. Only smaller aid donors, such as Canada, the Netherlands, and Norway, pledged additional financial assistance.

Successful policy reform and economic rehabilitation in Africa will require substantial political will—not just on the part of African governments, but of foreign donors also. It will be a tragedy if, at a time when many African governments have expressed a willingness to make the painful policy decisions necessary to rehabilitate their economies, the international community fails to provide the requisite external support.

■ NOTES

1. See, for instance, Carlos Diaz-Alejandro in Albert Fishlow et al., *Rich and Poor Nations in the World Economy* (New York: McGraw Hill, 1978).

2. For further discussion of self-reliant strategies, see Johan Galtung, Peter O'Brien, and Roy Preiswerk, eds., *Self-Reliance: A Strategy for Development* (London: Bogle-L'Ouverture, 1980).

3. William J. Foltz, *From French West Africa to the Mali Federation* (New Haven: Yale University Press, 1965); Colin Leys and Cranford Pratt, eds., *A New Deal in Central Africa* (New York: Praeger, 1961).

4. For more detailed discussion, see John Ravenhill, "Regional Integration and Development in Africa: Lessons from the East African Community," *Journal of Commonwealth and Comparative Politics* 17, no. 3 (November 1979), and Christian P. Potholm and Richard Fredland, eds., *Integration and Disintegration in East Africa* (Lanham, Md.: University Press of America, 1980). For the earlier years, see Donald

Rothchild, ed., *Politics of Integration* (Nairobi: East African Publishing House, 1968).

5. Steven Langdon and Lynn K. Mytelka, "Africa in the Changing World Economy," in Colin Legum et al., *Africa in the 1980s* (New York: McGraw Hill, 1979); Peter Robson, *Integration, Development and Equity* (London: George Allen and Unwin, 1983).

6. Robson, *Integration, Development and Equity,* pp. 120–121.

7. Ibid, p. 35.

8. Possible incompatibilities between ECOWAS and CEAO are discussed in S.K.B. Asante, "ECOWAS/CEAO: Conflict and Cooperation in West Africa," in Ralph I. Onwuka and Amadu Sesay, eds., *The Future of Regionalism in Africa* (London: Macmillan, 1985), Chapter 5.

9. Michael Clough and John Ravenhill, "Regional Cooperation in Southern Africa: The Southern African Development Coordination Conference," in Michael Clough, ed., *Changing Realities in Southern Africa* (Berkeley: Institute of International Studies, University of California, 1982), Chapter Five.

10. A useful listing of African cooperative institutions is found in Olatunde J.C.B. Ojo, D. K. Orwa, and C.M.B. Utete, *African International Relations* (London: Longman, 1985), Chapter 10.

11. For further discussion, see John Ravenhill, "The OAU and Economic Cooperation: Irresolute Resolutions," in Yassin el-Ayouty and I. William Zartman, eds., *The OAU After Twenty Years* (New York: Praeger, 1984), and John Ravenhill, "Collective Self-Reliance or Collective Self-Delusion? Is the Lagos Plan a Viable Alternative?" in John Ravenhill, ed., *Africa in Economic Crisis* (New York: Columbia University Press, 1986), Chapter 4.

12. Among the most useful recent comprehensive surveys are Andrew Coulson, *Tanzania: A Political Economy* (Oxford: Clarendon Press, 1982); and Goran Hyden, *Beyond Ujamaa in Tanzania* (Berkeley: University of California Press, 1980).

13. This section draws heavily on Thomas M. Biersteker, "Self-Reliance in Theory and Practice in Tanzanian Trade Relations," in Ravenhill, *Africa in Economic Crisis.*

14. The phrase appears in the memorandum that Algeria submitted to the Sixth Special Session of the United Nations; published by the Algerian government as *Petroleum, Raw Materials and Development* (Algiers, 1974), p. 10.

15. The text of the National Charter may be found in *Notes et études documentaires,* 4348–4350 (Paris: La Documentation Française, 28 December 1976). The quote appears on p. 72.

16. For further discussion, see Robert Mortimer, "Development and Autonomy: The Algerian Approach," *TransAfrica Forum* (Winter 1987).

17. Data derived from Leslie L. Rood, "Foreign Investment in African Manufacturing," *Journal of Modern African Studies* 13, no. 1 (January 1975): 23.

18. A useful overview of the contending theoretical perspectives on TNCs is found in Thomas J. Biersteker, *Distortion or Development? Contending Perspectives on the Multinational Corporation* (Cambridge: MIT Press, 1978).

19. See the discussion in Donald Rothchild and Robert L. Curry, Jr., *Scarcity, Choice, and Public Policy in Middle Africa* (Berkeley: University of California Press, 1978), pp. 158–160.

20. An excellent case study is Steven Langdon's "Multinational Corporations, Taste Transfer and Underdevelopment," *Review of African Political Economy,* no. 2 (1975), pp. 12–35.

21. F. N. Burton and Hisashi Inoue, "Expropriations of Foreign-Owned Firms in Developing Countries: A Cross-National Analysis," *Journal of World Trade Law* 18, no. 5 (September-October 1984): 396–414.

22. Reginald Herbold Green, "Industrialization in Tanzania," in Martin Fransman, ed., *Industry and Accumulation in Africa* (London: Heinemann, 1982), p. 86.

23. Michael Adejugbe, "The Myths and Realities of Nigeria's Business Indigenization," *Development and Change* 15, no. 4 (October 1984): 577–592.

24. Thomas J. Biersteker, "The Illusion of State Power," *Journal of Peace Research* 17, no. 3 (1980).

25. For a more detailed exposition of this argument, see Theodore H. Moran, *Multinational Corporations and the Politics of Dependence* (Princeton, N.J.: Princeton University Press, 1974).

26. Rothchild and Curry, *Scarcity, Choice, and Public Policy,* pp. 168 ff.

27. Paul Bennell, "Industrial Class Formation in Ghana: Some Empirical Observations," *Development and Change* 15, no. 4 (October 1984): 607.

28. John Ravenhill, *Collective Clientelism: The Lomé Conventions and North-South Relations* (New York: Columbia University Press, 1985), Chapter 3.

29. Frederick Cooper, "Africa and the World Economy," *African Studies Review* 24, no. 2/3 (1981): 51.

30. Stephen D. Krasner, *Structural Conflict* (Berkeley: University of California Press, 1985).

31. On the pre-Lomé relationship between Africa and the EEC, see I. William Zartman, *The Politics of Trade Negotiations Between Africa and the European Economic Community: The Weak Confront the Strong* (Princeton, N.J.: Princeton University Press, 1971).

32. This section draws heavily on Ravenhill, *Collective Clientelism.*

33. The agricultural products of Morocco, Tunisia, and Algeria, unlike those of tropical Africa, are often directly competitive with those of other Mediterranean countries, both inside and outside the community. Algeria enjoyed inherited advantages for several years by virtue of the fact that it was treated as part of France in 1957 when the Treaty of Rome was signed. Not until the 1970s did the Maghreb states complete "cooperative agreements" with the Common Market that accord them preferences over nonmembers but also impose quotas on various export items.

34. Joanna Moss and John Ravenhill, "Trade Developments During the First Lomé Convention," *World Development* 10, no. 10 (October 1982).

35. John Ravenhill, "What Is To Be Done for Third World Commodity Exporters? An Evaluation of the STABEX Scheme," *International Organization* 38, no. 3 (Summer 1984): 537–574.

36. Data on growth rates from World Bank, *Toward Sustained Development* (Washington, D.C.: World Bank, 1984). Data on exports (which exclude Nigeria) from International Monetary Fund, *World Economic Outlook April 1987* (Washington, D.C.: IMF, 1987).

37. For further discussion of Africa's debt problems, see Thomas M. Callaghy, "The Political Economy of African Debt: The Case of Zaire," in Ravenhill, *Africa in Economic Crisis,* pp. 307–346.

38. For a discussion of the potential problems with dependence on aid, see Rothchild and Curry, *Scarcity, Choice and Public Policy,* pp. 274 ff.

39. Gerald K. Helleiner, *The IMF and Africa in the 1980s,* Princeton Essays in International Finance No. 152 (July 1983).

40. An early examination of the perils of dependency on the IMF is Ronald T. Libby, "External Co-optation of a Less Developed Country's Policy Making: The Case of Ghana, 1969–72," *World Politics* 29, no. 1 (October 1976): 67–89.

41. A. W. Clausen, Foreword to World Bank, *Financing Adjustment with Growth* (Washington, D.C.: World Bank, 1986), p. v.

Part 4

INTERNATIONAL RELATIONS

11

Inter-African Relations

Africa has been prolific in the production of states. Home to 10 percent of the world's population and occupying about 20 percent of its landmass, the continent contains roughly one-third of the world's states. Over fifty territorial units have been carved out of the deserts, highlands, forests, and savannahs of the continent and its neighboring islands. From the Mediterranean to the Cape, Africa presents an intriguing mosaic of states whose relations are complex and diverse.

Africa would thus appear to be the expression par excellence of the state system in which modern international relations takes place. Like the rest of the world's states, those of Africa compete with one another to defend their national interests. Tensions among governments and frictions across borders abound in this environment of multiple sovereignties. Alliances and counteralliances have been forged and dissolved here as elsewhere in the state system. Yet, if the inter-African system has reproduced many of the familiar features of international politics, it has distinctive and unique attributes as well.

The great originality of inter-African diplomacy lies in the endeavor to manage African politics on a continental scale. A conception of African unity, historically rooted in a pan-Africanism that originated outside Africa, has significantly influenced inter-African relations. The institutional expression of this concept is the Organization of African Unity, which was founded in 1963 after the first wave of accessions to independence. The OAU has experienced more failures than successes, but it remains a focal point for collective initiatives and for conflict management. The attempt to construct solidarity at the continental level is not a sentimental illusion but rather a reasoned response to Africa's dependent position in the global economic system. African leaders are conscious

303

of the utility of cooperation at the same time that they have found cooperation difficult to achieve in practice.

A multitude of states with diverse national conditions, yet a commonality of purpose in the pursuit of economic development—these constitute the thesis and antithesis of a distinctive African dialectic of international relations. In this chapter, we shall examine this dualistic quality of interstate relations in Africa. We begin at the regional level and progress toward the continental level. We shall see, however, that regional disputes, such as the wars in Western Sahara and in Chad, have rapidly escalated to the continental level. Conversely, we shall discover that continental cleavages have sometimes exacerbated local disputes as between Zaire and Angola.

The heterogeneity of African regimes has contributed to inter-African rivalry. Because they are susceptible to external influence, African governments have accorded high priority to foreign policy. Most have focused on their proximate geopolitical environment, but a few states such as Algeria, Libya, and Nigeria have aspired to more ambitious diplomacies. During the 1960s, Egypt, Ghana, and Ethiopia played particularly active roles in African affairs. These activist states have generally taken the lead in promoting continental-scale conceptions of African politics. In defining their own interests in continental terms, they have contributed to the "continentalization" of African affairs.

For analytic purposes, we shall initially identify three geopolitical subsystems that have emerged as distinct arenas of inter-African relations. These three systems cut across the older subunits that divided Africa according to colonial administrations. They have been demarcated more by political interactions—both competitive and cooperative—since independence than by patterns of trade or cultural orientation. The first subsystem is trans-Saharan Africa, a large northerly bloc that is joined (rather than divided) by the Sahara desert. Trans-Saharan Africa includes the Mediterranean states of predominantly Arab culture from Morocco to Egypt, the largely Muslim states that stretch from Mauritania to Sudan and on to the Horn, and the West African coastal states from Senegal to Nigeria. Under colonial rule, these states were divided among French North Africa (or the Maghreb), French West Africa, part of French Equatorial Africa (Chad), numerous British dependencies, a Portuguese colony, a Spanish colony, areas under Italian control, and the independent states of Liberia and Ethiopia. Numerous factors, including Libyan adventurism and the prolonged conflicts in Western Sahara and the Horn, have made the northern tier into a geopolitical unit of intricate calculations and maneuvers.

The second band, Central Africa, extends from Cameroon and Gabon in the west to Kenya on the east coast. It also embraces a body of states that were parts of diverse colonial domains—French, Belgian, British, and Spanish. This central belt is physically dominated by Zaire, whose internal troubles have made it the site of numerous interventions, both inter- and extra-African. On a lesser scale, turmoil in Uganda has also sparked intervention. This zone astride the equator is of considerable geopolitical significance to both the states to its north and to its south. African diplomacy has time and again focused on this central region, especially its Zairian heartland.

Third, we can designate southern Africa as the area south of Zaire and Kenya to Capetown, a region still overshadowed by the military might of the minority government of South Africa. International politics in this subsystem has centered around the issues of liberation from Portuguese rule (until 1975), white settler rule in Rhodesia/Zimbabwe (until 1980), and apartheid in South Africa and Namibia. Thus, the independent states of the southern tier have dubbed themselves Front Line States in their confrontation with South African power. Tanzania has been an important actor in the Front Line group, which is why we place it in this third subdivision.

As active as Tanzania has been in the southern subsystem, it has also been much involved with its neighbors to the north, Kenya and Uganda. Located at a juncture connecting the central and southern regions, Tanzania is geopolitically engaged with both. Its dual involvement exemplifies that these subsystems are the component parts of an ever-evolving continental system. Although each geopolitical zone has its distinctive strategic character, the stronger or more ambitious states in each zone seek to influence events wherever they see their interests at stake.

The distance from north to south across Africa exceeds 5,000 miles (8,200 km); from east to west at the widest points is almost as great (about 4,700 miles or 7,800 km). The continent is thus 20 percent larger than North and Central America combined. What is surprising, therefore, is not that unity has been difficult to achieve but rather that the fifty states of this vast expanse have concerned themselves with one another as much as they have. Our intention is to examine these interactions as expressions of the policy goals of the numerous state actors on the continent. In keeping with our theme of political choice, we shall analyze inter-African politics in Africa as foreign policy choices. For most African governments, foreign policy, like other policy, must be conducted under constraints of scarcity: a shortage of skilled personnel, limited resources to establish embassies or to gather information about external events. These factors impel African states to concentrate their diplomatic activity on continental affairs, contributing to the intensity of inter-African relations.

One may discern four rough periods in inter-African relations since 1960, the "year of independence" (pre-1960 events serving as a suggestive prelude). The first was a turbulent phase of multiple rivalries. Diplomatic coalitions, often designated by the cities in which they held conferences—the Casablanca bloc, the Brazzaville group, the Monrovia group—came together to form competing camps. This period came to an end with the formation of the OAU in May 1963. During the second period, which ran from mid-1963 until 1970, states nominally acknowledged the continental authority of the new OAU, but there persisted considerable jockeying to define the direction of the continental system. A series of crises over Zaire, the Unilateral Declaration of Independence by Rhodesia's white minority, and the secession of Biafra from Nigeria still continued to divide states; potential rivals to the OAU, such as the franco-phone Afro-Malagasy Common Organization (OCAM), took form but never gained real substance.

The third period, 1970 to 1975, saw the upsurge of a spirit of solidarity and militance behind the idea of a New International Economic Order; conferences of the Nonaligned Movement in Lusaka (1970), Algiers (1973), and Dakar (1975) punctuated this period, which was marked by strong identification with OPEC and a widespread break of diplomatic ties with Israel. This phase of relative solidarity gave way to a resurgence of divisive conflicts by late 1975 or early 1976. Angola's civil war and the Moroccan-Algerian tensions over Western Sahara ushered in the fourth period, which has been further perturbed by events in Chad, in the Horn, and in Shaba Province of Zaire, as well as by economic crisis throughout the continent. This succession of crises almost destroyed the OAU in 1982–1983. Whether it is possible to discern an end to this harsh fourth period and the beginnings of a fifth, more benign phase is a question that we shall return to in the conclusion of this chapter.

■ TRANS-SAHARAN AFRICA

The Sahara is a vast, forbidding environment sparsely populated by nomadic peoples. It appears to constitute a formidable barrier between the peoples of its northern and southern "shores." Throughout history, however, traders have traversed the Sahara in caravans, and today its expanses are shared by almost a dozen sovereign states. The conflicts and issues that have arisen in parcels of this enormous territory, notably concerning Chad and Western Sahara, have had significant repercussions upon international relations throughout the continent. Arab North Africa and black West Africa have been drawn into a set of issues that delineate a single geopolitical theater.[1]

Yet, the civil war in Chad and the clash between Morocco and the Algerian-supported Polisario Front (Frente Popular para la Liberación de Saguia el-Hamra y Rio de Oro) over what was once called Spanish Sahara would not have engaged so many other states had it not been for the ambitious diplomacy of certain key states. Algeria and Libya have both undertaken unusually active foreign policies in Africa. Morocco has become deeply involved in continental politics, largely in response to Algeria's reaction to its irredentist policies. Other major trans-Saharan actors include Nigeria, Africa's most populous state, and Egypt, which aspired to a broad Third World leadership role under Gamal Abdel Nasser. During limited periods the leaders of Ghana, Côte d'Ivoire, Senegal, and Ethiopia have exercised wide influence on regional and continental affairs. We shall begin our study of international relations in trans-Saharan Africa by examining the foreign policy objectives of these activist states.

☐ Algeria

Algeria was deeply immersed in inter-African politics long before it became independent in 1962. Indeed, it was the long war for independence that plunged the Algerian nationalists of the 1950s into intense relations with the "fraternal" states of Arab and black Africa. The diplomatic demands of the struggle against France obliged the Algerians to solicit every possible source of support for their cause, and they saw anticolonial solidarity as a crucial potential force. Having turned first to the Arab world and Asia, Algeria next sought the opportunity to participate in the early Conferences of Independent African States. Algeria's policy goal was to win further Third World backing for its own cause of independence. Its bid for support in turn posed policy issues for other African states.

The first Conference of Independent African States was organized by Kwame Nkrumah in 1958, only a year after Ghana's independence. The Accra conference may be viewed as the point of departure for modern inter-African relations. It brought together three Sub-Saharan states—Ghana, Liberia, and Ethiopia—and five North African states—Morocco, Tunisia, Libya, Egypt, and Sudan. The guiding force behind the meeting was Nkrumah's commitment to pan-Africanism. He saw the conference as a platform for his notions of African unity rooted in what he called the "African personality." These ideas accordingly found their way into the conference's final declaration alongside resolutions condemning "racialism" in South Africa and colonialism in any form. In these, one sees early formulations of the anticolonial and antiapartheid themes that have remained sources of consensus in collective African diplomacy.

For Algeria, the Accra conference and a follow-up meeting in Addis Ababa in 1960 were precious opportunities to censure France and to win international recognition. The National Liberation Front (FLN) thus devoted major attention to these early African forums. It expected the African states to rally to its cause once they entered the United Nations, where Algeria's informal representatives were seeking a resolution demanding a referendum on Algerian self-determination.

The 1960 General Assembly session was the first for over a dozen former French colonies. Both Algeria and France severely pressured these new states to support their respective positions, France being steadfastly opposed to any UN-mandated referendum. The newly independent francophone states were caught in a squeeze, reluctant to oppose their French patron, President Charles de Gaulle, but embarrassed to vote against Algeria's position. After deliberating in Abidjan, the francophones decided to vote against the call for a referendum and merely in favor of negotiations between France and the FLN. The Algerians were bitterly disappointed by the failure of these African governments to grant them unqualified support. They became all the more determined to play a forceful role in inter-African affairs on behalf of their vision of what independence ought to mean.

Another major event in 1960 likewise contributed to Algeria's engagement in continental politics—namely, the "Congo crisis." Within days of the independence of the Belgian Congo (now Zaire), army mutiny, Belgian intervention, the secession of the mineral-rich Katanga Province, and generalized instability brought the new state to its knees. Prime Minister Patrice Lumumba, the leader of the major nationalist party, called upon the United Nations to prop up his reeling country, and the Security Council duly dispatched a force known as ONUC (after the French acronym for United Nations Operation in the Congo). The UN force played a controversial role in a series of events that led to the overthrow of Lumumba in September 1960. Algeria reacted with outrage to what it called "a conspiracy of the western powers to implant neo-colonialism in Africa."[2]

The rupture of the Congo into warring factions was a major factor in stirring a series of inter-African meetings that divided Africa into two camps. The first of these assembled most of the francophone states in Brazzaville in December 1960. The Brazzaville group, having previously abandoned the FLN, now urged a Round Table Conference to negotiate a political settlement to the strife across the river in the Congo. This position tacitly supported the Congolese factions that had overthrown Lumumba, a stance that further dismayed the Algerians. The meeting also decided to create a more permanent grouping under the title Union of African States and Madagascar (UAM), a group composed solely of former French colonies.

This arrangement provoked a counterreaction from seven other states that met in Casablanca, Morocco, in January 1961. The expression "Casablanca bloc" was coined to designate this association of Algeria, Morocco, Egypt, Ghana, Guinea, Mali, and (somewhat mysteriously in light of its conservative orientation under King Idris) Libya. In fact, the Casablanca conferees were far from being a "bloc," but their meeting highlighted an early cleavage between more conservative and more radical orientations toward world politics. The Casablanca states backed the FLN and supported Lumumba. The Algerian war and the Congo crisis both raised questions about African policy toward continuing European influence on the continent. The Casablanca and Brazzaville groupings as such proved short-lived, but the policy issues have proven perennial matters in inter-African debate.

At independence in mid-1962, Algeria promptly adopted a policy of prominent support to liberation movements around the continent. Its first president, Ahmed Ben Bella, initially also took an interest in opposition movements in states such as Niger, Cameroon, and Chad, whose governments had been tepid in their support of the FLN. Soon, however, Ben Bella ventured that a continental organization might be the most promising means by which to reshape African affairs.

The Organization of African Unity was to be the prime instrument of this strategy. Algeria became one of the most active promoters of the founding conference of the OAU in 1963. As Immanuel Wallerstein points out, the creation of the OAU transformed the concept of African unity (or pan-Africanism) from the mobilizational theme of a social movement into an alliance of governing elites—or, to put it slightly differently, into the foundation for a state system in Africa.[3] Algeria, however, did not immediately recognize this, seeking instead to use the new organization to effect radical change in 1964 when a struggle for power again flared in the Congo.

Conflict erupted in the Congo when Moise Tshombe was named prime minister. Tshombe had been the leader of the Katanga secession that had contributed to Lumumba's downfall. Tshombe, in turn, had been defeated in 1962 and banished from the Congo. His sudden return at a moment when the centrist Congolese government was facing serious armed resistance from Lumumba's political heirs prompted Algeria to mount a diplomatic campaign in the OAU to isolate and undermine Tshombe. The first phase of this campaign succeeded as Tshombe was barred from the July 1964 OAU summit. In August, when Tshombe resorted to South African mercenaries and Western military aid to quell the insurgents, Algeria, acting in concert with Mali, called for a special session of the OAU's Council of Ministers to condemn this maneuver. Algeria sought OAU intervention to depose Tshombe and aid potential allies to come to power. When the OAU council did convene, however, there was no consensus to oust Tshombe; the best that the OAU interventionists could get was formation of a "conciliation committee" (whose own efforts were subsequently thwarted by a Western military intervention in November 1964).

Algeria's attempt to utilize the OAU in this manner nevertheless revealed a dynamic approach to inter-African politics. Declaring that "it is no longer Katanga that threatens Congolese unity, it is the whole Congo that has become the Katanga of Africa,"[4] Ben Bella defended a broad conception of Algeria's African interests. Algeria sought through its African policy to encourage the emergence of like-minded forces committed to a genuinely independent Africa. The conception of continental solidarity implicit in Algeria's support of liberation movements and the Congolese rebels has continued to mark Algerian policy, making Algiers an important actor in a host of disputes that have erupted between Afro-Marxist or socialist states and others around the continent.

This Algerian impact will be evident as we examine some of these cases in the rest of this chapter. Suffice it to say here that Algeria has consistently championed the idea of an Africa free from undue reliance upon the former colonial powers. As an oil and natural gas producer, Algeria has the material resources to conduct an ambitious diplomacy. Whenever leftist governments have replaced conservative ones, Algeria has been quick to consolidate ties. Thus, for example, Algeria promptly signed economic agreements with Benin and with Madagascar when radical officers came to power in these states that had formerly maintained very close ties with France. Similarly, Algeria was among the first to offer aid and technical assistance to Guinea-Bissau, Angola, and Mozambique when these states gained independence from Portugal. It has, moreover, maintained close lines of communication with the geographically distant Front Line States (as illustrated, for example, by the extensive southern

Africa tour of President Chadli Benjedid in 1981). These material bonds and ideological commitments are the expression of an Algerian outlook that represents a major presence in inter-African relations.

☐ Libya

Like Algeria, Libya has the resource base to exercise influence beyond its borders. Unlike Algeria, it did not have an extended period of diplomatic struggle for independence; rather it entered the state system quite painlessly in 1951 as a traditional monarchy. Only with the overthrow of the monarchy by Colonel Muammar Qaddafi in 1969 did Libya emerge as a prominent actor in inter-African affairs. But Qaddafi has made up for lost time.

The military officers who seized power as the Revolutionary Command Council (RCC) saw themselves primarily as Arab nationalists. Their model was Nasserist Egypt, and their early foreign policy was oriented toward the Arab world, particularly the cause of the Palestinians. Qaddafi's African policy began largely as an effort to counter Israeli influence in black Africa. Later as Egyptian-Libyan relations deteriorated after the death of Nasser, counterbalancing Egypt also became a policy goal. Moreover, as the Sanusi brotherhood (a Muslim religious order) of southern Libya had proselytized widely throughout the Sahara, it was easy to perceive states to the south, such as Chad and Niger, as candidates for a Libyan sphere of influence.

Qaddafi first wooed Niger by generous grants of aid (some $100 million) during the early 1970s. He succeeded in establishing quite cordial relations with Niger's first president, Hamani Diori, culminating in a state visit in March 1974. Only a month later, the military overthrew the Diori government, souring relations between the two states. Since then, Libya has resorted to more subversive tactics by encouraging Niger's northern Toubou and Tuareg populations to enter into dissidence.

Coercion through intervention has been central to Libya's Chad policy from the outset. Of all Libya's African initiatives, the engagement in Chad has had the most impact upon the inter-African system as a whole. Shortly after coming to power, the RCC began to aid Frolinat (Front pour la Liberation Nationale du Tchad), a northern-based oppositional movement that was waging a civil war against the southern-based government of François Tombalbaye in Ndjaména. Like many of the francophone states, the Tombalbaye government had good relations with Israel. Libya's primary goal in aiding the rebels was to exert pressure upon Tombalbaye to sever relations with Israel. In 1972 a deal was struck: Libya agreed to suspend its aid to Frolinat, and Tombalbaye broke diplomatic relations with Tel Aviv. Libya sweetened the deal by extending financial aid to the Tombalbaye government—although Chad apparently paid a further price in the form of acquiescence in another matter, Libya's occupation of the uranium-rich Aouzou strip, a contested area along Chad's northern border.[5] Libya could count this early venture into trans-Saharan politics a policy success.

Qaddafi perceived another opportunity to pursue his anti-Israel campaign when Idi Amin seized power in Uganda, a state with which Israel had developed especially close relations. When Israel refused Amin's exorbitant requests for new military aid, the dictator expelled the Israeli diplomats and advisors. In return, Libya dispatched a small military detachment a few months later when rebel forces backed by Tanzania sought to overthrow Amin. Qaddafi's gesture sealed a close relationship that lasted until 1979, when once again Libya sent troops in an attempt, this time unsuccessful, to rescue Amin from a second clash with Tanzania. The Ugandan connection later offered Tripoli a possible source of leverage upon Sudan as its relations with Khartoum deteriorated. The initial goal, however, was to oust Israeli influence.

Libya was successful in this anti-Israel diplomacy in both Uganda and Chad. By the end of 1973, for reasons that had less to do with Libyan policy, the objective of splitting black Africa and Israel was largely achieved. The entire Israeli-African relationship was transformed by the repercussions of the October 1973 Arab-Israeli war and the attendant OPEC oil price increases. The prospect that Arab oil would become more valuable than Israeli technical assistance led the majority of African governments to break formal ties with Israel. But this setback to Israel did not change the balance of power in the Middle East. Accordingly, Libya began to broaden its conception of the transformations that it sought to achieve.

Anti-Zionism was transmuted into a broader antiimperialism. Libya increasingly perceived the world as divided into two camps—those attached by one manner or another to the ex-colonial powers of Europe and their U.S. ally (protector of Israel) and those committed to eradicating Western influence. When Africa split dramatically into two camps over the Angolan question, Qaddafi took note of the pattern of francophone and certain Arab states (Morocco, Tunisia, Egypt, Sudan) that voted against the Marxist MPLA. As he saw it, these Arab and black African governments were guilty of colluding with U.S. purposes in Africa and the Middle East. This analysis incited Qaddafi to step up his support to groups opposed for one reason or another to the governments of what he considered the pro-Western camp.

This Libyan policy had ramifications for all of trans-Saharan Africa. For Niger, as already suggested, Libyan meddling took the form of stirring up disaffected Toubous and Tuaregs. Similarly, Libya gave support to opposition elements in Mali and Senegal. Distributing arms here and there about the Sahara, Qaddafi cultivated such notions as an "Islamic Legion," a "United States of the Sahel," or an independent "Saharan Republic." Libya's Saharan ambitions extended well beyond the official national map that it issued showing Libya incorporating some 7,000 square miles (18,000 square km) of Niger, a like-sized chunk of Algeria, and the entire 27,000-square-mile (70,000-square-km) Aouzou strip.[6] Magnified by Libyan aid to the Polisario Front in Western Sahara, Libya's far-reaching Saharan policy raised anxiety in such distant capitals as Abidjan, which had friendly ties with most of the target states.

To the east as well, Libya was involved in tense relations with Egypt and Sudan. There were frontier incidents after the reopening of the Suez Canal in 1975 and a brief border flare-up in July 1977, presumably attributable to Egypt's rapprochement with the United States for the sake of the recovery of Sinai. As Nimeiri of Sudan followed Anwar Sadat's lead, Qaddafi took an interest in toppling him. This objective, in turn, encouraged Libya to enhance its ties with Ethiopia and Uganda, Sudan's eastern and southern neighbors. Qaddafi's Uganda policy was one of the connecting links between the trans-Saharan and the central zones.

At the heart of this vast network of Libyan inter-African relations lay crippled Chad, a victim of its own internal divisions as well as Libya's ambitions. Tombalbaye had been deposed in 1975 by the army, which placed General Félix Malloum in power. About the same time, Frolinat split into several factions, the most powerful of which was led by Hissene Habré. Before long Goukouni Oueddei split with Habré to form his own dissident group. Goukouni turned primarily in the direction of Tripoli for support, while Habré and Malloum eventually made common cause against him. As Chad shattered into even more factions, both the OAU and the most immediately concerned neighboring governments tried to piece the country back together again. A diplomatic conference in Kano, Nigeria, led to a precarious Transitional National Union Government (GUNT) of no less than eleven groupings under Goukouni's leadership with Habré as minister of defense. This collage came unglued in early 1980, as Habré and Goukouni clashed again. Goukouni signed a defense agreement with Libya that threw some sixty-five hundred regular Libyan army forces into the battle for Ndjaména. After a decade of covert intervention throughout the region, Libya moved openly to secure an ally in power in December 1980.

The success (though short-lived) of the Libyan operation in Chad set off alarm signals from one end of trans-Saharan Africa to the other. Libya's African revisionism and overall orientation (Soviet arms, support of the Iranian revolution, militance on Middle East issues) unsettled a host of moderate governments from Senegal to Togo and Nigeria along the western shoulder of the continent. We shall return to the further developments of the Chadian civil war later in this chapter. For the moment, it suffices to underline the tumultuous impact of Libya upon the trans-Saharan subsystem.

☐ Nigeria

Nigeria is Africa's most populous country. It also has substantial quantities of oil. Like Algeria and Libya, it is a member of OPEC and like them it has sought to influence and shape its regional and continental environment. Although not a Saharan state, Nigerian interests have led it to develop an important role in the northern tier as well as beyond it. Yet, Nigeria was slow to assume the role that its power resources appeared to hold out to it. Despite the grandiose statement of its first foreign Minister, who declared in 1960, "Our country is the largest single unit in Africa . . . we are not going to abdicate the position in which God Almighty has placed us. . . . The whole black continent is looking up to this country to liberate it from thralldom,"[7] Nigeria pursued a rather modest foreign policy until the mid 1970s. Although it did send a military contingent to the Congo as part of the UN operation, otherwise the country's early leaders were sufficiently absorbed by domestic politics to steer clear of continental initiatives. Prime Minister Tafawa Balewa limited his efforts through 1965 to debunking the unity proposals of Ghana's Nkrumah. Then military coups and the Biafra secession stunned the country, obliging Nigeria to limit its diplomacy to the requirements of the civil war.

Only after containing the secession did Nigeria begin to exert itself as an African power—in part to settle some scores from the civil war period. Although most African states had abstained from recognizing the Biafra rebels, a few states under French influence, such as Côte d'Ivoire, Dahomey (now Benin), and Gabon, supported the secessionist cause. Nigeria thus came to view French influence in West Africa as a threat to its national integrity; accordingly, it devised a long-term strategy to reduce France's role in the region. With oil revenues gushing into the treasury, Nigeria could readily imagine itself as the economic core of a huge West African hinterland. Nigerian economic integrationists like Adebayo Adedeji, then serving as commissioner for economic development, pressed the idea of a West African common market as a lever to pry French neocolonial influence out of Nigeria's potential hinterland.

Nigeria thus embarked upon a sustained diplomatic offensive to create the Economic Community of West African States. According to Olatunde Ojo, "It took Nigerian leadership, extensive efforts in national coalition formation, and even more intensive and difficult regional negotiations and coalition formation to get ECOWAS inaugurated."[8] The decision to work for a regional common market was an important step in redefining West African geopolitical space, for it implicated Lagos in matters beyond economic cooperation.

In assuming a leadership posture in the region, Nigeria had to respond to security concerns as well. As Niger, Mali, Senegal, and Côte d'Ivoire all were uneasy about Libyan policies and feared the broad destabilizing effects from the collapse of Chad, Nigeria projected itself into the various efforts to mediate a Chadian settlement. It sponsored a series of meetings in Kano and Lagos designed to work out a compromise. Moreover, as part of the first Kano accord, Nigeria dispatched a peacekeeping force to Chad that became more involved than the Chadians wanted; later, it briefly imposed an oil embargo to bring pressure upon the local parties. These interventions were signs of a more activist diplomacy, of which ECOWAS leadership was but one component.

The broad policy of diplomatic activism had become more pronounced after the overthrow of General Yacubu Gowon in 1975, which brought to power Murtala Mohammed. When Mohammed was killed in an abortive coup, General Olusegun Obasanjo succeeded him. The Mohammed/Obasanjo government (1975–1979) generally expanded the conception of Nigeria's interests in

Africa, most notably in southern Africa. An early expression of this "Afro-centric activism," as Timothy Shaw calls it,[9] was Lagos's decision to recognize the leftist MPLA government in Angola. We have already noted that the struggle for power in Angola was one of the major polarizing issues in inter-African affairs. In associating itself with the more radical states on the Angolan question, the post-Gowon leaders sought to give Nigerian foreign policy a more militant orientation.

Under Obasanjo, Nigeria assumed a place as virtually a sixth member of the southern group of Front Line States (originally comprising Tanzania, Zambia, Mozambique, Angola, and Botswana). The southern African policy was a logical extension of the drive to build a structure of influence in western Africa. At the core of both initiatives was a nationalist "Africa-for-the-Africans" impulse rooted in the knowledge that Nigeria was potentially Africa's greatest power. Afrocentrism implied the expulsion of non-African influence from the continent: that of France from its immediate regional environment; that of Portugal, Great Britain, and European settlers from the unliberated south. In a continent purged of the vestiges of the colonial era, Nigeria's human and petro-chemical resources would have room for their full development. The continent as a whole would assume its rightful place in global affairs and Nigeria's voice would be extremely important in representing Africa. Regional leadership accorded Nigeria continental (and global) credibility, whereas continental activism reinforced its legitimacy at the regional level. The two subsystems, trans-Saharan and southern, were linked in a praxis that went beyond an abstract pan-Africanism.

As we deal later with southern Africa as a subsystem, this is not the place to examine in detail Nigeria's specific Front Line initiatives. Suffice it to note here that the Obasanjo government put its weight behind pressure on Western governments, notably those of the United States and Great Britain, to assist in the decolonization of Rhodesia and Namibia. It exerted power most directly by nationalizing British Petroleum assets on the eve of the 1979 Commonwealth conference in Lusaka that was to formulate a policy on Rhodesia. In these initiatives, Nigeria spurred the process that brought Robert Mugabe's Patriotic Front to power. Nigeria insisted on its right to be consulted as a Front Line State despite its geographical distance from the "front line." The cultivation of national prestige was an integral component of this southern strategy.

When the 1979 election brought the Shehu Shagari government to power, the new administration, although less militant in tone, sought to continue along essentially the same lines of regional and continental prestige. The new president's first trip abroad was to Monrovia to participate in the OAU's ad hoc committee seeking a settlement in Western Sahara. He announced his government's willingness to participate if necessary in a Saharan peacekeeping force. Nigeria also proposed to take the lead in establishing an ECOWAS defense force. These gestures implied an intent to act as the regional hegemon. In a similar vein, Shagari acted to exclude the new Liberian leader, Sergeant Samuel Doe, who had just seized power in a particularly bloody coup, from OAU and ECOWAS sessions in the spring of 1980, just as the Obasanjo government had cut off oil deliveries to Ghana the year before in order to coerce the new Rawlings government. In all these instances, successive Nigerian leaders sought to control events in the regional environment, which it increasingly perceived as its sphere of influence.

Nigeria has thus emerged as the third major actor in the trans-Saharan system. It has backed its claim to regional leadership with financial commitments, such as contributions to the completion of the trans-Saharan highway (this route, which will one day connect Algiers and Lagos, is itself a manifestation of the development of a trans-Saharan system) and the road from Lagos to Cotonou in Benin. These contributions to regional infrastructure are part of a drive to enhance trade so as to translate the ECOWAS concept into economic reality. The convening in Lagos of the OAU's economic summit in 1980 applied this regional aspiration to the continent as a whole. It was appropriate that Nigeria should host this occasion, for the ambitious Nigerian diplomacy of the late 1970s and early 1980s was premised on its emergent economic strength. The subsequent collapse of oil prices and the return of political instability slowed Lagos's push for continental leadership, but Africa's most populous country remains a consequential actor, especially in the trans-Saharan subsystem.

☐ Other Trans-Saharan Actors

Algeria, Libya, and Nigeria are the three actors that have done most to constitute the entity that we call trans-Sahara. Other states, however, have been prominent actors at one or another time or on specific issues. A brief review of their most important policies will show how they have also contributed to the contemporary pattern of interactions. We examine Nasser's Egypt, Nkrumah's Ghana, and the policies of Côte d'Ivoire, Senegal, Tunisia, and Morocco under their long-lived leaders, Houphouët-Boigny, Senghor, Bourguiba, and Hassan II.

During the mid-1950s, Cairo became one of the havens for African nationalists from both Arab and black Africa. Egypt had a geopolitical stake in the Nile Valley. The British, after all, had gone into East Africa in the nineteenth century in the name of protecting the headwaters of the Nile. But Nasser's motivation was actually more ideological than geopolitical. As a progressive nationalist, he wanted to see other nationalist movements come to power. Toward this end, Nasser created a Supreme Committee to Supervise African Affairs and another organ called the African Association and established the headquarters of the Afro-Asian Peoples' Solidarity Organization (AAPSO) in Cairo. These agencies enhanced Nasser's prestige in black Africa and in the Third World in general, projecting an image of nationalist assertion around the man who nationalized the Suez Canal. The northern gatekeeper hoped to line up other like-minded troops behind his leadership.

Nasser's policy was manifest in many activities on the continent, but the focal point proved to be the Congo crisis. He interpreted the events in the Congo much as the Algerians did—namely, as an attempt by the West to wrest control of the newly independent state from Prime Minister Lumumba. Egypt promptly sent technicians and medical personnel to aid the faltering Lumumba government and subsequently committed troops to the UN force, only to be dismayed by its failure to protect Lumumba. Upon the ouster of Lumumba, Egypt took the lead in channeling aid to the pro-Lumumba faction holding out in Stanley-ville in the east. In 1964, when the second round of turbulence broke out, Nasser tried again to shore up the rebels.

Twice thwarted, Nasser began to draw back from deep involvement in Africa in about 1965. The means that Egypt could bring to bear in distant places were in the final analysis rather limited compared to those of the Western powers that were competing with Egypt in the Congo. Nasser was sufficiently pragmatic to acknowledge limitations on his capabilities; moreover, Middle Eastern politics reclaimed almost all his diplomatic attention. As one of Africa's largest states and as a crossroads, Egypt is necessarily involved in continental affairs, but it has not exercised the active role that Nasser once envisaged.

Throughout the period during which Nasser was particularly oriented toward Africa, he had a major rival for the mantle of continental leadership. This was Kwame Nkrumah, whose prestige as the head of the first Sub-Saharan state to negotiate independence was enormous. Steeped in the pan-Africanist tradition, Nkrumah promptly set about to organize inter-African relations. "I am necessarily as much concerned with the problems of all the different countries which make up our great continent as I am with those of Ghana," wrote Nkrumah in his *Africa Must Unite,* and he acted upon this presumption from the earliest days of independence.[10]

His first initiative was to convene the Conference of Independent African States (CIAS), for which he meticulously laid the diplomatic groundwork from August 1957 through April 1958. He sent personal envoys in advance to all seven of the invited states in order to "anticipate difficult issues on the agenda."[11] Nonetheless, the conference had a tough time coming to agreement on some of these "difficult issues," notably the conflicting policy priorities of Ghana and Egypt. Egypt wanted a militant stand on the Algerian question, whereas Ghana did not want North Africa to be the focus of the proceedings; Ghana proposed a liberation fund for black Africa, whereas Egypt was content with an existing AAPSO fund. Most important, Ghana wanted support for creation of a permanent secretariat to assure continued coordination on matters of common interest to the independent African states. Egypt, backed by Liberia, which was already suspicious of Ghanaian activism, downplayed the idea, proposing instead that consultations at the United Nations would suffice. To Nkrumah's disappointment, no secretariat was established, but the CIAS did serve to launch Ghana on its ambitious pan-African diplomacy.

Nkrumah recognized quickly that independent African states were neither his only nor his best policy framework. He thus poured funds into a second gathering known as the All African Peoples Conference (AAPC), a meeting of parties and nationalist movements, not of independent governments. Convening in December 1958, "the conference was ideally timed to meet the needs and mood of a rebellious continent." To this conference, W. Scott Thompson attributes

> much of the strength on which Nkrumah was able to draw in later years. He remained within the castle (seat of government in Accra) throughout most of the proceedings, consulting, reconciling, advising delegates; he was never too conspicuous. He dominated the conference all the more by such tactics. Thereafter he had a network of admirers throughout the continent, some of whom, like Kenneth Kaunda, were to remain loyal even after being assailed by Ghanaian organizations.[12]

The AAPC did serve briefly as a vehicle of Nkrumah's vision of uniting Africa. Yet, as Thompson suggests, Nkrumah had admirers rather than followers, essentially because his vision of a federated Africa clashed with the very country-focused nationalism that he inspired. In the final analysis, Nkrumah was slower than Nasser to recognize that each new state's national identity must be respected. In his own drive to move beyond nationalism to continental union, Nkrumah ultimately alienated the good will that his support for independence had won him.

When Guinea broke abruptly from France in September 1958, Nkrumah moved swiftly to embrace Sekou Touré as an ally. In November, the two states announced an agreement to constitute "the nucleus of a Union of West African States."[13] Two years later, Mali briefly associated itself with the "union." In fact, however, independence was rapidly undermining Nkrumah's dream, as newly sovereign states, intent to consolidate national power, expressed their disdain for anyone who "makes the mistake of feeling that he is a Messiah who has got a mission to lead Africa."[14] The impact of the Congo crisis was a further major blow to the Ghanaian leader's crusade for unity.

Ghana began to follow developments in the Congo closely as early as 1958, when Patrice Lumumba attended the AAPC conference in Accra. Nkrumah urged Lumumba to demand independence and offered technical assistance to smooth the transition. Even though the two countries were over 1,000 miles (1,650 km) distant from one another, Nkrumah harbored hopes of an eventual Ghana-Congo union. When the disorder began, Ghana was the first to send military forces. These promptly became embroiled in a controversy over their action in disarming some Congolese units. The Ghanaian contingent walked a tightrope between the wishes of the Lumumba government and the need of UN Secretary-General Dag Hammarskjold to maintain broad international backing for ONUC. Lumumba lost trust in the Ghanaians, and Nkrumah, in turn, lost any real leverage over the course of events. Like Egypt, Ghana did not have adequate resources to control the course of events in the Congo. Although

Nkrumah maintained an extremely innovative and unconventional inter-African policy until his overthrow in 1966, the events of 1960 largely revealed that it was a diplomacy beyond his means.

Activism in pursuit of unity often took the form of subversion. Thompson has suggested that Nkrumah "equated obstinate heads of state, who would not surrender their 'petty national sovereignty' (as he called it), with Ashanti chiefs, and thus as candidates for destoolment."[15] Nkrumah's neighbors to the east and west were understandably wary of such designs. To the east, Togo warded off Ghanaian efforts to exploit the idea of Ewe reunification, but the frontier between the countries was a site of frequent incidents and perpetual tension for several years. On the western border, Nkrumah toyed with a group of Sanwi separatists at odds with the government of Côte d'Ivoire. Here he faced a covert counteroffensive of destabilization from a major rival, Felix Houphouët-Boigny, who had no intention of being "destooled."[16]

Côte d'Ivoire under Houphouët has not pursued an energetic African policy, but it is nevertheless one of the major states in the region. Houphouët made a famous wager with Nkrumah in 1957, betting that the conservative Côte d'Ivoire would be economically better off in ten years than its newly independent neighbor. Within the framework of his own continued close ties with France, Houphouët was extremely careful to create a zone of security around his country as a safeguard to winning his bet. Thus, Côte d'Ivoire took the lead in creating a politico-economic organization called the Conseil de l'Entente, which brought three other French colonies into its orbit: Upper Volta (now Burkina Faso), Niger, and Dahomey (now Benin). Although the Conseil was originally conceived to counter a Senegalese project of regional federation, it served through the 1960s essentially as a barrier to contain Ghana as well as to assure the Ivorian cocoa and coffee plantations a supply of cheap labor from Upper Volta.

Houphouët's foreign policy has been preeminently oriented toward maintaining ties among the francophone states. In 1960 he took the lead in creating the UAM. When this was disbanded after the founding of the OAU, he laid the groundwork for a new francophone regrouping, the Afro-Malagasy Common Organization. Founded in 1965 in the aftermath of the second Congo crisis, OCAM resketched the lines of division between moderates and radicals as well as reaffirmed the notion of a francophone alliance (all the original members were francophone states). The formal organization sputtered along for several years without ever acquiring much diplomatic force, but its presence reflected an orientation that has weighed heavily in inter-African relations under the impulse of states like the Côte d'Ivoire. As OCAM declined, Houphouët backed yet another francophone regrouping, the Economic Community of West Africa (see Chapter 10).

Senegal's influence in inter-African relations has stemmed from the eminence of its leaders, Leopold Sedar Senghor, an internationally acclaimed poet who governed from 1960 to 1980, and Abdou Diouf, a highly respected administrator. Because Dakar served as the capital of the entire colonial federation of French West Africa (AOF), Senghor sought to retain a West African federal structure after independence. The best that he could achieve was a federal union with Mali, which disintegrated almost immediately. But Senghor persisted, eventually succeeding in regrouping four of the former AOF territories in the Organization of Senegal River States (later refashioned as the Senegal River Development Organization, or OMVS). In addition to Mali, Mauritania and Guinea are members of the OMVS. Senegal's historical affiliation with Mauritania in the AOF has stamped Senegalese diplomacy with a northward orientation that took on renewed saliency when Mauritania became embroiled in the Western Sahara dispute.

Senegal has also been closely involved in the affairs of tiny Gambia, the fingerlike entity poking into Senegal's midsection. Senghor mildly encouraged the integration of British Gambia into Senegal but did not oppose eventual Gambian independence in 1965, opting instead for a policy of close cooperation, which has gradually produced a sense of a Senegambian security community. In 1980 Senghor dispatched troops to Gambia to thwart an attempted coup that the Gambian authorities attributed to Libyan subversion. Senghor's efforts to construct these regional cooperative arrangements coexisted with his most ambitious commitment to *la francophonie,* (the French-speaking world) which he understood as an association for technical and economic cooperation in which all French-speaking peoples (in Europe, Asia, and the Americas as well as in Africa) would join. Although a francophone agency was created in 1970, it never achieved Senghor's far-reaching ideal, but it did serve to establish Senegal as an actor of mark in global and inter-African affairs.

 confederate in 80s

One of Senghor's closest associates—and, indeed, actually the initiator—in the francophone project was Tunisia's Habib Bourguiba. Tunisia was the first of the Maghreb states to pursue an active policy in Sub-Saharan Africa. Although subsequently overshadowed by the initiatives of Libya, Algeria, and Morocco, Tunisia's early attraction southward is another component of the trans-Saharan system. Bourguiba attended the ceremonies marking the independence of Ghana in 1957 and declared that "the trip to Ghana was for me truly a discovery, that of the great African continent from which we were long cut off and with which we hope to reestablish our historical ties of exchange. . . . It is important that Tunisians . . . pay attention to the huge act of gestation of the African continent. We can not let ourselves be overwhelmed by the pace of events."[17]

Bourguiba understood that Tunisia was caught up in the processes of political change that were beginning to sweep across the continent. He saw his own country as a relay station between Mediterranean (Western) civilization and the emergent regimes to the south. As the Tunisian scholar Mohsen Toumi astutely observes: "Fundamentally [Bourguiba's] attitude toward black Africa derives from a larger set of assumptions: solidarity with the western world."[18] Tunisia pursued a policy of support to moderate African governments as a way of protecting its own pro-Western orientation. Tunisia and Senegal ("heirs of the same legacies,"[19] as Bourguiba put it during his state visit to Senegal in 1965) have closely coordinated their policies on African questions. The Tunis-Dakar axis is another manifestation of durable trans-Saharan ties.

At the other end of the Maghreb, Morocco's African policy has been harnessed to a rare goal, the recovery of precolonial lands. In laying claim to Mauritania, Morocco bucked a widely prevailing consensus—namely, to recognize colonial borders as the framework for transferring sovereignty to Africans. So long as Morocco seriously pursued the goal of reclaiming Mauritania, it found itself virtually isolated. King Hassan refused to attend the founding conference of the OAU because Mauritania's president was present; then Morocco hesitated four months before signing the charter.

A brief border war with Algeria in October 1963 obliged Morocco to cultivate some alliances. Morocco's general pro-Western orientation was akin to that of Tunisia, Senegal, and Côte d'Ivoire, all three of which were firmly committed to Mauritania's right to exist. Thus, King Hassan moved away from his Mauritanian claim in order to solidify his standing with Bourguiba, Senghor, and Houphouët. Even so, as Mohammed Bouzidi observes, Morocco maintained only a limited number of embassies in black Africa and could count upon only "a limited number of African friends" when once again it became embroiled in a serious dispute.[20] A few years after officially recognizing Mauritania in 1970, Morocco set about to gain control over Western Sahara, an ambition that hurled it to the very center of inter-African politics.

The Western Sahara dispute is one of several divisive issues (the Congo crisis, civil wars in Angola and Nigeria, the hostilities in Chad and the Horn) that have had continentwide repercussions. It has contributed to the forging of a trans-Saharan subsystem because states have been obliged to become involved with one another over the matter. However ironic it may seem, the struggle over this arid and inhospitable stretch of land, one of the last remnants of the colonial order, has greatly intensified the network of interconnections across the northern third of the continent.

☐ Trans-Saharan Conflicts and Connections

The Western Saharan issue has involved virtually every African state via its impact upon the OAU. At the regional level, the interconnections are especially intricate because each of the principal adversaries has its own set of networks. Fundamentally, the conflict has involved Morocco and the Saharawi rebels, but Mauritania, Algeria, and Libya have all been significantly involved as well. Each direct participant called upon its allies for diplomatic support, embroiling most trans-Saharan states in the conflict in one manner or another.

The dispute had its origins in the same historical interpretation that had earlier prompted Morocco to claim Mauritania. Some of the nomadic clans of Western Sahara had paid fealty to Moroccan sultans in the eighteenth and nineteenth centuries. Rabat thus concluded that the territory colonized by Spain since 1884 was historically Moroccan. King Hassan, shaky on his throne after two attempted coups in 1971 and 1972, staked his regime upon recovering these Saharan "provinces." Yet, by the 1970s, indigenous leaders had called for independence and established a liberation movement called the Polisario Front. Algeria, which had long championed the cause of liberation movements throughout Africa, gave support to Polisario. On geopolitical grounds, Algeria had no desire to see extension of Moroccan sovereignty another 500 miles (800 km) down the Atlantic coast. Algiers invoked the principle of self-determination, confident that the Saharawi people would elect independence rather than integration into Morocco—if given the chance. Libya's initial goal in supporting the Polisario guerrillas was essentially to thwart King Hassan, whose Western orientation Libya deplored: Having overthrown one monarch, Qaddafi had no inhibitions about dethroning another. (Although supporting its war effort, Qaddafi, the confirmed Arab unionist, advised Polisario to form a confederation with Mauritania.)

These conflicting notions came into sharp clash in 1975, when King Hassan organized the "Green March," a massive mobilization of some three hundred and fifty thousand unarmed Moroccan citizens who crossed the border brandishing flags and the Koran. The Spanish were dumbfounded by this maneuver and capitulated in the Tripartite Agreement, by which they turned over their colonial administration to Morocco and Mauritania (the latter getting the impoverished southern third of the Spanish holdings). Polisario for its part organized a large-scale exodus from the territory into Algeria, where the Saharawis set up camps around Tindouf. Since then the Polisario guerrillas have been resisting the Moroccan-Mauritanian takeover both militarily and diplomatically.

On the military front, Polisario succeeded in knocking Mauritania from the battlefield (the military overthrew President Mokhtar Ould Daddah in July 1978 and signed a peace treaty in 1979). Morocco has been a more determined adversary, digging in to defend roughly one-sixth of the territory, the "useful triangle" in the northwest where the major towns and the phosphate mines are located. On the diplomatic plane, Algeria and Polisario have steadily gained ground behind the principle of self-determination, creating strains within the OAU since 1976. Both sides have exerted strong pressure on the other African states to support their cause, making the matter a continental as well as regional issue.

The dispute has been before the OAU since 1976. After proposals to convene a special summit meeting devoted to the problem failed to materialize, the OAU turned the problem over to a Committee of Wisemen in 1978. The "sages" were the heads of state of Mali, Guinea, Côte d'Ivoire, Nigeria, Tanzania and Sudan. A year later, at the Monrovia summit, this committee proposed a ceasefire and a referendum to determine the will of the Saharawis. Upon approval of this recommendation, the Moroccan delegation walked out of the conference in protest and set about to dissuade the OAU from persisting in this path.

Morocco's tactic was to call in some IOU's from a number of friends, such as Zaire (for military assistance during the Shaba uprisings), Guinea (for aiding the Guinean-French rapprochement), and Egypt (tacit support of the Camp David Accords). Hassan also appealed to Senghor of Senegal, who was disposed to worry about an Algerian bid for hegemony in the Sahel, and to Tunisia, with its interest in balancing Algeria. Committed conservatives like Côte d'Ivoire and Gabon could also be relied upon. In this manner, Morocco was able to line up some dozen states willing to threaten a walkout from the OAU if Moroccan interests were unduly manhandled.

The threat first came into play at the 1980 summit in Freetown. By this time the issue had taken a slightly different form. To counter Morocco's annexation, Polisario had formed its own government of what it called the Saharan Arab Democratic Republic (SADR) in 1976. By 1980, twenty-six African states, or one more than half of the OAU's total membership, had recognized the SADR. They presumably had the votes to admit the SADR to the OAU if they wished. Several states, notably those that had most recently fought for their own independence, such as Zimbabwe and Mozambique, called for admission of the Saharawis. Morocco first raised a procedural objection, arguing that the OAU Charter provides only for the admission of sovereign, independent states; as the SADR did not meet these prerequisites, a two-thirds majority vote would be required to amend the charter. Behind this legalistic ploy, however, lay Morocco's real argument: that it could enlist enough supporters in a walkout to cripple the OAU. The supporters of Polisario, reluctant to provoke such a split, agreed to drop the admission question when Morocco expressed its willingness to cooperate with the Committee of Wisemen.

These developments from 1976 to 1980 well illustrate how a local conflict in northwestern Africa gradually engaged a large number of African governments. This "continentalization" of the issue reflected again the perennial split between radicals and moderates. By and large, francophone and Arab moderates supported Morocco, whereas the radicals rallied to Polisario's cause alongside Algeria. That Morocco was dependent upon French and U.S. weaponry (and Saudi financing) to wage the war increased the radicals' devotion to the cause of self-determination. The issue took on continental significance, not only because the OAU was obliged to deal with it, but also because of global alignments that it implied. Continental and global implications in turn enhanced the saliency of the issue for the regional governments.

The Committee of Wisemen dutifully continued its efforts but could not persuade Morocco to sit down at the bargaining table with Polisario. As more and more states became irked at Moroccan obstructionism, the support for admitting the SADR grew. Moreover, riots over food prices and unemployment in the war-torn economy rocked Casablanca in June 1981. Hassan was obliged to make a conciliatory gesture at the 1981 Nairobi summit. In a rare move, the king personally led his delegation to Nairobi to announce his readiness to permit a "controlled referendum" in the former Spanish colony. Algeria welcomed the Moroccan offer as a "first step in the search for peace"[21] and proposed that

Morocco withdraw its troops and administration as a second step. The heads of state voted down the latter proposal, restricting themselves to the creation of a new implementation committee to work out the arrangements for a cease-fire and referendum. The new committee had the same membership as the Committee of Wisemen plus Kenya's President arap Moi, incoming chairman of the OAU.

Kenya then set to work organizing two sessions of the new committee in August 1981 and February 1982. No progress was made at these sessions, the main stumbling point being Morocco's refusal to negotiate directly with the Polisario Front. Frustrated by the deadlock, Algeria brought pressure upon OAU Secretary-General Edem Kodjo to try something new. Kodjo obligingly issued credentials to the SADR delegation to attend the annual administrative meeting of the organization. Via this diplomatic coup, Polisario hoped to strengthen its hand by occupying a seat at the OAU. Morocco, however, stormed out of the meeting, sweeping eighteen other members along with it,[22] and the OAU faced a major crisis because it no longer had the two-thirds quorum necessary to conduct business.

The paralysis of the OAU over the Western Saharan question reproduced the major cleavage that has marked inter-African relations since the 1960s. Many of the states that have generally relied on the West for support stuck by Morocco, whereas those that have looked toward the socialist world backed the Polisario Front. Morocco could stymie the OAU by rallying the bulk of the francophone states and the Arab moderates that together constituted a blocking third. Most of these states had no immediate stake in the outcome in Western Sahara; even less were they persuaded of Morocco's historical sovereignty over the land. Their motivation in joining Morocco was their consciousness of a network of like-minded governments with a mutual interest in supporting one another. The solidarity of the conservative states was a form of collective security. Their walkout demonstrated that almost twenty years of OAU activity had not transcended the radical-moderate cleavage; by the same token, it showed that the OAU could function only by accommodating the viewpoint of the moderate camp.

The states that had recognized the SADR were themselves a relatively heterogeneous group.[23] Although most of the socialist-oriented states (Algeria, Libya, Ethiopia, Angola, Mozambique, Tanzania) were in these ranks, so were such states as Botswana, Lesotho, Swaziland, Togo, and Mali. They certainly did not constitute a "bloc," but they were a body of states more inclined to challenge the structural legacy of imperialism. Both the decolonization factor and Morocco's reliance on Western military support persuaded these countries to back Algeria's position of self-determination. Their willingness to do that in turn accentuated the cleavage in inter-African affairs. So long as individual pairs of radicals versus moderates (that is, Algeria versus Morocco) come into conflict over local issues, the continental cleavage is likely to characterize the inter-African system.

The Western Saharan case is not the only trans-Saharan conflict to affect the larger continental system. The civil war in Chad has likewise hobbled the OAU. We have already seen that Libya sent troops into Chad in 1980. Under French pressure, Libya withdrew them in 1981. For Goukouni Oueddei, the Libyan withdrawal was to be compensated by a contingent of OAU troops to protect his government from his rival, Hissene Habré, who had reconstituted his own forces with Western help during his exile in the Sudan. OAU "peace-keepers" (from Nigeria, Senegal, and Zaire) were duly deployed, but their mandate was unclear. Goukouni sought an active military role that was, in fact, beyond the means of the OAU force. For its part, the OAU urged Goukouni's GUNT to negotiate a new political settlement with Habré. Goukouni refused, and Habré's men stormed back into power in June 1982. Goukouni then fled the capital to regroup again in the north. The inability of the OAU to impose or police a settlement on the ground in Chad was apparent. Moreover, the Chadian strife compounded the disarray in an organization already rocked by the Western Sahara crisis. An attempt to convene the OAU in Tripoli in November failed when host government Libya refused admission to the Habré government. This exclusion prompted another boycott that reinforced the cleavage in inter-African affairs.

In a more direct bid to remove Habré, Libya again sent troops into Chad in mid-1983. In this second round, France intervened directly by positioning 3,000 French troops across the country at the fifteenth (and later the sixteenth) parallel. The French involvement, urged by the United States but also by Senegal and Côte d'Ivoire, was a move to reassure the francophone moderates by foiling Libya's objectives in Chad. The French intervention did stabilize the military situation but at the cost of a virtual de facto partition of the country. Although OAU mediators sought periodically to bring the competing factions to the bargaining table, the stalemate held firm until December 1986, when fighting erupted again.

Elements of Goukouni's men rebelled against Libyan tutelage (Goukouni himself, moreover, was being detained in Libya). Habré seized the opportunity to carry the battle across the sixteenth parallel in an attempt to reunite the country and succeeded in regaining control over the oasis town of Fada in the north. In March 1987, Habré launched a second offensive that routed the remaining Libyan forces; but the Aouzou strip remained under Libyan control, and Goukouni still enjoyed some diplomatic support (notably in Algeria). Habré's military success brought a respite from rather than an end to Chad's tribulations.

Like Western Sahara, Chad would hardly appear to be worth all the commotion that it has caused. The country is poor and sparsely populated, but it borders on six other countries and constitutes a door into black Africa for Libya. Geopolitics, like nature, abhors a vacuum; thus, states as distant from Chad as Senegal and Zaire were willing to join Nigeria (which has a short northeastern border with Chad) in seeking to reconcile the competing factions in order to contain Libyan expansion. The vacuum in Chad has, therefore, had the effect of stimulating a stronger regional consciousness throughout trans-Sahara.

Likewise, the dispatch of troops from Zaire to the short-lived OAU force illustrates that Central African states have also felt the repercussions of Chad's civil war. Cameroon has seen refugees crossing its border, and Kenya became involved during its tenure in the OAU chairmanship. Like the Congo crisis of the 1960s, the Chadian imbroglio has effected linkages between trans-Saharan and Central Africa.

☐ Ethiopia and the Politics of the Horn

Much the same is true about the final foyer of conflict in the northern zone. The Horn of Africa, the great bulge of the continent projecting into the Indian Ocean, contains the hostile pair of Ethiopia and Somalia as well as Africa's largest territory, Sudan, and one of its tiniest, the Republic of Djibouti. Ethiopia, the most densely populated of the four countries, is an indigenous imperial state that incorporates two highly contested regions, the province of Eritrea, which has been struggling for independence, and the Ogaden, which is claimed by Somalia. These two fierce disputes in this strategic area on the Red Sea and the Indian Ocean have made the Horn the site of explosive tensions and frequent external intervention.

Sharing the Red Sea coastline but also the Nile and the desert, Sudan is the hinterland of the Horn and the transit point to the rest of trans-Saharan Africa. Whereas the Arab north has historically been oriented toward Egypt, the southern Sudan is populated by black people, many of whom are Christian. Armed revolt in the south has plagued the central government and provided incentives for Ethiopia (and others) to meddle. Moreover, drought in Ethiopia and civil war in Chad and Ethiopia have periodically driven refugees from these states into Sudan. Its long borders with Egypt, Chad, and Ethiopia and its lesser borders with such tension spots as Libya, Uganda, and Zaire explain Sudan's geopolitical significance and its involvement in a host of issues.

As an imperial state, Ethiopia's central policy concern has been to preserve the integrity of its borders. As Christopher Clapham puts it, "For as far back as records reach—at least 500 years—control of the local periphery has been, in its own view, the historic mission or manifest destiny of the Ethiopian state."[24] In recent times, under Emperor Haile Selassie, Ethiopia expanded to absorb the territory of Eritrea, which had fallen under Italian control in 1890. As Eritrea had twice been the pathway for Italian campaigns against Ethiopia, control of this outlet to the Red Sea was of great value to Addis Ababa. Proceeding by stages, Ethiopia succeeded in attaching Eritrea, first under a federal arrangement from 1952 to 1962 and then by outright annexation. Many Eritreans, however, did not wish to be incorporated into the Ethiopian state, and they began a struggle for independence in 1961 under the banner of the Eritrean Liberation Front (ELF). The war has been going on ever since.

Likewise, Ethiopia has historically sought control of the Ogaden, roughly speaking the eastern spearhead of territory that thrusts into Somalia. Ethiopian Emperor Menelik conquered this territory in the last decade of the nineteenth century; it was then taken by Italy in the 1930s and subsequently occupied by Great Britain during World War II (when Italy's colonies on the Horn fell). In 1948 Britain withdrew, allowing Ethiopia to reassert its rule over the Somali population that lived there. The Somalis along the coast bitterly resented the British move, and the seeds of future conflict were sown.

Haile Selassie thus had two dissident groups to worry about. He conceived a diplomatic response to this situation that was tactically brilliant. His greatest asset, he realized, was symbolic, for he was heir to a dynasty that had been the only African elite successfully to resist the imposition of colonialism. Having ascended to the throne in 1930 (after a fourteen-year regency), Selassie had made a famous speech at the League of Nations in 1936 defending Ethiopia's right to independence. His kingdom was the symbol of resistance to colonialism, and he was indisputably the elder statesman of African leaders. Selassie astutely exploited this image as the rest of Africa acceded to independence.

When the UN Economic Commission for Africa was formed in 1958, Ethiopia welcomed its headquarters to Addis Ababa. In 1960 Selassie was host to the second Conference of Independent African States, laying the groundwork for his greatest diplomatic coup: the founding of the OAU at Addis Ababa in 1963. The emperor was well placed to promote the ideal of African unity, for he had the advantage of neutrality between formerly British and formerly French Africa and between Arab and black Africa, and he had not been prominently involved in the split between moderates and radicals. Although other leaders, like Kwame Nkrumah, had taken the lead in promoting African unity, Selassie seized the opportunity to host the founding conference and to offer the Ethiopian capital as its site. Of particular utility to Ethiopia was the key charter provision calling for respect of the existing African boundaries.[25] Virtually every African government had some fear of ethnic or regional dissidence. The charter adopted by the thirty-two independent states in May 1963 reinforced the Ethiopian position and enhanced the prestige of Haile Selassie.

Once the OAU headquarters were located in Addis Ababa, the Ethiopian ruler was well placed to preside benevolently over continental matters. When fighting flared along the Algerian-Moroccan border in October 1963, for example, Selassie was called upon to serve as a mediator. In turn, Ethiopia called upon the OAU to uphold the status quo during clashes in the Ogaden border region in 1964 and 1965. Haile Selassie's role of senior statesman and the frequent sessions of OAU council meetings in Addis Ababa provided the Ethiopians a kind of diplomatic moral stature that neutralized Somali and Eritrean claims against the empire. Coupled with a long-standing reliance upon U.S. military supplies and economic assistance, Ethiopia had the means to assure its territorial integrity up to the end of Haile Selassie's reign. Internal tensions arising out of domestic misrule were more important in the overthrow of the emperor in 1974 than were issues of foreign policy.

The period following the fall of Haile Selassie was marked by a fascinating mix of inter-African policy continuity combined with a dramatic reversal of extra-African alliances. The military committee (the *derg*) that took power was as determined as the emperor to hold on to Eritrea and the Ogaden. But it was also committed to a policy of land reform that disrupted the countryside; the crumbling of the old order unleashed new expressions of ethnic separatism. The revolutionary officers cracked down on various dissident groups, causing the United States to protest human rights violations and to grow wary of the overall course of the revolution. In these circumstances, the United States was not eager to continue to arm the Ethiopians, who began to look elsewhere.

Conversely, so did the Somalis. From 1969, when Mohammed Siad Barre had seized power in Somalia, until the mid-1970s, Somalia had relied upon the Soviet Union for support in its domestic development and foreign policy. By 1974, when the two governments signed a twenty-year treaty of friendship and cooperation, Somalia appeared to have become the Soviets' favored client in black Africa. Somali policy was in good measure the mirror image of Ethiopia's; when conditions changed, it reversed itself. So long as Ethiopia was supported by the United States, strains in the Soviet-Somali relationship could be glossed over. But, in fact, the Soviets had never been willing to unleash the irredentist Somalis; thus, as Robert Gorman observes, once "it became obvious that Ethiopia, at least in name, had embraced socialist dogma, it became increasingly difficult for both Somalia and the USSR to hide their differences."[26] Somalia denounced its treaty with the Soviets and veered Westward in 1977, ever in search of its primary objective, the recovery of the Ogaden.

The reversal of alliances was effected, moreover, in the heat of battle, as Somali forces entered the Ogaden in July 1977. The Somali move was opportunistic, relying upon a perception that Ethiopia was crumbling under the weight of a new Eritrean offensive in the north and domestic turmoil elsewhere. Somalia took note as well of the fact that Sudan, which had previously practiced a policy of neutrality toward the Eritrean conflict, was now aiding the nationalists and other opponents of the *derg*. (Sudan's switch was part of the overall pattern of shifting alliances: As Ethiopia moved left, Addis Ababa became friendlier with Qaddafi—Nimeiri's nemesis. Suspecting Libyan and Ethiopian complicity in a foiled coup attempt in 1976, Nimeiri countered on the Eritrean front.) Somalia did not actually declare war or even admit the presence of its own troops in the Ogaden; its official version was that the hostilities were between the Western Somali Liberation Front (WSLF), a movement of the indigenous Somali population of the Ogaden, and the Ethiopian military. By October 1977, the combined Somali/WSLF offensive controlled over 90 percent of the Ogaden. Somalia's short-term calculation of Ethiopian disarray was accurate, but Siad Barre miscalculated Ethiopian determination and the Soviets' willingness to rebuild Ethiopia's military strength. For their part, the Soviets decided that Ethiopia was worth more than Somalia; and although the West was happy to win back Somalia, it was not ready to endorse Somali irredentism (for much the same reasons that had motivated Soviet caution on this matter).

Thus, Soviet aid, bolstered by Cuban troops, eventually restored the territorial status quo ante in the Horn. The student of inter-African relations cannot help but be struck by the paradox of the Horn. On the one hand, we see the unswerving determination of the local actors to pursue their goals by whatever means are available. On the other hand, we see how dependent the local actors are upon foreign support. In order to pursue its primary goal of territorial integrity, Ethiopia devised a new military supply relationship when the old one faltered. Somalia, in turn, was obliged to swap patrons. The Soviet Union, we might add, did make a valiant attempt to reconcile the adversaries in the name of common socialist values, but neither side would compromise, obliging the Soviets to choose their partner. The African states had the freedom to realign rather than the resources to deal autonomously with their problem.

Sudan has not been directly involved in the Ogaden conflict but has been intermittently involved in the Eritrean secession, or the struggle for the Red Sea. Since the establishment of the Ethiopian-Eritrean federation in 1952, Sudan has been a natural haven for nationalist exiles from neighboring Eritrea. Throughout the 1960s, as fighting intensified in the province, Sudanese support for the Eritreans waxed and waned; Muslim sympathizers pressed the government to aid their Eritrean counterparts, but this exposed the Sudanese to counterintervention by Ethiopia in the southern Sudan, where Khartoum likewise faced a secessionist movement. In 1972 both parties agreed to desist from interference in one another's secessions. This agreement held until 1976, when the emergent Libyan-Ethiopian alignment prompted Nimeiri to reopen the Sudanese-Eritrean connection. Once again Libyan policy prompted far-flung reactions.

Common antagonism with Ethiopia provided grounds for Sudan and Somalia to cultivate friendly relations. During the late 1970s and 1980s, after their respective flirtations with the East, both states, accompanied also by Egypt, moved into the camp of the African moderates. Sudan's willingness to provide sanctuary (and to channel arms) to the anti-Libyan forces in the Chadian civil war was, of course, consistent with this stance. From a different perspective, one can see that Nimeiri had to choose between Egypt and Libya and opted for Sudan's traditional partner on the Nile, thereby creating tensions along the Libyan-Ethiopian axis. After the coup against Nimeiri in 1985 (and faced with a renewal of dissidence in the southern sector of the country), the new leadership sought to improve relations with these states in order to reduce their propensity to intervene in Sudanese affairs. Thus, the flow and counterflow of pressure entered a new stage.

The Horn, therefore, is not at all a self-contained system. Rather, the unresolved conflicts there have repercussions throughout the continent and continually invite extracontinental intervention. Such intervention is not reserved to the great powers but includes several Middle Eastern states as well (most notably Saudi Arabia, Syria, and Iraq). In the mid-1980s, these geopolitical instabilities were further complicated by a devastating drought that crippled already feeble economies. The dual disasters of starvation and refugee flows did nothing to resolve the underlying conflicts that have made the Horn a perennial trouble spot.

The vast trans-Saharan region with its activist states and its unresolved conflicts has been, therefore, a major theater of inter-African relations.[27] Its issues and actors have generated camps and countercamps within and beyond the zone. Not every government in this expanse is intensely involved in every issue, but the interconnections are sufficiently thick that an assassination in Egypt can cause grave concern in Côte d'Ivoire, and both Senegalese and Somalis react to Libyan policies. And, in numerous ways, the activism of the trans-Saharan states has also impinged upon Central Africa.

■ CENTRAL AFRICA

The band that we call Central Africa is geographically dominated by Zaire. Around Zaire is deployed a semicircle of relatively lightly populated states including the People's Republic of Congo, Gabon, Cameroon, Central African Republic, Uganda, Rwanda, and Burundi. With the exception of Uganda, this area was subject to French and Belgian colonial rule, and these states have been associated in the various francophone groupings that we have already discussed—*la francophonie* is thus one form of linkage between Central and trans-Saharan Africa. The other major actor in this central band is Kenya, the most prosperous of the East African economies. Under the leadership of Jomo Kenyatta until 1978, Kenya pursued a basically pro-Western foreign policy as an inducement to foreign investment. Kenya's economic policies caused some tensions with Tanzania and Uganda, but otherwise it maintained a rather low profile in inter-African affairs. Like Ethiopia, Kenya also had to worry about Somali nationalism, for Somalia laid claim to Kenya's North Eastern Province, which like Ogaden contained a large number of ethnic Somalis. Kenyatta addressed this matter right after independence by a classic move, a treaty with Ethiopia against Somali irredentism. The treaty handily survived the change of government in Ethiopia in the mid-1970s. The shifting alignments of its various neighbors have left Kenya unperturbed in its pursuit of economic growth through foreign investment. But global pressures emanating from the proximity of the Horn to the Saudi Arabian oil fields have drawn Kenyatta's successor, Daniel arap Moi, more tightly into the Western camp.

With the partial exception of Zaire, none of the states of the central zone has assumed a major role in inter-African relations. Although this equatorial band might appear to be a buffer zone between the wars of trans-Sahara and the liberation politics of southern Africa, it is perhaps even more a buffeted zone that registers the political shock waves from the adjacent subsystems. We know already that its Zairian heartland has been the object of multiple rivalries. But these states have not failed to use what means they have to influence their external environments.

☐ Zaire's Protracted Malaise

The Congo crises of the early 1960s had their prolongations in the Shaba crises of the latter 1970s; external debt, internal corruption, and a host of foreign dependencies have extended Zaire's malaise into the mid-1980s. Even more than Chad, Zaire has had a turbulent postindependence history that has polarized the rest of Africa. Despite its unsettled situation, Zaire plunged into the struggle for power among Angola's competing liberation movements in 1975, compounding its domestic difficulties. In the midst of this turmoil, Mobutu Sese Seko managed to navigate a foreign policy course that helped to maintain him in power over two decades. As Crawford Young puts it, "the very bonds of economic dependency have been used with virtuosity."[28]

Mobutu took power in 1965 at the end of the first round of crises that we have already discussed as inter-African issues. The complex tripartite struggle for power between Lumumba, Joseph Kasavubu, and the Katanga secessionists opened the country to multiple interventions and ceaseless controversy. Throughout this five-year period, the competing Congolese factions sought external support from fellow Africans and from extra-African patrons. The West and the African moderates ultimately succeeded in keeping pro-Western elements in power. Mobutu inherited this situation and never significantly departed from this general orientation. Mobutu shored up his ties to the West, nevertheless playing Belgium, France, and the United States off against one another to gain a modicum of maneuvering room. He maintained participation in OCAM, the vehicle of the pro-Western francophones, for several years. In the early 1970s, Mobutu initiated a brief venture in the direction of a more radical policy, visiting Romania and China, signing a military training agreement with North Korea, breaking with Israel and Taiwan, and nationalizing some foreign companies. He also traveled widely throughout Africa, visiting many African states in pursuit of a continental-scale diplomacy; in 1973, for example, he paid calls in no less than fourteen African countries. These gestures did not signify any real break with the past, however. Motubu's ambitions for a more independent image were short-lived, as pressures emanating from events in Angola pushed him back into the embrace of the moderates and the West.

Zaire shares some 1,500 (2,500 km) miles of border with Angola. Moreover, northern Angola is populated by Bakongo people, the dominant ethnic group in lower Zaire. Zaire had had a role in the Angolan liberation movement from the outset of armed resistance to Portuguese rule in 1961. Zaire favored the National Front for the Liberation of Angola (FNLA) under Holden Roberto over the Marxist-oriented MPLA led by Agostino Neto. This preference "paralleled that held by the United States and China, which were, for somewhat different reasons, convinced that the MPLA was under Soviet influence. As Angola moved toward civil war, both governments collaborated with Zaire, though not with each other, in reinforcing the FNLA's military capabilities."[29] Mobutu's policy goal was to assure Roberto at least a foothold in a coalition government after Portuguese withdrawal. Zaire's rather modest ability to achieve this goal was quite overwhelmed by the flood of other interventions that the last round of the struggle for power in Angola released.

In mid-1975, Mobutu made the fateful decision to intervene directly in Angola alongside the FNLA. Presumably encouraged by the CIA, which had long financed Holden Roberto and which had just received the go-ahead for covert military action, Zaire sent a company of commandos and armored cars into combat in Angola.[30] Over the next two months, Mobutu committed another four battalions of paratroopers to the FNLA cause. At the same time, South African forces moved across Angola's southern border in support of the FNLA and of another contender, UNITA, led by Jonas Savimbi. Had the MPLA stood alone against these forces, Mobutu's venture might have succeeded. But the MPLA had allies as well. Once Cuban troops and Soviet arms joined the fray, the military situation was reversed. The Cubans helped the MPLA to drive out the FNLA-Zairian force, and Mobutu had to come to terms with a Marxist government in Luanda.

For Zaire, the episode was even more humiliating politically than militarily. Mobutu's effort to establish an independent and progressive image was shattered by the apparent alliance with South Africa (not to speak of the CIA). His pretension to influence the course of events even in the contiguous environment proved a fiasco. He was obliged to disengage and to "normalize" relations with the MPLA government by declaring that he had merely been fighting against "Portuguese colonialism." Worst of all, however, the episode left the Angolans ill disposed to Zaire's leader and not unsympathetic to his opponents, certain of whom were camped in northeastern Angola near the border with Shaba (formerly Katanga) Province. Rather than shoring up his regional environment, Mobutu had in fact weakened it. The result was even greater dependence upon external protectors.

The Shaba front deteriorated in March 1977 when opponents of the Mobutu regime infiltrated from Angola and took control of several localities. Zaire claimed that it was being invaded by five thousand Cuban-led Katangese mercenaries from Angola and sent out an alarm to Washington and Paris. In reality, although the incursion enjoyed the tacit support of the Angolan government (which was still being harassed by the FNLA), it was more indicative of a regime crisis than of a foreign threat. Yet, whatever the mix of causes, the crisis was real and Mobutu needed help. The new Carter administration was not eager to get involved, but the French government saw an opportunity to improve its position in the former Belgian sphere in conjunction with another ally-in-need, Morocco. King Hassan, in turn, was willing to supply troops to shore up an African government that had backed Morocco on the Western Sahara issue. French planes transported Moroccan soldiers and materiel to the front, and the rebel forces slipped back into the countryside or across the border. The threat "appeared to have come and gone as quickly as the afternoon showers common to Shaba province,"[31] but in fact a more violent storm lay ahead in Shaba II.

The second round began in May 1978 much as the first with rebel forces reentering the copper zone. This time, however, they succeeded in seizing the important mining town of Kolwezi where some twenty-five hundred Europeans worked. Once again, the Mobutu government had to appeal to external sources to redress a situation that the Zairian army could not handle. With European lives presumed in danger, France and Belgium dispatched their own forces into the contested zone. French Foreign Legionnaires engaged in a bloody battle over Kolwezi that took some eight hundred lives. The rebels were beaten back, but once again Zaire became the site of bitter controversy over Western intervention and the character of Mobutu's dependent regime. Zaire could only reinforce its ties with the francophone moderates and meekly work out a modus vivendi on noninterference with Angola.

The French were reluctant to withdraw without establishing more durable security arrangements. Once again, they mobilized the Moroccans, who provided the bulk of an inter-African peacekeeping force that also included smaller contingents from Senegal, Togo, Gabon, the Central African Republic, and Egypt. The reinsertion of Zaire into the francophone family was clear. Although outspoken leaders like Tanzania's Nyerere deplored the rescue of Mobutu, his allies acquiesced in the salvage operation. Shaba II was remarkably reminiscent of Stanleyville 1964; the Zaire of 1978 was as porous as the Congo of 1964, and the African alignments surrounding the issues were remarkably stable.

The inter-African force remained in Shaba for about a year, but Mobutu remained conscious of his political debt to the participant states for several years thereafter. Most prominently, Zaire became Morocco's most fervent defender on the Western Sahara question. Elsewhere, Zaire reciprocated the support of the Central African Republic by sending troops to crush student demonstrations there. It supplied a contingent to the OAU force that was deployed in Chad in an effort to reduce Libyan influence in that country, an undertaking earnestly desired by Mobutu's African allies in Senegal and Togo. Zaire consistently supported Egypt on the Camp David Accords and eventually renewed diplomatic ties with Israel, a project that many of the black African moderates tacitly supported. In this manner, Zaire gradually refurbished its standing in moderate Africa even if the political foundation of the regime remained fragile.

Earlier, we saw how the Western Sahara dispute broke the OAU apart in February 1982. Zaire stood fast by Morocco through 1982 as two attempts to overcome the boycott by Morocco's supporters failed. By 1983 a compromise (voluntary withdrawal from the meetings by the Western Saharans) allowed the OAU to resume its sessions. In 1984, the compromise broke down in the face of Moroccan intransigence and growing support for the Polisario's SADR. When the November 1984 summit formally seated the SADR, Zaire alone joined Morocco in leaving the organization (Morocco withdrew from the OAU, whereas Zaire officially "suspended" its participation). Thus, the Rabat-Kinshasa axis remained firm while the rest of Africa elected to carry on without them. Zaire's fidelity to Morocco was impressive, although its willingness to leave the OAU was consistent with a different project that appealed to Mobutu.

This project was the proposal to abandon the OAU and found a new "League of Black Africa," which Mobutu advanced in 1984. Nobody paid much attention to Mobutu's appeal to dissociate black Africa from Arab Africa. Despite the fact that disputes in the northern tier had caused major divisions within the OAU, there remained a broad consensus that the organization was needed. Nor were the cleavages in the OAU a function of differences between Arab and black states; on the contrary, as Mobutu in particular had good reason to appreciate, inter-African coalitions and linkages reflected alignments that extended beyond Africa. By the same token, they reflected Africa's dependency in world politics. However limited its means, the OAU symbolized a strategy for overcoming this dependent status. Thus, whatever dream Mobutu may have cherished to lead a League of Black Africa was not to be realized. His gesture to King Hassan in November simply underlined his previous dependence on Moroccan aid.

Virtual isolation at the continental level, vulnerability to insurrection at the regional level, financial dependency at the global level—in all these ways, Zaire was revealed as a giant with feet of clay. This sprawling land lying in the center of Africa might well have seemed the logical core of a Central African common market. Indeed, Zaire had sought to build a customs union encompassing such states as Central African Republic, Chad, Gabon, and the People's Republic of Congo. This scheme never achieved much substance, as Zaire inspired little confidence and each of the smaller states of the region sought other, more reassuring partners. For states like Central African Republic and Gabon, France remained the major patron long after independence. The Central African Republic, especially during the days when the tyrannical Jean-Bedel Bokassa pursued Napoleonic fantasies, was a grim case of external dependency and internal misrule (much like Uganda under Idi Amin). Gabon had more attractive options by virtue of its oil resources, which led it into OPEC membership. But the sparsely populated equatorial country had little infrastructure other than the offshore rigs, and it was content to follow the lead of more prominent francophone states (Côte d'Ivoire, Senegal, Cameroon) on most matters.

Of Zaire's northern neighbors, only the People's Republic of Congo broke out of the moderate francophone pattern toward an orientation closer to that of the progressive states. Recriminations occasionally arose between Brazzaville, which lies just across the Congo River from Kinshasa, and the Zairian government over the former's toleration of oppositional activity against Zaire. Yet, the frontier with the Congo never gave rise to incidents comparable to the Shaba episodes, and the two states' relations remained strained but not prone to violence. The tensions between Congo-Brazzaville and its larger ex-namesake were symptomatic of the fragmented nature of what might have become a Zaire-dominated subsystem under other circumstances. Instead the single most in-fluential political actor throughout the region was France.

☐ Cameroon and Kenya

Only two states across Central Africa have had relatively successful develop-ment experiences, but neither has mounted a very active inter-African policy. Cameroon and Kenya may be seen as the "peripheral powers" on the western and eastern coasts of the zone. Cameroon has a modest oil-exporting capability, and its agricultural development programs have done well; as a result, it has one of the higher per capita incomes on the continent. It has not ventured much beyond the confines of the francophone group, however, despite the fact that part of the country was once under British rule. Under the rather conservative leadership of Ahmadou Ahidjo for two decades, the government was initially wary of radical opposition forces that enjoyed some external support in Ghana and Guinea. Thus, Cameroon elected to emphasize its ties with the moderate states in organizations like OCAM. The French connection was likewise re-assuring with regard to occasional tensions along the border with Nigeria. Here as well, prudence has prevailed, Cameroon cautiously maintaining a policy of support to the Nigerian federal government during the Biafran secession, from 1967 to 1970. To do otherwise would have invited Nigerian countermeasures to be sure; but at a most fundamental level, it would have violated Cameroon's traditional practice of maintaining a low profile in inter-African affairs.

Likewise, Cameroon's counterpart on the east coast, Kenya, has followed a policy that has been "cautious from the day that she gained her indepen-dence."[32] Aside from the issue of Somali irredentism, Kenyan foreign policy has been principally directed to its economic relations with Uganda and Tan-zania, its partners in the East African Community (as discussed in Chapter 10). Kenya's thoroughgoing commitment to capitalist development, including strong encouragement of foreign investment, was a policy that placed higher priority upon national development than upon regional integration.[33] In choos-ing heavy reliance on external capital, Kenya adopted an orientation that dis-counted the importance of inter-African relations.

Kenya, nonetheless, could not ignore Somalia as the Somali ethnic claims extended across the length of their common border. Britain had decided in 1963 to attach what was called the Northern Frontier District (where some two hundred forty thousand Somalis lived) to Kenya. Kenya thus inherited a dis-puted frontier and local hostilities (known as the *shifta* war), to which it re-sponded by means of a pact with Ethiopia. This treaty was not affected by the coup in Ethiopia, as "the threat posed to Kenya by Somalia's territorial claim was far more serious than the ideological orientation of the Ethiopian regime."[34] Yet, the main thrust of Somali irredentism has always been directed against "Greater Ethiopia," and as Somalia recognized that the *shifta* war was un-winnable and that Kenya was a desirable economic partner, Kenyan-Somali relations gradually improved. This rapprochement was especially pronounced during the 1980s, as both countries moved into a closer relationship with the United States—in part because of Ethiopia's growing ties with the Soviet Union and in part because of larger geopolitical pressures (notably the U.S. scheme for a Rapid Deployment Force, which we discuss more fully in Chapter 12).

Circumstances briefly thrust Kenya into a more visible continental role in 1981–1983 following the OAU summit meeting in Nairobi. As chairman of the organization, Daniel arap Moi found himself at the center of two major disputes—concerning Western Sahara and Chad. He was designated to chair the implementation committee, which the Nairobi summit set up to work out procedures for the mandated referendum on Western Sahara. Likewise, he was called upon to oversee arrangements for the short-lived OAU force in Chad. Kenya's good offices proved inadequate to settle these intractable conflicts, however, and arap Moi, moreover, had to confront an attempted coup at home. Kenya turned back upon its immediate regional environment and local security needs, matters on which the United States was willing to help. An external patron, in other words, appeared the surest guarantor against domestic and regional upheavals.

The Kenyan case confirms the most striking attribute of Central Africa as a whole—namely, the resort to external supporters. In contrast to trans-Saharan Africa, where several states mounted quite active independent diplomacies at one or another period, the states of Central Africa at best can maneuver among alternative patrons. With the temporary exception of Zaire, these states have not aspired to leadership roles in continental affairs. The reasons are obvious: None of them has power resources comparable to Algeria, Libya, or Nigeria. Even the best endowed, Zaire, is a fragile construct. Given their limited resources, these states have attended to their local environments far more than to the continental environment. As a general rule, this has meant integrating their respective economies into the global economy rather than seeking to challenge their position by organizing Africa into a coherent unit.

But if the governments of Central Africa have rarely sought the mantle of continental leadership, they are no less obliged than others to formulate a foreign policy, no matter how constrained. As relatively weak states, the external environment impinges upon them in substantial ways. Their strategy has been to call upon external patrons—France, the United States, the Soviet Union, Great Britain—for protection rather than to pursue some version of the model of continental self-reliance proffered by one or another of the activist states. Still, the common framework of the OAU—however battered—does engage every African state to some degree in a common enterprise. To the extent that the inter-African system has broken into two camps, most of these states have entered the moderate camp. The struggle in and over Zaire epitomizes the victory of pro-Western social forces across the central zone. A more radical process of change, however, has occurred in the third major subdivision of the continent. The issues and actors of southern Africa, moreover, exercise moral pressures upon all the rest of Africa. We must turn now to the southern African subsystem to complete our analysis of inter-African relations.

■ SOUTHERN AFRICA

Inter-African relations in the southern subsystem have been primarily concerned with the still incomplete agenda of liberation from colonial and minority rule. Of the southern states, only the island of Madagascar belonged to the 1960 generation of independence. At the founding conference in 1963, the OAU established a Liberation Committee to channel support to the peoples of southern Africa. The headquarters of this body was placed in Dar es Salaam, capital of Tanzania, the only independent state in the region at the time. By 1965, when the white settlers of Rhodesia (now Zimbabwe) issued their Unilateral Declaration of Independence, (UDI), only Zambia and Malawi had joined the ranks of African self-rule. Whereas Malawi opted for a policy of accommodation with white power, Tanzania and Zambia became significantly involved with the liberation movements of Zimbabwe, Angola, Mozambique, Namibia, and South Africa.

The entire southern African subsystem is dominated by the military might of South Africa, the ultimate bastion of minority rule on the continent. Until 1975, South Africa was aligned with Portugal as it clung futilely to Angola and Mozambique. The withdrawal of Portugal substantially altered the regional environment, but Angola and Mozambique, in turn, have had to confront the reality of Pretoria's economic and military capability. Even the independence of Zimbabwe in 1980 has not overturned the pattern of South African hegemony. Most exposed of all to South African power are the former British protectorates of Botswana, Lesotho, and Swaziland.

The common adversary in the south gives the southern subsystem a rather different character from those of Central and trans-Saharan Africa. Policymaking has been dominated by decolonization and by security issues to a much greater degree than elsewhere. The black-governed states have drawn together in such collective arrangements as the Front Line States and the Southern African Development Coordination Conference (SADCC). But these associations cannot obscure the fact that the different members have often pursued dissimilar policies in dealing with South Africa and with competing national liberation movements. Although issues of liberation politics have been a constant in regional decision making, the governments of southern Africa have faced a changing policy environment, especially over the decade 1975–1985. Portugal's decolonization, the termination of UDI, the ongoing pressure for Namibian independence, and, since 1976, the turbulence within South Africa demonstrate that the southern subsystem is in flux.

☐ Tanzania and Zambia: The First Front Line

Because of its central location and its borders with four territories engaged in anticolonial struggles (Angola, Namibia, Zimbabwe, Mozambique), Zambia has been as directly involved in regional politics as any state could be. On geopolitical grounds, Zambia had no choice other than to deal with a host of security issues thrust upon it by its embattled environment. Tanzania, on the other hand, had a broader range of options and might have been expected to orient its diplomacy primarily toward an East African community. One of the most interesting features of Tanzanian foreign policy has been its choice of a southern orientation. Many factors contribute to explain this choice, including disillusionment with developments in Kenya and Uganda, but none was more important than Nyerere's belief that ideologically sympathetic regimes coming to power in Mozambique and elsewhere across the south would enhance Tanzania's ability to pursue socialism and self-reliance. Because differing rationales lay behind the two countries' policies, the Tanzania-Zambia relationship was not always free of disagreement, but they generally viewed one another as partners in the enterprise of confronting minority power.

In its overall posture, Tanzania has been a maverick in inter-African relations. Two episodes especially illustrate Nyerere's willingness to buck the tide: his recognition of Biafra during the Nigerian civil war and his refusal to recognize the Idi Amin government in Uganda. In both cases, Tanzania violated OAU norms of noninterference or respect for colonial borders. In the former case, Tanzania's support for the principle of Biafran self-determination had little practical impact. In the latter case, however, Nyerere backed Ugandan exiles loyal to his friend, Milton Obote, in efforts to overthrow Amin; although a first attempt failed in 1972, a later campaign (brought on by Amin's ill-considered sortie into northern Tanzania in 1978) succeeded when Nyerere committed his own troops to the fray. With Uganda in a shambles from the despotic Amin's policies, Tanzania continued to exert influence until Obote was eventually restored to power. This involvement in hapless Uganda, one of the rare instances of a successful inter-African military intervention, was exceptional also in its northward thrust, for the most prominent characteristic of Tanzanian foreign policy has been its southern orientation.

The border with Mozambique was the immediate source of Tanzanian involvement in liberation politics. Tanzania welcomed the creation of the Front for the Liberation of Mozambique in the early 1960s and offered it headquarters in Dar es Salaam. This offer was a practical commitment to a movement pledged to socialism as well as anticolonialism, and Tanzania consistently backed the primacy of the FRELIMO leadership against other contenders when splits in the nationalist movement occurred. Tanzania did what it could, in other words, to assure the triumph of an ideologically sympathetic movement on its southern flank. By hosting the OAU Liberation Committee, the Tanzanians committed themselves to an activist policy across the rest of the south.

A primary component of this policy was partnership with Zambia upon its independence in 1964. Zambia was especially exposed to the many pressures in the region. Its landlocked copperbelt was dependent upon rail lines through Portuguese and South African territory for access to the sea. Rhodesia supplied virtually all its industrial energy. In these circumstances, it was little wonder that Zambia had an "obsessive preoccupation" with the liberation of southern Africa.[35] President Kenneth Kaunda fully shared Nyerere's moral indignation over minority rule, and the two leaders formed an extraordinary working relationship, meeting no less than seventy-one times over the years 1964–1974.[36] They collaborated in the construction of road, rail, and pipeline links in order to extricate Zambia from the stranglehold upon its transport options. The TanZam partnership constituted a significant new axis in inter-African relations, but the immediate pressures upon the two governments remained unequal as illustrated in their differing responses to the crisis created by UDI in November 1965.

For Zambia, the policy dilemma was how to persuade the British government to prevent a seizure of power by the white settlers of Southern Rhodesia. Kaunda went so far as to offer British Prime Minister Harold Wilson military bases in Zambia to deter a breakaway by the settler government under Ian Smith. Lacking adequate military resources of his own, Kaunda felt obliged to seek his goal through collaboration with London, which ignored his offers and his advice.

Once deterrence failed, Zambia took the lead in an African/Third World campaign to pressure Great Britain to end the rebellion. Although Britain accepted its formal responsibility to do so, it insisted that economic sanctions were the correct means. Other African governments, notably Tanzania, disagreed with Zambia over diplomatic tactics. The OAU met shortly after UDI and passed a resolution calling upon all African governments to break diplomatic relations with London if Prime Minister Wilson did not promptly use military force against the breakaway regime; likewise, it requested governments to make military advisors available to study the feasibility of a joint African force. But Zambia was opposed to both these approaches for compelling reasons. A multilateral OAU force would be cumbersome and expensive, and the logistics of the operation would make Zambia vulnerable to retaliation. Kaunda was convinced that only British troops could move quickly enough while avoiding a racial confrontation. Thus, he opposed breaking with Britain at the same time that he attacked Wilson's reluctance to employ force. Tanzania, on the other hand, did sever diplomatic relations.[37] This divergence in policy was an early indication of tactical differences that would from time to time separate the two states in their liberation policies.

Why have these two relatively like-minded states behaved differently? Geopolitics explains some of the discrepancy, but the nature of domestic elites is also pertinent. The Zambian policymaking elite contained competing factions of "national politicians" and "technocrats."[38] The former espoused thoroughgoing support of liberation causes, whereas the latter advocated cooperative relations with South Africa and with foreign investors in the mining industry. Zambian foreign policy has fluctuated as one or the other group held sway or as Kaunda tried to compromise between their competing preferences. Regarding UDI but more generally as well, Kaunda sought a middle ground between these two policy groups. The Tanzanian elite (which to be sure had less to risk) was somewhat more homogeneous in its ideological commitments—both on economic and liberation issues. Its foreign policy was more systematically "liberationist."

Kaunda was also influenced by a belief that South Africa might be persuaded not to assist the Smith secessionist government. Over the years, Kaunda has fluctuated between outspoken denunciation of apartheid and quiet overtures toward accommodation with South African leaders. In dealing with UDI as in dealing with South Africa, Zambia has experienced great frustration. Despite a cautious pragmatism, the price to Zambia of economic sanctions was very high. Kaunda asserted in 1978 that twelve years of redirected trade, transport, and military preparedness cost the country $6 billion, the equivalent of two years of GNP.[39]

As it became obvious that Great Britain would not employ military force and that economic sanctions would not suffice, the focus shifted to guerrilla warfare conducted by the Zimbabweans. Once again Zambia and Tanzania had to make policy decisions about whom to support between two principal contenders, the Zimbabwe African National Union (ZANU) led by Robert Mugabe and the Zimbabwe African People's Union (ZAPU) led by Joshua Nkomo. The split in the Rhodesian nationalist movement predated UDI and reflected both ethnic and ideological divisions and differing international linkages. Zambia decided in 1964 that ZAPU had the greater internal support and generally remained faithful to Nkomo. Meanwhile ZANU won the favor of a range of backers that included China, North Korea, Algeria, Mozambique, and the Palestine Liberation Organization (PLO). Tanzania came to the conclusion that ZANU was the more effective liberation force. Although both states encouraged the two movements to come together—and eventually succeeded in creating the coalition Patriotic Front, in 1976—they nevertheless disagreed in their approach to Zimbabwean nationalism.

Both states, it should be stressed, offered facilities to most of the movements combatting minority rule in southern Africa. Lusaka's Liberation Center had a generally open door policy, and Dar es Salaam harbored all those recognized by the OAU Liberation Committee. Still, each state was inclined to support most vigorously the group or leadership that it saw as most congenial to its long-term interests. Tanzania particularly desired to see leftist movements accede to power, whereas Zambia preferred moderate nationalists. More exposed to South African power and more fully integrated into the southern African mineral production economy, Zambia walked a tightrope, seeking decolonization with minimal destabilization. Both sought to channel the process of change in accordance with their own security concerns in a volatile environment, all the more so as the violence expanded in the Portuguese colonies.

☐ The Dual Struggle for Angola and Mozambique

Nowhere was the rivalry for African recognition and control over liberation politics so intense as in Angola. The question of whom to support in Angola plagued other governments through the 1960s and burst into a profoundly divisive inter-African disagreement in 1975 as Portugal withdrew. More than any other case, the Angolan revolution illustrates how the future orientation of a state may become a stake for other states.

No sooner had the guerrilla war against Portugal begun in 1961, than a "salient pattern of . . . intrarevolutionary rivalry" was established.[40] Two parties with distinctive social bases had organized in the 1950s to oppose colonial rule. The MPLA was an urban movement, Marxist in intellectual orientation, multiracial but mainly Mbundu in its ethnic base. The UPA (Union of Angolan Peoples, which would subsequently reconstitute itself as the FNLA) by contrast was rural, ethnopopulist, uniracial, and ethnically Bakongo and Ovimbundu.[41] Even before the insurrection, the leaders of both groups were well known outside Angola, having attended the various anticolonial gatherings, such as the All-African People's Conference. From the very outset, the Angolan revolution was an international affair, as Angolan guerillas received training elsewhere in Africa. Algerians, for example, began training the FNLA recruits in Tunisia in 1961 even before the end of the Algerian war. But this was only half the story: Other Algerian military based in Morocco were giving comparable training to MPLA personnel. Although it was possible to have a foot in both camps at this early stage, over the years African governments would be pressed to choose between the Angolan contenders.

It was Holden Roberto's FNLA that initiated hostilities in 1961 in northern Angola, taking advantage of an operational base in Zaire. The MPLA hastened to open up its own theater of operations, but it faced greater logistical difficulties. Not until 1963, when a sympathetic regime came to power in Brazzaville, did the MPLA have comparable access to Angolan territory—namely, the Cabinda enclave (which is separated from the rest of Angola by part of Zaire, but which also borders the People's Republic of Congo to the north). Both anti-Portuguese movements, however, threw themselves equally into the battle for African recognition. For example, Mario de Andrade, a founder of the MPLA, traveled to Algiers in November 1962 to seek continuing support for his organization, which Ben Bella granted. Two months later, it was the turn of Holden Roberto, who likewise won a pledge from the Algerian leader. It is clear that Algeria wished to support the cause of Angolan independence, but this implied unifying the two movements, a diplomatic mission that Algeria undertook without success. By the summer of 1963, both movements were invited to present their cases for support before the newly formed OAU Liberation Committee. The FNLA was better organized at the time and was duly recognized. But the internecine battle continued, and the FNLA, which had formed a government-in-exile (called the Angolan Revolutionary Government in Exile or GRAE), suffered defections. At its 1964 meeting, the OAU reaffirmed its support of Roberto's movement but also recognized the MPLA as an authentic anticolonial force. Like the Algerians in 1963, the OAU tried to reconcile the two to no avail.

Over the succeeding decade, therefore, both movements maintained their own external relations. The MPLA, now under the leadership of Agostino Neto, cultivated friendly relations primarily with Marxist and other leftist governments, notably including Cuba. The FNLA enjoyed support mainly from the West and pro-Western governments. By the mid-1960s, a third actor appeared on the scene, mainly in southern and east-central Angola. The National Union for the Total Independence of Angola, or UNITA, was the creation of Jonas Savimbi, a "spellbinding orator" who had represented the southern Ovimbundu in the FNLA/GRAE.[42] Savimbi managed to pull together an underground group that carried out a few attacks against railroad lines; its impact was relatively limited from 1967 until 1974, when it suddenly emerged as a significant contender for power. There is some evidence that UNITA had established a working relationship with the Portuguese authorities against the MPLA in the later years of the war.[43] UNITA did not receive aid or recognition from the OAU, which channeled its aid preferentially to the MPLA over the period 1966–1972. The FNLA received modest aid from the OAU and bilaterally from Tunisia, Morocco, and Côte d'Ivoire—that is, governments friendly to its principal supporter, Zaire.

None of this aid was sufficient to defeat Portugal militarily, but the strain of the colonial war (being waged concurrently in Mozambique and Guinea-Bissau) took its political toll in Lisbon. The turning point for all three colonies came when a dissident faction in the Portuguese military toppled Portugal's right-wing government in April 1974. The officers' decision to negotiate with the African nationalists provoked a bitter struggle for power in Angola that once again brought to the fore the old cleavage between moderates and radicals in the inter-African system. These divisions were much exacerbated by extra-African intervention, which overwhelmed a noble OAU effort to reconcile the Angolan antagonists.

The civil war in Angola was much like the earlier Congo crises in its impact on inter-African politics. The question of who would govern Angola fitted into the larger structure of continental alliances and ideological affinities. Each government had its preference in the event that a nationalist coalition should prove impossible; but the OAU sought first to achieve Angolan unity. Thus the OAU brought together Neto, Roberto, and Savimbi to negotiate a common front in January 1975. They indeed signed a trilateral accord and then proceeded to negotiate an agreement with Portugal that fixed the date of independence for

November 11, 1975. In the meantime, elections were to determine the shape of the government. The OAU's good intentions went for naught, however, as the intra-revolutionary fratricide burst forth again with a little help from the United States and the Soviet Union. The former approved a covert grant of funds to the FNLA that emboldened it to attack MPLA offices in Luanda. The Soviets dispatched arms to the MPLA to help defend its popular stronghold in the politically crucial capital city. Savimbi, who had been the first to negotiate a cease-fire with the Portuguese in 1974, presented UNITA as an alternative to the Marxist MPLA, thereby engaging the aid of such odd partners as China and South Africa.

In June, the OAU once again tried to avert the looming civil war by bringing the three parties to the bargaining table. This temporary detente was shattered in July when the FNLA assisted by Zaire began an offensive. An OAU summit meeting at the end of that month deplored the bloodshed and appointed a commission to work for a coalition government. All African governments adhered to this posture right up to the appointed independence day in November. In October, however, a new element was injected into the struggle for power. South Africa, which had long held an operational sector in southeast Angola (under agreement with the Portuguese), began an offensive of its own. By mid-November the South African march penetrated some 500 miles northward, and the MPLA was squeezed between two hostile forces. At this point the MPLA launched an urgent appeal to Cuba for military assistance.

Although the Cuban intervention was controversial, South Africa's offensive was the kiss of death for the MPLA's rivals. The aggression provided the grounds for several states sympathetic to the MPLA to break ranks with the OAU policy by promptly recognizing the MPLA government.[44] These same states also encouraged Havana to respond to the MPLA call for help. States friendly to the FNLA meanwhile called for an extraordinary OAU summit that revealed an Africa evenly divided into two camps.

Twenty-two states sponsored a resolution calling for withdrawal of all African and non-African states, a cease-fire among the Angolan combatants, and an agreement to set up a National Union Government. The other twenty-two submitted a counterresolution calling for military aid to the MPLA in the face of what they called "incontrovertible evidence about the blatant interference of imperialist forces seeking to dictate to Africa."[45] The groupings behind each resolution reflected almost perfectly the configurations that we have previously observed. Backing the FNLA were most of the francophone states: Senegal, Ivory Coast, Upper Volta, Togo, Cameroon, Gabon, Central African Republic, Zaire, Rwanda, and their northerly associates Tunisia, Morocco, Mauritania, and Egypt; the smaller West Africans—Gambia, Sierra Leone, and Libera—and the southern African dependencies Botswana, Lesotho, Swaziland, and Malawi; and perhaps less predictably Kenya and Zambia (Kaunda having previously backed the MPLA). By and large, these were states closely tied to one or another Western power. The coalition behind the second resolution was somewhat more heterogeneous. Its most consistent leaders were Algeria and Tanzania, both active promoters of socialism and aid to liberation movements. Libya (since Qaddafi), Guinea, and Ghana were generally to be found at their sides and Mali was often influenced by Algeria. Benin, Congo, Burundi, and Madagascar formed a category of sorts, all francophone states in which military coups had introduced a more radical orientation. The four other ex-Portuguese territories (Mozambique, Guinea-Bissau, Cape Verde, and Sao Tomé and Principe) were the newest recruits to this grouping and the small ex-Spanish colony of Equatorial Guinea voted with them. So did the Indian Ocean mini-states of Mauritius and the Comoro Islands, then under mildly leftist governments. Likewise Sudan, Somalia, and Chad were all in leftist phases. One can see that these states tended to be more dispersed, and many of them had little geopolitical weight. This group was bolstered, however, by Nigeria, which had reacted furiously to the South African invasion—more than any other government, Nigeria reversed an earlier suspicion of the MPLA in response to Pretoria's intervention.[46]

The summit met for three days without breaking the twenty-two/twenty-two stalemate. More than a decade after its creation and with half-again as many members, the organization still reproduced the pattern of radicals versus moderates that it had been founded to transcend. The deadlock precluded any action by the OAU; indeed it revealed graphically the limitations of the organization when squarely confronted by the radical-moderate cleavage. The split vote exemplified a recurrent feature of the inter-African system, a pattern that had earlier been evident over Algeria and the Congo and subsequently would reappear over Western Sahara. Although changes of government have sometimes altered national affiliations, the general pattern has been quite durable because it reflects two persistent alternative visions of African development.

The hung jury at the OAU left the way open for the matter to be settled on the ground in Angola. The military tide turned toward the Cuban forces, and the MPLA secured its hold on Luanda. The MPLA was sufficiently in control to win widespread diplomatic recognition. Within a month of the deadlocked special summit, the next regular OAU session admitted Angola to the organization. The radicals gained a new partner, but the underlying pattern was only marginally reshaped.

Since 1976 Angola has generally identified itself with the radical camp, but its foreign policy concerns have centered on the immediate environment. At independence it felt isolated, surrounded by Zaire, Zambia, and, via Namibia, South Africa. Zambia was the first to improve relations by backing away from UNITA. After two rounds of fighting in Shaba province, Zaire also moved to a rapprochement with Angola in agreeing to close down FNLA offices in return for Angola's pledge to keep the anti-Mobutu ex-Katanga gendarmes under wraps. This left only the southern front, but this remained insecure. South Africa not only continued to sustain UNITA, but also carried out military strikes and even periodically occupied southern Angolan territory, ostensibly to counter SWAPO if not to destabilize the MPLA government as well. With its southern provinces essentially a war zone, Angola clung to its Cuban alliance and focused its diplomacy on the Front Line issues of Namibia and apartheid.

These issues equally confront Mozambique and Zimbabwe, the other new actors in the subcontinent. Mozambique acceded to independence shortly before Angola—under similar circumstances but without a civil war. Armed resistance to Portugal began in Mozambique in 1964 with precious support from other African governments, most notably Tanzania, Zambia, and Algeria. The former pair provided crucial logistic support by permitting bases in their territory that allowed FRELIMO to establish fronts in the north and northwest. Algeria (and to a lesser extent Nasser's Egypt) provided military training to the earliest guerrilla recruits including Samora Machel, who became Mozambique's first president twelve years later. Consistent with these alliances, FRELIMO developed a socialist ideology similar to that of the MPLA, but it managed to monopolize anticolonial legitimacy in a manner that was impossible for any party in Angola. Thus in 1974, the Armed Forces Movement faced a united adversary ready to assume power and prompt to declare its affiliation with progressive Africa.

No sooner was a transitional government set up than FRELIMO participated in the founding of the Front Line States organization in November 1974. As an original member along with Tanzania, Zambia, and Botswana, Mozambique gave the highest priority to assisting the struggle in Zimbabwe. By opening its 750-mile border and transferring weapons to the guerrillas, it transformed the logistics of the Rhodesian war. Like Zambia before it, Mozambique paid a heavy price economically and militarily for this solidarity.

In committing Mozambique to the overthrow of Ian Smith's Rhodesian Front, the Machel government chose to channel its aid primarily to ZANU rather than to ZAPU. Mozambique entered the network of inter-African relations with a set of historically determined preferences that extended beyond the southern theater. A sentiment of solidarity with Algeria, grounded in comparable national liberation experiences and concretized by Algeria's early assistance, created similar policy preferences among these partners at opposite ends of the continent. An Algiers-Maputo common approach became evident during the OAU's Angola debate and in subsequent alignments over Western Sahara, Shaba, and other matters. More broadly, the entry of the liberation movements of Portuguese Africa into the inter-African system created new linkages from North to South.

All the more so did the independence of Mozambique and Angola strengthen the Front Line States on the Rhodesian question—now it was the Smith regime that was virtually encircled. Moreover, the departure of Portugal made the United States and Britain much more interested in achieving a settlement. Backed by a strong African consensus, the Front Line States maintained diplomatic pressure on the West and likewise pressed the Zimbabweans to form a single bargaining agent, the Patriotic Front. This contributed to the independence of Zimbabwe in 1980 under a coalition government led by Mugabe's ZANU. Echoing an insight familiar to Zambia, Zimbabwe's foreign minister observed that "while nations are free to choose their friends, they cannot, however, choose their neighbors."[47] Zimbabwe's friends were largely in the progressive camp, and its impact at the OAU has been along those lines; its most prominent neighbor of course was South Africa.

Much like Zambia fifteen years earlier, Zimbabwe felt exposed to South African power. The Mugabe government has steered a narrow course between principle and practical constraints. It has denied the use of its territory for incursions across the border and has maintained South Africa as its number one trading partner. Still Zimbabwe's independence has made the Front Line grouping one country stronger. The period of 1975–1980 redefined the geopolitics of the southern tier without eliminating its residual focus on liberation politics.

□ The Final Bastion

The remaining major actor in the southern subsystem is of course South Africa. It stands defiantly as the regional hegemon, a formidable adversary to the Front Line States. Governed by an entrenched white minority, elaborately integrated into the global capitalist economy, it harbors the most powerful military establishment on the continent. Its apartheid policy has made the white regime a pariah state—in but not of Africa; and it has held on to South West Africa, or Namibia, in the face of global censure. South Africa's neighbors are obliged to reckon with its means of military and economic coercion, however much they contest its legitimacy and detest its racism. The South African government has alternately pursued policies of accommodation and confrontation in its relations with black Africa in seeking to deter them from assisting the African National Congress (ANC) and the South West African People's Organization (SWAPO).

We have seen that the regional environment has changed significantly since 1974. Even prior to that, the geopolitical pattern evolved as Botswana, Lesotho, and Swaziland acquired formal sovereignty. These three states had been known as High Commission Territories under British protection during the colonial period. Virtual geographic and economic hostages, these states have been constrained to a minor role in inter-African affairs, including the campaign against apartheid. Nonetheless, Botswana became a "pipeline for escaping refugees and political militants,"[48] and it was a founding member of the Front Line States. Lesotho and Swaziland have likewise harbored antiapartheid organizers, policies that have exposed them to punitive military strikes and economic coercion. Although all three joined SADCC, none has the means for a genuinely independent foreign policy, and thus they survive in tense coexistence with Pretoria. The great irony of South Africa is that its domestic policy of apartheid runs counter to its regional economic interests. What the South African economy needs is a regional market. So long as Portugal and Rhodesia were present in the subcontinent, this need was largely satisfied. As explained in

Chapter 10, the black governments sought to deprive white South Africa of this economic hinterland by creating SADCC.

Although South Africa has made occasional overtures to assist the neighboring black governments in economic development (such as its ill-starred 1979 "constellation" proposal for regional cooperation), its main instruments of influence have been subversion and coercion. We have seen that South Africa invaded Angola during the civil war. It has continued to carry out periodic incursions while channeling a steady flow of arms to Savimbi's opposition movement, UNITA. Likewise, it has underwritten the Mozambique National Resistance Movement (RENAMO), whose sabotage operations have wrought havoc on the Mozambican economy. Indeed, the Machel government felt constrained to sign in 1984 the Nkomati Accord, by which it agreed to cut back its support to the ANC in return for Pretoria's pledge of noninterference. Likewise, Angola negotiated a similar agreement, the Lusaka Accord. But South Africa has not honored either of these agreements, continuing its clandestine support of RENAMO and UNITA. Direct military strikes have been carried out against ANC offices in Lesotho, Botswana, and even Zambia.[49] Violent confrontation between South African military power and the Front Line is the current manifestation of the decolonization issue that has characterized the southern subsystem.

Namibia remains the final classic decolonization case. From the perspective of inter-African relations, Namibia has produced an easy consensus. A single movement, SWAPO, has enjoyed unanimous African backing, and a united Africa has pressed this matter before United Nations forums since the 1960s. Concerted international pressure seemed well on the way to achieving South African withdrawal until 1981, when the Reagan administration turned down the heat. The U.S. government linked settlement of the Namibian question to a withdrawal of Cuban troops from Angola. This linkage provided South Africa several years of respite, but the undisputed colonial status of Namibia makes indefinite South African control unlikely. Pretoria will no doubt eventually accept coexistence with an independent Namibia. So long as the final bastion refuses to share power at home, however, the southern African subsystem will contain unfinished business. (See Chapter 13 for further discussion of politics in South Africa.)

■ CONCLUSION

The inter-African system reveals a mix of competition and cooperation, of conflict and consensus. African governments have pursued their national interests much as others have in the state system. They have been attentive to the distribution of power on the continent and its implications for their security and welfare. Although wars have broken out between African states in numerous instances, direct military threats to security have not been the foremost feature of inter-African politics. The most intense conflicts have revolved around civil wars, or the struggle for power within states. The question "Who shall rule?" (such as in Zaire, or Angola, or Chad) has been the most persistent inter-African issue, because states (inside and outside Africa) have viewed these struggles in terms of the overall distribution of power on the continent. African governments have sought to shape the flow of events, sometimes by direct intervention, more often by forming diplomatic coalitions and by utilizing the instrument of the OAU.

Although there has not been any continental consensus on who shall rule, there has nonetheless been an underlying notion that all African governments should collaborate in addressing common problems. From this sentiment, the OAU was created in 1963. The decision to transcend the rivalries of the earliest phase of inter-African relations produced an institution that has somehow survived a host of battles. Its formal organization is unexceptional: Headquarters in Addis Ababa operated by a modest secretariat led by a secretary-general; a set of standing commissions on various economic, social, political, and administrative matters, of which the Liberation Committee has always been considered the most important; regular intergovernmental sessions at the ministerial level; and, as its principal organ, an annual meeting of heads of state. Each year a state is selected to chair the organization, thereby thrusting its leader to the forefront of continental politics; during 1986–1987, for example, Congo's President Denis Sassou Nguesso became momentarily a key figure in negotiations concerning Chad and Western Sahara. In this manner, the OAU draws lesser powers more fully into the inter-African system.

We have seen that the OAU has had little success in solving Africa's most salient conflicts. Its peacekeeping force failed to keep the peace in Chad; its implementation committee failed to implement anything in Western Sahara; its special session on Angola only dramatized an even split among Africa's governments. Yet, from 1963 through 1981, the organization did succeed in convening an annual summit conference. Even after the crises of 1982 broke this pattern, the member states discovered the means to resume the summitry in 1983.

The OAU has endured because it does serve a diplomatic need of the African states. It has successfully mediated some lesser disputes, and it has articulated a common position to the external world on apartheid and economic development issues. It has provided a framework for the generation of common economic strategies, such as the Lagos Plan of Action. Most important, however, it serves to keep lines of communication open on a continental scale.

The OAU has exemplified both the divisions of the inter-African system and the expressed will to act collectively for the welfare of Africa as a whole. The dominant pattern of inter-African politics has been for like-minded coalitions to form around competing notions of who shall rule. Each of the three regional zones has had specific issues that have primarily concerned the proximate states, but allegiances that cut across these zones have produced a continental network of interactions also. Although it is possible to discern different periods in the evolution of the system, the period since 1975 has looked not unlike the early pre-OAU period. Several of the most disruptive issues of the post-1975 period remained unresolved in 1987, and some—like Eritrea, southern Sudan, and southern Africa—have entered acute new phases. At the same time, the resuscitation of the OAU, talks on the Western Sahara question, signs of a possible reconciliation in Chad, and the very need to deal in common with Africa's economic crisis may serve to usher in a more peaceful period.

Concern with local and continental balances of power will remain a constant. One feature that especially marked the post-1975 period was an increased incidence of great power intervention on the continent. Avoiding external intervention was one of the objectives to which African governments aspired when they formed the OAU. This goal has remained elusive. External powers continue to influence the distribution of power on the African continent. We turn to this dimension of African international relations in Chapter 12. Whether African or extra-African power resources came into play, African governments have sought to enhance their interests by shaping their geopolitical environment.

■ NOTES

1. For an early analysis of the emergence of trans-Saharan geopolitics, see Robert A. Mortimer, "Politics in Trans-Saharan Africa," *Africa Report* 26, no. 3 (May-June 1981).

2. The quote is from the official nationalist newspaper, *El Moudjahid,* in its issue of 5 August 1960 (even before the actual fall of Lumumba).

3. Immanual Wallerstein, *Africa: The Politics of Unity* (New York: Random House, 1967).

4. *Le peuple* (Algiers), 26 November 1964.

5. René Otayek, "La Libye révolutionnaire au sud du Sahara," *Maghreb Machrek* 94 (October-December 1981): 27.

6. Hervé Bleuchot, "La politique africaine de la Libye," in *Annuaire de l'Afrique du nord, 1978* (Paris: Conseil National de la Recherche Scientifique 1979), p. 76.

7. Cited in Timothy Shaw and Orobola Fasehun, "Nigeria in the World System: Alternative Approaches, Explanations, and Projections," in Timothy Shaw and Olajide Aluko, eds., *Nigerian Foreign Policy: Alternative Perceptions and Projections* (New York: St. Martin's Press, 1983), p. 205.

8. Olatunde Ojo, "Nigeria and the Formation of ECOWAS," *International Organization* 34, no. 4 (Autumn 1980). See also his chapter, "Nigeria," in Timothy Shaw and Olajide Aluko, eds., *The Political Economy of African Foreign Policy* (New York: St. Martin's Press, 1984).

9. Timothy Shaw, "Nigeria in the International System," in I. William Zartman, ed., *The Political Economy of Nigeria* (New York: Praeger 1983), p. 213.

10. Kwame Nkrumah, *Africa Must Unite* (New York: International Publishers, 1970), p. xii.

11. The phrase is from Ako Adjei, one of the envoys along with George Padmore, the Jamaican pan-Africanist who advised Nkrumah in this period, as cited in W. Scott Thompson, *Ghana's Foreign Policy, 1957–1966* (Princeton: Princeton University Press, 1969), p. 33.

12. Ibid., p. 61.

13. Ibid., p. 57. In May 1959 a more elaborate declaration used the language "Union of Independent African States" opening the arrangement to "all independent African States or Federations." See the text in Legum, *Pan-Africanism* (New York: Praeger, 1962), p. 160.

14. Y. M. Sule, leader of the Nigerian delegation at the Second Conference of Independent African States, as cited in Colin Legum, *Pan-Africanism*, p. 174.

15. Thompson, *Ghana's Foreign Policy*, p. 5.

16. Jacques Baulin, a French aide to Houphouët, has revealed that Houphouët carried out his own destablization campaign against Ghana and Guinea. See his *La politique africaine d'Houphouet-Boigny* (Paris: Editions Eurofor, 1980).

17. Mohsen Toumi, "La politique africaine de la Tunisie," in *Annuaire de l'Afrique du nord, 1978*, p. 115.

18. Ibid., p. 118.

19. Ibid., p. 126.

20. Mohammed Bouzidi, "Le Maroc et l'Afrique sub-saharienne," in *Annuaire de l'Afrique du nord, 1978*, p. 109.

21. *New York Times*, 27 June 1981.

22. The protesters were Cameroon, the Central African Republic, Comoros, Djibouti, Equatorial Guinea, Gabon, Gambia, Guinea, Côte d'Ivoire, Liberia, Mauritius, Morocco, Niger, Senegal, Somalia, Sudan, Tunisia, Upper Volta, and Zaire. See John Damis, "The OAU and the Sahara," in Yassin el-Ayouty and I. William Zartman, eds., *The OAU After Twenty Years* (New York: Praeger, 1984), for a thorough account of the OAU's handling of this issue.

23. The twenty-six states that recognized the SADR in February 1982 were: Algeria, Angola, Benin, Botswana, Burundi, Cape Verde, Chad, Congo, Ethiopia, Ghana, Guinea-Bissau, Lesotho, Libya, Madagascar, Mali, Mozambique, Rwanda, Sao Tomé and Principe, Seychelles, Sierra Leone, Swaziland, Tanzania, Togo, Uganda, Zambia, and Zimbabwe.

24. Christopher Clapham, "Ethiopia," in Shaw and Aluko, *The Political Economy of African Foreign Policy*, p. 80.

25. Article III, provision 3 calls for "respect for the sovereignty and territorial integrity of each State."

26. Robert F. Gorman, *Political Conflict on the Horn of Africa* (New York: Praeger, 1981), p. 55.

27. Our account has focused on the most far-reaching and prolonged clashes. Other problem areas could be added, such as the tensions between Senegal, Côte d'Ivoire, and Guinea throughout the 1960s; the strains between Nigeria and Ghana over the expulsion of Ghanaian workers; sporadic border closings; or the frontier dispute between Mali and Burkina Faso that erupted into war in December 1985. The latter dispute was resolved by a ruling of the International Court of Justice in December 1986.

28. Crawford Young, "Zaire: The Unending Crisis," *Foreign Affairs* 57, no. 1 (Fall 1978): 177.

29. Crawford Young, "The Portuguese Coup and Zaire's Southern Africa Policy," in John Seiler, ed., *Southern Africa Since the Portuguese Coup* (Boulder, Colo.: Westview Press, 1980), p. 204.

30. An authoritative account of U.S. policy is Nathaniel Davis, "The Angola Decision of 1975: A Personal Memoir," *Foreign Affairs* 57, no. 1 (Fall 1978). Davis was assistant secretary of state for African affairs in 1975 until he resigned over the decision to intervene militarily.

31. Galen Hull, "Zaire: Internationalizing the Shaba Conflict," *Africa Report* (July-August 1977), p. 9.

32. John Okumu, "Kenya's Foreign Policy," in Olajide Aluko, *The Foreign*

Policies of African States (London: Hodder and Stoughton, 1977), p. 138.

33. Richard Fredland stresses Kenya's "extreme addiction to capitalism" in "Who Killed the East African Community?" in Christian Potholm and Richard Fredland, eds., *Integration and Disintegration in East Africa* (Lanham, Maryland: University Press of America, 1980), p. 75.

34. Vincent B. Khapoya, "Kenya," in Shaw and Aluko, *The Political Economy of African Foreign Policy,* p. 155.

35. Douglas G. Anglin and Timothy Shaw, *Zambia's Foreign Policy* (Boulder, Colo.: Westview Press, 1979), p. 16.

36. Ibid., p. 189.

37. Only nine governments actually ever implemented the OAU resolution. They were Algeria, Egypt, Sudan, Mauritania, Ghana, Guinea, Mali, People's Republic of Congo, and Tanzania.

38. Marcia Burdette, "Zambia," in Shaw and Aluko, *The Political Economy of African Foreign Policy,* pp. 325–326.

39. Anglin and Shaw, *Zambia's Foreign Policy,* p. 35.

40. John A. Marcum, *The Angolan Revolution,* vol. 2, *Exile Politics and Guerrilla Warfare (1962–1976)* (Cambridge: MIT Press, 1978), p. 9.

41. Ibid., p. 50. Marcum notes as well that the ethnic divisions were reinforced by different religious sectarian affiliations.

42. Ibid., p. 247.

43. See Michal Wolfers and Jane Bergerol, *Angola in the Storm* (London: Zed Press, 1983), for an attempt to document this.

44. They were Algeria, Congo, Guinea, Somalia, and four former Portuguese colonies whose independence preceded that of Angola: Mozambique, Guinea-Bissau, Cape Verde, and Sao Tomé and Principe.

45. *Africa Contemporary Record,* vol. 8 (1975–1976), p. A73.

46. Nigeria's position (and Algeria's) no doubt influenced that of Niger, which provided the final pro-MPLA vote, departing from its customary affiliation with the francophones. (Uganda and Ethiopia abstained.)

47. Cited in Ken Good, "Zimbabwe," in Shaw and Aluko, *The Political Economy of African Foreign Policy,* p. 364.

48. Bernard Magubane, "Botswana, Lesotho, and Swaziland: South Africa's Hostages in Revolt," in Thomas M. Callaghy, ed., *South Africa in Southern Africa* (New York: Praeger, 1983), p. 357.

49. In this regard, Pretoria even advanced its own version of the Monroe Doctrine, claiming a "special responsibility" to police southern Africa. See Callaghy, *South Africa in Southern Africa,* pp. 4–5.

12

Africa in World Politics

A century after the 1885 Congress of Berlin, which carved the continent up into European zones of colonization, Africa remains of substantial interest to external powers. During the sixteenth century, the slave trade began to integrate black Africa into the global division of labor, but most of Africa was not incorporated into the global political system until the latter part of the nineteenth century. As Ronald Robinson and John Gallagher show in their classic *Africa and the Victorians,* Africa acquired new strategic significance after the opening of the Suez Canal made control of Egypt an important stake in British imperial policy. The scramble for Africa was triggered by Britain's response to Egyptian nationalism. Colonialism, in turn, was terminated by African nationalism after a relatively short historical period.

The legacy of imperialism nevertheless remains a strong influence upon Africa's place in contemporary world politics. France and Great Britain were, of course, the continent's most intrepid colonizers, while other European states claimed lesser shares. France remains a very influential actor in African affairs and has taken the lead in fashioning a close economic relationship between Africa and the entire European Economic Community. Since World War II, the two global superpowers have gradually increased their involvement in Africa. (On a more modest scale, so has China.) For the Soviet Union, decolonization represented an opportunity to forge friendly ties with the new states, especially where strong antiimperialist movements emerged. For the United States, African independence posed the challenge of keeping the former European colonies inside the Western orbit of influence. Just as the Congo crisis of 1960 was one of the major issues in inter-African relations, it also marked a considerable intensification of East-West rivalry on the continent. U.S. policy has often been dominated by the fear of Soviet gains; whether these fears are well founded has been a source of much debate among policy analysts.

Soviet-U.S. competition has been the most significant change in the external environment facing African states. Changes in the Third World, however, have also had an impact upon African foreign policies. The emergence of such organizations as the Nonaligned Movement and the Group of 77 has provided a framework for Third World collective diplomacy in which African states have participated energetically. African governments have sought to develop more extensive relations with other developing states in Latin American and Asia. Ties with the Arab world are particularly intricate for geographic, cultural, and economic reasons. The North African states are, of course, part of the Arab world, and many black African states have significant Muslim populations. Especially since OPEC, with its strong Arab contingent, asserted itself as a force in the global economy, the notion of an Afro-Arab partnership has received considerable attention. Together, the states of Africa and the Middle East constitute the geographic and political core of the Third World coalition that has tried to reshape the North-South relationship. Thus, African states, which individually can wield little power in international politics, have been particularly attracted to the strategy of acting collectively with other developing states. Yet, there is abundant evidence of the difficulty of Africa, Asia, and Latin America coordinating their policies toward the North when regional and national interests vary. African states must balance individual and collective interests as best they can in coping with an external environment containing stronger actors than themselves.

Africa is an important strategic arena in contemporary world politics. The great powers are interested in the distribution of power and they seek zones of influence on the continent. African elites facing pressing domestic problems and conflicts often turn to external patrons for support; and African economies are tied into a global division of labor that is highly constraining. In this chapter, we examine the interaction between African states and the major powers. We identify the interests that non-African actors have sought to advance in Africa and examine the policies of the African governments vis-à-vis these external powers. Our objective will be to understand how the rest of the world looks from an Afrocentric perspective.

The broad picture that is discernible from this perspective is the dialectic between African autonomy and external interventionism. Africans have sought to enhance their freedom of action while the great powers have intervened in accordance with their own agendas. Africa's interests in autonomy and economic development have been subordinated to the globalist logic of great power rivalry. The overall pattern is one of cycles of confrontation and quiescence. An early round of confrontation surrounded the Congo crises; the latter 1960s were a relatively subdued period. The mid-1970s saw a renewal of competitive turbulence, as the oil shock, the fall of Emperor Haile Selassie, the withdrawal of Portugal, and the reappearance of French air power all sent tremors across the continent. In the mid-1980s, hostilities over Libya and unrest in South Africa raised tensions at one end of the continent and the other. The economic crisis of the 1980s, moreover, has provided additional leverage for Western pressure on African governments. Arresting Africa's economic decline is a precondition for reasserting African political autonomy.

■ AFRICA AND EUROPE

☐ France

Plus ça change, plus c' est la même chose: Time and again, observers have been struck by the extraordinary continuity of French policy in Africa. The reasons for this continuity are quite straightforward. The African empire was one of the great exploits of French history. Especially since 1830, when an expeditionary force set foot in Algeria, Africa has loomed very large in the French imagination and worldview. By the end of the nineteenth century, France claimed control of vast expanses of the Sahara, the Sahel, and posts along the Atlantic coast stretching to the Congo in the south. Over the next twenty years, France gained a protectorate over much of Morocco and mandates over Togo and most of Cameroon. This extensive overseas domain was crucial to the fortunes of the Free French under General Charles de Gaulle during World War II. When President de Gaulle subsequently presided over the decolonization of this empire, he took great care to preserve a close relationship with *l'Afrique française*.

France fought two terrible colonial wars, in Indochina and then in Algeria. De Gaulle, who came to power in 1958 in a country ravaged by the war in Algeria, chose not to resist decolonization in black Africa. Rather, he turned over local political power to a generation of African leaders who had represented their territories in the French National Assembly. With the exception of Guinea-Conakry, whose leader Sekou Touré broke with France in 1958, all the colonies of French West and Equatorial Africa plus Madagascar acceded to independence in 1960 under leaders like Leopold Senghor and Felix Houphouët-Boigny who had strong attachments to France. Culturally, economically, militarily, and thus politically, the newly independent francophone states remained bound to the metropole, and successive French presidents since de Gaulle have cultivated and even extended this sphere of influence.

All the French colonies were relatively small in population. The largest by far were Algeria and Morocco in the Maghreb; the Sub-Saharan territories, therefore, were generally quite economically dependent. France's strategy was to maintain maximal influence in these states via financial and technical aid combined with highly personalized relations with the leaders. As Tamar Golan puts it (in her well-titled piece "How Can France Do Everything That It Does in Africa—and Get Away with It?"), de Gaulle and his successors have nurtured an atmosphere of "club" and "family" that has offered prestige to the elites of the francophone states.[1] Landlocked countries like Chad and Central African Republic, countries in need of infrastructure like Gabon and Côte d'Ivoire, sparsely populated countries like Mauritania and Niger, very small countries like Togo and Djibouti all have relied on the link for technology, education, communications, internal security, and even administrative personnel. These were the perquisites of membership in the club, however paternalistic the family has appeared to stronger states like Nigeria and Algeria.

De Gaulle's cult of national dignity and presidential authority appealed to many of the leaders of fragile newly independent states. Gaullist France cultivated this affinity by supplying the technical advisors and teachers that these new governments needed to build a state apparatus and provide basic services. The French astutely named this dependent relationship *"la coopération"*; it assured the flow of French goods into these markets and protected the environment for French capital investment. By supporting a common currency—the CFA franc—Paris assured tight financial links and a measure of monetary stability throughout the entire francophone community (only Guinea and Mali tried to establish their own money, and both eventually sought admission to the franc zone). Likewise, France maintained military bases, supplied arms, and trained the military and the police; military coups have rarely yielded any significant change in relations with France. Not only has France been a major military supplier to the francophone club, but its weapons sales to other states (Libya, Nigeria, Kenya, Somalia, South Africa) have ranked it the foremost Western arms merchant (second only to the Soviet Union) on the continent.

Under de Gaulle, all these arrangements were overseen by his special advisor on African affairs, Jacques Foccart, a rather shadowy figure from the intelligence services. Foccart's position, discretely sheltered in the president's office, was typical of the highly personalized relationship between the francophone leaders and the French government. When de Gaulle stepped down in 1969, Georges Pompidou kept Foccart in office to manifest his intention for continuity in Franco-African affairs. Only when Valéry Giscard d'Estaing became president in 1974 was Foccart removed, only to be replaced by a new aide (René Journiac) who continued the practice of special attention to the African leaders. Nor did the socialist government of François Mitterrand see fit to change this special relationship. Mitterrand's choice of a trusted associate, Guy Penne, as his personal emissary to Africa revealed how deeply ingrained this approach to the former empire has become. Indeed, when the Gaullist Jacques Chirac became French prime minister in 1986, for African expertise he called upon none other than—Jacques Foccart. Africa is important to France's claim to be a global power. The francophone elites, in turn, have become accustomed to this privileged treatment at the highest level of the French government. Such treatment accords them a visibility and international recognition that would be difficult to acquire elsewise. In return for France's flattering attention, they have reserved an open door for French influence.

What looks like cooperation to some appears as neocolonialism to others. What France has managed to "get away with" has been a series of interventions in the weaker states and a record of propping up conservative regimes.[2] In 1964, French troops reversed a coup d'état against the government of Gabon's Leon M'Ba. Gabon, now a relatively wealthy country thanks to minerals and offshore oil, epitomizes what critics call the *chasse gardée* (or private hunting preserve). France has stood by Omar Bongo, the autocratic successor of M'Ba, in spite of violations of democratic rights and dubious expenditures of oil revenues. The Central African Republic became quite literally Giscard d'Estaing's private hunting ground, as he cultivated a close tie with the brutal dictator, Jean-Bedel Bokassa. French suppliers raked in fabulous sums when Bokassa crowned himself as "emperor" in a grim parody of Napoleonic rule. Once support of Bokassa became too embarrassing to tolerate, the Central African army dethroned him with French complicity. The most prolonged French intervention came in Chad, to which Paris dispatched troops on several occasions during the endless civil war. The most audacious intervention, however, no doubt occurred in Zaire in 1978. Here Giscard's apparent affinity for pro-Western autocrats and his determination to spread French influence carried him beyond the frontiers of the old empire. During the second Shaba incursion, Giscard sent in the Foreign Legion to quell the disturbance and shore up the Mobutu government. These various operations were only the most overt expressions of France's capacity to exercise power in Africa.

The moderate francophones have welcomed this French role. Many of them have security agreements with France, and French troops are regularly based in Senegal, Côte d'Ivoire, Gabon, the Central African Republic, and Djibouti (the francophone outpost on the Horn). Their role is more to assure internal security than to defend against external threats. Only rarely have these bases been used in actual military operations; one of the few instances occurred when Giscard used the base near Dakar to fly missions against Polisario forces operating in Mauritania in the early part of the Western Sahara war. Yet, these attacks, carried out about the same time as the parachute drop into Shaba, revealed how extensive the French theater of operations in Africa actually was. An axis of strong French influence clearly extended from Paris to Rabat to Dakar to Abidjan to Libreville to Kinshasa. Another rougher line could be sketched from Corsica (whence the Legionnaires departed) to Tunis, Ndjaména, Bangui, and Kolwezi (where they landed). The Shaba campaign was the crowning episode in an effort to extend the French presence deeply into an area once dominated by Belgium, thereby to rival the more recent U.S. influence in Zaire. President Mobutu, for his part, gratefully accepted his recruitment into the club.

Although largely an extension of de Gaulle's conception of France's African vocation, Giscard's adventurism in Africa did draw considerable criticism in France. Whereas de Gaulle and Pompidou had projected a dignified relationship with partners of stature such as Senghor and Houphouët (Pompidou and

Senghor had actually been classmates in Paris in the 1920s), Giscard hob-nobbed with petty dictators like Bokassa and Bongo. Gaullists criticized the style more than the substance, at least until 1980, when they condemned Giscard's failure to thwart Qaddafi in Chad. The socialists offered a more funda-mental critique of interventionism, support for autocrats, indifference to human rights, arms sale to South Africa—in short of French alignment with the most retrograde governments in Africa. In contrast, the party's electoral platform stressed support for self-sustaining development and implied a new progressive orientation for France's Africa policy. Thus, when Mitterrand was elected in 1981 after twenty-three years of rightist government, observers in France and Africa wondered what changes might lie ahead.

In practice, little changed under Mitterrand, who himself had long been involved in the Franco-African network. Indeed, he had served as minister of overseas colonies during the Fourth Republic and had been instrumental in forg-ing an important parliamentary alliance with Houphouët-Boigny in those days of shifting governmental coalitions. Although Mitterrand spoke the language of innovation, he was prompt to reassure France's long-standing African partners, and he took care to include Houphouët's Côte d'Ivoire on his first state visit to black Africa. His principal gesture toward a broader and more progressive re-lationship with Africa was the nomination of Jean-Pierre Cot as minister of cooperation. Cot was known to favor a fresh approach characterized by such policies as "self-sufficiency in food, satisfaction of basic human needs, . . . multilateral aid and the globalization of French assistance, . . . humanitarian preoccupations, and distrust of the old guard."[3] Cot emphasized building rela-tions with the Front Line States, the former Portuguese colonies, and Ethiopia—all beyond the traditional francophone club. Meanwhile, however, Mitterrand's special advisor, Guy Penne, was assigned to cultivate the old guard.

Before the end of 1982, Cot was ousted from the government, but Penne was still in place (moreover, with Mitterrand's son Jean-Cristophe working in his office, the family ties had most assuredly won out). Most of the familiar patron-client relationships reasserted themselves as the socialists found them-selves meddling in Central African Republic, collaborating with Bongo's Gabon, sending soldiers to Chad, attending to King Hassan, and training marathoners from Djibouti. As the editor of the weekly *West Africa* observed in 1983, none of this should have come as much surprise. He notes that a close reading of the socialist program revealed that beyond the disdain for Giscard's safaris lay a policy "imbued with the idea that France's high profile in Africa should be maintained."[4]

One of the fascinating forums of this remarkable relationship is the Franco-African summit. Inaugurated in 1973 by Georges Pompidou, these meetings were converted into an annual institution under Giscard d'Estaing. Alternating between sites in France and in Africa, the summits have grown in participation from an original francophone core of ten states (plus France) in 1973 to thirty-eight participants (including some "observers") in 1983 and 1984. Giscard enlarged the circle to include Zaire in 1975 and such lusophone states as Guinea-Bissau and Cape Verde in 1976. He used the 1977 conference in Dakar to rehabilitate Senghor's old notion of Eurafrica and the 1978 session to call for an inter-African force to serve in crises such as Shaba. Mitterrand settled very comfortably into the summit institution while expanding it to even greater dimensions and utilizing it principally to orchestrate his Chad policy.[5] The November 1982 summit was particularly noteworthy in assembling thirty-six African delegations together with the president of France at a moment when the OAU was itself incapable of mustering a quorum! That France should be able to mount such a gathering each year is indicative not only of its special relationship with Africa but of the importance that its leaders, regardless of political complexion, accord to perpetuating the linkage.[6]

Geopolitics and history have determined this enduring French commitment to an active presence in Africa. As Algiers was in easy striking distance in 1830, so is Kolwezi and the Sahara in the 1980s. The forces that de Gaulle rallied in Brazzaville in 1940—and those that returned him to power from Algiers in 1958—have shaped a national consensus that perceives Africa as a French sphere of influence. The United States and (to a lesser extent) even the Soviet Union have acquiesced in this conception. What requires explanation is not so much these French policies as Africa's own considerable acquiescence in the maintenance of French economic and political interests.

Many factors contribute to explain African tolerance of the French presence, but they are most simply summed up by the concept of dependency. The states where French aid and influence loom largest are among the least developed on the continent. They are predominantly commodity exporters with relatively poor terms of trade. This weak economy supports an often bloated bureaucracy of privileged wage-earners whose position largely depends upon their command of the French language and technical skills acquired in francophone institutions. Cultural assimilation, ultimately the greatest triumph of French imperialism (even if limited to an elite), constitutes a durable bond between the ruling class and the former metropole. This link is reinforced by the political fragility of many of the francophone states, where ethnic divisions, sometimes reinforced by religious differences and regional fragmentation, render national unity precarious. Rising class tensions and splits between urban and rural interests increasingly challenge the ruling parties. Beleaguered rulers readily turn to external support systems for internal security, provision of technical skills, and financial bailouts. Chad, where French forces have come and gone for over twenty years of unrest and civil war, is perhaps the most extreme manifestation of dependency. Côte d'Ivoire, which lies at the other end of the spectrum economically and in terms of political stability, likewise has encouraged French private investors and technical personnel to stay in the country as guarantors of the regime.

For these states, France remains the most accessible and the most willing external partner. Even those governments that have shifted to the left in domestic ideology, such as Benin, Congo, and Madagascar, have retained military technical assistance agreements and have not left the franc zone. Moreover, even rebel Guinea ultimately returned to the fold because France was better able to provide knowledgeable assistance than was anyone else. Although a few deeply assimilated leaders, most notably Senghor and Bourguiba, romantically extolled the notion of *francophonie* as a distinctive cultural framework, most have simply found the French connection a practical necessity. In a world of scarce resources, France has offered the best deal to ruling elites facing a multitude of problems. Furthermore, the deal has looked attractive to newcomers like Zaire and the other former Belgian protectorates, Rwanda and Burundi, both of which, for example, have security agreements with France. Several other small dependent states, such as Guinea-Bissau, Cape Verde, Mauritius, Sierra Leone, and Liberia, have likewise sought to enter the "family."

There have, of course, been a few holdouts from this feast of Franco-African *fraternité*. The most serious challengers, as previously suggested, have been Algeria, Libya, and Nigeria. Algeria has tried with variable success at different periods to woo such states as Mali, Niger, and Mauritania away from the fold; the French intervention against Polisario was a particular affront drawing angry Algerian condemnation. Libya's most acute rivalry with France has been over Chad, but it has tried to exploit the Islamic connection in other French preserves as well. Nigeria has been most suspicious of France, as the French aided the Biafran secession, and is acutely aware of its encirclement by francophones. But even these competitors have an ambivalent relationship with Paris, for as de Gaulle perceived from the beginning, France offers an alternative of sorts to the superpowers. Algeria is still marked by an unmistakable Gallic imprint, and France is an obvious market for Algerian natural gas and migrant labor. Libya, likewise, seeks to avoid total dependence on U.S. oil technicians and Soviet military advisors. Nigeria sees commercial deals with French investors as a useful bargaining chip in regional affairs.

Hence France, whether under Gaullist, liberal, or socialist government, has been committed to an active role in Africa. Jean-Pierre Cot's brief fling in the Ministry of Cooperation revealed both the special assets that France enjoys and the constraints within which it must operate. In seeking to extend French influence to new horizons—Nigeria and Ethiopia, Kenya and Tanzania, Angola and Zimbabwe—Cot exploited the notion of a progressive, "Third Worldist" France standing up for Southern development in Northern circles. He wished to project France less as the patron of a group of francophone clients than as the champion of a new conception of North-South relations. This was, in effect, Mitterrand's version of the older Gaullist notion of French aid as an alternative to superpower hegemony. Even France's African rivals can sympathize with this notion of France's role on the continent.

The francophone core, nevertheless, reasserted itself as the foundation of French influence in Africa. Cot had to give way to Guy Penne lest the core group fragment and undermine the whole edifice. In this manner, Mitterrand remained well within the framework of his predecessors. Jean-François Bayart puts it best in explaining the residual continuity in French policy. It is not so much that Mitterrand has returned to an earlier scheme of things but rather that

> it would be more accurate to say that [Mitterrand's predecessors] have taken the road that Mr. Mitterrand opened in 1951 in managing the split between [Houphouët-Boigny's] African Democratic Rally and the French Communist Party. . . . The real continuity is older than claim the rightist parties, it flows from Mitterrand to General de Gaulle and his successors.[7]

If France is to pursue a global role, it must be rooted in Africa where the historical ties are deep and tangled. Gnarled as they are in ambiguity and ambivalence, these roots still nourish the French presence beyond the Mediterranean.

☐ The Idea of Eurafrica

No other European state has maintained an African policy comparable to that of France. Despite its extensive involvement in colonial Africa, Great Britain has played a declining role in African affairs since independence. Certainly London has remained an influential partner for such states as Nigeria, Kenya, and Zambia, and it has been a central player in southern African affairs, most notably regarding Rhodesia. Indeed, Britain has been embroiled in a series of crises, including the civil war in Nigeria and the expulsion of its Asian citizens from Uganda, that have required delicate policy decisions. Moreover, African issues have been crucial ones for the Commonwealth, Britain's favored instrument for the management of postcolonial relations. Yet, in fashioning the Commonwealth as their primary forum for Third World relations, both Labour and Conservative governments have elected to treat Africa as but one component of a larger scheme.

British policy was initially to channel change in ways that would least undermine its own investments and trade. Thus, for example, Britain joined with the other Western powers to undermine Lumumba and encourage the Katanga secession in 1960. By the end of the decade, however, British policy-makers saw their interests aligned with Nigeria's Federal Military Government against the Biafran secession. Despite an active lobby for Biafra in England, the British government supplied large quantities of arms to Lagos in order not to jeopardize its commercial preeminence there. The overall thrust of British policy, however, was away from Africa and toward Europe as it sought entry to the Common Market.

For fifteen years, from 1965 to 1980, British policy was burdensomely shackled to the Rhodesian issue. Several African governments broke diplomatic relations with London in 1966 over its unwillingness to apply force to unseat the minority government of Ian Smith. African governments turned their efforts to supporting a guerrilla resistance movement. By the late 1970s, Britain faced two hardy adversaries, black and white, contending for control over Rhodesia. Moreover, it confronted growing international pressure, notably from Nigeria, which had by then passed South Africa as Britain's foremost market in Africa, and from the United States, which under President Carter was eager to see majority rule. In these circumstances, a youthful Labour foreign secretary, David Owen, undertook a major negotiating effort between the Patriotic Front and the Smith forces. Spurred onward by a Commonwealth conference in Lusaka, Owen's successor, Lord Carrington, presided over the Lancaster House Conference (September–December 1979), which painstakingly produced a constitution and a cease-fire agreement. Ultimately, therefore, British diplomacy achieved a rare feat—negotiated settlement of a guerrilla war before either side was clearly defeated.

Britain's colonial legacy likewise entailed a significant stake in the economy of South Africa. These commercial interests have required a diplomatic balancing act between Commonwealth pressures for sanctions against Pretoria and pressures from British investors and exporters intent upon maintaining a strong economic presence in that country. Great Britain is first and foremost a trading nation, and its overall approach to Africa has been to do what is necessary to maintain markets. London has had its hands full reacting to political turmoil in Rhodesia, Nigeria, Uganda, and South Africa, leaving it little opportunity to challenge Paris as the preeminent European actor in Africa. More like Belgium than like France, it has accepted the European Community cadre (supplemented by the Commonwealth) as the framework for its evolving relations with Africa.

As a rising power, West Germany has expanded its ties, capturing a substantial share of the African arms market and opening up dynamic cultural centers in many African states in an effort to cultivate interests and links. Italy has sought to maintain a presence, notably in the Libyan arms bonanza, but it cannot project a major profile. Portugal fought the tide of independence until the mid-1970s before belatedly joining the era of decolonization. Like Britain, these Europeans have mainly elected to multilateralize their relations with Africa under the auspices of the EEC. Just as French relations with Africa have changed more in form than in substance, much the same may be said about the broader Eurafrican relationship. Nor is this surprising when one realizes that France has been the driving force behind the African policy of the EEC.

The Lomé Convention, which we examined in Chapter 10, is the principal instrument of this common European policy. Although Lomé III extends well beyond the continent, Africa remains the core area of an enduring geopolitical conception—namely, that Europe must preserve a sphere of influence to its south if it is to compete with the United States and the Soviet Union in global politics. This conception has not been limited to European strategists, as might be expected. African leaders have sometimes been more fervent Eurafricanists than have the Europeans themselves. No doubt, the best example is Leopold Senghor, the poet and theoretician of "negritude" who was president of Senegal from 1960 to 1980. Senghor had unusually deep personal roots in Europe. He had arrived in France as a student in 1928, earned the prestigious *agrégation* degree, taught school, and served in World War II before entering the French National Assembly in 1945 as a deputy from Senegal. By the late 1940s, he was a committed federalist, actively supporting unity in Europe, large federations in Africa, and ultimately a transcontinental federation. Senghor held an idealized vision of Eurafrican cooperation, yet underlying it was essentially the same rationale that appealed to the Europeans: It was a way of creating a third force in world politics capable of resisting the hegemony of the superpowers.[8]

Although Senghor would have preferred Eurafrica to national independence, the times were, of course, against this. Indeed, there was relatively little talk of Eurafrica through the 1960s, the decade of independence. Instead of federating, Africa and Europe negotiated over the terms of their economic relations in the two Yaoundé Conventions of 1963 and 1969. During the 1970s, however, the idea surfaced again in the context of the energy crisis and the fear of raw materials shortages. This time it was not so much the Senegalese leader as France's President Giscard d'Estaing who rehabilitated Senghor's old theme. At a moment of economic insecurity, in other words, Giscard evoked the complementarity of African resources and European technology that had figured in Senghor's thinking two decades earlier. (A third partner, Arab capital, figured in Giscard's version as well.) Whether emanating from Senghor or Giscard, Eurafrica was a symbolic term that sought to accord political legitimacy to an economic relationship that has been of great value to Europe. Senghor's idealistic version no doubt aspired to a more equitable partnership; Gescard's more cynical version hoped to persuade Africa that Europe was its best bet in the economic crisis.

Whatever its rhetorical intent, Eurafrica does describe a historically grounded political economic relationship of undeniable significance. Now that all four of the major colonial powers in Africa (France, Britain, Belgium, and, since January 1986, Portugal) are part of the Common Market, Europe will seek to maintain its economic presence and political influence through the multilateral framework of the European Commission. Each Lomé Convention has involved strenuous bargaining over the precise terms of the evolving economic relationship, but the grand lines of the relationship still reflect the pattern imposed during the colonial period. In this manner, Europe under French leadership exercises power in much of Africa and sees the continent as a crucial geopolitical extension of its own heartland. What the Europeans most fear, however, has been happening. The superpowers have become increasingly involved as new actors in African international relations. Although Europe (aside from France) has guarded the door of an essentially commercial exchange with its former empire, the superpower rivals have entered the continent via the door of political breakdowns.

■ SOVIET-U.S. COMPETITION IN AFRICA

The United States and the Soviet Union share an important attribute in common in African affairs. They are both relative newcomers to the continent. Their lack of experience and genuine knowledge has led both to make blunders in their African policies, but their military and economic capabilities suffice to make them actors to be reckoned with. Each has approached the continent in the light of its own rivalry; neither has been particularly attentive to African realities but, rather, has interpreted African interests in terms of containing the other. There is an asymmetry in their respective stances in that the United States is allied with the former colonial metropoles, whereas the Soviet Union has neither the advantages nor the drawbacks of partners. The Soviets enjoyed the rhetorical advantage of approaching the continent with a clear antiimperialist ideology. The United States, although laying claim to an anticolonial tradition, was generally content to defer to its European allies so long as the latter could maintain a stable presence in their spheres of influence. When they failed, as, for example, most dramatically in the Congo, the United States became much more visibly involved. Whether the United States was seconding or displacing its European ally, the concern was the same: to prevent Soviet influence, just as the Soviets strove to diminish Western influence.

Neither superpower simply allowed African nationalism to take its own course. The Soviets were more open to the notion of African nonalignment (because it implied some "disalignment" from the colonial order) than was the United States (for the same reason), but neither really believed in "Africa for the Africans."[9] Both tended to become involved in those states where the transition from colonialism to independence was most turbulent. Yet, it would be misleading to suggest that the great powers took all the initiatives. On the contrary, competing African leaders often looked abroad for support against internal factions or external enemies. The exigencies of domestic and regional struggles for power often opened the door to intervention. Sometimes, as the local context evolved, this door turned out to be a revolving one. The fact remains that the newcomers were poised on the threshold, ready to enter a new arena in their global competition.

□ Soviet Antiimperialism

Tsarist Russia pretty much lost out in the scramble for Africa. After Great Britain closed the Suez Canal to Russian ships during the Russo-Turkish War of 1877, Tsar Alexander III dreamed of revenge on the Nile. His plan was to secure a Russian presence on the Red Sea that would "thwart Britain's ambition to control a swath of imperial territory from the Cape of Good Hope to Cairo" and give Russia access to the headwaters of the Nile.[10] Although they never succeeded in their scheme for an Eritrean colony, the Russians did end up assisting Emperor Menelik II in defeating Britain's ally, Italy, at Adowa in 1896. This alliance of Coptic and Orthodox Christendom lasted until World War I and may even have won the tsar some trade-offs from the British in the Far East, but it left the Bolsheviks with a clean slate regarding Africa when they came to power. Indeed, the new Soviet regime's strongest asset in dealing with Africa was its ideological opposition to imperialism. From the outset, the revolutionary Soviet government championed the cause of national liberation in the colonial world. Africa was distant, however, and Lenin focused his early sympathies on nationalists in the immediate environment who could challenge British influence around the borders of the Soviet state. As Robert Legvold puts it, "for the first forty years of Soviet history . . . [Africa] stood on the outermost edge of Soviet consciousness."[11]

Only as the post–World War II wave of nationalism reached African shores did the Soviets begin to pay serious attention. The war in Algeria and its repercussions in Morocco, Tunisia, and Egypt; Nkrumah's push for independence in Ghana; Sekou Touré's sudden breakaway from France—all alerted Moscow to the opportunity to establish the presence that had eluded the tsars. The Soviets were attracted by targets of opportunity much more than by any coherent design. First Nasser appeared to be interested in Soviet support, then Sekou Touré looked eastward. The Soviets did their best to respond, but their early moves tended to be clumsy in an environment about which they knew little.

Egypt became the point of entry when Nasser sought weapons that a West protective of Israel denied him. Nasser's procurement of arms (from Czechoslovakia) led U.S. Secretary of State John Foster Dulles to renege on an earlier commitment to finance the Aswan Dam. Soviet Premier Nikita Khrushchev quickly offered to build the high dam and then backed Egypt during the Suez crisis of 1956. Western antipathy opened the first door for Soviet sympathy; the Egyptians in turn promised the Soviets further access to anticolonial leaders through a forum like the Afro-Asian People's Solidarity Organization. The Soviet presence in Cairo proved to be a slippery foothold as Nasser himself maneuvered about (before Sadat eventually totally reversed camps); despite Soviet arms and technical assistance, Nasser suppressed the small Egyptian Communist party and largely pursued his own aims. To a considerable extent, this pattern has been repeated time and again.

Guinea provided the first black African example of a target of opportunity. At first, the prospects looked even more propitious, because unlike the officer Nasser, Sekou Touré was a trade union leader who had had some contact with French communist cadres in "study groups" organized by the party in the colony. Moreover, the abrupt expulsion of Guinea from the French fold in 1958 rendered it particularly needy of external support. The Soviets were prompt to supply arms and economic credits and to invite Sekou Touré to Moscow, where he declared that "we are fighting imperialism and are therefore allies of the world that has chosen freedom and a place for all nations."[12] To the Soviets, Guinea appeared to be a vanguard country ushering in an era of revolutionary change. For a brief period, it became even more than Cairo a center for black

African militants from such colonies as Cameroon, Congo, Angola, Niger, and Côte d'Ivoire. But most of these radical nationalists never came to power (as moderate elements prevailed in most colonies), and Guinean-Soviet relations soured after a brief honeymoon. The Guineans became disillusioned with the quality of Soviet aid and trade (one notorious incident involved the shipment of snowplows to tropical Conakry) and intervention in domestic affairs by an overly zealous ambassador. Sekou Touré brusquely expelled the Soviet diplomat, leaving the Soviet policymakers "gun-shy and suspicious" and henceforth wary of the "unpredictability of African personalities and events."[13]

The rapid pace of African events nevertheless opened up other opportunities for Soviet diplomacy. The assassination of Lumumba and the ideological cleavage over the Congo led other governments to seek Soviet support. New candidates for socialist honors appeared on the scene, such as Modibo Keita of Mali and Kwame Nkrumah, as he began to pursue a more radical vision. Similarly, when Algeria came to independence under the romantic socialism of Ahmed Ben Bella, Soviet optimism rekindled. Yet, what became increasingly evident was that the Soviet Union's highest priority was simply to establish a diplomatic presence on the widest scale possible. Although the Soviets might have their African favorites, they desired satisfactory working relations with such states as Senegal, Nigeria, Côte d'Ivoire, and Liberia. Their goal was more to be recognized as a great power in dialogue with African states than to subvert the conservative governments in power.

Indeed, China took the Soviet leadership to task for its alleged betrayal of the national liberation revolution in Africa. The Soviets, in fact, were engaged in a dual rivalry for influence on the continent with both China and the United States. China, for example, succeeded in establishing a more substantial role in Tanzania than the Soviets could achieve. Chinese Premier Chou En-lai conducted a triumphal tour of progressive African states in 1964, presenting China as a revolutionary model. At the same time, the United States was succeeding in thwarting the radicals from achieving power in the Congo. In this context, the Soviets had little choice but to back leaders who professed socialism in order to establish their own credibility as an actor in African affairs.

Throughout the 1960s, however, the Soviet Union had relatively little to show for its efforts. Ben Bella was overthrown in 1965, Nkrumah in 1966, and Modibo Keita in 1968; Sekou Touré, largely discredited by oppressive policies at home, drifted back toward France. Conservative leaders like Senghor and Houphouët-Boigny proved to have more staying power. Looking for whatever partners they might find, the Soviets responded readily to the Nigerian military government's appeal for weapons during the Biafran secession. By the end of the decade, in other words, the Soviet Union's most active ally in West Africa was not a revolutionary regime but a centrist government in need of arms. The relationship revealed two major facets of Soviet policy: pragmatism in the choice of governmental partners and a reliance upon arms deliveries as its principal instrument of influence in Africa.

Over the next decade, the Soviet Union established itself as the world's leading arms dealer in Sub-Saharan Africa. From 1975 to 1979 alone, Soviet arms sales to Africa rocketed to about $3.4 billion, a fifteenfold increase over the period from 1965 to 1974; and during 1980–1983, a like amount ($3.87 billion) was again transferred. The bulk of this supply, however, has gone to only two states, Ethiopia and Angola, new targets of opportunity made available by local conflicts. Beleaguered governments, both subject to internal rebellion and external attack, turned to the Soviet Union (and its allies) in order to survive. To be sure, the MPLA had long considered itself a Marxist party and the Ethiopian *derg* eventually convinced itself of the same, but in both cases Soviet access was largely attributable to dire straits and a lack of alternatives.

The collapse of Portuguese colonialism ushered in this new era of Soviet involvement in continental affairs. Although leftist regimes had come to power periodically (in Congo, Benin, and Madagascar, for example) the abrupt emergence of three new governments professing Marxism (Guinea-Bissau and Mozambique as well as Angola) was unprecedented. The situation in Angola, moreover, took on the dimensions of an obligation—if the Soviets could not defend the MPLA, their reputation as a power in Africa would be dashed. The Soviet Union had long-standing ties to the MPLA as a liberation movement reaching back to the early 1960s. But even in these circumstances, the Soviet government proceeded very cautiously, for it was divided in its assessment of the stakes and the risks of intervention. Its initial policy objective was essentially to secure a place for the MPLA in a coalition government with UNITA and the FNLA.

Jiri Valenta, an expert on Soviet decision making, concludes that Moscow decided to "go for broke" in Angola only after the U.S.-Chinese interventions.[14] Until then, policymakers in both the Ministry of Foreign Affairs and the Ministry of Defense opposed intervention, arguing that it would endanger détente and could prove to be very expensive, as they harbored doubts about the MPLA's ability to prevail. The U.S. involvement, however, unleashed the critics of détente on the eve of the Twenty-fifth Communist Party Congress, placing Leonid Brezhnev in a difficult position. Valenta argues that irresolution on Angola made Brezhnev politically vulnerable at home. He continues: "A tough stand, on the other hand, afforded Brezhnev and his supporters a convenient demonstration to critics at home and abroad that détente was not a 'one-way street,' that the USSR did not 'betray' the revolutionary forces in the Third World, and that Angola would not become another Chile."[15]

A second major factor that reinforced Soviet resolve was Cuban policy. Castro's support for the MPLA was more intense than the Soviet Union's. Agostino Neto had visited Havana on numerous occasions over the years of the liberation struggle, and he and Castro shared a common ideological outlook. Castro perceived Angola as a test of Cuban revolutionary commitment and believed that he could enhance Cuban prestige in Third World affairs by rallying to the MPLA cause. Although the Cubans, of course, relied on Soviet material and logistical support, Cuba was not so much the proxy as the prod of the Soviet Union. For Cuba the stakes were clear cut: a gain or a defeat of progressive forces in the Third World.

Valenta's analysis of the Angolan intervention leads him to conclude that there is no Soviet "master plan vis-à-vis Africa."[16] On the contrary, as David Albright puts it, Soviet policy has been reactive and opportunistic: "Key Soviet initiatives have come in response to developments and trends in the African countries themselves and to the behavior of other major outside powers."[17] The scale of the Soviet commitment to Angola went well beyond its previous engagements because Soviet prestige was at stake in a way that it never had been in Guinea or the Congo. The pattern was essentially the same, however— namely, to capitalize upon changing conditions as the old colonial order crumbled. By the same token, the longer-term outcome has been quite similar. The Angolan leaders have become wary of the Soviet presence. Economically, the Soviet Union has little to offer, and the Angolans have continued to rely on Western oil companies to exploit their major resource. Meddling in domestic affairs in Angola got the Soviet embassy in trouble as it did in Guinea; and even in foreign policy, the Angolans recognized that they had to deal with the United States in order to achieve their goals regarding Namibia and South Africa. Having seized the opportunity of the Angolan civil war, the Soviet Union has been able to hang on in Luanda largely by the grace of South Africa's continuing incursions into Angola and hard line on Namibia.

Mozambique was the East African counterpart of Angola. FRELIMO declared itself a Marxist-Leninist party in 1977, the outcome of a process of ideological evolution during the anticolonial war. The government concluded a Treaty of Friendship and Cooperation with the Soviet Union at about the same time. Engaged in active support of the Patriotic Front in Zimbabwe and the African National Congress in South Africa, it needed military aid, which the Soviets could supply. Embattled even after its independence, it appeared a primary candidate for client status. Called upon by the Mozambicans to support their development, the Soviets responded as best they could, dispatching Bulgarian agronomists, East German engineers, Cuban sugar specialists, and Soviet factory managers to provide technical assistance. For their efforts, the Soviets requested a naval base on the Indian Ocean. Mozambique refused. In this instance, one might have wondered whether it was not the Soviet Union that was the "target of opportunity."

Certainly the Soviet government could only welcome the emergence of an ideologically friendly government in Maputo. The entire southern African theater is an area ripe for change and for winning friends by opposing apartheid. When South Africa strikes across its borders, as it did against Mozambique early in 1981, the Soviets must show the flag; when it underwrites armed opposition, as in its support of the National Resistance Movement, the Soviets are virtually obliged to provide weaponry. Thus, Mozambique received some $250 million worth of armaments over the period 1978–1982 (significantly less than

such states as Libya, Ethiopia, or Angola). Likewise, official exchanges between the two Marxist-Leninist parties have been frequent, but none of this has
prevented Mozambique from widening its range of diplomatic and economic
relations.

In Mozambique, as elsewhere, the Soviets ran afoul of their relatively
limited capacity to provide aid and investment beyond the military sector. President Machel traveled to France and Great Britain in 1983 and to the United
States in 1985 in search of new trade and finance; in between, he suffered the
ignominy of signing a nonaggression pact, the Nkomati Accord, with South Africa. Soviet assistance, in other words, proved inadequate to control RENAMO
destabilization. At the same time, it is clear that Soviet support is crucial to the
campaign of the Front Line States to overthrow apartheid rule in Namibia and
South Africa. African abhorrence of white dominance virtually requires the
Soviets to play a role in southern Africa.

The Horn of Africa is perhaps the only part of Sub-Saharan Africa in which
the Soviets have an active strategic interest. Lying on the Red Sea route from
the Mediterranean to the Indian Ocean, the Horn constitutes the southern
periphery of the Middle East. From the Soviet perspective, it is desirable that
the Red Sea not become a conservative Arab lake; hence, they have consistently
sought a diplomatic presence in the region. Even while feudalism reigned in
Ethiopia, the Soviet Union sought to improve relations with Emperor Haile
Selassie through the 1960s. They hopped on the bandwagons of Nimeiri in
Sudan and Siad Barre in Somalia when these military men seized power.
Somalia appeared well on its way to becoming the major Soviet client in black
Africa (it received some $180 million in arms deliveries and a major buildup of
naval installations at Berbera) until the coup in Ethiopia revised this outlook.
As the leftward-drifting *derg* made overtures to them, the Soviets changed
camps. States do not have friends, they might have explained, only interests.
By 1977, Ethiopia looked like a better bet (bigger, better situated, more influen-
tial, and arguably more ideologically reliable than the Somalis).

To be sure, the Soviet government, assisted by Fidel Castro, first made a
valiant effort to reconcile Ethiopia and Somalia. From Moscow the logic of a
solution appeared simple: Both states (as well as the Eritrean nationalists, who
were to be part of the deal) embraced a socialist ideology—secessionist and irredentist sentiments ought to give way to a federation in the name of the overriding goal of socialism. The logic, moreover, coincided admirably with Soviet
interests. Castro managed to bring Siad and Mengistu together at a meeting in
Aden (likewise a candidate for the federation in the grand design), but Somalia
argued that self-determination for the Ogaden (and Eritrea) should precede federation. Ethiopia preferred just the opposite. The logic of socialism failed to
prevail over that of nationalism, forcing the Soviets to choose between partners.

Even then the Soviet policymakers still tried optimistically to keep a foot in
both camps, offering Ethiopia arms and Somalia spare parts. They left it to Siad
Barre to denounce the Treaty of Friendship and Cooperation in November 1977

before finally undertaking a massive airlift of weaponry and Cuban troops into Addis Ababa. The Soviet shift was really *faute de mieux*; having alienated Somalia, the Soviets could not allow the dismemberment of Ethiopia. As Marina Ottaway observes, the "new alliance with Mengistu was of little use if it only meant presiding over the disintegration of Ethiopia."[18]

Ethiopia's military needs far outstripped those of earlier clients. From 1977 to 1980, the Soviets supplied nearly $2 billion worth of arms, almost quadruple what Angola purchased and more than ten times what they had supplied to Somalia over the previous decade. This military support, backed by Cuban soldiers, turned the tide in the Ogaden and much of Eritrea. There were in the mid-1980s an estimated four thousand Soviet military and technical advisors, one thousand East German security and intelligence personnel, and a thirteen-thousand-strong Cuban troop contingent still in the country. This commitment to the maintenance of the Ethiopian state and regime has become the major Soviet engagement in black Africa. A friendly government in Ethiopia represents a positive evolution in what the Soviets call the correlation of international forces.

A combination of internal turbulence and conflict with Somalia made Ethiopia dependent upon an external patron. Although they scored an easy hit upon this target of opportunity, the Soviets by the same shot implicated themselves in an ongoing match whose outcome is uncertain. Their main goal has become to secure the political reliability of their new partner in the Horn. Toward this end, they have persistently pressed Mengistu to form a proper vanguard party. In 1984, ten years after the overthrow of the emperor, the *derg* finally founded the Workers' Party of Ethiopia (WPE). Communist officials hailed this as an advance toward more authentic revolutionary organization, but observers noted that many members of the WPE's Central Committee wore officers' caps in the *derg*. The Ethiopian military may prove more loyal than Nasser or Siad Barre or Sekou Touré, but the fact remains that the Soviets are serving Ethiopian national purposes more than vice-versa. Frictions over the role of the party and the quality and quantity of Soviet economic aid (especially during the drought and famine of the mid-1980s) have arisen, but the relationship appears durable so long as Ethiopia is insecure about Eritrea and the Ogaden. For its part, the Soviet Union has executed the classic great power maneuver of inserting military capability into a strife-ridden area.

In exchange for Soviet aid, the Ethiopians have permitted the Soviet navy to establish a major servicing facility in the Dahlak Islands off the Eritrean coast (in effect replacing the one foregone at Berbera). In this manner, Soviet vessels have enhanced their operating capabilities in the Indian Ocean, waters of both strategic and commercial significance. Friendly ports of call are crucial to any naval power, and the admirals have no doubt had their say in shaping African policy. On balance, however, harbors appear to be a by-product of political opportunities rather than a major determinant of Soviet policy.

What is true of the Indian Ocean is likewise true of the Mediterranean. The area is obviously of strategic interest to the Soviet Union, and North Africa was the site of the earliest Soviet engagements on the continent. In North Africa as elsewhere, nonetheless, the record shows the Soviet Union reacting to local leaders' appeals. As an early practitioner of the art of playing East against West, Nasser turned to the communist world for arms. Fifteen years later, as Egypt veered back toward the West under Sadat, Libya's Qaddafi sought Nasser's mantle as pan-Arab leader and similarly armed his military with Soviet equipment. In each instance, the Soviet Union has enjoyed at best a touchy relationship with its North African partner. What Moscow has provided, in effect, has been the means by which these states have pursued relatively independent foreign policies.

Khrushchev considered Nasser to be one of the major Third World leaders. Thus, he backed him at Suez in 1956, as later Brezhnev would agree to rearm him after the disastrous Six-Day War in 1967. Until Sadat's reversal of alliances after the 1973 war, Egypt was by far the major recipient of Soviet arms—in fact, it received more arms than all the rest of Africa combined! To be sure, Soviet aid to Egypt was more a function of its Middle Eastern than its African policy. Most important of all, however, was Nasser's desire to free himself of dependency upon the West. Thus, despite Nasser's harsh treatment of the Egyptian communists and despite his more markedly nationalist than socialist orientation, the Soviets judged his regime to be worthy of support. The relationship did entail access to submarine-servicing facilities in Alexandria (which Sadat closed in 1976); while this was of considerable utility to the Soviet navy, it was not the rationale for the relationship. It was a side-payment in the larger deal by which the Soviets underwrote Egyptian antiimperialism.

Libya has replaced Egypt in this regard. Long before Qaddafi appeared on the scene, the Soviet Union somewhat half-heartedly proposed that it assume trusteeship responsibility over Libya after World War II. Instead, Libya was rather quickly granted independence under a conservative monarchy that accepted the United States and Great Britain as protectors. The discovery of oil subsequently gave the country potential influence, but King Idris had few international ambitions. The United States enjoyed the use of Wheelus Air Force Base, but otherwise nobody paid much attention to the country. Colonel Qaddafi's 1969 coup abruptly changed the givens of the situation; he ejected the Americans from Wheelus and embarked upon a foreign policy hostile to U.S. influence in both the Middle East and Africa. Especially after the death of Nasser in 1970, the Soviets could hardly ignore this new revolutionary regime. Qaddafi did not have the stature of Nasser, but alternatively he did have plenty of petrodollars. Libyan activism not only disconcerted the West, but it poured hard currency into the Soviet treasury. The Soviets have not hesitated to sell Qaddafi what he has ordered.

Thus Libya's 55,000-person army, the largest per capita force in Africa, has no less than 2,900 tanks (Egypt by comparison has 2,100 tanks for its army of 340,000, which is Africa's largest in absolute terms). Overall, Libya has the highest ratio of armaments to soldiers in the world, a very costly arsenal valued at about $12 billion, roughly two-thirds of which was purchased from the Soviet arms industry (which still leaves a pretty penny for other suppliers, such as France and Great Britain). Through this arms buildup, most of which is apparently in storage, Libya has displaced Egypt as the major African recipient of Soviet weaponry, far outstripping Ethiopia and Angola as well. Libya's maverick status is distinctive, yet the same pattern of policy may be discerned in all these "client" relationships. In each case, a regime that has broken with the past has called upon the Soviet Union for assistance. In each instance, the Soviet government has responded to the call in the name of antiimperialist solidarity. What was primarily at stake from the Soviet perspective was its own reputation as a great power capable of assisting radical forces.

The Soviet-Libyan relationship is aptly characterized by Ellen Laipson as an "alliance at arm's length." Noting that the two states share convergent objectives on many matters, she proposes that the Soviets "may see Libya more as a wealthy trading partner than as a reliable political ally."[19] Qaddafi has refused Soviet requests for bases on Libyan soil; only in 1981, when relations heated up with the Reagan administration, did he grant naval visiting rights. The Libyan leader is ideologically a pan-Muslim activist, certainly not a Marxist. The Soviets, in turn, gave only the faintest endorsement to Libyan involvement in the Chadian civil war, and they are aware that Qaddafi's destabilization activities elsewhere have been largely counterproductive. No doubt Soviet strategists perceive Libyan territory as a valuable staging point for potential operations in the Middle East or Africa and as a naval servicing facility. Through the mid-1980s, however, they had been unable to replicate the strategic access that they had earlier enjoyed in Egypt. Although Qaddafi's agenda was not their own, the Soviets found the military supply relationship a satisfactory instrument for maintaining a presence.

Far more than their backing of Ethiopia and Angola, the Soviets' Libyan connection is fraught with the risk of dangerous confrontation with the United States. Libyan-U.S. relations became highly charged during the 1980s. From an early clash over the Gulf of Sidra in August 1981 to the U.S. air attack upon Libyan territory in April 1986, the Reagan administration sought to bring down Muammar Qaddafi. These policies greatly increased Qaddafi's reliance upon the Soviet tie, and Moscow demonstrated its willingness to meet Libyan needs by providing SAM-5 missiles, however ineffectively they may have performed during the 1986 hostilities. Conflict in North Africa, with its linkages to the Middle East, has long been one of the potential perils of the superpower rivalry. One must presume that neither superpower considers a Libyan provocation worth unleashing major war; but so long as both superpowers pursue spheres of influence in the region, the risk will nonetheless remain.

Through 1985, the Soviet role in North Africa has been essentially as an arms merchant and a political guarantor. This has been as true of Soviet relations with Algeria as with Egypt and Libya. In the Maghreb, however, the Soviets have never become involved on the same scale. During the Algerian war, Khrushchev was extremely cautious in his contacts with the FLN. The reasons for Soviet restraint stemmed from European, not African concerns. Khrushchev saw in President de Gaulle a potential challenger to U.S. hegemony in Western Europe. For fear of alienating de Gaulle, the Soviets maintained a low profile on the Algerian question. Only when de Gaulle himself had come to terms with Algerian nationalism did the Soviets venture closer ties.

Algeria encouraged technical assistance, and the Soviets aided them to set up an oil engineering institute and a steel plant, but here as elsewhere the major bond became arms sales. Recognizing Algeria as an influential leader in Third World affairs, they maintained a cordial relationship but never acquired any leverage over Algerian decision making. If anything, Boumedienne challenged the Soviet Union to prove itself the balancer of U.S. power, especially in the Middle East. Algeria increased its arms purchases substantially once the conflict with Morocco over Western Sahara began, but the Soviets refrained from fully endorsing the Algerian position. They preferred a more ambiguous policy that allowed them to maintain a profitable economic arrangement with Morocco in the phosphate industry. Despite the fact that Algeria ranks third among African states (behind Libya and Egypt) in overall arms deliveries from Soviet stockpiles, the Soviet Union has never acquired any significant foothold in the country.

Soviet policy in Africa, it is apparent, has focused on the Mediterranean states. The bulk of Soviet arms transfers have gone to the northern tier of Algeria, Libya, and Egypt. Since 1955, Soviet influence has waxed and waned in this region intimately connected to the Middle East. The Soviet presence in Sub-Saharan Africa has been modest. Even during the period of severe strife in Angola and Ethiopia, only 10 percent of total Soviet arms transfers went to black Africa and 90 percent of that was concentrated in five states. The Soviets became engaged south of the Sahara principally on behalf of movements expressing the intention to build socialist societies. Although there is no doubt that geopolitical competition with the West is one motive of Soviet policy, the best explanation of the growing Soviet role, as Robert Grey argues, has been the call "to help defend the threatened 'states of socialist orientation.'"[20]

The postwar era has been a tumultuous period in African history. The Soviet Union has become caught up in these processes of change and has seized opportunities where they have appeared. Nor is this turbulence about to end, especially in southernmost Africa. The Soviet Union has become the foremost arms supplier to SWAPO and the ANC. These policies have prompted the South African government to proclaim that they are under assault from global communism. But Soviet influence within the ANC is modest and exists largely by default. The actual outlay of weapons has not been very great, just enough to keep the ANC going; indeed, some observers conjecture that the Soviets are content simply to watch the situation fester as an example of the evils of capitalism. By supporting the ANC, the Soviet Union has nonetheless aligned itself with the likely course of history; in simplest terms, the Soviet Union has nothing to lose from the overthrow of white rule. Change and the potential for further change have forced the Soviet leaders to become engaged in the African arena. They have suffered setbacks, but they have also demonstrated the capacity to project power—essentially military capability—onto distant shores. In the turmoil of the postcolonial era, the Soviet Union has acted like other historic great powers, becoming entangled here and overextended there, because it dares not leave the field to other competitors. Like the others, it will not leave the field so long as it has the means to stay.

☐ U.S. Anticommunism

Like the Soviet Union, the United States knew little of Africa when decolonization began. Through normal channels of diplomatic and commercial relations and through aid programs, it acquired a minimal foothold on the continent. Perhaps the most original feature of the U.S. approach to Africa has been the Peace Corps, which has provided a distinctive brand of grass-roots people-to-people technical assistance. Indeed, service in the Peace Corps has probably produced the largest body of Americans with a sound understanding of Africa's development problems. Top policymakers, on the other hand, have rarely had direct contact with Africa. Only in its seventh year in office, for example, did the Reagan administration for the first time send its secretary of state to black Africa, and other administrations rarely did much better. As a consequence, U.S. policy has often rested upon flimsy knowledge and stereotypes.

The United States observed the passing of colonialism in Africa with a mix of approval and apprehension. On the one hand, the U.S. heritage was anticolonial; the national instinct was to applaud the advance from European rule to self-government. On the other hand, African nationalism emerged during the cold war and challenged the hegemony of the Western alliance on the continent. As European control receded, some U.S. policymakers worried about the political evolution of the continent. Vice President Richard Nixon was present to celebrate Ghana's independence in 1957—after all, Kwame Nkrumah had studied in the United States before emerging as the leader of Ghanaian nationalism. Yet, anticolonialism was an unpredictable force, as the Ghanaian pan-Africanist himself turned out to be; rather than whole-hearted support of independence across Africa, U.S. policy leaned toward damage limitation. When the Congo erupted in disorder in 1960, the Eisenhower administration feared major damage to Western interests. Much of U.S. policy since then has been influenced by what Henry Jackson calls the "Congo syndrome."[21]

We have seen, in Chapter 11, how the Congo crisis catalyzed divisions within Africa. By the same token, East and West differed sharply over who should govern the rich but unstable ex-Belgian preserve. At the center of this controversy was the passionate and charismatic Patrice Lumumba,[22] fervently committed to the territorial integrity of his country, which was immediately threatened by Belgian intervention and the secession of Katanga Province. Although his government turned first to the United States for aid in quelling the secession (aid that was refused), Lumumba was deeply mistrusted in Washington, notably by the CIA, which promptly established a station in Leopoldville that hatched a plot to assassinate him. The Eisenhower administration elected to deal with the Congo crisis through the United Nations, an approach initially supported by the Soviet Union and most Third World governments as well. Moscow assumed that ONUC would assist Premier Lumumba in restoring control over the country; Washington hoped that the UN presence would allow pro-Western factions to assert themselves (and, by the same token, render unilateral Soviet intervention difficult). The outcome bore out U.S. hopes. First President Kasavubu and next Colonel Mobutu challenged Lumumba's authority; the UN force abetted Mobutu's coup; Lumumba was cut off from his power base, subsequently taken into custody by Mobutu's army, and then transferred to Katanga where he was murdered. With the help of Lumumba's internal enemies, the CIA got what it wanted; this grim episode marked the U.S. entry into significant involvement in postcolonial Africa. The Congo syndrome, the fear of radical nationalism in Africa, had already taken hold.

The perception of Africa as part of a "global East-West chessboard"[23] has largely governed U.S. policy since the Congo crisis. Although there have always been critics of this globalist approach, they have rarely prevailed in policy debate. Democratic administrations have sometimes cautiously challenged this orthodoxy, but the anticommunist impulse has remained strong. The Carter administration made the strongest effort to deal with Africa in regional rather than globalist terms, but it was seriously divided within; when Carter's national security advisor, Zbigniew Brzezinski, declared that "SALT lies buried in the sands of Ogaden," he revealed the irrepressible propensity to situate African issues on the Soviet-U.S. chessboard. As a result, the United States has often been supportive of reactionary and repressive regimes so long as they appeared staunchly anticommunist.

U.S. policy toward the Congo illustrates this proposition all too well. Even after the death of Lumumba, the United States remained concerned that his followers would seize power. The State Department and the CIA remained actively involved in Leopoldville in support of pro-Western centrists like Cyrille Adoula, whom the Kennedy administration deemed better suited to contain the leftists. In order to strengthen the Adoula government, Kennedy collaborated with the UN operation to end the Katanga secession. By mid-1964, however, with the departure of ONUC, civil war flared again, and the United States flew to the support of the central government now led by the ex-secessionist Moise Tshombe. Authorizing mercenary forces and a Belgian paratroop drop into Stanleyville, U.S. officials rescued the Tshombe government in 1964; when it appeared in 1965 that Tshombe was losing political control, the CIA encouraged Mobutu to carry out his second coup.[24] Zaire became a major recipient of economic aid and the second largest U.S. arms client in black Africa. Despite a dubious record on political rights and economic management, Mobutu was hailed as a "good friend" and wise leader for whom U.S. officials professed "a warm spot in our hearts."[25]

Such warmth was fueled by cobalt, copper, and other mineral resources, but especially by Zaire's sprawling strategic dimensions. The corruption of the Mobutu regime was deemed tolerable so long as it kept Zaire in the Western camp. Under Carter, the United States distanced itself somewhat from Mobutu but supported France in its Shaba rescue operations—the critical objective was not so much direct U.S. influence as securing the government's Western orientation. Belgium failed in this task, and the United States reacted accordingly.

Indeed, until 1975, the United States refrained from substantial involvement elsewhere in black Africa so long as French or British influence appeared adequate. When the Nigerian civil war erupted, Secretary of State Dean Rusk frankly declared that this was Britain's sphere of influence; likewise, the United States largely deferred to British policy regarding Rhodesia. Thus, the only major U.S. involvement during the 1960s was in Ethiopia, bereft of a European guarantor. Haile Selassie, like Mobutu, was a profligate and autocratic ruler whom the United States found an acceptable partner. To be sure, the emperor astutely exploited the symbolism of Ethiopia's long-standing independence from direct European rule. As host to the OAU and Africa's senior statesman, he enjoyed international prestige. Ethiopia became a major recipient of U.S. economic and military aid; indeed, before it became the number one Soviet arms client in black Africa, it had the distinction of being the number one U.S. client! The United States set up a major communications station at Kagnew (in Eritrea) that was useful in monitoring the Middle East, Africa, and the Indian Ocean. U.S. policy was to support the regime for its virtue of being anticommunist. The deposition of Haile Selassie was a rude blow, but the United States initially hoped to retain influence with the new military leadership. Arms flowed unabated during the postcoup transitional period until it became apparent that the left wing of the army was in control. When Mengistu reversed alliances, the United States discovered Somalia. U.S. policy in the Horn was generally comparable to that in Zaire, its objective to contain Soviet influence by aiding a friendly autocrat.

The changes in the Horn occurred in the midst of other major events that pushed Africa much higher among U.S. foreign policy concerns. Just as the withdrawal of Portugal changed Soviet opportunities, so too did it jolt U.S. policymakers into heightened awareness of the instabilities of southern Africa. If SALT was eventually to decay in Ogaden, Soviet-U.S. détente was first shaken by the conflict over Angola. Secretary of State Henry Kissinger interpreted the struggle for power there as a Soviet-U.S. confrontation; declaring détente "indivisible," Kissinger warned the Soviet Union against any response to his decision to release CIA funds to the FNLA. He thereby transformed an intra-Angolan battle into a cold war proxy battleground.

Earlier U.S. policy toward Angola typified U.S. ambivalence toward African nationalism. Under President Kennedy, the government initiated modest and discrete assistance to Holden Roberto, at the time widely perceived as the most authoritative Angolan leader. Kennedy, who in 1957 had distinguished himself on the Senate floor by a speech in favor of Algerian independence, did not want to handcuff U.S. policy to Portuguese anachronism. The Johnson administration cut back on this aid in deference to Portugal (whose Azore Islands provided a mid-Atlantic link on military flights to the Middle East), and the Nixon administration terminated it altogether. Arguing that "the whites are here to stay" throughout southern Africa, Kissinger advised Nixon to "relax political isolation and economic restrictions on the white states."[26] From Kennedy's to Kissinger's analysis lay a considerable gulf, but neither saw Angola as a major theater until Kissinger rediscovered the FNLA.

Kissinger's intervention in Angola was a huge fiasco. He miscalculated the capability of the FNLA, misjudged the local situation, and gravely underestimated the reaction of Cuba and the Soviet Union. Kissinger professed disbelief that his authorization of $300,000 of covert aid ("to buy bicycles [and] paper clips") could have sparked the Soviet aid that subsequently alarmed him. Yet, as Gerald Bender argues "the aid indicated that the United States had decided to meddle in Angolan affairs even before the transitional government had an opportunity to prove whether or not it could work" and reinforced "the large amounts of support which China [and Zaire] had been giving to the FNLA at the same time."[27] Once the fighting escalated, Kissinger overruled the objections of the State Department's Africa Bureau and pushed through a major increase in (still covert) aid to the FNLA and, at this point, to UNITA as well. Bender demonstrates that there was no significant difference in the overall amount of the combined external assistance—Soviet and Cuban, on the one hand; U.S., French, British, Belgian, Chinese, and South African, on the other—to the warring parties between July and October 1975. As we have seen, the difference on the external scale ultimately turned upon the willingness of Cuba to send troops. Kissinger's proxy failed him; his globalist analysis merely succeeded in creating a military solution to a situation that probably could have been resolved diplomatically.

The U.S. decision to intervene, however futilely, in Angola stemmed from the same fear of communism capturing African nationalism that had motivated Eisenhower's policy in the Congo. Kissinger had little genuine knowledge of Africa and overrode those who had more. He subsequently ran into a congressional roadblock in the form of the Clark Amendment, which forbade further aid to those who opposed the MPLA. Although this amendment did not prevent the right wing from cherishing Jonas Savimbi (who was honored in Washington as recently as January 1986), it prevented serious U.S. destabilization of the MPLA government. The debacle in Angola did alert Kissinger to the fact that southern Africa was not the stable bastion of white supremacy that he had imagined.

U.S. policy toward Rhodesia/Zimbabwe began to shift as a result. Until

1976 the United States had given little attention to the conflict there, limiting itself to a posture of generally backing British policy toward the breakaway Smith regime. Even this policy was severely compromised by the 1971 passage of the Byrd Amendment, which had the dubious effect of setting the United States in violation of United Nations sanctions against Rhodesia. Ostensibly a measure to avert U.S. dependence upon the Soviet Union for strategic minerals, the real intent of the Byrd Amendment (sponsored by an old-guard conservative senator from Virginia) was to help Ian Smith by the importation of Rhodesian chrome. Anthony Lake shows that the Nixon administration did nothing to deter this legislation despite its harmful impact upon U.S. relations with Africa.[28] Kissinger traveled to Zambia in 1976 to usher in, as he put it, "a new era in American policy" devoted to "self-determination, majority rule, equal rights, and human dignity." Racial justice, Kissinger now stated, was "not simply a matter of foreign policy but an imperative of our own moral heritage."[29] This newfound sensitivity was, in fact, a tribute to the changing balance of power in southern Africa; the secretary of state undertook one of his patented exercises in shuttle diplomacy in September. The package that he negotiated with Ian Smith unraveled quickly, and Kissinger was denied a final diplomatic coup; nor was he entitled to one on the basis of his African policy. On the contrary, the shift revealed how ill chosen the Nixon-Ford southern Africa policy had been. By counting on Portuguese and Rhodesian colonialism as bulwarks against communism, U.S. policy misread both power and principle.

More genuinely than Henry Kissinger, it was the Carter administration that ushered in a new era of southern African policy. UN Ambassador Andrew Young gave Africa high priority. Leaving a Rhodesian settlement primarily to British responsibility, he zeroed in on the Namibia issue. Both Vice President Walter Mondale and Secretary of State Cyrus Vance exerted pressure on Pretoria to accept Namibian independence; Young worked at the United Nations to secure Resolution 435, which called for a UN presence to monitor a transition to self-government there. This was the most sustained U.S. engagement on behalf of majority rule in southern Africa; it came from an administration that shelved the global chessboard in favor of a regional analysis. This policy eventually succeeded in moving the South African government to a negotiating conference in January 1981. Here, however, the process stopped, for the November 1980 election had relieved the pressure on South Africa.

Instead, the old era returned in the retailored garb of "constructive engagement," a policy proposal that earned Chester Crocker the job of assistant secretary of state for African affairs in the Reagan administration. Crocker offered an amended version of "the whites are here to stay" argument. According to Crocker, the Afrikaners faced an "awesome political dilemma" in the face of which it was not the place of the United States to choose between black and white.[30] In theory, constructive engagement was to encourage South Africa gradually toward racial equality and self-rule in Namibia; in practice, Crocker linked the withdrawal of South Africa from Namibia to the withdrawal of Cuban troops from Angola. Once again, U.S. priorities reverted to the specter of communism in Africa. In its sympathy for the awesome plight of the Afrikaners and its antipathy for the harassed Angolans (subject both to direct South African attack and indirect South African subversion via UNITA), the Reagan administration turned back the clock to the vintage Kissinger era.

Crocker's solicitude for South Africa, in fact, had even deeper roots in U.S. policy. As early as 1950, a State Department official observing southern Africa declared it "gratifying to single out a region of ten million square miles in which no significant inroads have been made by communism, and to be able to characterize the area as relatively stable and secure."[31] This relative stability was perceived as a valuable strategic asset, protecting the Cape Route and assuring access to harbors, communications bases, and minerals. South African administration of Namibia was an integral component of this apparent oasis of Western security. Through the 1950s, the United States was reluctant to disturb the status quo, even abstaining on General Assembly resolutions condemning apartheid. The Kennedy administration changed the rhetoric and voted for a voluntary arms embargo in 1963, but only after negotiating a weapons sale in return for a space-tracking station in 1962. Backsliding occurred under the Johnson administration, which was loathe to jeopardize the Cape passage for "ships en route to and from Viet-Nam waters."[32] Although apartheid has been a considerable embarrassment to U.S. policymakers, the realpolitik of anticommunism has overwhelmed moral qualms.

The Carter administration's emphasis on human rights produced the only serious attempt to dissociate the United States from South Africa. Carter's policy focused particularly upon Namibia as the most likely issue on which to make progress. Since 1966, the United States had formally endorsed Namibia's right to independence under UN stewardship, but in practice Namibian rights remained hostage to the larger concern to accommodate Pretoria. A mild case of the Congo syndrome afflicted Washington insofar as the South West African People's Organization was concerned. Like other liberation movements, SWAPO received some aid from the Soviet Union. During the Carter years, SWAPO was treated as a legitimate representative of Namibian opinion, and it in turn cooperated with the Western effort to implement Resolution 435. The Carter interlude demonstrated that U.S. pressure could have some impact upon South African policy. The return of globalist thinking to the White House in 1981, however, once again checked Namibian independence on the strategic chessboard. The Cuba-Namibia linkage realigned Washington with Pretoria in the view of Africans.

U.S. willingness to accommodate South Africa is in part attributable to economic interests. Many U.S. corporations have invested in the country, especially since the 1960s; nearly $3 billion in direct capital investment by 1983 constituted by far the largest U.S. holdings anywhere on the continent. Another $4 billion worth of annual trade is likewise significant. Investment and trade have certainly served to shore up the white government, but they do not suffice to explain U.S. policy. Rather, the United States has been soft on apartheid because the South African regime is hard on communism. However abhorrent the racial legislation of the Afrikaners, white rule has been perceived as a lesser evil than the prospect of Soviet influence. The fear of communist gains—the Congo syndrome—has shaped U.S. policy on southern Africa quite consistently, constructive engagement being merely the most recent expression of this outlook. Strong protests by antiapartheid groups did convince Congress to pass economic sanctions over President Reagan's veto in 1986; likewise, Secretary of State George Shultz met with ANC leader Oliver Tambo in 1987. The violence in South Africa (see Chapter 13) ultimately overwhelmed constructive engagement, but the Reagan administration failed to produce any clear alternative vision.

The commitments to Mobutu, Haile Selassie, Savimbi, and Pieter W. Botha establish a pattern that is replicated in trans-Saharan Africa as well. Although the United States has been relatively less involved in this region where French influence has remained strong, it has addressed the area as another cold war battleground. The crucial arena for the United States has been the northern tier of Arab states from Morocco to Egypt; here, as elsewhere, it has worried about radical regimes—initially that of Nasser, then that of Ben Bella, but especially that of Qaddafi. The corollary has been to assist friendly regimes: The heftiest aid has gone to Nasser's successors, Sadat and Hosni Mubarak, and to King Hassan of Morocco, especially once he became embroiled in the war over Western Sahara.

U.S. relations with Nasser's Egypt were often stormy, more as as consequence of Nasser's Middle Eastern than his African policies. But the United States acknowledged Nasser as an independent leader, comparable in stature to Nehru of India and Tito of Yugoslavia. However exasperating Nasser's policies, however extensive Soviet aid became, U.S. policymakers did not see him as primarily a Soviet puppet; over the Nasser years, the United States watched warily from a respectful distance. The relationship changed dramatically under Sadat, not immediately in 1970 nor even in 1972 when Sadat expelled the Soviet military advisors; on the contrary, Sadat had to go to war in 1973 to seize Kissinger's attention. Once Kissinger embarked upon shuttle diplomacy in the Middle East, however, the United States became extremely solicitous of Egypt's welfare. Sadat became convinced that he needed the United States to achieve his aims in the Sinai, and the United States poured military and economic aid into Cairo so that he would not change his mind. Sadat's spectacular journey to Jerusalem in 1977 and the Camp David Agreement of 1978 made the U.S. commitment even stronger.

Egypt's reversal of alliances was akin to and roughly contemporaneous with that of Ethiopia. The United States responded to Egypt's wants much as the Soviet Union did to Ethiopia's. In each case, the superpower disbursed aid for the sake of influence; in each instance, the African state sought to secure vital goals through external support. Sadat's shift to a pro-Western orientation was especially welcome in light of other events that reduced Western influence in the large Middle Eastern–Mediterranean region. Of paramount concern to U.S. policymakers were the fall of the shah of Iran, the Soviet intervention in Afghanistan, the possible vulnerability of oil sources, and the growing activism of Qaddafi's Libya. Sadat's willingness to cooperate with the U.S. Rapid Deployment Force was a strategic windfall in these circumstances.

Whereas the United States had grudgingly respected Nasser, it terribly distrusted his political stepchild, Qaddafi. It is not surprising that U.S.–Libyan relations have been strained. Qaddafi's antipathy to Israel and to Sadat's diplomacy and his excursions into the Sahara run directly counter to U.S. preferences. What is surprising is that the United States has paid so much attention to his adventures and misadventures; especially since 1981, the Reagan administration has treated a thorn in its side like a dagger at its throat. Despite its arms stockpile, Libya has limited means to change its external environment. Its short-lived gains in Chad, in themselves relatively meager, were more attributable to Chad's woeful weakness than to Libyan might. Its intervention in Uganda was a fiasco, nor have its periodic threats against Egypt, Tunisia, or Sudan had much effect. U.S. diplomats invested energy in encouraging a boycott of the 1982 OAU summit scheduled for Tripoli; perhaps the effort was worth the frustration it caused Qaddafi. In 1985, the *Washington Post* reported that President Reagan had approved a CIA plan to overthrow the Qaddafi government, precisely the kind of news to rally other governments around Libya; later, all U.S. nationals were ordered out of the country. The attention lavished upon Libya has been disproportionate to its capabilities.

Although Qaddafi's immediate neighbors have often been perplexed or irritated by his policies, they have found their own methods to deal with him. The most startling example of this phenomenon was the Treaty of Oujda signed by Morocco and Libya in August 1984. For years Libyan radio had been insulting the Moroccan king and urging his overthrow; for good measure, Libya supplied arms to Polisario. Yet, when the two regimes found themselves diplomatically isolated, the good king (as viewed in Washington) signed a pact with the bad colonel. U.S. oversimplification of regional dynamics had apparently left Washington unprepared for this local readjustment. (The treaty lasted for two years before new diplomatic pressures ruptured it.)

The U.S. government has long considered Morocco worthy of support. Although primarily in the French sphere of influence, Morocco accorded the United States valuable naval and communications bases until the early 1960s. Relations remained cordial after their withdrawal, and in the early 1970s the United States extended substantial credits for a major renovation of Morocco's military. This occurred on the eve of the king's march into Western Sahara; it seems unlikely that the United States anticipated Hassan's Saharan escapade. Once apprised, however, Kissinger gave a green light to the Green March. He reasoned that the king should not be thwarted in a project that promised—if successfully executed—to secure Hassan's shaky hold upon power. This initial tilt in favor of Morocco's ambitions has set the direction of U.S. policy since 1975.

The conflict over Western Sahara highlighted again the propensity to support friendly governments in dubious circumstances. Moroccan annexation of the former Spanish colony hardly accorded with the recognized norm of self-determination. Indeed, for this reason the United States has not officially recognized Morocco's claim to sovereignty over the territory. U.S. critics of Moroccan policy questioned whether U.S. arms should be used in what Senator Dick Clark calls a "conflict of questionable legitimacy."[33] Yet, even the Carter administration, which displayed some reticence about supporting the violation of Saharawi rights, ended up shipping arms to Morocco. Jolted by the overthrow of the shah of Iran, Carter yielded to the argument that Moroccan defeat would endanger U.S. interests. The Reagan administration shared none of its predecessor's qualms and threw itself wholeheartedly behind Morocco.

To assert that an independent Western Sahara would be harmful to U.S. interests is unconvincing. The issue has not been the fate of Western Sahara but rather the fate of the Moroccan monarchy. Morocco, like South Africa, is a strategically valuable asset to the West. Its position at the gateway to the Mediterranean and en route to the Gulf (for the Rapid Deployment Force, subsequently renamed the Central Command) is attractive on the East-West chessboard. In this perspective, Hassan's stakes became U.S. stakes, for he appeared the most reliable guarantor of pro-Western policies.

Sympathy for the king took its toll upon U.S. relations with Algeria, which never have been very good in any case. Policy toward Algeria illustrates quite well some of the shortcomings of the globalist approach to Africa. When inserted onto the global chessboard, Algeria looks like a Soviet gain: For a long time, it acquired most of its armaments from Moscow, and it pursued a vigorous antiimperialist foreign policy, loudly criticizing U.S. policy in Vietnam, in Central America, in the Middle East, in the Congo, Angola, and South Africa. Yet, as we have seen, Soviet interests do not determine Algerian policy, nor has the Soviet Union acquired significant strategic advantages there. Moreover, Algeria's trade patterns are virtually entirely with the West, and for a period in the late 1970s the United States was its major trading partner (for exports of oil and natural gas). The globalist model can make little sense of these data. The regionalist model readily attributes Algerian support of national liberation movements to its own historical experience, its engagement behind Polisario to the immediate geopolitical environment, and its trade pattern to economic pragmatism. Algeria is a radical nationalist regime with which the United States should be able to do business diplomatically as well as economically (as was demonstrated graphically by Algerian mediation during the Iranian hostage crisis). The dominance of globalist over regionalist analysis, however, had made such pragmatic relations difficult to achieve.

As we saw in Chapter 11, the wars in Western Sahara and Chad became major issues in African international relations. The instabilities triggered by these conflicts affected many states in trans-Saharan Africa and beyond. They challenged the diplomatic ingenuity of Africans and others to come up with fresh approaches to evolving power relations on the continent. The U.S. government neglected to bring much fresh thought to these problems in trans-Saharan Africa. Just as earlier it approached difficult transitions in the Congo/Zaire and Angola with simple models of East-West competition, so too did U.S. policy toward the Maghreb settle for simplified categories of friends and enemies. The elevation of King Hassan to the status of guardian of Western interests in northern Africa actually constrained U.S. options. The policy was perfectly representative, however, of the anticommunist guideline that has generally governed the U.S. approach to Africa.

Soviet and U.S. strategic policies, therefore, look quite like mirror images. The United States has tried to contain Soviet influence, whereas the Soviet Union has sought to establish a presence in the wake of colonial rule. Both states have sought to channel the changes of the postcolonial era in directions favorable to their own interests. The Soviets have capitalized upon antiimperialist sentiment when they could, and the Americans have all too often invested in conservative regimes. Neither superpower has demonstrated much inclination to leave "Africa to the Africans," whereas both have largely respected France's residual sphere of influence. All three have exercised the classic role of great powers toward weak states, intervening in an environment highly susceptible to external influence, sometimes directly and sometimes through proxies. But the African governments, in turn, have used their juridical authority to control access to their systems in order to maximize their own bargaining power vis-à-vis their external supporters. African insecurities and rivalries have exposed the continent to substantial foreign influence, but the outsiders do not have free rein (let alone reign).

Economic dependency, the legacy of Africa's incorporation into the global economy during the imperialist era, remains a major determinant of the constraints upon African governments. Access to resources, markets, and investment opportunities are an important part of external calculations, especially on the part of Europe. By the same token, economic fragility is a major reason that African elites call upon extra-African patrons. The fact remains that the major foreign interventions—in Congo/Zaire, in Ethiopia, in Chad, Morocco, and elsewhere—have all occurred in the context of political crises (secession, civil war, annexation) and breakdowns. Perhaps one should distinguish between crisis intervention and the sort of "permanent intervention" that France has carried out in Côte d'Ivoire or Gabon or Djibouti. The latter does reflect an essentially economic form of dependence. Crisis intervention often entails economic stress, but economic interests do not suffice to explain these cases. The strategic rivalry of East and West and the willingness of competing African elites to exploit that rivalry are required to explain these more spectacular episodes of impingement upon the continent.

■ CONCLUSION:
AFRICA AMONG THE LESSER POWERS

In this chapter, we have focused upon unequal relationships between African states and various great powers. The Europeans and the superpowers are not, of course, the only external actors to pursue interests in Africa. We have looked very briefly at Chinese policy in Africa. China has wooed African leaders assiduously and has been a significant donor of economic aid. During the 1970s, for example, China committed $1.8 billion in assistance to Africa, nearly twice what the Soviet Union extended over the same period (arms transfers excluded). The largest portion of this aid went to Tanzania and Zambia to build the TanZam railroad. Long active in southern Africa, during the 1980s China increased its profile in West Africa. China has been involved in Africa primarily to counter the Soviet Union, which it has characterized as the "tiger" entering Africa at the very moment that the Western "wolf" was being repelled.[34] Chinese activity, for example in Angola, has occasionally served to trigger Soviet countermoves, but its overall impact upon African affairs has been relatively limited.

Much the same generalization applies to other external actors such as Japan, Canada, the Scandinavians, and Israel. As elsewhere in the world, Japan has profitably extended its markets in Africa but has otherwise been only marginally involved. Canada has developed a constructive and respected aid program relying largely upon Québecois citizens to win friends in francophone Africa. The Swedes have given particular attention to struggling democracies like Botswana and to populist governments like that of Nyerere, more out of conscience about Northern obligations to development than any other motive. Politically, Israel has been the most deeply involved of these secondary powers. It established substantial aid programs in over thirty black African countries, exporting Israeli expertise in agriculture, cooperatives, water management, engineering, and security training. As Michael Curtis observes, "For Israel this set of relationships meant enlarging its circle of international contacts with the hope that African countries would support—or at least not oppose—Israel's struggle for existence."[35] Israel was quite successful in cultivating such contacts until the Six-Day War; after 1967, Arab pressure focusing on the issue of Israeli occupation of Egyptian territory began to erode Israel's ties. The Yom Kippur war and its repercussions upon oil politics virtually wiped out Israel's diplomatic network, largely nullifying its investment in African solidarity at the United Nations. The aid and trade relationship did not entirely disappear, however, and by the 1980s a new lower-profile presence was back in place. Israel's efforts to win back friends in black Africa have been jeopardized by limited but imprudent military and economic ties with South Africa.

Just as Israel sought to win friends in Africa, so have the Arab states of the Middle East. In many ways, their task was much easier. As eight African states are actually members of the Arab League, Afro-Arab solidarity is an obvious notion. Moreover, many other African societies have large Muslim populations.

Over the past decade, the number of black Africans making the religious pilgrimage to Mecca has grown steadily. The establishment of the Islamic Conference has provided a forum for closer contacts. These cultural ties create affinities that such Middle Eastern actors as Saudi Arabia have exploited. King Faisal, for example, traveled to Guinea and Mali (as well as to Tunisia and Morocco) in 1966 and invited the presidents of Niger and Sudan to his country the same year. This diplomatic offensive toward Muslim communities in Africa was a precursor of much more active efforts to court African leaders in the 1970s. OPEC diplomacy after 1973 added a new dimension to the Afro-Arab relationship, as both sets of parties adjusted to new economic conditions. Brimming coffers in Saudi Arabia, Kuwait, and the Emirates created opportunities for and expectations of enhanced Afro-Arab solidarity.

Such expectations were only partly met. New financial institutions, such as the Arab Bank for Economic Development in Africa, the Arab-African Technical Assistance Fund, the Islamic Development Bank, and the OPEC Special Fund, were established. So too were bilateral Saudi and Kuwaiti aid programs. But the bulk of the disbursements went to a small number of Arabo-Muslim states (Egypt receiving the lion's share).[36] An Afro-Arab summit was convened in March 1977 in recognition of the dissatisfaction of many African governments, and new pledges of assistance were extended. Nevertheless, the aid flow never achieved proportions adequate to sustain a major new Afro-Arab connection. For the African scholar Dunstan Wai, African hopes of Arab largesse proved to be "misplaced optimism"; for the Arab donors, neither material interest nor sentiment of solidarity motivated a larger-scale involvement in Africa.[37]

Of the Middle Eastern governments, only Saudi Arabia has become a significant actor in African affairs, pursuing specific national interests in the Horn and in northwest Africa. In the Horn, the Saudis have adopted Somalia since its break with the Soviet Union. Saudi Arabia purchases most of Somalia's livestock exports and has given large amounts of aid for military and other needs. Likewise, the Saudi government has meddled in the complex Eritrean conflict supporting Muslim elements hostile to the *derg*. Its largest commitment, however, has been to Morocco for which it has picked up much of the bill of the Saharan war. The Saudi throne harbors a strong concern for the welfare of its fellow monarch as another conservative force in Arab world affairs. The Saudi political investment in Morocco is designed to balance Algeria as that in the Horn is designed to contain Ethiopia. For the Saudis, the chessboard is regional rather than global, but their efforts have largely reinforced Western preferences.

Though on a lesser scale, the Saudis have become involved in Africa for much the same reasons as France, the Soviet Union, or the United States. They have committed resources to help people whom they view as friendly to their own interests. Such is the overall pattern of Africa's place in world politics. Africa has been an arena of competition in which stronger powers have intervened militarily and economically with relative ease. In most cases, African governments, or embattled elites within African countries, have sought external support, and the stronger powers have often hastened to respond to their friends in need.

Economic scarcity and political fragility have made Africa vulnerable to foreign influence. Because the external powers act competitively, however, African actors have been able to retain some margin for maneuver. The distribution of power in the North is sufficiently different from what it was in the heyday of imperialism to permit Africa greater freedom than it formerly had. Although Africa clearly remains subject to foreign intervention, many African governments do have the means at least to regulate the ebb and flow of external influence.

African governments would, of course, prefer to have more impact upon the external environment than they presently have. The only feasible means to this end is collective action. This was one of the main reasons that African states created the OAU in 1963. The OAU has served in some instances to articulate common African positions, notably on decolonization and apartheid, that have had influence on the policies of external powers. On many issues, however, the OAU has been divided and its influence accordingly neutralized. In any case, the OAU is a necessary but not a sufficient instrument to promote collective African interests. The charter of the OAU (Article III, section 7) explicitly commits the member states to a policy of nonalignment. Participation in the activity of the Nonaligned Movement and of the related Group of 77 has proven to be the principal means by which African states have sought to achieve a voice in international decision making.

Africa's role in the evolution of the NAM has been substantial. Four of the eight summit meetings of this Third World organization have been held on African soil. Twenty-five Asian, African, Latin American, and Mediterranean states formed the NAM in 1961; of these, eleven were African governments. The founding meeting was held in Belgrade, at the initiative of Yugoslavia's President Josip Broz Tito, and focused its attention upon the dangers of the cold war and nuclear testing. The next three summits, however, took place in Africa and shifted the focus of the movement to issues of decolonization and international economic reform. When the second summit convened in Cairo in 1964, nineteen more African governments participated, in accordance with the OAU's charter principle of nonalignment. Well over half the membership (which climbed to a total of forty-seven) was African, and the conference resolutions focused less on cold war mediation than on the evils of superpower intervention in the Third World and the need to promote Third World economic development.

Tanzania and Zambia hosted the next two meetings, which firmly established the NAM as the principal vehicle of Third World collective diplomacy. President Nyerere urged the nonaligned states to return to the practice of regular meetings by calling a preparatory meeting in Dar es Salaam in April 1970. This conference led to the third summit meeting, held in Lusaka five months later. Here President Kaunda placed southern African issues (Angola, Mozambique, Rhodesia, Namibia, South Africa) at the center of the nonaligned agenda. The

Lusaka meeting also issued a Declaration on Nonalignment and Economic Progress, which identified the structural constraints upon development that hampered African and other Third World economies. Economic issues, in turn, occupied an important place at the subsequent summit meeting held in Algiers in 1973 (which gave rise, as we saw in Chapter 10, to the NIEO resolutions). African states thus seized upon the organizational framework of the larger NAM to bring their policy concerns to the attention of the more powerful governments of the industrial North.

The NAM was also instrumental in creating the other major vehicle of collective southern diplomacy, the Group of 77; the nonaligned sponsored the initiative that gave rise to the 1964 conference at which the Group of 77 took form. African governments have played a key role in sustaining Group of 77 activities. African diplomats, like Kenneth Dadzie of Ghana and Akporode Clark of Nigeria, have provided leadership within the Group. Key meetings have taken place in Algiers and Arusha, that in Arusha aptly devoted to the strategy of Third World collective self-reliance.

In 1986, the NAM returned to Africa to hold its eighth summit. This time the site was Harare in independent Zimbabwe; coupled with a prior foreign ministers' session in Luanda, the Harare summit symbolized the progress that Africa has made in the overthrow of colonialism. But the unfinished business of majority rule in Namibia and South Africa remained before the 1986 meeting, which pledged itself to the creation of an Africa Fund to assist the Front Line States against the adverse effects of retaliation from South Africa. The presidency of the movement passed to Robert Mugabe of Zimbabwe, who expressed his intention to utilize the organization to its fullest potential on the South African question. For Mugabe, as for other African leaders, the NAM has the great virtue of being a movement of relative equals that can challenge the heritage of manifestly unequal relations that has prevailed historically in Africa as it has prevailed more generally in North-South relations.

The United Nations is, in principle, an organization founded upon the premise of equality. It is accordingly a forum to which African policymakers have given much attention. As its inception, the UN had but four African members (Egypt, Ethiopia, Liberia, and South Africa), but since 1960 Africa has been an integral part of a Third World majority in the General Assembly. Africa now controls, by gentleman's agreement, two nonpermanent seats on the Security Council. Concerting their positions in the United Nations, generally with the support of Asian and Latin American states, Africans have used UN resolutions to bring sanctions against Southern Rhodesia, an arms embargo against South Africa, and recognition to SWAPO as the legitimate representative of the Namibian people as well as to mobilize support on a host of other political and economic issues. As small states with limited means for diplomatic representation, Africans have found the United Nations system a very convenient framework for diplomacy.

Nevertheless, the United Nations merely mirrors the power relations that have rendered Africa vulnerable to intervention and economically dependent. African states have little choice but to devise strategies of empowerment. The ideals of African unity institutionalized in the OAU and of Third World solidarity through the NAM both express a vision of power through collective diplomacy that is compelling but elusive. The very diversity and heterogeneity of African regimes that we have observed constitutes yet another constraint upon African decision making. However elusive the goal of a much more broadly based collective African stance, African leaders are bound to strive in this direction. They understand the consequences of unequal power relations too well not to work for a movement of equals.

■ NOTES

1. Tamar Golan, "A Certain Mystery: How Can France Do Everything That It Does in Africa—and Get Away with It?" *African Affairs* 80 (January 1981): 3–11.

2. For a table listing major and minor direct military interventions, see Edward Kolodziez and Bokanga Lokulutu, "Security Interests and French Arms-Transfer Policy in Sub-Saharan Africa," in Bruce E. Arlinghaus, ed., *Arms for Africa* (Lexington, Massachusetts: Lexington Books, 1983), p. 138.

3. Jean-François Bayart, *La politique africaine de François Mitterrand* (Paris: Karthala, 1984), p. 27.

4. Kaye Whiteman, "President Mitterrand and Africa," *African Affairs* 82 (July 1983): 330.

5. Giscard had agreed to hold the 1981 summit in Kinshasa, Zaire, a venue of some embarrassment to Mitterrand who had criticized Giscard's close ties to the Mobutu regime. On the pretext that the first Franco-African summit of his term ought to be held in France, Mitterrand succeeded in evading Kinshasa—if only for a year. By 1982, *raison d'état* had reconciled Mitterrand to maintaining the tie with Zaire.

6. The very growth in participation eventually annoyed the original partners. By 1985, the French decided to devote the first day of the conference *exclusively* to the francophone states, thereby to perpetuate an inner circle. It is noteworthy that Morocco attended for the first time in 1985 as a useful way to compensate for its boycott of the OAU. The institution evidently served a wide range of diplomatic needs.

7. Bayart, *La politique africaine,* p. 52.

8. See Chapter 31, "The Creation of Eurafrica," in Jacques Louis Hymans, *Leopold Sédar Senghor: An Intellectual Biography* (Edinburgh: Edinburgh University Press, 1971), pp. 164–166. One might note that Senghor's support of federation in Africa reflected the interest of Dakar as administrative capital of French West Africa.

9. Despite the fact that John F. Kennedy's assistant secretary of state for African affairs, G. Mennen Williams, enthusiastically adopted this slogan.

10. Edward T. Wilson, "Russia's Historic Stake in Black Africa," in David E. Albright, ed., *Communism in Africa* (Bloomington: Indiana University Press, 1980), p. 71.

11. Robert Legvold, *Soviet Policy in West Africa* (Cambridge: Harvard University Press, 1970), p. 1.

12. Ibid., p. 65.

13. Ibid., p. 129.

14. Jiri Valenta, "Soviet Decision-Making on the Intervention in Angola," in Albright, *Communism in Africa,* p. 102.

15. Ibid., pp. 109–110.

16. Ibid., p. 116.

17. David E. Albright, "Moscow's African Policy of the 1970s," in Albright, *Communism in Africa,* p. 58.

18. Marina Ottaway, *Soviet and American Influence in the Horn of Africa* (New York: Praeger, 1982), p. 114.

19. Ellen Laipson, "Libya and the Soviet Union: Alliance at Arm's Length," in Walter Laqueur, ed., *The Pattern of Soviet Conduct in the Third World* (New York: Praeger, 1983), p. 133.

20. Robert Grey, "The Soviet Presence in Africa: An Analysis of Goals," *Journal of Modern African Studies* 22 (September 1984): 527.

21. Henry Jackson, *From the Congo to Soweto* (New York: Morrow, 1982), p. 55.

22. Clare Timberlake, the first U.S. ambassador to the Congo, is reported to have remarked that "if Lumumba had walked into any gathering of Congolese politicians as a waiter with a tray on his head he would have come out as Prime Minister," according to Conor Cruise O'Brien, *To Katanga and Back* (New York: Grosset and Dunlap, 1966), p. 94. See O'Brien and Steven R. Weissman, *American Foreign Policy in the Congo* (Ithaca, N.Y.: Cornell University Press, 1974), for thorough accounts of U.S. and UN policy.

23. The term is from Helen Kitchen, *U.S. Interests in Africa* (New York: Praeger, 1983), p. 2. See also Donald Rothchild and John Ravenhill "Subordinating African Issues to Global Logic: Reagan Confronts Political Complexity," in Kenneth Oye, Robert J. Lieber, and Donald Rothchild, eds., *Eagle Resurgent?* (Boston: Little, Brown, 1987).

24. Steven Weissman, "The CIA and US Policy in Zaire and Angola," in René Lemarchand, ed., *American Policy in Southern Africa* (Washington, D.C.: University Press of America, 1978), p. 394.

25. Testimony to the Senate by the deputy assistant secretary of state for African affairs in 1975, as cited by Weissman, ibid., p. 395.

26. The quotations are from National Security Study Memorandum 39 and an accompanying document submitted to Nixon in January 1970, as cited in Gerald Bender, "Kissinger in Angola: Anatomy of Failure," in Lemarchand, *American Policy in Southern Africa,* p. 68.

27. Ibid., pp. 76–77.

28. Anthony Lake, *The "Tar Baby" Option: American Policy Toward Southern Rhodesia* (New York: Columbia University Press, 1976); one of the classics on the bureaucratic politics of U.S. foreign policy decision making, this book is likewise one of the best studies of U.S. policy toward southern Africa.

29. U.S., Department of State, *Department of State Bulletin* 74, no. 1927 (May 31, 1976): 5673–5674.

30. The quoted phrase appears in Chester Crocker, "South Africa: Strategy for Change," *Foreign Affairs* 59, no. 2 (Winter 1980-1981), p. 350.

31. Cited by Allen D. Cooper, *U.S. Economic Power and Political Influence in Namibia, 1700–1982* (Boulder, Colo.: Westview Press, 1982), p. 33. The speaker was George McGhee, assistant secretary of state for Near Eastern and African affairs.

32. The quotation is from a 1966 speech by Assistant Secretary Williams, cited in Cooper, *U.S. Economic Power,* p. 40.

33. Cited in Tony Hodges, "At Odds with Self-Determination: The United States and Western Sahara," in Gerald Bender, James Coleman, and Richard Sklar, eds., *African Crisis Areas and U.S. Foreign Policy* (Berkeley: University of California Press, 1985), p. 266.

34. George T. Yu, "Sino-Soviet Rivalry in Africa," in Albright, *Communism in Africa,* p. 181.

35. Michael Curtis, "Africa, Israel, and the Middle East," *Middle East Review* 17, no. 4 (Summer 1985): 7.

36. Victor T. LeVine and Timothy W. Luke, *The Arab-African Connection: Political and Economic Realities* (Boulder, Colo.: Westview Press, 1979), pp. 24–25.

37. Dunstan M. Wai, "African-Arab Relations: Interdependence or Misplaced Optimism," *Journal of Modern African Studies* 21, no. 2 (June 1983), pp. 187–213.

Part 5

POLITICAL FUTURES

13

South Africa: The Politics of Incipient Civil War

In May 1986, the South African air force carried out bombing raids against the capitals of Zambia, Zimbabwe, and Botswana. These attacks were a stark reminder that the government of South Africa is virtually at war with the rest of the continent. Specifically targeted at external offices of the African National Congress, the bombardments were desperate attempts to contain resistance to apartheid inside and outside the Republic of South Africa. The air strikes did nothing to stem the surge of unrest that has swept across South Africa, claiming over twenty-three hundred lives since 1984; on the contrary, in June 1986, President Pieter W. Botha decreed a state of emergency in the troubled land. South Africa was unmistakably in the throes of a grim societal crisis that verged on conditions of civil war.

The whites of South Africa number about 5 million out of a total population of 32 million. The minority has succeeded in holding onto power, making South Africa the anomaly in modern African affairs. The crisis of the mid-1980s, however, is subjecting the system of minority rule to great internal strain and to unprecedented external scrutiny. The South African situation has become a major international issue, not only for its African neighbors, but for other states as well. In the United States, for example, the issue of U.S. policy toward the South African regime and its challengers has assumed major importance. For all these reasons, we devote this chapter to the case of South Africa.

The scale of European settlement and its deep historical roots set South Africa apart. Observers have noted a *laager, or fortress, mentality* in white South African society. The regime is indeed under siege as the majority population, cantoned in ghettos and so-called homelands, seeks to assert its elemental human rights. Violence is the hallmark of this divided society—institutionalized in white dominance and a police state, on the one hand; often spontaneous in the protests and riots of the disfranchised, on the other. Moreover, armed resistance is increasingly being organized by black nationalists against the formidable power of the South African state. The dual society, in other words, has become a battleground.

However anomalous its system of white domination, South Africa's incorporation into the global economy, its multiethnic character, and the emergence and radicalization of a national liberation movement have much in common with other African societies that we have studied. Algeria and Rhodesia may suggest rough parallels to the South African case; for South Africa's black majority, it is clear, the liquidation of the colonial order elsewhere in Africa provides the model for their own political aspirations.

In this chapter, we analyze South Africa using the concepts and organizational format that we have already applied to other African countries. In examining societal structures, we focus on the organization of social life into minority and majority groupings. Our study of the state necessarily emphasizes the concentration of the instruments of coercion in white hands alongside the creative proliferation of associational forms (occupational, youth, religious, and cultural groups) in black society. The political process in this dual society is energized by the conflicting ideologies of apartheid and liberation; the clash between the "center" and the majority is over the very rules of the game. We shall examine one recent instance of public policymaking—namely, the constitutional revision of 1984—in order to illustrate the more fundamental issue of the struggle for control of the state. The economy likewise poses unique issues; compared to other African countries, South Africa is relatively developed economically. Wealth has been accumulated largely through the exploitation of cheap black labor; the issue today is the redistribution of political power and the products of South Africa's mines and factories via the creation of participatory political institutions.

■ STATE AND SOCIETY IN SOUTH AFRICA

Throughout the continent, Africans struggle with the legacy of alien rule and involuntary incorporation into the world economy. Although South Africa shares this heritage, the fact that the colonizers came earlier and still exercise power makes all the difference. The first European settlers arrived in 1652 to establish a "refreshment station" for the Dutch East India Company on the Cape of Good Hope. There they encountered a peaceful, pastoral people, the Khoikhoin, who had long been grazing their cattle in the Cape region. The Dutch imperiously asserted a "right of conquest" when the Khoikhoin chiefs came to complain of the depredations of the early settlers. Governor Jan Van Riebeeck recorded their poignant query in his diary in 1660: "They asked if they would be allowed to do such a thing supposing they went to Holland."[1]

We know, of course, that the peoples of southern Africa never sought to colonize Europe. Instead, settlers backed by Europe's superior military means gradually claimed more and more territory around the Cape. By the end of the seventeenth century, some of the settlers had already begun to think of themselves as a distinct people, "Afrikaners," who regarded the Cape as their permanent home. Although the white population numbered only about fifty-four hundred persons a century after their first settlement, today's multiracial society was already dimly perceptible long before colonialism arrived elsewhere in Africa.[2]

The Cape Colony subsequently tempted the British during the imperial rivalries of the Napoleonic wars. Great Britain took possession of the colony from the Dutch in 1806, triggering what Bernard Magubane calls an "uninterrupted series of wars" against both Africans and Afrikaners over the course of the following century.[3] It was the British far more than the Boers who transformed the South African economy by the introduction of capitalist agriculture. The appropriation of land was doubly pernicious for the Zulus, the Xhosa, the Sotho, the Swazi, and the other African peoples of the hinterland. Not only did the British wage war against them to secure land, but British expansion also drove the earlier Dutch settlers inland on what they came to celebrate as the Great Trek. Then, in the final third of the nineteenth century, diamonds (discovered at Kimberly in 1867) and gold (discovered at Johannesburg in 1886) spurred the full-scale integration of the subcontinent into the global economy. Tensions between the British and Dutch rivals for control over African resources culminated in the Anglo-Boer War of 1899–1902, which confirmed British hegemony.

The modern political order was instituted in 1910 when the colonies of the Cape, Natal, the Transvaal, and the Orange Free State were united to form the Union of South Africa. Britain granted internal self-rule to the white colonists, but the new parliamentary system excluded virtually all of the black population. In 1931, the Union became a sovereign member of the British Commonwealth. In transferring power to the minority, Britain sanctioned the regime of white supremacy that deprived Africans of political rights in their own country and treated the black population essentially as a pool of cheap labor. Even the modest scruples of European colonial administrations were stripped away. Under this racially exclusive parliamentary system, political parties representing different economic, linguistic, and cultural segments of the white population competed for power. In 1948, a coalition representing the most militantly racist element of Afrikaner nationalism narrowly won a parliamentary majority. Reorganized as the National party (NP) in 1951, the Afrikaners have been in power for nearly four decades, implementing their ideology of apartheid. We shall see that control of the state has been a source of economic patronage for the Afrikaners, who thus hold a strong vested interest in retaining power.

Literally translated, *apartheid* means "apartness." As an ideology, it is exclusionary in its very meaning. Like other ideologies, it expressed an understanding of the past and a vision of the future society. The theorists of apartheid drew upon a legacy of cultural nationalists who believed in a God-given mission of the Afrikaner people. The Afrikaans language, the Calvinism of the Dutch Reformed theology, and the tales of the Great Trek bestowed a sentiment of unique identity whose destiny apartheid was meant to protect. The theory called for the "separate development in accordance with their respective inherent characteristics" of South Africa's diverse peoples. In the words of its apologists, separateness expressed "the desire of the Afrikaner people to find a lasting and ethically just solution to the Union's color problem in general, and the native question in particular." In practice, separate development rationalized a project of racial domination and material privilege.[4]

The whites who govern South Africa in 1987 constitute about one-sixth of the total population. Their racial legislation divides the rest of the people into three categories: Asians, or people mainly of Indian and Pakistani background, who number about 1 million, or 3 percent of the population; 3 million Coloreds, or people of mixed racial descent, who constitute another 9 percent; and Africans, or indigenous peoples, whose 23 million constitute 73 percent of the total population. The National party government elaborated a complex system of laws that established varying rights for these different racially designated groups. Central to the scheme was the concept of "Bantu homelands," essentially ethnic reserves set aside for the black Africans. According to the theory of separate development, blacks were to be considered citizens of these ethnic enclaves whether they lived there or not, thereby removing any obligation to provide them with political rights outside the homeland. About 13 percent of the national territory (generally the poorest land) was thus set aside as home for 73 percent of the population. The government carved out ten such "bantustans" and eventually purported to grant independence to four of them (Transkei, Ciskei, Bophuthatswana, and Venda), although no other country has ever accorded these entities recognition. What the bantustans actually represent, of course, is a claim by the white minority to decentralize responsibility for these overcrowded and poverty-stricken areas while excluding blacks from political participation at the center. In 1985, President Botha proposed to restore South African citizenship to blacks who permanently reside in the urban areas outside the homelands. Although abolishing the fiction of homeland citizenship for urban Africans, this reform still leaves black political rights very narrowly circumscribed. In effect, it merely acknowledges the necessity of a black urban labor force.

A system so blatantly constructed upon racism necessarily requires strong instruments of enforcement. After a century of incessant warfare, the first three prime ministers of the South African state (Louis Botha, Jan Smuts, and J.B.M. Hertzog) were all generals. The prime minister (now president) since 1978, P. W. Botha was minister of defense for twelve years before assuming power (under institutional changes in the early 1980s, the title of the head of the government became "president"). A strong military and strong police force have been constant factors in the regime, the police for a long time the dominant security instrument of the state. As Philip Frankel observes, the two forces often worked in tandem:

> In general the police have been in the forefront in combatting political unrest since the establishment of the Union, black political unrest in particular. Nevertheless there are numerous instances in twentieth-century South African history where the Defense Force has been used, either alone or in conjunction with the police in quelling domestic insurrections on the part of either blacks or whites. . . . there is in fact an entire tradition of the police and military being used on an interchangeable inter-external basis to defend the interests of the South African state.[5]

The police force has nearly tripled in size since 1960 in order to carry out its primary functions of riot control and enforcement of "pass laws" (which have regulated the movements of blacks in one or another form since 1760!).[6] A specialized Security Police agency exists with authority to arrest, detain, interrogate (and, as considerable evidence indicates, to torture) political opponents of the regime. There is also a separate National Intelligence Service, successor to the Bureau of State Security (BOSS), whose mission was to infiltrate and disable black political organizations; at one time, the BOSS's director was held to be "the second most powerful man in the country."[7]

Under President Botha, the military has displaced the police as the most powerful institution within the state. The military budget has increased seventy-fold from 1960 to 1983, representing about 5 percent of GNP by the 1980s.[8] Likewise, the number of military personnel, including various reserve forces, has grown from 78,000 to 494,000, a more than sixfold increase from 1960 to the early 1980s. This massive expenditure has produced a growing military participation in political and social affairs. The South African sociologist Philip Frankel argues that "the current militarization of South African society, [and] the growth of the garrison state with its accompanying siege culture" have broken down the distinction "between the civil and military sectors of society as the military extends its web into national education, the scientific and business communities and finally . . . the highest of public decision-making bodies and state councils."[9] The militarization of South African society is comparable to the intervention of the military elsewhere in Africa, but it stems from the racial cleavage rather than from economic weakness and the breakdown of civilian institutions. The growing role of the South African military is attributable to two factors: the changing external environment (as discussed in Chapter 11) and the radicalization of black organizations.

Most Afrikaners are members of the Dutch Reformed Church, a conservative body of Calvinist inspiration that has historically upheld racial segregation. This church's role has been important in justifying apartheid for many devout Afrikaners. More elitist and perhaps even more influential has been the Afrikaner Broederbond, a secret organization founded in 1918 to promote Afrikaner interests by imbuing its members with ethnic discipline and solidarity. Recruiting teachers, clergy, prominent farmers, and businesspeople, the

Broederbond in turn provided a significant component of the leadership of the National party; in 1972, for example, virtually the entire cabinet as well as three-fourths of the NP members of parliament came from the ranks of the Broederbond.[10] These interlocking institutions underlie the power structure that blacks are contesting.

■ POLITICAL DISSENT IN A DUAL SOCIETY

Politics within the black population are effectively still in the nationalist, or anticolonial (colonialism being "internal" here), phase. Rough analogues to the South African situation are found in the national liberation experiences of Algeria and Zimbabwe. In Algeria, the settlers composed about 10 percent of the population and exercised strong pressure upon the French government to resist Algerian nationalism. The Algerian *colons* (colonists), however, were not completely independent agents; they required metropolitan resources and public opinion to wage their war against the FLN, external support that they eventually lost. In Rhodesia/Zimbabwe, the relatively large settler group (about 6 percent of the population) did declare its independence of Great Britain and fought ZANU and ZAPU for some fifteen years. But the Rhodesian whites also lacked adequate resources to contain the liberation movements, especially after the opening of the Mozambican front. In both cases, the nationalist movements were able to unseat their adversaries. South Africa's colonial regime is both stronger and more determined than those faced by the Algerian Provisional Government or the Patriotic Front. Its defense industry is highly developed, and it is close to self-sufficiency in arms and energy production; even so, its military stockpile has been enhanced by purchases abroad. It has a presumptive nuclear capacity. These factors certainly set the South African case apart. Nonetheless, protest and resistance have grown steadily under the auspices of nationalist organizations. Black nationalism has a long history dating back to the early years of the twentieth century.

As already suggested, the nineteenth century was a violent period of conflict for South Africa, as Xhosa, Sotho, and Zulu kingdoms fought futilely against the better-armed conquerors. Edward Roux suggests that the poll tax rebellion in Natal in 1906 marked the turning point between the period of ethnically based wars and a second phase in which political organizations sought to mobilize blacks as a national group.[11] The African National Congress, which remains the backbone of African opposition to apartheid, held its founding meeting in 1912. The meeting was convened by a young African lawyer, P. Ka I Seme, who had studied in the United States, and who spoke the classic language of Third World nationalism:

> We have discovered that in the land of our birth Africans are treated as hewers of wood and drawers of water. The white people of this country have formed

what is known as the Union of South Africa—a union in which we have no voice in making of laws and no part in their administration. We have called you, therefore, to this conference so that we can devise ways and means of forming our national unity, and defending our rights and privileges.[12]

This early nationalist idealism, however, was fated to confront a regime stubbornly determined to control black labor as hewers of diamonds and drawers of gold.

Although intellectuals like Seme continued to play a leadership role in the ANC, labor organizers like Clements Kadalie, who formed the Industrial and Commercial Workers Union in 1919, may have had an even greater impact upon black political consciousness, for Africans were being drawn into the white-controlled economy in ever-growing numbers. Spurred by the riches extracted from the mines, the economy developed much more rapidly in South Africa than elsewhere on the continent. Industrialization and urbanization shattered the traditional social system; by 1939, there were 800,000 Africans employed in manufacturing and mining—a scale of social change unmatched in African history. Unions and a small Communist party thus emerged as important political actors; organized labor, although persecuted by the regime, has thus been a more important social force in South Africa than elsewhere in Africa.

Although blacks were drawn inexorably into the modern economic sector, the white government stringently controlled their lives by such legislation as the Land Act (restricting their property rights), the Native Administration Act (restricting freedom of speech and according wide authority to a Native Affairs Department), the Riotous Assemblies Act (restricting freedom of association), and a host of other bills that legalized racial discrimination at every turn. Despite this segregation, an increasingly diverse body of black teachers, clergy, lawyers, and journalists took form in the shadow of the racist laws. This black elite articulated the grievances of the mass of the population, keeping alive the spirit of political protest in the face of ever-increasing harshness.

Until the end of World War II, the ANC pursued a very moderate program of reform that stressed nonviolent demonstrations as a means of change. Several factors radicalized the movement in the following years: the brutal repression of a mineworkers' strike in 1946, the election of the NP in 1948, and the model of emergent African nationalism elsewhere in the continent. The development of an ever-broader nationalist coalition took place in South Africa during the late 1940s and 1950s much as it did elsewhere on the continent. When the government clamped down upon one type of organization, another pushed forward from a different sector (labor, churches, students) to assert basic human rights.

The ANC called for African self-determination in its 1949 Program of Action (PA). In conjunction with the South African Indian Congress and the South African Communist party, it sponsored a "Freedom Day Strike" on 1 May 1950. These were the same kinds of political action that led to independence elsewhere in Africa, although under the most inhospitable conditions. In South Africa, such activities provoked the NP government to pass the Suppression of

Communism Act, which defined communism broadly enough to cover most forms of opposition to apartheid. In turn, the ANC initiated a Campaign for the Defiance of Unjust Laws, which involved peaceful demonstrations against the whole battery of pass, curfew, residency, and censorship laws. Thousands were arrested, greatly enhancing the reputation of the ANC, which concurrently broadened its base by allying with Indian and Colored associations and the Congress of Trade Unions.

Together these groups drafted the Freedom Charter in 1955, a call for equal rights, which the government treated as a "blueprint" for a communist state. The Freedom Charter still stands as the basic platform of the ANC. Drafted by a multiracial coalition, it held out in simple eloquence a vision of a nonracial, democratic state:

> We, the people of South Africa, declare for all our country and the world to know:
> That South Africa belongs to all who live in it, black and white, and that no government can justly claim authority, unless it is based on the will of all the people. . . .
> And therefore, we, the people of South Africa, black and white together—equals, countrymen and brothers—adopt this Freedom Charter. And we pledge ourselves to strive together, sparing nothing of our strength and courage, until the democratic changes set out here have been won.[13]

It is a measure of the determination of both sides that the ANC continued to strive thirty years later for the basic premise of equality: one person, one vote. The reaction of the white government was to arrest and detain ANC leaders for about a year; upon their release, such leaders as Nobel Peace Prize recipient Albert Luthuli and Oliver Tambo mounted a campaign against the pass laws, which they called "the main pillar of our oppression and exploitation."[14] It was during this campaign that the police killed sixty-eight demonstrators in the notorious Sharpeville massacre. In this state-sanctioned massacre, the Afrikaner regime bluntly displayed that it would not yield to nationalism. The authorities then banned the ANC and the Pan-Africanist Congress (PAC), a new nationalist formation that had recently broken from the ANC. (The PAC objected to the inclusion of the Indians and white antiapartheid militants, including communists, in the multiracial ANC. Although the idea of black "exclusivism" divided the nationalist forces into competing factions for several years, the ANC has prevailed as the preeminent nationalist organization.)

By forcing these nationalist movements underground, the Afrikaner government suppressed essentially peaceful forms of opposition, only to unleash more violent resistance and to spur new organizational initiatives. On the one hand, the ANC authorized armed struggle by creating the Umkhonto we Sizwe, or "Spear of the Nation." Lawyer and long-standing ANC activist Nelson Mandela became head of this clandestine military organ, and his colleague Oliver Tambo went into exile to direct an external wing of the ANC. The capture of Mandela and other underground leaders such as Walter Sisulu and Govan Mbeki gravely damaged the internal operations of the ANC, but the imprisoned Mandela has become a worldwide symbol of African protest. Abroad, the ANC became closely aligned with such liberation movements as FRELIMO, the MPLA, SWAPO, and ZAPU and gradually reconstructed a capability for sabotage attacks inside South Africa. Since 1976, guerrillas of the Umkhonto we Sizwe have carried out attacks against numerous military, police, and economic installations.[15] Both its external recognition and its underground network within the country have made the ANC the leading force in contemporary nationalist politics, one that the government will have to negotiate with if a stable and enduring peace is to materialize.

☐ Social Groupings

The indignities of apartheid have politicized many other sectors of black society, especially in the face of the ban on normal political activities. Organized labor is potentially a very powerful force in light of the dependence of the economic system upon black labor. Africans began to organize unions in the 1920s. They had limited impact, however, as the country's labor legislation long did not recognize the black unions as agents in collective bargaining. Although not formally prohibited, the unions existed in a grey zone, some operating essentially as allies of the ANC and advocating its nonracial policies, others focusing purely on labor issues; some of the latter unions insisted upon exclusively black membership. As the economic role of black labor continued to grow, the white government decided to introduce new labor legislation in the late 1970s. Its purpose was to regulate the black unions more closely but also to recognize them formally as bargaining agents.

Labor activity has expanded considerably under the new legislation. Two large federations emerged in the late 1970s and early 1980s. One was the Federation of South African Trade Unions (FOSATU), which grouped together some ninety-four thousand workers in the metal, chemical, transport, food, paper, textile, and automobile sectors. These affiliated unions endorsed a position of nonracial membership: They were open to all workers including whites, Coloreds, and Indians, as well as blacks. A competing federation grounded in the racially exclusive unions (many of which had been formed as black branches of white unions) also formed under the title Council of Unions of South Africa (CUSA). Under the new labor law, CUSA undertook to organize the critical mining sector, and by 1985 the National Union of Mineworkers (NUM) had become the country's largest trade union, registering two hundred fifty thousand members.

The general secretary of the NUM is Cyril Ramaphosa, a lawyer and former student leader turned labor organizer. Having forged the NUM under CUSA auspices, Ramaphosa took the lead in December 1985 in forming a new and larger federation, the Congress of South African Trade Unions (COSATU). Bringing together thirty-two unions with some five hundred thousand members, COSATU was at its birth the largest labor federation in South African history. The new federation named Elijah Barayi, a vice president of the NUM, as its first head. The choice of Barayi, who had formerly been active in the ANC alongside Nelson Mandela, was politically significant. Although South African law forbids COSATU from associating itself directly with the ANC, the new confederation tacitly aligned itself with important ANC principles. On the one hand, it embraced the ANC's multiracial ideology in leaving behind CUSA. On the other, it endorsed the notion that labor issues cannot be isolated from the broader political objectives for which the ANC stands. As Ramaphosa declared at COSATU's founding convention, "Working class issues are political issues. . . . We have to make a link between economic and political issues. We all agree that the struggle on the shop floor cannot be separated from the wider political issues."[16] The organization of mineworkers (whose previous union had been shattered in the suppression of their 1946 strike) and the rapid growth of labor federations represent a significant new force that can challenge the power relations in the society. We have seen that labor unions have been important components of nationalist movements elsewhere on the continent. Their role in a more industrialized South Africa is potentially even greater, as was evident during the NUM strike in 1987.

Numerous other community associations have likewise sprung up around the churches, youth and student groups, women's groups, and various professional and cultural organizations. The churches have produced such well-known opponents of apartheid as Desmond Tutu, the Anglican archbishop, and Allan Boesak, president of the World Alliance of Reformed Churches. In 1978 Bishop Tutu became secretary-general of the South Africa Council of Churches (SACC), a coordinating body representing both black and white denominations that support the "Message to the People of South Africa" adopted in 1968 declaring that "apartheid, with its attendant hardships, [is a doctrine] truly hostile to Christianity."[17] The Dutch Reformed Church (to which most Afrikaners belong) is not associated with SACC. The council has supported conscientious objection to military service and divestment of foreign firms from the South African economy. Numerous members of the clergy have been banned, but the churches have remained a significant source of dissent.

Like the unions and the churches, the schools have provided an important framework for political action. Both high school and university students have become increasingly politicized in protest against the educational policies of the white government. Discrimination in education is one of the ugliest hallmarks of apartheid. In 1979, for example, per pupil expenditure on the education of black Africans was one-tenth that for whites. This translated into a pupil-teacher ratio of 19:1 in white schools as compared to 47:1 in schools for Africans.[18] Educational issues (among others) sparked young people to set off the Soweto uprising of 1976. In 1979, high school students organized the Congress of South African Students (COSAS), which spurred student activism and played an important role in the unrest of the 1980s. Like earlier trade unions,

COSAS was never officially recognized by the government up to the time that it was banned in 1985. But COSAS and its predecessor organizations have created a practice of youth militance that the government is unlikely to squelch.

University students have also been instrumental in challenging the apartheid order. Student leader Steve Biko organized the South African Students' Organization (SASO) in 1968, breaking away from the white-dominated student union. SASO and Biko were instrumental in developing an ideological position known as "black consciousness," which had a significant impact in the 1970s. Stressing black solidarity (by which was understood Africans, Coloreds, and Asians), the Black Consciousness Movement (BCM) distinguished itself from the ANC's class analysis and nonracial approach. For a time, the white government tolerated SASO and the BCM as compatible with its own theory of "separate development." But SASO's militant nationalism, its elaboration of a black liberation theology, and its linkage to the black labor unions and to the secondary schools all assured an eventual clash. After Soweto, SASO and several other BCM-affiliated organizations were banned. Biko himself was arrested and died (presumably killed) in detention.

A successor to SASO appeared promptly under the new name of Azanian Students' Organization (AZASO). (The term "Azania," initially adopted by the Pan-Africanist Congress to denote South Africa, generally implies ideological sympathy with the PAC or BCM. Thus, for example, the Azanian People's Organization, AZAPO, sprung up in the wake of the original BCM.) For tactical reasons, AZASO has chosen to focus its demands on educational policy. For example, it has drafted an Education Charter (inspired by the Freedom Charter of the 1950s) calling for an end to discrimination in education. Like other organized black groups, its fundamental purpose is to challenge the structure of white political dominance. Originally much influenced by black consciousness, AZASO (like COSAS) has moved closer and closer to the ANC position during the 1980s. The most militant BCM currents, however, continue to distinguish themselves from the ANC.

The activities of these diverse voluntary associations—students, labor, church groups, parents' associations, and others—are the channels through which the African majority deals with the white power structure. These grassroots associations have formed a network of linkages that is difficult for even a very arbitrary government to control. Whether expressed in terms of black consciousness or a common struggle for equity and justice, these organizations express the majority view. That the most significant organizations have been rallying around the themes and analysis of the ANC, that Nelson Mandela has emerged as the symbol of African political rights—these are signs that the ANC is the main political force with which the Afrikaners must ultimately deal.

☐ Ethnic Enclaves

Instead, the white government has tried to channel black political expression into the artificial bounds of the homelands. The "solution" of banishing blacks to these bantustans has been a notorious failure if for no other reason than it is contradicted by the need for black labor in the mines and factories of white South Africa. By establishing the homelands, however, the minority regime has created another framework for black political activity. Within this framework, some traditional leaders have been able to develop power bases that should not be neglected as components of the South African political process.

The best known of the homeland politicians is Chief Gatsha Buthelezi who is ruler of Kwa Zulu. As the grandson of the last king of an independent Zulu state, Buthelezi enjoys traditional political legitimacy. He has formed a mass organization called Inkatha, which functions rather like the party in some of the one-party states elsewhere in Africa. Inkatha has described itself as "custodian of the ideals of the ANC" but is, in fact, largely in competition with the ANC for the loyalty of Zulu people.[19] Buthelezi has contended that the nominal autonomy granted under the bantustan scheme allows Africans to develop skills and resources that will ultimately increase their political leverage. Although this is a controversial position among black South Africans, most of whom condemn the entire bantustan framework, the role of social forces like the Inkatha movement must be acknowledged. They organize people around ethnic identity and certain statelike functions in the enclaves that apartheid has set aside for blacks. It is clear that the reserves cannot be considered liberated territories, but they are reflections of the ethnic and regional interests that we have observed as political factors in other African societies.

Alongside these organized movements exist more spontaneous forms of protest and violence. The uprising in Soweto in 1976 signaled a new level of popular resistance to the regime. On 16 June 1976, about fifteen thousand schoolchildren converged on a Soweto secondary school to protest a government decree that math and social studies courses be conducted in Afrikaans. The police fired on the demonstrators, igniting the spark of a "virtual communal insurrection" of rioting, arson, barricades, and attacks on police.[20] Several months of disorder and strikes that spread across the country eventually left at least 575 dead and 2,389 wounded, according to the official government report. Analysts have variously attributed the specific causes of the revolt to the spread of black consciousness ideology, the rise of working-class militance, and the contradictions between the system's growing need for educated skilled labor and its repressive political arrangements. No doubt each of these variables contributes some part of the explanation. Most simply put, white dominance itself has created an insurrectionary situation: Institutionalized violence has led to a spiraling of counterviolence and state violence.

Thus, nine years after Soweto, disorder erupted again in 1985. The Botha government cracked down by declaring a state of emergency, but the violence

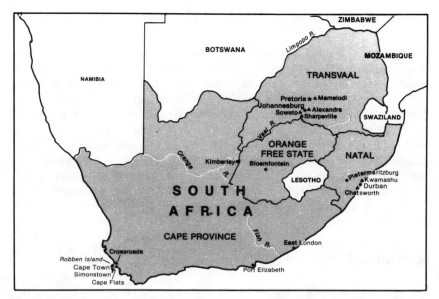

South Africa (Reprinted from the Study Commission on U.S. Policy Toward Southern Africa, *South Africa: Time Running Out,* © 1981 by University of California Press/Foreign Policy Study Foundation.)

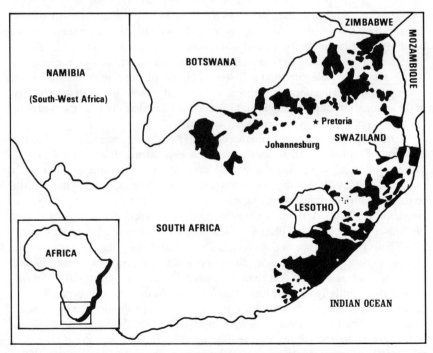

South Africa's Bantustans (Reprinted from Wayne C. McWilliams and Harry Piotrowski, *The World Since 1945,* © 1988 by Lynne Rienner Publishers.)

has not been contained. Observers have been struck by the fury of the young people, who have executed black collaborators mercilessly.[21] Such outbreaks of popular retribution are the continuing signs of the spiral of repression and insurrectionary anger that apartheid has wrought. In the face of all this unrest, the Botha government finally advanced cosmetic reforms, only to be met by a die-hard reaction from the right wing of the white community. In the summer of 1986, National party ministers and politicians were hooted down by extremist elements bent upon absolute resistance to change. The specter of a white vigilante movement, akin to the Secret Army Organization that emerged among the *colons* of Algeria in the final months of the Algerian war, has arisen in the troubled country. The regime is now under challenge on all sides.

■ PUBLIC POLICY AND POPULAR PROTEST

By 1986, it made more sense to interpret South African events as an incipient state of civil war rather than as an evolving political system. The state is itself at war with the majority of its population. What might elsewhere be considered issues of public policy are in South Africa the occasion for revolutionary mobilization. Such was the case in 1976 when an ostensible matter of educational policy triggered the Soweto uprising. Essentially the same scenario has been repeated in the 1980s around ostensible constitutional issues. The Botha government's proposals to create new parliamentary institutions—namely, an Indian House of Delegates and a Coloured House of Representatives—served essentially to fuel the popular outbreaks of the mid-1980s. We shall look briefly at these constitutional revisions and other recent developments as examples of the public policy process in South Africa.

The white government announced in 1977 that it intended to examine the question of including other races in national governance. It appointed a Commission of Inquiry and then a special council to make proposals for such changes. In May 1983, the government formally submitted a Constitution Bill to the all-white parliament calling for new Colored and Indian chambers. No provision for black African representation was included. Such a scheme was obviously unacceptable to blacks as well as to most Coloreds and Indians.

These proposals spurred Reverend Boesak to call for the formation of an umbrella group of diverse associations opposed to the proposed constitutional revisions. In this manner was born the United Democratic Front (UDF) in August 1983; initially some four hundred community-based organizations (unions, churches, youth groups, women's groups, professional and cultural bodies) declared their affiliation with the UDF.[22] The UDF grew to embrace some seven hundred groups representing nearly 3 million persons of all races, making it the largest single opposition group since the crackdowns of the 1950s. A smaller group representative of the black exclusivist vein of nationalism called the National Forum (NF) also took form. With broad grass-roots support, the UDF and the NF launched a campaign of rallies and mass meetings to mobilize opposition to the constitutional proposals. Protest spilled over into many other issue areas: wages, housing, education—in short, all the indignities of the white dominance system. Activism against the sham parliament gave vent to anger over the powerlessness of the majority.

From the perspective of the government, much of this activity was irrelevant. Despite the obvious popular dissent, the proposed changes were approved, first by a National party convention, then by the white parliament, and finally by the white electorate in a referendum held in November 1983. The next step was less simple. The government fixed August 1984 as the date for electing members to the newly created Colored and Indian chambers, but the UDF coalition called upon these two communities to boycott the election. The UDF won this round, as only 17 percent of the eligible voters actually cast ballots. Despite this popular rejection, the government inaugurated the new tricameral legislature with great fanfare in January 1985. What the Botha government had actually achieved was to provoke a mood of crisis.

On the one hand, the new institutions lacked legitimacy. Together, the Indian House of Representatives with its 45 members and the Coloured House of Deputies with its 85 members have little power alongside the 178-member White House of Assembly. Moreover, the tricameral parliament actually had less power than the old parliament had, for the new constitution actually shifted effective power from the legislative branch to the executive branch. The chief executive is now called state president, and decision-making power is firmly lodged in that office and another organ of recent creation, the State Security Council, which has largely supplanted the role of the cabinet. On the other hand, people had been mobilized to express their outrage at a process of "reform" that failed to address the real issue—namely, the representation of the black majority in the political system.

The activism unleashed by the constitutional proposals did not subside but turned increasingly in the direction of violent clashes. Rent strikes, school boycotts, and acts of violence against blacks perceived as collaborators (police officers or officials on government-sponsored black community councils) all contributed to a growing climate of unrest. Then, in March 1985, on the twenty-fifth anniversary of the Sharpeville massacre, police fired into a crowd of peaceful mourners engaged in a funeral march in Uitenhage. The Uitenhage incident further inflamed popular opinion, as did the murder of four prominent UDF activists. Political violence had become a daily event by mid-1985, claiming some eight hundred lives in the year following the imposition of the institutional reforms. In July 1985, the government declared a state of emergency, under which thousands of people were detained including UDF founder Allan Boesak. More than a quarter of those detained were children under the age of sixteen. Even such draconian measures did little to still the unrest in the land;

the government briefly suspended the emergency decree only to reimpose it as the tenth anniversary of the Soweto disorders approached in June 1986. In February 1988, the government banned the activities of the UDF and numerous other antiapartheid organizations.

Thus did the Botha government's attempt to coopt Coloreds and Indians into the system of minority rule trigger a period of sustained unrest. The government in 1986 advanced a new scheme for black political participation in a National Council, an advisory body open to moderates—namely, people without affiliation to the ANC. What the years of agitation have really shown, however, is that more and more black people support the basic concept of one person, one vote for which the ANC stands. Influential corporate leaders have acknowledged that the ANC must be recognized as representative of black opinion. In an unprecedented gesture, these leaders flew to Lusaka, Zambia, early in 1986 to confer with the ANC leadership. Further talks took place in July 1987, and the white parliamentary opposition, the Progressive Federal party (PFP), urged the government to negotiate with the ANC. The apparently inexorable rise of protest, violence, and unrest has stirred a sense of imminent breakdown that such voices seek to avert. The advocates of negotiation must contend with the neofascist Afrikaner Resistance Movement, which has been unflinching in its devotion to the *laager*. These militant rightists gained enough seats in the May 1987 whites-only election to displace the PFP as the official opposition party in the white chamber of parliament. Harassed on all sides, the Botha government has been unable to stem the drift toward civil war. It has lost control over the violence that it unleashed.

■ THE POLITICAL ECONOMY OF APARTHEID IN THE WORLD ECONOMY

Like its political system, South Africa's economy is also an anomaly on the continent. Its GNP of $70 billion (in 1984) exceeded that of such states as Denmark and Austria, and it has become one of the top fifteen trading countries in the world. The rapid growth of the South African economy over the past century is attributable to its extraordinary endowment in mineral resources, the availability of cheap black labor, and foreign finance. Investors, especially in Great Britain, poured large sums into the mining industry, in this manner incorporating South Africa into the global capitalist economy more rapidly and on a larger scale than other countries in Africa.

The road of South African economic development was cut with diamonds and paved with gold. In 1867 the colonial secretary exultantly displayed one of the newly discovered gems to the Cape House of Assembly and declared, "Gentlemen, this is the rock on which the future success of South Africa will be built."[23] Empire-builders like Cecil Rhodes rushed to open up the interior of the country, and diamond exports rose within a few years to over to £1.5 million annually. But diamonds proved to be but the "dress rehearsal" for the gold rush that began in 1886.[24]

The city of Johannesburg shot up as the mine shafts bored down. Output expanded very rapidly as forty-four mines, very largely financed by foreign capital, were already in operation by 1888. Gold production soon outstripped diamond earnings, and by the turn of the century South Africa had become the world's foremost exporter of gold. Railroads and energy were required as well; coal deposits were conveniently situated near the goldfields, and over 2,000 miles (3,400 km) of railways were laid from 1890 to 1899. Although the Anglo-Boer War briefly interrupted this phenomenal economic expansion, the mining boom had transformed a previously agrarian economy by the end of the nineteenth century.

The third crucial element in the boom was black African labor. As D. Hobart Houghton observes, "During the fifty years from 1862–1912, the number of persons employed in mining had risen from practically zero to 325,000 and they formed the first large body of wage-paid workers in the country."[25] Nearly 90 percent of these workers were blacks recruited from all over southern Africa who generally served six- to eighteen-month tours of labor before returning to their families. As essentially migrant laborers, they were poorly paid and poorly organized alongside the white miners who held the better jobs. Exploitation of their labor reaped the profits that eventually built such huge conglomerates as the Anglo-American Corporation. For a long time, the largest share of the dividends of the mining industry were transferred abroad. But even with this expatriation of profits, mining laid the groundwork for the third stage of the South African economy, the beginning of local manufacturing.

Local industry responded first to the needs of the mining sector; shops producing dynamite and miners' boots found a ready local market. The outbreak of World War I provided a further stimulus, as supply disruptions created opportunities for import-substitution industries. A rise in the price of gold in the 1930s further spurred national industrial development, and then World War II allowed another spurt into heavier sectors like iron and steel. Overall, the value of manufacturing output more than doubled from 1939 to 1945, and the industrial labor force took in over a hundred thousand new nonwhite workers.[26]

Much of the capital for industrial enterprise still came from abroad or from settlers of English origin. The Anglo South Africans rather than the Boers were much more likely to be engaged in the sectors of finance, mining, and large industry. Only during the investment surge of the 1930s did the Afrikaner bourgeoisie begin to move into small industry. Economic structures reflected, in other words, the divisions within the white community that led to the 1948 triumph of the National party as well as the deeper cleavage between black and white.

The election of 1948 had significant economic consequences insofar as the whites were concerned. The National victory depended upon a coalition of the largely rural Afrikaner bourgeoisie and the predominantly Afrikaner white working class. The NP government embarked upon an expansion of the public sector that created many new employment opportunities for Afrikaners. The state set up new public enterprises in such sectors as energy utilities, armaments, chemicals, railways, and harbors. South African Railways and Harbors, for example, grew to employ a very large number of Afrikaners, as did the police, the post office, and the civil service. By the mid-1980s, no less than 40 percent of the adult Afrikaner population worked for the state, constituting a substantial body with a vested interest in white power.[27] Government credits and Afrikaner-controlled financial institutions boosted Afrikaner participation in the private sector, and the parastatals provided upgraded opportunities for managerial status in the society. As Hermann Giliomee concludes, under NP rule, state capitalism emerged as the Afrikaner approach to economic development.[28] Economically as well as politically, the state has become a major interventionary force.

Control of the state was instrumental as well in allowing the Afrikaner elite to diversify the flow of foreign capital into the country. Attracting new investment became a major challenge for the regime after the Sharpeville crisis in 1960. The violence at Sharpeville seriously undermined investor confidence in the country; a substantial flight of capital over the following year depressed Pretoria's reserves. The government succeeded, however, in restoring order and then undertook a major bid for foreign technology. Multinational corporations in Germany, France, Japan, and especially the United States overcame their hesitations and began to pump new financial resources into the system. This influx of new capital gave the economy a tremendous boost; after the monetary decline of 1960-1961, the end of the decade saw a doubling of total foreign investment.

What attracted foreign corporations was the high rate of profit largely attributable to a cheap supply of labor. A U.S. business magazine observed in 1972 that "the Republic of South Africa has always been regarded by foreign investors as a gold mine, one of those rare and refreshing places where profits are great and problems small. Capital is not threatened by political instability or nationalization. Labor is cheap, the market booming, the currency hard and convertible. . . . Returns on . . . investment have been romping home at something like 19% a year."[29] Most major U.S. firms made substantial investments in the country during the 1960s, making the United States the second largest foreign investor after Great Britain. Among the U.S. giants that acquired significant holdings were General Motors, Ford, Chrysler, Texaco, Mobil, ITT, General Electric, Firestone, Goodyear, IBM, and Union Carbide. This surge of investment largely in the manufacturing sector lifted South Africa into the company of the most advanced industrial economies. It greatly enhanced the power and the self-sufficiency of the white minority government; in other words, it fortified the *laager*.

The dynamism of the South African economy was undeniable; its flaw was equally apparent. Economic development is a two-edged sword, for as more Africans entered the advanced industrial economy, their political consciousness and their organizational opportunities inevitably rose. So too did their resentment of the maldistribution of the national product. Economic growth unaccompanied by economic equity was inherently destabilizing.

To the extent that South Africa has prospered through foreign investment, it is vulnerable to the withdrawal of that investment. And, in fact, many U.S. multinational firms, including General Motors, Eastman Kodak, General Electric, IBM, Dow Chemical, and Coca Cola, have announced a total or partial withdrawal from that country. To be sure, the growth of the 1960s and 1970s enables contemporary South Africa to produce much more than dynamite and miners' boots; it can produce sophisticated weapons, automobiles, energy, communications, and as many police officers' boots as it wishes. Yet, the fact remains that the South African economy has become accustomed to the steady input of technology and capital from abroad. This external support has been called into question in the mid-1980s as the antiapartheid movement abroad has gained political momentum.

The South African government is aware of its vulnerability to the loss of investment and the technological expertise that it brings. It has passed a law that makes it a crime to advocate divestment. Nevertheless, opponents of apartheid both inside and outside the country have called for divestment and other types of economic sanctions in order to bring pressure for change. The movement for divestment began slowly in the early 1970s and grew modestly over the next decade. By 1986, as the political crisis inside South Africa became apparent, the public mood abroad became increasingly supportive of economic sanctions. During 1986, the Commonwealth, the EEC, and the United States all approved new and stiffer sanctions (including bans on imports of South African goods and on new investments). These measures impose real costs upon the South African economy but are unlikely in the short term to ruin it.

Economic sanctions take time to exert a strong impact. Their efficacy depends both on the ability of South African business and government to evade them and the determination of other governments to enforce them. Pretoria is already devoting considerable resources to techniques of sanctions-busting. Economic pressure is a necessary but not a sufficient instrument to effect change. Assistance to the Front Line States and sustained diplomatic pressure upon the white government to negotiate with representative black leaders including the ANC are also necessary to avert "a much greater descent into violence."[30]

■ TRANSITION THROUGH VIOLENCE OR NEGOTIATION?

The persistence of quasi-colonial modes of politics into the contemporary era distinguishes South Africa. In terms of political structures, the state is harshly at odds with the societal majority. Class lines overlap very strongly with racial cleavage. In terms of political process, the system presents a distinct variant of what we have called mass conflict. The growing pressure for political change has ignited acts of rebellion against the internal colonizer. Forced political transition is under way, leaving the parties to choose between more intensified violence and negotiated change.

South Africa is a diverse multiracial multiethnic society with a complex set of laws, institutions, and social forces. But the problem that is tearing the country apart is very simple to state: A minority in control of the means of coercion has deprived the majority of normal political rights. In December 1986, seven months after the bombing of its neighbors, six months after reinstituting the state of emergency, the Botha government drastically tightened controls on political expression and news reporting and carried out a further round of political arrests. The government decree specifically prohibited calls to lift the state of emergency, thereby rendering illegal a UDF-sponsored campaign called "Christmas against the emergency." These measures, President Botha gravely announced, were necessary to stave off "revolutionary violence."[31] The white leader intended no irony in condemning black church leaders and community leaders for advocating a Christmas without political oppression. The tragic irony lay in his commitment to the regime that produced the turmoil.

It is not impossible to imagine solutions to the strife in South Africa. As we have stressed in this text, governments and peoples frequently face political choices. Africa's recent political history presents a range of precedents from which the antagonists in South Africa might choose. Bargaining and negotiation worked in Kenya, leaving the state and civil service largely intact at independence. Successful bargaining also occurred between the French government and the Algerian FLN, but the local settlers rejected the bargain in an orgy of violence that resulted in their mass exodus. A negotiated settlement was eventually struck under British auspices in Rhodesia, but the South African government has rebuffed the Commonwealth Group's effort to play a comparable role. As suggested above, the ANC's Freedom Charter still holds out the framework for a negotiated settlement between majority and minority. The landscape has been bleak, not because of the lack of alternatives, but because the minority regime has chosen defiance.

■ NOTES

1. Cited in Bernard Magubane, *The Political Economy of Race and Class in South Africa* (New York: Monthly Review Press, 1979), pp. 28, 27.

2. See the chapter by Leonard Guelke in Richard Elphick and Hermann Giliomee, eds., *The Shaping of South African Society, 1652–1820* (Cape Town: Longman, 1979), for details on the early settler population.

3. Magubane, *The Political Economy*, p. 36.

4. The quotations are from N. J. Rhoodie and H. J. Venter, *Apartheid* (Cape Town: Haum, 1960). See also T. Dunbar Moodie, *The Rise of Afrikanerdom: Power, Apartheid, and the Afrikaner Civil Religion* (Berkeley: University of California Press, 1975), and Heribert Adam and Kogila Moodley, *South Africa Without Apartheid: Dismantling Racial Domination* (Berkeley: University of California Press, 1986), who argue that "even many apartheid apologists hardly believe in it themselves and merely sell it as the only solution available."

5. Philip H. Frankel, *Pretoria's Praetorians* (Cambridge: Cambridge University Press, 1984), pp. 101–102.

6. In 1986, the government announced the abolition of the pass laws, but enacted new measures that continue to regulate the movements and residency conditions of blacks.

7. Rob Davies, Dan O'Meara, and Sipho Dlamini, *The Struggle for South Africa* (London: Zed Press, 1984), p. 194.

8. Ibid., p. 179.

9. Frankel, *Pretoria's Praetorians,* p. xxii.

10. Hermann Giliomee, "The National Party and the Afrikaner Broederbond," in Robert M. Price and Carl G. Rosberg, eds., *The Apartheid Regime* (Berkeley: Institute of International Studies, 1980), p. 39.

11. Edward Roux, *Time Longer than Rope* (Madison: University of Wisconsin Press, 1964), Chapter 9.

12. Magubane, *The Political Economy*, p. 273.

13. The text of the Freedom Charter appears in the Commonwealth Group of Eminent Persons, *Mission to South Africa: The Commonwealth Report* (Harmondsworth: Penguin Books, 1986), pp. 157–160.

14. Magubane, *The Political Economy*, p. 305.

15. See Davies, O'Meara, and Dlamini, *The Struggle for South Africa*, pp. 34–35, 288–290, for details on the Umkhonto we Sizwe.

16. *Africa Report* 31 (March-April 1986): 10. See the interviews with Ramaphosa and Barayi in this number.

17. Davies, O'Meara, and Dlamini, *The Struggle for South Africa*, p. 421.

18. Leonard Thompson and Andrew Prior, *South African Politics* (New Haven: Yale University Press, 1982), p. 119. The ratio in schools reserved for Coloreds was 29:1 and for Asians 26:1. More recent figures indicate very little change: 1,500 rands ($600) per white child, 170 ($18) per African.

19. Tom Lodge, *Black Politics in South Africa Since 1945* (London: Longman, 1983), p. 351. See M. Gatsha Buthelezi, *Power Is Ours* (New York: Books in Focus, 1979), for a collection of speeches.

20. Lodge, *Black Politics,* p. 328.

21. See, for example, Conor Cruise O'Brien, "What Can Become of South Africa?" *Atlantic* 257, no. 3 (March 1986), pp. 41-68.

22. Sylvia Vollenhoven, "South Africa at the Crossroads," *Third World Quarterly* 8, no. 2 (April 1986): 488.

23. Cited in D. Hobart Houghton, "Economic Development, 1865–1965," in Monica Wilson and Leonard Thompson, eds., *The Oxford History of South Africa,* vol. 2 (Oxford: Oxford University Press, 1971), p. 11.

24. Ibid., p. 13

25. Ibid., p. 19

26. Ibid., p. 36

27. Pauline Baker, "Facing Up to Apartheid," *Foreign Policy* 64 (Fall 1986): 54.

28. Heribert Adam and Hermann Giliomee, *Ethnic Power Mobilized* (New Haven: Yale University Press, 1979).

29. John Blashill, "The Proper Role of U.S. Corporations in South Africa," *Fortune* (July 1972), p. 49.

30. Such is the conclusion of Malcolm Fraser and Olusegun Obasanjo, "What To Do About South Africa," *Foreign Affairs* 65, no. 1 (Fall 1986): 157. Fraser and Obasanjo were co-chairmen of the Commonwealth Eminent Persons Group that spent six months attempting to encourage political dialogue in South Africa. See also their report, *Mission to South Africa*. For a careful analysis of the effectiveness of different types of economic sanctions, see Charles M. Becker, "Economic Sanctions Against South Africa," *World Politics* 39, no. 2 (January 1987), pp. 147–173.

31. *New York Times,* 13 December 1986.

14

Africa Toward the Year 2000

"Vibrant," "fluid," "rich," "complex": These are some of the terms that we have used to describe contemporary African politics. Despite the economic and social problems faced by most African governments, the continent is characterized by a tremendous political vitality. Indeed, the very difficulties that Africans have faced since independence have prompted experimentation with new political forms and directions. We hope that the political choice approach that we have presented in this book has provided readers with a concept that captures the diversity of contemporary African politics. Our approach is far from deterministic. Although recognizing the severe constraints under which most African governments function, we have emphasized that alternative options exist. Policy decisions have led not only to markedly different forms of regime but also to different economic structures and patterns of relations with foreign actors. Consequently, it is often misleading to talk in generalized terms about Africa as if it were a single entity—there are many Africas.

The fluidity of African politics and the variety of responses to constraints that have emerged since independence make any effort to predict the future—even over the relatively brief period until the turn of the next century—extremely hazardous. Old certainties have disappeared. The naive optimism expressed by some modernization theorists would find little echo in contemporary perspectives on Africa. On the other hand, the pessimism and determinancy of underdevelopment theories have increasingly been recognized as inadequate for conveying the richness and diversity of the African experience. In our final chapter, we continue to emphasize the centrality of choice in African politics. Rather than attempting to specify outcomes, we shall identify some of the major dimensions on which change may be expected and pose questions as to which directions that change might take.

Only thirty years have passed since the first black African country gained its independence. Although the popular saying is that a week is a long time in politics, thirty years is a relatively short period in political history. This is especially so when placed in the context of the centuries over which the states of Asia and Western Europe were consolidated or, indeed, the long period between the independence of the United States and the introduction of universal adult suffrage. It should come as no surprise, therefore, that African states have only traveled a short distance toward solving the enormous problems of state and nation-building identified by theorists of modernization in the 1960s. State capabilities for penetrating society and carrying into effect policies decided at the center remain weak; government is often characterized by personal rule. Nevertheless, state institutions have become an integral part of daily life on the continent.

The problems faced by Africans in the 1980s—whether these take the form of deteriorating commodity prices, population growth, shortage of land, or pressure from international agencies—sap limited state resources in a relentless manner. We can expect the gap between resource availability and the demands made on them to close only slowly. On the basis of aggregate economic performance since independence, the average African in 2087 will have a real income per capita of only $770 in today's money. This level of income, approximately that of contemporary Zimbabwe, is of course well below the per capita income enjoyed today in Latin America and many countries of Asia. Although some African states may experience windfalls that afford them some breathing space—as oil has done for Nigeria since the mid-1970s—the impact of such windfalls is likely to be only temporary and may indeed complicate the process of development by creating unrealistic expectations and encouraging extravagant expenditure.

Given the continuing dilemmas confronting African countries, some governments have had remarkable success in the pursuit of their objectives. Their achievements have to be placed in the context of their limited inheritance at independence and the constraints, both domestic and international, that they have subsequently faced. There have been significant advances in the fields of education and health care. In the political realm, rules and procedures for conflict management have gradually but steadily been established. Some African regimes—most notably Algeria, Cameroon, Mozambique, and Tanzania—have ably managed the difficult task of political succession (which has proven problematic even for the more institutionalized Marxist-Leninist regimes of Eastern Europe and Asia). African states have become active actors on the international stage, playing an important role in the Nonaligned Movement and at the United Nations. No secessionist movement has achieved its goals. Despite the complexities of their borders, African states (with a few exceptions such as Chad/Libya, Mali/Burkina Faso, and Tanzania/Uganda) have been adept at avoiding disputes over boundary issues. The continent's leaders and organizations responded maturely and creatively to the economic crises that beset Africa in the first half of the 1980s.

Although the economic malaise that characterizes much of contemporary Africa should not blind us to the very real accomplishments since independence, it would be naive to pretend that costly failures—in economic, political, and social terms—have not occurred. The lessons of mistaken policies, such as forced industrialization or the attempt to coerce the population into communal farming, should by now be sufficiently deeply inscribed on the minds of Africa's leaders that repetition will be avoided. Failures elsewhere have certainly made some policy paths much less attractive. In the early 1970s, for instance, Tanzania's strategy of self-reliance was widely praised and suggested as a model for other states to emulate. Today, few commentators would prescribe this course because the ineffective way in which aspects of this policy have been implemented has largely discredited the whole strategy. In these and other instances in which faulty implementation has damaged the credibility of otherwise potentially sound strategies, there may well be a risk of succumbing to the old proverbial danger of throwing the baby out with the bathwater.

One thing is certain. The ideal, "traditional" society, much beloved by theorists of modernization, has no counterpart in contemporary Africa. The continent has, of course, been penetrated by international traders for centuries, leaving few areas untouched by external influences. Processes of economic differentiation and class formation were well under way long before independence. Despite economic setbacks in the last decade, these trends are continuing and may be expected to increase in the remainder of this century. Problems in agricultural production may well lead to more experiments with large-scale capital-intensive farming that will accentuate issues of land tenure that have already emerged in some countries; Ghana, Kenya, Nigeria, and Zimbabwe are some of the most notable examples.

The days when Africans could display their dissatisfaction with government policies by pursuing an "exit" option—a retreat into subsistence farming—may well, in many countries, be less feasible. This narrowing of options has significant implications, not merely for the already rapid rate of urban growth and the emergence of a landless proletariat, but also for political participation and the forms of political conflict. Although a growing land shortage may enhance the ability of governments to "capture" the peasantry, it may also generate new economic and social forces. Major changes can be expected in social relations if access to the land is lost by the children of existing farmers: The roles of the village and of extended families, of such importance in the social and political life of many parts of Africa, might alter significantly. Continuing industrialization will accelerate the process of class formation: Whether the horizontal ties of class relations will become more important than the vertical links of patron-client relations remains to be seen. Will Africa's elites become self-perpetuating as a result of their children's privileged access to scarce educational resources?

In the political realm, the search for formulae for greater institutionaliza-tion is likely to continue. African states since independence have experimented with a wide array of regime types—from personal dictatorships and bureau-cratic regimes to Marxist-Leninist parties, populist governments, and multi-party democracies. The problem of establishing a tradition of responsible government remains. The next few years will witness the disappearance of the handful of survivors of the independence generation that still hold power. Will their departure from the political scene be handled successfully, as appears to have happened in Algeria and Senegal, or will it be the precipitant of a new round of military involvement in politics, as occurred in Guinea after the death of Sekou Touré? How will new leaders create a new foundation for legitimacy now that the status of "father of the nation" is no longer available?

What mechanisms of political accountability will be devised? Will the years until the turn of the century see the revival of political parties on the Afri-can continent? It is certain that the 1980s have witnessed the founding of more parties than at any time since the last years of the nationalist period. But will these parties become anything more than hollow shells? Will there be more Marxist-Leninist parties along the lines of those of Ethiopia, Angola, and Mozambique, or were these parties the outgrowth of particular political circum-stances—the revolutionary overthrow of a feudal ruling elite, on the one hand, and wars of national liberation, on the other? Will public demands for greater participation lead to an extension of multiparty systems (will the pluralism of African societies come to be reflected in their party systems?), or will there be more of the populist institutional arrangements of direct participation—"social inclusion"—that came to the fore in the 1980s in countries such as Burkina Faso and Ghana? Will it be possible to design other channels of representation and participation?

How will political transitions take place? It is safe to predict that the mili-tary will continue to play a major role in African politics in the remaining years of this century. Will more states succumb to military intervention? Have those countries that have not experienced a military coup been blessed with favorable background factors, found a successful formula for containing military inter-vention, or just been plain lucky? Can any government other than one domi-nated by the military hold together a country as diverse and politically divided as Nigeria? Will military governments be more successful than in the past in disciplining their own forces and in reducing the level of corruption? Will other states collapse into various warring factions in the same manner as Chad and Uganda in the 1980s or were these experiences the product of a particular com-bination of ethnic, geographical, and historical characteristics? The experiences of Chad and Uganda have shown that the road back from state collapse is long and painful.

How will changing economic and political conditions affect social organi-zation? We can expect that frameworks will continue to be redefined as urbanization progresses. Ethnicity will remain a powerful latent force that may be mobilized for political purposes. We have shown how some governments have handled their ethnic and regional problems in a creative manner through various policies such as ethnic balancing. Urban-rural and interregional inequalities are almost certain to be exacerbated as economic development progresses. Will governments be able to continue to pursue innovative politics of regional and ethnic equity in an era of extreme scarcity of resources? Will one response to scarcity be the revival of ethnic activity, as appears to be occurring in Kenya, or will demands be channeled through various class and interest groups?

Continuing conflict over resource allocation and disillusionment with the formal political process may also be expected to encourage the activities of voluntary organizations. Will these take the form primarily of groups whose principal purpose is to lobby governments, or of organizations such as syncretist churches that offer a vent for frustrations largely outside the official political realm? Will the Islamic revival that has taken place in the 1980s in West Africa continue and assume increasingly political overtones? Will we see the emergence in Africa before the end of the century of an Islamic fundamentalist state comparable to that of Khomeini's Iran? Will the rise of Islam conflict with the growing political role of women on the continent and the increasing awareness among women in the general population of their disadvantaged position? Will international agencies succeed in their professed goal of improving the situation of women in what continue to be patriarchal societies?

What are the prospects that the African state will become more effective? There is little hope that significantly increased resources will become available: If the state is to enhance its capacity for policy implementation, then existing resources must be used more creatively and efficiently. Most observers assert that a significant reason why African states have been ineffective is that the implementation of policymaking is distorted by sectional interests. How can the penetrative capacity of African states be facilitated while decision-making procedures are opened to closer public scrutiny? Early optimism that military governments would be able to resist pressures from special interests soon faded as it became obvious that they were as divided as the wider societies from which they were drawn. Similarly, Africa's handful of Marxist-Leninist parties have not succeeded as effectively as their Eastern European counterparts in turning themselves into organizational weapons that can overcome social divisions.

African countries seem certain to have to live with greatly increased interference by the World Bank and the International Monetary Fund. What will be the relationship between these international organizations and African governments? Will external agencies be important catalysts in forcing policy change, or will their activities invoke resistance from governments seeking to assert their sovereignty? An argument is often made that external agencies can be of major assistance to governments that wish to introduce reform yet lack the domestic support to do so. By appearing to impose policy change from outside, external agencies may enable governments to pursue the policy reforms they desire without undermining the foundations of their domestic supports. On the other hand, international actors may seek to impose changes that African leaders perceive to be too costly. All the evidence suggests that these agencies can most successfully promote reform when they are "leaning on an open door"— that is, when governments are already sympathetic toward the measures demanded.

Recent responses to external demands suggest that many African governments are willing, given the dire economic circumstances in which they find themselves, to attempt to pursue the policy changes demanded by the World Bank. Yet, significant vested interests are often threatened. Although some policies that African governments pursued since independence may well have been faulty in economic terms, they have often been chosen because they serve desired political ends. Economic rationality and political rationality are not always identical. Parastatal organizations, for example, are frequently perceived to be overstaffed. Such overstaffing is costly in economic terms, but from a political perspective overstaffing may avoid unrest generated by unemployed secondary-school leavers or may offer governments the opportunity to provide patronage to their supporters. African governments will have to be convinced that it is in their long-term political as well as economic interests to introduce policy reforms. Carrots can obviously be provided by the international community by linking increased financial support to such reforms. One question that may well prove decisive for the prospects of achieving the changes that international agencies are advocating is whether the international community will provide sufficient financial assistance to make a reform strategy attractive. Initial responses on the part of industrialized countries give little reason for optimism.

International agencies such as the World Bank and the IMF call for a greater reliance on market mechanisms to achieve a more efficient allocation of resources. Many commentators, however, question whether markets actually function effectively in Africa, where they are often dominated by a few large transnational corporations and information is far from perfect. There is also considerable controversy over the advocacy by international agencies of a reduced role for the state in African economies. Although many accept that the state has overextended itself, critics of the World Bank believe that it has misread twentieth-century economic history in general—and the recent experience of the newly industrializing countries in particular—in failing to perceive the leading role that the state has played in fostering economic growth through such devices as selective protectionism, the regulation of foreign enterprises, and the promotion of exports. Few would accept either the feasibility or the wisdom of the withdrawal of the African state from the economic arena. But will the adoption of policies that emphasize market forces render African economies in the remainder of this century even more vulnerable to international influences and weaken the bargaining positions of African governments with transnational actors just at the time when these governments are becoming more effective negotiators? Will decentralization of state activities, as advocated by many advisors, increase the effectiveness of the state or merely render it more vulnerable to capture by regional patron-client networks?

In the realm of international relations, will Africa become a battleground for the superpowers? Or will there be a more sophisticated realization on the part of the superpowers that most conflicts on the continent are over issues far removed from the global chessboard of East-West relations? It appears that differential economic growth in Africa will be translated into changes in the continent's military balance. Will this lead to an increase in transborder adventurism, to growing interference in the domestic political affairs of neighboring states? Will differential economic performances facilitate the growth of regional cooperation by making it easier for the relatively well-off to subsidize services for poorer partners? Or will it intensify interstate jealousies and complicate the task of regional integration? Will Africa's regions become more clearly defined or will the interactions that we have described in Chapter 11 become more genuinely continental, making any definition of regions more complex?

Finally, there is the issue of South Africa's future. In 1977, a well-known book posed the question: How Long Will South Africa Survive?[1] We are no closer to being able to provide an answer. The growth of internal violence and the divestment by Western corporations have been clear signals that the pace of change is accelerating. But we do not know whether the outcome will be achieved through a negotiated settlement or a terrible bloody conflict that has the potential to draw in the superpowers. What pressure will the United States attempt to bring to bear on South Africa in the future? Under the Reagan administration, eight years were largely wasted in the futile policy of "constructive engagement." Only popular pressure on Congress prompted the United States to level economic sanctions against the Republic of South Africa. Will a future administration increase the pressure and attempt to play a more active role? Will the Soviet Union become tempted to intervene in support of Marxist-Leninist regimes in neighboring black African states if South Africa intensifies its campaign of terror against them? Will white power crumble from within, as professionals and others with scarce skills "vote with their feet" and emigrate? Will the splits in white politics that emerged in the campaign for the 1987 general election lead to a more moderate government willing to enter into negotiations for a power-sharing arrangement with blacks or to retreat into the *laager* behind the right-wing, military-dominated government? Will black leaders be able to put their divisions behind them and form a cohesive nationalist movement? What will be the future of the ANC when its aging leadership departs from the scene?

We do not pretend to have the answers to these and other questions we have posed. We can only hope that the ideas that we have presented in this book have provided readers with a basis from which to undertake a better-informed consideration of the alternative paths that African countries might take and the various answers that will emerge to these questions. But we can be sure that there will be new strategies adopted, new solutions devised by imaginative peoples and their leaders. That is why the study of contemporary African politics is so exciting.

■ NOTES

1. R. W. Johnson, *How Long Will South Africa Survive?* (New York: Oxford University Press, 1977).

■ Appendix 1. Acronyms

AAPC	All African Peoples Conference
AAPSO	Afro-Asian Peoples' Solidarity Organization
ACP Group	African, Caribbean, and Pacific Group
AEF	Afrique Equatoriale Française (French Equatorial Africa)
AIDS	Acquired Immune Deficiency Syndrome
ANC	African National Congress
AOF	Afrique Occidentale Français (French West Africa)
AZAPO	Azanian Peoples' Organization
AZASO	Azanian Students' Organization
BCM	Black Consciousness Movement
BOSS	Bureau of State Security
CCM	Chama Cha Mapinduzi
CEAO	Economic Community of West Africa
CFA	African Financial Community
CIA	Central Intelligence Agency
CIAS	Conference of Independent States
COSAS	Congress of South African Students
COSATU	Congress of South African Trade Unions
CPP	Convention People's party
CUSA	Council of Unions of South Africa
DAC	Development Assistance Committee
ECA	Economic Commission for Africa
ECOWAS	Economic Community of West African States
EEC	European Economic Community
ELF	Eritrean Liberation Front
FLN	National Liberation Front
FNLA	National Front for the Liberation of Angola
FOSATU	Federation of South African Trade Unions
FRELIMO	Front for the Liberation of Mozambique
Frolinat	Front pour la Liberation Nationale du Tchad
GRAE	Angolan Revolutionary Government in Exile
GUNT	Transitional National Union Government
IMF	International Monetary Fund
ISI	import-substituting industrialization
KANU	Kenya African National Union
LDCs	less-developed countries
MPLA	Popular Movement for the Liberation of Angola
NAM	Nonaligned Movement
NANS	National Association of Nigerian Students
NF	National Forum
NICs	newly industrializing countries
NIEO	New International Economic Order
NP	National Party
NUGS	National Union of Ghanaian Students
NUM	National Union of Mineworkers

OAU	Organization of African Unity
OCAM	Afro-Malagasy Common Organization
OECD	Organization for Economic Cooperation and Development
OMVS	Organization pour la Mise en Valeur du Fleuve Sénégal (Organization for the Development of the Senegal River)
ONUC	United Nations Operation in the Congo
OPEC	Organization of Petroleum Exporting Countries
PA	Program of Action
PAC	Pan-Africanist Congress
PDG	Parti Democratique de Guinée
PFP	Progressive Federal party
PLO	Palestine Liberation Organization
PMAC	Provisional Military Administrative Council
PNDC	Provisional National Defense Council
Polisario Front	Frente Popular para la Liberacion de Saguia el Hamra y Rio de Oro
PTA	Preferential Trade Area
RCC	Revolutionary Command Council
RENAMO	Mozambique National Resistance Movement
SACC	South African Council of Churches
SADCC	South African Development Coordination Conference
SADR	Saharan Arab Democratic Republic
SALT	Strategic Arms Limitation Treaty
SASO	South African Students' Organization
SONATRACH	Société Nationale de Transports et de Commercialisation des Hydrocarbures
STABEX	Stabilization of Export Earnings Scheme
SWAPO	South West African People's Organization
TANU	Tanzanian African National Union
TNCs	transnational corporations
UAM	Union of African States and Madagascar
UDAO	Customs Union of West Africa
UDEAO	Customs Union of West African States
UDF	United Democratic Front
UDI	Unilateral Declaration of Independence
UNCTAD	United Nations Conference on Trade and Development
UNESCO	United Nations Educational, Scientific, and Cultural Organization
UNIDO	United Nations Industrial Development Organization
UNITA	National Union for the Total Independence of Angola
UPA	Union of Angolan Peoples
WPE	Workers' Party of Ethiopia
WSLF	Western Somali Liberation Front
ZANU	Zimbabwe African National Union
ZAPU	Zimbabwe African People's Union
ZNP	Zanzibar Nationalist Party

■ Appendix 2.   Basic Political Data

Country and Date of Independence	Capital City	Rulers Since Independence	Political Parties
Algeria 3 July 1962	Algiers	1. Ahmed Ben Bella, president, 1962–June 1965 2. Col. Houari Boumedienne, president, June 1965– December 1978 3. Col. Benjedid Chadli, president, February 1979–	National Liberation Front (FLN)
Angola 11 November 1975	Luanda	1. Antonio Agostinho Neto, founding president, 1975–10 September 1979 2. José Eduardo dos Santos, president, 20 September 1979–	Popular Movement for the Liberation of Angola (MPLA)
Benin 1 August 1960 (formerly Republic of Dahomey 1960– 1975)	Porto Novo	1. Hubert Maga, president, 31 December 1960– 28 October 1963 2. Col. (later Gen.) Christophe Soglo, president, 28 October 1963–January 1964 3. Sourou Migan Apithy, president, January 1964– 29 November 1965 4. Tahirou Congacou, president 29 November 1965– 22 December 1965 5. Gen. Christophe Soglo, president, 22 December 1965– 16 December 1967 6. Lt. Col. Alphonse Alley, president, 16 December 1967– July 1968 7. Emile-Derin Zinsou (civilian), president, July 1968– 10 December 1969 8. Lt. Col. Paul Emile de Souza, president, 10 December 1969– May 1972 9. Hubert Maga, president, May 1970–May 1972 10. Justin Ahomadegbe, president, May 1972–26 October 1972 11. Col. Mathieu Kerekou, president, October 1972–	Benin People's Revolutionary party (PRPB)
Botswana 30 September 1966	Gaborone	1. Sir Seretse Khana, 30 September 1966– 13 July 1980 2. Quett Masire, president 13 July 1980–	Botswana Democratic party Botswana People's party Botswana Independence party Botswana National party
Burkina Faso 5 August 1960 (formerly Upper Volta; renamed Burkina Faso, August 1984)	Ouagadougou	1. Maurice Yaméogo, president, April 1959– January 1966 2. Lt. Col. Sangoulé Lamizana, president, January 1966– 1980	None

Country and Date of Independence	Capital City	Rulers Since Independence	Political Parties
Burkina Faso (continued)		3. Col. Sayé Zerbo, 1980–1982 4. NCO coup, October 1982 5. Maj. Jean Baptiste Ouedraogo, president, January 1983–August 1983 6. Capt. Thomas Sankara, president, National Revolutionary Council (CNR), 1983–1987 7. Capt. Blaise Compaore, president, National Revolutionary Council, 1987–	
Burundi 1 July 1962	Bujumbura	1. (King) Mwami Mwambutsa II, 1915–1966. Prime ministers: André Muhirwa 1962–1963 Pierre Ngendandumwe, 1963 Albin Nyamoya, 1964–1965 Pierre Ngendandumwe, 1965 (assassinated, January 1965) Joseph Bamina, 1965 Leopold Biha, 1965 2. Mwami Ntare IV (deposed father, Mwambutsa II, as king). Capt. (later Col.) Michel Micombero, prime minister, 8 July 1966–29 November 1966 3. Micombero declares Burundi a republic, with himself as president, 29 November 1966–1 November 1976 4. Col. Jean-Baptiste Bagaza, president, November 1976–3 September 1987 5. Maj. Pierre Buyoya, Chairman, Military Committee for National Salvation, March 1987–	Parti de l'Unité et du Progrès National du Burundi (UPRONA)
Cameroon 1 January 1960 (1960–1961: Republic of East Cameroon; October 1961–1972: Federal Republic of Cameroono, composed of the East—former French trust territory—and West—part of former British trust territory; 1972–: United Cameroon Republic)	Yaoundé	1. Ahmadou Ahidjo, president, 5 May 1960–November 1982 2. Paul Biya, president, 1982–	National Cameroonian Union; renamed in March 1985; Rassemblement Democratique du Peuple Camerounais (RDPC)

Country and Date of Independence	Capital City	Rulers Since Independence	Political Parties
Cape Verde July 1975 (in federation with Guinea-Bissau, 1975–January 1981)	Praia	1. Aristides Pereira, president, 1975–	Partido Africano da Independencia de Cabo Verde (PAICV)
Central African Republic 13 August 1966 (1976–1979: Central African Empire)	Bangui	1. David Dacko (formerly prime minister), president, 17 November 1960– 31 December 1965 2. Coup led by Field Marshal Jean-Bedel Bokassa, 31 December 1965 3. Bokassa proclaimed "President for Life," 2 March 1972 4. Bokassa crowned emperor, 4 December 1977 5. Bokassa deposed in coup. David Dacko, president, 10 September 1979 6. Gen. André Kolingba established military regime, September 1981– (chairman of Military Com- mittee for National Recovery	Centrafrican Democratic Assembly (RDC)
Chad 11 August 1960	Ndjaména	1. Ngarta (formerly François) Tombalbaye, prime minister; head of state on independ- ence; president, 22 April 1962–13 April 1975 (killed in military coup) 2. Gen. Félix Malloum, president, April 1975–1979 3. Hissene Habré, appointed prime minister, August 1978 4. Malloum and Habré resign, 23 March 1979; Transitional Government of National Unity 5. Goukouni Oueddei, president 1979–1982 6. Hissene Habré, president, 1982–	Union Nationale pour l'Independence et la Révolution (UNIR)
Comoros July 1975	Moroni	1. Ahmed Abdallah, president July 1975–August 1975 2. Coup led by Ali Soilih, August, 1975; president, 1976–1978 3. Ahmed Abdallah, president, 1978–; reinstated in coup by mercenaries under Bob Denard.	National United Front National Council of the Institutions

Country and Date of Independence	Capital City	Rulers Since Independence	Political Parties
People's Republic of the Congo 15 August 1960	Brazzaville	1. Foulbert Youlou elected president under preindependence constitution, 21 November 1959 2. Military coup August 1963; Alphonse Massamba-Débat, president, 19 December 1963–4 September 1968 3. Governing National Revolutionary Council, 5 August 1968, chaired by Capt. Marien Ngouabi. Maj. Alfred Raoul, prime minister and temporary head of state, 5 September 1968–31 December 1968 4. Capt. Marien Ngouabi, president, December 1968–March 1977 5. Ngouabi assassinated, March 1977. Col. (later Brig. Gen. Joachim Yhombi-Opango, president, March 1977–5 February 1979 6. Col. Denis Sassou-Nguesso, president, 5 February 1979–	Congolese Workers' party (PCT)
Côte d'Ivoire 7 August 1960	Abidjan	1. Felix Houphouët-Boigny, prime minister, 1 May 1959; president, 27 November 1960–	Democratic Party of the Ivory Coast (PDCI)
Djibouti 27 June 1977	Dijbouti	1. Hassan Gouled, president, 24 June 1977–	Rassemblement Populaire pour le Progrès (RPP)
Arab Republic of Egypt October 1951	Cairo	1. King Farouk to 1952 2. Coup led by Col. Gamal Abdel Nasser and Abdul-al Hakim. Maj. Gen. Neguib, president, June 1953–November 1954 3. Nasser, head of state, 1954–1970 (president from 1956) 4. Col. Anwar Sadat, president, 1970–October 1981 5. Lt. Gen. Hosni Mubarak, president, 1981–	Liberal Socialist party National Democratic party National Progressive Unionist party New Wafd party Socialist Labour party Ummah party
Equaotiral Guinea 12 October 1968	Malabo	1. Francisco Macias Nguema, president, 29 September 1968–3 August 1979 2. Military coup led by Lt. Col. Teodoro Obiango Nguema Mbasogo, 3 August 1979 3. Lt. Col. Teodoro Obiango Nguema Mbasogo, president, 12 October 1980–	Democratic Party of Equatorial Guinea (PDGE) (September 1987)

426

Country and Date of Independence	Capital City	Rulers Since Independence	Political Parties
Ethiopia	Addis Ababa	1. Successio nof emperors 2. Emperor Haile Selassie, 1930–12 September 1974 3. Lt. Gen. Aman Andom, chairman PMAC (Provisional Military Administrative Council) until November 1974 4. Brig. Gen. Teferi Banti, chairman, PMAC. Power actually held by vice chairman Maj. (later Lt. Col.) Mengistu Haile Mariam and Lt. Col. Atnafu Abate. Banti killed, 3 February 1977. 5. Mengistu Haile Marian, chairman of PMAC, head of state, 1977–	Workers' Party of Ethiopia (WPE)
Gabon 17 August 1960	Libreville	1. Leon M'Ba, president, 1961–28 November 1967 2. Omar (formerly Albert-Bernard) Bongo, president, 29 November 1967–	Gabonese Democratic Party (PDG)
Gambia 18 February 1965	Banjul	1. Constitutional monarchy with Dawda Jawara, prime minister, 1965–1970 2. Gambia becomes a republic, April 1970. Dawda Jawara becomes first president, 24 April 1970–	National Liberation party National Convention party People's Progressive party United party
Ghana 6 March 1957	Accra	1. Constitutional monarchy, 1957–1960; Kwame Nkrumah, prime minister. Becomes republic, 1960; Nkrumah, president, 24 February 1966 2. Lt. Gen. Joseph Ankrah, chairman of National Loberation Council, February 1966–1969. Replaced, 1969, by Brig. Gen. Akwasi Afrifa 3. Competitive electoral politics: Kofi Busia, prime minister, September 1969–January 1972 4. Lt. Col. (later Gen.) Ignatius Kutu Acheampong, chairman of National Redemption Council, replaced by Supreme Military Council, 13 January 1972–5 July 1978 5. Lt. Gen. Frederik Akuffo, chairman of SUpreme Military COuncil, 5 July 1978–4 June 1979	None

Country and Date of Independence	Capital City	Rulers Since Independence	Political Parties
Ghana (continued)		6. Flight Lt. Jerry Rawlings, chairman of Armed Forces Revolutionary Council, 4 June 1979–September 1979 7. Dr. Hilla Limann, president, September 1979–December 1971 8. Flight Lt. Jerry Rawlings, chairman of the Provisional National Defence Council, December 1981–	
Guinea 2 October 1958	Conakry	1. Ahmed Sekou Touré, president, 1958–April 1984 2. Col. Lansana Conté, president, head of Comité Militaire de Redressement National, 1984–	None
Guinea-Bissau 10 September 1974	Bissau	1. Luiz De Almeida Cabral, president, 1974–1980 2. Gen. Joao Bernardo Vieira, president of the Council of State, head of government, 1980	African Party for the Independence of Guinea and Cape Verde Islands (PAIGC)
Kenya 12 December 1963	Nairobi	1. Constitutional monarchy, 1963–1964; Jomo Kenyatta, prime minister 2. Kenyatta, president, 1964–11 August 1978. 3. Succeeded by Daniel arap Moi, president, 1978–	Kenya African National Union (KANU)
Lesotho 4 October 1966	Maseru	1. Constitutional monarchy under King Motlotlehi Moshoeshoe II 2. Chief Lebua Jonathan seizes power in civilian coup, January 1970–January 1986 3. Maj. Gen. Justin Lekhanya, chairman, Military Council, 1986–	None
Liberia 1847	Monrovia	1. Until 1944, eighteen presidents 2. William V. S. Tubman, president, 1944–1971 3. William R. Tolbert, 1971–12 April 1980 4. M.Sgt. Samuel K. Doe, president, People's Redemption Council, 1980–	National Democratic party (NDP) Liberian Actio party (LAP) Liberian Unification party (LUP) Unity party (UP)

Country and Date of Independence	Capital City	Rulers Since Independence	Political Parties
Libya December 1951 (from March 1977, named Socialist People's Libyan Arab Jamahiriya)	Tripoli	1. King Idris, 1951–1969 2. Col. Muammar Mohammed Qaddafi, Leader of the Revolution, 1969–	None
Democratic Republic of Madagascar June 1960	Antananarivo	1. Philibert Tsiranana, president, 1960–May 1972 2. Gen. Gabriel Ramanantsoa, president, 1972–February 1975 3. Col. Ratsimandrava, February 1975 (assassinated) 4. Gen. Gilles Andria Mahazo, National Military Directorate, February 1975 5. Lt. Comdr. Didier Ratsiraka, president, March 1975–	Front National pour la Défense de la Revolution Socialiste Malgache (FNDR)
Malawi 6 July 1964	Lilongwe	1. Constitutional monarchy, Ngwasi Dr. Hastings Kamuzu Banda, prime minister, 1964–1966 2. Banda, president, 1966 3. Ngwasi Dr. Hastings Kamuzu Banda, "President for Life," July 1971–	Malawi Congress party
Mali 22 September 1960 (20 June 1960: independence of Mali Federation) (4 April 1959–20 August 1960: Mali Federation, with Senegal)	Bamako	1. Modibo Keita, president of Mali Federation; president of Soudan government, 15 April 1959; president of Mali, 1960–1968 2. Lt. (later Brig. Gen.) Moussa Traoré, chairman of Military Committee of National Liberation, November 1968–June 1979 3. Gen. Moussa Traoré, president, 19 June 1979–	Union Démocratique du Peuple Malien (UDPM)
Islamic Republic of Mauritania 28 November 1960	Nouakchott	1. Mokhtar Ould Daddah, president, 1961–10 July 1978 2. Lt. Col. Mustapha Ould Mohammed Salek, president of Comité Militaire de Redressement National (CMRN), 10 July 1978–6 April 1979 3. Lt. Col. Ahmed Ould Bouceif, prime minister, 6 April 1979–27 May 1979 (assassinated) 4. Lt. Col. Mohammed Khouna Haidalla, prime minister appointed by Salek, 31 May 1979	Mauritanian People's party (PPM)

Country and Date of Independence	Capital City	Rulers Since Independence	Political Parties
Islamic Republic of Mauritania (continued)		5. CMSN (formerly CMRN) forces Salek to resign, June 1979. Lt. Col. Mohammed Mahmoud Ould Louly, president, June 1979–January 1980 6. Haidalla ousts Louly, 4 January 1980. Becomes president, head of state, and chairman of CMSN, 1980–1984 7. Col. Maawiya Ould Sid'Ahmed Taya, president of the Republic, chairman of the Military Commottee for National Salvation, 1984–	
Mauritius March 1968	Port Louis	1. Seewoosegur Ramgoolam, prime minister, 1968–1982 2. Anerood Jugauth, prime minister, 1982–	Comité d'Action Musulman (CAM) Independent Forward Bloc (IFB) Mauritian Labour party (MLP) Mauritius People's Progressive party Mouvement Militant Mauricien (MMM) Mouvement Socialiste Mauricien (MSM)
Morocco March 1956	Rabat	1. King Mohammed V, to 1961 2. King Hassan II, 1961–	Istiqlal Mouvement Populaire (MP) Mouvement Populaire Constitutionnel et Democratique (MPCD) Organisation de l'Action Democratique et Populaire Parti de l'Action Parti du Centre Social Parti Democratique pour l'Independence Parti National Democrate (PLP) Parti Liberal Progressiste (PLP) Parti National pour l'Unité et la Solidarité Parti du Progrès et du Socialisme (PPS) Rassemblement National des Independents (RNI) Union Constiutionnelle (UC) Union Nationale des Forces Populaires (UNFP) Union Socialiste des Forces Populaires (USFP)

Country and Date of Independence	Capital City	Rulers Since Independence	Political Parties
Mozambique 25 June 1975	Maputo	1. Samora Moisés Machel, president, 1975–1986 2. Joaquim Alberto Chissano, president, 1986–	Front for the Liberation of Mozambique (FRELIMO)
Niger 8 August 1960	Niamey	1. Hamani Diori, president, 1960–15 April 1974 2. Maj. Gen. Seyni Kountché, head of state, president of Supreme Military Council, 1974–1987 3. Col. Ali Seibou, president of Supreme Military Council, head of State, 1987–	None
Nigeria 1 October 1960	Lagos	1. Abubakar Tafewa Balewa, prime minister, 1960–1966; Nnamdi Azikiwe, president, 1963–1966 2. Gen. Johnson Aguiyi Ironsi, head of Federal Military Government, January 1966–July 1966 3. Lt. Col. Yakubu Gowon, head of Federal Military Government, July 1966–29 July 1975 4. Brig. Gen. Murtala Mohammed, chief of Supreme Military Council, 29 July 1975–13 February 1976 5. Lt. Gen. Olusegun Obasanjo, 13 February 1976–October 1979 6. Alhaji Shehu Shagari, president, October 1979–December 1983 7. Maj. Gen. Mohammed Buhari, December 1983–August 1985 8. Maj. Gen. Ibrahim Babangida, president, August 1985–	All parties banned since 1984
Rwanda 1 July 1962	Kigali	1. Grégoire Kayibanda, president, 1961–5 July 1973 2. Maj. Gen. Juvénal Habyarimana, president, 5 July 1973–	Mouvement Revolutionaire National pour le Développement (MRND)
Saharan Arab Democratic Republic (SADR) (Western Sahara) February 1982 (admitted as 51st member of OAU)	Not applicable	1. Mohammed Abdelaziz, president, 1982–	Frente Popular para la Liberación de Saguia el Hamra y Rio de Oro—Frente Polisario (Polisario Front)

Country and Date of Independence	Capital City	Rulers Since Independence	Political Parties
Sao Tomé and Principe July 1975	Sào Tomé	1. Dr. Manuel Pinto de Costa, president, 1975–	Movement for the Liberatio nof Sao Tomé and Principe
Senegal 20 August 1960 (14 April 1959– 20 August 1960: Mali Federation)	Dakar	1. Léopold Sédar Senghor, president, 1960–January 1981 2. Abdou Diouf, president, January 1981–	Senegal Democratic party (PDS) Senegalese National Democratic Assembly (RND) Parti Socialiste Senegalais (PS)
Seychelles June 1976	Port Victoria	1. James Mancham, president, June 1976–June 1977 2. Albert René, president, June 1977–	Seychelles People's Progressive Front (SPPF)
Sierra Leone 27 April 1961	Freetown	1. Sir Milton Margai, prime minister, 1961–1964 2. Sir Albert Margai, prime minister, 1964–1967 3. Lt. Col. Andrew Juxon-Smith, chairman of National Reformation Council, March 1967–April 1968 4. Siaka Probyn Stevens, prime minister, April 1968 5. Stevens becomes president of Republic, April 1971–October 1985 6. Maj. Gen. Dr. Joseph Saidu Momoh, president, 1985–	All People's Congress (APC)
Somalia 1 July 1960	Mogadishu	1. Aden Abdulla Osman, president, 1960–1967; Abdirashid Ali Shirmarke, prime minister, 1960–1964; Abdirazak Hussein, prime minister, 1964–1967 2. Abdirashid Ali Shirmarke, president, 1967–1969; Mohammed Ibrahim Egal, prime minister, 1967–1969 3. Maj. Gen. Mohammed Siad Barre, president, 1969–	Aomali Revolutionary Socialist party (SRSP)
South Africa 31 May 1961	Pretoria	1. Dr. Hendrik Verwoerd, prime minister, 1958–1966 2. B. J. Vorster, president and prime minister, 1966–1978 3. Pieter W. Botha, prime mnister, then president, 1978–	Afrikaanse Weerstands-beweging (AWB) Azanian People's Organi-zation (AZAPO) Conservative Party of South Africa (CPSA) Democratic Workers' party (DWP) Freedom party Ferstigte Nasionale party (HNP)

Appendix 2. Continued

Country and Date of Independence	Capital City	Rulers Since Independence	Political Parties
South Africa			Labour Party of South Africa National party (NP) National People's party New Freedom Party of Southern Africa New Republic party People's Congress party Progressive Federal party (PFP) Progressive Independent party Reformed Freedom party Solidarity party South African Black Alliance
Sudan 1 January 1956	Khartoum	1. Ismail al-Azhari, prime minister, 1956 2. Abdulla Khalil, prime minister, 1956–1958 3. Lt. Gen. Ibrahim Abboud, prime minister, 1958–1964 4. Sir el-Khalim el-Khalifah, prime minister, 1964–1965 5. Muhamman Ahmad Mahgoub, prime minister, 1965–1966 6. Sayed Siddick El Mahdi, prime minister, 1966–1967 7. Muhammed Ahmad Mahgoub, prime minister, 1967–1969 8. Abubakr Awadallah, prime minister, 1969 9. Field Marshal Gaafar Mohammed Nimeiri, president, May 1969–April 1985 10. Coup, 6 April 1985. Lt. Gen. Abdel Rahman Swar al Dahab, chairman, Transitional Military Council 11. Ahmed Ali el Mirghani, president, Supreme Council, 1986–	Principal parties: Baath party Communist party Democratic Unionist party Muslim Brotherhood National Alliance for Salvatio n(NAS) National Congress party National Islamic Front Nationalist Unionist party Southern Sudanese Political Association Sudan African National Union (SANU) Sudanese National party Umma party
Swaziland 9 September 1968	Mbabane	1. King Sobhuza II, 1922–September 1982; Queen Mother Dzeliwe, regent, September 1982. Deposed August 1983. Prince Mahhosetive named as future king, King Mswati III, 1986–	Imbokoovo National Movement (INM)
Tanzania 9 December 1961 (of Tanganyika) December 1963 (of Zanzibar)	Dodoma	1. Julius Nyerere, prime minister, December 1961–January 1962 2. Rashidi M. Kawa, prime minister, January 1962–December 1962	Chama Cha Mapinduzi (CCM)

Country and Date of Independence	Capital City	Rulers Since Independence	Political Parties
Tanzania (continued) (Tanganyika joined with Zanzibar to form United Republic of Tanzania in April 1964)		3. Tanzania becomes a republic, December 1962; Julius Nyerere, president, December 1962–November 1985 4. Ali Hassan Mwinyi, president, 1985–	
Togo 12 April 1960	Lomé	1. Sylvanus Olympio, president 1960–13 January 1963 2. Military coup, January 1963, led by Sgt. (later Gen.) Etienne Eyadema. Nicholas Grunitzky, president, 1963–January 1967 3. Col. Kleber Dadjo, chairman od Comité de Réconciliation Nationale (CRN), January–April 1967 (bloodless coup) 4. Gen. Gnassingbé Eyadema, president, April 1967–	Rassemblement du Peuple Togolais (RPT)
Tunisia March 1956	Tunis	1. Habib Bourguiba, prime minister, 1956–July 1957 2. July 1957, becomes a republic. Habib Bourguiba, president, 1957–1987 3. November 1987, Zine el el Abidine Ben Ali accedes to the presidency, 1987–	Mouvement de l'Unité Populaire (MUP) Mouvement des Democrates Socialistes (MDS) Parti Communiste Tunisien (PCT) Parti Socialiste Destourien (PSD) Rassemblement Socialiste Tunisien (RST)
Uganda 9 October 1962	Kampala	1. Apollo Milton Obote, 1962–1971 (prime minister until 1966; then president) 2. Maj. Gen. Idi Amin, president, 1971–April 1979 3. Yusuf Lule, president, Provisional Government, April–June 1979 4. Godfrey Binaisa, chairman of Military Commission of Ugandan National Liberation Front (UNLF) and president, June 1979–May 1980 5. Paulo Mwanga, chairman, UNLF, May–December 1980 6. Obote, president, December 1980–July 1985 7. Coup led by Lt. Gen. Tito Okello of Uganda National Liberation Army; president, July 1985–January 1986 8. Yoweri Museveni of National Resistance Army (NRA), president, January 1986–	Political parties were ordered to suspend active operations following accession to power of the National Resistance Movement (NRM). The NRM government includes representatives of: Conservative party (CP) Democratic party (DP) National Resistance Movement (NRM) (the military wing of this is the NRA) National Liberal party Uganda Freedom Movement Uganda Patriotic Movement Uganda People's Congress

Country and Date of Independence	Capital City	Rulers Since Independence	Political Parties
Zaire 30 June 1960 (formerly Congo-Kinshasa; named Zaire in October 1971)	Kinshasa	1. Patrice Lumumba, prime minister, June–September 1960; Joseph Kasavubu, president, 1960–1965 2. Col. Joseph Mobutu suspends constitution, September 1960. College of Commissioners rules until February 1961 3. Joseph Ileo, prime minister, February–August 1961 4. Cyrille Adoula, prime minister, August 1961–July 1964 5. Moise Tshombe, prime minister, July 1964–October 1965 6. Evariste Kimba, prime minister, October–November 1965 7. Military coup led by Gen. Mobutu Sese Seko Ngendu Wa Zabanda, president, 1965–	The Popular Movement of the Revolution (MPR)
Zambia 24 October 1964	Lusaka	1. Kenneth Kaunda, president, 1964	United Naitonal Independence party (UNIP)
Zimbabwe 18 April 1980	Harare	1. Canaan Banana, president, head of state, 1980; Robert Mugabe, prime minister, 1980	Conservative Alliance of Zimbabwe (CAZ) Independent Zimbabwe Group National Democratic Union Patriotic Front–Zimbabwe African People's Union (PF-ZAPU) United African National Council (UANC) United National Federal party (UNFP) Zimbabwe African National Union–Patriotic Front (ZANU-PF) Zimbabwe African National Union–Sithole (ZANU-S) Zimbabwe Democratic party Zimbabwe National Front

Sources:
Africa Contemporary Record... Annual Survey and Documents 1983–84, New York: Africana Publishing Company, 1985
Africa Research Bulletin: Political Series, Exeter: Africa Research Limited, February-September, 1987
Africa South of the Sahara 1987, London: Europa Publications Limited, 1986
Europa Yearbook: A World Survey, London: Europa Publications, 1986 and 1987
Foltz, William J. and Bienen, Henry S., *Arms and the African: Military Influences on Africa's International Relations*, New Haven: Yale University Press for the Council on Foreign Relations, 1985
Jackson, Robert H. and Rosberg, Carl G., *Personal Rule in Black Africa: Prince, Autocrat, Prophet, Tyrant*, Los Angeles: University of California Press, 1982
Keesing's Record of World Events, London: Longman, January -July 1987
The Statesman's Yearbook, London: Macmillan, 1987–88

■ Index

■ About the Book and the Authors

This introduction to African politics and society depicts in broad strokes the complexities, diversities, and intricate dynamics of the African world since independence. The authors provide a basic knowledge of political events and of major problems, processes, and trends. Their effort to relate the various historical, political, social, economic, and international constraints of the environment to the political choices made in Africa today is a major contribution to our understanding of the multiple forces at work on the continent.

Naomi Chazan is a senior lecturer in political science and African studies at the Hebrew University of Jerusalem. Robert Mortimer is professor in the Department of Political Science at Haverford College. John Ravenhill is senior lecturer in the Department of Government at the University of Sydney. Donald Rothchild is professor of political science at the University of California, Davis.